PERFORMING LITERATURE

oral interpretation & drama studies

for Christian Schools®

Teacher's Edition

Diana Smith

BJU PRESS
GREENVILLE, SOUTH CAROLINA

First, *Performing Literature* is professional-quality training. The text assumes that many students do not have prior experience performing or even reading dramatic literature. The text balances academic materials such as terms and concepts with performance projects. This could be likened to a piano lesson that includes music theory and study of composers in addition to "how to play" instruction.

Secondly, *Performing Literature* is user-friendly. Clear definitions of terms and concepts, and chapter overviews and reviews appear in every chapter. Project assignments include rubrics for evaluation, and appendices contain numerous resources for performance materials.

Finally, *Performing Literature* is flexible. Students may study this material in various settings: home education (family setting or local group) or conventional classroom as a requirement or elective course. Though not every feature of the book will be ideal for every situation, *Performing Literature* does have something for everyone.

A trained speech teacher should find this text to be a resourceful tool, helping him

---

The Teacher's Edition

The purpose of this book is to help you make the student text materials come alive for your students. View this edition as a toolbox from which you will select tools as you construct a course that suits your students, your resources, and your teaching style. These features include items in the Student Edition as well as in this Teacher's Edition.

Student Edition Features
Chapter Overview

This preview presents the concepts the students should learn (*know*), the skills they should develop (*grow*), and the performance activity(ies) they should do (*show*).

Activity Boxes

These activities are individual study and performance-related projects that include questions for the student to answer. They may be used during your teaching session or assigned as independent work.

Definitions

These marginal notes summarize each boldface term in the text.

"Big Picture" Boxes

Summaries of key ideas appear with the corresponding portion of the text.

Review Pages

Review questions and a list of terms appear at the end of each chapter's textual portion.

teach what he already knows. An educator with little or no formal speech background should find enough helpful advice in the Teacher's Edition to allow him to teach speech as professionally as he does his primary subject. The home educator will find helpful hints for adapting group activities to a class of one or two as well as creating performance opportunities when your classroom does not have a built-in audience.

Purpose of the Text

The text is designed to develop the following long-term goals: communication skills, self-discipline, teamwork, and leadership. These elements are conveyed through subjects as diverse as storytelling, interpretation of poetry, readers theater, and acting. As the course instructor, you are the academic guide as well as the forensics coach and play director for your students. Set forth goals for yourself and your students this semester. A course that involves cocurricular activities such as a school play/program creates a special ministry opportunity for the teacher. Seek to be an example in these four areas—communication, self-discipline, teamwork, and leadership—when working with students in and out of class. They will learn as much from your example as they

This textbook was written by members of the faculty and staff of Bob Jones University. Standing for the "old-time-religion" and the absolute authority of the Bible since 1927, Bob Jones University is the world's leading Fundamentalist Christian university. The staff of the University is devoted to educating Christian men and women to be servants of Jesus Christ in all walks of life.

Providing unparalleled academic excellence, Bob Jones University prepares its students through its offering of over one hundred majors, while its fervent spiritual emphasis prepares their minds and hearts for service and devotion to the Lord Jesus Christ.

If you would like more information about the spiritual and academic opportunities available at Bob Jones University, please call
1-800-BJ-AND-ME (1-800-252-6363).
www.bju.edu

"The Line-Gang" by Robert Frost from *The Poetry of Robert Frost* edited by Edward Connery Lathem. Copyright 1916, ©1969 by Henry Holt and Co., copyright 1944 by Robert Frost. Reprinted by permission of Henry Holt and Company, LLC.
The White Cliffs by Alice D. Miller, copyright 1940 by Alice Duer Miller. Copyright © renewed 1967 by Denning Miller. Used by permission of Coward-McCann, Inc., a division of Penguin Putnam Inc.

NOTE:
The fact that materials produced by other publishers may be referred to in this volume does not constitute an endorsement by Bob Jones University Press of the content or theological position of materials produced by such publishers. The position of Bob Jones University Press, and of the University itself, is well known. Any references and ancillary materials are listed as an aid to the student or the teacher and in an attempt to maintain the accepted academic standards of the publishing industry.

PERFORMING LITERATURE: ORAL INTERPRETATION AND DRAMA STUDIES for Christian Schools® Teacher's Edition
Diana Tobbe Smith, M.A.

Contributor: Brock T. Miller, M.A.
Consultants: David Carroll Burke, M.A., Ph.D.
Corretta Johnson Grass, M.A.
Doris Fisher Harris, M.A.
Terri L. Koontz
William C. Moose, M.A.
Betty S. Panosian, M.A.
Laura S. Pratt, M.A.
Linda Pierce St. John, M.A.
Project Coordinator: Kathryn Martin

Editors: Melissa Vogdes Moore
Robert E. Grass
Book and Cover Design: Joseph Tyrpak
Composition: Carol Anne Ingalls
Jennifer Hearing
Photo Acquisition: David John Palmer
Joyce Gordon Landis
Cover Photo: Unusual Films

Produced in cooperation with the Bob Jones University School of Fine Arts
for Christian Schools is a registered trademark of Bob Jones University Press.

Project and Assignment Pages

The requirements for each major performance project are explained in phases of preparation, practice, and performance.

Dramatistic Analysis

A list of seven or eight questions helps the student evaluate the literature used in each project. Grade the student's written analysis based on quality of thought and thoroughness more than on mechanics.

Workshop Evaluations

Some projects recommend a workshop (graded rehearsal). A simple form is included when needed and should be completed in class.

Project Evaluations (Rubrics)

Because each project involves different requirements, features, and skills, each evaluation form is unique to its corresponding project. Write as many comments as possible during and immediately following each performance. Train the students to expect a

two- to three-minute lull between speeches and insist they wait quietly.

Teacher's Edition Features

The side margin includes a chapter introduction, outline, and goals, as well as specific lesson motivators, lesson objectives, and additional notes. Many chapters also include a project description and a discussion of the evaluation form for that project.

The bottom margin includes a lesson plan, a list of teaching materials that could serve as homework assignments,

CONTENTS

do from this book; undoubtedly even more.

Planning the Course

Performing Literature is designed to support a one- or two-semester course. If the teaching schedule is followed with a standard-sized class of fifteen to sixteen students, the course may be completed in one semester. With fewer students, more time may be given to the optional activities while still completing the material in half a school year.

However, if you wish to include the production of a school play as part of the study, a two-semester approach is advisable. One semester will not be adequate to incorporate play rehearsals and production-planning activities in class. If a one-semester course is your only possibility, plan to rehearse and prepare the play as an after-school cocurricular activity. Ideally, your rehearsal process would not begin until about one-third of the course is complete.

and alternative projects for the home school setting.

Side Margin Notes

Chapter Introduction

The introduction contains pertinent background or fundamental information.

Chapter Outline

Major sections are listed as Roman numerals with subsections under each. These major sections correspond to the topics listed in the lesson plan.

Chapter Goals

This box presents the essential concepts of the chapter.

Lesson Motivator

A clear purpose for each lesson is presented in the lesson motivator to facilitate preparing your lesson plan.

Lesson Objectives

The lesson objectives box gives behavioral objectives specific to that topic. The teacher is encouraged to teach with these objectives in mind.

Assessment

Participation in class discussions, quizzes, and oral presentations are common forms of assessment. Sample assessments are given in the first two chapters.

Additional Notes

These notes give additional information to enhance and clarify ideas presented in the student text.

Project Description

The project description allows you to preview the assignment. You as the

Your Challenge

This type of course has the potential to aid students in many ways. Requiring a high level of participation, it gets *everyone* involved—definitely a good habit to develop. Learning to communicate publicly can develop confidence balanced with dependence on the Lord. Performing literature can foster a lifelong love of good literature. Your challenge as a teacher is to wisely lead, to encourage, and to fairly evaluate each student.

THE CHALLENGE AHEAD

Perhaps you are taking this course in hopes of becoming a fine storyteller or actor. You may have even competed in a fine arts contest previously and wish to improve your skills. This book is designed to guide you toward those goals. You will examine the elements of a story and evaluate the philosophy of selections of literature. Theory and technique combine to instruct you in presenting narratives, poetry, stories, monologues, acting scenes, readers theater, radio broadcasts, biographies, and more. Each project includes "how-to" instructions. Since your progress will be clearly evident on each assignment, you should find this course very rewarding.

Even though improving interpretation and acting skills is a valuable and worthwhile pursuit, you will find many academic advantages resulting from this study that extend beyond the discipline of drama. Performing various types of literature improves comprehension of and appreciation for literature as a whole. Commun-

Henry V *by William Shakespeare (Bob Jones University Classic Players)*

teacher may override any requirements that do not suit your situation.

Bottom Margin Notes

Lesson Plan

The lesson plan table suggests some activities to amplify each section of the student text and to provide one or more means of assessment.

Lesson plan columns are described as follows.

LESSON DESCRIPTION—sections of the textbook and assessment to be taught. The first page of each section is also provided.

RECOMMENDED PRESENTATION—suggested teaching materials to present, designated by location (ST for student text and TE for teacher's edition).

PERFORMANCE PROJECTS/WRITTEN ASSIGNMENTS—activities and outside-of-class work, including improvisations, projects, and journal assignments.

Teaching Materials

A list of suggested materials is included to allow you to plan ahead for necessary items.

Discussion Questions

Possible discussion questions are included throughout the text.

Performer's Journal

Appendix A contains journal assignments for some

icating publicly improves poise and concentration. Practicing for a dramatic performance improves self-discipline. Storytelling involves outlining plot, which improves organizational skills. Presenting memorized and extemporaneous projects improves memorization skills greatly. Some projects even provide opportunity to develop teamwork skills. Though not an exhaustive list, these benefits show the many skills you can refine during this course of study.

What Is Expected of You in This Course?

Your primary obligation is to practice what you learn. Regardless of your talent or level of experience, you need to focus on applying knowledge gained through this textbook and your teacher's lessons each time you approach a performance project.

You will learn the following skills:

- Writing
    Creative/inventive—through activities such as improvisation and playwriting
    Critical—through self- and peer-performance evaluation as well as analysis of literature

- Comprehension
    Literal—What does it mean?
    Interpretive—How can I communicate the meaning?
    Appreciative—How does the meaning change me?
    Critical—How does the meaning influence society/philosophy?

- Performance skills
    Communication with the audience
    Interpretation
    Characterization—Who is this person?

- Acting
    Dramatic intentions—What does a "line" do?
    Ensemble chemistry—How do we become a team?

- Radio broadcasting
    Commercials
    Dramatic segments

- Production Concepts

Some of these areas may sound more exciting to you than others. However, the projects are designed to build your skills, increase your appreciation of literature, and introduce you to a variety of dramatic elements. Let the projects that seem less natural for you expand your horizons.

chapters. Writing brief paragraphs of self-evaluation and recording observations can increase learning retention and improve higher-level thinking skills.

Projects
Most of the projects in this text are related directly to refining acting skills. Improvisations and acting games that may be performed in class are labeled as activities.

Bible Study
Memory verses, biblical principles, and discussions are provided to aid you in making biblical application.

Home School
Many of the projects, assignments, and classroom activities are usable for home educators; however, some specific activities and suggestions are included that will help you tailor the program to your situation.

Quick Write
Quick Write activities give the students a break from the routine with short writing projects.

UNIT

Hamlet *by William Shakespeare (Bob Jones University Classic Players)*

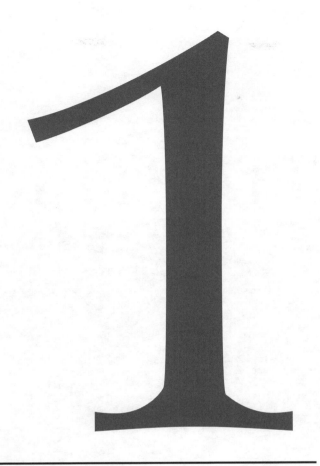

PREPARATION

To be, or not to be, that is the question:
Whether 'tis nobler in the mind to suffer
The slings and arrows of outrageous fortune,
Or to take arms against a sea of troubles,
And by opposing, end them.

Unit 1 presents many foundational concepts and therefore does not include any major performance projects. You will cover four chapters of textual material foundational to the rest of the course. Because of this theory emphasis, use of improvisations and acting games is strongly recommended during this first portion of the course.

Students shouldn't perceive that they have enrolled in a lecture course. Both the enthusiast and the timid wallflower need to be assured that this really is a performance course.

In subsequent units, the class activities and other small projects are woven into the text in preparation for the major project in each chapter.

Some students and parents may be skeptical about a drama class, favoring a more "academic" course. This unit may help you alleviate their concerns. You can assure them that this course is designed to refine the communication skills of Christian young people for the Lord's service, not to foster the careers of would-be Hollywood stars.

Chapter 1 Introduction

This chapter was designed to relate performance to the previous experiences of the students. You won't necessarily need to complete all suggested activities to be clear and effective. The numerous activities provide options for the teacher to tailor the course to specific needs, interests, and resources of the class.

Chapter 1 Outline

CHAPTER 1

Lesson Plan

Suggested homework is in **boldface.**

Lesson Description	Recommended Presentation	Performance Projects/ Written Assignments
Course introduction	Review class rules; describe expectations	
I. Everyday Life (p. 5) II. As We Grow (p. 9)	ST—Keyword Stories TE—Seven Ages Parodies; Read *Jungle Book* chapter; Using Good Sense; Scenarios for Evaluation	**TE—Assign "Create a Career" improvisation**
III. Formal Performance (p. 13)	TE—Message; Community Performances	
Assessment	Chapter quiz	Create a Career performance
Suggested teaching time: 5-6 class periods		

The Role of Drama

All the world's a stage
And all the men and women merely players.

Chapter 1 Goals

The student will be able to

1. Understand that real life has dramatic elements.
2. Understand that drama reflects real life.

Lesson Motivator

The rising popularity of docudramas and biography demonstrates a renewed awareness of the inherent drama of life. Not all heroes are named Prince Charming. Some are neighbors who rise to the occasion in an emergency. Some are parents. Some are teachers. Society as a whole is obviously fascinated with careers that include adventure or even danger. The number of books and television programs featuring police officers, detectives, lawyers, emergency room personnel, and the like prove that fact. We find the trials and tribulations of ordinary people interesting and often humorous because we can so easily relate to their dilemmas.

For students who will one day teach, preach, write, or even parent, seeing the drama in life will be a great benefit. Teachers and preachers (and other communicators such as lawyers) draw illustrations from everyday life to explain the ideas they seek to communicate. Writers—from journalists to novelists—do much the

Teaching Materials

- A copy of *The Jungle Book*
- Objects for Using Good Sense
- Blank paper to evaluate Create a Career

same, but in print. Since parents are the primary teachers of their children, they too must be able to evaluate action and real-life roles. Indeed, they must teach their children how to fill various roles such as student, peer leader, and, one day, parent.

Though brief, this section discussing drama in everyday life and in stages of development and growth should help you introduce these ideas to your students. Emphasize the importance of understanding drama as well as other academic disciplines in view of life as a whole.

OVERVIEW

Know—*Concepts*

Contexts of drama
 Daily activities
 Development from childhood to adulthood
 Formal performance
Formal performance shares many characteristics with daily experience.
Formal performance can be distinguished by its design elements.

Grow—*Interpretation Skills*

Mimicry
Role-playing

Show—*Performance*

Keyword stories

As You Like It by William Shakespeare (Bob Jones University Classic Players)

definition

Drama *refers to a theatrical production or a selection of literature intended for performance as well as life events marked by action and emotion.*

What do you think of when you hear the word **drama?** Do you think of last year's school play? Maybe televised "docu-dramas" come to mind—the real-life story of a Holocaust survivor or something similar. Maybe you even think of a classmate everyone describes as being "dramatic."

All of these things *do* represent elements of drama. But drama is something more, something beyond this list. The most famous English playwright of all time, William Shakespeare, often commented on drama as an integral part of life. In Shakespeare's play *As You Like It,* the wry commentator Jaques (JAY kweez) declares:

> *All the world's a stage*
> *And all the men and women merely players.*
> *They have their exits and their entrances*
> *And one man in his time plays many parts.*

This famous passage may help you grasp the concepts discussed in this first chapter. It is not enough for you to learn *how* to successfully perform a dramatic reading or comic duo-acting scene for a state competition. Make it your goal to

---

All the World's a Stage

Read the following *As You Like It* monologue to the class, suggesting each "age" through your interpretation. Don't be afraid of letting the monologue be humorous. Jaques is so melancholy that audiences generally do laugh at him (depending on the actor's interpretation). With this exercise, you can engage the students' minds and set a positive tone for the class.

All the world's a stage,
And all the men and women merely players;
They have their exits and their entrances;
And one man in his time plays many parts,
His acts being seven ages. At first the infant
Mewling and puking in the nurse's arms.
Then the whining schoolboy, with his satchel
And shining morning face, creeping like snail
Unwillingly to school. And then the lover,
Sighing like furnace, with a woeful ballad
Made to his mistress' eyebrow. Then a soldier,
Full of strange oaths, and bearded like the pard [leopard],

Jealous in honour, sudden and quick in quarrel,
Seeking the bubble reputation
Even in the cannon's mouth. And then the justice,
In fair round belly with good capon lined,
With eyes severe, and beard of formal cut,
Full of wise saws and modern instances;
And so he plays his part. The sixth age shifts
Into the lean and slippered pantaloon,
With spectacles on nose and pouch on side,
His youthful hose, well saved, a world too wide
For his shrunk shank; and his big manly voice,

understand what the material means and why it matters. Even if you don't take first place in competitions after taking this course, you should gain something not dependent upon talent or experience: an understanding of dramatic performance and—more importantly—the drama called life.

EVERYDAY LIFE

Drama is all around us—in the literature we read, in events and objects we observe, and in how we live and grow. It is as much a part of our daily activities as eating or sleeping. Consider the following examples.

Reading: A Writer-to-Reader Experience

Literature is one avenue by which we experience drama. Carefully read the passage below, imagining yourself in the Indian jungle on a moonlit night.

Father Wolf listened, and below in the valley that ran down to a little river he heard the dry, angry, snarly, singsong whine of a tiger who has caught nothing and does not care if all the jungle knows it. . . .

Then there was a howl—an untigerish howl—from Shere Khan.

"He has missed," said Mother Wolf. "What is it?" . . .

Directly in front of him, holding on by a low branch, stood a naked brown baby who could just walk—as soft and as dimpled a little atom as ever came to a wolf's cave at night. He looked up into Father Wolf's face, and laughed.

"Is that a man's cub?" said Mother Wolf. "I have never seen one. Bring it here. . . . Now, was there ever a wolf that could boast of a man's cub among her children?"

"I have heard now and again of such a thing, but never in our Pack or in my time," said Father Wolf. "He is altogether without hair, and I could kill him with a touch of my foot. But see, he looks up and is not afraid."

The moonlight was blocked out of the mouth of the cave, for Shere Khan's great

square head and shoulders were thrust into the entrance. Tabaqui, behind him, was squeaking: "My lord, my lord, it went in here!"

"Shere Khan does us great honor," said Father Wolf, but his eyes were very angry. "What does Shere Khan need?"

"My quarry. A man's cub went this way," said Shere Khan. "Its parents have run off. Give it to me." . . .

THE ROLE OF DRAMA 5

Many students mistakenly believe that a good dramatic reading is one that makes people cry. This idea is not necessarily true and may lead to choosing weak literature.

Furthermore, a good humorous interpretation piece does not necessarily have to make the audience roll in the aisles. Steer your students away from choosing "skit" material for comic duo scenes or humorous interpretation. Skits are appropriate in settings such as youth group meetings or summer camp, but for study in this class or for performance in a fine arts competition, more challenging material is suggested. See Appendix F for examples of good literature for dramatic or humorous interpretation categories. Choose well-known playwrights or well-known literature for material in the duo-acting category.

The Jungle Book

Consider reading to the students a chapter of Kipling's *The Jungle Book* or inviting a guest storyteller to perform in class.

Enjoying Literature

"Some books are to be tasted, others to be swallowed, and some few to be chewed and digested."

—Francis Bacon

Turning again toward childish treble, pipes
And whistles in his sound. Last scene of all,
That ends this strange eventful history,
Is second childishness and mere oblivion,
Sans [without] teeth, sans eyes, sans taste,
  sans everything.

—*As You Like It*, Act II, Scene 7

Seven Ages Parodies

Have the students form two teams. Each team will invent and perform its own "ages." A possible choice would be the seven

ages of teenagers (begin with the excited thirteen-year-old and conclude with the sophisticated nineteen-year-old). Encourage creativity. Students could also do this activity independently.

Everyday Life/As We Grow

God's Design in Daily Activities

Ask one of your students to read Ecclesiastes 3:1-14 aloud. Explain to your students that God has a sovereign design behind every activity of our lives, including drama. (There are many Bible reading activities in which it is recommended that you ask a student to read aloud. Encourage the

"The Wolves are a free people," said Father Wolf. "They take orders from the Head of the Pack, and not from any striped cattle-killer. The man's cub is ours—to kill if we choose." . . .

The tiger's roar filled the cave with thunder. Mother Wolf shook herself clear of the cubs and sprang forward, her eyes, like two green moons in the darkness, facing the blazing eyes of Shere Khan.

"And it is I, Raksha . . . who answers. The man's cub is mine, Lungri—mine to me! He shall not be killed. He shall live to run with the Pack and to hunt with the Pack; and in the end, look you, hunter of little naked cubs—frog-eater—fish-killer—he shall hunt thee! . . . Go!" . . .

Father Wolf looked on amazed. He had almost forgotten the days when Mother Wolf ran with the pack . . .

Shere Khan might have faced Father Wolf, but he could not stand up against Mother Wolf, for he knew that where he was she had all the advantage of the ground, and would fight to the death. So he backed out of the cave mouth growling, and when he was clear he shouted, "Each dog barks in his own yard! We will see what the Pack will say to this fostering of man-cubs. The cub is mine, and to my teeth he will come in the end, O bush-tailed thieves!"

Mother Wolf threw herself down panting among the cubs, and Father Wolf said to her gravely: "Shere Khan speaks this much truth. The cub must be shown to the Pack. Wilt thou still keep him, Mother?"

"Keep him!" she gasped. . . . "Assuredly I will keep him. Lie still, little frog. O thou Mowgli—for Mowgli the Frog I will call thee—the time will come when thou wilt hunt Shere Khan as he has hunted thee."

—Rudyard Kipling, *The Jungle Book*

You, the reader, may have found yourself tensing when Shere Khan blotted out the moonlight in the mouth of the cave. You may have shared in Father Wolf's admiration for Mother Wolf, defending the "man's cub."

Evidenced by the vast amount of literature and action features depicting far-off lands, people, and animals, adventure stories are very popular. In *The Jungle Book* the reader journeys to the mysterious and wonderful jungle world that lives in the pages of Kipling's epic tale.

The adventure of literature introduces us to experiences that we wouldn't ever have otherwise. Also, in literature we see how the protagonist's (main character's) actions lead to certain consequences. We see his reactions to his opponent, the antagonist. Consider the wisdom of the following statement: "Learn from experience—preferably other people's."

The Main Characters

- *Protagonist:* the main character in a play
- *Antagonist:* the major opponent of the main character

Literature helps us learn. In the comfort of an overstuffed chair, we can safely read of savage animals, daring stunts such as tightrope walking over the Niagara River, criminal court cases, and many other events. We benefit from the lessons learned by the protagonist.

---

students to read with sufficient volume and dynamic emphasis. Reading the Bible aloud well is not particularly easy, and these activities can provide good practice for your students.)

Choices, Choices

Yes, the protagonist's actions do lead to certain consequences. Ask your students to give examples of Bible characters who experienced positive or negative consequences as a result of certain actions or choices they made. (*Answers may include Noah, Abraham, Joseph, Caleb, David, Solomon, Nehemiah, and Daniel—positive; Adam, Esau, Achan, Samson, Saul, David, Solomon, Jonah—negative.*)

Ask one of your students to read I Corinthians 10:1-12 aloud. Explain to the students that the Lord wants us to learn from the examples of those who have gone before us.

Observing: A Firsthand Experience

Of course, reading is not our only means of learning. We all employ our senses to learn about the world around us. We analyze sensory details to understand people, places, and events. In the following humorous poem, what important *idea* do the six men not "see"?

It was six men of Indostan
To learning much inclined,
Who went to see the Elephant
Though all of them were blind,
That each by observation
Might satisfy his mind.

The First approached the Elephant
And, happening to fall
Against his broad and sturdy side,
At once began to bawl:
"God bless me, but the Elephant
Is very like a wall!"

The Second, feeling the tusk,
Cried, "Ho! what have we here
So very round and smooth and sharp?
To me 'tis very clear
This wonder of an Elephant
Is very like a spear!"

The Third approached the animal
And, happening to take
The squirming trunk within his hands,
Thus boldly up he spake:
"I see," quoth he, "The Elephant
Is very like a snake!"

The Fourth reached out an eager hand,
And felt about the knee:
"What most the wondrous beast is like
Is very plain," quoth he;
"'Tis clear enough the Elephant
Is very like a tree!"

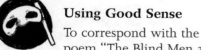

Using Good Sense

To correspond with the poem "The Blind Men and the Elephant," have students practice using their senses without the aid of sight. Bring in interesting tactile objects and hide each in a box or brown bag. Samples might include a seashell, Silly Putty, an open container of pudding or gelatin, marbles, Gummy Bears, and jacks. Have several or all students take a turn blindly reaching into the bag to touch a mystery item. Have the student give a twenty- to thirty-second impromptu pantomime, to convey what he thinks the object is. Then reveal what was in the bag.

The Fifth, who chanced to touch the ear,
Said, "Even the blindest man
Can tell what this resembles most;
Deny the fact who can:
This marvel of an elephant
Is very like a fan!"

The Sixth no sooner had begun
About the beast to grope
Than, seizing on the swinging tail
That fell within his scope,
"I see," quoth he, "the Elephant
Is very like a rope!"

And so these men of
*   Indostan*
Disputed loud and long,
Each in his own opinion
Exceeding stiff and strong.
Though each was partly in the right,
They all were in the wrong!

—John Godfrey Saxe, "The Blind Men and the Elephant"

Despite poetic description, these men could not grasp or convey the big picture. They were all missing something. Write below how these men might have formed a clearer picture of the elephant.

> *They could have better understood by communicating with each other, by using other senses (elephants smell different from walls and spears!), and especially by more thoroughly investigating the elephant.*

We often employ multiple senses to fully comprehend and retain ideas. Consequently, preschool and elementary-school children listen to songs about everything from the alphabet to multiplication tables, as well as use movement while singing songs such as "Head and shoulders, knees and toes, knees and toes, knees and toes . . ."

At the high-school level, teachers may use overhead transparencies, slides, or computer aids to convey subordination of ideas and organization. They may show charts, graphs, and video clips. Literature class, among other classes, often involves students reading aloud to one another. Why? Because hearing a boy on the fourth row, even if he is rather embarrassed, reading the part of Romeo while a girl on the second row blushes through Juliet's lines provides more clarity and understanding of the story than a silent reading might.

8   CHAPTER 1

Reading Aloud: A Reader-to-Hearer Experience

And so we read aloud. Essentially, that is the purpose of this book: reading aloud. The differences among the specific activities of storytelling, interpretation, readers theater, acting, and other theater arts are only in technique or environment. All of these activities hold in common the act of orally presenting words from a printed page. Sometimes we perform the actions of the story and omit the spoken word (pantomime); at other times we use only the dialogue combined with action, allowing the scenery and movement to fill in the description (play-acting). But even then we have the same goal as the oral reader—bringing drama to life.

Read the following verse (James 3:1) silently:

> *My brethren, be not many masters, knowing that we shall receive the greater condemnation.*

Now read it aloud, emphasizing the words in all capital letters and pausing where marked.

> *My brethren, BE not many / MASTERS, knowing that WE SHALL RECEIVE the greater CONDEMNATION.*

When first reading the verse silently, we may get the impression that we should avoid being something called "many masters." Obviously that seems confusing or even preposterous. However, when a skilled and thoughtful reader emphasizes the keywords and pauses briefly before "masters," it is suddenly clear that not many people should take the office of "master" or what we would call a leadership role. The justification given for the instruction now makes sense too—since a leader has extra responsibility, he or she has extra accountability before God.

AS WE GROW

Our performance experiences begin when we gasp our first dramatic breath and continue until we sigh our last.

Childhood

Picture a toddler, precariously balanced on the front half of his small chubby feet and his tall mother behind saying, "Follow Daddy." Immediately the child echoes, "Fa-whoa datty." The toddler's **mimicry**—imitating his mother's words and his father's actions—was natural.

Mimicry is a primary means of learning. A child learns his native tongue within a few short years without formal training through mimicry. Mimicry is also a technique used by actors to create action and characters on stage. It is the means by which we grasp vocal intonations such as sarcasm and character-specific manners such as diction, dialect, and gestures. These skills will be discussed more thoroughly in future chapters.

*D*efinition

Mimicry is the act of imitating or copying the voice or actions of another.

The Bible Out Loud

Encourage your students to read the Bible aloud as they have their daily devotional time. This will help to clear away mental distractions as well as aid in gaining a clearer understanding of the message. This also applies when reading other literature, such as Shakespeare or Milton.

Phrasing Scripture

Another verse that is often phrased incorrectly is Luke 2:16: "And they CAME with HASTE, / and found MARY, / and JOSEPH, / and the BABE / LYING in a MANGER." (As if Mary, Joseph, and baby Jesus are *all* lying in the manger.) Who is lying in the manger? (baby Jesus) The message is clearer when read: "And they CAME with HASTE, / and found MARY, and JOSEPH, // and the BABE LYING in a MANGER."

Mime, Pantomime, and Mimicry

Mimicry is the act of imitating or copying. Though the term *mimicry* is never applied directly to an acting form, two related words are used: *mime* and *pantomime*. The *American Heritage Dictionary* uses these words interchangeably, but some scholars make a small distinction. They use the word *pantomime* to refer to any use of bodily action to communicate silently (like charades). The word *mime* is then reserved for artistic, rehearsed performance by a costumed mime. The terms *mime* and *pantomime* will be used throughout the book with these distinctions.

Keyword Stories

You may want to organize this activity in cooperation with an elementary teacher in your school (or school system) or another home schooling family. If this is not feasible, perhaps give extra credit (homework points) to any student with enough initiative to try the project with neighborhood or Sunday school children.

definition

Role-play, simply put, means to act out a role.

In addition to mimicry, children enact roles **(role-play)**. Jill, about two and a half at the time, seemed quite intent as she pushed a toy shopping cart around and around the room, stopping periodically to comfort or discipline her "pet" giraffe, who was propped up in the child seat of the cart.

"What are you doing, Jill?" asked an observer.
"Takin' da baby to da store."
She then spoke encouragingly to her giraffe about purchasing Oreo cookies.

What might you guess about this little girl's mom, based on this scenario? Her mom probably takes her grocery shopping and sometimes even buys cookies for a treat.

Both mimicry and role-playing (even in the case of make-believe) are natural, everyday versions of dramatic performance. When you and your elementary-school friends played "house" or "school" or "office," you were using mimicry and role-playing.

Keyword Stories

With younger siblings, neighborhood children, or perhaps children in your church, read or tell a simple story such as the biblical account of Jonah. To better understand mimicry, have the children perform a certain action, word, or sound every time they hear a particular *keyword*. Ideally, write out or practice telling the story, intentionally repeating the keywords frequently.

Example: Each time you say "Jonah," the children echo, "Listen, Jonah, listen" and when you mention the sea, they could imitate the swishing sound of the water. For "Joppa," have the boys shout, "Wrong way, Jonah" and for the wind, have the girls blow a sustained "Whoosh."

Have the children listen to the story and then assign parts. Let them act out the parts of the story as you read or tell it a second time. If you do not have access to a group of children aged four to seven, your peers can perform these tasks instead. Just use your imagination!

When the story is finished, the children should be receptive to a clear lesson from Jonah's life. When you discuss the importance of obedience, the audience has a clear illustration with which to relate.

Scenarios for Evaluation

Read the following scenarios to the class and ask them to identify the type of situation described. They may choose from mimicry, role-playing, social roles, and positive or negative stereotypes.

1. An ad campaign for mayor proclaims Ernest Schaub as "a candidate who represents courage and defense of liberty—one who has faithfully served his community as a lawyer and as a search and rescue volunteer." (*best answers: social role or positive stereotype*)

2. At lunch, Peter entertains everyone at the table with an impersonation of the morning's guest speaker, a local dietician. (*best answer: mimicry*)

3. "I'm not surprised that Rusty had a fender-bender, since he's a teenager." (*best answer: negative stereotype*)

4. Children playing "office" or "school" together. (*best answer: role-playing*)

Preparing to tell the story

1. What story will you tell? _____

2. What is the theme or lesson? _____

   _____

3. List the keywords (characters, places, actions, or ideas) you will repeat and assign an action or chant for the children to perform each time you say that word.

   _____   _____

   _____   _____

   _____   _____

   _____   _____

Reviewing the results

4. How did the children respond to your instructions? _____

   _____

5. What word/action assignments worked well? _____

   _____

6. What word/action assignments would you change if you told this story again?

   _____

   _____

Adulthood

If it seems that acting is nothing more than childhood games, consider the many ways adults act.

Social Roles

The second Sunday in May brings a special activity to Community Bible Church. The pastor begins with his announcements. Then with a broad smile he mentions, "This is a very special day." He continues by asking every mother in the room to stand. The ushers stroll about, distributing carnations and bookmarks to each mother present. The pastor asks those with certain numbers of children and/or grandchildren to remain standing until one lady can be honored for having

THE ROLE OF DRAMA 11

Create a Career

Assign students to prepare an improvisation outside of class time. Each student should think of a career that he can portray in two to three minutes. He should practice a precise pantomime of the daily activities of this employee character. The student should avoid oversimplifying or performing stereotypical actions such as a doctor listening to someone's heart. You may want to restrict their selection away from certain careers such as "doctor" and "teacher." Encourage creativity. Students should rehearse their pantomime about eight times. This can be counted as a quiz grade.

Tell students to view this assignment as a performance opportunity, not just a game of charades. Speed and generalizations are appropriate for a game, but only attention to detail will improve their performance skills.

Evaluate each student on a scale of one to five in the following areas:

1. Actions were deliberate and carefully planned.
2. Actions were realistic, not melodramatic.
3. Actions were complete—no hesitancy or abruptness.
4. Pantomime was believable.

As time permits, supply the class with the following sample descriptions, contrasting a weak plan and a strong plan for this activity.

When I Grow Up . . .

It is fascinating to ask young children what they want to be when they grow up. Most boys want to be policemen, firefighters, soldiers, or even garbage men, while many girls aspire to be mothers, nurses, teachers, or even truck drivers. In general, children are attracted to what is introduced to their sphere of knowledge and experience. Rarely do children desire to be college professors, lawyers, or chemists, unless, of course, their parents are in one of these professions.

Little boys are generally attracted to action, adventure, and noise. They don't view higher education, law, or chemistry as exciting professions.

Stereotypes

The text emphasizes that negative stereotypes should be avoided because generalities are often unfair and inaccurate. Positive stereotypes can be harmful when overgeneralization occurs. Making assumptions can make one vulnerable to those who are not what they seem to be. For example, children often associate the word *stranger* with a person who seems scary, not merely a person they don't know. Be sure students understand that the text is encouraging them to support positive associations with various roles but not to naively trust someone based on a few details. They must always be "wise as serpents."

the most children and another for having the most grandchildren. Thus, one small church honors a segment of its population for their hard work that often goes almost unnoticed. These women have filled or enacted a **social role,** as we all do.

 definition

*A **social role** is a part enacted in everyday life.*

***Stereotypes** are conventional views of groups.*

Right now, you play the role of high-school student and perhaps any number of other roles, such as soccer player or student body officer. Perhaps you have a part-time job in which you are a baby sitter or a grocery store clerk. These are all social roles.

Many of the decisions we make concerning a career stem from our perception of social roles. Liam, a child in Janiece's toddler Sunday school class, aspires to be a "fie-weh-fie-tuh" (firefighter). It doesn't matter what the lesson is about—if Liam hears a siren in the street, his head snaps in the direction of the sound. The fire truck's color, its urgent speed, the siren's power to divide traffic like the parting of the Red Sea, and the lure of adventure thrill Liam to the limits of his three-year-old experience.

Now that you are approaching adulthood and independence, you've no doubt changed your view of careers. Academic experience over the last decade has unlocked many doors of opportunity to you. The Introduction to Art course you took last year may have revealed ability in calligraphy or three-dimensional art design. An after-school job may have confirmed your interest in business or sales. In college or technical training, you will likely find your niche, even if it isn't apparent now.

Social Expectations

As you take on a role, certain behaviors will be expected of you. Some may argue that social expectations are merely **stereotypes.** Stereotypes may be positive or negative. Some positive stereotypes equate law officers with justice and courage, physicians with compassion, business workers with professionalism, and administrators with respectability. Negative stereotypes may falsely associate politicians with mudslinging, automotive dealers with deceit, and road-crew workers with laziness.

These negative stereotypes are harmful because they are sweeping generalizations that can set bad precedents. Human nature naturally tends to fulfill what is expected. If a parent repeatedly comments that his son is lazy and will amount to nothing in life, that young man is a candidate for depression and apathy. Clearly harmful, negative stereotypes should be rejected wholeheartedly.

 12 CHAPTER 1

Example of a weak improvisation

Career: Flight Attendant

Action: Demonstrate the safety instructions routine.

Example of a strong improvisation

Career: Flight Attendant

Action: Be seated in a chair directly facing the audience. Mime removing a seat belt and directing "passengers" to the front exit. Straighten up the cabin, looking for litter, pillows, and so on.

Greet oncoming passengers. Walk down the aisle, shutting overhead compartments and checking for safety belts. Bring a magazine to a passenger. Direct someone to the lavatory. Demonstrate the safety instructions.

Obviously, the second example is far more thorough. It is also less obvious. Encourage the students to be thorough in planning their improvisations so that they are precise. Also, encourage them to avoid oversimplifying their career, making it too easy for their classmates

to guess, as would be the case for the first example.

Do You Stereotype?

Have one of your students read Romans 12:9-10 aloud. Remind the students that we must love our Christian brethren sincerely. (Dissimulation could also be translated "hypocrisy.") Warn your students that Christians can participate in negative stereotyping just as easily as non-Christians participate in it. Ask the

On the other hand, positive stereotypes do overlap with true social expectations. Consider the following story:

Jessie's dad was a U.S. Army Reservist. Practically speaking, that meant he worked a civilian job most of the time and worked for the army only some weekends and two weeks in the summer. Jessie never went to a military base until she was eleven years old. Large posters hanging from the ceiling of the commissary caught Jessie's attention. They pictured a serviceman in uniform with an attractive woman and a small boy. The picture seemed very patriotic.

AMERICAN PRIDE

Support Our Troops

As her parents left the store, Jessie noticed two different women, one of whom was noticeably pregnant. Two teenage boys were loading their groceries for them. Though Jessie had seen "bag boys" at the store back home, they had never been this helpful, or neat in appearance, or courteous. Like scouts, these commissary workers nodded politely and said, "Yes, ma'am," and "No, ma'am."

The next time Jessie went to the grocery store with her mom that summer, she wished those boys tossing their food into bags could have seen the guys at the commissary. Maybe they would bag groceries differently.

It may be stereotypical to say that scouts and soldiers are noble, brave, and courteous, but this attitude is edifying. Since it emphasizes positive characteristics such as honor, respect, and service, such a stereotype serves as a model for ideal behavior.

FORMAL PERFORMANCE

Picture the following scenario: A young actor enters, dressed all in black. The barren stage features only a couple of black wooden boxes. Tipping his chin down slightly and lowering his brow, the actor glowers at the audience, skulking forward to a crouched position near the front of the stage, mere inches from the first row of the audience.

In a low, resonant voice, he begins to unfold his tale. As he speaks, every muscle in his body seems to respond to each new idea and emotion.

Drama
Everyday Life
• Childhood: mimicry and role-playing
• Adulthood: social roles and social expectations
Formal Performance
• Conceptualizing
• Planning
• Structure

Lesson Motivator

This section is by no means an exhaustive explanation of formal performance. Its main purpose is to compare and contrast formal interpretation and acting with the dramatic elements found in everyday life. Of course, there are various shared qualities as well as distinctions.

Lesson Objectives

The student will be able to

1. Discuss the characteristics of drama.

2. Recognize the distinctive characteristics of formal performance.

Sample Assessments

The student will

1. Evaluate a selection of literature, identifying and classifying each element of drama identified in the text.

2. Describe which of those elements are characteristic of real life and which are exclusive to drama.

Use Your Imagination

Why the barren stage, simple costume, and ordinary boxes? The actor wants the audience to concentrate on the literature so that images are created in their minds. Storytellers often keep performances very simple in order to highlight the literature.

students to name some ways in which negative stereotyping is practiced in their environment. (*Possible answers include teachers are slave drivers; preachers are boring; cheerleaders are snobs; principals are heartless; junior-high students are immature, and so on.*)

Sovereign Design

When telling a friend about an event that occurred earlier that day or week, one might impersonate the voices or mannerisms of each person in the narrative.

However, this task is seldom if ever rehearsed or even planned ahead of time. The same could be said of many other occurrences of drama in everyday life. Formal performance, however, is always planned and rehearsed. The planning results in set design, lighting, and so on. The rehearsing results in blocking (stage positions and movement) and interpretation on the part of the actors. The text refers to this entire effect as *design*.

For the Christian, creation and all of history reflect God's design. Man fills his role, acting within the framework of God's design. Jonathan Edwards said, "It was particularly affecting to me to think that the earth remained the same through all these changes upon the surface; the same spots of ground, the same mountains and valleys where those things were done, remaining just as they were, though the actors ceased." The drama of life does have design, though in a different way. The actor

Set Design

The young actor used the barren stage, simple costume, and ordinary boxes because he had designed his performance in that way. He could have adorned his stage with rustic tables and benches and dressed in coat and mail while holding a sword and shield.

Worldview

This topic will be developed in much greater detail in Chapter 3. If time permits, you may wish to begin developing the discernment skills of your students. Emphasize the following ideas to the students.

1. A worldview (viewpoint) is a filtering lens for viewing reality, and the only proper lens for the Christian is the Word of God.

2. Performing a story or play with the wrong philosophy may have tragic results, since explanations and disclaimers are difficult to tack on to an evening of entertainment. In contrast, the same story or play may be appropriate reading in the framework of a Christian educational environment, where needed explanation may be given.

To Communicate or Not to Communicate

Many communication experts believe that a person cannot *not* communicate; consequently, he is constantly communicating, whether he

---

Now Grendel came, from his crags of mist
Across the moor; he was curst of God.
The murderous prowler meant to surprise
In the high-built hall his human prey.
He stalked 'neath the clouds, till steep before him
The home of revelry rose in his path,
The gold-hall of heroes, the gaily adorned. . . .
     The door gave way,
Though fastened with bolts, when his fist fell on it. . . .
     Then forward he hastened,
Sprang at the hero, and seized him at rest;
Fiercely clutching him with fiendish claw.

 —Beowulf

Snarling and jeering movements, in addition to the actor's vocal characterization, dramatic pauses, and intensity hold the audience spellbound from the opening lines to the last.

Formal performance shares many characteristics with the drama of real life, but it is distinct in that it possesses *design*. This design includes conceptualizing and planning as well as structure, such as the script.

Shared Characteristics

Formal performance has several elements that overlap with real-life role-playing, but these elements are more refined in formal performance. These shared characteristics include philosophy, message, audience, and time frame.

> ### Shared Characteristics
> - Philosophy: worldview that determines overall production
> - Message: content of the literature
> - Audience: specifically chosen beforehand
> - Time frame: as it occurs

Philosophy

You don't need to take a philosophy course to have a life philosophy. In fact, your life philosophy, or belief system, begins to develop before you even start kindergarten. What you believe determines how you view the world and carries over into how you behave.

definition

Worldview is a philosophical viewpoint—the lens through which life is viewed.

Actions result from choices, and choices stem from your basic **worldview.** Some actions seem rote. Perhaps you would argue that you brush your teeth or walk your dog out of habit alone, but even these little things you do each day reflect your worldview or philosophy of life.

From brushing your teeth to applying for college or writing a speech for an important event, choices you make

14 CHAPTER 1

---

anticipates a cue, but man walks by faith (Hab. 2:4; Rom. 1:17; II Cor. 5:7; Gal. 3:11; Heb. 10:38). The stage set must be constructed for each production, but God's brilliant design has magnificently served as a backdrop to all of history. The play's cast and crew answer to a director, but mankind answers to God, the all wise.

Remind students of the security they may find in God's sovereign power. Unlike a human director, nothing takes Him by surprise, and no detail escapes His eye.

PRESENTATION

Formal Performance

Perspectives

Discuss Ellen's faulty viewpoint. Whom does the Bible command to care for widows and fatherless minors according to James 1:27? (Christians ["Pure religion . . ."]) How

should a man gain his daily bread? (*Gen. 3:19 instructs man to get bread through his own work [labor] and even before the fall of man, Adam and Eve had a job—keeping the garden and overseeing the animals. [Gen. 2:15]*) You could also discuss other faulty viewpoints. What biblical principles are violated by physician-assisted suicide? (*Refer to Gen. 2:7—God gave man a soul with the breath of life, setting man apart from the rest of creation. Also, He formed man in His own image [Gen. 1:27]. Of course, "Thou shalt not kill"*

each day reflect your personal philosophy. If you go to bed without brushing your teeth, you make a statement, albeit a minor one, about your response to I Corinthians 6:19, which teaches:

> *What? know ye not that your body is the temple of the Holy Ghost which is in you, which ye have of God, and ye are not your own?*

In other areas of life, ask yourself: To what causes do I donate money or time? Once I'm eighteen, how will I vote? Will I vote?

Your definition of a term varies based on personal philosophy. Compassion to Lydia may mean nurturing baby birds fallen from a nest or visiting a terminally ill person to bring encouragement. To Ellen, the public welfare system represents compassion.

Christians view the world in light of God's Word, whereas others depend on human knowledge as a reference point for their philosophy. This subject of philosophy will be discussed more thoroughly in Chapter 2.

Message

Tightly intertwined with philosophy, the message outflows from the communicator, whether speaker, writer, or performer. **Message,** simply put, is what is communicated. Ideally, the message is received and understood as the communicator intends.

Your friend Blake calls to say he just got two tickets to your favorite team's championship game. Your pulse races as you contemplate attending. How do you communicate the message of your gratitude and excitement? Do you shriek into the phone; wait in breathless silence; or say with a sneer, "Wait till my little sister finds out—"? What if Blake sent an e-mail? Maybe you would create an emphatic reply such as this:

Go Pioneers!!!!   No Kidding???   *This is grrreat!*

If he told you on the way into the school gym, you might high-five or (try to) dunk a basketball to express your enthusiasm.

Definition

Message refers to content—the ideas and feelings being conveyed.

likes it or not. Whether someone is talking, not talking, yawning, laughing, crying, sneering, sleeping, concentrating, nodding, whispering, yelling, singing, whistling, humming, or almost anything else, communication is taking place. Of course, this idea can be carried to an absurd level, but most activities of life send a message to which someone will assign a meaning.

Emotion Versus Idea

Different situations call for different ways to communicate your emotions and ideas. In literature and drama, the message may emphasize one of these over the other. Evaluate the following samples, determining whether the main message conveys an *emotion* or an *idea.* Explain your answer.

[Ex. 20:13] is the sixth commandment. Many other passages further support this truth.)

Message

Discussion topic: Why are sermons sometimes called "messages"? Consider the "messages" to the churches, recorded in Revelation 2 and 3. What parallels exist between a preacher's message and these messages? Prompt students to evaluate areas such as purpose and content.

Purpose: Both groups of messages serve to convey truth about God and His gospel (doctrine, reproof, correction, and instruction in righteousness).

Content: Both feature facts but include an appropriate amount of emotional content. (Fact—"Thou art neither cold nor hot" Rev. 3:15; Feeling—"So then because thou art lukewarm . . . I will spue thee out of my mouth" [literally—your behavior makes me sick] Rev. 3:16). Not only do these parallels explain calling sermons messages, but

they also show how these Bible messages are models for communicating. A good message of any sort needs an important purpose and usually balances facts with emotional content. In Revelation 3, the facts could have been presented as (1) you lack zeal in your Christianity and (2) this displeases God. However, God chose to share His heart with His audience. Consequently, the facts are clearer and the rebuke is strengthened.

> *Blessed is the man that walketh not in the counsel of the ungodly, nor standeth in the way of sinners, nor sitteth in the seat of the scornful. But his delight is in the law of the Lord; and in his law doth he meditate day and night. And he shall be like a tree planted by the rivers of water, that bringeth forth his fruit in his season; his leaf also shall not wither; and whatsoever he doeth shall prosper. (Psalm 1:1-3)*

1. Is the main message an emotion or an idea? Pick one. Why?

   Idea. Though very descriptive, the psalmist is revealing a fact, a cause-effect relationship between a man and his level of prosperity. If he rejects evil (verse 1) and delights in God's law (verse 2), God will bless him (verse 3).

> *As the hart panteth after the water brooks, so panteth my soul after thee, O God. My soul thirsteth for God, for the living God: when shall I come and appear before God? My tears have been my meat day and night, while they continually say unto me, Where is thy God? (Psalm 42:1-3)*

2. Is the main message an emotion or an idea? Pick one. Why?

   Emotion. The fact the psalmist wished to convey might be summarized, "My need of God is so apparent, I constantly seek Him and desire to commune with Him." The feelings he is experiencing surround this fact, expressed through simile ("as the hart panteth . . ."), synecdoche, or a symbolic use of a part for the whole ("meat" for "sustenance"), and so on. Note: Students do not need to specify the literary terms; a description of the ideas is acceptable.

Whether emphasizing emotions or ideas or balancing both, formal performance has a specific message. Before you perform a selection or even practice it, you need to determine what that specific message is. How can you communicate it if you do not understand it yourself? Don't be a performer who aims at the vague or unspecific, for as someone once said, "If you aim at nothing, you will surely hit it."

Audience

Communication requires an **audience**—a receiver of the message. If communication is effective, the audience understands what the communicator thinks and feels; whether the audience holds the same opinion is another matter.

In formal performance, the message often seeks to sway the audience to the viewpoint of the author or performer. The message may be quite effective due to the diversity of tools employed. These tools include empathy, humor, memorability, and interest. Though these tools will be discussed more thoroughly in future chapters, as you begin reading literature to choose for performance, be aware of these qualities and their persuasiveness.

A message is geared to a **target audience.** For example, a drama about the prodigal son may target its message specifically to Christians who have walked away from fellowship with God, or perhaps to religious people who are prideful and unforgiving toward an erring brother. The focus will increase the effectiveness either way.

Time Frame

Every telling of a story, reading of a poem, and performance of a dramatic script occurs during a limited period of time. When you read *Jane Eyre* or *A Tale of Two Cities*, you can stop at any moment, insert a bookmark, lay the book down, and go for a walk or pop some popcorn. You may come back in ten minutes or ten days, and the book will still be there. You might even reread part of it. Not so with a play. If you get up and leave during a play, you miss the event. For that matter, if you fall asleep after supper and don't leave in time to arrive when the play begins, you miss it. Drama is a live event with clear implications for the audience. In future chapters we will look at how live performance influences acting and producing.

The Distinctive Characteristic: Design

Formal performance sets itself apart from any drama in day-to-day living because formal performance possesses **design.**

Usually the playwright is the first to work on a play. He organizes and researches as needed and writes and revises the play script. This script will provide a framework for future productions. He must understand the setting, characters, and plot to successfully develop his story. A World War II play set in Iceland during the 1800s wouldn't work, would it?

Of course the director must have a vision for the production as a whole. He studies the playwright's work and related materials. He learns about the time period and culture depicted. Once he has a mental picture of how the play should be produced, he meets with designers and conveys that vision to them.

definition

*The **audience** receives the message.*

*The **target audience** is the specific person or group for whom the message is intended.*

***Design** means that study, planning, and artistry are intentional components of the product.*

Process or Event

Refer to Chapter 1 in *Sound Speech: Public Speaking and Communication Studies* for Christian Schools (BJU Press). Communication is described as "a process, not an event." Here, performance is defined not as an entity but an event. Students may see this as contradictory. While we communicate through various means each day, a drama or even the telling of a story occurs in a span of time. Performances do have a beginning and an end. They cannot be "paused" like a video or "put down" and later "picked up and reread" like a book.

THE ROLE OF DRAMA 17

An Excellent Work of Art

Ask one of your students to read Exodus 31:1-11 aloud. Explain to your students that God gave Bezaleel special interest and skill in artistry and craftsmanship in order to construct the tabernacle and its contents for God's purposes. We should look at formal performance in this way. Encourage your students that God may have given some of them special interest and skill in areas of dramatic production including acting, set design, set construction, makeup, costuming, and sound. Challenge them to use their abilities in an excellent way for the glory of God.

The set, lighting, makeup, and costume designers must work together to develop the director's mental picture or sketches into a physical representation. The designers must function as a team. A play with an ornate realistic set would not make sense with abstract costume design or makeup. Likewise, the lighting must support all other design elements. A scene in a Victorian banquet hall would not look right if lit with streams of sunlight partially shaded by leaves!

Finally, the actors must understand their roles and make clear choices about interpretation and tactics. Their style must agree with the style of the production. The actors should complete the picture.

The entire cast and crew form a team of people who realize the playwright's text and the director's vision as a unified work of art.

CONCLUSION

In this chapter we have seen that drama is a part of life as we learn and grow. Roles we play begin with childhood games and lead to very significant and integral parts of society in the form of professional and social roles. We have also considered the qualities of formal drama.

As you proceed in your study, be aware of the drama in your everyday life. The more you observe, the better storyteller and actor you will become. In addition, Christians can become more effective Christian witnesses and counselors through a better understanding of people by developing their communication skills, viewing their talents as a gift from God, and seeking opportunities to use them in service to Him.

Community Performances

Now that the students have had opportunity to experience drama and understand the basic premise—mirroring life—you may wish to plan a field trip. If you can preview any local performances sponsored by community groups or even a story hour in a local library, consider securing permission to take students to that activity. Exercise discretion about the type of material presented as well as the reputation of the sponsoring group.

Terms to Know

drama	worldview
mimicry	message
role-play	audience
social role	target audience
stereotypes	design

Ideas to Understand

Multiple Choice: **Choose the best answer.**

___B___ 1. Which of the following is *not* a characteristic of both daily life roles and stage roles?

    A. audience   C. message

    B. design   D. philosophy

True/False: **Write True or False for each statement. If false, cross out the word or words that make it incorrect and write in the word or words that make it true.**

___True___ 2. Literature is one of the ways we experience drama.

___True___ 3. Acting is part of everyday life.

___False___ 4. Mimicry is not acting. **not** *(Mimicry is a way we "act" in everyday life and is a useful tool in formal acting situations for skills such as characterization.)*

___True___ 5. Everyone plays multiple roles in everyday life.

___False___ 6. A focus group is the part of the audience for whom a message is intended. ~~**focus group**~~ **target audience**

Planning the First Quiz

The emphasis of any performance course (such as music, art, or speech) should be on performing. However, there is nothing more practical than good theory. Consider weighting grades to favor performance assignments over written work, but do not neglect written work altogether. Quizzes should force students to review the major terms and ideas without requiring a great deal of time. The review page in each chapter should provide the teacher with a springboard for creating tests and quizzes.

Chapter 2
Introduction

Ninth-grade literature studies are the springboard for this chapter. You will find it helpful to acquaint yourself with the approach to teaching plot used by your school's ninth-grade literature teacher. He probably uses Freytag's pyramid but may apply terms differently than this text does. (See notes on Plot.)

The improvisational activities for this chapter have a twofold purpose: to help students apply head knowledge of plot structure to dramatic activities and to introduce them to the whole experience of dramatic communication. Just as a child learns to converse fluently before studying the syntax and usage of his language, so too the actor must begin by acting. After experiencing several improvisational activities, specific techniques can be incorporated within that context of usage. Even though the students will use letters and/or music rather than normal dialogue to communicate, guide them toward communicating real thoughts and feelings sincerely.

Chapter 2 Outline

Introduction

Elements of a story
  A. Conflict
      The major dramatic
      question

Lesson Plan
Suggested homework is in **boldface.**

Lesson Description	Recommended Presentation	Performance Projects/ Written Assignments
Elements of a Story (p. 23)	TE—Read *Cyrano*, Act V; Act out a portion of *Cyrano*	
TE—Basics of Communicating a Story	TE—Partner Improvisations; Improvisations and Games	**ST—Assign Story Without Words and/or Sing Your Story**
Performance practice	In-class rehearsal of story projects	
Assessment	Chapter quiz	Story Without Words and/or Sing Your Story performances **ST—Assign Journal 1**
Suggested teaching time: 5-6 class periods		

Dramatic Structure

This shape is the strongest and most stable supporting structure known to man.

Chapter 2 Goals

The student will be able to

1. Understand the elements of a story.
2. Present a clear plot through at least one of the improvisational projects included in the chapter.

Lesson Motivator

Though students should already be familiar with the elements of a story from their literature courses, guide them in applying the ideas to this discipline. A good storyteller or actor will have a clear understanding of his characters and the conflicts they face. An inexperienced actor attempts to "learn" a story or a role without clear understanding of these elements. The result is a weak delivery and rote memory that may fail him in a moment of nervousness. Though this section is partially review, don't take too cursory an approach to it.

Teaching Materials

- Copies of *Cyrano de Bergerac* by Edmond Rostand (available in FUNDAMENTALS OF LITERATURE for *Christian Schools*, BJU Press)
- Simple props for the improvisations, such as a small table, two or three chairs, and a pitch pipe or musical instrument

Though some of this material should be a review from literature class, several new terms are included that apply to dramatic works. As you teach these concepts, help the students to see that the elements of a story are integral to their understanding of the story's message. The message reflects the story's philosophy.

Weatherproof

Good structure always stands the test of time. Standing up to wind is one thing, but a structure as tall as the Gateway Arch is a sitting duck for lightning strikes. Never fear—the arch is able to withstand many lightning strikes each year, thanks to the installation of insulated lightning rods that are grounded into bedrock.

OVERVIEW

Know—*Concepts*

Elements of a story
   Conflict
   Exposition
   Characters
   Plot
Parts of plot

Grow—*Interpretation Skills*

Basics of communicating a story

Show—*Performance*

Story Without Words
Sing Your Story

Constructed in the early 1960s, the Gateway Arch in St. Louis contains an observation deck over six hundred feet in the air. Visitors can see as far as thirty miles on a clear day. The panoramic vista encompasses a portion of the Mississippi River and part of Illinois to the east as well as the city of St. Louis to the west. Though it resembles a slender ribbon on the horizon, the arch contains 886 tons of stainless steel. Each section of the arch is an equilateral triangle. The triangle sections at the base measure fifty-four feet per side, but those at the top measure only seventeen feet per side. As with the construction of any arch, the center section, or keystone, was added last. Jacks forced the two legs of the arch to open from two feet to eight so the keystone could be inserted. Once the keystone was in place, the jacks were removed, allowing the two legs to clamp it in place.

> This shape is the strongest and most stable supporting structure known to man. It is so strong that the bridge [of the arch] sways only eighteen inches in winds of 150 miles per hour.
>
> —Ron Tagliapietra, *The Seven Wonders of the World*

Structural design is really the keystone to all of the technological wonders of the world, whether speaking of the arch, the Akashi-Kaikyo Bridge in Japan, or the

How's Your Structure?

Just as excellent structural design is the key to the strength and support of large buildings and bridges, excellent structural design is the key to the strength and support of our spiritual lives. Ask your students to name some ways in which we can make sure that our spiritual lives have excellent structural design. (*Answers should include salvation, love for Jesus Christ, Bible reading, prayer, brotherly love, Christian service, and avoidance of sin.*)

CN Tower in Toronto. Excellent engineering makes these marvels possible. Likewise, structure is the backbone of every dramatic and narrative literature selection.

No doubt you've studied the elements of a story and the parts of a plot in a literature course. Here we will review those ideas and make some specific applications to drama.

ELEMENTS OF A STORY

theme or message. As a performer of literature, you must decide beforehand what sort of message you want to present.

As you read selections to look for a competition piece or a story to perform, you will probably not find the theme clearly labeled up front. Instead, you will have to read carefully, noting the elements of the story—conflict, exposition, characters, and plot—and then determine what theme supports those elements.

Philosophy, mentioned in Chapter 1, is discussed in much more detail in Chapter 3. However, before identifying the philosophy of a story, you must determine its **theme.** Authors begin writing a story with a certain

definition

Theme is the message of a story, poem, or play.

Conflict refers to the meeting of opposing forces.

Conflict

Every story must have **conflict** in order to appeal to its audience. When two opposing forces clash, conflict exists. Categories of conflict, according to the type of opposition faced by the protagonist, include all of the following: the protagonist against another person, against himself, against society as a whole, against the forces of nature, or against deity.

From a story you've read or a play you've seen, list an example after each type of conflict.

"You don't really want my lunch, do you, Hurricane?" Is this Man vs. Man or Man vs. Nature?

1. Man vs. Man   *Answers will vary.* _____

2. Man vs. Himself   *Answers will vary.* _____

3. Man vs. Society   *Answers will vary.* _____

4. Man vs. Nature   *Answers will vary.* _____

5. Man vs. God or the gods (Greek legends)   *Answers will vary.* _____

DRAMATIC STRUCTURE **23**

PRESENTATION

Elements of a Story

The Real Corruption

The message one chooses to send is very significant. Most people realize that much of the drama produced by Broadway and Hollywood is full of moral corruption, but the corruption isn't limited to these production giants. Even some community theaters showcase morally corrupt productions. The obvious objectionable elements in mainstream theater productions are most likely just symptoms of the real corruption—the message that the directors and producers choose to send. Remind your students that we need to run all of our production choices through the litmus test of Philippians 4:8: "Finally, brethren, whatsoever things are true, whatsoever things are honest, whatsoever things are just, whatsoever things are pure, whatsoever things are lovely, whatsoever things are of good report; if there be any virtue, and if there be any praise, think on these things." Encourage your students to memorize this verse or assign it to be memorized as part of their grade.

Theme, Theme, Theme!

Performance preparation is never complete without a definite knowledge of the theme of the literature being used.

Types of Conflict

If a student struggles to identify a story for a particular type of conflict, direct his attention to the stories he has studied recently in literature class.

The Major Dramatic Question

Which best describes the MDQ of *Romeo and Juliet*? The MDQ of Romeo and Juliet ("Will Romeo and Juliet successfully create peace between the Capulets and the Montagues?") is a man versus man conflict. Some students may have seen or read the play with the premise that the feud affected the whole town. In this scenario, they may perceive that "everyone" was against Romeo and Juliet's love. In this case, man versus society would be an acceptable answer.

A Child Bride

In Shakespeare's day, age thirteen was the youngest at which a girl could legally marry. Juliet is only two weeks and a few days away from her fourteenth birthday when she marries Romeo. However, both of them die within three days of the event—certainly not

The Major Dramatic Question

The **major dramatic question (MDQ)** is the heart of the conflict. Although the phrase is generally associated with drama it applies to other literature as well.

definition

The major dramatic question (MDQ) is the key question presenting the central conflict of a story, poem, or play.

Exposition introduces the characters, plot, setting, and circumstances.

If you were writing the short story or play, you would first pose a significant question for your main character. An author or playwright would never just start writing a story, making it up as he went, unless he wanted to create a "yarn," or tall tale. (Even this form tends toward better quality when skillfully planned.)

Instead, the author decides what the main character wants but presently cannot obtain. Romeo and Juliet want their families to get along so they can marry and live happily ever after. The MDQ (major dramatic question) is "Will they successfully create peace between the Capulets and the Montagues?" They attempt several actions in an effort to create peace. In the end, they are successful in bringing the families together, but it is too late for them to enjoy that success. The climax of any story occurs when the MDQ is answered.

Romeo and Juliet by William Shakespeare (Bob Jones University Classic Players)

From the types of conflict listed above, which best describes the MDQ of *Romeo and Juliet*? <u>Man vs. Man (see margin for further explanation)</u>

Exposition

Exposition explains and describes characters, plot, setting, and circumstances. In most short stories and novels, the exposition serves as introductory material to the selection. Because of this, exposition may be included with plot when studying literature. In drama, however, exposition may be minimal and interspersed throughout the play. The conflict often begins within moments of the curtain rising. Since a play has a set, costumes, and sound, the audience may use its own senses of sight and hearing to obtain information. In other words, the playwright doesn't spend the first ten minutes describing the scene, since you're looking at it. Of course, the reader of fiction must rely on exposition for such details.

24 CHAPTER 2

Characters

Characters are perhaps the most obvious elements of a story. When you ask, "Who is the story about?" we reply, "the characters." The people, animals, fantasy creatures, or personified abstractions who participate in the action, directly or indirectly, are the characters of the story.

Characters may evoke our sympathies or our scorn. An author may cause the audience to appreciate the struggles and personal trats of a character. When you read a story, ask yourself, "With whom do my sympathies lie?" Then evaluate whether that character deserves your admiration.

Definition

Characters are any people, animals, fantasy creatures, or personified abstractions involved with the story.

What a Character!

Human characters abound, but you may or may not be familiar with non-human characters. Here are a few titles you might want to explore. Some will be on your reading level; others might serve as good material to read to a young friend.

ANIMALS	FANTASY CREATURES	PERSONIFIED ABSTRACTIONS
Charlotte's Web, E. B. White	The Chronicles of Narnia, C. S. Lewis	*Everyman*, Anonymous
The Trumpet of the Swan, E. B. White	*The Hobbit*, J. R. R. Tolkien	"The Masque of the Red Death," Edgar Allan Poe
Uncle Remus stories— "Brer Rabbit," "Brer Fox," etc., Joel Chandler Harris	*The Lord of The Rings* trilogy, J. R. R. Tolkien	*A Christmas Carol*, Charles Dickens
The Adventures of Peter Rabbit, Beatrix Potter	"The Legend of Sleepy Hollow," Washington Irving	*The Pilgrim's Progress*, John Bunyan
The Adventures of Winnie-the-Pooh, A. A. Milne	*Paul Bunyan, the Giant Lumberjack*, Traditional	"The Erl-King," Johann Wolfgang von Goethe

You may be able to name the nonhuman characters in many of these stories. Besides the short stories, novels, and play listed above, countless children's fables and allegories use nonhuman characters. "The Tortoise and the Hare," "Androcles and the Lion," and *Pinocchio* allow people to distance themselves from the story to be able to see their human failings and learn from them. The Bible itself presents numerous parables conveying lessons through stories about symbolic characters. Christ speaks of a shepherd seeking one lost sheep, while ninety-nine are safe in the fold. Nathan tells King David about a man stealing a neighbor's lamb to depict

an endorsement of hasty decisions about young love.

What a Character!

If you wish to discuss the stories in the character box, various characters from each story are listed below.

ANIMAL CHARACTERS

Charlotte's Web—Charlotte the spider, Wilbur the pig

The Trumpet of the Swan—Louis and Serena, swans

"The Tar Baby"—Brer Rabbit, Brer Fox

The Adventures of Peter Rabbit—Flopsy, Mopsy, Cotton-tail, Peter

The Adventures of Winnie-the-Pooh—Pooh Bear, Tigger, Kanga, Rabbit, Owl

FANTASY CREATURES

The Chronicles of Narnia—Mr. Tumnus the Faun, Puddleglum the Marsh-wiggle, Reepicheep the two-foot-tall mouse

The Hobbit and *The Lord of the Rings* trilogy—hobbits, elves, dwarves

"The Legend of Sleepy Hollow"— the headless horseman

Paul Bunyan, the Giant Lumberjack—Babe the blue ox

PERSONIFIED ABSTRACTIONS

Everyman (a medieval morality play)—Everyman, Fellowship, Knowledge, Good-deeds, Death

---

Discernment

"With whom do my sympathies lie?" Explain to the students that the ability to discern positive or negative influences is one of the most important abilities they can possess. Ask one of the students to read Proverbs 1:1-5 aloud. Impress upon the students that they can learn this crucial ability of discernment by studying the Book of Proverbs.

Cyrano de Bergerac
Introduction to *Cyrano*.

Edmond Rostand's heroic comedy *Cyrano de Bergerac* (1897) is partly based on historical fact. The real Cyrano (1619-55) was not a Gascon, like Rostand's main character, but a native of Paris, educated in Bergerac, Gascony. A soldier for ten years, twice severely wounded, Cyrano turned to a literary career. As a writer he showed extraordinary gifts. The great play-

wright Molière (1622-73) borrowed heavily from one of his two plays. Cyrano's swaggering Bohemian lifestyle, imaginative genius, and over-sized nose are the main historical ingredients of Rostand's heroic character.

On these basic elements Rostand elaborated considerably. His Cyrano excels as poet, critic, fighter, and friend. He has no equal with either sword or pen, and his poetic eloquence comes spontaneously. His one defect—his ridiculously large nose—he regards with

David's sin against his neighbor and his neighbor's wife. In both of these stories, an animal represents a person in order to communicate certain characteristics of that person.

If you have read some of the above-mentioned or other similar stories, what lessons have you learned from them?

Plot

Think about the last time you told a story to your friends at lunch. As you spoke, details raced through your mind—actions, sensory images, and emotions. Here is one student's story.

This morning, I left home a little before the sun came up to throw the newspapers to the houses near my home. My bike gears were catching again. *I'll have to work on them this afternoon,* I thought. I left the driveway, banging over a manhole cover. The smell of Mrs. Gomez's pancakes drifted across the street. Mr. Hauser's black schnauzer, Bear, sniffed the trash and recycling bins. I guess he was looking for breakfast. The air was chilly, so I pulled my sweater tighter around me. Lots more leaves had fallen since yesterday, covering the lawn and car. That meant I would have to rake again this afternoon.

The Deerbornes' white house with blue shutters was all lit up, and a violin was making sounds that resembled sobbing. I felt its pain. . . .

definition

Story refers to all of the details of an event.

Plot includes details of the story that create suspense while emphasizing conflict.

On and on the speaker drones a detailed account of his morning. It might take more time to tell this story than it took for the events to occur! Surely you didn't recount your morning this way.

Plot Versus Story

The term **story** best describes everything that happened, whether factual or fictitious. **Plot,** however, is not *everything* that happened, but rather the events that form a

extreme sensitivity and, seemingly, with genuine pride. In only one area of his life does he let it dishearten him. Because of his face, he hesitates to woo the only woman he has ever loved—his cousin, the beautiful, witty Roxane.

Plot Summary. Two soldiers love Roxane—Cyrano and Christian. Cyrano has the wit and talent to charm her, but Christian is handsome. Cyrano thinks he cannot win Roxane's heart for himself because of his ridiculously large nose. He agrees to be Christian's pen

and poet. Roxane, won by the beautiful sentiments Cyrano expresses, marries Christian. He and Cyrano leave for battle as soon as the ceremony is performed. The letters Roxane receives from her husband (Cyrano's words) so inspire her that she braves the battle scene to visit Christian. She tells him that his letters have shown his soul to her and that she could love him even if he were ugly. Christian realizes that Roxane loves Cyrano, not him. He insists that Cyrano reveal the truth to

her and let her choose between them. Before Cyrano can say that it was he who came to her balcony and he who penned those letters, Christian is mortally wounded in battle. In friendship, Cyrano feels he cannot reveal the truth to Roxane. He whispers to Christian that he did tell Roxane and that she still loves Christian. Christian dies, and Roxane mourns for him.

Act V—Cyrano's Gazette. *Cyrano* is printed in FUNDAMENTALS OF LITERATURE for *Christian Schools* (BJU Press). Read a

meaningful sequence. All details and events in a plot fit together like puzzle pieces, inherently connected to each surrounding piece to complete the picture.

The basic components of plot are stasis, inciting incident, rising action, crisis, climax, falling action, and denouement (day noo MAHN) or resolution.

> **Plot Versus Story**
> - The sequence of events versus everything that happens

Stasis

Let's get back to the newspaper-route story above. What was wrong with it? First of all, nothing out of the ordinary occurred. It was just a recounting of daily routine. When nothing of any importance is happening, the situation is called **stasis.** Stasis means life is tranquil. It also means your story is boring! Are there characters? Yes! Has action occurred? Well, maybe it has, but not the kind of action that compels you to keep reading. The story does include some clear descriptions, but still there is *no plot.*

Secondly, notice that the details included sound much like a zealous diary entry—blow-by-blow detail with little purpose. No doubt you've heard people tell stories that wandered aimlessly.

In a story that opens with exposition, stasis accurately describes the scenario until some sort of upset occurs. In a play, the curtain rises on a world in stasis, but only momentarily. In Shakespeare's *Hamlet*, for instance, the first words spoken introduce an intrusion upon the stasis in Denmark. A watchman who is arriving to work the night shift fearfully asks, "Who's there?" Obviously, the guard who works the evening shift would normally be there, but the night watchman is suspicious and fearful.

Stasis is a time of inactivity or a condition of stability.

*The **inciting incident** is the event that introduces conflict to the story.*

Inciting Incident

The **inciting incident** describes an event that hurdles the world of stasis into motion. The nervous watchman in *Hamlet* reveals fear in the first line. Immediately the audience realizes that "something is rotten in the state of Denmark." With every line following, this fact becomes more obvious. This first upset in any story, narrative poem, or play is that story's inciting incident.

What if the newspaper-route story began like this instead?

---

portion of this act aloud, having the students who read each part act out what they are saying. If your class is small or time is very limited, work only on the portion from Cyrano's entrance to his announcement of his wound. As time allows, you may wish to incorporate more of the class by doing a longer segment that includes many characters. Afterward, ask the students the following questions.

1. Did we create adequate suspense that built to the climax? (*Answers will vary, based on the level of performance and previous student experience with acting out drama.*)

2. What thoughts and feelings did you experience when Roxane discovered that it was really Cyrano who loved her with such beautiful expression, not Christian? (*Answers will vary but may include distress and pity.*)

3. Did you sympathize with Cyrano's dilemma? When did his inner struggle become apparent in your mind? (*Cyrano is a noble hero, worthy of* our sympathy. Depending on the amount of the scene performed, students may indicate various points of realization—whenever they come to understand that Cyrano's great conflict was not a sword fight or even a war but a conflict between fidelity in friendship to Christian and love for Roxane.*)

I left home before sunrise to throw the newspapers to the houses near my home. Mr. Hauser's black schnauzer, Bear, sniffed the trash and recycling bins, looking for breakfast. Nearing the Deerbornes' house, I cringed at the sound of a violin making a sobbing noise. Right after this "music" began, Bear started barking rapidly like a firing squad. Aggravated by the sound of the violin, Bear bolted through shrubs and darted in front of my bike's path. My tires screeched as I flew over the handlebars. On my way over, I noticed that the Deerbornes' cat, Meow, had fled the whining violin inside only to encounter a worse terror outside. Bear "introduced" himself to Meow as a mud puddle broke my fall.

1. What is the inciting incident in the story above? _Bear hears and dislikes the violin music._

2. What action directly results from the inciting incident? _Bear barks and runs around._

3. How does that action influence the main character? _He loses control of his bike._

While this piece still doesn't make the bestseller list, it does have some obvious contrasts to the first version. This time the world does *not* remain in stasis. There is an intrusion on the peaceful, tranquil, expected course of events. The intrusion, or inciting incident, is followed by a conflict, and then another. In fewer words, far more action occurs. And so the plot thickens!

definition

Rising action refers collectively to the conflicts that lead to the story's crisis.

The term crisis is sometimes used to denote the significant turning point in the plot.

Rising Action

The numerous conflicts that lead up to the crisis compose the **rising action.** In fiction the rising action may account for half or more of the story, while in drama it may occupy nearly all of the story. One intrusion is not plot by itself. The inciting incident must be followed by one conflict after another until one great conflict, the crisis, comes.

Crisis and Climax

The terms *crisis* and *climax* are sometimes used interchangeably because they overlap in some cases. To be specific, a **crisis** is a turning point in a conflict. That

28　CHAPTER 2

Crisis and Climax

Even if your students are well grounded in the elements of a story from literature class, be sure to adequately cover this section on crisis and climax. These words will be used throughout the book, and the students need to clearly differentiate between them.

Partner Improvisations

Introduction. This activity will help prepare students for the Story Without Words project. (See Improvisations and Games for additional information about improvisation.)

Directions. Assign each student a partner. Communicate the facts below to the correct partner in each pair to the exclusion of the other team member and the rest of the class. Scenarios may be repeated, but do not tell students they have been assigned to the same scenario. If you double-assign a scenario to students of a different gender, the scenes will end up being quite different anyway. For example, Scenario 1 (below) would be influenced by whether it is "Daddy's little girl" asking, or a son asking his mom, or a same-sex situation.

Scenario 1—Parent and son or daughter

Partner A: You want your eleven-year-old son/daughter to do homework. He/she must be ready for the science fair in just a week, and he/she has a quiz in math tomorrow.

Partner B: You are eleven years old, and today is the first sunny day after three rainy days. Your friend next door wants you to play basketball. Try to get permission to play—at least until supper is ready.

Cyrano de Bergerac *by Edmund Rostand (Bob Jones University Classic Players)*

means a story or play may have numerous crises, because a subplot would have a crisis or two and the main plot may have several. For the purpose of our study, we will label only the most prominent clash as the crisis of the story. In Rostand's *Cyrano de Bergerac*, the members of the audience have known from the beginning that Cyrano loves Roxane. They have watched his poetry and style capture her affections while the credit went to Christian, who is actually clumsy with words and love. In the final scene, Cyrano knows he is dying from a wound, and he begins "reading" Roxane's treasured letter. The quality of his voice and his empathy catch her attention, and then he continues "reading" when darkness falls.

"How can you read now? It is dark . . ." Roxane asks, knowing the answer already. His "reading" has revealed to her that he is the true author. Cyrano realizes his fourteen-year secret has been discovered. This is the crisis moment.

When all of the suspense builds and emotion is at its highest point, the story has reached the **climax.** Cyrano begins protesting Roxane's conclusion, though he knows she is correct. In a beautiful speech, she gently scolds him for never telling her of his love:

> Ah!
> Why have you kept silent these fourteen years,
> Knowing he had no part in this letter—
> Knowing the tears were yours?

The climax. What will our hero do? How will he answer? The members of the audience have seen a turn in the action a few moments earlier, when Roxane guesses the truth. Now they experience maximum suspense as Cyrano finally speaks, referring to stains on the letter:

> "The blood was his."

With four words, the hero reveals his purpose for all action over the past fourteen years. Fidelity in friendship. Honor above self. Then he freely reveals facts to Roxane that the audience has already known—he is dying. He tells his love this day because it is his last.

D*efinition*

Climax usually indicates the moment of highest emotion or suspense.

Crisis vs. Climax

- Crisis: the most prominent clash; turning point
- Climax: the moment of highest suspense

DRAMATIC STRUCTURE　29

Scenario 2—Best friends

Partner A: You really want to go skiing with your youth group this weekend. However, you've never skied before, and don't want to go without your best friend.

Partner B: You have to sing in a recital in a week but seem to be getting a sore throat. You are trying to stay out of the cold weather as much as possible.

Scenario 3—Siblings

Partner A: You are the eldest child in your family, and you love building intricate models of famous ships. You are nearly finished with your greatest masterpiece.

Partner B: You are seven years old. You just found a stray kitten caught in some fallen debris behind your house. You need help from your older brother/sister to free the kitten.

Scenario 4—Teacher and student

Partner A: Your student has turned in several late, poorly done assignments during the first few weeks of class. Now he/she has another late paper.

Partner B: Your dad travels a great deal, but he has actually been around several times lately. He has tried to do fun things with you to make up for the time he's been away. You're having difficulty getting your homework done on time. Today you are turning in another late assignment.

Plot Structure

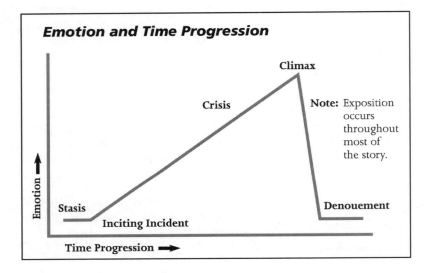

Falling Action

In fiction, an unresolved segment of the story often remains after the crisis. From the turning point of action comes a completion of the action known as the **falling action.** Often in drama, the falling action and climax compose the final moments of the play.

Denouement

What could be more annoying in the middle of a good story than the words, "To be continued . . ."? As much as we enjoy a good story with suspense and excitement, we also enjoy a sense of relief in seeing the conflict resolved. When the main conflict is resolved, the world settles back into stasis again, though perhaps a very different stasis than before. The world of the story or play is at rest. This is called the **denouement,** or resolution.

CONCLUSION

For some of you, considering the elements of a story was a review from English class, but you need to keep these concepts fresh in your mind as you read Chapter 3, "Navigating Thought." The better you understand the structure of a piece, the clearer the meaning will be. Imagine the plot of each story you read to be like the Gateway Arch. The MDQ functions as the keystone of the story. The philosophy of the story, as you will see in Chapter 3, serves as the design.

In the improvisation projects for this chapter, specifically concentrate on the structure of the action. You will greatly benefit, since focusing on the plot structure will help you remember your improvisation more easily.

© 2002 BJU Press. Reproduction prohibited.

Lesson Objectives

The student will be able to

1. Construct a suspenseful plot.

2. Communicate a story saying only the letters of the alphabet.

3. Communicate a story through singing.

4. Evaluate his own work as well as the work of his peers.

Sample Assessments

The student will

1. Outline a plot for each improvisation project.

2. Effectively communicate a story without words.

3. Effectively communicate a story in song.

4. Give oral feedback in class discussion, evaluating the performances.

5. Write a brief paragraph of self-critique in his journal. (Journal 1)

Terms to Know

theme	inciting incident
conflict	rising action
major dramatic question (MDQ)	crisis
exposition	climax
characters	falling action
story	denouement (resolution)
plot	stasis

Ideas to Understand

Multiple Choice: **Choose the best answer.**

_C_ 1. Any of the following could be a character in a story *except*

   A. a family pet.   D. Red Death.
   B. a hobbit.   E. all of these.
   C. lion taming.

_D_ 2. When a story opens, life is in a state called

   A. denouement.   C. stillness.
   B. exposition.   D. stasis.

_C_ 3. The plot is set in motion by the

   A. dramatic intrusion.   C. inciting incident.
   B. exposition.   D. rising action.

True/False: **Write True or False for each statement. If false, cross out the word or words that make it incorrect and write in the word or words that make it true.**

True 4. Crisis and climax may occur at the same moment.

True 5. "Story" refers to all details of an event, whereas the plot contains only specific details.

True 6. Rising action precedes the crisis, but falling action follows it.

Short Answer

7. To discern a story's philosophy, you must first determine _the theme or message_ .

32

Communicating a Story

In this chapter, you learned what makes a good plot. Now it's time to put that knowledge to work. Your teacher may assign you either one or both of the projects described below. Use your creativity to make your "story" the best it can be.

Story Without Words

Every student will need a partner. With your partner, decide on a plot for your improvisation. You can base it on something that has really happened to one of you, or it can be completely fictitious. When you have decided on a plot, outline it on the assignment sheet. Using your outline, practice acting out your story together once or twice. Your story should not last longer than two minutes, so be sure to time your practices.

Now that you are comfortable with the basic idea of the scene, stop using real words to speak to each other. Instead, communicate with letters only. A sample dialogue might begin as shown below (intonation is suggested by the arrows).

As you practice using just letters, don't try to use any pattern or try to memorize what you do one time rather than another time. Just concentrate on creating the plot without getting sidetracked.

CHARLIE: A   b   c.
            (You should go.)
BETSY: D, d   d   a   b.
            (Charlie, you don't know what you're saying.)
CHARLIE: D d,   B.   H   g   a   b.
            (Please listen, Betsy. Think of what this would mean to them.)
BETSY: (moves away) D   f   t!
            (Leave me alone!)
CHARLIE: A—a   b   c?
            (Oh—so that's the way you're gonna be?)
BETSY: M   n   o,   C.   M   n   o.
            (You don't understand, Charlie. You just don't understand.)

Sing Your Story

This activity may work best with groups of three or four students. Work with your partners to think of a plot for a scene that might suit a musical or an opera. The scene may be very comic or very tragic, but musicals are seldom in between. Work out a basic outline of the plot on the assignment sheet. Then assign one or more characters to each group member and begin rehearsing with speaking lines. After practicing two or three times, rehearse singing your lines. Don't be concerned about melody or poetry. Definitely don't try to sing a real song. For each word, simply sing a note that suits the idea.

Your "script," which might *not* be recorded on paper, could resemble the text below:

SETTING: A moonlit garden
ANTONIO: *(Calling from a distance)* My dear, dear, darling Angelina! Are you waiting for me in the garden tonight as you always are?

Basics of Communicating a Story

These projects should be viewed as more of a pretest or diagnostic test than as a major project for the course. Assess each student's current skill level, strengths, and weaknesses so that you will know how to coach each one throughout the course.

Projects

Though these two projects are grouped together at the close of the chapter, you may wish to assign one at the beginning and one at the end. The first project would then serve as a diagnostic pretest, measuring what the student already knows about plot. The second would be a progress report, measuring the amount of learning that has occurred. "Story Without Words" would be more manageable as a pretest than "Sing Your Story."

Story Without Words

Regardless of when you assign this project, you will want to have the students experiment with speaking in letters informally before having them work on the actual project. In initial practices, you may wish to limit the students to just a few letters such as A, B, C, D, E, F, and G. Then they won't become distracted by selecting letters that seem meaningful. Instead, they can focus solely on communicating action.

PRESENTATION
Communicating a Story

Improvisations and Games

The following discussion should lead directly into the first activity described below. You may find it preferable not to have students trying to take notes while you discuss improvisation. Either prepare a half-sheet handout to replace notes they would have taken themselves or allow a couple of minutes for them to make notes at the conclusion of the activities.

Discussion. *Improvisation* means to make something up as you go along. In real life, improvising may suggest lack of preparation or lack of materials. In art, it can mean creativity and even genius. Improvisation is a great way to improve your thinking skills—creativity, spontaneity, and problem-solving. In the context of this course, improvisation refers to a dramatic activity that is spontaneous or carefully planned but always created by the student using his imagination. Acting with a script is not improvisation. The teacher provides a basic purpose, scenario, or rule and allows the students to brainstorm for ideas. Improvisations may involve individual or group activities. Each will require flexibility and much participation. Many will be pantomimed action, but some will involve non-memorized text. Avoid conveying to the students that improvisations are mere exercises leading up to "real" performance activities.

Have the students evaluate their projects after each pair performs its scene. They should ask questions such as

1. Was there a clear sense of conflict?

2. Could you follow the plot easily?

3. Did the actors make the relationship between the characters evident?

4. What clues did you use to reveal those details?

Sing Your Story

For this project, you may wish to bring a pitch pipe or instrument to class to introduce the idea of music as a form of communication. You might use the sample script provided for the students as a springboard for a class activity. Be sure to allow students some class time to rehearse their scenes together. They should be able to practice simultaneously, ignoring the other scenes being rehearsed. However, some students will need more supervision to keep them from wasting time. In that case, you could have each team rehearse in front of the class with you serving as coach.

Assignment Sheet

The assignment sheet is designed to guide students through a simple process for preparing an oral presentation. Each sheet may be counted as a homework

ANGELINA: (Looking in a wishing well—oblivious to his voice) Antonio! Antonio! Antonio! Antonio! Oh, how I long to see your lovely face. (Observing her own reflection) Ah, such a lovely, lovely face!

ANTONIO: (To the audience) My sweet little darling Angelina is so very shy. She's meek and sweet and very humble too. Never does she flirt or sigh as other young girls do. My darling Angelina.

ANGELINA: Where is my darling Antonio? He has a very bad habit of being late when meeting me in the garden. Surely Papa will catch him eventually, and then what will I do?

ANTONIO: (Catches sight of Angelina, who is again admiring her reflection in the well) My lovely angel! (To the audience) I will creep up behind her and surprise her. (He does.)

It might sound something like this.

One Moonlit Night

Not only will whole-hearted participation in the improvisation develop their skills for more structured performances, but they will also have the opportunity to create a moment of drama that would not otherwise exist. Also, the students will make discoveries that a textbook could not teach, and they will remember those lessons, having personally experienced them.

The Rest of the Story

Assign the students to work in small groups to further the story (write a script). Then members of each small group should practice acting out their original ending. Have each group present its piece, including an original title such as "Disaster on a Moonlit Night" or "Moonlit Madness" or "The Ballad of Two Rather Self-Centered Admirers."

Your student could work independently to further the story. He could then perform both characters, which may even heighten the comedy.

Plot Improvisations Assignment Sheet

Story Without Words

Names _____

Story title _____

Characters _____

Climax _____

Plot _____

Inciting incident _____

    I.

        A.

        B.

    II.

        A.

        B.

   III. (Climax)

Resolution _____

Sing Your Story

Names _____

Story title _____

Characters _____

Climax _____

Plot _____

Inciting incident _____

    I.

        A.

        B.

    II.

        A.

        B.

   III. (Climax)

Resolution _____

DRAMATIC STRUCTURE 35

grade or incorporated into the grade for the oral part of the assignment. However, the written work should equal only a fourth to a third of the overall grade in the course.

The more feedback you can give students on their written work, the more they should be able to improve their oral work during their own practice times. Consequently, you will find much benefit in giving thorough comments on these early assignments. Late in the course, you will have less time to write.

If you wish to give an objective score on the written work, it would be appropriate to make note of point values and criteria in the margin on your copy of the sheet and then explain them to the class before assigning these first projects.

Evaluation Forms

Grading

More details will be provided concerning evaluations in later chapters. For these projects, work to give specific, concrete suggestions on the students' evaluations. Comments such as "weak" or "effective" are not helpful by themselves for a beginning student. Instead, try to write comments such as "pace was lagging" or "gestures aided message." On the other hand, do not try to write complete sentences if a phrase will do the job. Unlike grading written work outside of class, grading a performance means a very limited amount of time. Better to give helpful comments than a well-crafted essay that neglects important feedback details.

Planning a Performance Day

A good performance day will include the following elements: a prompt and encouraging opening, brief warm-ups, clear explanation of procedures, well-paced performances, and helpful feedback. (For basic warm-ups, consult "Warming Up to Acting," pp. 241-42 in Chapter 10 of the student text.)

Consider incorporating the following suggestions:

- Begin on time.
- Since students will be nervous, some will be especially chatty, while others will panic silently. For everyone's benefit, be especially firm about classroom decorum.
- Encourage the students at the beginning of the hour by sharing a Bible verse such as Jeremiah 1:9 or I Peter 5:7. Also remind them that you are there to help them improve, not to attack them.
- Make time for warm-ups. For these first projects, it should be adequate to have students stand and stretch to relieve some tension and call out a phrase or two to help

STORY WITHOUT WORDS EVALUATION

Students _____ Scene _____
Story Title _____
Characters _____

Note: You are ranked on a scale of 1-5, 1 being the lowest and 5 being the highest.

ELEMENT	COMMENTS	RANK
Inciting incident		
Plot continuity		
Climax		
Resolution		
Creativity		
Using letters, rather than real words		
Comments for individuals		**SCORE**

✂ -

SING YOUR STORY EVALUATION

Students _____ Scene _____
Story Title _____
Characters _____

Note: You are ranked on a scale of 1-5, 1 being the lowest and 5 being the highest.

ELEMENT	COMMENTS	RANK
Inciting incident		
Plot continuity		
Climax		
Resolution		
Creativity		
Singing rather than speaking		
Comments for individuals		**SCORE**

them think in terms of "performance volume" instead of the indoor, conversational volume they should use during most classes.

- Explain your procedure clearly and succinctly. You may want the students to submit their evaluation forms at the beginning of class so they do not have anything on their desks that might become distracting. Another option would be to have students submit their forms just before their performances so you don't have to sort the forms.

- Remind the students to be quiet between performances so you can take a minute or two to finish up your comments.

- Be sure to keep the pace up. Avoid writing for many minutes after the first speaker or scene so that you end up rushing through performances at the end of the class period.

- Make a goal of allowing a minute or two before the bell rings to comment about the performances. On a day when someone performs poorly or makes a silly error, it's especially important to end on a positive note.

Chapter 3
Introduction

Chapter 3 challenges students to analyze the philosophy (worldview) of a piece of literature. Philosophy is a weighty discussion for the first unit of a high-school textbook. However, in drama class students make some choices about selections of literature for performance in class and competition. Wisdom must become a compass to guide them.

The American entertainment industry has anesthetized the sensibilities of its patrons. True discernment in the secular world is arguably nonexistent. Among religious and conservative groups, it is often sadly lacking as well. Consider using the Bible study notes about discernment as part of your introductory lesson.

Chapter 3 Outline

Introduction

I. Philosophy
   A. Worldview
      1. Habit
      2. Ethics
   B. Christian worldview
   C. Humanistic worldview
   D. Moral tone
II. Discernment
III. Analysis
   A. Introduction
   B. "How Much Land Does a Man Need?" (a folktale)
Conclusion

CHAPTER 3

Lesson Plan
Suggested homework is in **boldface.**

Lesson Description	Recommended Presentation	Performance Projects/ Written Assignments
I. Philosophy (p. 41)	TE—Evaluation Project; Judgment Call	
II. Discernment (p. 46)		
III. Analysis (p. 47)	ST—"How Much Land Does a Man Need?" (story and evaluation questions)	TE—Pantomime Project
Assessment	Chapter quiz	**ST—Assign Journal 2**
Suggested teaching time: 3-4 class periods		

Navigating Thought

I believe in Christianity as I believe that the sun has risen, not only because I see it but because I see everything by it.

Teaching Materials

- Multiple copies of your school's literature textbook on the grade level of the majority of your students.

Interdisciplinary studies (optional)

- A compass, similar to the diagram provided on page 47.

A Navigator's Dream!—or Nightmare

There are many sailboat races, but one is particularly intriguing and arguably the toughest—the Vendee Globe. The Vendee Globe sailboat race pits some of the most talented sailors in the world in a nonstop, 25,000-mile sailing marathon around the globe. Only one sailor inhabits each boat in the journey across four oceans. The sailboats are equipped with some of the most sophisticated communication and guidance devices available. In 2001 Frenchman Michel Desjoyeaux set a new record of 93 days, smashing the previous record of 105 days set in 1997 by a fellow Frenchman. The race begins and ends on the west coast of France. Certainly, these sailors must make much preparation for a journey of this magnitude. They must know the course and be as prepared as possible to deal with the many dangers of the high seas.

Lesson Motivator

Every person, regardless of career goals or intent to pursue college training, must deal with conflicting philosophies in modern culture. Humanism is the most pervasive philosophy that stands diametrically opposed to Christianity. A preacher once defined humanism as looking for answers within. Steer your students away from this

OVERVIEW

Know—*Concepts*
Worldview
   Christian worldview
   Humanistic worldview
Moral tone

Grow—*Critical Thinking Skills*
Discernment

Show—*Analysis*
"How Much Land Does a Man Need?"
  by Leo Tolstoy

It is our business, as readers of literature, to know what we like. It is our business, as Christians, as well as readers of literature, to know what we ought to like.

—T. S. Eliot

In Chapter 1, we looked at the various components shared by everyday life and formal drama as well as drama's distinguishing element—design. Because one of the shared elements, **philosophy,** holds such a significant bearing on your understanding of literature, on your effectiveness in communicating it, and on your Christian testimony, we will look at philosophy in much greater detail in this chapter.

In many ways, trying to find your way through the numerous false, godless philosophies popular in today's society while on your quest for truth will be much like traveling. Just as sailors use the sun and stars as well as maps and a compass to navigate their course, you will navigate thought, guided by your philosophy or worldview.

definition

Philosophy refers to a belief system.

40 CHAPTER 3

Check Your Compass

Ask your students by what means the Israelites were led through the wilderness after their release from Egypt. (*God led them by day in a pillar of cloud and by night in a pillar of fire* [Exod. 13:21-22].) Remind your students that just as God guided the Israelites by the pillars of cloud and fire, so He guides us by His Word. Our philosophy of life must begin and end with God.

PHILOSOPHY

Imagine the following scenario: your after-school job is as a sales associate at a retail store. You soon hear a buzz on the sales floor about the upcoming "Storewide Annual Meeting." The weekend arrives, and so do you—at 8 A.M. on a Saturday, no less! The "meeting" begins with a huge breakfast buffet. Afterward, nearly two hundred people crowd into an assembly room. Mary Gonzalez, the regional vice president, speaks about her vision for the company's future. "We are providing more than clothing and household products. We are providing for families. . . . Our name should be equated with trust and dependability. . . . Our priority is not sales, but people! . . . Customer satisfaction does not refer to that which is adequate, but to that which is excellent."

Several heartwarming stories later, you realize what was really meant by the "Storewide Annual Meeting": your employer paid you to sit through a four-hour program, hoping you would embrace the company's philosophy, including its goals and values. Just as a company has a philosophy that governs its decisions, every individual has a life philosophy (belief system) that guides his personal choices.

Worldview

I believe in Christianity as I believe that the sun has risen, not only because I see it but because I see everything by it.

—C. S. Lewis

In Chapter 1, we defined worldview as a philosophical viewpoint—the lens through which life is viewed. Your actions result from choices, and choices stem from your basic worldview. This is not to say that a human is a robot, programmed with a course of action. Man does have a free will, but there are at least two ways in which our personal life philosophies govern us.

Habit

Habit is the first area influenced by your worldview. Can being taught something as a child, such as making your bed each morning, make you a better student? Indirectly, yes. A child taught habits of neatness, such as bed-making, putting toys away often, or taking out the trash, learns the importance of self-discipline and order. He will be more likely to keep up with schoolwork and properly care for his personal belongings as he grows up. This value, passed along from a parent, can become part of the child's philosophy and habit.

Ethics

The second area involves personal ethics. Suppose you're having friends over on a Friday for a pizza party. You stop by a local grocery store for some soda and

deceitful concept and direct their thoughts toward God's Word. Only Scripture can answer the difficult questions we face concerning morality and ethics because only Scripture is infallible. No human, regardless of how noble or moral, can serve as a benchmark on such issues.

For this course, students should focus on identifying a philosophy by its tenets and then avoid performing any work that opposes Christianity, since a performance can be interpreted as an endorsement. Obviously the students will benefit more if they can apply principles of discernment to all areas of life.

> **Lesson objectives**
>
> *The student will be able to*
>
> 1. Define worldview, Christian worldview, humanism, and moral tone.
>
> 2. Evaluate philosophy in a selection of fiction or drama.
>
> 3. Discern what elements disqualify a work from being performable by a believer.

PRESENTATION

Philosophy

Judgment Call

For this topic, more than any other in the course, be aware of current events and news issues that might serve as a springboard for discussion. You may wish to bring in several editorials or articles on controversial issues so the students can discuss and evaluate the situation. Emphasize that a Christian can serve the Lord by participating in the affairs of his community, but he must be discerning to serve effectively. Help the students see that even neighborhood watch programs, highway cleanup groups, and organizations opposing vices such as drug use and drunk driving are governed by philosophies. Students must begin preparing now to be wise leaders tomorrow.

Gray Areas

Explain to the students that God's Word provides principles that give us wisdom in handling any "gray area" that we face. As proof for this, ask one of your students to read II Timothy 3:16-17 aloud. Remind the students that the Bible is our only rule for faith and practice.

The Big Picture

One great teacher of the Bible put it this way: "Wisdom is life lived from God's perspective."

several bags of chips. You realize after you check out that you paid only for the chips. Somehow, the cashier didn't scan all of the items. Will you argue to yourself, "I didn't try to get this soft drink for free. It wasn't stealing; it was a store error. I don't owe anything since the cashier made the mistake"? Or will you go pay for the items?

In the space provided below, write the Bible principles applicable to this situation. List one or more references to support each principle.

Answers will vary but may include don't steal (Exod. 20:15); don't tell lies (Col. 3:9; James 3:14); be a good testimony (I Tim. 4:12); and be a light shining before men (Matt. 5:16).

In our society today, more and more lines of distinction between right and wrong are blurring. A Christian must be responsible. He must be so immersed in the truth of God's Word that even "gray areas" can be handled wisely.

Remember too that what you put into your mind will greatly influence what comes out in your life. A simple rule to remember is GIGO—garbage in, garbage out. If you allow the garbage of sinful culture to enter your life through your eyes and ears into your mind, it will corrupt your heart.

Worldview

- Your worldview influences your habits and ethics.

Christian Worldview

Life is not divided into the secular and the sacred. For the Christian, everything is sacred.

—Bob Jones Sr.

Often a philosophy of life that promotes morality, respect, and other basic Judeo-Christian values is labeled a "Christian worldview." Although far more extensive than these traditional values, Christian beliefs do include them.

definition

Moral worldview embraces justice and respect for authority, esteeming goodness while depicting evil as repulsive.

Christian worldview sees life through the lens of God's Word.

For clarity, this text will refer to this very generalized "Christian worldview" by the term **moral worldview.** Moral worldview will encompass ideas such as (1) we are subject to authority and order established by God as well as by the human government; (2) true justice rewards good and punishes evil; and (3) goodness seems appealing, while sin is clearly dangerous and undesirable.

Many people in our society sincerely embrace this moral worldview, especially while they are rearing young children. They speak of traditional family values, morality, and virtue. Though these beliefs are not bad, they do not represent true Christianity. A true **Christian worldview** seeks to compare everything to God's Word. Any discrep-

Sacred? Secular?

Ask your students to read and think about Bob Jones Sr.'s quotation carefully. Ask them to name what implications that truth has on their lives presently, and what implications that truth will have on their lives as they consider colleges, majors, careers, marriage, and so on. (*Answers may include—I should consider school, athletics, work, nursing home ministry, youth group activities, and so on as spiritual work that I am doing*

for God. I need to prayerfully consider colleges, majors, careers, and marriage because all of these will have a great effect on my future spiritual life.)

ancy between the worldview of a specific selection of literature and the Word of God shows a fault in the former because the Word is infallible (perfect and complete). A Christian not only seeks morality but also has a biblical view of God, life, death, heaven, and hell.

Humanistic Worldview

Then said his wife unto him [Job], Dost thou still retain thine integrity? curse God, and die. But he said unto her, Thou speakest as one of the foolish women speaketh. What? shall we receive good at the hand of God, and shall we not receive evil? In all this did not Job sin with his lips. (Job 2:9-10)

Obviously any view that opposes biblical values constitutes a non-Christian worldview. Think about Job's wife. Based on her response, does she appear to have a biblical view of who God is? Obviously not. Job's poignant reply correctly labels her faulty worldview as foolishness.

Whenever Christians face physical or financial problems, they have a good opportunity to demonstrate a Christian worldview by responding biblically. That is really what Christians mean when they say, "Pray that so-and-so has a good testimony to his doctor."

In a **humanistic worldview,** personal opinion and conscience establish the boundaries of belief and activity. Personal welfare and convenience are preeminent. Most of the literature you will read while in high school will fit one of these two worldviews: Christian or humanistic.

Humanism in literature can be very subtle. There may not be any offensive language or improper activities, such as smoking or drinking. The hero or heroine may be presented very nobly. However, if the message of the story exalts man rather than God, it is humanistic.

One example is Celeste Responti's play *I Never Saw Another Butterfly*, the story of a child who survived Nazi ghettos and labor camps but lost her parents, brother, friends, and a beloved teacher to death. The play concludes heroically with the woman,

Definition

Humanistic worldview sees man as the source of all things—all strength is human strength, and all nobility stems from human achievement.

I Never Saw Another Butterfly by Celeste Responti. Rasha: "I hear and I remember."

NAVIGATING THOUGHT 43

Authorial Intent

Make sure your students realize the importance of interpreting literature according to the author's intent. Most authors would not mind someone's cutting an oath or a minor detail from their work, but their message is *their* message, not yours. If you do not agree with the author, don't perform his work! There are other stories, other plays, and other poems to perform. An unsaved author who learns that a so-called Christian school changed the ending of his or her play will no doubt view the school's actions as arrogant and assuming. What a terrible testimony! If an unsaved student sees this dishonesty, he too may be turned away from receiving the truth. Make it your goal to evangelize people, not to Christianize published works.

Combating Humanism

Assign or encourage your students to memorize James 4:13-17. The self-reliant humanist says, "We will go into such a city, and continue there a year, and buy and sell, and get gain." He makes his plans with no thought of God. The God-centered person says, "If the Lord will, we shall live, and do this, or that."

Man Exalting Himself over God

The humanistic attitude of exalting man over God is clearly seen in the poem "Invictus" by William Ernest Henley. The first and fourth stanzas are given. The whole poem can be found on the Internet or in an anthology at a library.

Out of the night that covers me,
Black as the Pit from pole to pole,
I thank whatever gods may be
For my unconquerable soul.

. . . .

It matters not how strait the gate,
How charged with punishments the scroll,
I am the master of my fate:
I am the captain of my soul.

Although Henley probably wrote the poem to show that he would not give in to great physical maladies that wracked his body, the poem clearly shows a self-reliant attitude that is void of any submission to or acknowledgment of the sovereignty of God. Ask your

Rasha (RAZH uh), as an adult reflecting on these events and stating, "My name is Rasha—I am a Jew; I survived Terezin—not alone, and not afraid." Notice the use of first-person pronouns. This self-emphasis helps delineate the theme. Since none of the characters in this story are born-again believers, this is the noblest message that *could* be asserted—human courage has sustaining power in adverse circumstances.

However, a Christian facing this situation can declare that faith in God sustains far better, as seen in Corrie ten Boom's autobiography, *The Hiding Place*.

Believers in Bondage

The following story summarizes Corrie ten Boom's life testimony, *The Hiding Place*.

At the Ravensbruck concentration camp, Corrie ten Boom and her sister, Betsie, lived in a huge barrack room meant to house four hundred people, though now there were fourteen hundred prisoners in it. Here they slept on dirty straw mattresses crawling with fleas.

The prisoners worked at heavy manual labor all day but were given only a potato and soup at lunch with more watery soup and bread in the evening.

At the end of each day, Corrie and Betsie read their Dutch Bible. Slowly, more and more women came to join them, some translating the Dutch into several other languages. The guards never came into the barracks to stop them because of the fleas. The women thanked God for fleas!

Though Corrie's father and Betsie both died in prison, Corrie lived to realize Betsie's vision that there would one day be a house for people hurt by the Nazis and a camp in which bitter, angry former prisoners could learn about God's love and forgiveness. Corrie also traveled and spoke repeatedly until her death in 1983.

Some literature has a moral worldview even though a born-again believer did not write it. Historically, countless people have embraced morality without a personal knowledge of Jesus Christ. Many literary works teach truths about our world without opposing the Word of God. A wise Christian will seek the Holy Spirit's guidance when selecting literature and will make prayerful decisions about studying and performing such literature.

Many scholars and critics identify themselves according to their worldview. Examples range from Marxism to feminism to Freudianism to postmodernism.

---

students to name some ways in which they see individuals or groups practice this self-reliant humanism.
(Answers may include the following: thinking that more funding will solve social ills, thinking that fame and fortune will bring happiness, thinking that "it's every man for himself," and so on.)

Types of Worldviews

- The Christian worldview embraces biblical values.
- Non-Christian worldviews oppose biblical values.

Not only do these men and women influence culture through their lectures and literary critiques, but some of them also write fiction and drama that propagates their ideals. If you study literature and drama on the collegiate level or independently, you will soon encounter these philosophies.

Though this text will not discuss the tenets of these philosophies, the remainder of this chapter discusses tools to help you evaluate philosophical viewpoints.

Moral Tone

Closely related to worldview, **moral tone** describes the moral nature of the story. When reading a piece of literature for performance, you must evaluate whether the tone is moral or immoral. Usually the key is the story's ending. Did evil or good deeds characterize the protagonist? If the answer is "evil," then was he or she punished? Did he or she repent or receive forgiveness? If the answer is "good," did the author portray that character heroically, or did he mock the "good guy"? These answers determine whether or not the selection is a **moral story.** For the purpose of your study this semester, think of philosophy as the ideas behind a story's theme, and the moral tone as the resulting impression given to the reader.

The moral tone of a story relates to the primary elements of a story: conflict, exposition, characters, and plot. These can be evaluated with simple questions.

Definition

Moral tone refers to the moral or immoral quality of a piece of literature.

A moral story depicts evil as bad, with evil characters ultimately receiving punishment, while good is viewed positively, with good characters being rewarded.

QUESTION	ANSWER	
	Moral tone	**Immoral tone**
Does the conflict make you sympathize with evil actions?	No—evil is portrayed as dangerous with reciprocal consequences.	Yes—at least part of the action evokes sympathy toward wrongdoing.
Does the story encourage you to like noble, moral characters?	Yes—the "good guy" is a hero, and the "bad guy" is a villain.	No—a rebel or perhaps a fool might be a key figure. ("The fool hath said in his heart, There is no God" Psalm 14:1.)
Is evil punished and good rewarded in the end?	Yes—justice is served.	No—evil is flaunted or excused and good is mocked.
Does the theme conflict with a truth of the Bible?	No—the central message supports a moral worldview.	Yes—the story adds to or takes away from the truth.

Moral Tone

This box is an excellent source for thought-provoking quiz or test questions. Examples: Evaluate the following statements and label each *moral tone* or *immoral tone.*

1. A rebellious character appears heroic.
2. The reader or audience member admires an honest and wise person.

Moral Tone in Scripture

Encourage your students as they read the Bible each day to notice the moral tone of the narratives in Scripture. You may want to discuss the moral tone found in various well-known Bible narratives such as Adam and Eve, Noah and the ark, David and Goliath, Saul's incomplete obedience in I Samuel 15, and Samson. (For instance, in the account of David and Goliath, young David trusted God and triumphed over the arrogant Philistine giant who mocked God's people.)

Evaluation Project

Select several short selections from whatever literature textbook is grade level for the majority of your class. Read each selection together and ask each of the four questions listed in the question/answer box given in the Moral Tone section of the chapter.

Lesson Motivator

Inspire your students to pursue good judgment. Scripture repeatedly emphasizes the need for wisdom, particularly in the Book of Proverbs. Of course, one of the most famous Bible characters—King Solomon—asked for wisdom from God. God placed such high value on Solomon's choice that He gave him material blessings as well. Proverbs 3 extols wisdom's value as "more precious than rubies" (v. 15), a source of "length of days" and "riches and honour" (v. 16), as well as "pleasantness" and "peace" (v. 17) and a "tree of life" (v. 18).

Lesson Objectives

The student will be able to

1. Connect the abstract concepts of philosophy with concrete images.

2. Write a personal creed to express convictions and beliefs.

If you aren't certain about a story's moral tone, ask your parents and teachers to help you evaluate it. Throughout this course you will have many opportunities to evaluate literature selections.

DISCERNMENT

Jesus, Savior, pilot me
Over life's tempestuous sea;
Unknown waves before me roll,
Hiding rock and treacherous shoal.
Chart and compass come from Thee;
Jesus, Savior, pilot me.

When at last I near the shore,
And the fearful breakers roar
'Twixt me and the peaceful rest,
Then, while leaning on Thy breast,
May I hear Thee say to me,
"Fear not, I will pilot thee."

—Edward Hopper, "Jesus, Savior, Pilot Me"

Though this hymn text describes a spiritual journey in life, it reflects well the speaker's and performer's need for the right guide. Pastor Hopper's words, first published in 1871, were intended to strike a chord with the sailors who frequented his small church in the New York harbor area, the Church of Sea and Land. Hopper found inspiration for the text in the Gospel account of Christ calming the Sea of Galilee in the presence of His fearful disciples (Matt. 8:23-27). It may seem that spiritual storms cannot have much to do with drama, but nothing could be further from the truth. As a navigator of thought, you will explore a short story, play, novel, or poem. The author has laid out a course with the plot. The destination is the resolution or denouement, discussed in Chapter 2.

Just as the navigator's compass clarifies direction, your philosophy directs you. In navigating with a real compass in the physical world, an accurate needle points to the North Pole. Think of Christian worldview as a well-magnetized needle. The humanistic worldview can be likened to a needle being drawn away to the wrong magnetic field or distracted by nearby attractions. The Christian's worldview needle will point toward Truth.

PRESENTATION

Discernment

Get Wisdom

It is a disappointment if a student completes this course without improved communication skills. It is a tragedy if he leaves without increased discernment. Take this opportunity to challenge the students with what the Bible has to say about seeking wisdom in Proverbs 4:5-7 and 16:16.

Interdisciplinary Studies

If time permits and your student seems interested in navigation, which is used metaphorically in this chapter, the following discussion provides an interesting cross-disciplinary study. The navigation metaphor employed here creates a bridge between this course and a course in physical science or world studies.

The History of Navigation

Every civilization uses and will continue to use navigation skills to travel, hunt, hike, and explore. The compass is a navigational tool containing a permanent magnet, generally shaped like an arrow, that is free to rotate on a spindle. The magnet aligns with the earth's north-south magnetic field lines.

The compass has long been a valued tool of navigation. As early as A.D. 80, Chinese literature states that magnetized

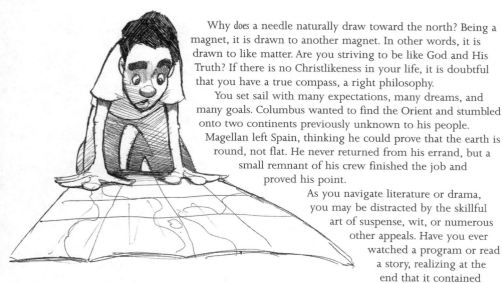

Why *does* a needle naturally draw toward the north? Being a magnet, it is drawn to another magnet. In other words, it is drawn to like matter. Are you striving to be like God and His Truth? If there is no Christlikeness in your life, it is doubtful that you have a true compass, a right philosophy.

You set sail with many expectations, many dreams, and many goals. Columbus wanted to find the Orient and stumbled onto two continents previously unknown to his people. Magellan left Spain, thinking he could prove that the earth is round, not flat. He never returned from his errand, but a small remnant of his crew finished the job and proved his point.

As you navigate literature or drama, you may be distracted by the skillful art of suspense, wit, or numerous other appeals. Have you ever watched a program or read a story, realizing at the end that it contained elements that *should* have offended you; but because you laughed so much or because it was so exciting, you didn't notice? The more you *know* God, the more discerning you will be in these situations.

> *Beware lest any man spoil you through philosophy and vain deceit, after the tradition of men, after the rudiments of the world, and not after Christ.* (Colossians 2:8)

This verse in Colossians is a powerful warning. It could also be translated, "See to it that no one takes you captive through his philosophy . . . according to men's traditions . . . rather than according to Christ." If a ship's pilot is aware of shallow water, rocks, or other obstacles nearby, he can safely avoid these dangers, unless the ship gets captured in a current. A Christian can be caught in the currents of complacency or ignorance when evaluating ideas. Ultimately this can lead to shipwreck.

ANALYSIS

Discernment takes time to develop. In the following pages, you will have the opportunity to evaluate a story with two worldviews presented. Use the tools presented in this chapter to evaluate the major dramatic question. Determine which worldview is presented as true.

Lesson Motivator

The simple fable included in this chapter should serve to demonstrate both moral worldview and humanism. Students need to recognize that a moral story often depicts a character with a faulty worldview. Such stories have tragic endings because a central figure comes to his demise. Help your students see that because Pakhom makes wrong choices, he is not admirable. Yet his story is worth reading because we can learn from him and avoid his mistakes.

Lesson objectives

The student will be able to

1. Contrast a character's philosophy with the worldview presented by the author.
2. Describe the dangers of choosing to live by a non-Christian worldview.

---

stone was used to find direction, but mariners probably didn't use lodestone, a magnetized rock, until the twelfth century. Prior to this primitive "compass," seafarers depended on the positions of heavenly bodies, landmarks, and knowledge of regional wind patterns. By 1522, sea navigation would prove that the earth was indeed round, when a fraction of Magellan's original crew arrived back in Spain.

Using a Compass

Determine which direction you wish to travel (north, southwest, etc.) using a map if necessary. Turn the compass housing dial until that direction is lined up with the direction-of-travel arrow. Turn not just the compass but your whole body until the red end of the compass needle points north. Now your direction-of-

travel arrow is pointing in the direction you need to travel.

A compass may misguide you for several reasons. Obviously, it can be used incorrectly. For example, if the needle is aligned north-south but the red end is toward "south" on the compass housing dial, you will go in the exact opposite direction you intend. These types of problems may be avoided simply by careful attention to detail.

Introduction

In Genesis 3, a new character enters the scene. Appearing as a serpent, Satan approaches the first woman, Eve, and appeals to her "wanter." Eve listens to Satan's deceptive story and chooses to rebel, taking something that was not meant for her. From that day until the present, mankind has battled greed and covetousness.

In Matthew 4, Satan has the audacity to approach Christ with a similar offer:

> *Again, the devil taketh him up into an exceeding high mountain, and sheweth him all the kingdoms of the world, and the glory of them; And saith unto him, All these things will I give thee, if thou wilt fall down and worship me. (Matthew 4:8-9)*

Though all of creation belongs to God, Satan hopes to appeal to Christ's humanity. Christ rejects the offer and its condition to worship Satan. Regardless of his appearance, neither Satan's nature nor his goals have changed from when he beguiled Eve in the garden. He wants glory, so he appeals to the "wanter" instinct in men to turn them from God to himself.

Numerous works of fiction have sprung from this basic theme of Satan's tempting men with greed. The classic tale of Faust, which appears in several versions including a drama and an opera, depicts a man tempted by Satan. American author Stephen Vincent Benét wrote "The Devil and Daniel Webster" in which Jabez Stone bargains away his soul in exchange for success, wealth, and marriage. Leo Tolstoy, the Russian author of *War and Peace*, develops this same theme using a Russian peasant named Pakhom as his protagonist and land as the object of desire. Read Tolstoy's story to discover its worldview.

How Much Land Does a Man Need?

Summary

The story opens with Pakhom's sister-in-law mocking their poverty and simple living. Pakhom wishes aloud that he could become a landowner, insisting that he wouldn't fear any man or even the Devil himself. The Devil hears him and plots to tempt him.

Pakhom and his wife scrape together enough money to buy some land from the Barina (landowner). For a time, Pakhom is quite pleased with his land. Before long, however, Pakhom begins to have difficulty with trespassers. He tries to be patient, but soon he begins to fine the peasants as the Barina had fined him.

A traveling peasant asks to stay with Pakhom's family one night. This stranger tells Pakhom about generous portions of land beyond the Volga. The land is inexpensive and very fertile. Pakhom sells all that he has and moves his family to the new settlement in the spring. Pakhom finds himself ten times better off than he had been.

Soon Pakhom becomes discontented because by law he cannot raise wheat every year in the same field but has to leave it fallow. He finds a landowner who needs to sell; Pakhom offers fifteen hundred rubles for

---

Secondly, being a magnet, the compass needle may be disturbed by nearby magnetic fields surrounding metal objects, mineral deposits, electric motors, and so on. Avoid these objects to avoid their interference.

Finally, the needle may deviate, not due to a nearby magnetic field, but simply because of one's geographic location. In other words, when navigating the Pacific, one would encounter different variables than he would find in the Atlantic, and vice versa.

 PRESENTATION

Analysis

"How Much Land Does a Man Need?"

Not only can you teach worldview from this selection, but you can also assess the students' understanding of the other elements of drama by leading them in a class discussion.

Plot Summary. Pakhom, a Russian peasant, becomes dissatisfied with his situation, envying the wealth of others. Through a series of events, he finally offers one thousand rubles for all the land he can walk around from sunup to sundown. As he walks, his greed overtakes him and he tries to get more and more. As the daylight grows short, he realizes how exhausted he has become. He reaches his starting point to make his claim, but collapses dead from the exertion. His servant buries him. All the

thirteen hundred acres. Just before they agree upon this sale, a passing dealer stops at Pakhom's house to buy feed. He tells Pakhom he has just returned from the land of the Bashkírs where he bought thirteen thousand acres for just one thousand rubles. The dealer insists that you had only to befriend the Starshina (chief) and give the Bashkírs some gifts to be able to obtain such a bargain. Pakhom is delighted to think he can buy ten times more land for only one thousand rubles.

Pakhom inquired how to get to the place, and as soon as the tradesman had left him, he prepared to go there himself. He left his wife to look after the homestead, and started on his journey, taking a servant with him. They stopped at a town on their way and bought a case of tea, some wine, and other presents, as the tradesman had advised. On the seventh day of travel, they came to a place where the Bashkírs had pitched their tents. It was all just as the tradesman had said. The people lived on the steppes by a river, in felt-covered tents. They neither tilled the ground, nor ate bread. Their cattle and horses grazed in herds on the steppe. The colts were tethered behind the tents, and the mares were driven to them twice a day. The mares were milked, and from the milk, kumiss was made. It was the women who prepared kumiss, and they also made cheese. As far as the men were concerned, drinking kumiss and tea, eating mutton, and playing on their pipes was all they cared about.

As soon as they saw Pakhom, they gathered around him, bringing an interpreter. Pakhom told them he had come about some land. The Bashkírs led Pakhom into one of the best tents, where they made him sit on some down cushions placed on a carpet, while they sat round him. They gave him tea and kumiss and had a sheep killed and gave him mutton to eat. Pakhom took presents out of his cart and distributed them among the Bashkírs, and divided amongst them the tea. The Bashkírs were delighted. They talked a great deal among themselves, and then told the interpreter to translate.

"They wish to tell you," said the interpreter, "that they like you, and that it is our custom to do all we can to please a guest and to repay him for his gifts. You have given us presents, now tell us which of the things we possess please you best, that we may present them to you."

"What pleases me best here," answered Pakhom, "is your land. Our land is crowded, and the soil is exhausted; but you have plenty of land and it is good land. I never saw the like of it."

The interpreter translated. The Bashkírs talked among themselves for a while. Then they were silent and looked at Pakhom while the interpreter said:

"They wish me to tell you that in return for your presents they will gladly give you as much land as you want. You have only to point it out with your hand and it is yours."

The Bashkírs talked again for a while and began to argue. Pakhom asked what they were arguing about, and the interpreter told him that some of them thought they ought to ask their Starshina about the land and not act in his absence, while others thought there was no need to wait for his return.

While the Bashkírs were arguing, a man in a large fox-fur cap appeared on the scene. They all became silent and rose to their feet. The interpreter said, "This is our Starshina himself."

Pakhom immediately fetched the best dressing-gown and five pounds of tea,

land he really needed was six feet—head to toe.

Throughout the story, various characters enter the scene, spurring Pakhom's greedy quest. The night before his walk, Pakhom dreams that each of these wicked men represents temptation.

Discussion. This intriguing folktale depicts a sobering end to a man's greed.

Reading this story to the students or reading it aloud together would be an ideal opportunity to hone their evaluation skills.

Contrasting Selection

If you have a mature group of students, you may wish to contrast Tolstoy's work with Stephen Vincent Benét's short story "The Devil and Daniel Webster," which has a similar theme but a non-Christian viewpoint.

In Benét's work, the character Daniel Webster poses as a defense attorney for Jabez Stone, a man who promised his soul to the Devil in exchange for ten years of wealth, power, and finally the opportunity to marry. Though Christ's atoning work is not depicted and Jabez does not repent, Webster appeals to the "jury's" love of freedom, and Jabez is pardoned. You could explain this to the students, guiding them to see the faulty philosophy. Emphasize the difference between evaluating such a work in class

and offered these to the Starshína. The Starshína accepted them, and seated himself in the place of honor. The Bashkírs at once began telling him something. The Starshína listened for a while, then made a sign with his head for them to be silent, and addressing himself to Pakhóm, said in Russian: "Well, let it be so. Choose whatever piece of land you like; we have plenty of it."

"Thank you for your kind words," Pakhóm said. "You have much land, and I only want a little. But I should like to be sure which bit is mine. Could it not be measured and made over to me? Life and death are in God's hands. You good people give it to me, but your children might wish to take it away again."

"You are quite right," said the Starshína. "We will make it over to you."

"I heard that a dealer had been here," continued Pakhóm, "and that you gave him a little land, too, and signed title-deeds to that effect. I should like to have it done in the same way."

The Starshína understood.

"Yes," replied he, "that can be done quite easily. We have a scribe, and we will go to town with you and have the deed properly sealed."

"And what will be the price?" asked Pakhóm.

"Our price is always the same: one thousand rubles a day."

Pakhóm did not understand. "A day? What measure is that? How many acres would that be?"

"We do not know how to reckon it out," said the Starshína. "We sell it by the day. As much as you can go round on your feet in a day is yours, and the price is one thousand rubles a day."

Pakhóm was surprised. "But in a day you can get round a large tract of land," he said.

The Starshína laughed.

"It will all be yours!" said he. "But there is one condition: If you don't return on the same day to the spot whence you started, your money is lost."

"But how am I to mark the way that I have gone?"

"Why, we shall go to any spot you like, and stay there. You must start from that spot and make your round, taking a spade with you. Wherever you think necessary, make a mark. At every turning, dig a hole and pile up the turf; then afterwards we will go round with a plough from hole to hole. You may make as large a circuit as you please, but before the sun sets you must return to the place you started from. All the land you cover will be yours."

Pakhóm was delighted. It was decided to start early next morning. They gave Pakhóm a feather-bed to sleep on, and the Bashkírs dispersed for the night, promising to assemble the next morning at daybreak and ride out before sunrise to the appointed spot.

Pakhóm lay on the feather-bed, but could not sleep. He kept thinking about the land.

"What a large tract I will mark off!" thought he. "I can easily do thirty-five miles in a day. The days are long now, and within a circuit of thirty-five miles what a lot of land there will be! I will sell the poorer land, or let it to peasants, but I'll pick out the best and farm it. I will buy two ox-teams, and hire two more laborers. About a hundred and fifty acres shall be plough-land, and I will pasture cattle on the rest."

Pakhóm lay awake all night, and dozed off only just before dawn. Hardly were his eyes closed when he had a dream. He thought he was lying in that same tent, and heard somebody chuck-

50 CHAPTER 3

and producing a play version. An audience may be harmed by watching a story portray the impossible: redemption without repentance or the remission of sins. They may so greatly empathize with Jabez, noting that his new bride even prayed for him and thinking "our God is forgiving," and so forth, that they completely miss the discrepancies with the truth of Scripture. Make certain the students understand that when the sympathetic character escapes justice, the story is immoral. Refer again to the definition of moral tone.

Pantomime Project

After reading "How Much Land Does a Man Need?" assign students the following roles: Pakhom, the servant, the Starshína, and two or three Bashkírs. Have them pantomime the final scene of the story as you or another student reads the final page or two. Make it your goal to end with an image as is depicted in the photograph: the servant with his spade, standing over Pakhom's body.

ling outside. He wondered who it could be, and rose and went out and he saw the Starshina sitting in front of the tent holding his sides and rolling about with laughter. Going nearer to the Starshina, Pakhom asked: "What are you laughing at?" But he saw that it was no longer the Starshina, but the dealer who had told him about this land. Just as Pakhom was going to ask, "Have you been here long?" he saw that it was not the dealer, but the peasant who had come up from the Volga, long ago, to Pakhom's old home.

Then he saw that it was not the peasant either, but the Devil himself sitting there, and before him lay a man barefoot, dressed raggedly, with a face white as a sheet. Pakhom looked more attentively only to see that the man was himself! He awoke horror-struck.

"What things one does dream," he thought.

Looking round he saw through the open door that the dawn was breaking. He got up, roused his servant, bade him harness, and went to call the Bashkírs.

The Bashkírs got ready and they all started: some mounted on horses, and some in carts. Pakhom drove in his own small cart with his servant, and took a spade with him. When they reached the steppe, the morning red was beginning to kindle. They ascended a hillock and dismounting from their carts and their horses, gathered in one spot. The Starshina came up to Pakhom and stretching out his arm towards the plain.

"See," said he, "all this, as far as your eye can reach, is ours. You may have any part of it you like."

Pakhom's eyes glistened: it was all virgin soil, as flat as the palm of your hand, as black as the seed of a poppy.

The Starshina took off his fox-fur cap, placed it on the ground and said: "This will be the mark. Start from here, and return here again. All the land you walk around shall be yours."

Pakhom took out his money and put it on the cap. He then put a little bag of bread into the breast of his coat, and tied a flask of water to his girdle. Drawing up the tops of his boots, he took the spade from his man and stood ready to start. He considered for some moments which way he had better go—it was tempting everywhere. He turned his face to the east, stretched himself and waited for the sun to appear above the rim.

"I must lose no time," he thought, "and it is easier walking while it is still cool."

The sun's rays had hardly flashed above the horizon, before Pakhom, carrying the spade over his shoulder went down into the steppe.

Pakhom started walking neither slowly nor quickly. After having gone a thousand yards he stopped, dug a hole, and placed pieces of turf one on another to make it more visible. Then he went on; and now that he had walked off his stiffness he quickened his pace. After a while he dug another hole.

Pakhom looked back. The hillock could be distinctly seen in the sunlight. At a rough guess Pakhom concluded that he had walked three miles. It was growing warmer; he took off his under-coat, flung it across his shoulder, and went on again. It had grown quite warm now; he looked at the sun; it was time to think of breakfast.

"The first shift is done, but there are four in a day, and it is too soon yet to turn. But I will just take off my boots," said he to himself.

He sat down, took off his boots, stuck them into his girdle, and went on. It was easy walking now.

"I will go on for another three miles," thought he, "and then turn to the left.

NAVIGATING THOUGHT 51

This spot is so fine that it would be a pity to lose it. The further one goes, the better the land seems."

He went straight on for a while, and when he looked round, the hillock was scarcely visible and the people on it looked like black ants.

"Ah," thought Pakhom, "I have gone far enough in this direction, it is time to turn. Besides I am in a regular sweat, and very thirsty."

He untied his flask, had a drink, and then turned sharply to the left. He went on and on; the grass was high, and it was very hot.

Pakhom began to grow tired: he looked at the sun and saw that it was noon.

"Well," he thought, "I must have a rest."

He sat down, and ate some bread and drank some water; but he did not lie down, thinking that if he did he might fall asleep. After sitting a little while, he went on again. At first he walked easily: the food had strengthened him; but it had become terribly hot, and he felt sleepy; still he went on, thinking: "An hour to suffer, a life-time to live."

He went a long way in this direction also, and was about to turn to the left again, when he perceived a damp hollow: "It would be a pity to leave that out," he thought. "Flax would do well there." So he went on past the hollow, and dug a hole on the other side of it before he turned the corner. Pakhom looked towards the hillock. The heat made the air hazy: it seemed to be quivering, and through the haze the people on the hillock could scarcely be seen.

"Ah!" thought Pakhom, "I have made the sides too long; I must make this one shorter." And he went along the third side stepping faster. He looked at the sun: it was nearly half way to the horizon, and he had not yet done two miles of the third side of the square. He was still ten miles from the goal.

"No," he thought, "though it will make my land lop-sided, I must hurry back in a straight line now. I might go too far, and as it is I have a great deal of land."

So Pakhom hurriedly dug a hole, and turned straight towards the hillock.

Pakhom now walked with difficulty. His bare feet were cut and bruised, and his legs began to fail. He longed to rest, yet the sun waits for no man.

"Oh dear," he thought, "if only I have not blundered trying for too much! What if I am too late?"

Pakhom began running, threw away his coat, his boots, his flask, and his cap, and kept only the spade which he used as a support.

"What shall I do," he thought again, "I have grasped too much. I can't get there before the sun sets."

And this fear made him still more breathless. Pakhom went on running, his soaking shirt and trousers stuck to him, and his mouth was parched. His breast was working like a blacksmith's bellows, his heart was beating like a hammer, and his legs were giving way as if they did not belong to him. Pakhom was seized with terror that he could die of the strain.

Though afraid of death, he could not stop. "After having run all that way they will call me a fool if I stop now," thought he. And he ran on and on, and heard the Bashkírs yelling and shouting to him, and their cries inflamed his heart still more. He gathered his last strength and ran on.

The sun was close to the rim, and cloaked in mist looked large and red as blood. Now, yes now, it was about to set! The sun was quite low, but he was also quite near his aim. Pakhom could already see the people on the hillock waving their arms to hurry him up. He could see the fox-fur cap on the ground, and the money on it, and the Starshina sitting on the ground holding his sides. And Pakhom remembered his dream.

"There is plenty of land," thought he, "but will God let me live on it? I have lost my life, I have lost my life! I shall never reach that spot!"

Pakhom looked at the sun, which had reached the earth: one side of it had already disappeared. With all his remaining strength he rushed on, bending his body forward so that his legs could hardly follow fast enough to keep him from falling. Just as he reached the hillock it suddenly grew dark. He looked up—the sun had already set! He gave a cry: "All my labor has been in vain," thought he, and was about to stop, but he heard the Bashkírs still shouting, for they on the hillock could still see the sun. He took a long breath and ran up the hillock. It was still light there. He reached the top and saw the cap. Before it sat the Starshina laughing and holding his sides.

Again Pakhom remembered his dream, and he uttered a cry: his legs gave way beneath him, he fell forward and reached the cap with his hands.

"Ah, that's a fine fellow!" exclaimed the Starshina. "He has gained much land!"

Pakhom's servant came running up and tried to raise him, but he saw that blood was running from his mouth.

Pakhom was dead.

The servant cried out, but the Starshina remained sitting on his haunches—laughing, and holding his hands to his sides.

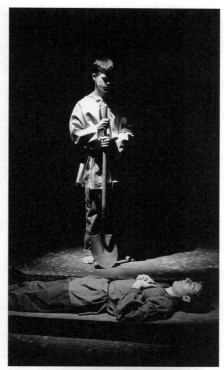

Profit? *by Nathan Vanburen, adapted from "How Much Land Does a Man Need?" by Leo Tolstoy*

At length he got up, took a spade and threw it to the servant.

"Bury him," was all he said.

The Bashkírs left. Only the servant remained. He dug a grave long enough for Pakhom, and buried him in it. Six feet from his head to his heels was all he needed.

—Leo Tolstoy, "How Much Land Does a Man Need?"

Analyze the Story

Answer the following questions about the plot of the story.

1. Who is the protagonist? <u>Pakhom</u>

___B___ 2. Which of the following best represents his philosophy?
   A. Being a landowner is for the birds.
   B. Owning land will make me happy. It will bring me independence, wealth, and respect.
   C. Wanting more than what you have is foolish.
   D. None of the above.

3. Who is the antagonist? <u>the Evil One (Satan)</u>

4. What is the major dramatic question? <u>Answers may vary. Will Pakhom ever get enough land? / How much land does a man need?</u>

5. How is the MDQ answered? <u>He will never have enough because greed is never satisfied. / All a man really requires is six feet in which to be buried.</u>

6. What is the theme? <u>Answers will vary but should relate to the following: Greed never pays off. / Possessions cannot bring contentment.</u>

7. Compare the philosophy of the story with Pakhom's philosophy. (See question 2.) Are they the same? If not, explain how they are different.
   <u>Answers may vary. The philosophy of the story is presented by the narrator, who gives little warnings throughout the story that Pakhom is in danger. The narrator does nothing to mask or lessen the impact of Pakhom's tragic end. The reader must see the consequences of foolishness.</u>

8. Do we see the events through the eyes of the protagonist or an omniscient narrator? <u>through an omniscient narrator</u>

Answer the following questions about the tone of the story.
(Answers will vary but should reflect the ideas in the answers provided.)

9. Does the story encourage you to admire noble, moral characters?
   <u>Two very minor characters, Pakhom's wife and servant seem to be good people. However, Tolstoy gives little insight into either of them. Otherwise, there aren't noble, moral characters to admire. The main character is selfish. The story does not</u>

encourage the reader to admire Pakhom. At best, you feel sorry for him.

10. Does the conflict make you sympathize with evil actions? *No. Because Pakhom dies in pursuing more land, the reader does not want to follow his example.*

11. Is evil punished and good rewarded in the end? *Yes. Pakhom's greed is punished. No character earns a reward, however.*

12. Does the theme conflict with a truth of the Bible? *No. Pakhom's personal philosophy conflicts with Scripture, but the theme does not.*

Answer the following questions about performing this story.

___C___ 13. Which of the following worldviews best represents the story as a whole?
   A. Christian worldview   C. moral worldview
   B. humanistic worldview   D. none of the above

14. Could you perform this story? Why or why not? *Yes. Answers will vary but may include that this story presents a good lesson. It supports biblical principles such as "the wages of sin is death" (Romans 6:23) and "the love of money is the root of all evil" (I Tim. 6:10).*

15. Could a Christian perform this story if Pakhom's choices were presented as wise choices? Why or why not? *No. Answers will vary but may include that Pakhom is a tragic figure. He makes wrong choices. Christians do not want to follow his example of greed.*

NAVIGATING THOUGHT   55

CONCLUSION

A preacher once said, "If you are not content with what you have, you will never be content with what you think you want." Pakhom had the same problem that all people have had since the Garden of Eden—wanting. His philosophy of materialism led him to his destruction. Materialism sets the worldview needle pointing in the wrong direction for seeking contentment. It invariably draws man away to fool's gold.

Pakhom demonstrated a slow progression away from contentment. This tendency of the natural man is outlined in Psalm 1. Notice how the danger increases as the man is described as becoming more and more comfortable with bad counsel. First he is walking, then presumably standing still, and finally sitting down.

> *Blessed is the man that walketh not in the counsel of the ungodly, nor standeth in the way of sinners, nor sitteth in the seat of the scornful. But his delight is in the law of the Lord; and in his law doth he meditate day and night. . . . The ungodly are not so: but are like the chaff which the wind driveth away. . . . The way of the ungodly shall perish.*

Pakhom learned his lesson the hard way. Unknowingly, he struck a bargain with the Evil One. You can choose to learn by observation rather than experience. As readers of literature, oral interpreters, and actors, you must decide on what foundation you stand. Whose counsel will you follow?

> *Thy word have I hid in mine heart, that I might not sin against thee. O how love I thy law! it is my meditation all the day. (Psalm 119:11, 97)*

As this chapter closes, your journey has just begun. Keep your tools at hand and use them frequently. If you have a clear focus on your ultimate destination, an alert mind, and a prayerful heart, God can provide discernment for you. James 1 promises, "If any of you lack wisdom, let him ask of God, that giveth to all men liberally." Claim that promise!

Are You Content?

Ask your students to name some material things that teenagers typically desire. (*Answers may include clothes, shoes, cars, money, and so on.*)

Ask them how the desire for these "things" could lead to a life of discontentment. (*Answers may include always wanting more, always wanting the best, always wanting the latest, and so on.*)

CHAPTER 3 REVIEW

question 3
Some humanistic stories may be appropriate if they contain worthwhile themes that feature characters who don't know God but present some moral principles.

Terms to Know

philosophy   humanistic worldview
moral worldview   moral tone
Christian worldview   moral story

Ideas to Understand

Multiple Choice: **Choose the best answer.**

__B__ 1. Respect for authority and good triumphing over evil characterize all of the following *except*
   A. Christian worldview.   D. moral worldview.
   B. humanism.   E. all of these.
   C. moral tone.

__E__ 2. Our personal philosophy is revealed in all of these *except*
   A. attitudes.   D. responses to situations.
   B. ethics.   E. all of these.
   C. habits.

True/False: **Write True or False for each statement. If false, cross out the word or words that make it incorrect and write in the word or words that make it true.**

__False__ 3. All humanistic stories are "un-performable" due to their content. ~~All~~ *Only some*

Short Answer

4. Give an example of a method that might distract you from noticing offensive elements when watching a film or reading a book. *humor, suspense, etc.*

5. If a business wants to communicate its goals, priorities, and ideas, it will present its *philosophy* .

NAVIGATING THOUGHT 57

Chapter 4
Introduction

Chapter 4 is the last chapter of foundational study in this course, emphasizing literature comprehension and analysis in preparation for each project hereafter.

Too often a student enters a selection in competitions without really understanding its message. A teacher or other coach instructs him on specific aspects of delivery but perhaps never requires the student to learn anything about the background of the author or the context of the selection. The student competitor is incapable of making his own performance choices because he understands too little of what his piece means.

Use this chapter as your starting block for a challenge you will revisit throughout the course. Insist that students analyze each selection they wish to perform. Require them to evaluate the worldview as well. Analyzing a performance selection before selecting it should become second nature—like fastening one's seatbelt before driving. This habit will serve a similar purpose—protection. Through analysis and evaluation, students can safely avoid performing a selection with the wrong message or misinterpreting the literature.

Lesson Plan
Suggested homework is in **boldface.**

Lesson Description	Recommended Presentation	Performance Projects/ Written Assignments
I. Reading Comprehension (p. 63)	ST—Reading Quiz; all *White Cliffs* activity boxes TE—Lady Jean	TE—The Last Line
II. Reading Techniques (p. 73)	TE—Word Choice Counts	TE—Comic or Tragic?; Emotion in Action
III. Dramatistic Analysis (p. 79)	TE—A Sample to Analyze	
Assessment	Chapter quiz or unit test	**ST—Assign Journal 3**
Suggested teaching time: 5-6 class periods		

Reading with Understanding

I have loved England, dearly and deeply,
Since that first morning, shining and pure,
The white cliffs of Dover, I saw rising steeply
Out of the sea that once made her secure.

Teaching Materials

- Several samples of shape poems
- A copy of "The Bells" by Edgar Allan Poe
- Basic furniture for scenes (a couple of chairs or a bench and perhaps a small table or desk)
- Slips of paper that could be put in a hat (a small file box, a cardboard box, or a bowl could be substituted for the hat)
- Copies of the stage directions from the Teacher's Edition

OVERVIEW

Know—*Concepts*

Reading comprehension
Denotative meaning
Connotative meaning

Grow—*Interpretation Skills*

Reading techniques
Prose
Poetry
Drama

Show—*Performance*

Dramatistic analysis

As you wait for your dentist's assistant to call your name, you scan the waiting room for something to occupy your time. Your eyes light upon the magazine rack. You skim over pictures of a "Death-by-Chocolate" layer cake and complementary titles such as "Running Your Way to a Thinner, Leaner You" and "Fifty Weight-Loss Tips." Finally, you pick up a decorating magazine featuring low-cost ways to give a bedroom a facelift. It seems impossible that your parents have finally agreed that you may redecorate your bedroom. Now that Erin is in college and the room is finally all yours, the pink flowers have got to go.

Knowing that you have just a few minutes until your name is called, you flip through the pages, trying to find the article. Color photos show several vastly different rooms, all in shades of blue, this season's preferred color. One room is Victorian with at least six differently patterned fabrics in view. The next is country—a wood-framed bed and nightstand. Calico-clad teddy bears adorn a wooden chair in the corner. Yet another depicts what you would label a cool, contemporary style—wrought-iron furniture and a steel-blue comforter. Nothing interests you there, so you flip to the next photo collage, this time depicting a variety of furniture arrangements. You flip again and read several paragraphs. Then your name is called. Returning the magazine to the rack, you think, "That was a waste of time." Okay, rewind. What went wrong? Why didn't you get what you wanted out of your reading? Possibly, the article was weak on content. However, it's also possible that you didn't read with understanding.

You may be asking, "Do I have to read every detail to read with understanding?" If that were true, in this situation you couldn't because your time was limited. Actually, the opposite is true. You must learn to skim, speed-reading what doesn't apply and absorbing what does. Just looking at pictures is fun, but you may not learn anything.

If you could look at the article again, you might find information such as an outlook on decorating. The designer interviewed in the article suggests making your room a place for you to be yourself. The designer also suggests planning the room to fit your work and leisure activities. Do you like to read? Put a comfortable chair near your bookcase; don't bury the books in an inaccessible corner. Do you enjoy listening to music while drawing or doing homework? An affordable stereo and CD tower within reach would be ideal. And so on.

Do you realize these ideas can be obtained in the article's subtitles and topic sentences? In the time it took you to look at the pictures and read a few disjointed portions, you could have been absorbing these main ideas and forming your own mental picture! Does that mean you should ignore photos and artwork? Absolutely not. But chances are, most of us could improve our reading habits.

Reading Quiz: **Circle the letter that best describes your reading style.**

1. When I read textbooks, I usually
   A. read every word, writing terms and other notes in my notebook (or highlighting and underlining the text if I own the book).
   B. look for bold terms or terms in the margin and study them.
   C. read the summary.
   D. read the headings and terms carefully before briskly reading the chapter text.
   E. other: _____

2. When I read a work of fiction, I generally
   A. read beginning to end, almost without sleep or food.
   B. read the last chapter first to figure out "who-dun-it" or read until I can guess what will happen and move on to another book or activity.
   C. read one chapter this year, another the year after, etc.
   D. read for a moderate length of time and skim back over a page or two when returning to the book several days later.
   E. other: _____

Reading with Understanding 61

Reading Resolutions

Encourage your students to develop good reading habits in general. Encourage them to limit the number of books that they read at one time (one or two at a time instead of four or five), to read two to three classics a year, and to read the Bible through every year. For those who want a challenge, the Bible can be read straight through without stopping in as few as seventy-two hours. Encourage them to read one book every two weeks, make sure their reading area is well lighted, take a speed-reading course if one becomes available, and make up a reading list, checking off books as they go. And last but not least—challenge them not to read the last page first!

Reading Quiz

Please note that question 3 will not be applicable to all students. They may skip it if they don't have a workplace.

Also, point out to the students that attitude plays an important role in their effectiveness in reading skills.

Three for Three

If you have magazines at home on topics such as home decorating, cooking, architecture, antique furniture, gardening, or another very visual subject, collect several short or mid-length articles (3-6 pages). Bring several to class. Allow students to work in groups of about three. Limit their time to approximately three minutes. Instruct them to take a page or two per person, skim for about two minutes, and then quietly discuss what they learned. Allow several or all groups to appoint a spokesman to present a brief summary of the article to the rest of the class. Ask students if they found the skimming and collaborating helpful.

Your student can collect these articles and skim them, writing a brief synopsis of a few of them. He could also present his synopsis orally, either as a presentation (public-speaking style) or a discussion (less formal).

3. When I read an article or pamphlet at my workplace, my general attitude might best be described as follows:

A. "Nothing else matters beyond this article."

B. "What's this about? Oh, I already know about that. I don't really need to read it."

C. "I've got that article somewhere. I'm getting to it, really I am."

D. "I was introduced to safety procedures during orientation week, but I should probably review and remind myself of the exits, etc."

E. other: _____

4. When I read for pleasure, my general attitude might best be described as follows:

A. "Do not disturb."

B. "I have better things to do with my time."

C. "I don't have time to read unless it's required. I wish I did."

D. "Reading gives me a change of pace, and sometimes I learn very helpful information."

E. other: _____

5. When purchasing a new electronic product, I

A. read the directions immediately, even if I have other things I probably ought to be doing.

B. skim the directions and start attempting to assemble or use the product.

C. eventually say, "There were directions in the box? I didn't see them!"

D. quickly but completely read the directions, making mental note of key ideas. I refer to the directions as needed.

E. other: _____

What answer did you most often give?

If you tended to answer *A*, you are probably a very zealous and hard-working person. You may discover, however, that your approach becomes so time consuming that you fail to get your homework done or have to study constantly to get it done.

If you most often answered *B*, you are decisive, perhaps to the point of judging too quickly. You need to avoid being too confident that you know what facts are important right from the beginning.

If you often circled *C*, you may be disorganized or lack interest. Be careful about both of these problems since they are harmful to success in your education and career.

If you answered D most or all of the time, you are developing some good reading habits and should already be on the road to academic and professional success.

If you usually answered E, evaluate your tone and actions in comparison with the descriptions above. Do any of these fit you?

What difference do our reading habits make? All the difference in the world! On an exam, time constraints restrict your opportunity to read and understand directions and questions. No doubt you've graded another student's paper and realized that he misunderstood or ignored the directions. The worksheet said, "Mark the following statements *True* or *False* and correct the false statements in the right margin." Your friend Nevin skipped the directions, confident that a True-False quiz was quite standard; now he will lose partial credit, not because he didn't know the answers, but because he failed to read one sentence!

Outside the academic world, the dangers are even higher than grades. Ignoring directions might get you to the wrong part of the airport, just in time to miss your international flight, or onto a one-way street—the wrong way. Consider how much it would affect your life if your doctor were careless about medical details he read and gave the wrong diagnosis for a problem! You could end up with the wrong medicine.

In this chapter, we will discuss comprehension, reading techniques for each genre (ZHAN ruh), or type of literature, and questions asked by good storytellers and performers.

READING COMPREHENSION

I have loved England, dearly and deeply,
Since that first morning, shining and pure,
The white cliffs of Dover, I saw rising steeply
Out of the sea that once made her secure.

—Alice Duer Miller, *The White Cliffs*

You probably didn't have to look up any words in the dictionary when you read this excerpt. The vocabulary is all quite familiar. But did you really understand it? Without context and analysis, the opening lines of Miller's World War I poem may seem elusive or vague. What does love of England have to do with the cliffs on Dover Beach? How did the sea provide security, and how was that security threatened or ended? You should be able to answer these questions after reading the following section.

Lesson Motivator
Many people enjoy reading because they understand and may even relate to the author's message. Effective reading is not passive absorption comparable to most television viewing. It is much more similar to a good conversation—sending and receiving ideas and feelings. Even though the reader does not reply to the author, he responds to the author's message. A significant part of oral interpretation and acting is sharing with the audience your personal response to a piece of literature.

Obviously the interpreter or actor cannot respond to that which he does not understand. Reading comprehension, then, is key to excellence in dramatic performance. This idea will be developed further in future chapters.

Lesson Objectives
The student will be able to

1. Define *denotation* and *connotation*.
2. Explore the meaning of poetry excerpts based on denotation, connotation, context, and experience.

The White Cliffs
Alice D. Miller's poem is well worth reading in its entirety. If you wish to share the entire selection with the class, preview the text first. The poem does contain a few

Understanding literature goes far beyond knowing vocabulary words, though ignoring the meaning of new terms definitely hinders comprehension. In this section, let's consider several short portions from this poem and try to understand the message the poet wished to communicate.

Denotative Meaning

Begin with the basics when approaching a piece of literature. Are there words you don't know or whose meanings don't make sense to you in this context? If so, what denotative definitions should you look for? **Denotative meaning** refers to the definitions of a given word contained in the dictionary.

Denotative meaning refers to the literal, dictionary definitions of words or phrases.

If you're helping your dad hang a new picture on the wall and he asks you to get a *level* for him, you might think to yourself, *Doesn't level mean floor—first floor, second floor, and so on?* Then you think about the word *level* used as an adjective and realize that you want to hang the picture *level*, not crooked. Still, if you are not familiar with the tool known as a *level*, a measuring stick with liquid and air encased in tubes, you'd have a hard time finding it in the garage, wouldn't you?

Dictionary Usage

In another passage from Miller's poem, the narrator, Susan Dunne, describes the family home of Johnnie (her future husband).

> *A red brick **manor house** in Devon,*
> *In a **beechwood** of old gray trees,*
> *Ivy climbing to the clustered chimneys,*
> *Rustling in the wet south breeze.*
> *Gardens trampled down by **Cromwell**'s army,*
> *Orchards of apple trees and pear,*
> ***Casements** that had looked for the **Armada,***
> *And a ghost on the stairs.*

Give the denotative (dictionary) definitions for words in boldface.

1. manor house <u>*may refer to a lord's residence or the main home on an estate*</u>

64   CHAPTER 4

PRESENTATION
Reading Comprehension

Lady Jean

Present the following facts to the students.

1. Lady Jean, Johnnie's mother, is described in the next excerpt. His father is deceased.

2. Throughout its generations, Johnnie's family has experienced Cromwell's overthrow and the battle with the Spanish Armada and may have lost family members in battle.

3. Two of Lady Jean's three sons will soon die fighting in World War I.

Ask students how they think these facts might explain the "ghost on the stairs." (*Answers will vary but should relate to the idea that such a house would hold a great deal of ambiance from its history.*)

The Last Line

Introduction. If the students understand the extent to which the reader and actor interpret words, they will be more motivated to diligently analyze a text for the author's intent. After completing this activity, ask questions about the importance of knowing what message was intended.

2. beechwood _a forest or grove of beech trees (Beech trees have smooth gray bark and nuts inside burs.)_

3. Cromwell _Oliver Cromwell led the Parliamentarian victory over the monarchy during the English Civil War (1642-49)._

4. Casements _window frames that open on hinges_

5. Armada _a fleet of warships_

6. Explain what specific Armada this may refer to. (If you are not familiar with British history, consult a world history text or teacher for help.)
The "Armada" refers to Spain's naval forces that attacked England during the reign of Elizabeth I.

7. What do you know about Johnnie's family, based on this selection?
Their house was very old. We might suppose that his family had some ruling power at some point in time or at least wealth and social influence.

8. Why might a manor house have "clustered chimneys"?
A building more than three hundred years old (today, four hundred years old) would lack technology to efficiently heat more than one or two rooms with one fireplace. Wealthy people often had fireplaces in each of several rooms and a wood-burning stove for cooking, as well as a heat source for servants' quarters.

9. Lines 5 and 7 describe historical events. What significance do these events bear on our knowledge of Johnnie's family?
Johnnie's family must be old and well established since both events occurred two to three centuries before the lifetime of the current occupants. Speculation suggests that Johnnie's family values highly its heritage and is loyal to the throne.

10. How do you think the narrator, Susan, perceives Johnnie's home? What are her feelings?
Possible answers include pride, intimidation, respect, awe, and love.

Instructions. Write the following list of sentences on separate slips of paper and allow students, in small groups, to select one from a hat.

"So, I guess this is 'goodbye.'"

"Always remember our summer here."

"Your carriage awaits, my liege."

"Will I ever see you again?"

"That was the last school bell—ever."

"I hope you can hear me, for you must know that you are forgiven."

"Maybe next time you'll remember not to do that."

"Make no mistake, you have not heard the last from me."

"It seems that life is indeed a bowl of cherries, for here we are in the pits."

"What do you mean you dropped the key?"

"Another case is solved. Another day's work is done."

You may want to include other sentences of your choosing.

Give the students about ten minutes to create two- or three-person scenes that climax with the line they selected. Have each pair or group present its scene for the class. Scenes should last about two to three minutes and have a great deal of purposeful action.

Discussion. After completing the improvisations, discuss how the context they created largely determined the meaning of that final line. Using one or two of the lines selected as an example, ask the class to brainstorm for other

Now reread the eight lines of poetry. How has your impression changed? Better understanding of the meaning of words transforms this excerpt from a vague catalogue of details to a poignant and clear description of far more than just a building. Now you should understand something of Johnnie's family within the walls of its home, as well as its society.

Connotative Meaning

Connotative meaning makes the difference between a house and a home. It is the reason that hearing your friend's name makes you smile but the name of someone who has treated you cruelly makes you wince. Think back to when a younger brother was born, and your mom might have suggested a completely normal name like Phil or Jeff; but since your dad once had a dishonest neighbor by that name, your parents probably chose a different name.

definition

Connotative meaning ascribes meaning to a word because of personal emotion or experience in a certain context.

Connotation does not limit its influence to the spoken word. If Lauren hears from a mutual friend that Paul might ask her to the junior-senior banquet, and then after lunch he smiles and nods to her in the hallway, his friendliness will carry connotative meaning it would not have had before.

All in Context

The next excerpt from *The White Cliffs* describes the narrator's future mother-in-law. This time, you will not encounter many new words but instead much new meaning and insight into Lady Jean's character.

Johnnie's mother, the Lady Jean,
Child of a penniless Scottish peer,
Was handsome, worn, high-colored, lean
With eyes like Johnnie's—more blue and clear—
Like bubbles of glass in her fine tanned face.
Quiet, she was, and so at ease,
So perfectly sure of her rightful place
In the world that she felt no need to please.
I did not like her—she made me feel
Talkative, restless, unsure, as if
I were a cross between parrot and eel.
I thought her blank and cold and stiff.

1. Look up the word *peer*. What definition suits the word in this context?

    a nobleman

66   CHAPTER 4

---

scenarios that would reach a different conclusion but could still employ that sentence. For example, one group might draw "That was the last school bell—ever" and improvise a scene about a teacher of fifty years retiring. Other possibilities include elated high-school or college seniors who are anticipating their graduation ceremony in two days or even elementary students (to whom the summer is an endless expanse of time) expressing the same joy.

Also discuss how each student's background experiences influenced his first impression of his group's line. What else prompted the idea? How did they arrive at the scenario they created?

A student studying independently might draft a rough outline of a scene and then interpret both roles. This should not be a meticulous, time-consuming task.

Impose the same time limits as given in the activity above.

Get to Know Yourself—Connotatively

Call out the following words slowly or put them on the overhead so that the students can concentrate on them: mission field, money, God, clothes, summer camp, television, church, music, parents, video games, athletics, friends, brothers, and sisters. After the students have heard or seen

2. What is the topic of the first five lines?

Lady Jean's appearance—she is beautiful and noble.

3. What impression does this description give the reader?

It reflects something of her character and experience. Her nobility is deeply bred.

Neither money nor lack of money has had much bearing on her attitude about her

position in life.

4. What is the topic of lines 6 to 8?

her confident attitude

5. List your own adjectives that could also describe the topic of lines 6 to 8.

proud, self-assured, dignified, etc.

6. Read your list of adjectives and then reread the three lines of poetry. Which conveys Lady Jean's personality more effectively, the lines in the poem or your list of adjectives that summarize them? Defend your answer.

Description of action is clearer than a list of adjectives we cannot necessarily

picture or relate to. We believe what we see even more than what we hear.

7. Why does the narrator dislike Lady Jean?

Lady Jean makes her feel "talkative, restless, unsure," and the narrator thinks Lady

Jean is "blank and cold and stiff."

8. Is the narrator's opinion based on fact or feeling? Give a reason for your answer.

Feeling—nowhere has the narrator stated that Lady Jean took any actual actions

against her. Her dislikes are based on her own attitude. Though we convey attitude

through action, her response is primarily emotive.

9. Is there anything in the poem that suggests that the narrator may change her opinion in the future? Give a reason for your answer.

Since the narrator notices surface similarities between this woman and Johnnie

and has only a surface knowledge of Lady Jean at this point, it seems possible if not

likely that her attitude may change as they become better acquainted.

READING WITH UNDERSTANDING 67

the words sufficiently, tell them to choose one word and then write down every thought that comes to mind on that word for three minutes. Remind them that they can learn much about themselves by the connotative meaning they attach to words. You may wish to have the students include this in their journals.

Though these two portions of the poem are sequential, you needed a different approach to understand them. The description of the house included many terms unfamiliar to the typical American student. (If you were reared in England, such would not be the case.) However, once you understood the new vocabulary, the meaning was obvious. By contrast, the description of Lady Jean lacked new vocabulary but required careful thought, time, and analysis to fully grasp its message.

Context

In the example about the *level*, **context** determined which denotative meaning applied. With any word that has more than one definition, context determines meaning. However, context plays an even greater role in connotative meanings.

definition

Context refers to the setting or to surrounding elements.

Consider the simple sentence "I'm going home." Imagine that the last-period bell just rang, ending math class, and you have a test tomorrow. You need a score of 80 percent to remain academically eligible to play soccer. When you say to your friend, "I'm going home," what are you implying? Maybe this friend suggested that you two stop for ice cream after school. Now you are declaring—with the words "I'm going home"—"Sorry, but I need to study more than I need to eat ice cream."

Imagine now you've been to camp for six *long* weeks, and your parents will be arriving in the morning with your kid sister and your very own brown and white beagle. You might grab your camp counselor by the shoulders and shout, "I'm going home!" Though the words remain the same, these two situations depict opposite extremes of emotion, expectancy, and, no doubt, delivery style.

The following letter, addressed to Johnnie, is written by the narrator, Susan Dunne.

Dear John:
I'm going home. I write to say
Good-by. My boat train leaves at break of day;
It will be gone when this is in your hands.
I've had enough of lovely foreign lands,
Sightseeing, strangers, holiday, and play;
I'm going home to those who think the way
I think, and speak as I do. Will you try
To understand that this must be good-by?
We are both rooted deeply in the soil
Of our own countries. But I could not spoil
Our happy memories with the stress and strain
Of parting; if we never meet again,
Be sure I shall remember till I die
Your love, your laugh, your kindness.

68 CHAPTER 4

Context Is Crucial

Read Genesis 31:49 to your students. "The Lord watch between me and thee, when we are absent one from another." You might want to ask your students if they have ever heard that verse used in any particular situation. Explain to them that many dating couples and good friends have expressed this verse to one another preceding periods of absence from one another. However, if one reads the whole of Genesis 31, he will find that this saying was expressed between Laban and Jacob in a very tense moment as a promise not to harm each other. If it is important to know the meaning of a phrase within the context of a poem, how much more important it is to understand a Bible verse in the context of a chapter or book.

"I'm going home." Simple words you've used regularly for years, but notice how many different meanings they might carry! When you choose a selection to perform, remember that each phrase deserves consideration of the meaning within the context of the poem.

Experience

In public speaking, your roles as both speaker and listener are shaped by your own experiences. This is also true when reading literature and especially influential when you "read" to others, since your delivery as storyteller or actor interprets much of the meaning for the audience, which sees the literature through your eyes.

Correspondence Across the Atlantic

After Susan wrote Johnnie (the last excerpt), she changed her mind about returning to America and she married Johnnie. Evaluate the following two examples from *The White Cliffs* and answer the questions below each example.

"So, Susan, my dear," the letter began,
"You've fallen in love with an Englishman.
Well, they're a manly, attractive lot,
If you happen to like them, which I do not.
I am a Yankee through and through,
And I don't like them, or the things they do.
Whenever it's come to a knock-down fight
With us, they were wrong, and we were right;
If you don't believe me, cast your mind
Back over history, what do you find?
They certainly had no justification
For that maddening plan to impose taxation
Without any form of representation.
Your man may be all that a man should be,
Only don't you bring him back to me,
Saying he can't get decent tea—
He could have got his all right
In Boston Harbor a certain night,
When your great-grandmother—also a Sue—
Shook enough tea from her husband's shoe
To supply her house for a week or two.
The war of 1812 seems to me
About as just as a war could be, ...

READING WITH UNDERSTANDING 69

And you must remind them now and then
That other countries breed other men.
From all of which you will think me rather
Unjust. I am.

Your devoted
Father. ["]

1. What historic events does her father mention directly and indirectly?

   Though he directly mentions the War of 1812, he also alludes to the Boston

   Tea Party, 1773.

2. Describe and explain Susan's father's view of her new husband.

   Susan's father, Mr. Dunne, generalizes about the British because he has ancestors

   who experienced firsthand the conflicts relating to the American Revolution and the

   War of 1812. (Also, he seems to perceive the English as stuffy or perhaps trivial

   since they value niceties such as tea.)

   B   3. In what sense does he mean he's a "Yankee"?
       A. a fan of the New York Yankees
       B. an American
       C. a person from New England
       D. a person from a state north of the Mason-Dixon Line and east of the Mississippi River

4. Because of the time period and the context, you may feel very far removed from the situation. Make a modern comparison.

   Answers will vary, but a possible answer could include people of different

   religions marrying.

5. Notice the punctuation beginning with "I am" and ending with "Father." What dual impression do these words convey, simply because of the punctuation? (Write out a paraphrase of each meaning.)

   (1) He really is her devoted father. (2) He's certain she'll think he's unjust because

   it's true—he is.

This letter from home sends Susan's memory reeling back to her memories of childhood, as she relates in the next excerpt.

I read, and saw my home with sudden yearning—
The small white wooden house, the grass-green door,
My father's study with the fire burning,
And books piled on the floor.
I saw the moon-faced clock that told the hours,
The crimson Turkey carpet, worn and frayed,
The heavy dishes—gold with birds and flowers—
Fruits of the China trade.
I saw the jack-o-lanterns, friendly, frightening,
Shine from our gate posts every Halloween;
I saw the oak tree, shattered once by lightning,
Twisted, stripped clean.
I saw the Dioscuri—two black kittens,
Stalking relentlessly an empty spool;
I saw a little girl in scarlet mittens
Trudging through snow to school.

Description of Susan's Home

The fact that this excerpt mentions jack-o'-lanterns and Halloween is not an endorsement of celebrating Halloween. Permission could not have been obtained to print this excerpt if that portion had been omitted.

6. No doubt the term Turkey carpet is a new vocabulary word. This refers to an oriental rug that would feel soft like velvet. Also, Dioscuri refers to Castor and Pollux, twin brothers in Greek mythology. Are there other unfamiliar terms? If so, list and define them.

   Answers will vary.
   _____

   _____

7. Which of these last two excerpts seems more closely connected to your personal life experiences? Explain your answer.

   The more likely answer is that the student relates to the description of Susan's

   home with all its quirks and qualities.
   _____

8. In another part of the poem, the reader learns that Susan's home lacks a mother figure, while Johnnie's lacks a father. What other differences are evident in what you have read? Compare this description of Susan's childhood home to that of her husband's (the manor house).

   Historically speaking, Susan's house cannot be as old as Johnnie's. No doubt

   it is much smaller and far less expensive. It is cozy rather than elegant, friendly

   rather than austere.
   _____

   _____

READING WITH UNDERSTANDING 71

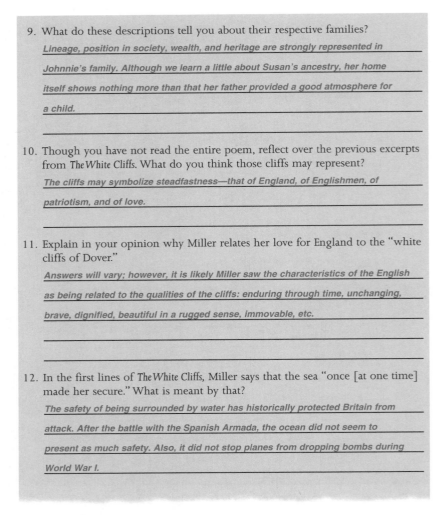

Encourage students to try performing from various genres and styles when they compete repeatedly. For example, if a student continually chooses heavy, emotional, dramatic literature, recommend a light humorous selection. This will stretch him in a direction in which he is probably not comfortable, but the experience will add another dimension to his ability. This also goes for students who continually choose humorous literature. Truly good performers can perform more than one kind of literature well.

Lesson Motivator

In addition to the high percentage of illiterate adults in modern society, many people who can read do not read well. They read too slowly to connect ideas or too quickly to absorb information. They may not read genres with any consideration of form. This section deals particularly with the latter challenge—reading genres appropriately. Encourage your students to experiment with the methods presented here. They should find reading various forms, particularly poetry, far less intimidating and much more enjoyable.

9. What do these descriptions tell you about their respective families?

Lineage, position in society, wealth, and heritage are strongly represented in Johnnie's family. Although we learn a little about Susan's ancestry, her home itself shows nothing more than that her father provided a good atmosphere for a child.

10. Though you have not read the entire poem, reflect over the previous excerpts from *The White Cliffs*. What do you think those cliffs may represent?

The cliffs may symbolize steadfastness—that of England, of Englishmen, of patriotism, and of love.

11. Explain in your opinion why Miller relates her love for England to the "white cliffs of Dover."

Answers will vary; however, it is likely Miller saw the characteristics of the English as being related to the qualities of the cliffs: enduring through time, unchanging, brave, dignified, beautiful in a rugged sense, immovable, etc.

12. In the first lines of *The White Cliffs*, Miller says that the sea "once [at one time] made her secure." What is meant by that?

The safety of being surrounded by water has historically protected Britain from attack. After the battle with the Spanish Armada, the ocean did not seem to present as much safety. Also, it did not stop planes from dropping bombs during World War I.

For a few of your projects in this course, you may feel most comfortable choosing literature that fits well within your realm of experience. However, you will benefit if you intentionally choose some works that have little or nothing to do with your previous experience.

Why choose such selections? Several benefits exist. When you study and perform a piece such as *The White Cliffs*, you learn much about English and American culture during the early twentieth century. In addition to the benefit of broadening your horizons, you as an oral reader gain enrichment from the emotional impact of a story depicting the lingering effects after a war as well as life during war: an ever-repeating phase of history you likely have not experienced. Also, a new setting helps you avoid responding by habit and assuming generalities.

READING TECHNIQUES

Now that we have studied reading comprehension, let's turn to a practical approach for reading each **genre** of literature. The three basic genres are prose, poetry, and drama. Prose includes all nondramatic, narrative literature; poetry, text in verse form or characterized by poetic devices; and drama, dramatic poems and play scripts intended for stage. All of these definitions will be discussed in further detail in the next three sections.

Definition

*A **genre** is a type of literature classified by style or purpose. Often literature is divided into three basic genres: prose, poetry, and drama.*

*****Prose** refers to the short story, novel, and biography as well as (in a broader sense) the essay, article, review, letter, and journal entry.*

Reading Prose

By far the most common and diverse genre, *prose* offers a host of exciting opportunities to the storyteller and actor. From actor Hal Holbrook performing the biography of Samuel Langhorne Clemens in his one-person show *Mark Twain Tonight!* to a chamber theater scripting of short stories like Guy de Maupassant's "The Necklace," prose continues to be a crowd pleaser. Today, even more so than in years past, prose is popular on stage. Solo actors perform journals, diaries, and letters; biographies become films or stage plays as "docu-drama" or historical fiction; and even old newspaper articles might be dramatized.

Three Basic Genres

- Prose
- Poetry
- Drama

Definition

The term **prose** refers to both form and content. The form of prose involves paragraph formatting and conversational diction through narration, exposition, and description. Nonfiction prose includes works such as letters, journals, essays, rhetoric, articles, biographies, histories, and textbooks. Fiction includes short stories or novels and could also be further classified by topic, such as "mystery."

The content of prose, being diverse, may best be defined by what it is not, or more specifically, by contrasting it with poetry and drama. For example, consider dialogue. Prose is not just spoken words like a script. In a play, nearly all of the words on the page are dialogue; whereas in prose, dialogue alternates with narration explaining and describing the action. Prose does not heavily feature poetic devices, such as alliteration and rhyme. That is not to say that prose must be altogether lacking in attention to words. Consider the following passages:

READING WITH UNDERSTANDING (73)

Lesson Objectives

The student will be able to

1. Define prose, poetry, and drama as genres.

2. Explain how each genre should be read to enhance understanding.

3. Contrast storytelling and memorized presentation of prose literature.

4. Define dramatic compression and identify the genre in which it is most often used.

5. Explain the role of imagination in reading any genre, particularly drama.

The Possibilities of Prose

Hal Holbrook has performed his one-person show *Mark Twain Tonight!* nearly 2000 times. He began the role at age 29 in 1954 and has since performed the role for forty-seven consecutive years. He's had other acting jobs as well.

It Reads Like Poetry

For an amazing display of imagery in a prose selection, read "Duty, Honor, Country," General Douglas MacArthur's famous farewell speech to the U.S. Military Academy at West Point. He delivered the speech on May 12, 1962, at age 82, just two years before his death. The speech can be found on the Internet.

PRESENTATION

Reading Technique

Word Choice Counts

The expression "lost in the translation" reflects the importance of wording. Read one or more of the excerpts on page 74 to the students or assign students to read them aloud. Have all students write for one to two minutes, creating a simplified summary of the text. Compare these summaries with the original, pointing out to the students the role that wording played in conveying meaning. You may have summaries such as this example for Kossuth's speech: "A place to live and legal rights sound really nice. Unfortunately I don't have either." Without the soaring rhetoric, the idea conveyed no longer seems profound.

Freedom and home: what heavenly music in those two words! Alas, I have no home; the freedom of my people is downtrodden.

　　—Louis Kossuth, "America's Welcome"

The credit belongs to the man who is actually in the arena; whose face is marred by dust and sweat and blood; who strives valiantly; who errs and comes short again and again . . . who at the best knows in the end the triumph of high achievement; and who at the worst, if he fails, at least fails while daring greatly.

　　—Theodore Roosevelt, "While Daring Greatly"

It was the best of times, it was the worst of times, it was the age of wisdom, it was the age of foolishness, it was the epoch of belief, it was the epoch of incredulity, it was the season of Light, it was the season of Darkness, it was the spring of hope, it was the winter of despair, we had everything before us, we had nothing before us, we were all going direct to Heaven, we were all going direct the other way—in short, the period was so far like the present period, that some of its noisiest authorities insisted on its being received, for good or for evil, in the superlative degree of comparison only.

　　—Charles Dickens, *A Tale of Two Cities*

As these and countless other examples testify, good prose uses words with great thought and precision, not abandoning all of the beauty of language to poetry.

Merit

When evaluating a selection of prose, begin by verifying its **merit**—literary and moral quality. If it isn't worthy of the audience, set it aside and keep searching. When looking for works with literary quality, consider classics first, winners of literary awards (mainly older works), and then selections recommended by reliable sources. At the end of this chapter, seven questions for a speaker/reader/performer to ask will help you better understand and evaluate literature. These same questions should help you determine merit too.

definition

Merit refers to the literary (artistic) and moral quality of a selection of literature.

Moral quality cannot be guaranteed by a simple formula. An author might write a harmless and even charming limerick but also have personal associations with offensive publications. If he has made a name for himself through the latter, avoid even referring to the good portions of his literature so as not to promote the author's lifestyle. Also, sometimes the title and even the story line may seem innocuous, but the underlying philosophy may teach the wrong lessons.

74　CHAPTER 4

Point of View

After determining the selection's worthiness, you must begin analyzing the actual text. One important trait of prose to consider is **point of view.** Authors of short stories and novels very carefully select a viewpoint character or narrative presence who interprets the events for the reader. You as an oral reader must understand this point of view to communicate the ideas and feelings of the selection.

Presentation Style: Story Reciting Versus Storytelling

As you continue your analysis (explained in detail at the end of this chapter), you must decide the form your presentation will take. In this course, that form will likely be assigned to you, but such may not always be the case. For example, if you wish to perform Mark Twain's story "The Celebrated Jumping Frog of Calaveras County," you must decide whether to use Twain's words or your own. The first style, often referred to as a "reading" or "monologue," may be better since Twain was such a master of comedy with his word choice. However, since this story and many other works of his have a conversational quality, the audience may never be the wiser for a bit of "storytelling."

Some stories seem better when almost completely performed in a "storyteller" mode, where your own words are thoroughly integrated with the author's. Storytelling is not an excuse not to memorize. In fact, effective storytelling requires an excellent vocabulary, quick thinking on your feet, and much practice to seamlessly blend yourself with the personality and style of the author or narrator. Well-refined storytelling skills are a great attribute to a man or woman in Christian ministry or business or education. Picture a politician who can effectively tell a story in the political arena and an opponent who cannot. If neither one's views are far from what you embrace, which one will you likely "hear out" and consider more carefully?

Story Reciting vs. Storytelling

- Story reciting: the author's own words
- Storytelling: one's own words integrated with the author's

The Greatest Storyteller

Encourage your students to look for ways to use storytelling in their current Christian service. We have the greatest example of an effective storyteller in Christ, who told approximately thirty-three recorded parables during His three-year ministry on the earth. Ask your students to name some of the parables that Christ told. (*Possible answers include the unmerciful servant [Matt. 18:21-35], the wicked husbandmen* [Matt. 21:33-44], *the marriage of the king's son* [Matt. 22:1-14], *the ten virgins* [Matt. 25:1-13], *the talents* [Matt. 25:14-30], *the good Samaritan* [Luke 10:29-37], *the great supper* [Luke 14:15-24], *the prodigal son* [Luke 15:11-32], *the Pharisee and the publican* [Luke 18:9-14], *and so on.*)

Divide your students into groups and have each group look up a parable to see how Jesus told it. The parables listed are some of the lengthier ones, and they can provide a lot of material for discussion. Have the students look for how Christ introduced the parable, what kinds of characters He used, how He introduced the characters, what kinds of settings He used, how He established the settings, how He developed the plot, how He concluded, how He drew applications, and so on.

Reading Poetry

When you hear the phrase *poetry reading*, no doubt your mind conjures up a specific image. Maybe you picture the last time you had to read in a group. You recall your stomach churning when you heard the teacher call your name to read. Maybe you have a more theatrical view. In your mind's eye, you see an eclectic group of people sipping lattes in a bookstore café, reading cryptic poems to one another while everyone nods thoughtfully.

If either one of these scenarios describes your current view of poetry reading, this course can change your mind forever. You will soon see how poetry may be presented as a solo reading, as an abstract group performance, or even as a dramatic scene.

Definition

What does a poem look like? What form does it take? Though numerous and varied exceptions exist, much **poetry** appears on the printed page in the form of lines composing verse, whether heroic, blank, or free verse. Sometimes, the text of a poem is even shaped like its topic. For instance, George Herbert's "Easter Wings," Maxine Kumin's "400 Meter Freestyle," and several of e. e. cummings's works are shape poems.

 definition

Poetry includes verse with rhyme and meter as well as free verse; it is characterized by poetic devices.

Dramatic compression refers to how much might be said briefly in a poem.

Popular poetic styles include the *sonnet*, which regulates the number of syllables per line; *ballad*, which also restricts the number of syllables; and *haiku*, Japanese verse of three lines. All of these prescribe a certain form. If you ignore line length or number of lines, you can call your work a sonnet; but without the right form, it is not a sonnet. If you write several paragraphs, you have not composed a haiku. Though poetry includes a great diversity of forms, it always has a form distinct from prose.

Secondly, poetry has a specific content or word choice. Poetry contains many poetic devices that you will learn about as you continue your literature studies. Some that you may already be familiar with include *rhyme*, *alliteration*, and *imagery*. Another term you should know is *onomatopoeia*, or using words that sound like their meaning.

These devices allow the poet to express in a few words what the essayist must explain in paragraphs. This is called **dramatic compression.**

Characteristics of Poetry
• Distinct form
• Specific content
Poetic devices
Dramatic compression

Portia on Mercy

In Shakespeare's *Merchant of Venice*, the lady Portia disguises herself as an attorney and pleads the case of *Antonio v. Shylock*, eloquently presenting fine rhetoric concerning mercy. Read the following excerpt and then answer the questions below.

Merchant of Venice *by William Shakespeare (Bob Jones University Classic Players).*
Portia: Be merciful. / Shylock: I stay here on my bond.

> *The quality of mercy is not strain'd,**
> *It droppeth as the gentle rain from heaven*
> *Upon the place beneath. It is twice blest:**
> *It blesseth him that gives and him that takes.*
> *'Tis mightiest in the mightiest, it becomes*
> *The thronéd monarch better than his crown.*
> *His sceptre shows the force of temporal power,*
> *The attribute to* awe and majesty,*
> *Wherein doth sit the dread and fear of kings;*
> *But mercy is above this sceptred sway,*
> *It is enthronéd in the hearts of kings,*
> *It is an attribute to* God himself:*
> *And earthly power doth then show likest God's*
> *When mercy seasons* justice.*

strain'd: obliged, forced

twice blest: provides two blessings

attribute to: visual sign of

an attribute to: the nature of, characteristic of

seasons: refines, modifies, flavors

1. Describe how this piece fits the first characteristic of poetry, form.

   The text appears in lines rather than in paragraphs.

2. Describe how this piece fits the second characteristic of poetry, content.

   Answers will vary but might include dramatic compression (an entire treatise on the subject of mercy is compressed into these few lines); poetic devices.

3. Of the above-mentioned poetic devices and others you've studied, which can you find in this selection? Give an example of one word or phrase from the poem and label the type of device it is.

   Possible answers: "Droppeth as the gentle rain . . ." is an example of simile.

   Kings are discussed as a symbol of power that is made greater by the attribute of mercy, etc.

Poetry in Drama

If time permits, consider reading the entire scene from *The Merchant of Venice* in which Portia's speech occurs (Act IV, Scene 1). Otherwise, share the summary below, asking students to imagine the speech in context. Afterward, discuss why Shakespeare might have chosen to write this speech in verse. (Many characters in the play speak in both prose and poetry, including Portia.)

Plot Summary

Having spent most of his resources, Bassanio must borrow money to properly court Portia. His generous friend Antonio agrees to borrow for Bassanio, promising the money-lender, Shylock, a pound of flesh if the money is not repaid as agreed upon. After Bassanio successfully solves a riddle and wins Portia's hand in marriage, the borrowed money must be repaid. Unfortunately, Bassanio is unable to pay, and Antonio suffers financial loss in his trade. When the two men go to court with Shylock, Portia disguises herself as a lawyer and speaks in defense of Antonio. Her speech emphasizes the Christian value of mercy. Shylock rejects the idea completely, demanding justice. Portia then presents him with more justice than he bargained for. If he must have a pound of Antonio's flesh, he must somehow take it without a

**"The Mountain Whip-
poorwill"**

Finding the Music

Poetry might be called the music of literature. Written for the ear, poems contain the best words in the best arrangement. Of course, hymn texts or nonsacred lyrics generally appear in verse form, but poetry's song is evident even when it is not paired with a tune.

In the following passage from American poet Stephen Vincent Benét, listen to the music of the words. Read it once or twice silently until you understand the ideas and then read it aloud to hear the music of the words.

Big Tom Sargeant was the first in line.
He could fiddle all the bugs off a sweet-potato vine.
He could fiddle down a 'possom from a mile-high tree,
He could fiddle up a whale from the bottom of the sea.
Yuh could hear hands spankin' till they spanked each other raw,
When he finished variations on "Turkey in the Straw."

Little Jimmy Weezer was the next to play;
He could fiddle all night, he could fiddle all day.
He could fiddle chills, he could fiddle fever,
He could make a fiddle rustle like a lowland river.
He could make a fiddle croon like a lovin' woman
And they clapped like thunder when he was
  finished strummin'.

Next came the ruck of the bob-tailed fiddlers,
The let's go easies and the fair-to-middlers.
The crowd was tired of their no-'count squealin'
When out in the center steps Old Dan Wheeling.

He fiddled high and he fiddled low,
(Listen, little whippoorwill, yuh got to spread yore
  wings!)
He fiddled and fiddled with a cherry-wood bow.
(Old Dan Wheeling's got bee honey in his strings.)
He fiddled the wind by the lonesome moon.
He fiddled a most almighty tune.
He started fiddling like a ghost
He ended fiddling like a host.
He fiddled north an' he fiddled south.
He fiddled the heart right out of yore mouth.

—Stephen Vincent Benét, "The Mountain Whippoorwill" or "How Hillbilly Jim Won the Great Fiddlers' Prize"

Could you hear the music? Notice how the line length, word choice, rhythm, and rhyme convey the local color of the Georgia fiddlers' show as well as the actual music of the fiddles. A writer would find it hard to communicate this story effectively in prose.

Reading Drama

Just when you thought you'd read it all, drama appears as a new fish altogether. Many an avid reader of novels and short stories (and perhaps even poetry) will pick up a play to read and then throw his hands up in despair, contending that the literature is incomprehensible. Why might this be?

A **play script,** unlike a story, novel, poem, or even the production of a play, is not a complete, knowable creature any more than a skeleton is a person. A play script contains the structure of the plot without the living essence of conflict. It is the bones of the characters without muscle or voice. How can a reader take this black-and-white, inanimate object and breathe full-color life into it?

Imagination is the singular key to reading a script intelligently. Though all literature demands the presence of imagination, nowhere is it more critical in application than in reading a script. Without this important key, the treasures of drama will be locked away as heirlooms might be in a trunk in the attic.

When reading a play script, follow this method: first, read just one scene, trying to understand the premise. Is this a comic situation in which I can laugh at people slipping on banana peels? Or is this tragic—a fatal fall? Then read to understand the characters. What is each one like? How do they relate to one another? A comment made friend to friend such as "I wouldn't do that if I were you" might be helpful advice. The same words uttered by someone robbing your house could be a severe threat.

Now start from the beginning and imagine the appearance, voice, personality, and style for each character as you read. Soon you will find the whole play enacted in your mind's eye.

Definition

*A **play script** is the skeletal structure of a plot without the living essence of conflict.*

DRAMATISTIC ANALYSIS

A speaker may be well informed, but if he hasn't thought out exactly what he wants to say today, to this audience, he has no business taking up other people's valuable time.

—Lee Iacocca, former president of Chrysler

The responsibility to prepare carefully for public speaking is obvious since you will be speaking your own words. You may think that you do not have that

---

Read Plays Aloud

Your students may find plays more enjoyable if read aloud. Unlike novelists, playwrights do not intend for their works to be enjoyed by a bookworm sitting beside a warm, crackling fire on a cold winter evening. Plays are intended to be spoken aloud by actors on a stage.

Lesson Motivator

Perhaps you have heard the expression, "Give a man a fish; feed him for a day. Teach him to fish; feed him for a lifetime." Considering that this text includes many selections of literature for students' projects, literature analysis could have been provided as well, saving students a great deal of homework time. However, they would leave the course lacking the ability to select literature on their own and intelligently evaluate it. Instead of handing them the finished product, this chapter is designed to provide both tools and methods simplified to be within the students' grasp.

Lesson Objectives

The student will be able to

1. Research background information using a library and/or Internet search.

2. Analyze a selection of literature by answering various questions concerning it.

Make It Live

If you have a copy of a play that you have seen or are quite familiar with, choose a brief section (1-2 pages) to show the students, allowing them to read it silently. Then read it aloud, dramatically interpreting the characters and stage directions. Discuss briefly how a thoughtful reading makes the story much more real and comprehensible.

An alternative activity would be finding a good audio book (fiction). Have the students read a page from the book and then play the recorded dramatization. Have them compare the two for clarity, interest, and style.

Comic or Tragic?

Instructions. Divide students into two teams. Present each of the following phrases to the entire class. Assign one team the task of thinking of a comic circum-

stance for the line. The other team will brainstorm for a serious circumstance for the same line.

1. You never know when a rope ladder will come in handy.
2. No one will find me in here.
3. Who's there?
4. Surprise!
5. Nice doggie. Good doggie, doggie.
6. I thought you were going to call the plumber.

responsibility with drama since you are performing someone else's words. However, if you do not understand what you present, you cannot possibly communicate the author's work effectively.

A play entitled *You Can't Take It with You* by George Kauffman and Moss Hart includes a waitress in a diner who claims to be the Russian Grand Duchess. One actress portrayed the role and then two years later discovered that this character was actually an allusion to a real person.

Perhaps you've heard of Anastasia Romanov. The Czar's family, including Anastasia and her siblings, were taken captive and later executed. However, when their skeletons were discovered many years later, two were missing—Anastasia's and a younger brother's. A woman living in the United States named Anna Anderson claimed that she was really Anastasia Romanov and had escaped, concealing her true identity for safety purposes. At the time when Kauffman and Hart wrote *You Can't Take It with You*, Anderson's claim to be Anastasia was a news topic. Apparently the playwrights thought Anderson's claim was far-fetched because they named a melodramatic, deluded waitress Olga Katrina. Anastasia's oldest sister, Olga Katrina, was indeed the Grand Duchess. However, no one could claim to be the long-lost Olga Katrina because there was conclusive evidence that she had been executed. Knowing this background obviously provides much help to the actress playing the part, especially in depth of characterization. If the audience can be made aware of the situation, the drama will be heightened.

The more you can learn about the author and the selection you perform, the better performance choices you can make. In addition, you will quickly enhance your perspective on historical events as you work on selections written during different time periods.

For the remainder of the chapter, we will discuss dramatistic analysis, a simple method of researching and evaluating performance selections.

Library Research

For some of you, darkening the doorway of the library is about as appealing as cleaning your room. However, learning to properly use library resources will reduce your library research time. Perhaps you will even someday enjoy going to the library. (Scary, isn't it?)

The following four questions, part of the **dramatistic analysis,** usually require library resources. If your selection is well known, you may be able to find comparable information on a reliable Internet site.

definition

*The **dramatistic analysis** consists of seven questions that aid in understanding and evaluating a selection of literature.*

Discussion. Afterward, discuss which lines worked easily for a comic scenario as well as a serious scenario. Did some lines seem inherently funny or serious? If so, would a change in diction influence that quality? (For example, would a paraphrase of the same general thought seem less bound to humor or sobriety?)

Have your student select one of the lines of dialogue above. Instruct him to brainstorm for a tragic scene that utilizes the line he chose. Then have him do the same for a comic scene. You may choose to have him improvise both scenes or just one scene. Encourage creativity as he creates multiple characters. One performer acting out several roles can make a serious scene very focused, very free from distraction. In comedy, the humor is often heightened as well.

Emotion in Action

Introduction. Most novice actors are eager to portray emotion. They read a description of their character, read their own lines, and decide they ought to act "snobby" or "scary" or "melancholy." Instead of letting action, both verbal and physical, convey the plot and character, they play a mood. Though the students have not yet studied acting techniques, they do understand how they express them-

Who Is the Speaker?

Sounds like a simple question, doesn't it? Believe it or not, it will likely warrant an entire paragraph answer. Imagine you are planning to perform a speech given by Abraham Lincoln. Begin with what you already know about Lincoln: his background, his career, and his place in history. Then research him. An encyclopedia is a good starting place. A biography from a reputable source is also appropriate. Does that mean you must read a six-volume biography about him, word for word? No. Instead, try to find a couple of short biographies and compare their contents for accuracy.

Take notes on what you read and then organize your ideas into one or two paragraphs. Each chapter in this text with an assignment that includes research also includes a dramatistic analysis worksheet for recording your research data.

Where Is the Speaker?

In most cases more than a biography will be needed to answer this question. Try to find a book or article about the actual speech, story, poem, or play you are performing. For nonfiction, such as a public speech, you will be researching historical facts. In fiction or drama, answer this question by focusing on the key figure in the story.

This question probes at more than just location, though that information should be included. The core issue is the situation or the environment. Abraham Lincoln once stood at the rear of a train car addressing the citizens of Springfield, Illinois, where he had practiced law and reared his children. He had just been elected president. Factions of abolitionists and slave owners as well as Unionists and secessionists were on the brink of a terrible conflict. Later he stood on a blood-drenched Pennsylvania battlefield without the knowledge that his simple commemorative speech would one day be among the most famous of all presidential addresses. From his Farewell Address in Springfield to the Gettysburg Address, the location at which Lincoln spoke played a huge role in the meaning and intent of his words.

In Shakespeare's *Merchant of Venice*, Portia and Nerissa are chattering ladies who critique suitors in one scene but later become attorneys in a court of law; the contrast is stunning. Not only do they change from having a social focus to being professional, but they also convincingly portray men, even before the eyes and ears of their own husbands.

When Is the Speaker Speaking?

First consider the time in relationship to other pertinent events. Perhaps your character delivers an urgent command with little time to persuade or coax. Read the following excerpt from Shakespeare's *Macbeth* as Lady Macbeth speaks.

---

selves in everyday life. This activity should instill the principle that emotion is most believably conveyed through action.

Instructions. Assign each set of stage directions below to a student volunteer. Allow the student a couple of minutes to read and reread the list of directions. Then each student should in turn act out the directions as a pantomime. (Permit occasional speaking.) Do not identify the emotion(s) named to the volunteer or the audience. After each

pantomime, have the class guess the scenario and then infer what emotion(s) the character experienced.

1. Basic scenario: Your older sister is in ICU after a car crash earlier that morning. (*sorrow, fear, disappointment, confusion, etc.*)

Action: You enter stage space as though you are walking down a hall, looking for her hospital room. You stop and read a sign on an invisible door. You enter slowly to find your sister attached

to many machines. You eventually pull up a chair near the bed. You study her face. You softly whisper her name. There is no response. You grasp the railing on the bed and call the name more loudly. No response. You lower your head to rest on your hands. Several seconds later, you reach out and brush her hand lightly, quickly withdrawing your hand. You stand. You walk around to the end of the bed and look into her face, noting each injury. You head for the door, intending to ask the nurses several

> To beguile the time,*
> Look like the time; bear welcome in your eye,
> Your hand, your tongue; look like th' innocent
>   flower,
> But be the serpent under't. He that's coming
> Must be provided for; and you shall put
> This night's great business* into my dispatch.*

beguile the time: deceive the world

great business: regicide—murdering King Duncan
dispatch: authority, command

Contrast Ebenezer Scrooge in Charles Dickens's *A Christmas Carol* before and after visits from the three spirits.

Before (speaking to his merry nephew)
"What's Christmas time to you but a time for paying bills without money; a time for finding yourself a year older, and not an hour richer . . . ? If I could work my will," said Scrooge, indignantly, "every idiot who goes about with 'Merry Christmas' on his lips should be boiled with his own pudding, and buried with a stake of holly through his heart."

After (speaking to the last spirit)
"I will honour Christmas in my heart, and try to keep it all the year. I will live in the Past, the Present, and the Future." . . .

Scrooge was better than his word. . . . And it was always said of him, that he knew how to keep Christmas well, if any man alive possessed the knowledge.

The time may also have a practical application. In the short story "The Scarlet Ibis" by James Hurst, the main character comes to a terrible realization concerning the fate of his little brother while in a forest in severe rain. As storyteller or actor, you could not convey this character effectively without considering the environmental factors of that moment.

To Whom Is the Speaker Speaking?

In public speaking, you need to tailor your message to your audience. Who is your audience? When you practice a speech, your audience might be your dog, but for an actual speech, you communicate a message to your listeners. **Audience** doesn't mean just the people in the chairs who are listening. Audience is anyone the speaker speaks to. If you are performing a short story, a character might address another character in dialogue. That other character is the audience for that line of dialogue. In short stories and plays, a character might address himself, another character, the **audience proper** (the people in the auditorium), or God.

definition

Audience refers to the person or group the speaker addresses.

Audience proper refers to the people seated in the auditorium.

questions about your sister. ("Brother" can be substituted for "sister.")

(Note: The student should fill in the gaps between the actions as he improvises. For example, he should turn a doorknob before entering the hospital room. These details have been omitted so the student can employ more creativity and thought.)

2. Basic scenario: A pleasant walk in the woods takes a turn for the worse. (*pain and fear, worry, hope, etc.*)

Action: You enter stage transporting a large backpack, whistling or humming. You love nature, so creating a leaf collection for science class is an enjoyable task. You turn when you hear a couple of birds chirping. Without watching where you are going, you slip on a rock. You lose your balance while wincing from a stabbing pain in your ankle. Your backpack seems twice as heavy as before. You look back down the trail, densely shadowed by trees. You try to stand, but collapse back to a seated position in pain.

You wiggle out of your backpack straps. You yell for help several times. You scan the surrounding area for a long twig that might serve as a walking stick. Finding one that looks promising, you try again to get to your feet. You look down at your backpack and then slowly creep toward the entrance you made at the beginning of the scene.

3. Basic scenario: The local bakery has a special on your favorite treat, Boston cream pie. However, you are trying to stick to a low-fat diet

Audience in Works of Fiction

In Shakespeare's classic romantic comedy *Much Ado About Nothing*, the Lady Beatrice entertains and gently ribs everyone from her cousin and uncle to the accommodating Prince Don Pedro himself. However, when Benedick, a soldier who apparently hurt her feelings in the past, becomes her audience, her cleverness turns to bitterness. With an acid tongue she banters words meant to slay the soldier's heart. Listen to the mockings.

Possible Audiences

- yourself
- another character onstage
- audience proper
- God

BEATRICE: I wonder that you will still be talking, Signior Benedick, nobody marks you.

BENEDICK: What, my dear Lady Disdain! are you yet living?

BEATRICE: Is it possible disdain should die while she hath such meet food to feed it as Signior Benedick? Courtesy itself must convert to disdain, if you come in her presence.

BENEDICK: Then is courtesy a turncoat. But it is certain that I am loved of all ladies, only you excepted; and I would I could find it in my heart that I had not a hard heart, for truly I love none.

BEATRICE: A dear happiness to women . . .

Beatrice has a different relationship to this audience than to any other, which influences her words, her delivery, and even her spirit. When at the close of the argument Benedick delivers his final blow and withdraws, not allowing Beatrice to retaliate, she complains that he "always ends with a jade's trick," implying that this is how he has treated her before.

Interestingly, as soon as Beatrice's concept of Benedick changes, the way she communicates with him changes. When she thinks he loves her, she speaks with caution rather than with stinging words.

To what sort of people did Lincoln speak at the Springfield railway station? To what sort of man did Lady Macbeth speak when she urged subtlety and preparation for a murder? Audience is an important part of the scene.

Evaluation

Now that you know the background facts, further evaluate the literature by asking the following questions: What is the speaker trying to communicate? How might he or she accomplish the communication goal? Even more practically, how will you communicate the speaker's ideas and feelings? What is the speaker's purpose? Examine both the text and your research to find these answers.

Jade Defined

Jade is a name given to horses that are of low breeding, worn-out, weary, bad-tempered, or even worthless or vicious. To apply this term to people was rather a jade's trick of her own.

READING WITH UNDERSTANDING 83

3. Basic scenario: The local bakery has a special on your favorite treat, Boston cream pie. However, you are trying to stick to a low-fat diet because you're training for the cross-country team. (*distress and indecision, excitement, panic, relief, etc.*)

Action: You are walking briskly down the street when you turn and see the bakery window full of delicious goodies. You look up and read a large sign advertising a one-day special on Boston cream pie and all cream-filled doughnuts. You remember your diet and turn to walk away. You turn again, smelling the aroma of fresh baked goods as another customer opens the door. You lean close to the window, peering longingly at the Boston cream pie. You suddenly spin about, looking to see if anyone involved with track and field is in sight. You look again in the window and then begin to walk away, fingering change in your pocket. You stop after a few steps and start counting your money. You try to be inconspicuous as you slip into the bakery shop. You order a pie and begin counting your change. Suddenly you look behind you and see the coach's wife browsing over French bread. You quickly pay and exit with the evidence, trying not to let her see you.

Discussion. After completing the improvisations, briefly discuss what principles may apply to understanding emotion from a reading of a script. What should the actor look for? (*Possible answers: verbal and physical action.*)

What Is Being Said?

Sarah and her family are visiting friends who live only about five hours' driving time from their own home. Despite this relative proximity, language and culture are different. Imagine the following scenario: Sarah's friend Emma joins her in the back yard and says in a most confidential tone, "Your brother's gettin' a growlin'." In utter bewilderment, Sarah stares as Emma continues, "I don't know what he's done, but he's gettin' it."

Emma might as well have been speaking a different language. Finally the message was deciphered: where Sarah lives, this same idea would be expressed, "Your brother's getting a lecture [because of wrongdoing]." Sarah was equally perplexed when Emma announced they couldn't have any pudding pops because "they're all." *All what?* Sarah wondered, not realizing this meant they were all gone.

Sometimes you will have to evaluate the actual words to make sure you understand them the way they were intended. The fable "The City Mouse and the Country Mouse" applies whether contrasting urban and rural dwellers, New Yorkers and Charlestonians, or people from different countries. Always study the context to make certain you are grasping the author's meaning.

How Is It Being Said?

Some speakers use poetic words; others use slang. Note the obvious differences in your delivery of these two inquiries:

[Rustic] "Hah y'all doin'?"

[British] "How d'you do, Sir?"

Style of **diction** will certainly influence your characterization and delivery! Be certain that you understand why a character speaks the way he does. Then work to convey that style, being true to the author's intent and fair to the character (avoid mocking the character or creating an unfair stereotype).

definition

Diction describes a speaker's word choice and style.

Also, the delivery might be influenced by any of the factors detailed above. If you were portraying Lady Macbeth and you knew someone might overhear your murderous plans with Macbeth, how would you speak? If you were certain that no servant was in earshot, would your method change?

Why Is It Being Said?

If you thoroughly answer every question up to this point and valiantly attempt to perform a selection based on the first six questions, you will still fail to be effective. It has been said that "A good speech is like a pencil. It must have a point."

This applies not just to a public speech, but to a dramatic reading, a poem, or a play. Without purpose, you might as well have remained silent. One might even say that the difference between an average performance and an outstanding per-

84 CHAPTER 4

PRESENTATION
Dramatistic Analysis

The Master Communicator

Encourage the students to study Christ's methods of spoken communication in their personal devotions. His primary audiences included His disciples, the religious leaders, and those who sought physical or spiritual healing. How did He address each group?

What Is Your Purpose?

Encourage your students to memorize or assign as part of their grade to memorize Philippians 3:7-8: "But what things were gain to me, those I counted loss for Christ. Yea doubtless, and I count all things but loss for the excellency of the knowledge of Christ Jesus my Lord: for whom I have suffered the loss of all things, and do count them but dung, that I may win Christ." We may never

accomplish as much as the apostle Paul did, but we can adopt for our lives his great purpose in life—loving and proclaiming Christ!

A Sample to Analyze

Introduction. *John Brown's Body* is a book-length poem by American author Stephen Vincent Benét, imaginatively chronicling the events and characters of the Civil War. Benét's work is a stirring tribute to the noble and courageous in every camp.

formance is not so much found in technique as in purpose. The technical merit could be very high in one performance, but if even the most gifted performer lacks a sense of purpose—a need to communicate the message—his attempt will not be excellent. The reverse is also true. Often a speaker will make technical errors such as vocalized pauses or nervous gestures. Though these distract from communication, zeal and sincerity will minimize the detraction.

Having a purpose allows mediocre people to do great things. For Christians this is a wonderful hope. Though Christians are clay vessels, if their life purpose is to pour out the fragrant truth of the gospel, they have not lived in vain. Sadly, many people in our society today perceive that their lives have no purpose, and so they live their lives that way—purposelessly.

Indeed, *why* is a question we ask as soon as we learn to speak. Many times we are disappointed not to find a clear answer. Sometimes our parents didn't tell us why when we were children, and sometimes God doesn't tell us why even now. However, you will usually be able to discover why the speaker is speaking.

When we discuss performing drama later in the text, we will revisit this idea. For now, concentrate on reading with a mind to figure out the speaker's motivation for his or her message.

CONCLUSION

In this chapter we've seen the importance of reading with understanding and then evaluating what we've read. When we read, we must have a goal in mind. Otherwise, we may skim words without gleaning the needed ideas.

Pay attention to both denotative and connotative meanings. Obviously we need a clear understanding of the literal, dictionary meaning of individual words. Perhaps more importantly, we must comprehend the meaning of the text as a whole unit in context. Context and our experiences influence our grasp of meaning, both denotative and connotative.

With reading technique, use specific approaches for each type of literature. Each genre has distinctive characteristics. Prose is distinguished by a narrator and his point of view in either word-for-word or storytelling style. Poetry emphasizes form and word choice. Drama, in play scripts, requires more imagination than other forms of literature because it is like an outline rather than a complete work. Evaluate the style (comic, tragic, etc.) and imagine the characters to make reading drama come alive.

Written analysis requires research and good thinking skills. You evaluate the speaker (who), the situation (where, when), the audience (to whom), and the message (what, how, why).

Throughout this course you will be reading many performance selections as well as listening to other students perform. Read, hear, and evaluate carefully. Don't avoid a selection just because of a few unfamiliar words or situations. Explore and experience as many selections of quality literature as you can.

READING WITH UNDERSTANDING 85

Instructions. Read the excerpts in Teacher's Appendix 3 to the class, urging them to picture each person speaking and each scene described. The appendix includes questions from the dramatistic analysis and sample answers. Encourage students toward discussion. This will set a precedent for their individual written work in future chapters.

question 4
Many words have multiple dictionary definitions, and the reader depends on the context to choose which one is intended by the author.

question 5
All communication, verbal and nonverbal, has connotation.

question 6
These are found primarily, but not exclusively, in poetry.

Terms to Know

denotative meaning	poetry
connotative meaning	dramatic compression
context	play script
genre	dramatistic analysis
prose	audience
merit	audience proper
point of view	diction

Ideas to Understand

Multiple Choice: **Choose the best answer.**

__B__ 1. Which of the following could effectively be conveyed through storytelling?
    A. drama   C. poetry
    B. fiction   D. all of these

__D__ 2. In which genre does dramatic compression usually occur?
    A. drama   D. poetry
    B. essay   E. all of these
    C. novel   F. none of these

__B__ 3. According to the text, what is the key to understanding a play?
    A. enthusiasm   C. research
    B. imagination   D. none of these

True/False: **Write** True **or** False **for each statement. If false, cross out the word or words that make it incorrect and write in the word or words that make it true.**

__False__ 4. Denotative meaning cannot change because of context, as connotative might.
    ~~cannot~~ can

__False__ 5. Connotation applies only to verbal communication. ~~only~~

__True__ 6. Prose does not feature much use of alliteration, meter, or rhyme.

__False__ 7. Short stories do not necessarily have a distinct, recognizable point of view, but most plays do. ~~short stories~~ plays; ~~plays~~ short stories

 CHAPTER 4

Short Answer

8. Think of two possible connotative meanings for this sentence: "I need help." Write below a one-sentence description of each context. Then in quotation marks, write paraphrases of the connotative meaning. *Answers will vary.*

Example:

context: You are working on geometry homework.

paraphrase: "I'm desperate to find a math genius; if I don't, I'll never get my homework done!" (This is what is implied when you say "I need help" in the context described above.)

context: _____

paraphrase: " _____ "

context: _____

paraphrase: " _____ "

READING WITH UNDERSTANDING   87

Unit 2 Introduction

Unit 2 features four major projects in solo performance. Despite the strong interest most students have in stage acting and interacting with other performers, studying solo performance before group performance generally helps them to refine their verbal communication skills, making them more effective actors when they do participate in a group performance. Also, the director will actually have time to coach the actors on their interaction, their stage movement, and the like rather than having to spend time helping them with basic textual meaning (or ignoring clear meaning altogether).

In this unit, students will present a narrative passage from the Bible using a manuscript, perform a sonnet from memory, create a stage character in a memorized one-minute monologue, and tell a short story in their own words.

Though these tasks involve related skills such as building suspense and vividly describing something, they also teach unique skills.

In the Scripture narrative project the students will gain experience handling a manuscript on stage.

Poetry presents an artistic challenge, since its meaning is so concentrated. Greater care is needed when delivering poetry. Since many

UNIT

Henry V *by William Shakespeare (Bob Jones University Classic Players)*

teachers, preachers, and other public speakers often include a poem in their speeches, handling poetry well is a valuable skill.

The monologue introduces the concept of creating a stage character. The project is also designed to acquaint students with the procedures and expectations at a play audition.

Finally, the storytelling project teaches students how to memorize ideas, rather than memorizing text verbatim. Though word-for-word memory sounds very professional in a dramatic reading contest, extemporaneous public speaking and storytelling are more practical and much more frequently used skills in adult life, both professional and personal. Extemporaneous speaking generally improves a student's overall academic work.

Enjoy this unit that focuses on the individual. Make it your goal to see each student make notable progress as a communicator through these projects.

SOLO PERFORMANCE

O God of battles! Steel my soldiers' hearts;
Possess them not with fear! Take from them now
The sense of reckoning, if th' opposed numbers
Pluck their hearts from them.

Chapter 5
Introduction

Most students who enroll in a course on oral interpretation or acting expect to study materials such as drama readings or lines from a play. The thought of sharing a Bible story might be completely foreign to them. As a Christian educator, you have the opportunity to show students the inherent value of God's Word in every aspect of life, including drama. We know that "The word of God is quick, and powerful, and sharper than any two-edged sword, piercing even to the dividing asunder of soul and spirit, and of the joints and marrow, and is a discerner of the thoughts and intents of the heart" (Heb. 4:12).

Certainly scriptural promises provide encouragement when students feel apprehensive about public communication. Additionally, the Bible truly is excellent literature and deserves to be studied and appreciated as such. Performing Bible stories or poetry has numerous benefits.

1. The performer benefits from studying (and memorizing) the passage.
2. The audience receives a profound blessing by hearing the Word.
3. The ideas in the passage are very understandable and memorable to both speaker and listener.

Lesson Plan
Suggested homework is in **boldface.**

Lesson Description	Recommended Presentation	Performance Projects/ Written Assignments
I. The Drama of the Ages (p. 93)	ST—Psalms in Verse; Scripting Practice TE—Reading Genres; What Makes a Classic; Prodigal Son Box	TE—Bible Story Improvisation **ST—Assign Scripture Narrative project.**
II. Interpretation Skills (p. 108)	ST—Subtextual Meaning TE—The Author's Ideas	TE—Context Improvisation
III. Standing Alone (p. 114)	Share I Peter 5:7 to help alleviate students' fears about communicating.	
Assessment	Chapter quiz	Scripture Narrative performances **ST—Assign Journal 4.**
Suggested Teaching Time: 6-8 class periods		

The Greatest Literature Book

Great literature is that kind of writing which, in addition to whatever other purposes it may serve, is characterized by aesthetic and artistic qualities.

Teaching Materials

- A Bible
- A visual aid for The Author's Ideas activity
- Various samples of literature for use with Reading Genres or What Makes a Classic
- Performance rubrics (students submit their own copy)

4. Effective communication of Scripture makes a Christian a more effective witness and teacher/preacher.

5. Performing Scripture can sometimes serve an evangelistic purpose. Many people who do not normally attend church will come to a dramatic program that presents a portion of scriptural narrative.

If you are personally convinced of the value of this project, you will easily motivate your students.

Chapter 5 Outline

Introduction

I. The drama of the ages
   A. What is a classic?
      1. Bible poetry
      2. Bible sermons and declamations
      3. Bible drama
   B. How can I present the Bible orally?
      1. Impromptu reading
      2. Find the drama
      3. Identify the plot
      4. Make a cutting
      5. Practice well

II. Interpretation skills
   A. Comprehension
      1. Vocabulary
      2. Context
      3. Theme
   B. Communication
      1. Thought units
      2. Phrases
      3. Emphasis and subordination
      4. Subtextual meaning
      5. Climax

III. Standing alone

OVERVIEW

Know—*Concepts*

Genres in the Bible

Grow—*Interpretation Skills*

Understanding the text
Thought units
Phrasing through use of pause,
   emphasis, and subordination
Subtextual meaning
Climax

Show—*Performance*

Dramatic narrative from the Bible

Then Joseph could not refrain himself before all them that stood by him; and he cried, Cause every man to go out from me. And there stood no man with him, while Joseph made himself known unto his brethren. And he wept aloud: and the Egyptians and the house of Pharaoh heard. And Joseph said unto his brethren, I am Joseph; doth my father yet live? And his brethren could not answer him; for they were troubled at his presence. And Joseph said unto his brethren, Come near to me, I pray you. And they came near. And he said, I am Joseph your brother, whom ye sold into Egypt. Now therefore be not grieved, nor angry with yourselves, that ye sold me hither: for God did send me before you to preserve life. ... So now it was not you that sent me hither, but God: and he hath made me a father to Pharaoh, and lord of all his house, and a ruler throughout all the land of Egypt.... And ye shall tell my father of all my glory in Egypt, and of all that ye have seen; and ye shall haste and

 Reading Genres

Select several examples of materials familiar to the students—paragraphs from last year's yearbook dedication, a student newspaper, a popular periodical, a story they may have read, a typical letter or e-mail, and so on. Read these brief examples, asking students to identify the genre. Ask them how they knew that a letter was a letter or a newspaper article was a newspaper article. Point out to the students that we have certain expectations for written communication, based on the genre. For example, newspaper article titles are always very concise rather than artistic. Some glossy periodicals feature opinion as much as or more than fact. Some publications are very professional or technical while others are conversational. Examine a number of styles.

bring down my father hither. And he fell upon his brother Benjamin's neck,
and wept; and Benjamin wept upon his neck. Moreover he kissed all his
brethren, and wept upon them: and after that his brethren talked with him.
(Genesis 45:1-5, 8, 13-15)

What book comes to mind when you read the words *The Greatest Literature Book?*
This literature book contains many stories both historical and fictitious, as well as
sermons and personal letters. Also, approximately one-third of this book is poetry.
This all-time bestseller is available in all major languages and numerous minor
languages.

You may have realized by now that this description refers to the Bible. Without
trivializing the sacredness of God's Word, we will study the Bible in this chapter as
the finest literature and performance material that has or will ever exist.

You will find several advantages of viewing the Bible as literature. First, identifying the genre of a biblical passage improves your understanding of that passage.
Though the Bible's source is divine, its form is very human. God knew His audience,
and He wrote to His audience in a way they would understand. He used the best
possible genre of literature for each portion of His message. If you know a text's
genre, you will understand what is literal and what is figurative.

Not only will you understand well what you read, but you'll also read aloud
more effectively. Practically speaking, you will need to read aloud from the Bible
many times in your life. Many people find reading aloud intimidating. Reading the
Bible aloud can be nerve-racking because of the diction of the translation, the unfamiliar names, or the social expectations of your peers. Whether in a small Bible
study class or as part of a church cantata, you have an important responsibility to
read well and communicate effectively.

In addition to improving comprehension, understanding the Bible as literature
provides increased appreciation—in other words, this will help Bible reading "come
alive" for you personally. This chapter is an opportunity to experience the joy and
blessings that come from reading God's Word to others, helping them better understand it.

THE DRAMA OF THE AGES

> *Great literature is that kind of writing which, in addition to whatever other*
> *purposes it may serve, is characterized by aesthetic and artistic qualities. It*
> *is peculiarly fitting, therefore, that so much of God's Word to us should be*
> *beautiful as well as true—reminding us that God created man with the*
> *wonderful and mysterious capability of responding with delight to beauty of*
> *many kinds.*
>
> —Calvin Linton

THE GREATEST LITERATURE BOOK 93

Even though the purpose of
this chapter is to prepare
students to effectively communicate Bible narrative,
their learning experience will
be greatly enhanced by seeing the big picture concerning the Bible as literature.
Once they consider the
qualities of each genre and
then identify a given passage
as a particular genre, their
understanding will improve
greatly. As the chapter explains, poetry is best understood when evaluated as
poetry, narrative as narrative,
and so on. This type of analysis should occur in studies of
other literature and music in
addition to Scripture. This
course will be more valuable
and more memorable when
integrated with other academic disciplines and daily
living.

Lesson Objectives

The student will be able to

1. Identify genres.
2. Identify plot structure
   in Bible narrative.
3. Cut a narrative to
   be suitable for oral
   reading.

Genre

Scholars have suggested a
diversity of labels for genres
in the Bible, including narrative history, genealogy, law,
chronicle, suspense, testimony, debate, hymn, poetry,
proverb, love song, sermon,
philosophical treatise,
prophecy, riddle, drama,

PRESENTATION
The Drama of the Ages

What Makes a Classic
Read the story of Joseph
aloud (from Genesis or an
illustrated Bible storybook) and/or an
excerpt from a classic work of fiction.
Discuss the appealing elements of each
story.

novel, biography, autobiography, fiction (parable), conversation, ecclesiastical epistle, personal letter, theological treatise, allegory, and creed.

Divinely Inspired Hymnbook

Churches today use various collections of hymns. Though many of these hymnbooks are excellent aids in worship, none can claim divine inspiration except one—the Book of Psalms in the Bible, sometimes called the Psalter. The Psalms give us the clearest doctrine about many important subjects, including Christ as the promised Messiah, who fulfilled the covenant God made with Adam, Abraham, David, and others.

Psalm 1

A common meter tune will accommodate the text of Psalm 1 from *The Bay Psalm Book*. Common meter has four lines per stanza with a syllable count of 8.6.8.6. Generally these are grouped into iambic feet, so the order would be "unstressed, stressed" four times in lines one and three, and three times in lines two and four. The traditional tune for "Amazing Grace" (NEW BRITAIN) is an example of common meter.

You may have heard the Bible referred to as "God's love letter." Indeed it is. God Himself reveals His heart to His creation. The Bible's primary subject is Jesus Christ, the Holy Son of God, member of the Trinity and coequal with the Father. Its great, timeless theme is God's plan for the redemption, sanctification, and eternal destination of man. Obviously no other story has more universal appeal than that!

What Is a Classic?

Many stories may be called **classics.** Titles range from children's literature like *Charlotte's Web* and *Where the Red Fern Grows* to famous adventures and romances such as *Great Expectations* and *Romeo and Juliet*. Hundreds of others could be included as well.

definition

Classic stories, sometimes called **classics,** *have universal appeal and a timeless plot.*

Universal appeal refers to the theme and characters in a selection that are compelling to most or all people.

Timeless stories do not become outdated. Though details may be connected to a specific time or place, the plot and the conflict surpass the details, continuing to be relevant.

Classic stories have **universal appeal.** Universal appeal refers to the theme and characters of a story. Universal literature depicts experiences and feelings common to all people. We all have known joy and sorrow, peace and fear, physical adventures and mental challenges.

In *Romeo and Juliet* we sympathize with the plight of the hero and heroine because young love is a popular universal theme. Consider *Great Expectations*, by Charles Dickens. You may pity an orphan who has a difficult home life and relate to the child's terror when an escaped convict demands a file and vittles. However, if you do not sympathize with Pip, you probably won't find that story appealing. You must comprehend Pip's dreams and obstacles to success before appreciating the story. Though the action is the same for any reader, the appeal of the character will influence each reader's interest level differently.

In addition to having universal appeal, classics are **timeless stories.** Many could easily be altered to fit a different place, time period, or culture without losing the impact of the story. The plot of *Julius Caesar* echoes through the centuries to the present—ambition, treachery, and assassination. Any time a plot hinges on this type of conflict, the story is timeless. Other timeless conflicts include jealousy, pride, and unrequited love.

In the next several sections, we will examine three genres from the Bible, focusing on how they might be presented.

Bible Poetry

The texts of many traditional hymns and gospel songs can be traced to Scripture passages, though some stem from sermons or personal experience. Perhaps in youth group you have sung choruses that are taken almost directly from verses in Psalms or Proverbs. If so, you are participating in a long tradition of singing from the Bible.

94   CHAPTER 5

Singing Psalm 100

Unlike Psalm 1 from *The Bay Psalm Book*, the following song from *The Scottish Psalter* has lines one and three rhymed as well as lines two and four. The first example adheres more tightly to the prose text whereas the second example emphasizes poetry more. Both accurately reflect the message of their respective psalms.

1 All people that on earth do dwell,
Sing to the Lord with cheerful voice;
2 Him serve with fear, his praise forth tell,
Come ye before him and rejoice.
3 The Lord ye know is God indeed,
Without our aid he did us make;
We are his flock, he doth us feed,
And for his sheep he doth us take.
4 O enter then his gates with praise,
Approach with joy his courts unto
Praise, laud and bless his Name always

For it is seemly so to do.
5 For why? the Lord our God is good,
His mercy is for ever sure;
His truth at all times firmly stood,
And shall from age to age endure.
—William Kethe

Psalm 100 from *The Scottish Psalter* can be sung to the tune LASST UNS ERFREUEN ("All Creatures of Our God and King") by simply including the "O praise him!" and "Alleluia!" phrases. The first two Bible verses combine into one

The first actual book to be printed in the United States was a **psalter,** called *The Bay Psalm Book.* This 1640 Psalter went through many editions, the first several of which included little or no music.

Read the example below and sing or hum a familiar tune, such as St. Agnes ("Jesus, the Very Thought of Thee"), trying to fit these words to it. You will sing through the tune once per verse.

D definition

*A **psalter** is a songbook of psalms set in poetic form.*

1 O blessed man, that in th' advice
Of wicked doth not walk
Nor stand in sinners' way nor sit
In chayre [chair] of scornfull folk.

2 But in the law of Jehova,
Is his longing delight;
And in his law doth meditate
By day and ere by night.

3 And he shall be like to a tree
Planted by water-rivers:
That in his season yields his fruit
And his leafe never withers.

4 And all he doth, shall prosper well,
The wicked are not so:
But they are like unto the chaffe
Which winde drives to and fro.

5 Therefore shall not ungodly men,
Rise to stand in the doome,
Nor shall the sinners with the just,
In their assemblie come.

6 For of the righteous men, the Lord
Acknowledgeth the way:
But the way of ungodly men,
Shall utterly decay.

—"Psalm 1" from *The Bay Psalm Book* (original spelling retained)

stanza, so the stanza numbers do not correlate with the Bible verses. The key of E-flat is appropriate for this tune.

1. All people that on earth do dwell,
Sing to the Lord with cheerful voice;
Alleluia, alleluia.
Him serve with fear, his praise forth tell,
Come ye before him and rejoice,
O praise him! O praise him!
Alleluia! Alleluia! Alleluia!

2. The Lord ye know is God indeed,
Without our aid he did us make;
Alleluia, alleluia.
We are his flock, he doth us feed,
And for his sheep he doth us take.
O praise him! O praise him!
Alleluia! Alleluia! Alleluia!

3. O enter then his gates with praise,
Approach with joy his courts unto
Alleluia, alleluia.
Praise, laud and bless his Name always

For it is seemly so to do.
O praise him! O praise him!
Alleluia! Alleluia! Alleluia!

4. For why? the Lord our God is good,
His mercy is for ever sure;
Alleluia, alleluia.
His truth at all times firmly stood,
And shall from age to age endure.
O praise him! O praise him!
Alleluia! Alleluia! Alleluia!

definition

The poetry books in the Bible are Psalms, Proverbs, Ecclesiastes, Song of Solomon, and Lamentations.

It's fairly easy to recognize Psalm 1 as a poem since it is written in lines with some rhyming words, and we know it was sung. However, all of the **poetry books in the Bible** (Psalms, Proverbs, Ecclesiastes, Song of Solomon, and Lamentations) feature poetry—Hebrew poetry. A Hebrew poem has different characteristics from an English poem. Rhyme is not a factor, nor is the number of syllables or regular meter. Instead, Hebrew poetry uses repetition, parallelism, comparisons, and contrasts. Some of these qualities are more difficult to detect when the Hebrew poetry is translated into English. The King James translators made special effort to repeatedly choose the same word, rather than an appropriate synonym, to help the reader be aware of deliberate repetitions and comparisons. The translators also tried to present the word order so that parallelism and contrasts would be as clear as possible. In addition to the poetry books named above, Moses' song (Deut. 32) and Mary's song, called the Magnificat (Luke 1:46-55), are beautiful poetry.

Psalms in Verse

Read the following two Psalms. Psalm 42 has been divided into stanzas by topic, similar to how you divide ideas into main points in public speaking. When one idea is a subordinate idea or an explanation to the idea preceding it, that second phrase is indented. For additional emphasis, some lines are indented twice. You should notice similarities between some pairs of lines indented twice.

Psalm 42
Hope Thou in God
To the chief Musician, Maschil, for the sons of Korah

As the hart panteth after the water brooks,
  So panteth my soul after thee, O God.
My soul thirsteth for God, for the living God:
  When shall I come and appear before God?

My tears have been my meat day and night,
  While they continually say unto me,
    Where is thy God?

When I remember these things,
  I pour out my soul in me:
For I had gone with the multitude,
  I went with them to the house of God,

Hymnody

Have your student choose a song from *The Bay Psalm Book*, *The Scottish Psalter*, or another Psalm book and find a tune in a hymnbook or on the Internet that is appropriate in cadence and style for that psalm. Sing the new hymn together. Discuss whether music makes the poetry and hence the Scripture more memorable.

Responsive Reading

If time permits, use the following performance activity in conjunction with the written poetry assignment.

Group students in pairs. Have them choose an arrangement of the poem and spend five to ten minutes reading it antiphonally or responsively, trying to assign "echo" lines to one reader.

Have each pair read in front of the class.

With the voice of joy and praise,
  With a multitude that kept holyday.
Why art thou cast down, O my soul?
  And why art thou disquieted in me?
    Hope thou in God:

For I shall yet praise him
  For the help of his countenance.

O my God, my soul is cast down within me:
  Therefore will I remember thee from the land of Jordan,
  And of the Hermonites, from the hill Mizar.

Deep calleth unto deep at the noise of thy waterspouts:
  All thy waves and thy billows are gone over me.
Yet the Lord will command his lovingkindness in the daytime,
  And in the night his song shall be with me,
  And my prayer unto the God of my life.

I will say unto God my rock,
  Why hast thou forgotten me?
  Why go I mourning because of the oppression of the enemy?
As with a sword in my bones,
  Mine enemies reproach me;
  While they say daily unto me,
    Where is thy God?

Why art thou cast down, O my soul?
  And why art thou disquieted within me?
    Hope thou in God:

For I shall yet praise him,
  Who is the health of my countenance,
    And my God.

1. What is the topic or theme of the poem? <u>*desire for God; evil can be*</u>
<u>*discouraging*</u>

2. What lesson does this poem teach? <u>*We need to desire God. When we are*</u>
<u>*discouraged by evil in this world, we need to think about God, placing our hope*</u>
<u>*in Him.*</u>

3. What title would you give to this poem?
<u>*Answers will vary but should reflect the topic or theme.*</u>

THE GREATEST LITERATURE BOOK **97**

4. Write each line that is repeated.

Where is thy God? / Why art thou cast down, O my soul? / And why art thou

disquieted in/within me? / Hope thou in God: / For I shall yet praise him.

5. Find examples of pairs of lines that are very similar. Write one pair.

Answers will vary but should include one of the following: (1) As the hart panteth

after the water brooks, / So panteth my soul after thee, O God. (2) For I had gone

with the multitude, / With a multitude that kept holyday. (3) Why art thou cast

down, O my soul? / O my God, my soul is cast down within me.

6. What ideas in this poem are contrasted? Give two examples.

day/night; sadness (cast down)/rejoicing and praise; thirst/abundance of water;

group worship/private worship

7. What ideas are compared? Give one example.

physical thirst of a hart (deer)/spiritual thirst of the author; tears/meat (food—in

this case symbolizing sustenance)

Now carefully read Psalm 43 (below). Look for repeating ideas that seem like a refrain. Notice which phrases serve to explain or reply to the previous phrase. Draw a line between the phrases at the point you will begin a new line. On scrap paper, experiment with how you might lay out the text of the psalm as a poem. When you are sure of what you want, write the poem on the lines below. Be sure to

1. Answer the questions about the poem.
2. Give your poem a title.
3. Capitalize the first letter of each new line.
4. Leave a space between each stanza (or draw a line if you need more room).
5. Indent phrases to clarify meaning and show the reader how the ideas fit together.

Psalm 43

Judge me, O God, and plead my cause against an ungodly nation: O deliver me from the deceitful and unjust man. For thou art the God of my strength: why dost thou cast me off? why go I mourning because of the oppression of the enemy? O send out thy light and thy truth: let them lead me; let them bring me unto thy holy hill, and to thy tabernacles. Then will I go unto the altar of God, unto God my exceeding joy: yea, upon the harp will I praise thee, O God my God. Why art thou cast down, O my soul? and why art thou disquieted within me? hope in God: for I shall yet praise him, who is the health of my countenance, and my God.

1. What is the topic or theme of the poem? <u>*asking for and praising God for*</u>
<u>*deliverance*</u>

2. What lesson does this poem teach? <u>*God provides hope and deliverance in the*</u>
<u>*midst of trial.*</u>

3. Several lines are similar to a previous line. Write two of these pairs.

   <u>*1. Why dost thou cast me off? / Why go I mourning . . .?*</u>

   <u>*2. Let them lead me; / Let them bring me unto thy holy hill, / and to thy tabernacles.*</u>

   <u>*3. Yea, upon the harp will I praise thee, / For I shall yet praise him,*</u>

   <u>*4. Why art thou cast down, O my soul? / And why art thou disquieted within me?*</u>

4. What ideas in this poem are contrasted? Give an example.

   <u>*mourning/exceeding joy; oppression/light and truth; being cast down*</u>
   <u>*(discouragement)/hoping in God*</u>

5. Write your poem below. *Answers will vary. Sample poem:*

   Title _____ *I Sing to My Deliverer* _____

   _____ *Judge me, O God,* _____

   _____ *And plead my cause against an ungodly nation:* _____

   _____ *O deliver me from the deceitful and unjust man.* _____

   _____ *For thou art the God of my strength:* _____

   _____

   _____ *Why dost thou cast me off?* _____

   _____ *Why go I mourning* _____

   _____ *Because of the oppression of the enemy?* _____

   _____

   _____

THE GREATEST LITERATURE BOOK **99**

A Whole Lot of Sermons

O send out thy light and thy truth:

Let them lead me;

Let them bring me unto thy holy hill,

And to thy tabernacles.

Then will I go unto the altar of God,

Unto God my exceeding joy:

Yea, upon the harp will I praise thee,

O God my God.

Why art thou cast down, O my soul?

And why art thou disquieted within me?

Hope in God:

For I shall yet praise him,

Who is the health of my countenance,

And my God.

Bible Sermons and Declamations

You may hear several sermons each week without realizing that the Bible contains sermons and persuasive speeches. In Ezekiel 33:1-20, God "preaches" to Ezekiel the message Ezekiel is supposed to give to the people. This is one of many sermons and announcements God gave to his prophets. By choosing to record His own words to the prophet rather than the prophet's sermon text, the divine source of the message is emphasized. God also reveals His preaching style.

The New Testament also contains many sermons preached by Christ and early church leaders. The Gospels record Christ's sermons, which include the Sermon on the Mount (Matt. 5–7; Luke 6), the Mission of the Disciples (Matt. 10:5-42; Mark 6:7-13; Luke 9:1-6), the Great Commandment (Matt. 22:33-40; Mark 12:28-34), the Condemnation of False Religious Teachers (Matt. 23:1-36; Mark 12:38-40; Luke 20:45-47), and the Great Commission (Matt. 28:18-20).

100 CHAPTER 5

Declare Truth

The description of Saul's (Paul's) conversion is found in Acts. In Acts 7:58–8:3 he's involved in persecuting believers, but Acts 9 records that he repents, trusts Christ for salvation, and begins preaching. His and other sermons appear below. If possible, have a male student read one aloud to the class. Consider offering extra credit points to male students who memorize a Bible sermon and fe-male students who memorize a Bible poem of comparable length and difficulty. If possible, provide an authentic situation in which to share the text—perhaps a school assembly or chapel or a youth program through the local church.

The Book of Acts presents a new type of sermon. Instead of hearing God speaking to His prophet or Christ Himself teaching, we hear the witness of Christ's followers after His ascension. The disciples preach what they have seen of God through their personal fellowship with Jesus Christ. Though many of these men were uneducated and fearful during the trial and crucifixion, they are now bold public orators, proclaiming Christ. Saul, a learned and respected leader, once persecuted Christians and stood by while Stephen was stoned to death. After meeting God, he had a new name and a new mission.

Some of the persuasive texts of Scripture were not delivered orally but in letters. Paul's Epistle to the Corinthians contains the most powerful, concise, and beautiful essay ever written on the subject of love (I Cor. 13).

All of these sermons and persuasive letters fully illustrate the principles of public speaking—verifying facts; using examples, stories, and personal experience; knowing your audience; and so on. These sermons and letters are models to which you should refer often.

Bible Drama

Perhaps you have been told stories of "a boy named David" and "Jesus feeding the five thousand" since you were old enough to pay attention to flannel-graph stories in children's church. These stories are not just for kids, however. All Bible stories transcend age groups when presented well.

The Bible stories about the characters listed in the chart are called **narrative drama.** These portions are often the easiest to understand at first reading and effectively appeal to a broad audience, including unsaved people. A children's Bible story-book often covers only narrative passages. Since the drama is emphasized, you may actually wish to skim an illustrated children's Bible storybook to help you in selecting a story.

Narrative drama refers to a dramatic story told with exposition, description, and dialogue.

Bible Character Chart

Encourage students to consult a study Bible, since some editions include notes on people of the Bible. Most study Bibles will list at least the occurrences of their names in a concordance. The students should read all passages pertaining to a character if at all possible. Of course, characters such as Moses, Joseph, Christ, and Paul are discussed in so many passages that it wouldn't be possible to read them all for one assignment. However, the more the students understand background circumstances and character, the better cuttings they can make, and the better narrative they can perform.

Quick Reference to Bible Narratives

BOOK	PRIMARY CHARACTERS
Genesis	Adam and Eve, Cain and Abel, Noah and his family, Abraham, Sarah, Isaac, Jacob, Rachel, Leah, Laban, Joseph
Exodus	Moses, Pharaoh, Pharaoh's daughter, Miriam, Aaron
Joshua	The spies, Joshua, Rahab
Judges	Deborah, Gideon, Samson and Delilah
Ruth	Naomi, Ruth, Boaz

Bible Sermons (A Sampling)

Speaker	Sermon	Audience	Summary	Reference
Joshua	"Choose You This Day Whom Ye Will Serve"	Israel	If you will not have God as your leader, choose now what pagan god you will follow. Joshua chooses the Lord.	Josh. 24:2-15
Nathan	"The Rich Man Takes the Poor Man's Lamb"	King David	Nathan speaks a parable that enrages King David. When Nathan reveals the parallel to the king's sin, David repents.	II Sam. 12:1-12
Christ	"Sermon on the Mount"	Disciples	Jesus presents the qualities that should characterize a believer.	Matt. 5–7
Peter	"Pentecost"	Jews and Gentiles	Peter preaches of the Resurrection of Christ, referring to David's prophecy in Psalm 16.	Acts 2:14-41
Stephen	"See What God Has Done!"	Sanhedrin	Accused of trying to destroy the Law, Stephen summarizes Israel's history, showing it to be a history of God's actions. He doesn't defend himself but teaches the truth about Jesus Christ.	Acts 7
Paul	"Sermon on Mars Hill"	Athenians	Paul sees that this city of idolatry carefully avoids accidentally missing a "god" in their worship by having an altar to the "unknown god." Paul seizes this opportunity to preach the true God.	Acts 17:16-34

BOOK	PRIMARY CHARACTERS
I and II Samuel	Hannah, Samuel, Eli and his sons, Saul, David
I Kings, I and II Chronicles	David, Solomon, Elijah, Ahab and Jezebel
II Kings	Elijah and Elisha, the Shunammite woman, Naaman
Esther	Esther, Haman, Mordecai
Job	Job, Job's wife, Job's three friends
Daniel	Daniel, Shadrach, Meshach, Abednego, Belshazzar, Darius
Hosea	Hosea and Gomer
Jonah	Jonah
Gospels	Mary, Joseph, Elisabeth, John, Jesus, the disciples, Mary, Martha, Lazarus, Zaccheus, the rich young ruler, the Samaritan woman, Pilate
Acts	Peter, Ananias and Sapphira, Stephen, Paul, Barnabas

How Can I Present the Bible Orally?

If called upon to read a passage of Scripture, you may not have an option about which text to read. When a teacher simply calls your name and asks you to read the next five or ten verses, you don't have time to practice reading the passage aloud or to look up unfamiliar words. But that doesn't mean you have to read poorly or in a monotone.

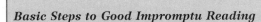

Basic Steps to Good Impromptu Reading

1. Skim quickly for extremely long or difficult-to-pronounce words. Don't be afraid to delay reading until you ask the teacher, "How do you say this?" or "What is this?"

2. Make sure your posture is correct, whether seated or standing.

3. If possible, face the direction of most of the audience. For example, if you are in the front of the room, stand and turn around. If the room is large or if the air conditioning or heating system is loud, always stand to aid projection.

4. Get a good deep breath before you begin. (Your audience should not hear you take this breath.)

Bible Story Improvisation

Assign small groups of students to improvise various Bible stories. (For ideas, consult the Quick Reference to Bible Narratives chart in the student text, pp. 101-2.) Urge them to focus on making the Bible characters real people with sincere reactions. Their exact wording should not be an issue.

Have your student select a Bible narrative to act out solo. Allow him to approach the assignment creatively. He could share the story, using a great deal of narration, or actually try to portray each character in a scene.

5. As you read, try to read fluidly without pausing until you reach a mark of punctuation.

6. Watch for question marks in advance so you can use your voice to ask the question rather than tell it.

7. Read the last phrase with a note of finality. Usually this can be communicated by a downward inflection on the last word or syllable.

8. If you stumble on a word, don't get flustered or give up. Clarify (if possible) and then continue.

Impromptu Reading

Even spur-of-the-moment reading can be thoughtful and clear. Read the following verses aloud, applying the steps listed above.

> *So Naaman came with his horses and with his chariot, and stood at the door of the house of Elisha. And Elisha sent a messenger unto him, saying, Go and wash in Jordan seven times, . . . and thou shalt be clean. But Naaman was wroth, and went away, and said, Behold, I thought, He will surely come out to me, and stand, and call on the name of the Lord his God, and strike his hand over the place, and recover the leper. Are not Abana and Pharpar, rivers of Damascus, better than all the waters of Israel? may I not wash in them, and be clean? So he turned and went away in a rage. (II Kings 5:9-12)*

What words might you need help pronouncing, if any? **Answers will vary but may**

include Abana (AB un nuh), Pharpar (FAR par), and Damascus (duh MAS kus).

No doubt applying so many steps to your reading process seemed like a great deal of work. However, you will find that with practice, it can become automatic. If you don't think you'll remember the steps, try reading aloud for your homework time or devotions this week and incorporate the steps then. Reviewing will help you retain the steps better.

Find the Drama

Now let's discuss a method to use when you will choose the passage of Scripture and will have time to practice. First of all, find the drama. Reading a genealogy aloud probably won't be dramatic! You must find *narrative* that

Presenting God's Word Dramatically
Primary Goals
• Find the drama.
• Identify the plot.
• Make a cutting.
• Practice well.

THE GREATEST LITERATURE BOOK 103

Cold Turkey Reading

Taking a series of chapters such as Mark 1–3, assign a portion of verses to each student to read aloud. Five to seven verses each should be sufficient for a ten- to fifteen-person class. More verses could be assigned for smaller classes. If you have an unusually large class, you could have half the students read one day and half the next or adjust as you see fit. Before the students read the verses aloud, have them look over the "Basic Steps to Good Impromptu Reading." (The first rule will not apply to this activity.) Use only one Bible translation (preferably the KJV because of its beautiful language and challenging syntax). Begin by having the first student read Mark 1:1-7 and proceed until each student has read his portion of verses. Tell your students that you are requiring them to demonstrate skills that they learned in the "Basic Steps to Good Impromptu Reading." Of course, be aware of any students who may have especially poor reading skills. You may want to plan ahead and pick out an easier section of verses for them so that there is no embarrassment on the day of the activity.

appeals to you personally. Is the story compelling? Are enough details included to create the drama? If the story occupies only a couple of lines or verses, it may not suit your needs. For example, the parable of the lost coin in Luke 15 is only a few verses. Though more detail could be imaginatively added to such a story for a devotional challenge or sermon, it would not be adequate for a Scripture reading alone. However, immediately following is the parable of the lost son, often called the parable of the prodigal son. "Lost" best describes the son's condition from the father's point of view, but "prodigal," which means wasteful, reckless, or extravagant, depicts his lifestyle. The story begins in Luke 15:11 and continues through verse 32, an adequate length to stand on its own.

Identify the Plot

The next step is to identify the plot. In the lost son parable, the plot structure is easily recognized. Read the story in Luke 15 before continuing.

The Parable of the Lost Son

PLOT ELEMENT	VERSES	CONTENT SUMMARY
Exposition	11-12	A man has two sons; the younger son asks for his inheritance.
Inciting Incident	13	The younger son leaves home.
Rising Action	13-16	This young man spends liberally and parties with the wrong crowd, all the while failing to plan for the future or to work. Finally, the money runs out and the friends disappear. The son must seek employment. The son eats the food of the swine he tends.
Crisis (turning point)	17-19	He "came to himself." He realizes that his choices have led to destruction. He repents of his foolishness.
(more) Rising Action	20	He humbly journeys back to his father's home. He arrives, planning to ask for forgiveness and for a job as a servant.
Climax	20-21	His father receives him with love and forgiveness. He is welcomed as a restored son, not as a servant or a slave.
Falling Action	22-30	A feast is prepared. The son is honored. The elder son complains that he has been slighted because he has received no honor.
Denouement	31-32	The father explains that the elder son will have all of the remaining inheritance. It was good to rejoice over his younger brother's homecoming.

104 CHAPTER 5

Prodigal Son Box

Many students will be able to identify the parts of plot concerning the lost son. However, most will take little notice of the story's subplot concerning the elder son. In class, have the students read Luke 15:1-2. Ask them to identify the background elements. Use questions from the dramatistic analysis such as "To whom is the speaker speaking?" Christ was ministering to the lost. The religious leaders were very self-righteous, and they rejected "sinners." They were upset with Christ for spending time with sinful people. They did not recognize that these people were coming to Christ on His terms. The sinners were seeking salvation. Christ gave the three parables about lost things to teach the religious leaders. The real lesson of the parable goes beyond the depiction of the gospel message. Though it beautifully shows how repentance can restore each of us to our Father, the real lesson involves the elder son. He has played the part of the "good kid." He has worked and been faithful to all that his father has asked of him. However, there is no evidence that he loves his father or that they have a personal relationship.

Beginning in verse 25, we see an angry, selfish youth who resents his brother terribly. Unlike his father, he is not happy to see his brother safe at home. He doesn't think about his brother's good or his father's joy. He thinks about himself. Like a child, he pouts, com-

Make a Cutting

Now that you have identified the plot, you must **make a cutting**—decide which verses to include in your reading. Several factors influence your cutting of a text. Time length will be your greatest concern. Of course, you will need to maintain clarity as well. When you read a paragraph, look for **tag lines** (he said, she said). Most of these can be cut unless there are several similar characters that might confuse the audience. Generally speaking, tag lines for dialogue by God and "the angel of the Lord" (Christ) are not deleted. Many audience members may take offense when an interpreter tries to "act out" God. There is never a good reason to offend sincere convictions. For most audiences, speaking God's dialogue as an indirect quotation would be better. In other words, tell about what God said rather than trying to portray Him.

Description of action is more effective if you convey it in your delivery instead of giving a report. The old adage is true—actions speak louder than words. If you say, "He was excited beyond imagination," but you look bored, your audience will believe what it sees first. Deliver the character's dialogue with excitement and cut the line of description.

Finally, cut extra details. Even the eloquence of Charles Dickens would become tedious if every description and detail were included in a performance. Dickens might spend three paragraphs describing the posture, movement, and appearance of your character. Treat that portion as stage directions, instructing you how to convey that character by means of your delivery. Then you won't need to actually say that text.

The example below, taken from Genesis 22:1-19, demonstrates how you might cut the story. Words appearing in brackets are added to the script as an aid to the reader but are not meant to be spoken. (Quotation marks have been added.)

> *And it came to pass after these things, that God did tempt Abraham, and said* ~~*unto him*~~*, "Abraham:"*
> ~~*and he said,*~~
>
> *[Abraham said] "Behold, here I am."*
>
> *And he said, "Take now thy son, thine only son Isaac, whom thou lovest, and get thee into the land of Moriah; and offer him there for a burnt offering upon one of the mountains which I will tell thee of."*
>
> *And Abraham rose up early in the morning, and saddled his ass, and took two of his young men with him, and Isaac his son, and clave the wood for the burnt offering, and rose up, and went unto the place of which God had told him. Then on the third day Abraham lifted up his eyes, and saw the place afar off.*
>
> ~~*And Abraham said unto his young men,*~~

efinition

*To **make a cutting**, you must select phrases, sentences, and paragraphs to include in the interpreter's script or "cutting."*

***Tag lines** identify the speaker in a line of dialogue.*

© 2002 BJU Press. Reproduction prohibited.

THE GREATEST LITERATURE BOOK 105

---

plaining that he's never been the center of attention at such a party. In his mind, he's the good son. He deserves this honor. His brother doesn't.

Interestingly, the father reminds him that he will eventually receive what is due him. He justifies the celebration of the younger brother's return. Here the story ends. Christ doesn't reveal whether or not the elder son repents of his selfishness and pride. Though in his father's home, he seems to be living as far from his father as his brother ever did.

The religious leaders claimed righteousness by their own good deeds. They spent much time in the house of God, but their hearts were in the same condition as the heart of this elder son. Discuss verses 25-32 as a separate plot structure about the struggles of the elder son. Help the students discover that the character who represents the Pharisees and scribes is the key figure in a second story. His story lacks the resolution and satisfaction of the other plot. We are left in dramatic suspense, wondering what will happen.

Good concluding questions:

1. What lesson does this parable teach lost people? (*Our heavenly Father is forgiving, and He delights to see us repent.*)

2. What lesson does it teach believers concerning witnessing? (*No one is too lowly or poor or sinful to come to*

The Greatest Literature Book 105

"Abide ye here with the ass; and I and the lad will go yonder and worship, and come again to you."

And Abraham took the wood of the burnt offering, and laid it upon Isaac his son; and he took the fire in his hand, and a knife; and they went both of them together.

~~*And Isaac spake unto Abraham his father, and said,*~~

[Isaac said] "My father:"

~~*and he said,*~~

[Abraham said] "Here am I, my son."

~~*and he said,*~~

[Isaac said] "Behold the fire and the wood: but where is the lamb for a burnt offering?"

~~*And Abraham said,*~~

[Abraham said] "My son, God will provide himself a lamb for a burnt offering:"

So they went both of them together. And they came to the place which God had told him of; and Abraham built an altar there, and laid the wood in order, ~~and~~ bound Isaac his son, and laid him on the altar upon the wood. And Abraham ~~stretched forth his hand, and~~ took the knife to slay his son.

And the angel of the Lord called unto him out of heaven, and said, "Abraham, Abraham:"

~~*and he said,*~~

[Abraham said] "Here am I."

~~*And he said,*~~

[The angel of the Lord said] "Lay not thine hand upon the lad, neither do thou any thing unto him: for now I know that thou fearest God, seeing thou hast not withheld thy son, thine only son from me."

And Abraham lifted up his eyes, and looked, and behold behind him a ram caught in a thicket by his horns: and Abraham ~~went and~~ took the ram, and offered him up for a burnt offering in the stead of his son. And Abraham called the name of that place Jehovah-jireh: as it is said to this day, In the mount of the Lord it shall be seen.

And the angel of the Lord called unto Abraham out of heaven the second time, And said,

"By myself have I sworn," saith the Lord, "for because thou hast done this thing, and hast not withheld thy son, thine only son: That in blessing I will bless thee, and in multiplying I will multiply thy seed as the stars of the heaven, and as the sand which is upon the sea shore; and thy seed

106 CHAPTER 5

Christ, so we should not discriminate when taking the gospel to them.)

3. What lesson did it present to the pious religious leaders? (Failing to rejoice over a repentant sinner is selfish and proud.)

shall possess the gate of his enemies; And in thy seed shall all the nations of the earth be blessed; because thou hast obeyed my voice."

So Abraham returned unto his young men, and they rose up and went together to Beersheba; and Abraham dwelt at Beersheba.

___D___ 1. What type of text has been cut most often?
   A. details and description
   B. dialogue
   C. primary actions
   D. tag lines

___A___ 2. What other element(s) has/have been cut?
   A. details and description
   B. dialogue
   C. primary actions
   D. tag lines

The cutting above is by no means the only right way to cut this story. Since it is not very long, you may be able to perform it entirely uncut. It is only an example of what can be done. Obviously, you want to avoid cutting details that are necessary for the story to make sense. Never cut so much that clarity is lost! Avoid assumptions about the audience's familiarity with the material. Some description and explanation can be crucial to effective communication.

Delivery cues are marginal notes on a script or speaking outline reminding the speaker to use a specific delivery element such as gesture, increase of intensity, or dramatic pause.

Scripting Practice

These principles apply to any nonpoetic literature. Usually you can and should cut most or all of the text that explains what you can easily convey with your delivery. Slightly different guidelines apply to cutting poetry, which will be discussed in a later chapter.

Cut the story below by crossing out the words you could show in your delivery and so do not need to say. If you wish to add **delivery cues,** do so with brackets this way: [Eagerly].

"What are you doing?" he asked eagerly.
Papa did not turn and look at Corey. "I'm going out with Edison."
Corey cupped his hands to his mouth. "Here, Eddie, here boy," he said and then whistled.
Edison came full gallop across the colorful leaf-strewn yard, his golden ears flapping and flopping against his head. His bark preceded him.
"Down, Eddie, down," cried Corey gleefully, as he vigorously petted Edison, half wrestling him to the ground. "We're going out with Papa."

Corey and Edison

This activity can help you explore the story about Corey and his dog. If you wish to perform or have a student in the class perform this little vignette, use the script below for practicing. Complete memorization should not be necessary.

COREY: (*Eagerly*) What are you doing?

PAPA: (*looking away*) I'm going out with Edison.

COREY: (*Cups hands; calls out*) Here, Eddie, (*Whistles*) here boy. (*Whistles again*)

Sound of a barking dog

COREY: Down, Eddie, down. (*Pantomimes petting dog*) We're going out with Papa. (*Looks up into Papa's face for a long moment*)

PAPA: No, Corey. Today, I'm going out with Edison alone. You must stay here.

COREY: (*Stands straighter; stops smiling*) But, Papa!

PAPA: (*Shakes his head*) No "but's" Corey. Go in the house so Edison won't see you and will go with me.

COREY: (*Looking down*) Yes, Papa. (*Walks slowly toward the low farmhouse door, glimpsing back only when Edison whines at being put in the pickup truck*)

Possible Script
Possible answer

[Corey, eagerly] "What are you doing?" he asked eagerly.

Papa did not turn and look at Corey.

[Papa looks away] "I'm going out with Edison."

Corey cupped his hands to his mouth.

[Corey cups hands; calls out] "Here, Eddie, [Whistles] here boy," [Whistles again] he said and then whistled.

Edison came full gallop across the colorful leaf-strewn yard, his golden ears flapping and flopping against his head. His bark preceded him.

[Gleefully] "Down, Eddie, down," cried Corey gleefully, as he vigorously petted Edison, half-wrestling him to the ground.

[Acts out petting dog]

"We're going out with Papa."

[Looks up, smiling]

Corey looked up into Papa's face. The lines were hard drawn there. He seemed much older than Corey remembered.

Papa spoke, [Papa, soberly] "No Corey. Today, I go out with Edison alone. You must stay here."

The smile fell from Corey's face as he stood up.

[Corey, stands straighter; stops smiling] "But, Papa!"

Papa shook his head ~~and said,~~ "No 'but's,' Corey. Go in the house so Edison won't whine when we leave."

~~Corey shifted his glance downward.~~

[Corey, looking down] "Yes, Papa," ~~he said and~~ (Corey) walked slowly toward the low farmhouse door, glimpsing back only when Edison whined at being put in the pickup truck without ~~Corey~~ (him) there.

Lesson Motivator

Obviously this section does not cover everything about interpretation skills. Rather, it should form a foundation on which students will build for the remainder of the course as well as in the future.

Even though the text introduces a few techniques in each chapter, avoid allowing students to focus wholly on those techniques. Communication is much more than methodology. Make it your goal to help your students see not just the parts but the whole. Compare speaking methods with the study of grammar. If a student spends an entire semester studying definitions of the parts of speech but never attempts to write essays, stories, or poems, his studies will profit him little. The grammar principles that he fails to relate with communication will not be memorable or useful in the future.

Corey looked up into Papa's face. The lines were hard drawn there. He seemed much older than Corey remembered.

Papa spoke, "No, Corey. Today, I go out with Edison alone. You must stay here."

The smile fell from Corey's face as he stood up. "But, Papa!"

Papa shook his head and said, "No 'but's,' Corey. Go in the house so Edison won't whine as we leave."

Corey shifted his glance downward. "Yes, Papa," he said and walked slowly toward the low farmhouse door, glimpsing back only when Edison whined at being put in the pickup truck without Corey there.

Practice Well

Now that you have found the drama, identified the plot, and made a good cutting, you are ready for the fourth step—practicing well. The last major section of this chapter provides the tools you need to practice your story and develop your skills, but it will be up to you to practice well.

INTERPRETATION SKILLS

Imagine that you are going to read the story of Abraham's test of faith for your project. Read that portion again. Then study the interpretation skills presented in this section.

Comprehension

I will not let meaningless words come out of my mouth.

Not just a good rule for speech class, the statement above is a good rule for life in general. Make this part of your creed and you will never regret it. It will earn you respect, trust, and friendship.

When communicating from the platform, your ethical responsibility is greatly increased. Because you are communicating to many people, you are even more accountable than you are in day-to-day conversations over lunch or at a ball game. For this reason, you must truly understand what you are saying and communicate it sincerely.

Understanding the Text
• *Vocabulary*—the words
• *Context*—the setting in history and in the text
• *Theme*—the lesson or moral the story teaches

Discussion. After the story, ask students to tell which communicated the story more completely to them: reading the dialogue and description or seeing and hearing it performed. (*Answers will vary.*) Discuss the reasons for their answers.

PRESENTATION

Interpretation Skills

Meaningless Words

Allow students a minute to ponder the meaning of the quotation "I will not let meaningless words come out of my mouth." Then instruct them to take out a sheet of paper and write down the words, phrases, and subject matter that they use that could be considered meaningless. Areas of meaninglessness could

include verbal clutter (uh, well, um), idle jokes and remarks, sarcasm, and so on. Give them three minutes or so to write. You may want to have the students include this in their journals.

Vocabulary

Since the last chapter dealt heavily with understanding words, we will not discuss vocabulary now. You can review if needed.

Context

Context may seem simple: determine where the sentence fits in the text or historical context. Sometimes the application is difficult. When you say, "He's a bear" because a grumpy person "growled" at you, you actually mean, "He's so grumpy and fierce; his behavior reminds me of that of a bear." Obviously it's easier to just say, "He's a bear." Context makes the meaning clear.

Unfortunately, the context is not always as clear to the reader or listener. This demonstrates another good reason to view God's Word as literature. If you read Christ's parables and prophecy the same way, you may end up being confused. They do not have the same context. Often those who argue that the Bible is irrelevant, illogical, or contradictory have evaluated ideas out of context. We need to be wise and discerning lest we fall into this trap.

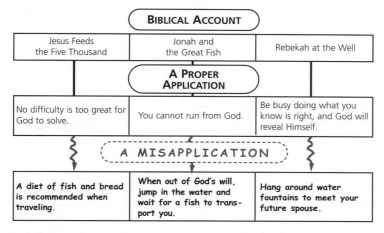

These are humorous examples, but atheists and agnostics make similar errors with serious consequences by ignoring context. Consider the following two verses:

> *Honour thy father and mother. (Ephesians 6:2)*

> *If any man come to me, and hate not his father, and mother, and wife, and children, and brethren, and sisters, yea, and his own life also, he cannot be my disciple. (Luke 14:26)*

Out of context, these verses seem to be contradictory ideas. In context, the first refers to showing respect and deference to parents. The second is a poetic device

---

As you instruct students concerning techniques such as phrasing, emphasis and subordination, and the skills taught in future chapters, keep the big picture in mind. Exercises provided in both the student text and the Teacher's Edition will help you accomplish this purpose. For example, the activity labeled "The Author's Ideas" is designed to introduce technique from a big-picture viewpoint. When students communicate their own ideas, they will generally phrase correctly and effectively subordinate less important ideas to the main ideas because their communication will be motivated by thought and understanding. If you then guide them through a process of reasoning, they will see that they must use the same technique in communicating the words of others. This approach prevents the technique of phrasing from degenerating into a rote task of drawing slash marks over marks of punctuation in order to receive a good homework grade. See the activity for further explanation.

Context Improvisation

Introduction. Use either four or six volunteers to perform the scene provided below. Provide a copy of the lines for each pair. It is likely that the pairs will produce quite different scenes, since the lines are rather ambiguous. Allow them several minutes to read over the lines in pairs, deciding how they will communicate those words. Encourage them to determine a very specific context for their scene. They should decide how these characters relate to their topic of conversation. Most importantly, they must decide what motivates each person—what each wants to see happen.

Instructions. When ready, have each pair perform the scene with script in hand. Have the class discuss how and to what extent context influenced the meaning of the scene.

1: You can't be serious.

2: Why do you say that?

1: Well, I thought that—

2: There are things you don't understand.

1: Apparently!

2: You're not upset, are you?

1: Why should I be?

2: I thought you would be.

1: No—no, I'm not.

2: That's good.

definition

Hyperbole is an extreme or excessive comparison used to strongly emphasize an idea.

A thought unit consists of a few sentences or paragraphs that express one main idea.

known as **hyperbole** (hye PUR buh lee), or an extreme comparison used for emphasis. Christ means that although His followers dearly love those closest to them, their commitment to Christ must make all other loves seem slight by comparison. He is also teaching the need to count the cost of discipleship before making a commitment. This is explained in verses 27 through 33. Context, then, is a crucial responsibility for the speaker.

Theme

Finally, evaluate the theme or message of the story. Consult a few commentaries when studying a Scripture passage, remembering that the Holy Spirit is the best guide to a believer's understanding. You will also want to use the questions in the dramatistic analysis (pp. 117-18) to determine the theme.

Communication

Now that you have a good grasp of the basic structure and content of your message, consider what you will communicate.

Thought Units

First, let's discuss a **thought unit.** Look at the excerpt from the Abraham story. How much of it would you consider to be expressing one idea? Do you think the paragraph below could be called a thought unit?

> *And Abraham took the wood of the burnt offering, and laid it upon Isaac his son; and he took the fire in his hand, and a knife; and they went both of them together.*

Identify the thought unit. Then decide what singular idea it expresses. If it doesn't seem to express a singular idea, perhaps you mislabeled several ideas as one thought unit. If so, further divide the paragraph. Then summarize the main idea with a mental title. (You probably don't need to write it down.) We could label the thought unit above "Abraham and Isaac continue their journey."

Main Elements for Communication

- Thought units—how the words fit together
- Phrases—groups of words and clauses that compose a thought unit
- Subtextual meaning—connotation
- Climax—peak of excitement

Phrases

Within each thought unit, consider which words fit into **phrases.** When playing a song on an instrument or when singing, you need to phrase words properly. If you just play notes in order with no sense of thought units or phrases, the listener

---

The Author's Ideas

Introduction. Usually students are instructed to "let punctuation be their guide" to phrasing and use of pause in oral reading. Though a useful and practical method, it will be most effectively applied if the student has a clear understanding of *why* punctuation often signals a pause. Without reminding students of the punctuation rule, conduct the following activity. Allow the students to deduce the rule from it.

Instructions. Provide an interesting photo or object for the class to examine visually. Make certain you choose something that is interesting and fun to describe. Allow the students two minutes to brainstorm, creating a list of words and phrases that describe your visual aid. Then allow another two minutes for them to rearrange these words and phrases into a simple paragraph.

Call time and then ask a student to read his paragraph aloud. Encourage him to really try to communicate effectively—

as if this were a competition, not just reading an answer aloud. Have the other students close their eyes to listen, trying to picture what the reader is describing. Ask the students to identify places that pause was used. Ask the reader why he paused in those places. He will likely answer that he was trying to group his ideas. Lead the class in discovering that we naturally pause at the end of a thought. Then further explain that punctuation is often a written expression of pause. Proceed to demonstrate marking for phrasing with

will have difficulty following the tune, and some of the beauty of the music will be lost. If you do not phrase well when singing, you will either run out of breath to support your voice or breathe at an awkward, inappropriate moment. Clarity and beauty are lost.

The same principle applies to the spoken word. Try reading the sentence below without stopping or phrasing any ideas by way of inflection or pausing.

> In the days when spinning-wheels hummed busily in the farmhouses and even great ladies clothed in their silk and thread-lace had their toy spinning-wheels of polished oak there might be seen in districts far away among the lanes or deep in the bosom of the hills certain pallid undersized men who by the side of the brawny country-folk looked like the remnants of a disinherited race.
> —George Eliot, *Silas Marner*

Are you out of breath? Most likely! Did this sentence make sense? Probably not. The opening of *Silas Marner* describes Silas himself, a reclusive weaver of the nineteenth century. The same single sentence is printed again below, this time with its punctuation. Read it aloud, pausing slightly at each comma and dash.

> In the days when spinning-wheels hummed busily in the farmhouses—and even great ladies, clothed in their silk and thread-lace, had their toy spinning-wheels of polished oak—there might be seen in districts far away among the lanes, or deep in the bosom of the hills, certain pallid undersized men, who, by the side of the brawny country-folk, looked like the remnants of a disinherited race.

Did the second reading make more sense? Probably so. A **pause,** however, is not the only way to set apart a phrase. No doubt you noticed when reading such a long, complex sentence that pausing was monotonous by the end. If it "gets old" after just a sentence, imagine performing an entire story written in such a style, using only pause! Additionally, since pause is frequently used to delineate the end of a phrase, it is very important *not* to, uh, pause, uh, in the middle, uh, of a phrase—whether or not it is vocalized (uh). It's very distracting, uh, don't you think?

Emphasis and Subordination

Now that you know what groups of words form phrases, you must decide how these phrases relate to each other. You may have difficulty sorting out how these ideas interrelate since the language is not modern. Try reading the paraphrase below.

*In oral communication, speakers use **phrases** to enhance the beauty and clarity of a message through the use of pause, emphasis, and subordination.*

*A **pause** is the space between words in spoken language.*

© 2002 BJU Press. Reproduction prohibited.

Suggested Reading

Silas Marner and other nineteenth-century novels provide excellent practice in phrasing since the sentence structure is often more formal and complex than modern fiction.

THE GREATEST LITERATURE BOOK (111)

---

slash marks, using an example of your choice.

Sample: A Century Plant Brainstorming List

green	fingers
yellow	reaching for light
snakes	pinpoints
grass	barbs
life	growth
waves	

Sample descriptive paragraph. Green and yellow snakelike fingers reach toward light—toward life. Each leaf, like a blade of grass, makes its own path of growth. In waves and curves, the plant grows from the soil toward the sun.

Conclusion. From this exercise, students should be able to conclude that phrasing ideas and using emphasis and subordination are natural and effective means of communicating thought. When they communicate their own ideas, they will not have to make a great effort to do this, but when communicating the ideas of others, these techniques will require forethought and practice.

Phrasing

Students of musical instruments or voice are taught to phrase music. Phrasing relates to tempo as well as to expression. A line of hymn text, for example, may last for four measures, but it must be played and sung as a single unit. The final note of a phrase is generally longer than its literal count because the vocalist must breathe. Beyond that practical reason, delineating phrases increases the effectiveness of communication from musician to listener.

Phrasing in speech operates on much the same premise and serves the same purpose.

Standing Alone

The need to cover the topic of communication apprehension will vary for every class. If most of your students are very quiet or inexperienced, use this topic to encourage and excite them about the prospect of successfully communicating ideas. If some of your students are overconfident or even just very experienced, make sure they understand the need to be courteous and sensitive to their less confident, less experienced peers. Nothing is more difficult for a nervous student than perceiving that an audience member is far superior and will hold that fact over his head.

Back when weavers spun thread and the rich used spinning-wheels as decorations, in rural areas you might see small, pale weavers who seemed to be a different race compared with the farmers, tanners, and smiths.

What is the main idea of this sentence? Try to write a sentence that begins with "Weavers" and summarizes this idea succinctly.

Sample answer: Weavers were an oddity in a distant culture.

A second means of phrasing is through **emphasis** and **subordination.** After you decide what the main clause is, use your voice to set it off and make other phrases less important. Look at our long sentence again. Experiment with a raised pitch range on superscript phrases and a lowered pitch range for subscript phrases. (You do not need to read a whole phrase at a particular pitch—just begin the phrase higher or lower.)

definition

Emphasis makes a word or phrase important and memorable through vocal variety—a change of intensity, volume, and pitch.

Subordination de-emphasizes a word or phrase through vocal variety—a change of intensity, volume, and pitch.

Subtext refers to connotation or underlying ideas.

In the days when spinning-wheels hummed busily in the farmhouses—$^{\text{and even great ladies,}}$ $_{\text{clothed in their silk and thread-}}$ $^{\text{had their toy spinning-wheels of polished oak—}}$there might be $_{\text{lace,}}$ seen $^{\text{in districts far away among the lanes,}}$ $_{\text{or deep in the bosom of the hills,}}$ certain pallid undersized men, who, $_{\text{by the side of the brawny}}$ country-folk, looked like the remnants of a disinherited race.

Now you have two methods for phrasing your thoughts: pause, and emphasis and subordination. You should be able to communicate with a reasonable level of clarity. Now we turn our discussion to subtextual meaning.

Subtextual Meaning

Evaluate the following nonsense dialogue to better understand the idea of **subtext.** Imagine that "1" is your mother and "2" is you. You want to go to a party with your friends but think you may still be grounded from last week. Read the lines with that situation in mind. Write in the blank by each line what you are communicating by describing your tone or writing a paraphrase. The first few are filled in for you as examples. Remember, in a performance you would still say the original dialogue, but you would try to convey the ideas in the blanks.

1: Are you going? *(Casually) You were going, weren't you?*

2: No. *As if you would let me—*

112 CHAPTER 5

1: Why not? *And where did you get that idea?* _____

2: I can't. *Answers will vary.* _____

1: I see. _____

2: Did you really think I would? _____

1: Well, I don't know. _____

2: You thought I could. _____

1: Did I? _____

2: Maybe. _____

Now imagine that "1" is your sibling and "2" is you. Your sibling knows you sprained your ankle and can't go ice skating with the youth group. He or she seems to be taunting you. Now write out the subtext in the blanks.

1: Are you going? _____

2: No. _____

1: Why not? _____

2: I can't. _____

1: I see. _____

2: Did you really think I would? _____

1: Well, I don't know. _____

2: You thought I could. _____

1: Did I? _____

2: Maybe. _____

Subtext really makes a difference, doesn't it? Someone once said, "Words mean more than what is set down on paper. It takes the human voice to infuse them with shades of deeper meaning." You must look at the context, the possible meanings of the words, and try to determine what the author meant to communicate. Only then can you deliver your lines, conveying the subtext properly.

Climax

Once you have phrased for clarity and conveyed subtextual meaning, you must develop a climax. Nothing is more disappointing than a story without a peak of excitement. "What was the point of that?" we ask. Your audience wants to experience the drama with the protagonist.

THE GREATEST LITERATURE BOOK (113)

Perhaps the best way to bolster the insecure while managing the overconfident is to focus on the importance of depending on the Lord for strength. Remind your students that we are all inadequate by our own merit. Only in Him can a believer be strong.

Lesson Objectives

The student will be able to

1. Recognize the term *communication apprehension,* equating it with stage fright.

2. Explain how to cope with fear when speaking or performing publicly.

Let us take a final look at the story of Abraham and Isaac. What is the climactic moment? Put yourself in Isaac's shoes. Your father asks you to take a long trip to make a special sacrifice but doesn't seem concerned about bringing any special sacrifice with him. No innocent lamb.

Did your father explain God's command when you reached the location of the sacrifice? Surely you submitted willingly as your elderly father bound you and laid you on the altar. What were you thinking? Your mind was flooded with promises, memories, hopes, and questions. You saw the knife above you, glistening in the sunlight. Then a voice. It was not a familiar voice. It was not your father, though he answered.

Intensity expresses internal emotions and ideas.

The climax occurs when God intervenes in the story's progress. Abraham and Isaac demonstrate their faith, and God demonstrates His faithfulness. As a storyteller, you must create this climax with your **intensity.**

Intensity is not something you can put on from the outside. You must experience it from within. You must be caught up in the moment yourself for your audience to sense that this is the big moment.

STANDING ALONE

As you approach this first major project, you may feel some butterflies. Remember these simple ideas. Stage fright, or *communication apprehension*, as it is sometimes called, is very common. Being a new actor and storyteller, you might not feel qualified to do a good job. You may feel uncomfortable with a new situation or with having to face an audience to which you don't relate. All eyes are upon you, and your stomach is performing a circus routine.

You must do your best to be prepared without expecting anything to be perfect. That means practicing properly. Also, don't forget to eliminate unnecessary tension in your body. Stretch, yawn, and breathe deeply to prepare your instrument.

Because man bears the image of God, he is infinitely more valuable to God than sparrows or lilies in the field. First Peter 5:7 speaks to believers, saying, "Casting all your care upon Him, for He careth for you." Fear should motivate prayer. If you come to the place that you know you can't do it, you are in the perfect position to trust God completely. He never leaves or forsakes His own!

114 CHAPTER 5

CHAPTER 5 REVIEW

Terms to Know

classics	make a cutting	pause
universal appeal	tag lines	emphasis
timeless stories	delivery cues	subordination
psalter	hyperbole	subtext
poetry books in the Bible	thought unit	intensity
narrative drama	phrases	

Ideas to Understand

Multiple Choice: **Choose the best answer.**

__A__ 1. A classic story is all of the following *except*
    A. dated.   C. universal in theme.
    B. timeless/enduring.   D. all of these.

__E__ 2. All of the following are poetry books *except*
    A. Ecclesiastes.   D. Proverbs.
    B. Lamentations.   E. Isaiah.
    C. Psalms.

True/False: **Write True or False for each statement. If false, cross out the word or words that make it incorrect and write in the word or words that make it true.**

__True__ 3. Some passages of Scripture are not suitable for dramatic presentation.

__False__ 4. A thought unit is the same as a phrase. *(is) not; or the student may make the following change: is the same as a phrase contains many phrases*

__False__ 5. Pause is the most effective means of phrasing ideas. *(is) not*

Short Answer

6. What term describes marginal notes about gestures, vocal emphasis, or another delivery element intended to remind the speaker of choices he has made?

    delivery cues _____

THE GREATEST LITERATURE BOOK **115**

---

question 5
Without emphasis and subordination, ideas still lack clarity and interest. Pause is not adequate alone and can be distracting when overused.

Scripture Narrative Project

Since this is the first major project, you will want to be especially thorough in reviewing the procedure and process given in the text. Depending on the size of the class and the length of your class period, you may need to develop a very precise routine for performance days.

Suggested Policies

You may find some of the following guidelines to be helpful in developing your own classroom policies for performance days.

1. Since dressier clothes generally improve conduct and atmosphere, consider requiring them for some or all projects. Be specific about your request.

2. Remember that a distraction or an interruption in any class inconveniences a teacher, but the situation is far more precarious on a class day in which students make presentations of any sort. It is unfair to have a student begin a speech or performance that cannot be completed before the end of the class period.

3. Assign a steep penalty (one to two letter-grade reduction) for being unprepared on the day assigned to speak. Many students perceive that it will not be a problem if they are unprepared on the appropriate day, as long as the next day or two are also set aside for performances. However, you will seldom find volunteers to perform a day sooner than expected without warning. Your semester schedule may fall irreparably behind without such a policy.

4. Between performances, you may or may not wish to permit talking. Performing can be quite nerve-racking and some students may be able to better relax and control their nerves if a break in tension occurs between performances. The possible negative results of permitting talking include distracting the next performer or disturbing neighboring classes with ever-growing volume. With a mature group of students, permit quiet talking between performances, stipulating that if you have to ask the class to quiet down more than once, they will lose this privilege.

Suggested Routine

Set a specific routine for handling the progression of the class. Students will perform better when they can proceed with confidence. Tailor the steps given below

Scripture Narrative Assignment Sheet

Prepare

Due Dates

_____ Select a narrative

_____ Teacher checks your manuscript

_____ Dramatistic analysis

_____ Title

_____ Introduction (thirty-second extemporaneous introduction you will deliver to lead into your script)

_____ Performance

Resubmit your manuscript after performing. Your teacher will consult it while grading your work.

Practice

Evaluate yourself on a scale of one to ten in each of the following areas, rating your current effectiveness in each skill. One is weak, five is moderate or adequate, and ten is excellent. Explain your evaluation.

_____ Phrasing _____

_____

_____ Emphasis (stress) _____

_____

_____ Subordination _____

_____

Set goals for each practice session, such as "developing phrasing" and "creating emphasis and subordination." Chart your progress here.

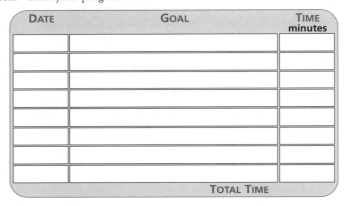

DATE	GOAL	TIME minutes
	TOTAL TIME	

Dramatistic Analysis of the Scripture Narrative

Title (include Scripture reference) _____

Passage _____
_____

Sources (list in bibliographical form) _____
_____
_____
_____

Research

1. **Who is the speaker?** (the main character, his background, his personality and nature, his purposes and goals, his strengths and weaknesses)

   _____
   _____
   _____
   _____

2. **Where is the speaker?** (physical location, circumstances—conflict)

   _____
   _____
   _____
   _____
   _____

3. **When is the speaker speaking?** (What is the time of the event in relationship to other pertinent events—what is the event before and after? Also, discuss the historical time period. Finally, where does this event fall in the action—is it a crisis moment?)

   _____
   _____
   _____
   _____
   _____
   _____

to suit your particular situation.

1. Open class with prayer. You may wish to rotate having students lead class in prayer—not from their seats but as if they were the teacher. This provides a real-life speaking opportunity.

2. Quickly make necessary announcements such as reading a list of names of those scheduled to speak that day and the next.

3. Remind students of the procedure for the first several performance days, until you are certain they have it memorized.

4. Double-check your workstation for whatever items you may need—pen or pencil, a stopwatch for any assignment you wish to time, a stapler, and so on.

5. Each student in turn should bring you his evaluation form and any other items due that day, such as an outline or dramatistic analysis. He should quietly proceed to the front of the classroom and wait calmly for you to signal him to begin. Usually a nod is an appropriate signal.

6. When the student finishes, he should quietly return to his seat. (Announce as class begins whether applause will be appropriate or not for that day's performances. Many teachers choose to permit applause, except in the case of a sacred presentation.)

The Evaluation Form

Some experienced teachers listen to speeches and performances, making comments on blank paper and assigning a subjective grade (or ranking, in the case of forensics).

Though this is a valid form of evaluation, most teachers and judges find it easier to be thorough and fair if they have a standard by which to measure the speaker or performer. A rubric or evaluation form provides this element of objectivity.

Notice that the student will be judged on his use of the three techniques taught in the chapter. Additionally, he will be judged on the elements of delivery most applicable to this project. Since this project includes the use of a manuscript, the rubric provides evaluation for the manuscript and the student's use of it on the platform. Of course you have the option of counting the student's written work as a separate homework grade if desired. Finally, the rubric provides an opportunity to make general comments about strengths and weaknesses.

7. Have the next performer remain in his seat until you call his name. Otherwise, he will be hovering over your desk while you are scrambling to make a few more notes concerning the last student's work. This is unfair to the student being graded and will make your task more difficult. Additionally, the next performer will remain more relaxed while seated than while waiting by your desk.

8. Above all else, work to establish an atmosphere conducive to concentration and confidence. Your students will thank you for it.

Project Checklist

For the Scripture Narrative Project, you will need to select due dates for each of the following components:

1. Choosing a dramatic narrative account

2. Dramatistic analysis

3. Assignment sheet

4. Manuscript

5. Performance

(The assignment sheet and manuscript could both be checked on the day the student speaks.)

4. **To whom is the speaker speaking?** (Who is the audience? Describe the audience members personally and in relationship to the speaker.)

_____

_____

_____

_____

_____

Evaluation

5. **What is being said?** (Summarize the message or theme.)

_____

_____

_____

_____

6. **How is it being said?** (diction, style, and delivery)

_____

_____

_____

_____

_____

7. **Why is it being said?** (purpose or goal)

_____

_____

_____

_____

_____

_____

Grading

Be careful not to get so caught up in deciding what level of performance the student has achieved in each area that you do not evaluate the performance as a whole. Did it communicate? Did the student do his or her best? What area needs the most improvement? What can you say to help the student improve on a future assignment?

You will notice that a grading scale is not provided. The rankings of one through four on each category are not intended to represent percentage points. A student who usually receives four points per category and communicates effectively should receive a grade in the A-range. Reserve the ranking of four for a truly excellent effort. Likewise, a student who receives two points in many categories and perhaps three or only one in some categories and communicates adequately is average and should receive a grade in the C-range.

Try to grade slightly low on early assignments, allowing even average students to improve their grades throughout the semester without ever assigning them a score higher than they really earned. Since grading speeches and performances is still a subjective task, you will find it much more difficult to "grade hard" on later assignments than on earlier ones.

For students who display quite a number of weaknesses on the first assignment, grade them fairly with only one

Name _____ Scripture Passage _____

	Interpretation	Comments	Pts.
Thought Units	**4** Clearly defined **3** Usually defined **2** Somewhat blurred together **1** Indistinct or confusing at times		
Phrasing	**4** Excellent stress and subordination **3** Most key phrases stressed **2** Some appropriate use of pause and subordination **1** Pause overused—relied too little on subordination		
Climax	**4** Memorable, powerful **3** Clear, effective **2** Lacked suspense **1** No noticeable peak of intensity		

	Delivery		
Poise	**4** Excellent emotional control **3** Good emotion to control nervousness **2** Noticeable nervousness **1** Nervousness obvious		
Bodily Action	**4** Aids communication **3** Usually enhances the message **2** Neither distracts from nor enhances the message **1** Distracts from the message		

	Manuscript		
Platform	**4** Handled professionally and gracefully **3** Handled smoothly **2** Used adequately **1** Used awkwardly		
Written	**4** (7-8 check marks) **3** (5-6 check marks) **2** (4 check marks) **1** (1-3 check marks)	___ Appropriate cuts in text Cut correctly for length ___ Bound correctly in folder Vocabulary has * and definition ___ Thought units in ( ) Phrases marked with / ___ Neat and legible overall Professional appearance	

You demonstrate good ability in . . .	You would benefit from more attention to . . .

Total Points _____   Grade _____

© 2002 BJU Press. Reproduction prohibited.

The Evaluation Form

The evaluation forms in this text should be tools, not rules for your grading process. For example, each project evaluation form includes a category for written work. You may wish to simplify your grade book by counting written work as a certain percentage of the project grade. However, many teachers like to have separate homework grades so students can clearly see what percentage of their overall course grade reflects oral work and what percentage reflects written. (A common breakdown is 60-65% oral, 35-40% homework, quizzes, and tests.) Either way, you can choose to record your comments about written work on the project evaluation form. Simply list a written score separately if desired.

Remember that the most valuable part of the evaluation is precise feedback from you. A comment such as "seemed confusing" will not aid the student. Instead, try "choppy phrasing—work to smooth this out to improve clarity." Then you have clearly identified a weakness and created a desired goal.

---

or two points per category, but don't overwhelm them with a shower of negative remarks in the "Comments" sections. Instead, decide which one or two areas are most in need of improvement and give specific advice on improvement in those areas. Even sandwich the negative comment between two encouraging remarks when possible. Never give back a paper with no positive feedback. Possibly include a note, "see me if you have questions," if you think the student will perceive his

grade to be too low and unfair. You can communicate more constructive criticism orally without discouraging a student than you can on paper. Your tone can soften your message.

Likewise, for students who have a real natural ability, be cautious about excessive praise. Give credit where credit is due and provide constructive criticism as well. Everyone has room for improvement.

If desired, you can return to an evaluation form later to add further notes and point values. This will also give you the opportunity to proofread your initial comments for clarity.

Chapter 6
Introduction

Had I the heavens' embroi-
dered cloths,
Enwrought with golden and
silver light,
The blue and the dim and the
dark cloths
Of night and light and the
half-light,
I would spread the cloths
under your feet:
But I, being poor, have only my
dreams;
I have spread my dreams
under your feet;
Tread softly because you tread
on my dreams.

> —William Butler Yeats,
> "He Wishes for the
> Cloths of Heaven"

Poetry is inherently theatrical. A playwright mirrors life on stage, while the poet mirrors life in print. As Hamlet unravels the mystery behind his father's death in a mere three hours, Yeats' narrator expresses utter devotion to his beloved with a brief eight lines of imagery.

You may meet with some resistance teaching poetry to high-school students. For one reason or another, poetry seldom attracts new admirers without encouragement from a teacher who will enthusiastically present its splendor and delights. Decide to be that kind of teacher and you will find many eager followers. When we agree to listen, poetry speaks to our innermost

Lesson Plan
Suggested homework is in **boldface.**

Lesson Description	Recommended Presentation	Performance Projects/ Written Assignments
I. Lyric Poetry (p. 124)	ST—Assign Dramatistic Analysis TE—More Precious Than Gold	TE—Haiku; Musical Metaphor **ST—Assign Sonnet project**
II. Figurative Language (p. 127)	TE—Name That Figure	
III. Interpretation of Lyric Poetry (p. 134)	TE—To Make Alive; An Unusual Ode	TE—Expressing Phrases; **Assign Act Abstract**
Assessment	Chapter quiz	Sonnet performance **ST—Assign Journal 5**
Suggested teaching time: 6-8 class periods		

"He Wishes for the Cloths of Heaven." Reprinted with the permission of Scribner, a Division of Simon & Schuster, Inc., from THE COLLECTED WORKS OF W. B. YEATS, VOLUME 1: THE POEMS, REVISED, edited by Richard J. Finneran. (New York: Scribner, 1997).

When I Consider How My Light Is Spent

O Prince of Peace! O Sharon's dewy Rose!

being and changes us. When we do not really listen, performance of poetry recedes into rote memorization and drudgery. This chapter is designed to help you and your students unlock the wealth of gems to be found in poetry. Savor the words. Relish the thoughts and feelings they represent.

Chapter 6 Outline

Teaching Materials

- Several selections of music for Haiku and/or Musical Metaphor
- Possibly a photo for Haiku
- Performance rubrics (students submit their own copy)

Millay's Sonnet

Though not a Christian, Millay presents a thought-provoking commentary on one of the two most significant events in the Christian calendar. Modern celebration of Christ's Advent indeed may appear superficial to those who cannot see with eyes of faith. To Millay, all who celebrated the Christian holiday were representatives of Christianity. Of course, many today celebrate Christmas as a time merely for family and generosity, excluding Christ entirely. The disgust and despair evidenced in the poem are not targeted at the Christian church specifically. Rather, Millay's commentary berates commercialism, selfishness, and hypocrisy. Encourage students to evaluate their own Christmas traditions. What motivates their activities? What attitude do they convey to the lost world around them? Would someone who observed only their families' Christmas celebrations agree with Millay's view?

OVERVIEW

Know—*Concepts*

Qualities of lyric poetry
Types of lyric poetry
Figurative language

Grow—*Interpretation Skills*

Aesthetic distance
Visualization
Word color
Vitalization

Show—*Performance*

Memorized presentation of a sonnet

For this your mother sweated in the cold,
For this you bled upon the bitter tree:
A yard of tinsel ribbon bought and sold;
A paper wreath; a day at home for me.
The merry bells ring out, the people kneel;
Up goes the man of God before the crowd;
With voice of honey and with eyes of steel
He drones your humble gospel to the proud.
Nobody listens. Less than the wind that blows
Are all your words to us you died to save.
O Prince of Peace!* O Sharon's dewy Rose!*
How mute* you lie within your vaulted grave.*
The stone the angel rolled away with tears*
Is back upon your mouth these two thousand years.

—Edna St. Vincent Millay, "To Jesus on His Birthday"

Prince of Peace: allusion to Isaiah 9:6: "For unto us a child is born, . . . and his name shall be called . . .The Prince of Peace."
Sharon's dewy Rose: allusion to Song of Solomon 2:1, which refers to Christ as "the rose of Sharon, and the lily of the valleys."
mute: silent, incapable of speech
vaulted grave: figuratively, enclosed chamber for burial
with tears: According to Matthew 28:2-8, an angel of the Lord moves the stone from the entrance to Christ's tomb and declares to the women who came to mourn that "He is not here: for He is risen" (v. 6). They depart joyfully to tell the news of Christ's Resurrection. Depiction of sorrow contradicts scriptural records.

What does this poem say to you? What mood does it create? Did the end come as a surprise? How do you feel after you read it? Another poet, Emily Dickinson, is famous for saying, "If I read a book and it makes my whole body so cold no fire can ever warm me, I know that it is poetry. If I feel physically as if the top of my head were taken off, I know that it is poetry. Is there any other way?"

PRESENTATION

Lyric Poetry

More Precious Than Gold

Introduction. Have a student read Psalm 19:7-10 aloud. Great lyric poems are like gems—small but valuable. However, God's Word, especially those Scripture passages that we have memorized, are more valuable to us than an abundance of pure gold. Ask your students to list the amazing properties of God's Word that are given in this passage. (*It converts [revives] the soul; it makes the simple wise; it gives joy to the heart; it gives light to the eyes; it endures forever; it is true [sure]; it is totally righteous.*)

Instructions. Ask your students to take out a sheet of paper and write down as many memorized Scripture passages as they can in three minutes or so. When they are finished, tell them that what they have in front of them is more valuable than pure gold. You may want the students to place this in their journals.

Some of the most powerful, memorable, and poignant literature in the English tongue can be found in poetry. Maybe you don't like poetry—or you think you don't like it. Do you remember the story of the blind men and the elephant in Chapter 1? The six men of Indostan each had confidence that an elephant was like a wall or a snake or a spear because they had discovered only one part of the elephant—his side or trunk or tusk. It's possible you have misconceptions about poetry because of limited experience. One person calls poetry sentimental, having read only mushy love poems. Another says it is boring because she read only ancient pieces she didn't understand.

Remember, the subjects and styles of poems are as varied as the authors who created them. Contrast "To Jesus on His Birthday" with Lewis Carroll's poem "Jabberwocky" (below) with its nonsense words and melodramatic adventure.

'Twas brillig, and the slithy toves
Did gyre and gimble in the wabe;
All mimsy were the borogoves,
And the mome raths outgrabe.

"Beware the Jabberwock, my son!
The jaws that bite, the claws that catch!
Beware the Jubjub bird, and shun
The frumious Bandersnatch!"

He took his vorpal sword in hand:
Long time the manxome foe he sought—
So rested he by the Tumtum tree,
And stood awhile in thought.

And, as in uffish thought he stood,
The Jabberwock, with eyes of flame,
Came whiffling through the tulgey wood,
And burbled as it came!

One, two! One, two! and through and through
The vorpal blade went snicker-snack!
He left it dead, and with its head
He went galumphing back.

"And hast thou slain the Jabberwock?
Come to my arms, my beamish boy!
O frabjous day! Callooh! Callay!"
He chortled in his joy.

'Twas brillig, and the slithy toves
Did gyre and gimble in the wabe;
All mimsy were the borogoves,
And the mome raths outgrabe.

WHEN I CONSIDER HOW MY LIGHT IS SPENT 123

Lesson Motivator

Though this text deals in greater detail with lyric poetry than either narrative or dramatic poetry, do not infer that lyric poetry is more valuable to performance or more important as a form.

In a high-school class, a short, memorized assignment is more practical than a long one. Since lyric poetry incorporates more poetic devices than other forms and is generally short, it is the most appropriate focus for this chapter.

For a forensics competition, a more experienced student of interpretation can and should select a narrative or dramatic poem. The story quality will be necessary in a competitive setting, and the length will better suit time requirements.

What is of great importance in this section is the explanations of the qualities of poetry and the purpose poetry serves. Your students will benefit from remembering the names of poetic devices, but it is more important for them to grasp *why* people write poetry and read it.

The earliest storytellers used verse to help them remember their tales. Today, many important ideas seem to need poetic expression. Whether a sympathy card with simple verse or an epithet tribute to a hero, we depend on poetic form to

The world of poetry offers something for everyone. Poetry may be grouped into three basic classifications: *lyric, narrative,* and *dramatic.* In this chapter, we will study lyric poetry, saving narrative and dramatic for Chapter 9, "From Page to Stage."

We'll also learn some principles of interpretation that prove especially useful in performing poetry. At the end of this chapter, you will have the opportunity to perform a sonnet of your choosing from Appendix C.

LYRIC POETRY

Lyric poetry consists of several fixed forms—the elegy, the ode, and the sonnet (perhaps the single most popular form of poetry). Many other forms such as haiku and free verse may also fall into this category, depending on their content. Though these types vary greatly in form, they do share one important quality that unites them as a classification.

Qualities of Lyric Poetry

All forms of **lyric poetry** present an emotional experience. They generally do not provide much background information; rather, they focus on sharing a moment with the reader. In addition to this element, most lyric poems are quite short, though there are exceptions to this rule.

definition

Lyric poetry presents an emotional experience and is generally short in length.

Being short, a lyric poem is usually dense in meaning. Look again at Millay's poem, "To Jesus on His Birthday." Could you express in a short paragraph what Millay is communicating with her sonnet? Probably not. You might be able to summarize, saying, "Jesus did so much for us, and all we do in return is take a day off from work and decorate." It loses something in the translation though, doesn't it! To effectively communicate in prose all that she conveys in verse might take pages; it might even be impossible.

Types of Lyric Poetry

As was mentioned above, various types of poems are classified as lyric. Several popular forms are explained below.

An *elegy* expresses grief. Its form varies, but usually it has elevated language to support the serious nature of its subject. Examples of well-known elegies include "Bells for John Whiteside's Daughter" by John Crowe Ransom, "Elegy Written in a Country Churchyard" by Thomas Gray, and "When Lilacs Last in the Dooryard Bloom'd," Walt Whitman's elegy on Abraham Lincoln.

Haiku

After reading about haiku on page 125, provide students with a brief musical recording or a scenic photo. Remind them that haiku seeks to capture a moment or a singular emotion. Allow two to three minutes for them to write a haiku based on what they have seen or heard. You may want the students to place this in their journals.

An Unusual Ode

Below is a poem by Thomas Gray, author of "Elegy Written in a Country Churchyard." The poem is titled and written as an "ode" but doesn't have the same somber tone most odes do. Read it aloud and ask the students to determine why he chose this form.

Ode on the Death of a Favourite Cat Drowned in a Tub of Goldfishes

'Twas on a lofty vase's side,
Where China's gayest art had dy'd
The azure flow'rs that blow;
Demurest of the tabby kind,
The pensive Selima, reclin'd,
Gazed on the lake below.
Her conscious tail her joy declar'd;
The fair round face, the snowy beard,
The velvet of her paws,
Her coat, that with the tortoise vies,
Her ears of jet, and emerald eyes,
She saw: and purr'd applause.

Moods in Lyric Poetry

Below is the opening stanza to Gray's poem, "Elegy Written in a Country Churchyard." Observe the mood as you read; then answer the questions.

> The curfew tolls the knell of parting day,
> The lowing herd wind* slowly o'er the lea,*
> The plowman homeward plods his weary way,
> And leaves the world to darkness and to me.

wind: a verb here, not a noun.
lea (LEE): meadow

Pick the correct contrast to describe the style of the poem.

1. Mood: tranquil or exciting _tranquil_
2. Attitude: cheerful or sad _sad_
3. Pace: slow, medium, or fast _slow_
4. Word choice: quick, crisp sounds or slow, smooth sounds _slow, smooth sounds_

An *ode* presents an exalted theme in a formal manner. Examples of odes include Gray's "Ode on the Spring" and John Keats's "Ode on a Grecian Urn." The main differences between elegies and odes are purpose and mood. Few odes are as somber as a typical elegy, and most are particularly grand in style.

Haiku, a Japanese form of poetry, has three lines in English with lines of five syllables, seven, and then five again. A haiku usually presents an image, like a snapshot.

> Evening darkens. Hunched
> On a withered bough, a crow.
> Autumn in the air.

> Lightning in the clouds!
> In the deeper dark is heard
> A night-heron's cry.

> —Bashō

The Sonnet

The *sonnet* is perhaps the most distinct and most popular type of lyric poetry. Every poetry anthology is sure to include sonnets from previous centuries as well as our own. A **sonnet** is most easily identified by the number of lines it contains. Most fourteen-line poems also have the other structural and content qualities of the sonnet. Usually a

*A **sonnet** is a fourteen-line poem generally written in iambic pentameter and one of two popular rhyme schemes: abba, abba, cdc, cdc or abab, cdcd, efef, gg.*

WHEN I CONSIDER HOW MY LIGHT IS SPENT 125

communicate important messages.

Lesson Objectives

The student will be able to

1. Define *lyric poetry.*
2. Name several types of lyric poetry.
3. Explain the purpose of poetic expression.

"Elegy Written in a Country Churchyard"

You might pose the following question to your students: What qualities of this poem create the mood it conveys? *(Answers may include the slow pace and slow, smooth sounds.)*

"On His Blindness"

Milton beautifully contrasts light, whose source is God, and the darkness of this world, depicting the depravity of man. Would God ask man to accomplish a task without providing the means? The answer given is that God has no need of man or even of the gifts He gave him. We serve Him best when we joyfully accept His will, whether or not His will includes our accomplishing a particular task.

Remind students that it is wise to submit our gifts and ourselves to God because we need His blessing on our lives, not because He lacks anything.

Still had she gaz'd; but 'midst the tide
Two angel forms were seen to glide,
The Genii of the stream;
Their scaly armour's Tyrian hue
Thro' richest purple to the view
Betray'd a golden gleam.
The hapless Nymph with wonder saw:
A whisker first and then a claw,
With many an ardent wish,
She stretch'd in vain to reach the prize.
What female heart can gold despise?
What cat's averse to fish?
Presumptuous Maid! with looks intent
Again she stretch'd, again she bent,

Nor knew the gulf between.
(Malignant Fate sat by, and smil'd)
The slipp'ry verge her feet beguil'd,
She tumbled headlong in.
Eight times emerging from the flood
She mew'd to ev'ry wat'ry god,
Some speedy aid to send.
No Dolphin came, no Nereid stirr'd;
Nor cruel Tom, nor Susan heard.
A Fav'rite has no friend!
From hence, ye Beauties, undeceiv'd,
Know, one false step is ne'er retriev'd,
And be with caution bold.
Not all that tempts your wand'ring eyes

And heedless hearts is lawful prize,
Nor all, that glisters, gold.

sonnet's meter is *iambic pentameter*, or lines of five *iambs*. An *iamb* consists of two consecutive syllables with the second being stressed rather than the first. The following lines by Emily Dickinson are an example of common meter (four iambic feet followed by three iambic feet). Emphasized syllables appear in all caps.

> We NEVer KNOW how HIGH we ARE
> Till WE are CALLED to RISE.

Though not all sonnets have this meter, most do.

A sonnet usually has a specific **rhyme scheme** or pattern of rhyme seen in the ending syllables of lines of poetry. The Italian *sonnet* groups the lines of the poem as follows: *abba, abba, cde, cde* (or a slight variation of this). An excellent example is John Milton's famous poem "On His Blindness."

definition

Rhyme scheme refers to the pattern of rhyme seen in the end words of lines of poetry.

When I consider how my light is spent,	*a*
Ere half my days, in this dark world and wide,	*b*
And that one Talent which is death to hide,	*b*
Lodg'd with me useless, though my Soul more bent	*a*
To serve therewith my Maker, and present	*a*
My true account, lest he returning chide,	*b*
"Doth God exact day-labour, light deny'd,"	*b*
I fondly ask; But patience, to prevent	*a*
That murmur, soon replies, "God doth not need	*c*
Either man's work or his own gifts; who best	*d*
Bear his mild yoke, they serve him best," His state	*e*
Is kingly. Thousands at his bidding speed	*c*
And post o'er Land and Ocean without rest:	*d*
They also serve who only stand and wait.	*e*

This form is seldom observed strictly in English since the English language lacks the abundance of rhyming words found in Italian. To further study this poem, see Appendix C.

The *English sonnet*, popularized by Shakespeare and his contemporaries, has a rhyme scheme of *abab, cdcd, efef, gg*. This rhyme scheme is easier for English poetry since only pairs of words rhyme rather than as many as four in the Italian sonnet. Shakespeare's Sonnet 18 is a good example of an English sonnet.

Shall I compare thee to a summer's day?	*a*
Thou art more lovely and more temperate:	*b*
Rough winds do shake the darling buds of May,	*a*
And summer's lease hath all too short a date:	*b*
Sometime too hot the eye of heaven shines,	*c*
And often is his gold complexion dimm'd;	*d*
And every fair from fair sometime declines,	*c*

126 CHAPTER 6

Questions

1. What is the cat a symbol of? (*vanity, arrogance, external beauty*)

2. What might you call the "moral of the story"? (*Answers will vary but may include: "All that glisters is not gold"; "a favored position means not having many friends"; and "a friend in need is a friend indeed."*)

3. To whom is the lesson addressed? (*"ye Beauties"—those who are vain about their beauty*)

4. Why do you think Gray chose the form of an ode for this subject? (*Answers will vary. Being "lofty," the form allows for mock seriousness, which makes the absurdity of the situation humorous [ironic].*)

You probably didn't have to read much past the title to guess that Gray wanted an elevated style to make his joke effective.

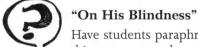

"On His Blindness"

Have students paraphrase this poem to explore the meaning. Tell students that "fondly" means "foolishly." Why does Milton consider his question foolish in hindsight? (*The poem states that "God doth not need / Either man's work or his own gifts."*) Have students look for the answer to this question in the final lines of the poem.

By chance, or nature's changing course, untrimm'd;   *d*
But thy eternal summer shall not fade,   *e*
Nor lose possession of that fair thou ow'st;   *f*
Nor shall Death brag thou wander'st in his shade,   *e*
When in eternal lines to time thou grow'st: *f*
So long as men can breathe or eyes can see,   *g*
So long lives this and this gives life to thee.   *g*

This sonnet also appears in Appendix C. You will want to study in detail whatever sonnet you choose for your project. Remember, not all sonnets have the same style. The poem at the opening of the chapter, "To Jesus on His Birthday," is also a sonnet, though it is very different in style from these two selections.

In summary, lyric poetry is very diverse in style but always expresses emotions and personal impressions of a topic. Though the language of some lyric poetry may deter you, don't give up! Well-written lyric poems are often like gems—small, but valuable.

FIGURATIVE LANGUAGE

In everyday conversation your friend might say, "I'm starving!" But he *really* means to say, "Breakfast was three hours ago, and I am very hungry for lunch." Such expressions are called **figurative language.** That particular "figure" is an example of *hyperbole,* which you studied in Chapter 5. Figurative language may be divided into three basic categories: *figures of thought, figures of speech,* and *figures of sound.*

Definition

Figurative language refers to words used in a nonliteral way.

A figure of thought is a poetic device used to compare one idea with another.

A simile is a comparison using the word like *or* as.

Figures of Thought

A **figure of thought** helps us convey many details briefly by referring the listener to a familiar object or situation. Rather than having to explain each characteristic of a friend, for instance, we might just say, "She's a peach." We don't mean that she hangs around in an orchard all day—the statement is not literal. Rather, the comparison tries to represent *personality* by associating it with something likable and sweet—a peach. The comparison ends there.

Simile and Metaphor

There are two types of comparison with which you need to be familiar in order to understand most lyric poems: *simile* and *metaphor.* A **simile** (SIM uh lee) compares two things using the word *like* or *as.* "Their house is as big as the Taj Mahal" is a simile. Some similes are so catchy that they become *clichés,* losing their

Lesson Motivator
On the high-school level, students need not make distinction among figures of thought, speech, and sound. They are discussed in these categories only for sake of clarity. Emphasize recognition and understanding of each specific figure instead. For example, it is more important for the student to distinguish between simile and metaphor than to identify both as figures of thought.

Lesson Objectives
The student will be able to

1. Understand uses of figurative language.

2. Define *simile, metaphor, metonymy, synecdoche, apostrophe, antithesis, parallelism, rhyme, onomatopoeia, alliteration, consonance,* and *assonance.*

Musical Metaphor

Introduction. Music is inherently lyrical. A march has a different effect on the listener than a waltz. The first would be appropriate as motivation for physical activity whereas the latter seems to fit best with a carousel ride on a breezy summer day. Like lyric poetry, music is more than a series of logical components—it is an expression of the soul.

Instructions. Play a recording of a musical selection of your choosing for the class. Have your students brainstorm for images that the music brings to their minds. Instruct each student to invent a pantomime to convey a singular image. Have each student perform and the other students guess what the image is. Possible music selections include *Moldau* by Smetana, "Moonlight Sonata" by Beethoven, any portion of *Peter and the Wolf* by Prokofiev, *Rodeo* (roh DAY oh) by Copland, and *The Carnival of the Animals* by Saint-Saëns.

Discussion. Ask various students to explain what motivated their pantomimes.

Tenor and Vehicle

If your students are already familiar with simile and metaphor, you may wish to add tenor and vehicle to their vocabulary list. However, these terms are not as important to the purpose of this course as are simile and metaphor.

freshness. Examples include: "quick as a wink," "sharp as a tack," and "hungry as a bear." If you find the text crowded with such clichés, don't select it for performance. Look for new, striking comparisons.

definition

*A **metaphor** is a word or expression that represents a distinctly different concept or action without asserting a comparison.*

***Metonymy** refers to an idea or an object by mentioning a related idea.*

A **metaphor** labels something directly without clarifying that it is making a comparison. In a love poem, John Frederick Nims writes about a woman "whose hands shipwreck vases." Of course he means she is clumsy, tending to break things. In a metaphor, the word used figuratively, such as "shipwreck" in the line above, is called a metaphoric *vehicle*. This simply means it is the device carrying the meaning. The idea represented, clumsiness, is called the *tenor*.

With simile and especially with metaphor, you must look at the context to determine the idea in the comparison. In Nims's poem about his clumsy wife, his title "Love Poem" is the first and most important clue to context for his choice of comparisons. The final stanza, which expresses his devotion and adoration, keeps the same style of comparison, suggesting not only that he loves a *real* woman who has faults but also that her unique personality merits such creative word choices. Vague greeting-card verse would not suffice.

Metonymy and Synecdoche

Even in everyday speech we constantly use one idea or object to mean something else. **Metonymy** (muh TAHN uh mee) refers to an idea or an object by mentioning a related idea. Consider the examples below.

As you can see, we use metonymy in order to condense the meaning—we communicate more while often saying less. An author's name easily suggests his writings. Symbols of office can easily be substituted for the individual—crown, throne, scepter, Oval Office, and so on.

METONYMY	
Figurative Expression	*Meaning*
I love Shakespeare.	I love the plays and poems written by Shakespeare.
The crown will prevail.	The king will prevail.
I'm a ball fan.	I enjoy being a spectator for athletic events, such as baseball and basketball.

PRESENTATION
Figurative Language

Name That Figure

Instructions. Divide your students into two teams if desired. Read each line below and have the teams (or individuals) identify each example's type of figurative language. Quiz and test questions might be drawn from the samples below.

Examples

"Devouring Time, blunt thou the lion's paws." (*apostrophe and personification*)

"O Sharon's dewy Rose!" (*apostrophe and metaphor*)

"Prayer, the Church's banquet." (*metaphor*)

"So when my tongue would speak her praises due" (*synecdoche*)

"[Canker-blooms] live unwooed and unrespected fade." (*personification*)

"[I speak] As an unperfect actor on the stage." (*simile*)

"With voice of honey" (*metaphor*)

"And when my pen would write her titles true" (*personification or metonymy*)

"He is trampling out the vintage where the grapes of wrath are stored" (*metaphor*)

"That thou lov'st mankind well, yet wilt not choose me, / And Satan hates me,

We can also relate two ideas or objects to one another by using a part to signify the whole. This is called **synecdoche** (sih NECK duh kee). The chart below gives several examples.

Synecdoche refers to using a part of something to signify the whole.

Personification describes an abstraction or inanimate object by giving it human characteristics.

definition

SYNECDOCHE	
Figurative Expression	*Meaning*
Count heads.	Count the people present.
She's a dear heart.	She's a dear person.
Many hands make light work.	Many people working with their hands make work easier.

In summary, metonymy uses a related object and synecdoche uses a part of the whole to represent the subject.

Personification

> *O wind, rend open the heat,*
> *cut apart the heat,*
> *rend it to tatters.*

These three lines compose the first stanza in a poem called "Heat" by Hilda Doolittle. They present another type of figure of thought called **personification,** which gives human attributes to abstractions or inanimate objects. The sonnet "Death Be Not Proud" also uses personification, as do "Ode on a Grecian Urn" and "Ode on the Spring." Personification appears in Scripture as well.

> *The mountains and the hills shall break forth before you into singing, and all the trees of the field shall clap their hands. (Isaiah 55:12)*

> *The heavens declare the glory of God; and the firmament sheweth his handywork. (Psalm 19:1)*

If the inanimate object or abstraction speaks or responds as a character in the literature, you will have to use your imagination to create a physical stance and

---

yet is loth to lose me." (*parallelism and antithesis*)

"That ribbon of highway" (*metaphor*)

"Now hard-fortuned Hamish, half blown of his breath with the height of the hill" (*alliteration*)

"All the world's a stage." (*metaphor*)

Divine Poetry

Read Psalm 42 to your students. Discuss why the poetry books in the Bible contain so much figurative language. Lead students to discover that comparing the abstract to the concrete makes the abstract more comprehensible. (*Depicting the hart [deer] panting for the water brook illustrates the psalmist's desire for God.*) Also, be sure the students realize that poetic devices—rhyme, alliteration, parallelism, and

antithesis in particular—make an idea more memorable.

vocal quality—perhaps even a personality for that personified character that is logical within the fictional setting.

In conclusion, remember that figures of thought convey nonliteral and very condensed meaning. Take time to really think about what you are reading when you find these devices in a selection. Otherwise, you won't be able to convey the full meaning to your audience.

Figures of Speech

Often the term *figure of speech* is used in a general sense to describe the devices explained in the last section. More specifically, a **figure of speech** alters primarily the arrangement of words rather than their meaning. Among other devices, figures of speech include *apostrophe, antithesis,* and *parellelism.*

definition

*A **figure of speech** does not try to alter the meaning of individual words for effect but rather arranges the words in a nonstandard manner.*

***Apostrophe** creates direct and explicit address either to an absent person or to an abstract or inanimate entity.*

***Antithesis** creates contrast or opposition in the meanings of contiguous phrases or clauses.*

***Parallelism** presents pairs of phrases possessing similar order or structure.*

Apostrophe

The poems "Heat" and "Death Be Not Proud" are examples of not only personification but also **apostrophe,** or speaking to an absent person, an abstraction, or an inanimate object. Since many sonnets address someone or something, apostrophe is commonly used. Another example is Edgar Allan Poe's "To Helen," in which he addresses Helen of Troy:

> *Helen, thy beauty is to me*
> *Like those Nicean barks of yore,*
> *That gently, o'er perfum'd sea,*
> *The weary way-worn wanderer bore*
> *To his own native shore.*

Of course, Poe could not actually speak to Helen of Troy since she is only a legendary character.

Apostrophe is used in Scripture as well. First Corinthians 15:55 says, "O death, where is thy sting? O grave, where is thy victory?"

Antithesis and Parallelism

The poetry in the Book of Proverbs, as well as many other poems, contains *antithesis* and *parallelism.* **Antithesis** (an TITH ih sis) contrasts ideas, while **parallelism** uses grammatical structure to point out the similarities or differences between two thoughts. Often antithesis and parallelism work together, as in the following examples:

130 CHAPTER 6

A soft answer turneth away wrath:
but grievous words stir up anger. (Proverbs 15:1)

A wise son maketh a glad father:
but a foolish son is the heaviness of his mother.

Treasures of wickedness profit nothing:
but righteousness delivereth from death.

He that gathereth in summer is a wise son:
but he that sleepeth in harvest is a son that causeth shame.

The memory of the just is blessed:
but the name of the wicked shall rot. (Proverbs 10:1, 2, 5, 7)

PARALLELISM
Each verse repeats the form of the first clause in the second clause.

	SUBJECT	**PREDICATE**	
	A soft answer	turneth away wrath:	
	but grievous words	stir up anger.	
	A wise son	maketh a glad father:	
	but a foolish son	is the heaviness of his mother.	
	Treasures of wickedness	profit nothing:	
	but righteousness	delivereth from death.	
	He that gathereth in summer	is a wise son:	
	but he that sleepeth in harvest	is a son that causeth shame.	
	The memory of the just	is blessed:	
	but the name of the wicked	shall rot.	

ANTITHESIS — Each verse has two subjects with opposite meanings. (left margin)

ANTITHESIS — Each verse has two predicates that show opposite results. (right margin)

Lyric poems tend to be persuasive or inspirational in nature. A wise poet refines his points (arguments) as efficiently as possible. Antithesis and parallelism are very useful means to that end. Also, the expression of thought or emotion about an object or person makes apostrophe a common occurrence.

These figures of speech will appear in many of the sonnets you and your classmates perform. Watch for these devices so you can apply good principles of interpretation when you perform lyric poetry.

WHEN I CONSIDER HOW MY LIGHT IS SPENT 131

Figures of Sound

While discussing poetry in Chapter 4, we mentioned finding the music of the poem. Poetry is indeed written for the ear. This task is accomplished by using one of the sound devices, sometimes called a *figure of sound*. The most familiar **figure of sound** in English poetry is *rhyme*. Children's verse seems wholly dependent upon it. What would be the appeal of "Hickory dickory, the mouse ran up the clock" or "Jack and Jennifer went up a hill"?

*A **figure of sound** is a device, such as rhyme or alliteration, that enhances meaning by deliberate use of words with certain sounds.*

***Rhyme** refers to having the last syllable of one word, beginning with a vowel sound, match that of another word.*

***Onomatopoeia** is the use of words whose sounds suggest or reinforce their meaning.*

***Alliteration** is the repetition of phonetic sounds in a phrase or sentence.*

Rhyme

Rhyme requires a similar end sound in two words. The similarity may be in either the last syllable or the last two syllables, but it always begins with a vowel sound. Therefore, *rain, pain, explain,* and *contain* are all rhyme words; but *rain* and *ran* are not because they do not share a vowel sound.

Onomatopoeia

Some words sound like what they represent. These words are *onomatopoetic*. **Onomatopoeia** (AHN uh MAT uh PEE uh) is inherently part of our language, and poetry tends to emphasize it. Comic strips often use words such as *ker-pow* and *bang* to convey sound.

Can you imagine a curtain "flickering" or a flame "fluttering"? Of course it makes better sense the other way around—a flickering flame and a fluttering curtain, right? Despite their similarity in meaning, these two words have different sound quality. "Flutter" seems too heavy for a flame, but paired with a curtain (fabric instead of light), it gives the impression of fluid movement. Onomatopoeia is one tool the poet can use to select the best words for his message.

Alliteration

Alliteration uses repetition of a sound through a phrase to point out an idea or to create a certain atmosphere. Contrast the effects of alliteration in the following two excerpts:

> Now hard-fortuned Hamish, half blown of his breath with the height of
>   the hill,
> Was white in the face when the ten-tined buck and the does
> Drew leaping to burn-ward; huskily rose
> His shouts, and his nether lip twitched, and his legs were o'er-weak for his
>   will.

> —Sidney Lanier, "The Revenge of Hamish"

This stanza gives the impression of being short of breath, doesn't it?

 CHAPTER 6

The tongue twister below is an energetic part of a comic opera. It too might leave you out of breath, but in the context of a comedy, the alliteration emphasizes the melodrama and humor as opposed to emphasizing details of the plot as in the first example.

> *To sit in solemn silence in a dull, dark dock,*
> *In a pestilential prison, with a life-long lock,*
> *Awaiting the sensation of a short, sharp shock,*
> *From a cheap and chippy chopper on a big black block!*
>
> —William Gilbert and Arthur Sullivan, *The Mikado*

Consonance and Assonance

Another sound device, **consonance** (KAHN suh nuns), involves repetition of consonant sounds in pairs. A classic example of consonance is found in W. H. Auden's work "O, Where Are You Going?" which includes the following word pairs: rider/reader, midden/madden, farer/fearer, looking/lacking, and hearer/horror.

Sometimes a similar effect is created with the use of vowels. This is called **assonance** (AS uh nuns). Assonance is probably more common, since vowels convey so much of the emotive quality of words and are easier to match than pairs of consonants. Alfred, Lord Tennyson makes extensive use of this device in his poem "The Lady of Shallot." Below are two examples.

> *Willows whiten, aspens quiver,*
> *Little breezes dusk and shiver*
> *Through the wave that runs forever*
> *By the island in the river*
> *Flowing down to Camelot.*

1. What vowel sound do you hear most often? _____ *short i* _____

> *Only reapers, reaping early*
> *In among the bearded barley,*
> *Hear a song that echoes cheerly*
> *From the river winding clearly,*
> *Down to tower'd Camelot.*

2. Which vowel is repeated in this portion? _____ *long e* _____

As you explore and study a sonnet for your project, watch for the figures of thought and figures of speech but listen for the figures of sound. Their music is part of the poem's message. Without the intonations and emotive force of figures of sound, a lyric poem could quickly become as dry as chalk.

D *definition*

Consonance is the repetition of a sequence of two or more consonants from one word to another.

Assonance is the repetition of identical or similar vowel sounds—especially in stressed syllables—in a sequence of nearby words.

WHEN I CONSIDER HOW MY LIGHT IS SPENT **133**

Lesson Motivator

Good interpretation of poetry develops appreciation even in those who were once hostile or indifferent to the genre. Poor interpretation of poetry is dull, lifeless, and even sing-songy—not very appealing to someone already opposed to poetry. The difference is more than delivery, though delivery makes a great difference. For the hearer, comprehension is greatly increased by effective interpretation.

Encourage your students who already have an interest in poetry to prioritize developing good technique so they can help others enjoy poetry too. Encourage those who are not poetry fans to realize that learning how to interpret a poem can be much more interesting than just silently reading poetry because they can better relate to the ideas and emotions presented.

Above all else, inspire students with the potential of interpreting poetry. Some of the most captivating adventures, the most thrilling mysteries, and the most beautiful romances are recorded in verse. Consider sharing some longer narrative poems with your students. Possible selections may be drawn from *Idylls of the King* or *Enoch Arden* by Alfred, Lord Tennyson; "Nightmare at Noon" by Stephen Vincent Benét; "The Highwayman" by Alfred Noyes; "The Fear" or

Just identifying figurative language is not sufficient. You must come to an understanding of why the author chose the devices he used. Why does Milton compare talent to light? Why does Shakespeare compare love to spring blooms? Answer these questions, and you are ready to share that piece of poetry with your audience.

INTERPRETATION OF LYRIC POETRY

Now you are ready to plunge into a lyric poem and interpret it orally for your audience. In the remainder of the chapter, we will discuss a few basic techniques for interpretation. Work to add these tools to your performer's toolbox; you will use them on many future projects.

An Approach to Lyric Poetry

1. Read the poem more slowly than other genres.
2. Present the poem indirectly (use *aesthetic distance*).
3. Visualize the imagery.
4. Color the words—especially descriptive action verbs and modifiers.
5. Vitalize (or animate) the text.

Remember the primary qualities of lyric poetry? Lyric poetry tends toward emotional content and brevity. These qualities influence how you must approach reading it aloud. First, read lyric poetry more slowly. A slower speed helps keep the heavy use of imagery and figurative language from overwhelming the audience. Secondly, present it with less directness. An indirect approach may include using a technique called *aesthetic distance*.

Aesthetic Distance

Aesthetic distance attempts to separate the fictional situation from the context of the performance. Contrast this with public speaking, in which you use eye contact to make each audience member feel as though you are speaking directly to him or her. Aesthetic distance tries to do just the opposite. Let's say you are presenting Elizabeth Barrett Browning's beautiful Sonnet 43 ("How do I love thee? Let me count the ways."). The speaker is Mrs. Browning, not you, and the audience is her husband rather than the other students. You can imagine why your looking directly at someone in the room might be rather confusing or even embarrassing.

definition

Aesthetic distance is a figurative, mental distancing, rather than a physical one—a sense of being separated from the situation to which one is responding.

This does *not* mean that you let your eyes wander or stare. Instead you imagine a fictitious audience (character) and "see" that person just a little higher than the heads of the audience. Speak to that

PRESENTATION
Interpretation of Poetry

Expressing Phrases

Have students take turns reading aloud each of the phrases given as examples in Name That Figure (TE p. 128). Work to express the images in each, using the techniques described in this chapter.

invisible "person," and your audience will feel as though they are listening in on a conversation rather than being spoken to. In some cases, that "person" you address will be the subject of apostrophe and personification.

In addition to direct address, aesthetic distance effectively communicates all description. When you see the details of the image in your mind, the audience pictures them as well.

Eagle Flight

Silently read the poem below several times, picturing what Tennyson describes. Then practice reading the poem aloud, using aesthetic distance. Your teacher may have you read it aloud.

> He clasps the crag with crooked hands;
> Close to the sun in lonely lands,
> Ring'd with the azure world, he stands.
>
> The wrinkled sea beneath him crawls;
> He watches from his mountain walls,
> And like a thunderbolt he falls.
>
> —Alfred, Lord Tennyson, "The Eagle"

Visualization

> Slowly, silently now the moon
> Walks the night in her silver shoon,*
> This way and that she peers and sees
> Silver fruit upon silver trees.
> One by one the casements catch
> Her beams beneath the silvery thatch;
> Couched in his kennel, like a log,
> With paws of silver sleeps the dog;
> From their shadowy cote* the white breasts peep
> Of doves in a silver-feathered sleep;
> A harvest mouse goes scampering by,
> With silver claws and a silver eye;
> And moveless fish in the water gleam,
> By silver reeds in a silver stream.
>
> —Walter de la Mare, "Silver"

shoon: *shining light; also shoes (archaic)*

cote: *a small building that shelters an animal*

"Home Burial" by Robert Frost; or "Sorab and Rustum" by Matthew Arnold.

Lesson Objectives

The student will be able to

1. Effectively use aesthetic distance, visualization, word color, and vitalization.
2. Appreciate the poetry contained in the chapter.

Devices in "The Eagle"

Draw your students' attention to the use of rhyme, assonance, and alliteration. They can interpret such a selection more effectively by identifying these poetic devices.

Visualization

Any time a story or description captivates our imagination, we naturally picture the situation and respond empathetically. Visualization means that the speaker chooses to concentrate and empathize enough to share his personal response with the listener. This technique should not be confused with New Age terminology.

Eyes of Understanding

Explain to the students that they have to open up their mind's eye to clearly see the images in a poem. When believers read the Bible, they must ask the Lord to open their eyes of understanding so that they will clearly see what the Lord has for them in His Word. Ask one of your students to read Ephesians 1:15-23 aloud.

Genuine Service

Explain to your class that just as performing poetry without a genuine desire to communicate meaning may be a total waste of time, so performing Christian service without a genuine heart of love will profit nothing (I Cor. 13:1-3). Many of your students are undoubtedly involved in nursing home services, bus ministry, choir, visitation, or children's ministry. Encourage them to participate in these activities with a heart of genuine love toward the Lord and those they serve. Have your students take out a sheet of paper and write down what spiritual weaknesses or potential spiritual weaknesses they see in their present Christian service. Encourage them to include Bible verses that apply to their situation. Give them about five minutes to work on this project. You may want the students to place this in their journals.

De la Mare's poem above contains a great deal of imagery. The only way the audience will see the beauty of the silver fruit or the tranquility of the dog with silver paws is if you as the speaker see these images vividly in your mind's eye.

Picturing imagery and responding to what you see through voice and body so that your audience understands is called **visualization.** For the interpreter, visualization includes a goal (audience understanding) and a means to that goal (personal response to imagery).

If you interpret literature for an audience without having this specific goal (helping that audience to understand the literature), you are likely to have several problems with your performance. You may tend to be melodramatic because you are thinking primarily about how you sound instead of concentrating on the message and the audience, or you may create so little mood that the audience quickly loses interest. Ways to prevent these problems include careful analysis before practicing, practicing with an audience (maybe your younger sister or your cat), and performing with the audience in mind.

definition

Visualization requires a personal response to imagery so that the audience is compelled to respond as well.

Types of Imagery

Visualization requires much practice for mastery. Reread the poem "Silver" below and then underline each image. Then write in the margin to which sense each image appeals. Of course the main senses are sight, hearing, smell, touch, and taste. Often a poem describes movement, not just a passive visual scene. Since the interpreter responds differently to movement than to descriptions of other visual elements such as color, light, shape, and size, mark action and movements as "action," not "sight."

The two lines below are done for you as a sample:

<u>Slowly, silently</u> now <u>the moon</u>	*action; hearing (quiet)*
<u>Walks the night</u> in her <u>silver shoon.</u>	*sight and action; sight (color)*

This way and that <u>she peers and sees</u>	**action**
<u>Silver fruit</u> upon <u>silver trees.</u>	**sight (color)**
One by one the <u>casements catch</u>	**action; sight (light)**
Her <u>beams</u> beneath the <u>silvery thatch;</u>	**action; sight**
<u>Couched</u> in his <u>kennel, like a log,</u>	**sight (color)**
With <u>paws of silver</u> sleeps the dog;	**sight; sight (color)**
From their <u>shadowy cote</u> the <u>white breasts peep</u>	**sight**
Of <u>doves</u> in a <u>silver-feathered sleep;</u>	**action**
A <u>harvest mouse</u> goes <u>scampering</u> by,	**both images—sight (color)**
With <u>silver claws</u> and a <u>silver eye;</u>	**action; sight**
And <u>moveless fish</u> in the water <u>gleam,</u>	**action; sight**
By <u>silver reeds</u> in a <u>silver stream</u>.	**both images—sight (color)**

Act Abstract

Instructions. From a short story or poem listed below, have your students select a personified character and create a dramatic sketch (like charades) of that character. If the character is not given lines of dialogue by the author, they may create their own as long as their lines are consistent with the style of the selection. The students may also choose to *pantomime* (act silently—communicate with gesture and facial expression) the character, even if there is written dialogue. Have them practice several times before presenting their characters in a minute or less. They should be prepared to present their improvisations in class.

Possible personified characters

Patience from "On His Blindness" by John Milton

Time from "Sonnet 19" by William Shakespeare

Red Death from "The Masque of the Red Death" by Edgar Allan Poe

Christmas Past, Christmas Present, or Christmas Yet to Come from *A Christmas Carol* by Charles Dickens

The main subject in any of the following poems by Percy Bysshe Shelley: "To Night," "The Cloud," "To a Skylark," and "Ode to the West Wind."

The sea in either "The Tide Rises, The Tide Falls" by Henry Wadsworth

Word Color

Not only do you need to visualize the imagery in your selection, but you also need to *color* your words. **Word color** refers to the mood of a particular word. Your voice must be that word's paintbrush, using force (volume), pitch, quality, and rate. In the activity above, you will note that the word *slowly* suggests a visual image. The moon moves slowly. How then should you color that word? Obviously you don't want a fast rate! Slow down your rate by elongating the vowel sound slightly. Let the "o" be very round and full and slo-o-ow. By contrast, the word *silently* needs a softening of volume. The vowel sounds especially should be light and soft. Be careful not to overdo this technique or your performance may become humorous—like a youth-night skit. Be subtle!

In a well-written piece, use of modifiers will be minimal and artful. Enjoy these adjectives and adverbs. Good literature has excellent word choices for its nouns and verbs. Your word color should clarify the nature of a noun, even to an audience member who is unfamiliar with that specific noun. Your word color of a verb is the muscle of its action. When you say, "He bolted for the door," your voice must convey the tense urgency and speed of the motion. By contrast, when you say, "He bolted the door," your voice needs to express the finality, force, and decisiveness of the act.

Word color creates the mood, developing the meaning of a word through its sound using force, pitch, quality, and rate.

Vitalization means to animate the text by concentrating on the ideas and sharing in the emotion while speaking.

Vitalization

Vitalization demands that you make the text come alive by appreciating the struggles of the characters or narrator in the selection and staying focused while presenting the text. Imagine someone trying to tell a scary tale but getting sidetracked or giggly—the suspense is broken. Likewise, a sad emotion cannot be communicated if the interpreter is mocking or otherwise "goofing off." Good dramatic communication requires composure, sincerity, and intensity.

THE VOCAL PAINTBRUSH: WORD COLOR		
Part of Speech	*Goal*	*Technique*
Nouns	Convey characteristics	Vocal quality suits the character; inflection suggests mood of a place, depicts images, etc.
Verbs	Reveal action	Voice mimics or suggests the qualities of the action
Adjectives and Adverbs	Create the mood of the environment	Voice reflects the same qualities being described

WHEN I CONSIDER HOW MY LIGHT IS SPENT 137

Longfellow or "Dover Beach" by Matthew Arnold

Spring in "Spring" by Dante Gabriel Rossetti

The moon in "Silver" by Walter de la Mare

Or any other personification in another work you've read

Have students complete the following before returning to class.

1. Character chosen
2. Title of the work
3. Author
4. Description of your dramatic sketch
5. What technique best helps you communicate your characters? (facial expression, vocal inflection, covert movement, overt bodily movement, gesture, etc.)

6. Number of practices: (Choose one) 1-2, 3-5, 7-9, 10+

Have students answer the following questions after performing their sketches.

1. T/F I practiced adequately to communicate clearly.
2. What worked well in your presentation?
3. What else might you do in the future to improve?

Putting Life into a Poem

The Robert Frost poem below, "The Line Gang," is one line short of a sonnet's fourteen-line standard and has an unusual rhyme scheme. It describes the process of putting together telephone lines. Read the poem several times until you understand the images and ideas. Then answer the questions. Finally, read it aloud, working to vitalize the text. Though you need not memorize this poem, be prepared if your teacher asks you to read it aloud.

Here come the line-gang pioneering by.	a
They throw a forest down less cut than broken.	b
They plant dead trees for living, and the dead	c
They string together with a living thread.	c
They string an instrument against the sky	a
Wherein words whether beaten out or spoken	b
Will run as hushed as when they were a thought.	d
But in no hush they string it: they go past	e
With shouts afar to pull the cable taut,	d
To hold it hard until they make it fast,	e
To ease away—they have it. With a laugh,	f
An oath* of towns that set the world at naught*	d
They bring the telephone and telegraph.	f

oath: promise
naught: nothing

1. Why do you think Frost says "pioneering" instead of simply "traveling" or "moving"? *They bring new technology with them.*

2. In what sense is the forest "broken"? *The natural beauty and growth of the forest have been damaged.*

3. What does Frost mean by "dead trees"? *telephone poles*

4. What is the "living thread"? *the wire, which will be "live" with electric signals*

5. What is ironic about the two ideas involving the word "hush"? *The purpose of the wire is to carry messages silently, but assembling the system is very noisy, disruptive work.*

6. How do you think Frost feels about this work of "progress"? *Answers will vary but should reflect Frost's skepticism. He seems to believe that this convenience will come at a great price—the peace, tranquility, and beauty of nature.*

To Make Alive

We can make a printed text come alive through our voice and body so that an audience enjoys the literature, but this is nothing compared to how God can take a person who is dead in his sins and make that person alive in Christ. Assign or encourage your students to memorize Ephesians 2:4-6: "But God, who is rich in mercy, for his great love wherewith he loved us, Even when we were dead in sins, hath quickened [made alive] us together with Christ, (by grace ye are saved;) And hath raised us up together, and made us sit together in heavenly places in Christ Jesus." You may wish to use this as an opportunity for sharing the gospel with students who are not believers.

7. Do you think Frost intentionally wrote his poem to be a little less than a sonnet (one line too short and a unique rhyme scheme)? If so, why?

Answers will vary. Frost may have wanted to convey an unsettled feeling. The

non-traditional length and awkward rhyme scheme are not typical of his style.

The reader feels that something is wrong. This reinforces Frost's message.

Review for Performance

In Chapter 5 we discussed emphasis and subordination. We used the term *thought unit* to describe the phrases that express one thought. A sonnet is designed more precisely than a narrative in that it expresses only one thought unit. Instead of marking the script for thought units, use parentheses to mark speech phrases to set them apart from the phrase or clause preceding or following them. They may be set apart with emphasis, subordination, intensity, pause, word color, aesthetic distance, or other interpretation techniques.

Memorization

Three techniques may help you memorize your sonnet: pick-up and put-down, paraphrase, and first-letter prompt. The pick-up and put-down method involves several steps. "Pick-up" refers to a focused read-aloud while slowly walking. Then you "put-down" your script. Without being overly scientific about it, retrace your steps physically while orally stumbling through your selection from beginning to end. No matter how many lines you're sure you've skipped, don't peek. Just get through to the end, remembering and saying as much as possible. Then you repeat the process. This time, each forgotten phrase will jump out at you, and when you put down the script a second and third time, you will remember much more. Most students find this technique to be the fastest and most reliable way to memorize paragraphs or even just main elements for storytelling purposes. By memorizing the whole selection at once, you will be less likely to have a memory lapse. If you do forget, you will be more likely to remember the next idea and be able to improvise.

Usually poetry is viewed so precisely that the idea of paraphrasing seems absurd or insulting. However, if you want to communicate the meaning, instead of just saying the words, paraphrasing each line during at least one of your practices will be very important. Also, if you memorize *ideas* rather than just aiming for rote memory of *words*, you will remember more quickly and longer.

If you still have difficulty remembering after ten or more repeated sessions of the pick-up and put-down method and paraphrasing, make a note card of first letters

WHEN I CONSIDER HOW MY LIGHT IS SPENT 139

to prompt you in between oral practices. The following example is the first-letter prompt for Milton's poem "On His Blindness."

> *W I c h m l i s, [When I consider how my light is spent,]*
> *E h m d, i t d w a w,*
> *A t o t w i d t h,*
> *L w m u, t m s m b*
> *T s t m M, a p*
> *M t a, l H r c,*
> *"D G e d-l; l d?*
> *I f a. B p, t p*
> *T m, s r: "G d n n*
> *E m w o H o g; w b*
> *B H m y, t s H b. H s*
> *I k: t a h b s,*
> *A p o l a o w r;*
> *T a s w o s a w.*

Notice that capitalization, line lengths, and punctuation are retained. This helps with clarity and phrasing. You may find this a good final review process for the sonnet project and a valuable tool for Scripture memory too.

CONCLUSION

In this chapter we've examined the form and content of lyric poetry. To present a complete thought or emotional experience in very few words, lyric poems employ figurative language. As an interpreter, you must carefully study the meaning of these poetic devices so that you can convey the author's message to the audience. To orally interpret a sonnet, use techniques such as aesthetic distance, visualization, word color, and vitalization. To perform literature from memory, use the techniques described at the end of this chapter.

Terms to Know

lyric poetry	synecdoche	onomatopoeia
sonnet	personification	alliteration
rhyme scheme	figure of speech	consonance
figurative language	apostrophe	assonance
figure of thought	antithesis	aesthetic distance
simile	parallelism	visualization
metaphor	figure of sound	word color
metonymy	rhyme	vitalization

Ideas to Understand

Multiple Choice: **Choose the best answer.**

__B__   1. All of the following are types of lyric poetry *except*
    A. elegy.   D. sonnet.
    B. epic.   E. all of these.
    C. ode.

__E__   2. Aesthetic distance may be used to effectively convey
    A. apostrophe.
    B. characters addressing one another.
    C. description.
    D. word color.
    E. all of these.

__E__   3. Simile and metaphor are types of
    A. figurative language.   D. poetic comparisons.
    B. figures of thought.   E. all of these.
    C. poetic devices.

__D__   4. Recommended methods of memorization do not include
    A. first-letter prompt.   C. pick-up, put-down.
    B. paraphrase.   D. one sentence at a time.

True/False: **Write** True **or** False **for each statement. If false, cross out the word or words that make it incorrect and write in the word or words that make it true.**

__True__   5. All types of lyric poetry convey emotional experiences.

__False__   6. Apostrophe and parallelism are often used together, especially in Hebrew poetry in the Old Testament. ~~Apostrophe~~ Antithesis

WHEN I CONSIDER HOW MY LIGHT IS SPENT   141

<u>_False_</u> 7. According to the text, sonnets no longer enjoy popularity with poets and readers as they did in Elizabethan and Victorian England. *no longer* **continue to**

<u>_True_</u> 8. Metonymy refers to something by using a closely related idea, whereas synecdoche refers to something by referring to part of that thing.

<u>_False_</u> 9. Apostrophe appears only in a poem containing personification. *only* **(may also address an absent person)**

Matching: **Match the following terms to corresponding examples and definitions.**

<u>_F_</u> 10. apostrophe   A. personal response to imagery in a selection

<u>_D_</u> 11. assonance   B. buzz, thwack, trot

<u>_G_</u> 12. consonance   C. animating the author's thoughts and ideas

<u>_B_</u> 13. onomatopoeia   D. "in the icy air of night"

<u>_H_</u> 14. personification   E. sounding happy when you say "happy"

<u>_A_</u> 15. visualization   F. "O grave, where is thy victory?"

<u>_C_</u> 16. vitalization   G. puddle/poodle

<u>_E_</u> 17. word color   H. "pebbles which the waves draw back, and fling"

142 CHAPTER 6

Dramatistic Analysis of the Sonnet

Title _____

Author _____

Sources (list in bibliographical form) _____

_____

_____

_____

Research

1. **Who is the speaker?** (background, personality and nature, his purposes and goals, his strengths and weaknesses)

   _____

   _____

   _____

   _____

   _____

2. **Where is the speaker?** (physical location, circumstances—conflict)

   _____

   _____

   _____

   _____

3. **When is the speaker speaking?** (What is the time of the event in relationship to other pertinent events—what is the event before and after? Also, discuss the historical time period. Finally, where does this event fall in the action—is it a crisis moment?)

   _____

   _____

   _____

   _____

   _____

WHEN I CONSIDER HOW MY LIGHT IS SPENT **143**

4. **To whom is the speaker speaking?** (Who is the audience? Describe the audience members personally and in relationship to the speaker.)

_____

_____

_____

_____

_____

 *Evaluation*

5. **What is being said?** (Summarize the message or theme.)

_____

_____

_____

_____

_____

6. **How is it being said?** (diction, style, and delivery)

_____

_____

_____

_____

_____

7. **Why is it being said?** (purpose or goal)

_____

_____

_____

_____

_____

144 CHAPTER 6

Sonnet Assignment Sheet

Prepare

Due Dates

——————— Sonnet selection

——————— Dramatistic analysis

——————— Title

——————— Author

——————— Introduction (write out, but do not memorize verbatim)

——————— Performance

Remember to mark your script and submit it to your teacher the day you perform.

Practice

Evaluate yourself on a scale of one to ten in each of the following areas, rating your current effectiveness in each skill. One is weak, five is moderate or adequate, and ten is excellent. Explain your evaluation. Sample explanations: "Phrasing has improved since the last project" or "I have difficulty not looking at the clock when I try to do aesthetic distance."

—————— Phrasing, stress, subordination ——————————————————————

—————— Aesthetic distance ————————————————————————————————

—————— Visualization ——————————————————————————————————————

Set goals for each practice session, such as "developing aesthetic distance" and "visualizing the text." Chart your progress here.

DATE	GOAL	TIME minutes
	TOTAL TIME	

The Sonnet Project

Appendix C includes several sonnets for student performance. Since students are instructed to include facts "about the writing of the poem, its purpose, or the author's life," biographical information is provided for you in the margin of Appendix C. Though not exhaustive, these sketches should facilitate grading the written work and the oral introduction.

The Appendix Selections

Use of sonnets from the appendix or from a high-school literature text would be most appropriate because those sonnets are chosen for a high-school readership. The appendix contains helpful notes to explain archaic words, allusions, and use of figurative language. Encourage students to make full use of these notes in order to avoid misinterpreting the selection.

Project Checklist

For the sonnet project, you will need to select due dates for each of the following components:

1. A specified number of sonnets read
2. Sonnet selected
3. Dramatistic analysis
4. Assignment sheet
5. Script
6. Performance

(Both the assignment sheet and script could be checked on the day the student speaks.)

The Evaluation Form

This chapter's evaluation form has several significant changes from the previous form. In the interpretation category, only *phrasing* has been retained. *Visualization*, *word color*, and *vitalization* have been added. Though not an actual category, also expect your students to begin employing the technique of *aesthetic distance*, which was introduced in this chapter.

Also note that *Manuscript* has been replaced with *Script*. The Scripture narrative project was read from manuscript, whereas this and future assignments are rehearsed with a script and then presented from memory or extemporaneously.

You may wish to collect these forms after students have time to read your comments and show their parents. By comparing with your comments from the last project, areas of improvement will be much more obvious. Since it is easier to see mistakes and weaknesses while evaluating a performance, comparing forms will help you be more fair and encouraging to your students.

Name _____ Sonnet _____

		Interpretation	Comments	Pts.
Phrasing		**4** Excellent stress and subordination **3** Most key phrases stressed **2** Some appropriate use of pause and subordination **1** Pause overused—relied too little on subordination		
Visualiza-tion		**4** Speaker responds strongly to the images. **3** Speaker responds to key images. **2** Speaker shows awareness of images. **1** Speaker lacks sensitivity to images.		
Word Color		**4** Compelling imagery **3** Mostly vivid imagery **2** Some clear imagery **1** Flat, uninteresting imagery		
Vitalization		**4** Used professionally and gracefully **3** Used smoothly **2** Used adequately **1** Used awkwardly		

		Delivery		
Poise		**4** Excellent emotional control **3** Good emotion to control nervousness **2** Noticeable nervousness **1** Nervousness obvious		
Bodily Action		**4** Aids communication **3** Usually enhances the message **2** Neither distracts from nor enhances the message **1** Distracts from the message		

Script

Written	**4** (5 check marks) **3** (4 check marks) **2** (3 check marks) **1** (1-2 check marks)	___ Pauses marked with / or // ___ Figurative language labeled in the margin ___ Figurative language underlined	Speech phrases in ( ) Legible, overall

You demonstrate good ability in . . .	You would benefit from more attention to . . .

Total Points _____   Grade _____

146 CHAPTER 6

ILLUSION

reality

O for a muse of FIRE

MIRROR

MASK

nature

TRUTH

drama

... an ever-fixed mark, that looks on tempests and is never shaken

... each man in his time plays many ...

MERCY is not strained; it droppeth as the gentle falling rain ... the quality of MERCY ...

... are the stuff DREAMS are made of ...

Chapter 7
Introduction

Some students have anxiously awaited a chapter devoted to stage acting. Chapter 7 introduces basic theory on acting and provides an assignment that can double as an audition. Chapter 10 will allow the students to take another step forward with a duo-acting scene. Chapters on readers theater and radio drama also provide opportunity for interaction between two or more performers.

All of these projects are preparatory to the production of a play. However, if a production is impossible, these projects can stand alone. The students will still be learning through situations that will improve their capacity to follow directions, work as a team, interpret literature, memorize scripts, and remain poised.

Even from the opportunity to audition—whether in a real-life situation or as a class project simulating the experience—students will gain much-needed skills for future college courses and job interviews.

If you have not yet had the opportunity to take your students to a local play production or another dramatic event, this would be an ideal time.

CHAPTER 7

Lesson Plan
Suggested homework is in **boldface**.

Lesson Description	Recommended Presentation	Performance Projects/ Written Assignments
I. Acting: What It Is Not (p. 151)	ST—Hamlet's Advice to the Players; Improve Your Improvisation	TE—Take Note **ST—Assign Monologue project**
II. Acting: What It Is (p. 154)	ST—Picture It TE—Believe What You See; Posture Poses	**ST—Details, Details** **TE—Stay Focused**
Assessment	Chapter quiz	Monologue performance **ST—Assign Journal 6**
Suggested teaching time: 6-7 class periods		

A Cast of One

A stiff silence falls over the half-empty auditorium . . .

Chapter 7 Goals

The student will be able to

1. Identify common misconceptions about acting.

2. Understand the components of acting.

3. Develop new interpretation skills.

Teaching Materials

- A challenging textbook excerpt— any subject
- A selection of vocal music (if Stay Focused project is completed in class)
- Performance rubrics (students submit their own copy)

OVERVIEW

Know—*Concepts*

Misconceptions of acting
Drama's frame of reference:
   comedy versus tragedy

Grow—*Interpretation Skills*

Observation
Characterization
Concentration
Realization
Illusion of the first time

Show—*Performance*

Audition monologue

A stiff silence falls over the half-empty auditorium as the director's voice is heard.

"Thank you all for coming this evening. Please submit your audition card to my assistant in the back row. Each actor will be called by name randomly and should perform for no longer than one minute. If my assistant calls 'time,' please stop immediately and make your exit. Are there any questions?"

Again, silence.

There were mountains of questions, but they would not be answered now. Questions such as "Will I get a part?" and "Who will play the lead?" and "Can I remember my lines?"

To be sure, there are as many butterflies and throbbing arteries right now as there will be on opening night itself.

The audition. A full house of spectators may not be more daunting than an audition. Actors fear failure while longing to succeed. That desire to succeed keeps actors coming back to auditions in spite of their nervousness.

In this chapter we will define acting, and you will have the opportunity to perform the type of literature used often in acting: the audition monologue. Though your project will be a one- to two-minute monologue, the principles will apply to any dramatic material, whether from a script, from prose, or from poetry.

150 CHAPTER 7

The tools you learn now will benefit you in competitive situations such as auditions and **forensics** competitions.

ACTING: WHAT IT IS NOT

Unfortunately, popular opinion is notorious for ascribing qualities necessary for acting that simply are not truly necessary. Common misconceptions include believing that beauty or physical strength equals acting ability, that acting requires a certain kind of personality, and that good acting is based on emotions.

Appearance

Broadway and Hollywood proclaim that physical appearance is the key to stardom. Though numerous men and women have found quick fame (a few have even enjoyed lasting fame) because of their appearance, good looks did *not* make them good actors. In many cases, good looks may have *prevented* them from becoming good actors. If fame comes quickly and easily without intense work, what *would* motivate an actor to develop skills or seek further training?

Even on the high-school level, directors and actors may easily fall into the pit of superficial casting: "He's the tallest, best-looking guy in school, so he gets the leading male role." There are several problems with this attitude. First of all, the best-looking fellow may not have the time, the talent, or the interest to perform the part well. Secondly, the young man who could soar with the role is very likely overlooked. A fellow who might have looked a little too thin or too solid, too short or too tall at an audition, might have the motivation and the focus to make the part really come alive.

In addition to lead roles, many supporting character roles demand a variety of physical builds. In a comedy, the chief of police may be a wiry, aged man of short stature supervising several rather large but bumbling officers. In a serious play, the chief may need a very commanding presence. Height may be beneficial to give that impression. Certainly it is not always needed, however. When a play is cast, there is no reason to assume, whether you are the director or an actor, that the principal roles must go to the popular or beautiful while others are permanently assigned to stage crew. Just as a beautiful frame cannot turn an average or poor painting into a great work of art, a pretty face does not make a performer. Nothing can replace training and talent. If you develop yourself, there should be a role out there for you.

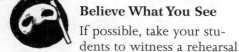

> **Good Acting Is Not Based On**
> - Appearance
> - Personality
> - Emotion

D *definition*

Forensics, in this context, refers to the organized public speaking, dramatic, and debate competitions held on local, state, and national levels.

Lesson Motivator

This chapter begins by discussing common misconceptions about acting. Students are likely to have preconceived ideas about the topic (acting) that conflict with what will be taught in this and other acting chapters. This section should not be time consuming to teach but is very important nonetheless.

> **Lesson Objective**
>
> *The student will be able to recognize that good acting is not appearance, personality, or emotion.*

Appearances Can Be Deceiving

If your students haven't participated in drama through church or another conservative organization, their perceptions may be based on whatever they know about secular TV and film productions, which emphasize physical appearance.

Explain that an attractive appearance can't make a good actor any more than a uniform makes a good police officer or a personal art studio makes an artist.

PRESENTATION

Acting: What It Is Not

Believe What You See

If possible, take your students to witness a rehearsal at a church youth group or school; even if it is a musical one (orchestra, band, choir, and so on), they can make some quick observations. First of all, a good performance results from hard work. There is no glamour in practicing the same symphonic work or church cantata dozens of times. Acting is no different. Also, a good ensemble includes people with different talents and styles. Everyone may admire the concertmaster, but the orchestra needs the oboe, drum, and cello to properly convey the majority of orchestral works.

If such a field trip is impossible, just discuss the ideas with your students.

Appearances

As with choosing actors, choosing friends based on looks, clothes, personality, or money can mean missing out on some very valuable friendships. Ask a student to read Romans 12:1-3 aloud. Encourage or assign your students to memorize this passage. Encourage them to make a personal, honest assessment of their friendships and motives.

Less of You

Not only does a memorable, extremely expressive personality tend to confine an actor to a certain type of character (type-casting), but the very personality that wins popularity among peers can prove a detriment to good characterization. A versatile actor is better equipped to fill diverse roles. Also, the actor who can set aside his personal traits, such as gestures, vocal patterns, and style of delivery, will create a more believable stage character.

Riding the Roller Coaster

More than other periods of life the teenage years are characterized by emotional roller coaster rides. Every fear, every joy, every heartache seems amplified. A teen is more likely to feel extremely awkward "playing opposite" someone. For instance, a seven-year-old girl playing "Mary" in a children's Christmas program will not be very concerned over which little boy is "Joseph." However, if fourteen- or fifteen-year-old students play these characters, they will be more realistic in appearance, but they might spend half of the rehearsal time feeling embarrassed. Additionally, stage fright or a personal crisis right before a public performance can be more traumatic for a teen than for a child or adult.

Personality

History shows that performers who came to the star scene on personality alone are forgotten as quickly as they gained their fame. Depending on personality to fulfill the demands of acting limits the actor to a certain type of role. A few performers *have* made history playing just one character. A good example is the stereotypical heroes of black-and-white western films. However, personality roles are rare. Generally speaking, an actor is called upon to play someone else, not himself.

The extent to which personality does make a difference on the stage is twofold. First, the actor must have a personality that is conducive to team effort. A play with one soaring eagle will never really fly. A truly great play has great actors delivering two lines as well as two hundred. Secondly, because many roles make demands on the emotions, the actor must have the capacity to feel deeply while controlling his feelings. Though all humans experience a wide range of emotion, many are unable or unwilling to convey great emotion publicly.

Emotion

Imagine a dramatic moment from a play you've seen—perhaps the moment that the character Mortimer Brewster finds a body in the window seat in *Arsenic and Old Lace* or when the character Emily relives her twelfth birthday in *Our Town*. Whether thinking of Mortimer's fear and confusion or Emily's wonder and despair, the key element is emotion. As human beings we love to feel deeply. Characters who provoke laughter or tears or dramatic suspense all hold the audience spellbound. The question then is not "Does acting involve emotion?" but "Who should feel it?"

Since most young performers approach their first stage role having been audience members many times before, they are likely to act based on the way things *seem* to the audience. However, this approach is doomed to failure. If the actor portraying Mortimer were genuinely scared, would he pull himself together enough to even show up for the performances—or even learn his lines, for that matter?

Arsenic and Old Lace by Joseph Kesselring. Mortimer (center) tries to protect his aunts from discovering the body in the window seat.

Perhaps you are saying that he shouldn't "feel" afraid until that scene comes. What about when that scene ends? An actor who is at the mercy of his own emotion will not make good decisions any more than a person controlled by emotion in any other situation. We often hear about "road rage." Any person governed by reason would not choose to wreck his car by running someone else off the road, but a person controlled by emotion (anger) might.

 "Great" Actors

Repeat the following line from the text: "A truly great play has great actors delivering two lines as well as two hundred." Ask a student to read Philippians 2:1-7 aloud. Verse three of this passage could also be translated as "Let nothing be done through selfish ambition or conceit." Ask your students to give some thoughtful answers to the following questions: Why aren't "great" actors usually content with a role containing two lines? What are some responses that would show the selfish ambition and envy that competing for a play role (especially a large one) can bring out in people? (*Possible answers:* "I want to be the star of the show"; "No one could play the lead part as well as I could"; "Everyone knows that I'm the best actor in the school"; "If my mom were a teacher, I'd get a big part too"; "He got the part because he's a senior"; "I'm a senior—I should get a better part than a sophomore.")

 High Emotion

Decision making in moments of high emotion sometimes results in negative consequences. Ask your students to give some examples. (*Possible answers: buying something that we can't really afford due to a high-pressured sales presentation; participating in sinful activities in order to please certain "friends"; verbally or physically attacking another person because we become irritated by him; and so on.*) Ask one of your students to read

When an actor studies a role carefully, sympathizing with the character he portrays, he will convey emotion to the audience. The audience can leave saying, "It was so real" without the actors emotionally battering themselves.

Good acting is *repeatable*; therefore, it must be planned and controlled. When telling stories about the experiences of others, you feel with them in their plight while the story occurs; but their grief, joy, or fear is not really your own. A similar situation must occur with the actor.

Just as the actor puts on clothes that belong to the character but never calls them his own or wears them to the grocery store, he also "puts on" the emotions and actions of the character. Hamlet gives some good advice (p. 155)—avoid tearing "a passion to … rags." Anything else is lunacy, not art.

Improve Your Improvisation

The situations listed below depict a character who would likely experience strong emotion. Select one hypothetical situation and improvise a solo scene based on it. Do not write a script of what you will say during your scene. It should be extemporaneous. Do write out below any plot details you need to perform your scene. The scene should last no longer than 1 1/2 to 2 minutes.

1. A student just found out he made the varsity team in a particular sport.

2. A new driver realizes he just backed over a trash can and scraped Dad's luxury car.

3. A ten-year-old realizes that his favorite pet is missing/has run away.

4. A senior just found out that his graduation gift from his parents is a cruise to Alaska.

5. You just got tickets to the Super Bowl, a World Series game, or an Olympic event unexpectedly.

6. You just received a very low score on an important test.

7. Pick a situation of your choosing.

Make notes about your scene in the space provided.

Character name (fictitious) _____

Character description (physical, emotional, etc.) _____

Primary emotion conveyed _____

Specific actions that show that emotion _____

Be attentive to all of your students in this area. Sometimes, the student who seems most confident is most prone to falter. Remind your students to be consumed with their message rather than their fears. Also, be sure to pray for each day's speakers as you open class that hour.

Be available to reassure the distressed student that his feelings are normal and reasonable. Offer encouragement and give the student time to regain composure before returning to class if necessary.

Galatians 5:16-26 aloud. Tell your students that the way to avoid making bad decisions in life is to "walk in the Spirit." Ask your students to name ways that they can know that they are walking in the Spirit. (*Answers should include that they are faithfully reading their Bibles, praying regularly, obeying godly counsel, avoiding sin, and so on.*)

Outline of plot

I. _____

_____

_____

II. _____

_____

_____

III. _____

_____

_____

ACTING: WHAT IT IS

Now that you understand what acting is not, let us consider what it is. In Chapter 1 we talked about how we perform roles in everyday life. Now we will limit our discussion to formal acting situations. In this chapter, the performance skills deal with how to approach acting. First we need to understand *frame of reference* and *interpretation*.

Hamlet's Advice to the Players

In this famous monologue, Prince Hamlet becomes an acting coach to a traveling band of actors who will soon perform a play for King Claudius. Each part of the advice is labeled individually. On the lines below, summarize each instruction in your own words. The first is done for you as an example.

1. "Speak the speech, I pray you, as I pronounced it to you, trippingly on the tongue: but if you mouth it as many of our players do, I had as lief the town-crier spoke my lines."

   Use good diction and don't sound as though you are mimicking.

   Answers will vary.

2. "Nor do not saw the air too much with your hands, thus, but use all gently,"

   Don't gesture too formally or melodramatically.

3. "for in the very torrent, tempest, and (as I may say) whirlwind of your passion, you must acquire and beget a temperance that may give it smoothness."

 CHAPTER 7

If you asked a dozen actors or acting teachers "What is acting?" you would hear a dozen different responses. What most professionals agree upon is that acting involves applying interpretation skills to a group performance and that really understanding your character means understanding the framework of the script. Even the most polished interpretation skills are wasted when a comedy is ignorantly staged as a tragedy or a serious drama is played melodramatically. Consequently, this section deals first with understanding the frame of reference of a selection.

Lesson Objectives

The student will be able to

1. Paraphrase Hamlet's famous speech giving advice to an acting troupe.

2. Explain the significance of frame of reference.

3. Observe everyday reactions as a guide for natural stage acting.

4. Concentrate while rehearsing and performing.

5. Employ imagination to draw the audience into the scenario.

6. Create the impression of spontaneity (illusion of the first time).

> O, it offends me to the soul to hear a robustious periwig-pated fellow tear a passion to tatters, to very rags. . . . I would have such a fellow whipt. . . . Pray you avoid it."
>
> *Use gestures and characterization conservatively.*

4. "Be not too tame neither, but let your own discretion be your tutor."

   Don't be too reserved about expressing yourself; just be reasonable.

5. "Suit the action to the word, the word to the action;"

   Make sure your actions are appropriate for the text.

6. "with this special observance, that you o'erstep not the modesty of nature:"

   Act naturally (not an affected or oratorical style).

7. "for any thing so o'erdone is [away] from the purpose of playing, whose end, both at the first and now, was and is, to hold as 'twere the mirror up to nature: to show virtue her feature, scorn her own image, and the very age and body of the time his form and pressure."

   Remember the purpose of drama—to make us think about real life ("nature") and evaluate it.

Frame of Reference

The first reading of Anton Chekhov's *The Cherry Orchard* has left many students utterly baffled. What a sad story! "Family loses beautiful estate after many generations." Sounds like a headline. What's so baffling is the playwright's own description on the title page: "A comedy in four acts." A comedy? Since when is it funny to lose your home? One might say that a story that is comedy on the Saturday matinee may be tragedy on the evening news. If a news report documents someone falling into a well, it is called an accident or tragedy. If one of the Three Stooges falls into a well, we laugh at him. The difference? **Frame of reference,** the viewpoint, the premise. The reason students may not understand *The Cherry Orchard* on a first reading is that they do not grasp the *frame of reference.* A story or play may have a comic frame of reference, a tragic frame of reference, or perhaps a combination of the two.

D*efinition*

*The **frame of reference** is the premise or basis of the story as given by the author or playwright.*

The Cherry Orchard

In his brilliant four-act play, Russian playwright and short story writer Anton Chekhov depicts an aristocratic family that seems to lack any common sense. A common man named Lopakhin repeatedly advises the family to manage their estate better, but they are concerned with trivial matters such as honoring a bookcase and discussing a guest who ate an entire bucket of pickles. In addition to their pettiness, they are poor listeners—constantly ignoring what others say to begin their own train of thought. *The Cherry Orchard* is comic because we do not sympathize with the family and because we do not perceive that losing their home will hurt them. If anything, perhaps losing a symbol of their station in life will remind them to behave more responsibly and practically. Since Lopakhin is an honest and hard worker, we are glad for him when he purchases the estate at an auction. The story has a happy ending.

Comedy

All I need to make a comedy is a park, a policeman and a pretty girl.

—Charlie Chaplin, My Autobiography

What makes a story funny? A comedian once said of comic film, "You show a banana peel on the sidewalk; then show a woman walking down the street, and then show the woman stepping over the banana peel and falling into a manhole—that is comedy." The audience laughs. Why? Because they didn't expect that. After seeing the banana peel and the woman, they expected the old "slip on a banana peel" trick. The course of events took them by surprise, and they laughed. *Incongruity* (or the unexpected) is often the reason something is funny. When someone tells a joke and you've heard the punch line or can easily guess it, the joke isn't very funny, is it? No incongruity, no laughter. **Comedy** can be defined as the unexpected or out-of-place character or plot that is likely to provoke laughter. In a broader sense, comedy includes all literature in which the main character has a happy ending. That may mean success, joy, or in some cases such as slapstick comedy, just survival.

Comedy *depicts characters and situations that are incongruous. Though some comedy focuses completely on humorous incidents, it encompasses all stories that have a happy or positive ending.*

Tragedy *depicts characters or situations with catastrophic problems leading to a sad or even disastrous conclusion.*

Tragedy

Perhaps the most famous description of tragedy comes from Aristotle, who asserted that **tragedy** involves "incidents arousing pity and fear." By this he suggested that a plot can be tragic. The protagonist, he said, is led into disaster by his "error of judgment," or tragic flaw. This refers to a tragic character.

Historically, tragedy depicted a great person such as a king or queen who faced insurmountable odds. The climax is a catastrophe that reverses the protagonist's situation from fortune to demise. One example is Macbeth, whose greed and pride prompt him to murder. His crime brings him temporary power and wealth, but in the end he is destroyed by his wrong choices. Modern tragedy has rejected the "restriction" of tragedy centering around great people; it depicts the trials and troubles of the common man.

A popular theme in tragedy involves questioning whether man is subject to fate or has a free will. The classic Greek character Oedipus (ED uh puhs) is a traditional tragic figure. He has high position and therefore power. He has a tragic

King Oedipus *by Sophocles.*
Jocasta defends her husband Oedipus to Creon.

156 CHAPTER 7

flaw—rash anger. Though he is wise enough to solve a riddle that rescues the people of Thebes (THEEBZ) from a plague, he is rash enough to kill a man who inconveniences him on the road. Later, Oedipus learns that he has fulfilled what had been predicted for his life—he has unknowingly killed the king of Thebes. One may argue that Oedipus was a victim of fate, saying that his crime wasn't his fault because he didn't know that the man was the king. However, he did choose to kill a man. Did he have to lose control of his temper? Oedipus had a free will; he had a choice. Only later did he greatly regret that wrong choice.

Summary

Of course, not all serious drama is truly tragic any more than all light-hearted selections are truly comic. The purpose of our discussion is not to develop classifications for every story and play ever written, but merely to understand the most common frames of reference. For the purpose of our study we will use the terms *tragedy* and *comedy* in the broadest sense—tragedies as stories with sad endings and comedies as stories with happy endings. (This approach is more common in the study of drama than in the study of nondramatic literature but may be applied to both.)

Interpretation

Everything you have learned in previous chapters on oral interpretation of narrative and poetry applies to the monologue—developing climax, phrasing, word color, and so on. In this chapter we will study *observation, characterization, concentration, realization,* and *the illusion of the first time.*

Observation

Every actor must be a student of human responses. What does a person do when someone hurts him, for example? How might one individual's response vary depending on who hurt him? Will he lash out verbally at a friend or cower from a bully? Will his silence speak volumes or his ranting and raving be unheard? Personality is only part of what determines human response. Character qualities such as self-discipline, one's position and rank, and circumstances will also influence the reaction.

Details, Details

At home, choose a simple task to complete. Possible tasks include:

1. Thoroughly washing and drying your hands

2. Putting on a coat

3. Slicing a banana

PRESENTATION

Acting: What It Is

Take Note

Assign the following as homework. Observe a group of people this week. This group may be intentionally gathered—a meeting, a rally, an auction, a service—or informally collected—a bus or train station, an airport, a checkout line in the supermarket. Discreetly observe a unique person in this group. If possible, take notes concerning repeatable characteristics (not hair color or the like). Then, at home, repeat the person's posture, movements, and so on. Be prepared to share your character with the class.

Characterization Notes

Teens often have difficulty playing elderly characters in a believable manner. Usually, they enact a mere parody of an elderly person—quavering voice, precarious walk, and stooped shoulders. Any of these may be appropriate but should not be substituted for character analysis. Observing grandparents or other elderly people in church or in town will provide ideas for believable characterization.

4. Making a bed

5. If you have a sister, combing her hair into a ponytail

6. A task you choose

While you perform this task, notice exactly how you move and in what order you move. Write below what you did with as much detail as possible. Then practice your actions until you can pantomime the entire scene. Be prepared for your teacher to have you share this pantomime.

_____

_____

_____

_____

_____

_____

_____

Characterization

If you want to be a good actor, you have to understand people—not just a few good friends but all sorts of people. If you portray a character without having insight into his motivation or response, your *characterization* will be two-dimensional at best or maybe even ridiculous. You don't have to "walk a mile" in the character's shoes to understand what his life is like. If that were true, only murderers could portray several of Shakespeare's title roles (Macbeth, Hamlet, etc.). Instead, try to understand a character by observing little similarities from various real-life people. For example, have you seen someone behave rashly? What did he do? How might his responses translate to this situation? How could you—as a performer—convey this?

Though we will study creating characters for the storytelling project and refining characterization for duo acting, you need to start developing characterization skills now by observing the world around you. Every person you know has unique characteristics. Each one has a unique vocal quality, manner of speech, pattern of facial expressions, characteristic movements, and so on. Remember the last time you did a skit in youth group or had a talent night or student body program? Perhaps a skit included people imitating a well-known figure. Maybe you have friends who impersonate people to entertain the lunch crowd over hamburgers. How do you know whom they are "performing"? Obviously, by their characterization. They imitate the vocal pattern or habitual gestures of that person. Even though

CHAPTER 7

Posture Poses

Instruct your students as follows. Each student will need a partner. With your partner, take turns demonstrating to each other a certain position you like to sit or stand in. Be specific. Do you cross your legs at the knee? The ankle? Do you stand with feet spread wide and toes pointed out? Do you like to sit "Indian-style"? After you can successfully mimic your partner and he can mimic you, return to your seat and wait for me to call "time." Now you will take turns presenting your character to the class.

After completing the activity, have students answer the questions below, possibly on paper to submit for a grade.

1. Whom did you portray? (student's name)

2. Describe exactly what you did physically to portray him. (For example, did you lean back in a chair?)

3. What character or personality qualities of the person did this posture convey?

they don't sound exactly like the other person, the characterization is strong enough for your imagination to supply the rest. Begin making characterization notes now for your own use. You will find them invaluable later.

Concentration

This may seem obvious, but good acting requires concentration—focused effort at attentiveness. If your teacher or director is speaking and you are whispering to a friend, you're going to miss something. When you are on stage, if you are daydreaming or otherwise occupied when a line is being delivered across the stage, you may miss a cue or distract the speaker. However, concentration in acting goes beyond the need to avoid "classroom" type distractions.

> ### Concentration
>
> **maintains . . .**
> - suspense for the audience.
> - characterization.
>
> **involves . . .**
> - focusing your attention.
> - maintaining your focus.

Compare dramatic performance and public speaking for a moment. If the public speaker loses his concentration, he might pause, fumble through notes, and then regain composure before proceeding. Of course this detracts from his message. In acting or storytelling, however, *suspense* is a key factor, as is *characterization*. Without concentration, suspense and characterization are lost, and so is the interest of the audience.

Concentration actually includes two basic tasks. First, you must focus your attention. When reading or practicing your script alone, study the dramatistic analysis and find a quiet place to work to help you accomplish the goal of focusing your attention. At a group rehearsal, your director may lead you in physical and vocal warm-ups to help you focus.

Secondly, you must maintain your focus throughout the acting activity. This requires determination, discipline, and practice. You can improve your acting ability by working to increase your attention span on everyday tasks such as homework, chores, and so on. The discipline you develop will carry into your acting.

Realization

The term *realization* may sound like some vague idea in a psychology book, but here its meaning is quite simple: the actor need not agree that the action *is* real but that it *could be* real. This is an important distinction whether you perform biography or fiction. If your character wants to be a famous baseball player, you must relate to his desire. If your character is painfully shy because of an overbearing family member, you must try to understand that character's struggles realistically, even if you are a friendly, cheerful person. If you portray Helen Keller in

The Miracle Worker *by William Gibson. Annie Sullivan teaches Helen Keller to communicate.*

Concentrating in Rehearsal

Even amateur actors find it relatively easy to concentrate when they have an audience present and blinding stage lights. What requires much discipline is concentrating when rehearsing. Of course, your students will have rehearsed many times without your direct supervision, but when you can set aside practice time in class, emphasize staying focused. If you develop a good habit in class, the students will be more likely to follow through on their own.

Stay Focused

Instructions. This project may be completed in class or for homework. Instruct students to read one page from a difficult textbook while listening to a recording of vocal music at normal volume—*not* turned down as faint background. (Tell them to ask their parents' permission before doing this at home!) When they finish that page, they should turn off the music and make notes of what they can remember from the reading. Then they should reread the page.

Discussion. Have students answer the following questions.

1. What effect did the music have on your ability to concentrate? Why do you think it affected you that way?

2. What facts did you notice or understand the second time after missing them the first time?

3. How could you avoid the potential for distraction during practice time?

4. What strategies could you use to concentrate in spite of distractions?

Conclusion. Encourage students to eliminate distractions when possible but to practice ignoring distractions periodically as well so that they will develop self-discipline in the area of concentration.

The Miracle Worker, you must imagine her world of darkness and silence. Otherwise, you cannot effectively communicate the struggles of that blind and deaf heroine.

One very important way to make the story "real" to yourself is to work for sensory recall. That means that as you observe real-life situations, you "memorize" sensory images. For example, Jenáe's mom always bakes cookies on weekday afternoons during the Christmas season. If Jenáe has good sensory recall, she will be able to remember the smell of those cookies even when they are not present. For most people, visual imagery seems to be the most memorable. Think of a sunset on the seashore you have seen or a view of a valley from a hiking trail. In Chapter 6, you learned about using aesthetic distance when describing something you wanted the audience to picture. The more sensory recall you develop, the more realistic the description. Likewise, the better your realization, the better you will use aesthetic distance in communicating with your audience.

Picture It

Find an event or picture to observe. List below the sensory imagery such as the smell, texture, or visual qualities.

_____

_____

_____

_____

Now, leave the room or remove the event/object from your location. Recreate each image in your mind until it seems real enough to you to be able to convey that image to another person.

Illusion of the First Time

Think of the last time you recited something from memory. Maybe it was a Bible verse or the pledge to the American flag. Did you think about what you were really saying? Perhaps you did, but many times we don't think about meaning when we recite. For the actor, memorization is necessary in most cases. Often anything less would hinder the message and its delivery. Unfortunately, memorization can present a problem. When you *recite* without creating an **illusion of the first time,** the audience is not drawn into the story. Observation, concentration, and realization are tasks you must complete before you can create this "illusion." Relate these ideas with the following formula:

Illusion of the first time refers to an audience's impression of spontaneity and "newness" created by the speaker's delivery style.

Discipline

Discipline is vital in acting but even more vital in our spiritual lives. Assign or encourage your students to memorize Proverbs 4:25-27: "Let thine eyes look right on, and let thine eyelids look straight before thee. Ponder the path of thy feet, and let all thy ways be established. Turn not to the right hand nor to the left: remove thy foot from evil."

> **observation + concentration + realization = illusion of the first time**

Each task becomes progressively more important in creating that illusion because it influences your acting more immediately. (Observation occurs before rehearsing; concentration occurs during rehearsal and performance; and realization begins in rehearsal and is heightened in performance.)

Review

As you approach performing a monologue, review the interpretation skills you learned in previous chapters. You will need to continue applying those tools on this project in addition to incorporating the new tools of observation, concentration, characterization, and realization.

CONCLUSION

In this chapter you have learned that acting is not appearance, personality, or emotion. In other words, acting is not superficial. Sometimes stardom is superficial, but good acting is always inherently genuine, well planned, and thoughtfully approached. Remember that acting must conform to the viewpoint of the playwright—comedy, tragedy, and so on. Also, acting involves interpretation skills. Along with the skills you have studied in previous chapters, acting requires stage characterization, concentration, and realization. Using these tools effectively allows you as an actor to create an illusion of the first time. You convey your dialogue and actions as a new occurrence rather than a recitation.

Becoming a good actor will not happen overnight. It won't even happen over time without persistence. You must practice using your tools—interpretation skills—until the audience sees only the art and not the artist, only the product, not the process.

Forensics Organizations

These and other organizations sponsor competition in various forensics categories.

- American Association of Christian Schools (A.A.C.S.) Fine Arts Competitions (state and national levels)

- Association of Christian Schools International (A.C.S.I.) Speech Meets (district only)

- Bob Jones University High School Festival & Preaching Contest (annual speech competitions as well as music, art, and preaching contests)

- National Forensics League (N.F.L.)

For contact information, refer to Teacher's Appendix 1.

Focus on Forensics

Speech Competitions

Each forensics organization will include any number of the following contests.

Debate requires thorough preparation and the ability to think clearly under pressure.

PUBLIC SPEAKING EVENTS

- Cross Examination Debate (CX)
- Lincoln-Douglas Debate (LD)
- Original Oratory (OO)
- Foreign and/or Domestic Extemporaneous Speaking (Extemp)
- Expository Speaking
- Impromptu Speaking

(See SOUND SPEECH for Christian Schools for details on these types of events.)

PERFORMANCE EVENTS

DRAMATIC INTERPRETATION OR DRAMATIC READING (DI)

- Genres: short stories, cuttings from novels and plays, dramatic monologues
- Content: strong climax, strong emotion, and serious material
- Length: six to ten minutes

Notes: Choose quality literature; avoid melodrama; remember that it is more difficult to portray numerous serious characters well than a few serious characters or numerous comic characters.

HUMOROUS INTERPRETATION (HI)

- Genres: short stories, cuttings from novels and plays, humorous monologues
- Content: comic characters and/or comic situations
- Length: six to ten minutes

Notes: Avoid standup comedy and topical jokes. (Topical jokes often contain local or temporary allusions to the news or events of the day.) Make sure the selection is suitable for your style of "funny." Are you a deadpan comic storyteller? Try the satire of Saki or Mark Twain. Do you like to tell tall tales? Consider selections such as "'Twas a Dark and Dreary Night" by Patrick McManus, "The Car We Had to Push" by James Thurber, or "The Ransom of Red Chief" by O. Henry. If you have comic acting experience, try a comic monologue from Shakespeare or another favorite playwright.

POETRY INTERPRETATION OR POETRY READING (OP)

- Genres: narrative poetry, dramatic poetry (may or may not be intended for the stage)

- Content: strong suspense, strong climax
- Length: six to ten minutes

Notes: Quality literature may be more important in this category than any other because weak poetry often has a singsongy quality that makes it difficult to prepare well. Also, weak poetry tends to be sentimental rather than realistically emotional.

RELIGIOUS READING

- Genre: short stories, biography, narratives, and monologues
- Content: should present a spiritual truth without being "preachy" or sentimental
- Length: six to ten minutes

Notes: Watch out for contrived or sentimental stories. Judges quickly tire of such entries. Biographies of Christian preachers, hymn writers, and missionaries are excellent resources.

ORAL READING OF SCRIPTURE

- Genre: Scripture narrative
- Content: dramatic or inspirational text (Most portions that meet time requirements are stories.)
- Length: six to ten minutes

Notes: Refer to Chapter 5 to review specific tips. Aim to compel your audience, not preach at or rebuke your listeners.

DUO (DUET) ACTING

- Genre: plays
- Content: may be humorous or dramatic
- Length: eight to twelve minutes

Notes: Because many entries in this category tend to be dramatic, a well-performed humorous scene may seem fresh and rewarding to the judges. Humorous scenes should depict comic characters or situations without imitating famous comedies. Also, avoid the level of exaggeration that may be workable for humorous interpretation. Dramatic scenes should have a climax and a sense of finality to conclude them.

IMPROVISED DUO (DUET) ACTING

- Genre: topics, not literature
- Content: competition-generated
- Length: four to seven minutes

Notes: Improvised Duo Acting is not currently included in all meets. This category requires a strong level of teamwork and quick thinking; includes thirty minutes of preparation time after the topic is drawn. Pre-tournament preparation includes creating characters, polishing your comic timing, and quickly developing interesting plots.

READERS THEATER OR CHAMBER THEATER

- Genre: dramatic or narrative prose or poetry adapted for group performance

A CAST OF ONE 163

- Content: any published literature with a strong plot and/or interesting imagery or sounds
- Length: ten to twelve minutes

Notes: Creativity is key in this event. Lines may be assigned to individuals, a portion of the group, or the entire group. Some performers may convey abstractions or help create environment. See Chapter 9 for more information.

Competitors

KNOW THE RULES

Regardless of the category you select, be sure to consult the specific guidelines for your school's competition.

Time limits are sometimes significantly shorter than what is listed here.

Some sections of oral interpretation events may have requirements concerning the amount of movement or type of dress (e.g., costumed or noncostumed).

DRESS FOR SUCCESS

Unless you have a good reason not to, you should dress professionally for the competition. Impress the judges.

Young men should wear a conservative tie and dress shirt. Some forensics meets may require a coat and tie.

Young ladies should choose dark and/or subdued colors and classic accessories rather then trendy styles.

FIRST IMPRESSIONS

You make them only once!

If your hair is an extremely trendy style, it may be a distraction. If it shadows your face in any way, you are forfeiting full use of one very important tool—facial expression.

Also, ladies in particular need to avoid brushing hair back or tucking it behind their ear repeatedly during a performance. This detracts from effective communication and conveys lack of forethought. (Use a clip or barrette!)

Remember that your manners will be visible too. Whispering during other competitors' selections, fidgeting, or showing other unruly behavior is a great way to rank last in the round.

Your sense of stage presence is established the first time the judges look at you, not when you finally reach the platform and pull yourself together. That means it's inadvisable to burst into the room and accost the judge or judges with some "urgent" question, straightening your tie while you talk.

LAST BUT NOT LEAST

Above all else, practice adequately and stay calm during the competition.

Christians can and should ask God to help them through each challenge and—most importantly—to help them glorify Him through their testimony. Good preparation and prayer are the keys to surviving the nail-biting moments until the final awards ceremony.

CHAPTER 7 REVIEW

Terms to Know

forensics

frame of reference

comedy

tragedy

illusion of the first time

Ideas to Understand

Multiple Choice: **Choose the best answer.**

___A___ 1. Good acting does *not* depend upon
   A. appearance.   D. B and C.
   B. concentration.   E. understanding the frame
   C. sensory recall.   of reference.

___B___ 2. All of the following are necessary to create the "illusion of the first time" *except*
   A. concentration.   C. observation.
   B. frame of reference. D. realization.

True/False: **Write True or False for each statement. If false, cross out the word or words that make it incorrect and write in the word or words that make it true.**

False 3. Comedy and tragedy cannot be mixed. ~~cannot~~ can

True 4. Actors must be students of human nature.

False 5. Characterization springs most directly from good concentration. ~~concentration~~ observation

Short Answer

6. Improving concentration helps maintain what two dramatic elements?
   <u>characterization and suspense</u>

7. Speech, drama, and debate competitions are called _____<u>forensics</u>_____ tournaments.

The Monologue Project

If you have access to an auditorium of some sort, this project is ideal for helping students with their ability to communicate in a larger space. Additionally, you could motivate students to further polish their performance by telling them they can audition for a school production using this assignment. If you make that an option, be sure to host your auditions within a couple of weeks after the due date so that they will not have to relearn the monologue.

Of course, if an auditorium is not available, you can certainly go to a spacious outdoor location (park, ball field, or playground) to practice projection, or you could focus more on interpretation skills by performing in your normal class setting.

Project Checklist

For the monologue project, you will need to select due dates for each of the following components:

1. Specified number of monologues read from Appendix D
2. Monologue selected
3. Dramatistic analysis
4. Assignment sheet
5. Script

(The assignment sheet and script could be checked on the day the student speaks.)

Monologue Assignment Sheet

Prepare

Due Dates

_____ Select a monologue

_____ Dramatistic analysis

_____ Performance

Remember to mark the script and submit it to your teacher!

Practice

Evaluate yourself on a scale of one to ten in each of the following areas, rating your current effectiveness in each skill. One is weak, five is moderate or adequate, and ten is excellent. Explain your evaluation.

_____ Observation _____

_____

_____ Concentration _____

_____

_____ Realization _____

_____

_____ Illusion of the first time _____

_____

Set goals for each practice session, such as "improve concentration." Chart your progress here.

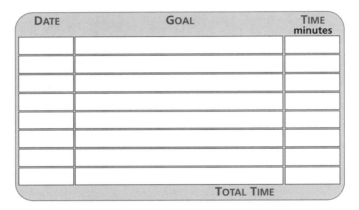

DATE	GOAL	TIME minutes
	TOTAL TIME	

 CHAPTER 7

Dramatistic Analysis of the Monologue

Title of play (or other selection)

_____

Author _____

Sources (list in bibliographical form)

_____

_____

_____

Research

1. **Who is the speaker?** (background, personality and nature, purposes and goals, strengths and weaknesses)

   _____

   _____

   _____

   _____

2. **Where is the speaker?** (physical location, circumstances—conflict)

   _____

   _____

   _____

   _____

3. **When is the speaker speaking?** (What is the time of the event in relationship to other pertinent events—what is the event before and after? Also, discuss the historical time period. Finally, where does this event fall in the action—is it a crisis moment?)

   _____

   _____

   _____

   _____

4. **To whom is the speaker speaking?** (Who is the audience? Describe the audience members personally and in relationship to the speaker.)

   _____

   _____

A CAST OF ONE 167

Appendix D

Do not view the provided selections as a restriction. If you find other valuable selections that suit your students, substitute or add them to the options. Some teachers require all students to perform the same selection or one of only two or three selections.

Repeating a selection makes memorization a little easier—especially if you allow the students to practice some in class. Even just hearing the words repeated on performance day can help. Also, students see that one selection can be handled in several ways with equal success. If you make this choice, be sure to encourage originality in style and then reward it on the evaluation form. You may find the students more motivated by competition this way.

Read through the selections in Appendix D before determining which format will work best for your students.

_____
_____

5. **What is being said?** (Summarize the message or theme.)

_____
_____
_____
_____
_____

6. **How is it being said?** (diction, style, and delivery)

_____
_____
_____
_____
_____
_____

7. **Why is it being said?** (purpose or goal)

_____
_____
_____
_____
_____

AUDITION CARD		
Name	**Grade**	**Age**
Audition selection		
Author		
Do you sing? Yes or No If yes, what part? S A T B		
What instruments, if any, do you play?		
What languages can you read and pronounce?		
Gender M or F Height Approximate weight Birthday		
Previous drama experience (nonacting)		
Previous acting experience		

168 CHAPTER 7

Name _____ Monologue _____

Interpretation		Comments	Pts.
Phrasing	**4** Excellent stress and subordination **3** Most key phrases stressed **2** Some appropriate use of pause and subordination **1** Pause overused—relied too little on subordination		
Characterization	**4** Strong evidence that observations have been incorporated into characterization **3** Clear characterization communicated **2** Adequate characterization communicated **1** Unclear or weak characterization		
Word Color	**4** Compelling imagery **3** Mostly vivid imagery **2** Some clear imagery **1** Flat, uninteresting imagery		
Illusion of First Time	**4** Effectively communicated by concentration and realization **3** Adequately conveyed **2** Not sustained **1** Unclear, not compelling		

Delivery			
Poise	**4** Excellent emotional control **3** Good emotion to control nervousness **2** Noticeable nervousness **1** Nervousness obvious		
Bodily Action	**4** Aids communication **3** Usually enhances the message **2** Neither distracts from nor enhances the message **1** Distracts from the message		

Script			
Written	**4** (7-8 check marks) **3** (5-6 check marks) **2** (4 check marks) **1** (1-3 check marks)	___ Appropriate cuts in text ___ Bound correctly in folder ___ Thought units in ( ) ___ Neat and legible, overall	Cut correctly for length Vocabulary has * and definition Phrases marked with / Professional appearance

You demonstrate good ability in . . .	You would benefit from more attention to . . .

Total Points _____   Grade _____

A CAST OF ONE 169

Evaluation Form

The evaluation form for the monologue is very similar to the form for the sonnet. You will note two changes: *visualization* and *vitalization* will be replaced with *characterization* and *illusion of the first time*. Of course, if a student's monologue includes a great deal of description, you will want to make comments about visualization as needed, perhaps in the section for word color. Commenting on energy level within the delivery categories can cover vitalization.

Since the monologues present a specific character speaking, the student's characterization will be very important in light of his overall performance. Also, each student should be working toward creating a sense that even his memorized communication is motivated at the moment of utterance, rather than practiced into monotony. Use the illusion of the first time category to evaluate this progress.

Chapter 8
Introduction

Picture the first time you heard an adventurous tale told around a campfire or at a childhood sleepover. In heightened anticipation, you failed to notice a mosquito biting your leg or a sense of thirst. Only the suspense was real. Would the hero escape from the cave before his lantern fuel was spent? Would the heroine win the first prize at the horse show?

If the story had an element of danger, the woods surrounding that campfire seemed to come alive. Every cricket and owl contributed to the atmosphere.

The storyteller slowly panned the little audience. His eyes met yours and then glanced away, as though he had seen the villain or hero through the trees. You felt compelled to snap your head in the direction of his gaze but feared to look.

That is the power of storytelling. A masterful storyteller can hold an audience spellbound. Even outdated or difficult material—when told well—can hold the attention of young and old.

Because modern culture is saturated with media, we may dismiss storytelling as passé. However, much of the appeal of film and television is the story. Encourage skeptical students that historians, politicians, teachers, preach-

Lesson Plan
Suggested homework is in **boldface.**

Lesson Description	Recommended Presentation	Performance Projects/ Written Assignments
I. Preparing Your Story (p. 173)	**ST—Read Me a Story** TE—Getting to Know You; A Carousel of Characters	**ST—Assign Storytelling project**
II. Practicing Your Story (p. 181)	TE—A Good Example	
Assessment	Chapter quiz	Storytelling performance **ST—Assign Journal 7**
Suggested teaching time: 6-7 class periods		

The Art of Storytelling

The country is India. A colonial official and his wife are giving a large dinner party.

ers, and many others en-
hance their vocation through
the skill of effective storytelling.

Chapter 8 Outline

Teaching Materials

- Blank paper if you wish to record your comments for A Good Example activity
- Performance rubrics (students submit their own copy)

OVERVIEW

Know—*Concepts*

Audience demographics: developmental needs
Adapting material to the situation
Organization

Grow—*Interpretation Skills*

Characterization
First- and third-person narration

Show—*Performance*

Extemporaneous storytelling

The country is India. A colonial official and his wife are giving a large dinner party. They are seated with their guests—army officers and government attachés and their wives, and a visiting American naturalist—in their spacious dining room, which has a bare marble floor, open rafters and wide glass doors opening onto a veranda.

A spirited discussion springs up between a young girl who insists that women have outgrown the jumping-on-a-chair-at-the-sight-of-a-mouse era and a colonel who says that they haven't.

"A woman's unfailing reaction in any crisis," the colonel says, "is to scream. And while a man may feel like it, he has that ounce more of nerve control than a woman has. And that last ounce is what counts."

The American does not join in the argument but watches the other guests. As he looks, he sees a strange expression come over the face of the hostess. She is staring straight ahead, her muscles contracting slightly. With a slight gesture she summons the native boy standing behind her chair and whispers to him. The boy's eyes widen: he quickly leaves the room.

Of the guests, none except the American notices this or sees the boy place a bowl of milk on the veranda just outside the open doors.

The American comes to with a start. In India, milk in a bowl means only one thing—bait for a snake. He realizes there must be a cobra in the room. He looks up at the rafters—the likeliest place—but they are bare. Three corners of the room are empty, and in the fourth the servants are waiting to serve the next course. There is only one place left—under the table.

His first impulse is to jump back and warn the others, but he knows the commotion would frighten the cobra into striking. He speaks quickly, the tone of his voice so arresting that it sobers everyone.

"I want to know just what control everyone at this table has. I will count to three hundred—that's five minutes—and not one of you is to move a muscle. Those who move will forfeit fifty rupees. Ready!"

The twenty people sit like stone images while he counts. He is saying, " . . . two hundred and eighty . . ." when, out of the corner of his eye, he sees the cobra emerge and make for the bowl of milk. Screams ring out as he jumps to slam the veranda doors safely shut.

"You were right, Colonel!" the host exclaims. "A man has just shown us an example of perfect control."

"Just a minute," the American says, turning to his hostess.

"Mrs. Wyynes, how did you know that cobra was in the room?"

A faint smile lights up the woman's face as she replies, "Because it was crawling across my foot."

—Mona Gardner, "The Dinner Party"

Suspense keeps the reader and the listener paying attention in a story such as "The Dinner Party." But what creates that suspense? Look at the story again. What clues point toward the surprise ending? In paragraph four our attention is directed toward the hostess. The author provides more details about her than about the other characters. This is the first indication that she is important to the current discussion about the "nerve control" of men versus women. The servant boy's response is a second clue. Step by step the author hints about the end of the story. In hindsight, these clues seem obvious; but when reading the story, they are subtle. The clues do not spoil the ending; they only make it plausible. Gardner clearly had her conclusion in mind with every sentence she wrote. Forethought was her tool in crafting an effective story. The oral storyteller must also plan ahead in order to succeed.

PREPARING YOUR STORY

The power of the narrator did not die with chivalry.
—Katherine Dunlap Cather

Cecilia was traveling in Central America with a mission team from her church. Though her Spanish was not good enough to say everything she wanted to express, she was finding it quite easy to communicate with children. So much could be said without worrying about perfect grammar skills. Then a six-year-old girl named Marie-José asked Cecilia to tell her a story. Much to her distress, Cecelia realized she was not prepared to express any children's story in Spanish. "Goldilocks" had never been the vocabulary theme in her *clasé de conversación*.

THE ART OF STORYTELLING 173

Forethought

Remind students that planning ahead is important, whether in their schoolwork, their schedules, or even in their recreation. For example, something as trivial as forgetting sunblock on an all-day picnic can have disastrous consequences. Not planning ahead on a big project generally spells disaster as well.

Encourage them to plan. However, remind the students that our plans are not always going to work out as we might desire. A Christian can rest assured that God has a plan for him—intended for his good and God's glory (Jer. 29:11).

Lesson Motivator

For many forms of communication in general—interpersonal, professional, even written—storytelling skills will be among the most practical your students can develop in this course. Any individual who can thoughtfully consider his audience and present a message tailored for that audience will be miles ahead of peers with the same level of knowledge because he can communicate what he knows.

PRESENTATION

Preparing Your Story

Getting to Know You

Have students discuss what age groups seem most intimidating to tell stories to. Try to solicit individual answers. (*Some students may feel comfortable with children but be horrified to be the narrator in a church Christmas program in front of adults. Others may feel comfortable only with peers, not children or adults.*)

Ask the students why they find some situations more nerve-racking. (*Answers may include feelings of inadequacy, inexperience, or lack of common ground.*)

Then ask the students to brainstorm for solutions. (*Answers may include learning more about each age group, getting some experience, and talking with a friend who does feel comfortable with that group.*)

Age Interests

This simple guide is very valuable, especially if the storyteller needs to communicate to an age group with whom he is not very familiar. However, remind students that the best stories are those that appeal to a broad audience. An elementary-school child can aurally comprehend a well-told story that would baffle him in print.

A storyteller may be called upon at a moment's notice to entertain friends or family. Familiarity with one or two well-written short stories allows him to delight an audience at a moment's notice.

Vocabulary is part of storytelling, even if you are speaking your first language. If your audience is young children, for example, word choice is important. A good storyteller strives to be adaptable to a wide variety of audiences.

Plan for the Audience

Every audience is unique. However, the needs of audiences can be grouped so that the speaker can quickly analyze the situation and adapt without knowing everyone in the audience personally. The speaker must consider the audience demographics and situation.

Demographics

If you have previously studied public speaking, you are already familiar with the term *demographics*, meaning the characteristics of a group. For storytelling, we will focus on two demographic elements: background knowledge and age group.

Background Knowledge

In the previous example about Cecelia and Marie-José, lack of vocabulary prevented the storyteller from communicating properly. Usually the vocabulary and contextual knowledge of the audience members will be the challenge. Just as Cecelia had no idea what sorts of legends or popular stories were familiar to Marie-José, you may not know enough about your potential audience's background knowledge.

Age Group

Preschoolers as well as kindergartners are fascinated by the world they can see, hear, touch, smell, and taste. They love crunching leaves and petting animals. They like to pretend to be the adults they know, such as a teacher or parent. Choose stories for this age group by topic, not just by simple vocabulary. Tell animal stories and imitate the sounds they make. Even have the children participate by creating the sound effects when they hear you say the corresponding animal. Tell stories about families and other familiar ideas.

Lower elementary-school students are developing their imaginations. Though some fairy tales are too gruesome to be appropriate, many fairy tales, tall tales, and legends delight young children. Traditional stories range from folk classics such as "Johnny Appleseed" to popular fairy tales such as "The Wild Swans" by Hans Christian Andersen.

Age Interests

- Ages six and under: sights and sounds of the world around them
- Lower elementary: imaginative stories such as tall tales and fairy tales
- Upper elementary through junior high: action, adventure, heroes
- Junior high and high school: ideals such as courage, loyalty, and romance

Note: These do overlap!

174 CHAPTER 8

The Higher Aim

Ask your students to name some possible higher aims of storytelling. (*Answers may include inspiring a love of literature, educating about distant peoples and lands, and inspiring the audience to do great things.*)

Beginning in the third or fourth grade and continuing until adolescence, children have a strong interest in stories that feature a central character. Recognize the importance of choosing a story in which the main character is a worthy hero. Children in this age group enjoy action and adventure stories. For example, if children are studying the American colonial period in class, they will love to hear a portion from *Johnny Tremain* by Esther Forbes.

With adolescence comes interest in ideals. Stories of courage, chivalry, loyalty, and love gain appeal. Stories including sentiment are more interesting than before. Reading stories that elevate these elements guides young people in developing worthy ideals.

> *The purpose of storytelling is not to merely entertain, although it does entertain, but that in addition to delighting young listeners, there must be a higher aim, of which the narrator never loses sight.*
>
> —Katherine Dunlap Cather

Of course, stories are not just for children or even for children and teens. Regardless of the age group, a good story has action, at least one sympathetic character, and a profitable theme. Told well, a story should be enjoyable to any audience, whether it includes a specific age group or a mix of children, teens, and adults.

Animals in Literature

Animals appear in literature in several ways. First, they may behave and be bound by natural laws while still filling central roles in the story. Many popular dog and horse stories fall into this category. Examples include the books *Old Yeller*, *Lassie Come-Home*, and *Black Beauty*. These stories are realistic.

Secondly, animals may live in an animal world but have human characteristics, such as the use of language. Examples include imaginative stories such as *Charlotte's Web*, in which a spider writes words in her web. With imaginative fiction, facts don't matter. What difference did it make to Fern that spiders can't spell?

Finally, animals may behave as humans—living in houses and driving cars. These stories also fall into the category of imaginative literature. Examples include "Little Red Riding Hood," "The Three Little Pigs," and *The Wind in the Willows*.

Animals in Literature

Have students find out how Balaam reacts to his talking donkey in Numbers 22:1-35. Ask one of your students to read the passage or split it up among your students. Note: This passage shows God's displeasure in Balaam's selfish desire for fame and wealth. Balaam really had no care to know God's will in this situation.

Situation

The situation, or circumstances, surrounding your storytelling influences your preparation and presentation. A loud fan or extreme temperature, a small group or a large audience, a formal setting or an informal one—all have consequences for any performer. But since you do not memorize your story verbatim, you can adapt more readily in various situations than someone reading or reciting a poem from memory.

Read Me a Story

Imagine you are invited to tell several stories to forty first and second graders. You have the option of taking them outdoors. The weather is quite warm, but there are shade trees. By the time you arrive, the children will have been sitting in class most of the day. Describe below what you would do in this situation.

1. What stories might you tell? _Answers will vary. Ideally, a tall tale, fairy tale, or fable would be used._

2. Would you go outside? Why or why not? _Answers will vary. Yes, depending on the available space. No, not wanting to deal with the distraction of being outside._

3. What specifically would you do to make the children comfortable so they could listen? _Answers will vary but may include the following: Instruct them to give their neighbors space—don't crowd, lean, or whisper._

4. What distractions could you anticipate and plan for? What would you do to handle them? _Answers will vary but may include any of the following: Some distractions, such as gnats, noises, or a strong breeze, will have to be ignored. Some distractions can be dealt with—don't play with or throw grass and keep your hands folded on your lap (so that you don't bother your neighbor)._

 Poise Practice

Help your students learn poise in distracting speaking situations. Assign familiar topics for a brief impromptu speech. Possible topics include "my favorite vacation," "why cats are superior to dogs" (or "why dogs are superior to cats"), and "the best restaurant in town." Without discussing poise beforehand, create a couple of distractions during each speech. You may want to call on your most confident and resilient speaker to go first. Try to do something different for each student so that he won't anticipate what you will do. Possible distractions include coughing, whispering, yawning, and opening a Velcro or three-ring binder. This speech should not be graded, except perhaps as part of a "participation" grade.

Choose the Literature

Now you know about your audience. What story should you choose? Several approaches may work for you. If you have very little time, try **brainstorming** for titles of stories with which you are already familiar that seem appropriate. Begin with a word or thought. Then write down whatever words or titles you associate with that thought.

If you have more time, you may still wish to begin by brainstorming, but then try a subject search by using a library catalog. Look especially for fiction and biography, both of which are indicated by call number and appear after the title. If possible, skim through numerous titles. Since short stories are printed in separate books for young children, you could walk through the juvenile section, reading titles as you go. For older students, generally only novels and biographies are bound individually. Short stories are published in magazines and anthologies (collections of stories bound together). Look through the title pages of these books for any stories that might interest you and your audience.

If you have access to a large library, check to see if the reference books include the *Masterplots* series. *Masterplots* are books containing plot summaries. Various editions focus on poetry, drama, and stories. In half an hour you can get the basic gist of dozens of selections. Select several that seem interesting to you and your audience. Look these up in the catalog to see if your library has holdings. Skim or read more than one option before you make up your mind. For those who prefer using the Internet, be sure to include a word such as "classics" in your search. Otherwise, you will have to wade through thousands of pages of stories written by children, amateurs, and unskilled writers. None of these would be appropriate for this assignment.

Definition

Brainstorming refers to making a quick list of anything that comes to mind about a subject. If done in a group, avoid criticizing any input since accuracy is not as important at this point.

Get Organized

For many of us, the very word *organize* may cause distress. Visions of neat drawers and daily planners haunt us. What can organization have to do with creativity or drama? Whether we want to admit it or not, organization has everything to do with the creative process. A creative work that lacks good order will either fail utterly or will be a quickly passing fad. Classics are crafted. They do not occur haphazardly, much less spontaneously.

Until now you have followed the structure of the literature you memorized for projects. Storytelling requires something

You can get good ideas for stories by . . .

- Brainstorming.
- Searching for a subject using the library catalog.
- Scanning titles on the shelves.
- Skimming title pages of anthologies.
- Reading *Masterplots*.
- Searching the Internet.

THE ART OF STORYTELLING 177

Books Still Exist

There is a growing tendency among students nowadays to think that the Internet is the only source for good information. Although the Internet is an efficient tool, remind students that libraries also contain very valuable tools for finding information. Don't rely solely on the Internet. Published material that stands the test of time is generally more reliable.

Internet material, like all research material, must be analyzed on the basis of source and purpose before it can be considered reliable.

Organization

If your students have previously studied public speaking, this section will partially be a review. However, organization is difficult for young students to apply consistently, and reviewing will not mean time wasted. Most students will find outlining easier for storytelling than for extemporaneous speech. The author has already engineered the story's framework and they need only identify it, whereas in an extemporaneous speech, the student must generate an outline from research and personal knowledge.

Apply Organization Outside the Classroom

Encourage your students to learn the benefits of organization while they are in school. They can organize

---

A Carousel of Characters

Introduction. Good storytelling requires a balance of organization and creativity. Have your students complete the improvisation below to practice relating these two demands of storytelling.

Instructions. This activity works best with at least six participants per group. If your class is small, you will not have to break up into groups at all. Choose one of the following topics for each group: circus or county fair, shopping mall, subway station, town square or city park, a ball stadium, or another "place" of your choice. Announce the topic and allow about 30 seconds for each student to invent a pantomime that relates. Possibilities include pantomiming a tightrope acrobat in the circus or a parent with a stroller in the mall. As soon as the group guesses a student's pantomime, he sits back down and the next student gives a pantomime. Require them to do a different character each time. When everyone is done, have the group organize their ideas into a miniscene that includes each character interacting in some way. Allow about five minutes of brainstorming and practice time before having the group perform.

their dresser drawers, closets, financial materials, desks, class notes, notebooks, lockers, and so on. Remind them that college life and a career will be less intimidating and more enjoyable if they start organizing their lives now.

Types of Outlines

This portion of the chapter depicts two different approaches to outlining the same story. At first it may seem like busy work to assign two outlines for one assignment. However, the outlines serve completely different purposes. The plot outline will assess the student's comprehension of the story. It should be thorough but concise.

The rehearsal outline should be as brief as or even sketchier than the example provided. The student needs to include only ideas that will prompt his recall of the story.

Outline Grading Tips

Major weaknesses in a student's outline are often closely tied to length.

Too short. If a student submits a plot outline that contains fewer than fifty or sixty words, he has probably skipped important details and/or not used sentences.

Too long. If either the plot outline or especially the rehearsal outline is more than a page and a half handwritten or one page typed,

more. Good storytelling demands that you *see* the structure as clearly as the author did in the writing process.

Outline the Plot

Let's begin with an outline of the plot of "The Dinner Party." You may add any details you believe are important by writing them in the margin near the appropriate point.

"The Dinner Party" by Mona Gardner

Plot Outline

Introduction: An official and his wife are hosting a dinner party in India.

I. A young girl and a colonel debate about the nerve control of men and women.

   A. She declares that women have overcome their reputation for jumping on a chair at the sight of a mouse.

   B. He insists they have not. He says they scream.

II. An American naturalist notices the furtive behavior of the hostess.

   A. The hostess is tense. She gives hushed instructions to a servant.

   B. The servant sets a bowl of milk on the veranda.

   C. The naturalist guesses that there is a cobra under the table and that the milk bowl is bait.

   D. The naturalist keeps everyone still by making a game of counting.

III. A cobra emerges from under the table and heads for the bait.

   A. The naturalist shuts the veranda doors, amid screams.

   B. The colonel boasts of the control of a man.

   C. The naturalist reveals that the hostess knew first.

Conclusion: The hostess reveals that the cobra crawled across her foot.

Notice that this sentence outline does not relate the descriptions or the dialogue, only the action. Action is the backbone of drama and narrative. Action is the starting place for you, the storyteller.

Look specifically now at the facts recorded as subpoints. What would happen to the story if you forgot one or more of them? The suspense would be weakened, wouldn't it? If you deleted several of these subpoints, the story might lose clarity. However, there would still be a story. In contrast, if the main points were lost, there would be no clear progression of action. The story itself would break down.

 178 CHAPTER 8

 Have your student create several different pantomimes instead of one. Then instruct him to brainstorm on paper for a mini-scene that would include those characters. Have him take the role of storyteller and share the scene he has created.

 The Main Points

"If the main points were lost, there would be no clear progression of action. The story itself would break down." This is a good analogy of the immature Christian. When a Christian begins neglecting Bible reading, prayer, reliance on Christ's strength, church attendance, and so on—the "main points" of his Christian life—his spiritual life soon becomes significantly weakened and

quite ineffective. If he keeps up this lifestyle, his spiritual life breaks down to a point at which he assumes a worldly way of life. Compare this with Psalm 1.

Plot Complications

After conflict is introduced by the inciting incident, events follow that lead up to the crisis. As a group, these events are called the rising action, as you learned in Chapter 2. Sometimes each one of these events is referred to individually as a **plot complication.** Each main point in your outline of a story should identify a separate plot complication.

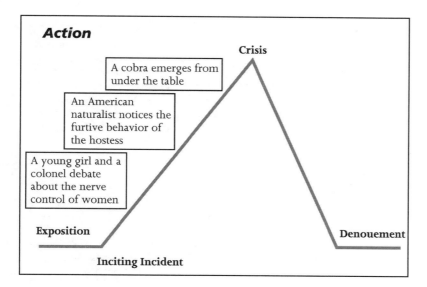

The Climax

To what event or thought does the story build? This dramatic peak must be clearly identified in your mind so you can convey the story effectively. Not identifying the climax might be equated with telling a joke but forgetting the punch line.

Tailor the Outline

Up to this point, your organization should be very objective. In other words, if someone else outlined the same story and you have both been conscientious, your outlines should be extremely similar. However, you as the storyteller are a unique artist. You must decide how you will actually tell the story.

the student has not really outlined at all. He or she has failed to discern between plot and extraneous detail. Unfortunately, this latter situation may occur with a student who generally excels in his written work. As a conscientious worker, he has falsely concluded that "more is better." Usually a low homework grade with thorough explanation is a swift cure. If you do not wish to assign a D or an F to a conscientious student who has overdone the assignment, perhaps allow him to rewrite the assignment for a small grade penalty, explaining that an outline is only the skeleton of the story, not all of the supporting detail. You are doing him a favor in the long run. He will save much time and energy on future writing assignments by learning to be *concise* as well as *complete*.

When Less Is Better

If the student is struggling to understand why less is better on outlines, ask him to recall the last time someone told him a story including so much detail that it seemed he would never get to the point. An outline with too much detail proves to be equally tedious.

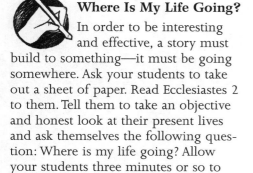

Where Is My Life Going?

In order to be interesting and effective, a story must build to something—it must be going somewhere. Ask your students to take out a sheet of paper. Read Ecclesiastes 2 to them. Tell them to take an objective and honest look at their present lives and ask themselves the following question: Where is my life going? Allow your students three minutes or so to write. Afterward, read Ecclesiastes

12:13-14 to them. You may want the students to place this in their journals.

Suit the Story

If the story is well worded, you will want to include many carefully chosen sentences in the author's own words, particularly excellent description or dialogue. Don't rob a story of its poetic quality.

On the other hand, you need not quote anything you can say just as well yourself. With some authors, the plot or characterization is rich, and the words are only a general way to describe them. However, the works of other authors may be difficult to convey without using at least some of their own words.

Suit Your Audience

Though a good story appeals to most people, not just a small segment of the population, you may need to modify a story for a particular audience. For example, what might you do to tell "The Dinner Party" to third- and fourth-grade students rather than teens and adults? Probably you would want to begin by creating a context in their minds. Research as needed to be able to add vivid details about British colonies in India. Be sure they understand the time period and culture from your introduction. In other words, give them the background that an adult would already have in his mind.

Suit Yourself

Use your outline as a tool rather than a crutch. Include details needed to trigger your memory—names of places, people, important dates, and so on. For the introduction and conclusion, you may want to select a few of the author's well-worded sentences, adding your own words as needed. Though you will submit a sentence outline to your teacher, you may want to practice from a keyword outline that has complete sentences for only brief, memorized parts. Consider the following example:

"The Dinner Party" by Mona Gardner

Rehearsal Outline

Introduction: The country is India during the British colonization. A colonial official and his wife are giving a large dinner party. They are seated with their guests—army officers and their wives, as well as a visiting American naturalist. The spacious dining room has a bare marble floor, open rafters, and wide glass doors opening onto a veranda.

I. Young girl and colonel debate.

 A. Girl—"Women don't jump on chairs."

 B. Colonel—"They do and they scream."

II. American naturalist notices hostess's behavior.

 A. Hostess—tense; she instructs servant.

B. Servant puts bowl on veranda.

C. Naturalist guesses about cobra bait and location.

D. Naturalist makes a game of counting—everyone keeps still.

III. Cobra emerges, heads for bait.

A. Naturalist shuts veranda door, amid screams.

B. Colonel boasts.

C. Naturalist reveals that the hostess knew first.

Conclusion: "Mrs. Wyynes, how did you know that cobra was in the room?" A faint smile lights up the woman's face as she replies, "Because it was crawling across my foot."

In addition to making a rehearsal outline, you can also add *delivery cues* to personalize your outline by writing notes to yourself in the margin of your rehearsal script or outline.

PRACTICING YOUR STORY

Practicing for storytelling is a challenge for performers at any level of expertise. Acting provides the motivation of at least a partner, if not the guidance of a director. Memorized interpretation can focus on phrasing and word color inherent to the author's wording. Storytelling focuses more on audience and audience response. How then do you practice it in a room by yourself? Impromptu storytelling may work at the lunch table for a few minutes, but it will seldom maintain audience attention for a longer span of time or properly convey the qualities of a selection of literature. This section describes some specific steps to help you make the most of your practice time.

Create Characters

After school one day, Philip began listlessly reading a book to his little sister Karis. It was not long before she tugged on his sleeve. "That's not right! You're not reading it right." Philip was puzzled. Karis, who had not learned any reading skills yet, took the book and began to "read" it for him. Her storytelling went something like this:

Christopher Robin saw Pooh stuck in the door.

(She mimics Christopher Robin's voice.) He says, "Siwy old bear."

Den Christopher Robin began to puw and puw. But Pooh was stiw stuck in the door. (She shrugs her shoulders.) He didn't come out.

Lesson Motivator
Practicing the storytelling assignment will be a different type of task than the other projects in this course. Students will not be trying to memorize verbatim. The closest parallel to this assignment is preparing an extemporaneous speech in which no notes will be used during final delivery. Students may find extemporaneous storytelling a little easier to remember than an informative speech because the story has forward motion in the plot. One thing leads to another. Plot does not characterize public speaking outlines in most cases. (Hence the use of memory devices such as alliterated main points.)

Whether your students have already studied public speaking or will do so in the future, seeing this parallel should aid their comprehension of the current assignment.

PRESENTATION
Practicing Your Story

A Good Example
Introduction. If stories are performed outside class, each student will enjoy a memorable personal learning experience in a real environment but will not benefit from observing his classmates. Whether you plan to have your students tell their stories in class or in an authentic setting such as an elementary-school class or school assembly, you may want to take time to coach some students through the rehearsal process as a teaching tool. Then students will be sure to learn from each other.

(Note: If your students perform for another class or an assembly for a grade, a preview is highly recommended. Either have each student perform in class first or meet with the students individually to hear their stories. This is the only means of being certain they are truly prepared to share their stories with an authentic audience.)

Instructions. You will probably not have time on this project to have a coaching session with every student. You may find it more manageable and equally productive to have only a couple of students (preferably students you know will respond well to feedback) volunteer for the task. Have the first student begin practicing his story in front of the class. Immediately begin providing oral feedback—don't wait for the

Lesson Objectives

The student will be able to

1. Rehearse storytelling using only an outline as a guide, instead of a script.

2. Rehearse storytelling without any notes.

3. Paraphrase a story thoroughly rather than reciting verbatim.

4. Create distinct characters in his chosen story.

5. Effectively use the dramatic "V" when appropriate.

Read More!

Encourage your students to read voraciously. This gives them a head start toward becoming good storytellers. The avid reader often has a larger vocabulary, greater ability in forming smooth oral sentences, and a more vivid, well-exercised imagination than the person who doesn't read much.

(She turns the page and then mimics Rabbit's voice.) Rabbit says, "Oh, dear, Pooh. What am I gonna do wid you?" Rabbit pushed and Christopher Robin puwed and puwed.

(She mimics Pooh.) Den Pooh says, "Oh, bodder."

Karis hands the book back to Philip. "Your turn, Phiwip."

Obviously Philip had assumed that reading a story to a child was the same as reading a high-school textbook or a magazine article. Karis had no trouble pointing out his mistake. She was not interested in the words but in the characters and their conflicts. She knew that they all had different voices and individual personalities. The storyteller is responsible to create characters, not just recite words.

For each character in the story, the storyteller must picture and then bring to life a distinct **characterization,** portraying each character physically, vocally, and emotionally. Characterization can be seen on a spectrum. At one end, the performer merely suggests the character and at the other, he attempts to be that character.

You must convey the body, posture, voice, personality, and emotional experience of each character in the story. You will need to present some characters more fully because the author has made them **round characters.** You do not need to develop **flat characters** as much.

definition

Characterization means conveying the character physically, vocally, and emotionally.

Round characters are fully developed, whereas flat characters are not described with much detail. Often the main characters are round, and supporting (minor) characters are flat.

Characterization for the storyteller is more difficult than for the actor. An actor portrays one character, often with the benefit of costume, makeup, and hairstyle. The storyteller must portray all characters through suggestion, while keeping them distinct. Also, the storyteller must shift fluidly from the physicality of the narrator to that of each character many times during a story. Portraying the entire cast and quickly shifting between characters are important characterization components for storytelling.

You must evaluate and understand each character. As a reader, remember that each character is described as the narrator views him. As in real life, opinions vary from person to person. Do not assume that the narrator's description is perfect or complete.

In order to have a complete view of a character, ask the following questions:

- What do other characters say about the character in question?
- What does the character do?
- How do other characters respond to him?

student to complete a long segment. This is not a performance, it's a practice session. Make a concrete suggestion such as "don't rush through that first sentence as if we are already familiar with the setting" or "speak more directly to the audience when you narrate." Then instruct the student to start again at the beginning or right before whatever portion the comment applies to. You may find it useful to have the student give you his outline during this coaching session so you can easily pro-

vide him a reference point for starting again. After one or two such ten-minute sessions, explain to the class that many of the same tips will help their stories as well.

Physical Characteristics

Once you understand a character, begin developing the physical characteristics. Every person has distinct movements and gestures that stem from habits, personality, and even circumstances. Also, each person has unique facial expressions and other covert movements. Being a good observer of people will help you develop different characters. For each character in your story, beginning with the central character, try to imagine the person in your mind. Have you seen or do you know someone who is like him or her?

> **Parallels to Public Speaking: The Speaker We See**
>
> - Posture: alignment of the head, the shoulders, and the back while standing or sitting
> - Stance: body position or attitude when standing
> - Walk: the particular way an individual moves when walking
> - Gesture: motion of the limbs used to communicate meaning
> - Facial expression: movement of the facial muscles into meaningful positions

Be careful not to overgeneralize. Don't portray all of your elderly characters as being frail. Obviously some are rightly characterized that way, but others are healthy and energetic. By overgeneralizing, you turn all of your characters into stock characters. Aim to create individuals instead.

Once you make specific choices about posture, stance, walk, gesture, and facial expression, you can practice that role. Work through your outline once, incorporating all of the physical characteristics of a particular character. This process need not take much time. For a main character, try to spend about fifteen minutes. A minor character could be rehearsed in less time.

When you feel comfortable suggesting each character's body and movement, practice through your outline several times, concentrating on switching smoothly from one character to another. These transitions will be important in maintaining your audience's **suspension of disbelief,** or willingness to pretend that the story is real. If your transitions seem awkward, you will distract your audience.

Suspension of disbelief occurs when the audience accepts fiction as real for the moment.

Vocal Characteristics

Now each character has a body but still needs a unique voice. The voice you give a character must be even more consistent than the bodily characteristics. Your audience will depend on the different character voices to follow the story. Whether or not you include tag lines (he said, she said), the audience will already have a character in mind because of the voice you use when delivering the dialogue.

One vocal issue is portraying gender. When a young man must portray a female character or vice versa, suggestion is more effective than complete embodiment. To suggest male characters, a woman should use pitches in the lower end of her natural vocal range. The sound should not be strained unless a comic effect is desired.

Be Creative but Careful

Although creativity is crucial when developing character voices, encourage your students to avoid using strained or throaty character voices. Students often use such voices to portray villains, bullies, animal characters, and elderly people. Encourage them to experiment with character voices that are not harmful to the vocal folds. Abusing the vocal folds over time can result in a permanently raspy, breathy, or crackly vocal quality.

Additionally, warn students that both cheerleaders and vocal spectators can easily abuse their vocal folds by harsh, strident screaming at ball games. Some students consider it noble to lose their voices from cheering. To cheer safely at ball games and use loud volume on stage, avoid the typical screaming effect that is caused by a tight, rigid throat. Instead, cheer and speak with a full, clear voice that is powered by a strong flow of air from the lungs. Vocal production is more fully discussed in Chapter 9 of *Sound Speech.*

THE ART OF STORYTELLING · 183

Likewise, men should use the upper end of their natural vocal range and avoid falsetto (extremely high pitches) unless a comic effect is called for.

Be creative when developing character voices. Make sure the voice is sensible for the character and his personality. Also be sure that the voice is distinct from your narrative voice and other characters' voices.

Basic Characterization Rules

Below are general guidelines for characters based on age and gender. Don't forget that personality, background, and circumstances can create an infinite number of variations on these characteristics. Use these ideas only as a starting point to develop your characters.

		GENDER		ADULT AGES		
		Male	**Female**	**Young**	**Middle-Aged**	**Elderly**
PHYSICAL	**Stance**	feet 10" apart	feet 6" apart	relaxed	dignified	uncertain
	Posture	shoulders back	shoulders down	erect	slightly bowed	bent over
	Gesture	from shoulder	from elbow	full	moderate	small
	Walk	full stride	half stride	energetic	smooth	slow
VOCAL	**Range**	low–moderate	moderate–high	higher	moderate	lower
	Inflection	fewer pitches	more pitches	modulated	steady	erratic
	Quality	full	clear	lively	resonant	dry, raspy

Children may seem to be caricatures of adults. Their movements are freer and more vivacious. Little girls tend to be giggly. They huddle in groups, hug, and whisper. Often little boys are animated and energetic. They may try to be "tough guys," but they still like to be hugged—especially if they are afraid or hurt. Some children are noisy, others shy. Some are loners, though most like to have at least one buddy. A few will be passive, but most are full of energy and action.

As you well know, teens encounter many changes that can prove awkward at times—changes in voice and sudden change in height, for example. Those who are leaders in athletics, academics, or music may influence their peers most during the teen years.

Know your characters well enough to present them honestly to the audience. If you make the characters real in the audience members' minds, you can evoke genuine laughter and tears over the quirks and failures of those characters.

Dramatic "V"

When you perform literature with more than one character, use a **dramatic "V."** Imagine two key characters in conversation. You have developed a posture and voice for each. When one speaks, the other is, presumably, listening. In order to convey this dialogue, use aesthetic distance, which you have already used in the past to convey description. By imagining the place you described over the heads of the audience members, allow them to look past you, picturing the scene in their minds. Aesthetic distance can also effectively convey dialogue.

When you portray a character, you must visualize the character you are addressing as standing in front of you at a realistic distance for your conversation. To help the audience differentiate between characters, choose a different focal point for each character. (See Figures 1 and 2.) The focal

point should reflect the character who is speaking rather than the listener since sometimes there will be multiple listeners. Examine the diagram below to see how the dramatic "V" could be used for the story "The Dinner Party."

Novices often misuse the dramatic "V." Common mistakes include looking too far to the right and left or making the technique more important than the characterization by noticeably shifting your focus. However, when used properly, this technique proves very effective.

Figure 1. Keep your focus narrow—never wider than the back wall of the room.

Figure 2. Additional variety of focus can be created on a vertical plane—taller characters conversing with shorter characters.

Narration

As a storyteller, you also have the goal of communicating narration. Narration always has a point of view, or viewpoint. Point of view, sometimes abbreviated P.O.V., generally falls into one of two categories: first person or third person.

First-Person Narration

Sometimes the narrator tells a story about his own life experience. This is called **first-person narration** and is found in autobiographies as well as in some fiction. The narrator is part of the story, referring to himself with the first-person pronouns I and me. You may need to create a unique characterization both physically and vocally apart from yourself for the first-person narrator.

THE ART OF STORYTELLING 185

Dramatic "V"
Angle of Focus

Usually, just a slight turn to the right and left is sufficient to differentiate between characters. If you are seeing only the student's profile when he is doing characterization, he has turned too far to the right and left and has wasted useful energy. A good rule for the interpreter is to visualize all the characters within the boundaries of the back corners of the room.

Level of Focus

Another common mistake is looking too high for characters, rather than at eye level. Exceptions would include portraying a child character speaking with an adult character, or other characters who would have noticeably different heights. Remind students to draw attention to the characters and not to the dramatic "V." Otherwise, the means becomes more important than the message.

Reality of Focus

As your students picture the character they are addressing, encourage them to focus on the imaginary eyes of the character. When we speak to each other in real life, we focus on the eyes. We need to do this with our characters also.

Coaching the Perfectionist

If some of your students sounded too memorized on the sonnet or monologue assignment, this is your chance to retrain them before they develop a bad habit. For this type of student, you may find the procedure below effective.

1. Coach them through a practice session before they've had time to memorize their outline verbatim.

2. Insist that they "stumble" through the story, telling what they do remember and not peeking to see what they've missed until they reach the end of the story.

3. Instruct them to read the outline not more than two to three times before trying again to tell the story without looking.

The student who sounds very memorized rather than spontaneous is usually focusing on rote memorization instead of communicating.

Once a student experiences successful communication without rote memory, he will be more willing to focus on communicating with memorized and extemporaneous assignments.

Third-Person Narration

Sometimes the narrator tells us about something that has happened to other characters. This is called **third-person narration.** Both biographies and fiction may use third-person narration. You may be able to be the narrator yourself—using your own voice and posture. When we tell stories to our friends, we generally serve as narrator, though we normally speak in first person for personal experience.

Dialogue

A final component of the story that involves the characters and sometimes the narrator is *dialogue*, the words spoken by the characters. Dialogue may be presented in one of two ways: direct dialogue or indirect dialogue.

Direct Dialogue

"Are you going to the store?" asked Frank.

In **direct dialogue,** the text is clearly spoken by the character. Often the author includes a tag line. As the storyteller, you may or may not include a tag line, depending on the frequency with which that character speaks. To convey direct dialogue, suggest the full presence of that character while speaking the text.

Indirect Dialogue

Frank asked if she would be going to the store.

In this case, the narrator is reporting the speech of a character. You may convey **indirect dialogue** in one of two ways. The obvious way is to maintain the personality of the narrator for the entire text. However, this may not seem to be the most natural method in oral storytelling. When we express a thought in daily conversation, we often mimic the person speaking, at least to some extent. You can do this when rehearsing and presenting indirect dialogue in a short story too. Begin the sentence above as the narrator but suggest the character when it would be appropriate. Compared to the suggested characterization used in direct dialogue, this characterization is more like hinting.

definition

Third-person narration means that the narrator is not part of the story.

Direct dialogue records the speech of a character as a separate sentence or phrase and marks that text with quotation marks.

Indirect dialogue involves the narrator reporting the character's speech.

Extemporaneous Style

Now that you've developed a good rehearsal outline and created characters, you need to practice the whole story. Your mode of delivery will be *extemporaneous.* The key for extemporaneous speech is to avoid focusing on the wording as you rehearse. Strive to be accurate about the ideas instead of the words. Well-rehearsed

 CHAPTER 8

extemporaneous speech can be very powerful, because the text has meaning for you. Focus on communicating effectively.

PARALLELS TO PUBLIC SPEAKING		
Mode of Delivery	Public Speaking	Performance
Memorized	Special occasion speeches	Poetry, acting, readings
Manuscript	Special occasion speeches, business reports	Scripture reading, readers theater
Extemporaneous	Speeches to inform, persuade, and inspire	Storytelling, skits
Impromptu	Group discussion	Storytelling, skits

CONCLUSION

Storytelling may be the most universally applicable skill you will learn in this course. As a high-school and college student, you will relate personal experiences with peers through storytelling. In fields such as writing, preaching, education, law, or business, professionals may illustrate ideas with stories. Parents teach their children literacy as well as many life lessons through storytelling. In some of these situations, you might not use all of the techniques presented in this chapter. However, mastering as many of them as possible gives you a better-equipped toolbox from which to choose.

Not only should you find storytelling skills very practical for your career and life, you should also find them very rewarding. The first time you share a suspenseful mystery or an uproariously funny yarn, you will understand the exhilaration that comes to one who holds the listeners' rapt attention and leaves them in awe.

A Worthwhile Skill for Ministry
Remind your students that they may be involved in children's ministries throughout their lives. Though a great blessing, children's ministries are very mentally and physically demanding. Storytelling skills make the task much easier. Children (of all ages) love a well-told story. Guaranteed!

THE ART OF STORYTELLING 187

Terms to Know

brainstorming	flat characters	third-person narration
plot complication	suspension of disbelief	direct dialogue
characterization	dramatic "V"	indirect dialogue
round characters	first-person narration	

Ideas to Understand

True/False: **Write** True **or** False **for each statement. If false, cross out the word or words that make it incorrect and write in the word or words that make it true.**

False 1. Preschool children enjoy imaginative stories. either ~~preschool~~ elementary or
~~imaginative stories~~ sights and sounds of the world around them

True 2. Junior-high students prefer hero-centered, action-packed stories.

False 3. The storyteller has less of an opportunity to adapt his material to his audience
than a reader of poetry. ~~less~~ more

True 4. Suggestion can be used with direct and indirect dialogue.

Short Answer

5. Collectively, what events are known as the rising action? _plot complications_

6. What term describes the speech of one character to another character? _dialogue_

7. What questions should you ask before forming a final concept of a character or developing
characterization? Give at least two. _What does the character do? How do other characters_
respond to the character's actions? What do other characters say about the character? What
does the narrator say about the character?

8. Explain how a storyteller portrays a character. _The storyteller portrays a character by creating_
a full presence of that character. The storyteller assumes the body, posture, voice, personality,
and emotional experience of the character.

Storytelling Assignment Sheet

Due Dates

_____ Select a Story

_____ My Situation and My Audience

_____ Outline

_____ Dramatistic analysis

_____ Performance

List your favorite stories below. Include author and appropriate audience. (Identify age group or other demographics.) List as number one the story you wish to perform for the assignment.

1. _____

2. _____

3. _____

Remember to mark your outline and bring it to your teacher.

Practice

Evaluate yourself on a scale of one to ten in each of the following areas, rating your current effectiveness in each skill. One is weak, five is moderate or adequate, and ten is excellent. Explain your evaluation.

_____ Characterization _____

_____ Dramatic "V" _____

_____ Creating Suspense _____

_____ Distinct Climax _____

Set goals for each practice session, such as "creating character voices." Chart your progress here.

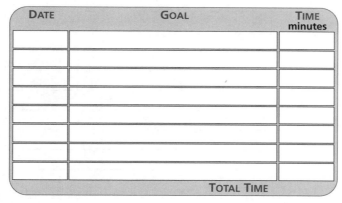

DATE	GOAL	TIME minutes
	TOTAL TIME	

THE ART OF STORYTELLING 189

The Storytelling Project

Since this project includes more written work than previous assignments, you will want to allow more days between giving the assignment and having students perform.

By this point in the course, you may wish to explain the project for the next chapter before the performances are completed in the current chapter. Have students make a selection before they begin reading the corresponding chapter. This overlap will help you make the most of your time.

Project Checklist

For the storytelling project, you will need to select due dates for each of the following components:

1. Specified number of short stories read
2. Short story selected
3. "My Situation and My Audience" worksheet
4. Plot outline
5. Dramatistic analysis
6. Assignment sheet
7. Rehearsal outline
8. Performance

(The assignment sheet and rehearsal outline could be checked on the day the student speaks.)

Appendix F
You may wish to add or delete stories from the list in the appendix before allowing your students to choose one.

If it would not cause an excessive homework burden, consider requiring each student to read several stories before making a final selection.

Performance Days
You may have completed performances for each of the last two projects in one class period each, but with a class of fifteen students, the short stories will require approximately three to four class periods.

My Situation and My Audience

1. WHERE will you give your story? What distractions could be present? What benefits does this location have? ——————————————

——————————————————————

——————————————————————

——————————————————————

——————————————————————

2. WHEN will you give your story? What challenges result from that time of day or time slot in the audience's schedule? ——————————————

——————————————————————

——————————————————————

——————————————————————

——————————————————————

3. WHO will be in your audience? What age group or age range will be represented? What particular interests might your listeners have? ——————————————

——————————————————————

——————————————————————

——————————————————————

——————————————————————

4. WHAT story do you plan to tell? (Give title and author.) ——————————————

——————————————————————

——————————————————————

——————————————————————

——————————————————————

5. WHY do you think this story is appropriate? ——————————————

——————————————————————

——————————————————————

——————————————————————

——————————————————————

 CHAPTER 8

Dramatistic Analysis of the Short Story

Title _____

Author _____

Sources (list in bibliographical form) _____

_____

_____

_____

Structure

1. **Whose story is it?** (personality and nature, purposes and goals, strengths and weaknesses of the central figure or figures)

   _____

   _____

   _____

   _____

   _____

   _____

   _____

2. **What are the circumstances?** (background, location, time, setting)

   _____

   _____

   _____

   _____

   _____

   _____

   _____

3. **What is the atmosphere of the story?** (mood)

   _____

   _____

   _____

   _____

   _____

   _____

THE ART OF STORYTELLING 191

4. **What is the climax of the story?**

_____

_____

_____

_____

_____

5. **What is the major dramatic question of the story?**

_____

_____

_____

_____

_____

Evaluation

6. **What is the theme of the story?** (the moral or central truth)

_____

_____

_____

_____

_____

7. **What are the worldview and tone?** (Refer to Chapter 3 if necessary.)

_____

_____

_____

_____

_____

8. **What is the purpose of the story?**

_____

_____

_____

_____

_____

Name _____ Story _____

Interpretation	Comments	Pts.
Narration **4** Clear viewpoint; compelling style **3** Clear viewpoint; acceptable style **2** Vague viewpoint; acceptable style **1** Weak viewpoint; weak style		
Characterization **4** Strong evidence that observations have been incorporated into characterization **3** Clear characterization communicated **2** Adequate characterization communicated **1** Unclear or weak characterization		
Word Color **4** Compelling imagery **3** Mostly vivid imagery **2** Some clear imagery **1** Flat, uninteresting imagery		
Illusion of First Time **4** Effectively communicated by concentration and realization **3** Adequately conveyed **2** Not sustained **1** Unclear, not compelling		

Delivery		
Poise **4** Excellent emotional control **3** Good emotion to control nervousness **2** Noticeable nervousness **1** Nervousness obvious		
Bodily Action **4** Aids communication **3** Usually enhances the message **2** Neither distracts from nor enhances the message **1** Distracts from the message		

Outline		
Written **4** (5 check marks) **3** (4 check marks) **2** (3 check marks) **1** (1-2 check marks)	— If used, delivery cues are used correctly — Main points accurately reflect primary plot complications	— Supporting points facilitate movement from one main point to the next — Introduction is well chosen — Conclusion is well chosen

You demonstrate good ability in . . .	You would benefit from more attention to . . .

Total Points _____   Grade _____

THE ART OF STORYTELLING **193**

The Evaluation Form

When comparing the evaluation form for the storytelling project with the form for the monologue project, you will find only two changes. First of all, *narration* has replaced *phrasing* in the interpretation section. Since students seldom struggle with phrasing in an extemporaneous setting, you may not need to make any comments about that feature. However, using the dramatic "V" and narration together will be a new and significant challenge. Secondly, note that a critique of the plot outline replaces a critique of the script.

Unit 3 Introduction

In Unit 3, students have the opportunity to participate in three vastly different projects that involve group interaction.

First, Chapter 9 teaches students about the various forms of readers theater, including chamber theater. Since Appendix G provides readers and chamber theater scripts, you will be able to lead students in exploring these forms.

In Chapter 10, students will work on an acting scene with a partner. If you have an odd number of students, you will need to substitute a three-person scene of your own choosing—perhaps from one of the plays already represented in Appendix H. Another option is to have one student perform in two scenes. Decide what suits your situation best.

Chapter 11 discusses radio broadcasting and playwriting. Unlike a school play, this project can provide a role in the production process for every student in your class. Though not a stage play, the radio segment allows students to learn many of the same skills—acting for an audience, creating sound effects, selecting appropriate music, and so on. If you want your students to have a real audience, air the segment over your school's public address system. You could even stage a behind-the-scenes production in which

CHAPTER 9 | Page to Stage

CHAPTER 10 | Romeo, Romeo, Dost Thou Know Thy Lines?

CHAPTER 11 | I Hear What You're Playing

Great Expectations by Charles Dickens, adapted by Robert Johanson
(Bob Jones University Classic Players)

a live audience watches students creating the segment as if they were touring a radio station during a production. Many find it intriguing and delightful to watch actors reading into microphones and to see the sound effects being made.

Unit 3 will require more class days than either of the first two units since the projects are more complex. While coaching your students in these group projects, you have a wonderful opportunity to get to know them better and cultivate camaraderie within the class.

GROUP PERFORMANCE

[Miss Havisham was] the strangest lady I have ever seen, or shall ever see. I saw that everything within my view which ought to be white, had been white long ago, and had lost its lustre, and was faded and yellow. I saw that the bride within the bridal dress had withered like the dress, and like the flowers, and had no brightness left but the brightness of her sunken eyes.

Chapter 9 Introduction

Traditionally, dramatic scripts have appeared on stage while poetry and prose were relegated to solo performance and private reading.

Readers theater departs from tradition by inventively staging all genres. The adapter identifies a dramatic or lyric quality in a selection and assigns speaking roles to facilitate the audience's understanding of that characteristic.

The readers theater performer seeks to engage an audience in the literature experience. The audience enjoys both hearing and seeing the story or poem.

In this chapter, you can teach appreciation of nondramatic literature through dramatic performance. Use the activities suggested in the marginal notes to guide your students through this unique dramatic art form.

CHAPTER 9

Lesson Plan
Suggested homework is in **boldface.**

Lesson Description	Recommended Presentation	Performance Projects/ Written Assignments
I. Understanding Readers Theater (p. 199)	TE—Love's True Meaning; First Impression	ST—Readers Theater Project **ST—Assign the Chamber Theater project**
II. Scripting Readers Theater (p. 201)	TE—Sparking Imagination; Be Adaptable	
III. Performing Readers Theater (p. 207)	TE—Work in Progress	Readers Theater workshop Chamber Theater workshop
Assessment	Chapter quiz	Readers Theater performance; **ST—Assign Journal 8;** Chamber Theater performance; **ST—Assign Journal 9**
Suggested teaching time: 9-10 class periods		

From Page to Stage

I give you the little white bird.

Teaching Materials

- Favorite poem or Scripture passage
- A transparency
- Highlighter pens in various colors
- Copies of a short poem or psalm
- A location appropriate for workshops—open space in your normal classroom or another more spacious location
- Workshop rubrics (students submit their own copy)
- Performance rubrics (students submit their own copy)

Love's True Meaning

Ask your students to name ways the world defines true love. (*Answers may include strong feelings toward someone, physical attraction, and butterflies in the stomach.*) If possible, obtain a copy of Sandburg's poem "Little Word, Little White Bird" to read to your students. This poem discusses the true nature of love compared to all of the flawed views that people have. Conclude by discussing the biblical view of love.

Have students read I Corinthians 13 aloud.

Chapter 9 Goals

The student will be able to

1. Understand readers theater as a form of dramatic communication.

2. Adapt a brief selection of literature into a readers theater script.

3. Communicate literature through readers theater performance.

OVERVIEW

Know—*Concepts*

Staging literature
    Readers theater
    Modified readers theater
    Chamber theater

Grow—*Interpretation Skills*

Choric speaking
Narration
Offstage focus and onstage focus

Show—*Performance*

Readers theater performance of a poem
Chamber theater performance of a short story
  or poem

The audience hushes to watch the final scene of the program. Five students are presenting Carl Sandburg's poem "Little Word, Little White Bird." Since the poem discusses the real meaning of love, each of the five students will take one side of the argument. A girl in an elegant, old-fashioned dress conveys lines in the poem that represent what love might mean to a young lady from Louisiana or Mississippi in the nineteenth century. Another young lady shares the theatrical and melodramatic images characteristic of a romance novel. A young man with the manners and clothing of a game-show host delivers lines that depict the commercial side of love. The fourth performer, another young man, represents the pessimist's viewpoint, constantly pointing out the dangers of love. The last performer is dressed all in white. She represents the voice of wisdom.

One young man tries to sell you roses while the other tries to discourage you completely. The southern belle speaks of romance and songbirds, while the dramatic girl describes love as a red, red rose. By the end of the poem, the young lady in white insists that "love is a little white bird" because it comes to you of its own choice. You can't hold it or force it to sing. You can't buy it or sell it and no amount of charm can earn it. When she concludes her argument, she lifts her hands together, suggesting that a small bird perched on her hands has just flown off. Though no props are used, many in the audience turn and look back, expecting to see that little white bird who brings the hushed song of love.

UNDERSTANDING READERS THEATER

The story above describes a *readers theater* presentation of poetry. In this chapter you will learn what readers theater is and what forms it includes. You will also learn about choosing and preparing materials for performance. At the end of the chapter, you will have the opportunity to participate in several types of readers theater.

Definition

After signing up to take Staging Literature as an elective, Heather asked several of her friends if they knew what readers theater was. Most of them had heard of readers theater and had at least a vague concept about it. Several of their descriptions are listed below:

- It's where actors read from scripts.
- People wear black clothes and sit on stools.
- Readers theater is fun and exciting—people share stories and poems. It's very creative.

Sometimes referred to as group interpretation or staged literature, **readers theater** simply means that readers—sometimes called oral interpreters, actors, or performers—are performing literature other than play scripts in the traditional sense.

Readers theater is the dramatic presentation of literature by readers.

Purpose

Many people who become interested in acting have been avid readers since childhood. Perhaps this background is what prompts actors and interpreters to think of new and creative ways to share some of their favorite literature.

Readers theater tries to turn stories into plays and poems into dramatic murals. Just as a lyric poem creates a mental snapshot that captures a feeling, thought, or moment, the readers theater performance depicts that image dramatically. The story at the beginning of the chapter is a good illustration of this. The audience is left with a singular impression.

Types of Readers Theater

The term *readers theater* actually includes several types of performances: *traditional readers theater*, *modified readers theater*, and *chamber theater*. These types are not completely separate. Picture them on a spectrum, blending seamlessly together. (See Figure 1.)

The Novice's Challenge
The novice may encounter several difficulties with readers theater. First of all, if he has never seen readers theater performed, he may have difficulty understanding the form. You may wish to inquire with local sources about any readers theater performances available in your area. Of course, the marginal notes in this text suggest various means of teaching the concepts.

Secondly, the novice often has difficulty thinking outside his own experiences. For example, he may falsely assume that a single narrator must deliver all narration or that characters can convey only dialogue. Readers theater often involves multiple narrators or even characters presenting narration in addition to dialogue. The scripts provided in Appendix G provide examples of various approaches to staging literature, including expressing abstractions.

PRESENTATION

Understanding Readers Theater

First Impression

Before defining readers theater, allow students two minutes to write their ideas about it. Have several students share the definitions they wrote. Discuss these ideas. Then ask the students the following questions. What was your definition based on? (*Answers will vary. Some students may have seen a competition or public performance. Others may be guessing completely.*) Has anyone actually participated in or viewed a readers theater performance? What was the setting? (*Answers may include church, forensics, tournaments, school, and community.*) What features about it do you recall? (*Possible answers include use of scripts, stools, offstage focus [performers looking at the audience], and narration.*) Discuss the variety of approaches to staging the literature that you have observed. If possible, compare dramatic segments in your church's cantatas with readers theater entries you and/or your students have seen at forensics meets.

Teaching Appreciation

Students learn by different means. Oral instructions, lecture, and expository reading communicate well to some students but confuse others who comprehend and remember only what they see or do. A picture or an action makes words and ideas accessible to them. Readers theater unifies these learning modes.

Readers theater challenges the student who understands and loves words to effectively communicate both the literature and his appreciation of it through visual means. This student has a head start on the project because compre-

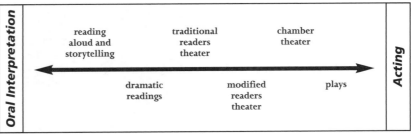

Figure 1. Performance Spectrum

Traditional Readers Theater

Traditional readers theater, usually just called readers theater, tries to convey literature in much the same way as a storyteller, but with multiple performers. Traditional readers theater has many or all of the following distinct characteristics:

Traditional readers theater generally always involves the use of scripts and always includes some or all of the narration in the literature being performed. Traditional readers theater may also include neutral costumes, use of stools or black boxes, and offstage focus.

Modified readers theater observes some of the conventions of traditional readers theater but makes some adjustments to suit the literature.

Chamber theater can be as fully dramatized as a play, retaining only a narrator from the conventions of readers theater.

- The readers hold scripts to create an association with the act of reading a story, though they may have the text mostly or completely memorized.
- Benches, stools, or black boxes may be used for furniture.
- Blocking, or changes in stage position, is minimal.
- The readers use offstage focus, directing their lines to the audience. (See Figure 2.) Even if two characters in the story are in dialogue, they speak without looking at one another. The effect is similar to that of a storyteller using the dramatic "V," discussed in Chapter 8.
- Costuming is often neutral or just suggests a character rather than being realistic.
- Action is described or pantomimed rather than actors using props realistically.

Modified Readers Theater

Modified readers theater maintains some but not all of the conventions of readers theater. For example, actors may sit on stools with scripts for part of the story but move about for certain scenes. Some forensics groups may not allow modified readers theater in a readers theater competition. Always check the competition handbook.

Chamber Theater

Chamber theater is at the other end of the spectrum, coming much closer to traditional acting. In fact, the only differences between a play scene and chamber

200 CHAPTER 9

theater may be the presence of a narrator and the source of the material, which is any kind of literature other than a play.

Actors may use traditional stage blocking and onstage focus, but with the narrator walking around the scene onstage. Chamber theater allows for abstract elements such as two performers playing the same character, but at different moments. In Robert Johanson's chamber theatrical production of Charles Dickens's *Great Expectations*, two actors portray the main character, Pip. One portrays the boy Pip. The other is both narrator and the adult Pip.

SCRIPTING READERS THEATER

Though some are available, you will not find many readers theater scripts on the market. One major reason is cost. Since a publishing house must pay the copyright holder (author or author's family) as well as the adapter, publishing such scripts is not very lucrative. However, this chapter contains some basic principles that will allow you to create scripts for your own classroom and competition use.

Materials for Presenting

First, you must choose appropriate material. It is generally not appropriate to take a play, sit on stools to read aloud, and call your effort readers theater. In some situations it may be acceptable to adapt a dated or classic play to make it more meaningful to a modern audience, but these situations are exceptions, not the rule.

Lyric Poetry

One possible type of appropriate literature is *lyric poetry*. As you learned in Chapter 6, lyric poetry uses figurative language to emphasize emotion and also seeks to leave a picture in the mind of the reader. When reading lyric poetry, much thought, time, and even multiple readings may be needed to grasp the poet's thought. For this reason, lyric poetry must be thoughtfully presented so the audience can absorb the ideas fast enough to keep up with the reading. Lyric poetry can often be staged effectively as traditional or modified readers theater, but not usually as chamber theater. Examples of lyric poetry scripts include "Be Still and Know" and "The Leaden Echo and the Golden Echo," found in Appendix G.

hension comes easily, but the requirement to stage the text may challenge him.

Also, readers theater creates a continuous visual illustration of the literature. Like a child's storybook, a readers theater performance constantly amplifies the text with "pictures"—stage pictures rather than drawings or photos.

Finally, readers theater provides participation. Literature can come alive for the student who sees only ink on paper. By participating in readers theater, the student experiences the ideas and emotions and then comprehends the literature.

PRESENTATION

Scripting Readers Theater

Sparking Imagination

One ideal way to introduce your students to readers theater is to allow them to experiment with a short selection of literature. You may choose to read one of your own favorite passages of Scripture or poems and then take about fifteen minutes to experiment with ways to read it as a group. Your "staging" of the piece could begin simply as a responsive reading. Make a transparency of the selection. Read one sentence or line of verse and have students read the next one together.

Repeat the exercise, experimenting with volume or vocal quality. If the selection includes characters, assign roles. If the selection might benefit from sound effects, assign some students to create them. For example, a story might be set in the forest or by the seaside. Students can easily mimic sounds typical of these locations.

If you do not wish to choose a selection of literature independently, try this same activity using a readers theater script from Appendix G. Rather than identifying the text as a readers theater script, simply read it aloud to the class as if it were a monologue. Then have your students turn to the script.

You may find that your students respond better if you use the two

Narrative Literature

Narrative literature refers to a story being told. Narrative prose includes most short stories, many novels, and some samples from other genres, such as letters. The major types of narrative poetry include *metric tales* such as Chaucer's *Canterbury Tales*, *epics* such as Homer's *Iliad* and *Odyssey*, and traditional *ballads* such as "Sir Patrick Spens" and "The Bonny Earl of Murray." Narrative prose will strongly resemble a play if staged as chamber theater. Some selections may be staged as readers theater, but modified readers theater tends to be more effective. Many stories seem limited by stools and scripts.

definition

Narrative literature presents a story.

Dramatic literature presents conflict without the aid of a narrator and includes much poetry as well as drama (plays).

Dramatic Literature

Dramatic literature encompasses all plays and certain types of poems. *Dramatic poetry* includes narratives and monologues in which a character faces conflict without the presence of a narrator. Examples include Robert Browning's "My Last Duchess," in which a character who is not the poet reveals the plot.

Principles for Adapting

To perform readers theater, you will likely need to make your own adaptation. The basic steps to follow include asking questions, developing a concept, and creating a script.

Ask Practical Questions

By asking practical questions, determine whether or not the literature will work onstage and what form to use. Later in the process, use aesthetic questions to make staging and performance choices. Use the questions below to guide you in evaluating a piece of literature you would like to adapt.

1. Can I present this text's philosophy without reservation?
   Hint: Unless the answer is "yes," you should move on to a different selection of literature.

2. Is the literature appropriate for the audience?
   Hint: Don't plan to perform a Greek myth at the elementary-school assembly or "The Little Engine That Could" for your peers.

3. Is there a narrative presence?
   Hint: Without some narration, your adaptation is a play, not readers theater. However, you don't necessarily have to have a separate narrator. Narration can be meaningfully assigned to many or all of the performers. Avoid random distribution just to help with memory work; such assignments would not be meaningful to the audience.

202   CHAPTER 9

---

traditional readers theater scripts provided ("Be Still and Know" and "The Leaden Echo and the Golden Echo") for experimentation in class. Then work on chamber theater scripts as full-fledged projects. Of course, you may wish to develop both categories into graded projects. If so, you could base your evaluation of the readers theater project on the rubric provided for the chamber theater project, making adjustments where needed.

Be Adaptable

Allow approximately fifteen minutes of class time for this activity. Divide the students into groups of four to six. Distribute a copy of a sonnet or psalm to each student and a master copy to one student. Everyone in a particular group should have the same selection from which to work. Provide multiple colors of highlighting pens so that each student in a group has his own color.

Allow each group a few minutes to brainstorm about how to script the selection. (You may need to appoint a team leader for each group.) Spend a few minutes with each group, participating in its discussion and moving the group members toward action. Instruct them to choose someone to speak each line, have that person read it aloud, and then decide if they like the line assignment. Every team member should highlight or underline his own lines on his copy. One team member should

4. Is there adequate text for character roles?

    Hint: Generally, you will need a reasonable portion of the text to be dialogue or some other type of interaction between characters in order to perform chamber theater. This will not be necessary for all readers theater.

5. What genre is this text?

    Hint: Choose from poetry, prose, or drama, including any other appropriate description such as *lyric* or *monologue*.

6. Can the staging of the text portray an abstraction more concretely?

    Hint: Some texts contain abstractions. If the abstraction is personified, such as Death in Poe's "Masque of the Red Death," the author has already made that abstraction a character. In readers theater, the director may have an actor or many actors portray an abstraction that is only described. For example, if a character in a story is afraid of something intangible or unknown, actors might try to convey the presence of that fear by using movement, voice, or both.

7. How many actors will I need?

    Hint: Remember this rule: more actors are not necessarily better. Many powerful performances involve two or three performers, not fifty. Even Shakespeare says to his audience, "Into a thousand parts divide one man," meaning, imagine that this one actor represents many men. Imagination is a powerful tool.

8. What special skills may the actors need?

    Hint: Do you need an actor who can convey a certain accent or dialect or maybe someone who can imitate certain sounds to create live sound effects?

9. What is the diction (word choice) of the text? What will I have to do to convey it?

    Hint: The diction of some poems may take a great deal more practice than some modern prose.

10. What figurative language or other literary elements must be considered?

    Hint: Be aware of the presence of simile, metaphor, irony, and other figurative language.

Develop a Concept

Every production should be designed and produced based on a **production concept.** This main idea will be developed in each facet of your production. If you are staging scenes from the novel *Jane Eyre,* for example, your concept might involve featuring the gothic (larger-than-life) elements. If so, your costumes, props, set, lighting, music, and acting style should all reflect that concept.

*D*efinition

*A **production concept** is the central idea for conveying meaning.*

FROM PAGE TO STAGE **203**

---

mark all lines in the color appropriate for the chosen reader on a master copy for you to check and grade if you choose.

Allow each group to share its work with the rest of the class. A participation grade would be appropriate but not necessary.

Provide a selection of literature for your student. Have him read it aloud several times and then create a script calling for three or more readers. If possible, have other family members or peers experiment with reading the script aloud.

If you are performing *Jane Eyre* with an emphasis on the thoughts of the characters, you will probably dispense with most of the visual elements. You might have pairs of readers convey each character, with both performers wearing a similar outfit, such as a gray dress. One would deliver Jane's spoken language and the other would share her thoughts with the audience.

Ideas for Production Concepts

LITERATURE	ELEMENT	PRODUCTION CONCEPT	EXPLANATION
"The Necklace" by Guy de Maupassant	Theme: pretentiousness, hypocrisy, discontentment	Wealth, luxury	Two narrators wearing tuxedoes appear on an elaborate set.
"The Celebrated Jumping Frog of Calaveras County" by Mark Twain	Subject: diversions of rural life	Hillbilly	Actors chew straw and wear brightly colored plaids and denim. The "frog" is a person squatting like a frog, wearing flippers (no frog costume).
Charlie and the Chocolate Factory by Roald Dahl	Characters: colorful; most having a single, distinctive trait	Characterization emphasized	Actors fully embody each character, though they assume multiple roles; an actor adds a prop for each character (hat, lollipop, etc.).

When you read a story to adapt, choose a significant element as your focus. In some stories, it will be appropriate to emphasize the theme; in others, the mood, plot, or characters. The production concept must be directly related to the content and meaning of the story. Otherwise, it will hinder the audience's understanding of the literature. The production concept must govern all choices about set, costume, lighting, and so on.

Create a Script

When creating a script, you may choose from several layouts, depending on your individual needs and abilities. One frequently used layout is modeled below. Regardless of layout, be sure to communicate ideas thoroughly yet concisely.

Principles for Adapting

1. Ask practical questions.
2. Develop a concept.
3. Create a script.

To be thorough, communicate your production concept, role assignments, basic staging suggestions, and any necessary stage directions. To be concise may be more difficult than it sounds. Proofread your script and have a friend do the same, crossing out the unnecessary words. Compare the following examples.

 CHAPTER 9

Too Sketchy

Title? Author? Adapter?
Too vague: What kind of park? What time of day is it? Is it crowded? What's the season or weather?

SCENE 1 A Park

MARCUS: Do you want to feed the ducks?

Who are these people? Are they siblings or husband and wife? Maybe father and daughter?

TIA: What are you talking about?

MARCUS: I brought some bread, and I just thought maybe—

TIA: You wanted to feed the ducks?

MARCUS: Here. Try it. It's fun.

TIA: This is dumb, Marcus.

MARCUS: Okay. You go home and feel sorry for yourself, and I'll feed the ducks.

TIA: That's not fair.

What do you think is going on in this scene? _**Possible answer: a tense discussion**_

What details seem to be lacking? _**Possible answer: description of the setting,**_
**description of characters, and stage directions**

Too Detailed

The overzealous adapter may get too wordy, too dictatorial.

Hand in Hand
by Sommer Daye
adapted by Jane Doe
One man, One woman

Hand in Hand is the story of Tia, a woman who lost much of her eyesight from head and neck injuries in a car crash. She spent close to a month healing and recently came home from the hospital after undergoing surgery. Marcus, her husband of three years, wants to help her enjoy life again. Her recent surgery has left her bandaged and embarrassed to go anywhere. Marcus has convinced her to go to a local park for some fresh air. They can go early so there won't be many people around.

Production concept: Set has enough obstacles that Tia must depend on Marcus to guide her. All stage pieces should be very simple, illustrating to the audience that trust is a simple choice, though sometimes difficult because of our human nature. Pantomime is recommended so the audience members participate imaginatively. This should help them focus on Tia's internal struggle.

FROM PAGE TO STAGE 205

SCENE 1 A city park in the springtime

It is early morning. The actors pretend to be able to smell the dewy grass. A jogger passes occasionally. Sounds of birds such as sparrows and ducks can be heard. Marcus slowly guides Tia to a park bench, where they sit down together.

MARCUS:	(*Turns to Tia as if she can see him and speaks imploringly*) Do you want to feed the ducks?	*How can Marcus turn "as if she can see him"?*
TIA:	(*Grudgingly*) What are you talking about? (*Turns slightly away*)	
MARCUS:	(*Reaches into his knapsack that is snapped and zippered shut from their walk*) I brought some bread, and I just thought maybe—	
TIA:	(*Cuts him off and speaks slightly sarcastically*) You wanted to feed the ducks?	*This stage direction is stating the obvious since Marcus's last sentence is a fragment punctuated with a dash.*
MARCUS:	(*Pantomimes handing her a piece of stale bread and smiles*) Here. Try it. It's fun.	
TIA:	(*Looks the other direction and sighs*) This is dumb, Marcus.	*A planned sigh will likely sound fake.*
MARCUS:	(*With resignation*) Okay. (*Stands and walks a few yards to the water's edge; pantomimes tossing bread to the ducks*) You go home and feel sorry for yourself, and I'll feed the ducks.	
TIA:	(*Sounding hurt*) That's not fair.	*Describe what actions to perform rather than how the actor should sound. For example, tell Tia to rebuke Marcus.*

What, if anything, about this version seemed awkward or difficult to use?

<u>Possible answer: the amount of description obscured the dialogue, and some stage</u>

<u>directions are difficult to follow.</u>

Thorough Yet Concise

Hand in Hand
by Sommer Daye
adapted by Jane Doe
One man, One woman

One frequently asked question is the number of roles in the play. Many plays list the number of men's and women's roles in a summary.

Dramatis Personae

TIA, legally blind from multiple injuries in a car crash
MARCUS, her husband of three years

Notice that characters are more easily understood with a brief description under dramatis personae than in a paragraph.

 CHAPTER 9

Background: Tia's face is bandaged from a recent surgery.

Production concept: Set has enough obstacles that Tia must depend on Marcus to guide her. All stage pieces should be very simple, illustrating to the audience that trust is a simple choice, though sometimes difficult because of our human nature. Pantomime is recommended so that the audience members participate imaginatively. This should help them focus on Tia's internal struggle.

Mentioning pantomime in the production concept instead of repeating it in every stage direction conveys it as an option rather than a mandate.

SCENE 1 A city park in springtime

It is early morning. A jogger passes occasionally. Sounds of birds can be heard. Marcus guides Tia to a park bench, where they sit down together.

Description is specific enough to be understood but allows for imagination on the part of the actors.

MARCUS:	Do you want to feed the ducks?
TIA:	What are you talking about?
MARCUS:	(*Reaches into his knapsack*) I brought some bread, and I just thought maybe—
TIA:	You wanted to feed the ducks?
MARCUS:	(*Hands her a piece of bread*) Here. Try it. It's fun.
TIA:	This is dumb, Marcus.
MARCUS:	Okay. (*Stands and walks a few yards to the water's edge. Tosses bread to the ducks.*) You go home and feel sorry for yourself, and I'll feed the ducks.
TIA:	That's not fair.
	(*Silence*)

Stage directions clarify important actions and identify needed props (whether real or pantomimed). Stage directions do not dictate tone of voice or attitude, which should come from the actor's characterization.

Summary

If you take part in creating a script, be sure to provide enough information to be clear. However, avoid overdoing it. Assume the actors will approach the script thoughtfully. Thoroughly and concisely communicate your ideas.

PERFORMING READERS THEATER

If you have never seen readers theater performed, it may be intimidating to think of participating. You will have the opportunity to participate in a practice activity before receiving a role assignment for your graded project. But first, consider the following techniques.

PRESENTATION

Performing Readers Theater

Work in Progress

Introduction. Workshops for Chapters 9-11 will involve coaching small groups. You will find it advantageous to establish a specific routine for class periods designated for workshops. A certain level of formality promotes classroom discipline. Balance good structure with enough flexibility to encourage participation and creativity. The goal is controlled, meaningful participation.

Process. Ways you might establish order include maintaining a typical opening to class time, reminding students of their expected conduct, and promptly enforcing classroom policies when needed. In other words, make sure your students do not equate leaving their desks and communicating in groups with recreation rather than a valuable learning process. To motivate good behavior, you may wish to grade students based on participation and conduct, averaging this grade into their overall homework score.

Of course, you will also need to establish an atmosphere conducive to participation. With some classes, the students' eagerness will motivate them whenever you designate time for the activity. However, with quieter, more reserved students, you may need to build rapport to encourage less-inhibited participation.

Lesson Motivator

Traditional readers theater may call for stylized delivery. For example, several readers might speak simultaneously or overlap one another. They might speak atonally or use carefully chosen pitches to convey an abstraction. Many of these techniques would be confusing in another setting, but when carefully rehearsed by oral readers who truly listen to each other, the effect is often impressive.

Chamber theater is often much more like a play. Delivery may be completely natural—conversational. Only the presence of a narrator reminds the audience that this story comes from prose or poetry rather than a play.

Modified readers theater falls in between these two.

The important thing is that the style of the performance match the mode of performance. If the scene is realistic and set in a modern living room, a chanting chorus will be distracting! If you use nonrealistic elements to convey more abstract or even "public speaking" segments of a script, aim to make the whole script theatrical. The resulting unity will improve the effectiveness of your communication. See the notes with the scripts in Appendix G for further information.

Techniques

You, the reader or interpreter, must use phrasing, emphasis, and subordination to communicate the basic ideas and the natural speech cadences. Use aesthetic distance, visualization, and word color to transport your audience to the world of the story. Vitalization helps maintain the audience's attention. Observation, concentration, and realization will help you to perform in a realistic and natural manner, as suits the literature. Illusion of the first time will be the natural product. You and the actors will make choices about how to handle first- or third-person narration as well as characterization.

In addition to the techniques of oral interpretation you have previously studied, readers theater may involve choric speaking, narrating, and offstage or onstage focus.

Choric Speaking

The use of a chorus—a group of speakers—characterized Greek drama, an early form of theater. The chorus commented on the story, approving or disapproving of the characters' actions. Though the chorus is no longer used in plays, the technique of speaking as a group may be used in readers theater. **Choric speaking** can create a dramatic effect if used well.

definition

In **choric speaking,** *several readers speak together.*

You could use choric speaking to perform short portions of text with significant sound quality or great importance. For example, if you staged Edgar Allan Poe's poem "The Bells," you might use choric speaking for phrases such as "the ringing and jingling" since these words convey many overlapping sounds. The variety of vocal tones in the group would emphasize the idea.

Narrating

A simple way to assign narration is to assign all necessary narrative passages to one actor and cut the rest. If the story is narrated by a distinct storyteller type of character and one of the performers can convey that personality, this choice is ideal. However, don't be limited to that choice. You could have two narrators to reflect multiple viewpoints or allow every actor to present narration related to his character.

Avoid assigning narration randomly. The assignment must be artistically meaningful. "Too much for one person to memorize" is not a good reason to divide narrative passages.

Interpretation Skills
• Thought units
• Phrasing
• Emphasis and subordination
• Aesthetic distance
• Visualization
• Word color
• Vitalization
• Observation
• Concentration
• Realization
• Illusion of the first time
• Characterization
• First- and third-person narration

Some simple techniques may prove useful in your classroom:

1. Meet in a different room larger than your typical classroom so you have adequate space to form groups and spread out. (Moving to the school's gym or auditorium may hold the added advantage of not disturbing other classes with noise.)

2. Prearrange several seating areas without desks. (Chairs, stools, or even a spacious bare floor are all preferable to desks.)

3. Use a few physical and vocal warm-ups at the beginning of class. (See Warming Up to Acting on pp. 241-42 for ideas.)

Most importantly, make workshops an opportunity for trial and error, a time for learning, not performing.

Feedback. Since workshops should not be weighted more than homework or quizzes, do not feel pressured to include large amounts of feedback. You may wish to give oral feedback during the workshop and simply make sketchy notes to remind the student of what you said. For group projects, focus on evaluating individual work at the workshop and then focus on the group effort for the final grade.

The narration in Frank Stockton's "The Lady or The Tiger?" can be meaningfully divided. Compare the first paragraph of the original text below to the first part of the script that follows. The entire script appears in Appendix G.

Original Text

In the very olden time there lived a semi-barbaric king, whose ideas, though somewhat polished and sharpened by the progressiveness of distant Latin neighbors, were still large, florid, and untrammeled, as became the half of him which was barbaric. He was a man of exuberant fancy, and, withal, of an authority so irresistible that, at his will, he turned his varied fancies into facts. He was greatly given to self-communing, and, when he and himself agreed upon anything, the thing was done. When every member of his domestic and political systems moved smoothly in its appointed course, his nature was bland and genial; but, whenever there was a little hitch, and some of his orbs got out of their orbits, he was blander and more genial still, for nothing pleased him so much as to make the crooked straight and crush down uneven places.

Dramatis Personae

NARRATOR 1 (N1), the voice of dignity
NARRATOR 2 (N2), the voice of the barbaric
THE KING
THE PRINCESS
THE YOUNG MAN, who dared to fall in love with the princess

Script

N1: In the very olden time there lived

KING: a semi-barbaric king,

N1: whose ideas, though somewhat polished and sharpened by the progressiveness of distant Latin neighbors,

N2: were still large, florid, and untrammeled,

KING: as became the half of him which was barbaric.

N2: He was a man of exuberant fancy, and, withal, of an authority so irresistible that, at his will, he turned his varied fancies into facts. He was greatly given to self-communing, and, when he and himself agreed upon anything, the thing was done.

N1: When every member of his domestic and political systems moved smoothly in its appointed course, his nature was bland and genial;

N2: but, whenever there was a little hitch, and some of his orbs got out of their orbits, he was blander and more genial still,

KING: for nothing pleased him so much as to make the crooked straight and crush down uneven places.

FROM PAGE TO STAGE 209

If one reader presented that entire paragraph, it might not hold the audience's attention. Dividing the narration allows the performers to emphasize different ideas. For example, the lines assigned to the king reveal his bold, confident style. Having two narrators helps feature the sense of conflict between what we may view as socially acceptable and what is acceptable to a "semi-barbaric" king.

Choosing the Focus

For your previous interpretation projects, you have used what is known in theater as **offstage focus.** As Figure 2 illustrates, if Carlos speaks to Greta, he should picture her above the heads of the audience members, directly in front of her stage location. The only time we might do this in real life is when we are facing a mirror and someone (perhaps a barber or sibling) behind us speaks to us and we reply, facing his mirror image rather than his face.

Though it may sound strange, offstage focus can be very powerful. The audience will have the impression of being in the middle of the conversation. In addition to sharing the actor's communication most completely with the audience, offstage focus is easy to stage and use consistently.

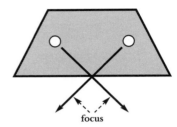

Figure 2. Offstage focus

definition

*In **offstage focus,** actors visualize their audience as a storyteller does with the dramatic "V."*

*In **onstage focus,** actors direct their dialogue to each other as we do in real life.*

Used in most plays and films, **onstage focus** refers to dialogue delivered as is typical in real life. Depending on the context, the speaker looks either at the listener or in his direction, and the listener usually looks at the speaker. The audience eavesdrops on the situation. This mode works well for a play or chamber theater scene set in a modern living room but wouldn't make sense in readers theater.

Offstage focus and onstage focus are often combined in modified readers theater and chamber theater. The example below is taken from "The Open Window" by Saki, scripted in Appendix G. The narrator makes observations, speaking to the audience as a storyteller or public speaker. Since Vera is addressing Framton Nuttel, she directs her comments to his mirror image. Nuttel both speaks to Vera and reveals his thoughts. His dialogue is delivered to Vera's mirror image and the rest is directed to the audience or aside.

NARRATOR: He made the last statement in a tone of distinct regret.

VERA: "Then you know practically nothing about my aunt?"

210 CHAPTER 9

NUTTEL:	"Only her name and address." He was wondering whether Mrs. Sappleton was in the married or widowed state. An undefinable something about the room seemed to suggest masculine habitation.
VERA:	"Her great tragedy happened just three years ago. That would be since your sister's time."
NUTTEL:	"Her tragedy?"
NARRATOR:	Somehow in this restful country spot tragedies seemed out of place.

Performance Choices

Now that you are familiar with some of the specialized techniques used in readers theater, you can begin making performance choices. First decide how to best convey your concept and then choose an environment for the literature.

Conveying Your Concept

If you use a script that suggests a production concept, try to incorporate it in every element. Consider the acting style— will the readers act realistically, using a conversational tone, or will they act in a stylized, theatrical manner? If you are producing a story such as the book *Cheaper by the Dozen*, which depicts the humorous conflicts of life in a large family, a natural acting style is appropriate. However, an outrageous comedy or a suspenseful story might call for stylized effects. Each of your sample scripts contains various suggestions for developing a concept.

> **Readers Theater Techniques**
> - Interpretation skills
> - Choric speaking
> - Narrating
> - Choosing the focus

Creating an Environment

The environment you create will likely be the first impression your audience has of your program. Since many theaters have stopped using curtains, the entire stage may have a preshow look for the audience to enjoy while being seated. This could involve specialized lighting, stylized props, and music or other sound effects. If a preshow set is used, it should convey something about the meaning of the production.

Set

The set itself will say a great deal to the audience. In some types of theater, grand spectacle is the emphasis. In readers theater and chamber theater, a more minimalist approach is usually preferred. A typical readers theater set uses various sizes of wooden boxes, stools, or simple chairs. For some chamber theater, a more illustrious set may be appropriate, as in a performance of "The Necklace," in which the conflict involves finery.

FROM PAGE TO STAGE 211

Perhaps the most important thing to remember when planning a readers theater set is that it doesn't need to be realistic, only sensible. For example, if you use an oblong black box to represent a sofa, pantomiming the use of a hand fan makes sense. If you use a real sofa, the pantomime will be interpreted as a mere gesture. Mixing styles causes confusion and sometimes humor, which is not always desirable.

Costumes

If you are performing traditional readers theater, neutral costumes are best. Possibilities include all black, black and white, or khaki and white. Even using these neutral colors can specify much about the setting of the story and the production concept. The garments could suggest a particular time period in history. For example, a modern story might use turtlenecks with monochromatic slacks or skirts. For an early nineteenth-century story, the women in the cast could wear neutral-colored empire-waist dresses; the men could wear black rubber boots over their slacks.

This approach is easier for ancient, biblical, and modern (1875 through the present) settings than for eras known for extreme styles. For example, not many of your friends will have anything that even resembles the ruffled collar worn in Elizabethan England!

Lighting

You may not have any options concerning lighting for performance and competition situations. If you put together a program for guests in your church or school auditorium, lighting could become very important. Even without sophisticated stage lights, you can create numerous effects by altering the level of light. Be creative with whatever resources you have at your disposal. For a Christmas story, actors could enter in the dark, carrying candles (battery-operated electric candles are the safest choice). For a program focusing on God's Word, consider borrowing several lamps or lanterns. Whatever choices you make concerning lighting, be sure they make sense and help carry the theme.

Sound

Some stories call for sound effects and wouldn't be complete without them. The British Broadcasting Company (BBC) sells an extensive digital sound library that will meet many theatrical needs. However, in readers theater, it can be very effective to create live sound effects. This possibility is suggested in several of the scripts in Appendix G.

You may also wish to incorporate music. If this is the case, plan far in advance of the performance so you have time to obtain permission.

 CHAPTER 9

Special Note

You may not play a copyrighted recording of music in a public performance without permission from the copyright holder. Of course, any music in public domain can be used freely. Remember that the song could be public domain, but if a musician recently recorded a new arrangement, that arrangement and the recording would be under copyright. If you purchase copies of sheet music, you have rights to perform that music live during the program, even for multiple performances. You may not perform the music live the first night and play a recording of it on succeeding nights.

Music can be a very powerful tool in drama. An appropriate selection can enhance the preshow as well as create atmosphere during the performance. The music should never overshadow the literature.

CONCLUSION

Readers theater is an exciting opportunity for creativity and teamwork. Patience, cooperation, and concentration will make your projects fun and rewarding for everyone. You will find the following selections for performance in Appendix G.

Traditional Readers Theater

- "Be Still and Know" adapted from Psalms 33, 46, 89, 93, 95, and 96
- "The Leaden Echo and the Golden Echo" by Gerard Manley Hopkins

Modified Readers Theater and Chamber Theater

- "The Lady or the Tiger?" by Frank Stockton
- "The Open Window" by Saki
- "The Blue Cross" by G. K. Chesterton

In each selection, you will see different possibilities for the art of readers theater. More than just doing an assignment, this is your chance to make the literature come alive for each member of the audience in a unique and rewarding fashion.

FROM PAGE TO STAGE 213

CHAPTER 9 REVIEW

Terms to Know

readers theater
traditional readers theater
modified readers theater
chamber theater
narrative literature

dramatic literature
production concept
choric speaking
offstage focus
onstage focus

Ideas to Understand

Multiple Choice: **Choose the best answer.**

_____F_____ 1. In readers theater and chamber theater, the text may come from
   A. biography, letters, and other similar materials.
   B. novels, short stories, and other prose fiction.
   C. plays.
   D. poetry.
   E. all of the above
   F. A, B, and D only

_____C_____ 2. Which of the following could best enhance your readers theater script?
   A. elaborate costumes   C. a well-integrated production concept
   B. professional stage lighting   D. none of these

True/False: **Write True or False for each statement. If false, cross out the word or words that make it incorrect and write in the word or words that make it true.**

_____False_____ 3. All readers theater is characterized by the use of scripts. ~~All~~ *Some*

_____True_____ 4. Traditional readers theater, modified readers theater, and chamber theater all must have narration.

_____False_____ 5. Narration must be delivered by a narrator. ~~must~~ *can* or ~~narrator~~ *any actor*

_____False_____ 6. Lyric poetry is ideal for chamber theater. ~~chamber~~ *readers*

_____False_____ 7. Choric speaking may be used only for narration. ~~only~~

_____True_____ 8. If one performer delivers the dialogue of a character and narration, he can use onstage focus for the dialogue and offstage focus for the narration to distinguish them.

Dramatistic Analysis of the Chamber Theater Selection

Title of play (or other selection) _____

Author _____

Sources (list in bibliographical form) _____

_____

_____

_____

Structure

1. **Whose story is it?** (personality and nature, purposes and goals, strengths and weaknesses of the central figure or figures)

_____

_____

_____

_____

_____

_____

2. **What are the circumstances?** (background, location, time, setting)

_____

_____

_____

_____

_____

_____

3. **What is the atmosphere of the story?** (mood)

_____

_____

_____

_____

_____

_____

FROM PAGE TO STAGE 215

4. **What is the climax of the story?**

_____

_____

_____

_____

_____

5. **What is the major dramatic question of the story?**

_____

_____

_____

_____

_____

Evaluation

6. **What is the theme of the story?** (the moral or central truth)

_____

_____

_____

_____

_____

7. **What is the worldview and tone?** (Refer to Chapter 3 if needed.)

_____

_____

_____

_____

_____

8. **What is the purpose of the story?**

_____

_____

_____

_____

216 CHAPTER 9

Chamber Theater Assignment Sheet

Prepare

Due Dates

_____ Workshop

_____ Dramatistic analysis

_____ Performance

Remember to mark the script and submit it to your teacher!

Practice

Evaluate yourself on a scale of one to ten in each of the following areas, rating your current effectiveness in each skill. One is weak, five is moderate or adequate, and ten is excellent. Explain your evaluation.

_____ Narration _____

_____

_____ Onstage Focus _____

_____

_____ Offstage Focus _____

_____

_____ Character Portrayal _____

_____

Set goals for each practice session such as "polish delivery of the narration." Chart your progress here. Include individual and group rehearsals.

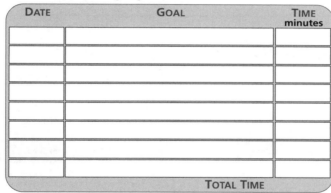

DATE	GOAL	TIME minutes
	TOTAL TIME	

FROM PAGE TO STAGE 217

The extent to which you develop the readers theater scripts as a project should be based on your class schedule and level of interest in staged literature. It may be equally appropriate to use the readers theater scripts as a complete project or perhaps just as a class exercise.

The chamber theater scripts should be given as much class time for workshops as you would give to rehearsing an equal-length portion of a play intended for public performance. Your students cannot be expected to meet with several other students outside class to rehearse. The most they can realistically do independently is review and memorize their lines and cues and strengthen their characterization. If you have kept a good pace throughout the semester, spending this extra time should not be a problem.

Performance Days

For a class of fifteen students, you will probably need most of a class period for the readers theater performances and a full class period for the chamber theater performances.

Project Checklist

For the readers theater and chamber theater projects, you will need to select due dates for each of the following components:

1. Readers theater role assignments
2. Readers theater roles studied
3. Readers theater workshop (date or dates should overlap with students' learning their roles)
4. Readers theater performance
5. Chamber theater role assignments
6. Dramatistic analysis
7. Chamber theater workshop (students should be very familiar with their lines)
8. Chamber theater roles memorized
9. Chamber theater performance

The Evaluation Form

When comparing the evaluation form for the chamber theater project with that of the storytelling project, you will note numerous differences. Only one category remains identical—narration. *Characterization* has been modified to *characters*, since this is a scene rather than a solo performance using the dramatic "V." Other new categories deal with teamwork: unity, focus, (group) energy level, communication, and staging. Also, instead of a category to rate the written work, an *Improvement* category appears at the bottom so each student can receive individual feedback.

The recommended approach to grade with this form is as follows: Make comments about a scene on one form, even though the scene may have four or five students involved. If you think you will forget individual comments, write them on separate paper. As soon as it is convenient, photocopy the rubric containing your comments for the whole scene— one for each student in that scene. Then write their names at the top and give individual comments in the last section. Each student's grade should primarily reflect the quality of the scene as a whole but include his individual effort as well.

Participants _____
Title of Scene _____

Teamwork		Comments	Pts.
Unity	4 Cast members function very well together 3 Cast members function reasonably well together 2 Some cast members work well together 1 Cast seems somewhat disjointed		
Focus	4 Concentration very evident, very focused 3 Good level of concentration 2 Lacking concentration 1 Little or no concentration—unfocused		
Energy	4 Excellent energy level; full of vitality 3 Adequate energy level 2 Inconsistent or low energy level 1 Inadequate energy level		
Focus	(Plot, conflict, exposition, theme, etc.) 4 All elements of the story clearly communicated 3 Most elements of the story communicated 2 Some elements of the story clear 1 Many elements not completely clear		
Staging	4 Creative, effective, and improved from workshop 3 Adequately effective 2 Does not complement the text 1 Distracts from communicating meaning		

Interpretation			
Narration	4 Clear viewpoint; compelling style 3 Clear viewpoint; acceptable style 2 Vague viewpoint; acceptable style 1 Weak viewpoint; weak style		
Characters	4 Distinct, lifelike characters 3 Varied characters 2 Characters sometimes superficial 1 Characters not distinct or believable		

Individual Work			
Improvement	4 Utilized feedback to improve significantly 3 Some improvement shown 2 Little change from workshop quality 1 No improvement shown		

You demonstrate good ability in . . .	You would benefit from more attention to . . .

Total Points _____   Grade _____

218 CHAPTER 9

READERS THEATER PRELIMINARY WORKSHOP EVALUATION

Name _____ Scene _____

Note: You are ranked on a scale of 1-5, 1 being the lowest and 5 being the highest.

ELEMENT	COMMENTS	RANK
Teamwork		
Energy		
Focus		
Communication		
Creativity		
Interpretation		

Comments for individuals

SCORE

- - - - - - - ✂ -

CHAMBER THEATER FINAL WORKSHOP EVALUATION

Name _____ Scene _____

Note: You are ranked on a scale of 1-5, 1 being the lowest and 5 being the highest.

ELEMENT	COMMENTS	RANK
Interpretation		
Characterization		
Memorization		
Response to Feedback		
Improvement		
Energy/ Enthusiasm		
Overall Preparedness		

Comments for individuals

SCORE

FROM PAGE TO STAGE 219

Chapter 10 Introduction

Chapters 7 and 9 prepared students for this study of duo acting. Auditioning and solo interpretation provided a performance basis while the interpersonal skills learned from participating in readers theater provided good teamwork experience for acting on stage.

Effective acting hinges on cooperation. Good actors are not like piano soloists in concert but like members of the orchestra who blend their instruments' voices with many others to produce what no individual instrument can create. Recognizably, if an orchestral work makes only minimal use of a feature such as percussion, and the percussionists distract either the other musicians during rehearsal or the audience during performance, they have greatly damaged the effort, though their official "role" was small. Likewise, a minor character or minor characters in a play can have the same effect. Of course, in both cases, if an individual or group with a principal role fails to function well, the effects can be even more disastrous.

This chapter is an opportunity for you to continue teaching an important life skill: working with others. In the home, workplace, church, and school, people must cooperate, or little can be accomplished.

CHAPTER 10

Lesson Plan
Suggested homework is in **boldface.**

Lesson Description	Recommended Presentation	Performance Projects/ Written Assignments
I. Stage wise (p. 223)	TE—Moving on Stage; Tic-Tac-Toe; Motivated Movement	**TE—Moving Words** **ST—Assign the Duo-acting project**
II. The ABCs of acting (p. 229)	ST—Brotherly Love; **Picture It; Evaluating Stage Directions; Earnest Characterization** TE—What a Character!; Character Metaphors	**ST—Assign Journal 10** Duo-acting workshop
Assessment	Chapter quiz	**ST—Assign Journal 11** Duo-acting performance
Suggested teaching time: 10-11 class periods		

Romeo, Romeo, Dost Thou Know Thy Lines?

Come, for the third, Laertes, you do but dally.

Teaching Materials
- Slips of paper (if desired, for the What a Character! activity)
- Workshop rubrics (students submit their own copy)
- Performance rubrics (students submit their own copy)

Chapter 10 Goals

The student will be able to

1. Identify the three types of stages.
2. Explain stage-blocking principles.
3. Recognize action in a scene.
4. Create a stage character.

Conflicts Through Cruel Words

The play *Macbeth* by William Shakespeare teaches many lessons, one of them from the treacherous Lady Macbeth: "What's done cannot be undone" (V. i. 68). Of course, Lady Macbeth speaks about the irreversible consequences of murder, but when we hurt our friends through demeaning language or sarcasm, indeed, "what's done cannot be undone." You may want to read James 3 aloud.

OVERVIEW

Know—*Concepts*

Stages
  Proscenium
  Arena
  Thrust
The ABCs of bringing life to your acting
  Action
  Background
  Characterization

Grow—*Interpretation Skills*

Acting verbs
Blocking
Acting chemistry

Show—*Performance*

Duo acting

Hamlet by William Shakespeare (Bob Jones University Classic Players)

At some point in time, you may have hurt a good friend. Afterward you could think of little to say to that person you once told everything to. Even reconciliation didn't erase the scars, though it restored the bond you shared.

In the play *Hamlet*, Prince Hamlet and Laertes were friends until something terrible happened. Laertes' father was eavesdropping on a conversation between Hamlet and his mother. Hamlet assumed that the spy was his uncle, his father's murderer. Without hesitation, Hamlet stabbed the spy, only to find he had mistaken the man's identity. Even though conflicts between school friends seem minor by comparison, the relationships and the people are much the same.

When you approach a script to perform, it's easy to notice the differences between the play's characters and your own experiences. The life of a prince, for example, seems so far removed from the life of the average student. Don't begin by focusing on what is different. On your first approach to a script, look for similarities to your own life and knowledge. Try to predict what will happen next as you read so that you will better understand the action of the story.

This chapter describes theater spaces and the staging used in each space. It then deals with the ABCs of bringing life to your acting: action, background, and characterization.

PRESENTATION

Stage Wise

Moving on Stage

Introduction. In front of an audience, nervousness can mean that simple, everyday tasks may require extra thought and effort to be completed naturally.

Instructions. Take time in class to practice the tasks described below. If your students have difficulty completing spe-cific tasks smoothly, repeat those tasks as part of your warm-up routine until they are proficient. Instruct your students as follows:

Standing—Work for correct posture unless the scene or character demands otherwise. The actor should be able to stand comfortably against a wall. Heels, shoulder blades, and the back of the head should be touching or nearly touching the wall. Weight should be evenly distributed over the arches of the feet. (See *Sound Speech*, Chapter 10, for more detailed information.)

Walking—Feet should not be turned in or out. The head should not precede the body. The energy behind each step should come from the thighs, with the back leg pushing the body forward onto the front leg. The heel should touch before the ball of the foot.

Sitting/rising—After approaching your chair, rather than turning and looking, sit casually when the back of your leg

STAGE WISE

As an acting student, you will need to understand basic stage positions, types of stages, and the blocking techniques for each. A stage has nine basic areas. Each area has a name that reflects the actor's point of view, not the audience's. Imagine that you are standing in the very center of a stage, facing the audience seating. Half of the space is behind you and half is in front of you. You are also standing halfway between the two side edges of the stage, which is appropriately designated *center stage* or *CS*. The area to your right is *stage right* and is divided into *upstage right* or *USR*, *center stage right* or *CSR*, and *downstage right* or *DSR*. *Downstage* is in front of you, closer to the audience, and *upstage* is behind you. The center portion and the left-hand portion of the stage are divided in the same way. (See Figure 1.) Familiarize yourself with these abbreviations, since they are often used in staging notes.

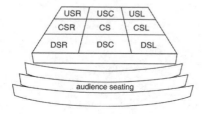

Figure 1. Stage Areas The abbreviations on the diagram frequently appear in written stage directions. For example, "Phil crosses DSL to confront the burglar." This should be spoken, "Phil crosses downstage left . . ." or "Phil crosses down left . . ."

Blocking

Novice directors and actors may view blocking as a mechanical requirement that has nothing to do with the art of acting. Actors are told to "always face the audience" and not to "stand in front of someone who is speaking." Although blocking involves some basic rules, it also involves art. In the context of drama, **blocking** refers to the relative positions and movements of actors on the stage set. Just as a photographer arranges his subject and chooses his angle and proximity, actors and directors block scenes in order to present powerful images to the audience. Good blocking creates a series of snapshots that tell the story of the play or opera as well as the text can. Some guidelines for blocking vary according to the type of stage and audience arrangement.

D definition

Blocking, when used as a noun, refers to the relative positions and movements of actors on the stage. As a verb, it refers to the process of choosing these positions and movements.

The Major Types of Stages

Though some stages do not fit into one of these categories, most professional stages are *proscenium, arena,* or *thrust* stages. Each is described and pictured below.

---

brushes the chair's edge. Generally speaking, avoid drawing attention to your action. Avoid sitting too far back in a soft piece of furniture; otherwise it will be awkward to rise gracefully. Always sit and rise with good posture unless your characterization demands otherwise.

Entering/exiting—You must assume your character before entering stage and maintain that role after your exit. Stay focused as you listen for your cue. Timing is crucial! For a group entrance,

the character who speaks first usually needs to enter first. Generally, you should confidently move to your first stage position upon entering. You may wish to cross to your exit location before completing your last line.

Opening/closing doors—Doors should be closed whenever they are not in use to avoid revealing the backstage area to the audience. Remember to keep yourself "open" to the audience by opening a door with your upstage hand when exiting.

Gestures—All stage gestures should appear natural but generally be planned. Extraneous movement is highly distracting. Gestures should never be sloppy or repeated many times unless a comic effect is needed. Imagine each gesture as having three components: movement away from the body, a specific position, and movement returning to the body. To suggest femininity and refinement, gestures should be detailed—finger and wrist movements are appropriate.

Lesson Motivator

Most of your students will be familiar with the proscenium stage, though they probably do not know the name. Arena and thrust stages might be quite new to them. Take time to discuss the photos and illustrations of each stage space. Nothing will better aid their understanding than a clear visual image of each type of stage. To almost as great an extent, studying pictures of blocking can open your students' eyes to the art of stage composition. Of course, two-dimensional depiction of blocking is not enough. You will need to get your students physically involved for their learning to be most effective. The suggested activities in this chapter should provide a good foundation for your teaching goals. Strong acting workshops will be necessary to complete the process.

Lesson Objectives

The student will be able to

1. Describe a proscenium stage.
2. Describe an arena stage.
3. Describe a thrust stage.
4. Define blocking.
5. Describe blocking appropriate for each type of stage.

It Looks So Natural!

Well-planned blocking is like a figure skater's routine. The audience watching may say, "It looks so easy!" Of course, figure skating is not easy. The skater made it look easy by planning and practicing well. Lack of preparation in such a sport can lead to disastrous consequences.

A good director will spend a great deal of time orchestrating the movement of the actors, who must, in turn, rehearse the movement numerous times. By opening night, the stage movement should seem motivated and natural—like real life. If the director doesn't insist on disciplined stage movement, a sloppy, awkward play production will usually follow.

Blocking That Communicates

Excellent blocking creates strong visual composition—an artistic element. More importantly, excellent blocking communicates. Remind your students that their first goal in using any performance technique is effective communication. One important principle to remember: keeping part of your face visible to the audience aids in properly communicating your message.

Blocking Basics

The following lists are not rules but *principles* to apply to your situation as needed. Remember that blocking must be both practical and artistic. Above all else, it must help you communicate your message.

More Emphatic/Effective	Less Emphatic/Effective
• Standing up	• Sitting
• Marching or walking with a confident stride	• Wandering
• Standing firmly	• Shifting your weight often
• Standing or moving in the upstage areas	• Standing or moving in the downstage areas
• Crossing in slightly curved lines	• Crossing in straight lines
• Crossing stage when delivering a speech	• Crossing stage while another character is speaking
• Gesturing with the arm that is farther from the audience	• Gesturing with the arm that is between you and the audience
• Face turned fully or partly toward the audience	• Face turned mostly or completely away from the audience

definition

*A **proscenium stage** presents the play's action on a stage visible to the audience through an arch or picture window.*

*The **proscenium arch** is a frame that separates the stage and the audience.*

The Proscenium Stage

A **proscenium stage** (pro SEE nee um) is located at one end of the room with the audience seating facing that stage. (See Figure 2.) A curved or rectangular frame called the **proscenium arch** separates the stage space and the audience seating. Usually a curtain is hung directly behind this arch.

Figure 2. The Proscenium Stage Notice that the proscenium arch creates a picture frame around the stage set. In most permanent theaters, the audience seating is on a rake, or slanted floor. The rake improves visibility for seats in the middle and back. Seating in the proscenium auditorium includes orchestra, or main floor, and possibly a balcony and boxes or tiers along the walls. The auditorium is referred to as the house or front of house.

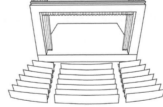

224 CHAPTER 10

Masculinity is better conveyed by free, full movements from the shoulder.

Tic-Tac-Toe

Introduction. Students will definitely need review and reinforcement to remember the principles presented in Blocking Basics. Ideally, you should complete this drill on a platform or stage.

Preparation. If only your classroom is available, move chairs to one end. On the available floor area, mark off the nine stage areas with masking or glow tape (lines that form a grid or at least a mark in the middle of each area). Divide the class into two teams (the Xs and the Os).

Procedure. Tell the students they can place an X or an O by correctly answering a question about effective blocking. When a correct answer is given, a member of that team may take his place on the "tic-tac-toe" board by identifying which stage area he wishes to occupy. If he fails to name a real stage area (i.e. "downstage left") or if he walks to a different area than he called, he forfeits the spot. The other team now has the opportunity to answer a question. If students frequently misidentify the areas of the stage or are unable to answer a good percentage of the questions, you may wish to play more than one time. (You may notice that the first questions require factual knowledge. The rest require application and evaluation.)

A proscenium stage allows the audience to see through an invisible "fourth wall" to the rest of a room or an outdoor scene. This creates a sense of detachment.

If an actor then speaks directly to the audience or steps in front of the proscenium arch, he has broken the fourth wall and has broken the audience's sense of distance from the action. Sometimes a clown or another character will deliver an *aside*, or a line to the audience. This reminds the audience members that they are not observing real action, but theater.

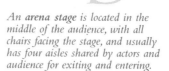

*An **arena stage** is located in the middle of the audience, with all chairs facing the stage, and usually has four aisles shared by actors and audience for exiting and entering.*

Christmas Vespers 2000.
The curtain rises to reveal a beautiful parlor. The mantle is trimmed with seasonal decorations. A tall evergreen, partially decorated with satin balls and white lights, stands in the middle of the room.

The Arena Stage

Arena stages place the actors in the center of the audience seating. This is similar to the athletic stadium concept, though the playing space is much smaller.

Also called theater-in-the-round, an **arena stage** allows the audience to surround the actors. For an actor who has never performed in this space, challenges include blocking, which is radically different from proscenium blocking, and the proximity of actors to the front row of the audience. Also, stage lights may partially illuminate the audience members, making them more a part of the actor's experience. (See Figure 3.)

Because of the effect of the fourth wall, proscenium stages are ideal for realistic stories. Realistic drama characterizes most film and television drama. Nonrealistic drama includes forms such as readers theater, in which the actors may directly address the audience. In realistic plays, characters usually speak to one another, not the audience.

Many operas and classic plays are produced in a proscenium-stage theater, an ideal form for a play or opera with an elaborate set. Although the arch may be missing, many schools and churches have auditoriums based on the same concept since it is appropriate for public speaking as well as musical and dramatic productions.

As You Like It by William Shakespeare.
The audience sits on all sides of a simple square stage with only two white urns, each containing several white hellium-filled balloons. A circle is painted on the floor.

ROMEO, ROMEO, DOST THOU KNOW THY LINES? 225

Questions. (True/False) Note: these questions all assume a proscenium stage—audience all facing the stage from one direction.

1. You should move from one area to another in a curved line. (*True*)

2. Since you need to be in the right place for your next line, you should move to that location while another actor is saying his line. (*False—such movement will be distracting to the audience. Move when you are speaking*

to reinforce your own words. If one person is moving and another is speaking, the audience is more likely to notice the movement than the speech.*)

3. Small movements such as shifting your weight help keep the scene natural rather than "too stiff." (*False—extraneous movement detracts from the scene and your speech.*)

4. Walking with a confident stride adds emphasis to a speech. (*True*)

5. The actor who is speaking with his face turned mostly or fully away

from the audience can effectively heighten suspense throughout a scene. (*False—the audience will not understand the words of a speaker who faces away from them. They will quickly lose interest in what he does as well.*)

6. Rising from a seated position calls attention to that actor. (*True*)

7. Being seated in a very visible place, such as a large throne, can be as emphatic as standing. (*True*)

8. If an actor is USR facing CSL, he should predominantly use his right

The New Globe

Staged as an authentic Elizabethan production, *Henry V* was one of the two opening productions in the New Globe's opening season in the summer of 1997. Costumes were Elizabethan period dress, and men played both male and female roles. The director was Richard Olivier, son of the renowned Shakespearean actor Sir Laurence Olivier.

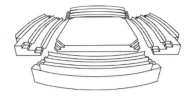

Figure 3. At first, audience members may find it startling to look past the actors and see another part of the audience. However, a well-staged play will soon consume their attention. By the end of a production in an arena theater the audience members feel that they have met the characters personally.

Practically speaking, an arena-stage set cannot include towering set pieces such as stairs, walls, or high furniture. The actors would be obstructed from the audience's view. Though furniture such as a desk or sofa may work, often very little furniture is used at all. Keep in mind that without a curtain it is more difficult to change the set between scenes. Plain chairs or benches can more easily suit various locations for different scenes than finely detailed furniture.

The Thrust Stage

Sometimes a stage protrudes out into the audience so audience members are seated around three sides of the stage. (See Figure 4.) This is known as a **thrust stage.** This type of theater space combines some of the qualities and benefits of proscenium and arena. Upstage, there is room for some spectacle such as tall scenery, furniture, and stairs

definition

*The **thrust stage** allows for audience seating on three sides, but retains one side that may be used for backdrops, as is typical of proscenium theater.*

Much Ado About Nothing *by William Shakespeare. Behind the proscenium, flats painted with white and gold jungle animals suggest portions of a wall (upper left corner). The floor is painted with "grass" and "cobblestone." Potted plants and two patio chairs dress the set.*

behind the proscenium arch. Of course, furniture used downstage must not block the audience's view of the action. Dramatic effects may be created as actors or objects upstage are lit from behind, making them appear in silhouette. Like the arena stage, much of the thrust stage is very close to the audience, creating an atmosphere in which the audience is very involved with the action.

Perhaps the most famous thrust stage was Shakespeare's Globe, which was rebuilt in the 1990s as The New Globe. Much of that stage protruded into the center of the seating. Some audience members paid a lower fee and had to stand throughout the performance, sometimes leaning on the edge of the stage. Wealthier patrons occupied three tiers of seating that surrounded the stage.

Figure 4. The thrust stage and audience seating.

226 CHAPTER 10

---

arm for gesturing. (*False—he needs to use his left arm so that he doesn't obstruct the audience's view of his face.*)

9. If numerous pairs of actors are simultaneously engaged in movements, such as fencing, and one actor stands perfectly still USC, that actor will go unnoticed by the audience. (*False—the stationary actor will be noticed because his action is different.*)

10. If a conversation is occurring principally in the center area of the stage, another character who is eavesdropping should enter upstage of the conversation and remain in a location visible to as much of the audience as possible. (*True*)

11. If about a dozen actors are watching two actors fence, the fencing actors can be in any stage area in which they are visible to the audience and still be the focal point for the audience. (*True*)

12. Picture a sofa CS, angled to face DSL. Two actors are seated on the sofa, looking at an actor seated in an armchair DSL. Another actor enters and stands full front near the US end of the sofa. This fourth actor has taken the focus. (*True*)

13. If a king is going to knight a soldier, he might stand upstage at an angle from where the soldier kneels facing him. (*True*)

14. If a mother character and a child character (child is seated downstage of mother) are seated on a bench facing DSR and the child

Specialized Blocking for Each Type of Stage

Though the general rules of blocking discussed in the Blocking Basics box (p. 224) apply to all stages, each type of stage has unique benefits and challenges for the staging process. These issues are explained below.

TYPES OF STAGES	
Stage	*Description*
Proscenium	"Fourth wall"; picture window; audience faces stage located at one end of the room
Arena	"Theater-in-the-round"; minimal scenery; actors are closer to the audience
Thrust	Retains proscenium arch but has audience on three sides of the stage; combines elements of proscenium and arena

Proscenium Blocking

When acting on the proscenium stage, you need to have at least part of your face toward the audience to be heard and understood. Therefore, if your partner has a big speech or an important line coming up and needs to be able to see you during this line, don't stand farther upstage than he stands. You would prevent him from being open to the audience proper. Study the following diagrams (Figures 5-8.) that depict strong proscenium blocking positions as well as potential weaknesses in the staging.

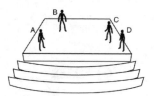

Figure 5. In this picture, actor B is the key figure in the scene. He may be delivering a long line or an informal speech.

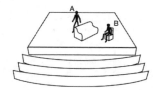

Figure 6. A living room scene. Here, actor A dominates the scene. Actor B is intimidated by actor A.

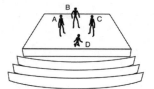

Figure 7. Actor D appears to be at the mercy of actors A, B, and C, perhaps in the context of war or persecution.

Figure 8. A kitchen scene. Here, actor A is dominant and may represent a parent of the person seated.

 ROMEO, ROMEO, DOST THOU KNOW THY LINES? **227**

---

character begins to cry, the mother character should use mainly her left hand to comfort the child. (*False—she needs to use her right hand or the audience's view will be obstructed.*)

15. If two characters are having an argument, they should both stand still because movement will weaken the verbal action. (*False—they can actually reinforce the argument through movement. Whoever has the "upper hand" on a given line should have the stronger stage position.*)

16. Six people are dining on stage. Two actors effectively enter from US to ambush the group. (*True*)

17. Stage directions call for two park benches and a slender tree for the setting of the play. Ideally, the benches should be placed parallel with the front of the stage for good visibility. (*False—an angle will create more visual interest and better blocking opportunities.*)

18. Your scene requires a kitchen table and four chairs—three of which

will be occupied simultaneously during the scene. The chair facing US should be the extra chair. (*True*)

If you need more questions, create your own scenarios or randomly read bulleted items from the "Blocking Basics" chart.

Lesson Motivator

Action and strong conflict are inherently dramatic. These ideas were introduced in the first unit of this text and will be discussed again in Chapter 11 in light of playwriting. It is most appropriate then that the "A" in the ABCs of acting is *action*. Action begins with a goal, often faces an obstacle, and results in conflict. This is true in life as well as on the stage. *Background* information has played a vital role since the first project. Each dramatistic analysis has featured questions concerning background. Finally, *characterization* is discussed in light of creating a stage role. Unlike creating characters in a dramatic "V," acting requires full embodiment. That does not imply that it is a more difficult task—just a different one. Let your students enjoy developing stock characters during the classroom activities since this will help them explore characterization possibilities with fewer inhibitions. However, for their workshop sessions, begin to steer them away from stock characters and toward more realistic, sincere characters. Certainly encourage a student who is already attempting greater depth of characterization for class activities. He will be one step ahead.

Now that you have seen several examples of proscenium blocking, consider how you might move from one position to another. This aspect of blocking is called **crossing**. When crossing, always remember to move in curved lines, not straight, and avoid being in a weak position, if possible. For example, don't walk in front of someone who is speaking or turn your back to the audience. These principles of crossing also apply to blocking on arena and thrust stages.

definition

Crossing means moving from one place to another onstage.

Arena Blocking

In arena blocking, actors in conversation stand farther apart than what is natural in real life. At first this seems awkward for an inexperienced actor, but soon many actors enjoy the style. On the arena stage, center stage is a weak position because only half of the audience can see your face. Standing in any corner facing center stage is an effective stage position. Make it your goal to have your face visible to as many audience members as possible. (See Figures 9-12.)

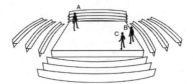

Figure 9. Either actor A or actors B and C were exiting when the other party called for his/their attention.

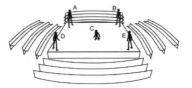

Figure 10. Here, actor C appears to be threatened by the other four actors.

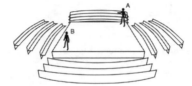

Figure 11. In this picture, either actor A is trying unsuccessfully to get the attention or forgiveness of actor B or actor A has asked actor B to report "what he can see" offstage.

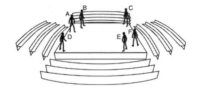

Figure 12. Actors A, B, E, and F might be pursuing or guarding actors C and D.

Thrust Blocking

When acting in the upstage area, many of the same rules apply from a proscenium stage. Keep in mind that the audience in the center seating section should not receive more emphasis than either side section.

228 CHAPTER 10

Use the previous questions to evaluate your student's understanding of blocking. Instead of creating a life-size tic-tac-toe board, draw one on a dry-erase board or on paper. Allow your student to place an X every time he gives a correct answer. You place an O when he answers incorrectly. You can still require him to verbally identify the stage area before placing his X. If he places the X in a different area, he forfeits that square and you should place an O.

Motivated Movement
Introduction. This activity can stand alone or be a technique for workshops. By limiting choices of movement, you can force students to concentrate on the motivation for the movement. This exercise is ideal for two actors but can easily be modified for three.

Instructions. Divide the class into pairs or casts of three. Assign approximately eight to ten lines from a play scene (Appendix H) to each cast. You may choose to use the same portion for each group. If using this technique for a workshop, simply have the students use a short portion from their own scene. Explain the rules of the exercise as follows:

1. You are standing on an invisible tightrope with your partner(s)— straight line for two, triangle for

When acting center stage or in any portion of stage near an audience, the principles of arena blocking apply. Often, you can communicate effectively by putting your back to the aisle you are standing closest to. (See Figures 13-16.)

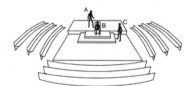

Figure 13. A throne room. Actor A portrays royalty, and actors B, C, and D are attendants listening to him.

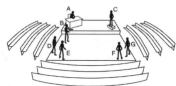

Figure 14. A throne room. Actor B is royalty or is claiming the throne. Actor C is addressing actor B but is showing appropriate response, though the two may be peers. Actor A may be guarding the throne or even ambushing actor B.

Figure 15. Actor D may be an investigator and actor A could be a police officer. Actors B and C are seeking help or being interviewed.

Figure 16. Actor A is a judge; B, a lawyer; C, the accused. Actors D, E, F, and G are spectators or accusers.

THE ABCs OF ACTING

Now that the stage is familiar to you, turn your attention toward the study of acting. In many ways, you will find acting similar to the interpretation skills you have already learned. Both employ imagination on the part of the performer and certainly on the part of the audience. Both try to create an illusion of that which does not exist. However, the interpreter *suggests* what the actor will seek to *embody*. The interpreter uses aesthetic distance to paint in minds; the actor often has the benefit of scenery and costume.

Some say that the interpreter's job is more difficult because he alone may be responsible to be the cast, crew, scenery, and so on. Others insist that acting is more challenging because the actor must walk in the character's shoes, so to speak. You may find one form more satisfying or enjoyable than the other.

three. Do not take this so literally that you pantomime a balancing act. Keep both feet on the floor and maintain normal posture.

2. On every new sentence or phrase, you have four major movement choices: (1) taking a step toward your partner, (2) taking a step away from your partner, (3) facing your partner, and (4) turning away from your partner. If your group has three, you can also change whom you are facing. You may also use two movements in combination. For example, you may turn away and take a step in that direction or remain facing your partner but still take a step away.

3. For each line, ask yourself: would my character be trying to get away from this other character or drawing closer to him/her?

An example. Read the example below to aid the students' understanding of the process. Notice that the dialogue is supplemented with recommended action—which is the goal of this exercise, as well as the action verb conveyed—which is discussed later in the chapter. The action verb is included here only as justification for the recommended physical action. If its presence seems confusing, skip it for the time being. Also remember that there are a variety of effective ways to convey most actions and emotions, not just the means suggested here.

You may wish to read just the actual dialogue aloud first and then read the

ACTING	INTERPRETATION
Performer and audience imagine	Performer and audience imagine
Tries to create an illusion of what does not exist	Tries to create an illusion of what does not exist
Seeks to embody	Seeks to suggest
Benefit of scenery and costume	Paints in audience's minds

Action

Imagine that you have entered a room during a lively discussion or a television program. You might say to someone there, "What's going on?" We expect that action has occurred and will continue. The same is true in music. No one listens to just one note for three and a half minutes and calls that a song. We expect a melody with forward motion. Athletic games also require action. Can you imagine a football game without it? Ticket sales would fall quite steeply, to say the least.

Action is a primary ingredient for all events. In order for events to occur, they must have action. In drama, as in life, action has three main components: goals, obstacles, and conflict.

Goals

In tales of the old West, the outlaw always wanted something, such as the money in the town bank. He had a goal. This goal by itself was not an action. However, all actions begin with a goal. I want a candy bar from a vending machine, or you want to meet your favorite mystery author. Leigh wants to be a neurosurgeon. We all have something in common—goals. When reading a play, try to understand the characters' goals.

First, determine a character's major goal for the entire play before evaluating momentary goals. For example, the bank robber's *major* goal is to get the loot. Additionally, each line conveys a smaller, *momentary* goal. If he says to a person in line at the bank, "Git outta my way," he is trying to *intimidate* that person. This builds up his "tough guy image." If he says, "I gotta gun here, so you better listen to me!" then he is trying to *scare* the people in the bank. "To scare" and "to intimidate" are actable goals, as are "to tease," "to excite," "to sadden," and "to cajole." For the purpose of our study, we will call these **acting verbs.** It is much easier to identify and then act out these momentary goals when you know the major goals.

 230 CHAPTER 10

---

dialogue again with the recommended actions. This will help students follow the scene better.

Character 1: Should I tell him? (*face and take one step forward—"to implore"*)

Character 2: How should I know? (*turn away but remain stationary—"to rebuke"*)

Character 1: I thought you could help me—advise me. I guess I was wrong. (*do not turn, but retreat a couple of steps—"to hurt" or "to discourage"*)

Character 2: I'm sorry. I just don't have all the answers anymore. (*turn and face Character 1—"to appease"*)

Character 1: Just when I needed you most. (*turn and walk several steps away—"to hurt" or "to manipulate"*)

Character 2: That's not fair and you know it! (*take a step toward Character 1—"to rebuke"*)

Character 1: Then what should I do? (*turn toward Character 2 quickly—"to intimidate" or "to challenge"*)

Character 2: Don't ask me. (*turn away—"to defy"*)

PRESENTATION

The ABCs of Acting

 Moving Words
Introduction. This activity could be completed in class or independently. Your students need to understand the connection

Brotherly Love

In the cutting below from *Cheaper by the Dozen*, by Frank B. Gilbreth and Ernestine Gilbreth Carey, all of the characters are siblings. Anne is the oldest child and Frank Jr. is her younger brother. Read this comic scene completely once. On a second reading, write a possible acting verb that identifies the goal of each line and is something you can do to someone. The verbs mentioned in the paragraph above are samples. If different sentences in the same line convey different goals, list more than one verb. Also, specify whom the action applies to. For example, for a line such as, "You know you lost the last race, Sarah. Why embarrass yourself again?" the acting verb might be "to discourage Sarah." The first two lines have been done for you.

Cheaper by the Dozen by Frank B. Gilbreth and Ernestine Gilbreth Carey, dramatized by Christopher Sergel

> The curtain rises and lights come up, revealing the living room of the Gilbreth home. It's an unusual room, for there are all sorts of charts, photographs, and maps on the walls. There are also an old telescope, a microscope, and other similar items. In many ways, the room seems ready for an illustrated lecture on almost any subject.

FRANK JR.: Hey, Anne—you had a phone call. It was a boy!

ANNE: Are you trying to tell the neighbors?

(She comes into the house through porch door.)

FRANK JR.: *(Delighted, pointing)* You're blushing!

(Frank Jr. turns to share the delicious news with his two younger brothers, Fred and Bill, who have started down the stairs.)

FRANK JR.: Hey, Fred—Bill—she's blushing! *(Back to Anne)* It was Larry Johnson.

ANNE: If you're teasing—

FRANK JR.: No, really.

(Anne is suddenly serious. Frank Jr. suppresses a giggle.)
He wants your notes on the Second Punic War.

(Fred and Bill have hurried up to peer at Anne. Now Fred turns to Frank Jr.)

FRED: *(Disappointed)* She isn't blushing.

---

between physical and verbal action. In real life, effective communicators reinforce their words with their physical action. On stage, the same should be true. Remind students that theater mirrors life.

Instructions. Have your students choose one of the scenarios below or invent their own. With a partner or alone, have them pantomime the story as realistically as if it were part of a play scene. The only difference should be absence of dialogue.

Scenario 1: (solo) You come to the kitchen looking for a snack and find a large container of chocolate chip cookies, freshly baked. Making sure that no one else is around, you take several, pour a glass of milk, and enjoy your snack. When you are almost finished, you hear someone coming. You hurry to "hide the evidence" and leave the kitchen before the other person arrives.

(duo) Proceed as above, but the second actor catches you trying to dispose of crumbs and pursues you around the

room in fury. Those cookies were intended for a party. The second actor indicates signs of that by pointing out packaged decorations on the table and so on.

Scenario 2: (solo) You are in the town library reading a book or searching on the computer. You read something very funny and accidentally laugh loudly. You immediately recognize that the librarian is glaring at you. You stifle your laughter and continue reading. What you are reading is so funny that

ANNE:	I hate, loathe and despise all of you.
	to hurt and rebuke her brothers
	(The two younger boys are astonished, and they look askance at Frank Jr.)
FRANK JR.:	(Explaining) She's hoping someone will go mad about her.
	to "egg on" or stir up Bill and Fred and to tease Anne
BILL:	(Incredulous) About her?
	to amaze himself
	(Frank Jr. nods.)
ANNE:	(Coldly, demanding) What's so ridiculous about that?
	to reprimand or intimidate Bill
BILL:	Nothing, only—
	to defend himself
ANNE:	If you've anything to say—
	to compel or to intimidate
BILL:	I just wouldn't think you'd have that sort of effect on anybody.
	to defend himself and to tease Anne
FRED:	And we've known you all our lives. (Being fair) Of course, some boy who doesn't know you so well—
	to assure Anne; to encourage Anne

By now, you should see that identifying the action for each line can be very challenging, but the task really improves comprehension of the scene and makes rehearsing the scene much easier.

Obstacles

Did the outlaw have the bank's money when the story began? Of course not. If he did, there would be no story. He is faced with an obstacle: the sheriff. Having no money would be the obstacle to my candy bar hope. If the author you want to meet has a book signing while you're out of town on vacation, you are faced with an obstacle. Anything that opposes a character's pursuit of a goal is an obstacle, not just visible barriers. Most goals in life have obstacles. All well-written drama contains obstacles.

Conflict

As was discussed in Chapter 2, *conflict* is a major element of a story. Two wills clash. Someone has a goal; someone or something presents an obstacle to that goal. Conflict results. When you read a play or a scene for the first time, look for the conflict. Conflict moves the muscle of action.

> **Action: Three Main Components**
>
> **Goals**
>   Characters have one major goal, many momentary goals.
> **Obstacles**
>   Obstacles are anything that opposes a character's pursuit of a goal.
> **Conflict**
>   Conflict occurs when an obstacle meets a goal.

this happens again. This time you quickly exit to avoid the librarian, who seems very upset with you.

(duo) Proceed as above, but have a second actor play the librarian and approach the laughing individual, first as a reprimand and then to ask the individual to leave.

Scenario 3: (solo) You are visiting a friend's home for the first time. A younger sibling comes to the door and leaves you in a casual living room alone while he calls your friend from another part of the house. You find yourself alone with an exotic pet. Respond to his curiosity about you and your movement.

(duo) Proceed as above, but this time, your friend enters just in time to "catch" the pet, which is pursuing you around the room. Make the chase lively!

Goals in Life

Ask your students to take out a sheet of paper. First, give them a minute to ponder their goals in life. Then give them three minutes to write three to five short-term goals and several long-term goals. Remind them to keep James 4:15 in mind as they write their goals: "For that ye ought to say, If the Lord will, we shall live, and do this, or that." Your students will need this paper for a later

Background

Obviously, not everything in a play will be just like your own experience. Even if this is your own biography on stage, it is still *not* your life; it is theater. Every story, including the story in every play, has a background. This background is an integral part of the action in presenting the plot. Think of the background as the skeleton that forms the story. The actions are the muscles that surround that skeleton. Background can be divided into two basic categories: previous action and current circumstances.

Previous Action

If you are playing in Shakespeare's *Henry V,* you must be aware that a great deal of action has occurred before Scene 1, both in factual history and in Shakespeare's other history plays. Much of the play will be lost to you if you have no knowledge of the previous action. For example, in the *Henry IV* plays, Prince Hal (Henry V's boyhood nickname) is depicted as a young man who wastes his time in Falstaff's company. When he ascends the throne, he rejects Falstaff's friendship. Though Falstaff never appears in the play *Henry V,* several scenes focus on his failing health, attributed to a broken heart. Lines such as "the king [Henry V] hath killed his heart" are baffling if you do not know about Hal's friendship with Falstaff.

This information can be obtained only through study. You should have at least a cursory knowledge of England's line of kings. Better still, you should know how Shakespeare depicted Henry and his father before this play.

You don't need to consult every source of material. Time doesn't permit that type of thoroughness. Some plays will need very little research in comparison to Shakespeare's works. You might choose a modern play that no one has summarized or critiqued or that is not based on a previous play.

The playwright may include an essay or at least a few paragraphs of notes to guide would-be directors and actors. These pages in the script are not a waste of your time. Read them! They may actually keep you from wasting time trying to make sense of the script.

Also, use textual clues, either in addition to research and the playwright's notes or instead of other resources if none are available. What subjects are discussed? For example, if World War II is mentioned, you should figure out what facts about it pertain to the story.

The play may contain *allusions,* or references to other events or works of literature. What allusions do you find in the script of your play? Characters' names, locations, and dialogue may all contain allusions. Make sure you truly understand what is going on in the story.

---

activity, "Obstacles to Goals." You may want the students to place this in their journals.

Obstacles to Goals

Ask your students to refer to their list from the "Goals in Life" exercise. Ask them to skim their list of short-term and long-term goals. Have them take out another sheet of paper. Tell them to pick out one of their long-term goals and write for two minutes on what obstacles they may face as they strive to fulfill that goal. You may want the students to place this in their journals.

What a Character!

Introduction. It has been said that "plot is character." Whether or not you agree, actions are a primary means of revealing personality, personal motivation, and so on. In other words, what you do reveals much about who you are. Have your students explore characterization by refining the actions that a particular character might perform.

Instructions. Below you will find a list of characters and a list of simple tasks. Randomly assign one character and one task to each student. If desired, you could write each on a slip of paper and allow them to draw one from each category. Remember, these are not group scenes. Interaction should be conveyed through pantomime only.

Picture It

Russia's great playwright Anton Chekhov wrote both stories and plays. Several of his most famous works are comedies, including the play *A Marriage Proposal*. In this play, a loud-mouthed, volatile man has a young-adult daughter with a temper and passionate disposition equal to his own. A neighbor visits and speaks first with the father, asking for permission to marry the daughter. The father is delighted that his daughter can marry a wealthy landowner. He calls the daughter and excuses himself. Meanwhile, the audience notices that the suitor is a very nervous, excitable person. While momentarily alone, he reasons aloud with himself that marriage will be good for him, with his weak heart. This girl is a good cook and a hard worker. She will be of great benefit to him, even if she is plain. Once the daughter appears, their conversation quickly turns into an argument over who owns the meadow land between the two family's properties. Both insist their families have owned the land for generations. The young man, shouting at this point, behaves as though his heart will jump right out of his suit. More chaos follows.

Below you will find a short cutting from *A Marriage Proposal: Western Style*, a play adapted by Tim Kelly from this famous comedy. This time, instead of a Russian countryside, the setting is the rustic American West. The mother is a slap-you-on-the-back type of cowgirl. The suitor is as nervous as ever. As you read, try to picture the action as well as the characters and scenery. Then answer the questions below.

LEM: I'll have a glass of the lemonade, if you don't mind.
to calm himself

MRS. TAUB: Help yourself. That's what it's there for.
to encourage Lem
(Lem moves to pitcher, pours a glass, gulps it down.)
Don't gulp. You'll get hiccups. (*Aside.*) If he's come to borrow money, I won't give him any. (*Directly.*) What's on your mind, Lem? Don't beat about the bush. Tell me.
to scold Lem; to assure or amuse the audience;
to encourage Lem

LEM: Uh . . . I, uh, have come to ask for the hand of, uh, your daughter.
to rouse or rally himself

MRS. TAUB: (*Delighted.*) You want to marry Natalie!
to excite Lem and herself

LEM: Yes, Ma'am.
to encourage or to assure Mrs. Taub

Allow several minutes for the students to brainstorm about presenting their characters. Their brainstorming should include improvisation. They should verbally and physically practice the role, ignoring the practice of their peers. Be sure to discipline a student who focuses on someone else's practice rather than his own. Have each student perform his character. At the end of the improvisation, the class should be able to identify both "who" and "what" about the scene.

Characters

refined household servant
elderly person with a cane
anxious business person
taxi driver
police officer
young parent leading a child by the hand
track star
department store salesperson
warehouse packer
maintenance worker
auto mechanic
fast-food restaurant cashier

student body officer
painter
tour guide
self-employed cosmetics consultant
campaigning politician
rancher
professional clown
pediatrician
heavy-weight champion
military officer
bum or hobo
others of your choosing

MRS. TAUB: You are the old-fashion boy. It's Natalie you should be talkin' to. (*Embraces him, kisses him.*) I've wanted this to happen for so long. I've always loved you like my own son. Why am I standin' here like a blockhead? (*Exits right, hurriedly.*) Natalie, Natalie!
to tease Lem; to delight Lem; to rebuke herself; to call Natalie

1. Describe a stage set that you think would be good for this scene.

   _____

   _____

   _____

   _____

2. Describe how you would present the characters in this scene (how you would costume them, for example). _____

   _____

   _____

   _____

3. What lines do you think would get the biggest laughs?

   _____

   _____

   _____

4. Did the presence of the suggested acting verbs help you better understand and picture the scene? Why or why not? _____

   _____

   _____

   _____

Current Circumstances

Knowing the previous action is part of understanding the background. You also must understand what is happening now and why it is happening. For most plays, especially modern works, your only source will be the text itself. Let's look at the two basic elements of the text: dialogue and stage directions.

Actions

raking leaves
beating cake batter
washing high windows
cleaning mud off car tires
ironing clothes
shopping for produce
straightening a messy desk
hunting for evidence of something
greeting a stranger
introducing one friend to another
shoveling snow

waxing a large tile floor with industrial equipment
riding a farm tractor
eating spaghetti in the presence of formally-attired guests
pinning a hem in a long skirt or slacks that someone is wearing
pruning roses
sawing a log
adjusting appearance before a job interview (hair, clothing, or possibly makeup)
beating dirt out of a welcome mat
arranging flowers

Discussion. Improve the value of this exercise by briefly discussing several specific pantomimes. What made them effective, memorable, and clear? How did each performer adapt his approach to the action based on the character he was assigned? (An elderly person with a cane certainly rakes leaves differently than an average high-school student.) Then have each student consider what he could have done differently or better.

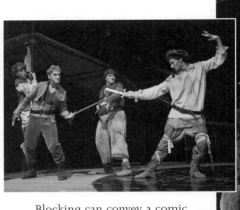

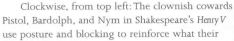

Blocking can convey a comic premise or a serious one. The composition depicting key moments may heighten the drama more than even the text itself.

Clockwise, from top left: The clownish cowards Pistol, Bardolph, and Nym in Shakespeare's *Henry V* use posture and blocking to reinforce what their costumes and dialogue already convey about their characters.

Use of two levels and dramatic down lighting create appropriate suspense for another scene in *Henry V* in which a thief is hanged.

Pip, the protagonist of *Great Expectations*, intercedes on behalf of his boyhood rival, Herbert Pocket. Magwitch's blocking makes the moment dramatic because it is clear that Herbert is at the mercy of his dagger.

In Charles Dickens's *Great Expectations*, adapted for stage by Robert Johanson, escaped convicts fight angrily in the marshes. Their blocking and use of props (prison chains) depict the immediacy and intensity of their conflict.

(All photos: Bob Jones University Classic Players)

236 CHAPTER 10

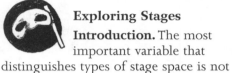

Exploring Stages

Introduction. The most important variable that distinguishes types of stage space is not the space for the actors but the location of the audience. If the entire audience is seated facing one direction, your stage will have to be designed and blocked as a proscenium stage, even if you have no proscenium arch or wall to separate backstage from the seating area. Likewise, if the seating surrounds half to three-quarters of the acting area, thrust scenery and blocking is needed. Of course, an audience that surrounds the stage requires arena blocking and no scenery high enough to obstruct their view from any angle.

To teach students how to respond to these three types of stage space, complete the activity below.

Instructions. Use your classroom chairs in various configurations to simulate the three types of stages if you do not have access to real examples of each type. Use the three-person scene provided in Teacher's Appendix 4 as a practice script. Use three students to block the scene for a proscenium audience. Other students should be scattered throughout the seating area. Instruct the students in the audience to raise their hands any time their view of important action is obstructed. When you reconfigure the chairs to create a thrust stage space, reblock the scene, possibly

Proximity and focus in blocking choices aid actors in conveying the story line as well as their characters' relationships to each other.

Clockwise, from top left: Stage lighting aids the blocking in creating stark contrasts of emotion in Diana Tobbe's *A World Twice Rich: Tales of Pericles the Prince*, adapted from Shakespeare's *Pericles*. The title character, Pericles, bids farewell to his beloved wife, Thaisa, as the nurse, Lychorida, soothes the newborn, Princess Marina.

Viola, disguised as a boy (Cesario), admires her master, Duke Orsino, who doesn't yet realize that his favorite servant is actually a shipwrecked heiress. This scene from Shakespeare's *Twelfth Night* simultaneously depicts a primary plot in the play—a love triangle that also includes the Lady Olivia (not shown), and the narrative role of Feste (top center), who freely comments insightfully on the behavior and foibles of his betters. (Bob Jones University Classic Players)

Blocking, aided by choice of props, establishes Sir Toby (far left), Sir Andrew, and Fabian as comic characters in this *Twelfth Night* scene. Viola's twin brother, Sebastian, defends himself against these strange men who mistake him for the boy Cesario. (Bob Jones University Classic Players)

Mr. Ribaldi claims the attention of his young voice pupil Bonnie in *Rigoletto: The Melody Within* (screenplay by Leo Paur; stage play by Jessica Nunez). This gentle move on Ribaldi's part contrasts with earlier raging to show multiple facets of his nature.

ROMEO, ROMEO, DOST THOU KNOW THY LINES? **237**

---

with different actors. Follow the same procedure for arena.

 If a sibling or other peer is available, assign one role to your student and one role to the other child, taking one role yourself. Complete the above activity, allowing time for discussion after each section. Ask questions such as "Do you think all of the audience members would have seen what was going on?"

and "How could we improve this scene's blocking for this type of stage?"

Dialogue

In nondramatic literature, dialogue is supplemented with narration, description, and exposition. In drama, dialogue carries most of the plot. With no narrator, each actor is highly responsible to convey the action through the dialogue. This may seem imposing, but in reality, we use words to convey action all the time.

Some things we say count as formal action. When we meaningfully say, "I'm sorry—I was wrong. Will you forgive me?" we have apologized. The words were an action. When we say, "I promise," we have made a vow, a commitment.

Though not always to such an extent, all meaningful dialogue has some intent to action. For example, "Do you need a ride?" may be making an offer to a friend who is walking several blocks to a store. "Help me!" could be a strong plea for assistance. Even an infant's cry urges you to do something. The baby cries because he wants something—milk, a toy, or attention. His goal may stump you, but his need is obvious.

As you read a play's dialogue, be constantly thinking about the actions motivating the words. By the end of your first reading of the scene, you should be able to tell a friend what happened, almost blow by blow. This is easier and more sensible than trying to repeat the actual dialogue.

Stage Directions

Stage directions include all of the information about the production as well as the instructions for the actors. Unfortunately, no other feature in all of drama has a worse reputation than stage directions.

definition

Stage directions include all production information and acting directions.

Some actors and directors have worked on plays with poorly written stage directions. They have also observed that classics such as Greek and Elizabethan dramas have few or no stage directions. Because of their experience, they have come to this conclusion: stage directions are worthless or even harmful. Although this may sound sensible, it is not true.

Greek and Elizabethan playwrights directed their own scripts. As directors, they gave oral instructions, so their plays didn't need written stage directions. Poorly written stage directions can generally be found in poorly written plays. If the stage directions are truly a waste of your time, the play may be as well.

Choose a well-written play and then trust the playwright to tell you how it can ideally be performed. If he can formulate a strong plot that is exciting to perform, he can provide useful stage directions. Consider a play about a rich, naïve young woman. Her fiancé never shows up when they are to be married. Years later, he returns and begs for her forgiveness. She agrees to elope with him. However, when the appointed time comes, she does not pack. She orders a servant to bolt the door. The man knocks. He calls her name. She breaks the thread on her embroidery, blows out the lights, and ascends the stairs. The play ends with him calling her name in desperation.

238 CHAPTER 10

Her actions as described in the stage directions are essential, controlling the end of the play completely. Well-written stage directions can do that. They convey action. Poorly written stage directions make unreasonable or useless demands on actors. Evaluate stage directions. If they further the plot or clarify interpretation, use them. If they suggest stage movement that is impossible on your stage set, try different blocking. Whatever you do, don't ignore a good playwright's directions entirely.

Evaluating Stage Directions

A strong stage direction is easily understood and proves helpful to the action of the play. A weak stage direction treats actors as mindless puppets or calls for action that might work on only one stage set. A weak stage direction may be controlling or just useless. Read the stage directions below and label each *strong* or *weak*.

1. He hides the rare coins. *strong* _____

2. She leans on the arm of the sofa, looking at him with raised eyebrows.
   weak _____

3. She does not answer. *strong* _____

4. Juliet drinks the potion. *strong* _____

5. He crosses to the front door, upstage left. *weak* _____

6. (A man is proposing marriage.) She yawns repeatedly. *strong* _____

Characterization

Your play script has clear structure (a skeleton) and motivated action (the muscles); now it needs characterization (the pulse). Remember, the novel reader can imagine the character's tone of voice. The storyteller's audience members can take the suggested characterization and further develop it in their minds. However, the theater audience must pretend that the actor *is* that character. The actor, then, has a great responsibility to characterize his role well.

Appropriate for the Role

In Oscar Wilde's play *The Importance of Being Earnest*, the manservant, Lane, has many lines such as "Yes, sir," "It never is, sir," and "Thank you, sir." These lines tell us about his character. The constant use of *sir* conveys something about his position in the household in comparison with the person with whom he speaks. The brevity conveys something about his nature in addition to emphasizing his position.

ROMEO, ROMEO, DOST THOU KNOW THY LINES? 239

Earnest Characterization

To learn more about a character's personality and how an actor might portray him, look at the other characters' lines. How do others describe him? How do others respond to him? How are they different from him? Read the two excerpts below and answer the questions that follow.

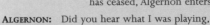

Scene: Morning-room in Algernon's flat in Half-Moon Street. The room is luxuriously and artistically furnished. The sound of a piano is heard in the adjoining room. Lane is arranging afternoon tea on the table and, after the music has ceased, Algernon enters.

ALGERNON: Did you hear what I was playing, Lane?

LANE: I didn't think it polite to listen, sir.

ALGERNON: I'm sorry for that, for your sake. I don't play accurately—anyone can play accurately—but I play with wonderful expression. As far as the piano is concerned, sentiment is my forte. I keep science for Life.

LANE: Yes, sir.

later

ALGERNON: Tomorrow, Lane, I'm going Bunburying [going to visit his fictitious friend Mr. Bunbury in order to escape activities he does not want to participate in].

LANE: Yes, sir.

ALGERNON: I shall probably not be back till Monday. You can put up my dress clothes and all the Bunbury suits . . .

LANE: Yes, sir.

ALGERNON: I hope tomorrow will be a fine day, Lane.

LANE: It never is, sir.

ALGERNON: Lane, you're a perfect pessimist.

LANE: I do my best to give satisfaction, sir.

*The Importance of Being Earnest
by Oscar Wilde*

1. Based on the fact that Lane *does* contribute to conversation, not just take orders, how would you describe his relationship with Algernon?

   They seem to be friends despite the difference in status.

2. Algernon seems to enjoy Lane's contribution to the conversation. What personality quality(ies) might cause Lane to speak shortly?

   He seems to be quiet and rather humorless.

3. Choose two sequential lines of Lane's dialogue. Write them in the space below. Describe the bodily movements and gestures you picture Lane using to communicate each line.

<u>Answers will vary but may include actions such as bowing the head slightly when</u>

<u>saying "Yes, sir" or maintaining an expressionless face and monotone quality.</u>

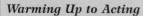

Warming Up to Acting

No one runs in a marathon without warming up first. We might run to catch a bus without preparing our bodies, but twenty-six miles is a different story. Public speakers, interpreters, and actors are in much the same position. Answering a question in class, reading a story to a child, or sharing a personal experience with your friends will not really need warming up to accomplish the task effectively. However, the longer the communication, the larger the audience, and the more movement involved, the more important warm-ups become.

Important reminder: be sure to find a place to warm up where you will not be seen or heard by the audience.

Benefits to Warming Up
- Reduces nervousness
- Improves clarity of thought
- Aids projection
- Improves use of body on the platform
- Makes diction clearer

Types of Warm-Ups
- *Movement*

If you are nervous or if you have been sitting still for a while before approaching the platform, a few basic stretches help loosen up your major muscle groups and relax you. Stretch your arms out to the sides and above your head. Relax your upper body forward from the waist up. Slowly roll from this slumped-over position until standing upright. Arm circles, neck rolls, and other relaxing stretches are also beneficial.

- *Posture and breathing*

Proper spinal alignment and appropriate physical stance are important for good posture. Some characters may require a deviation from ideal posture, but in general, start with normal, correct posture. (Your feet should be six to ten inches apart, knees loose, and pelvis tucked. In profile, your shoulders should be centered above the hips with your head back far

ROMEO, ROMEO, DOST THOU KNOW THY LINES? 241

enough to place the ears above the shoulder.) Also, for quickness of movement, keep your weight balanced over the arches of your feet, not leaning backward or forward.

Practicing good breathing is possible only after you achieve good posture. When sitting or standing tall or lying flat on your back, good breathing should be easy. If your body is slouched or bent over, you will lack breath support to speak or perform well. You may want to practice while lying on your back. Take deep breaths with either your hand or a book on your diaphragm, located right below your rib cage. If either your hand or the book moves up as you inhale and down as you exhale, you are breathing correctly. Work to fill your lungs on each breath. Obviously you won't take breaths this deep all the time, but you will take deeper breaths with less effort after this type of practice.

• *Voice*

Sometimes a person will describe his morning voice as "having a frog in his throat." When the voice goes unused, it may lack the quality and resonance it would otherwise have. This is equally true when a person switches from a low, conversational voice to projecting his voice for an audience. Often, humming with the mouth closed can improve the transition. Begin humming softly. Then slowly increase the volume and intensity. Call out brief words such as *hey* or *hi* with the intent of speaking to someone in the very back of the room.

• *Diction*

Even a public speaker with a small audience may need to use diction warm-ups. Even if you aren't nervous and don't need to project your voice very far, you can still get tongue-tied. Though not a guarantee, diction drills help most speakers dramatically. Practice several of the following phrases to improve your diction.

> *Blue blood, black blood*
> *She sells seashells by the seashore.*
> *The tip of the tongue, the teeth, the lips*
> *Aluminum, linoleum*
> *The wagon wheel wobbles wildly.*

You may find some of these warm-ups more helpful than others. For example, if you are a very relaxed person, the preliminary stretches may have little effect, but the diction drills may polish your communication. The more experienced the actor, the more refined the warm-up routine. As you rehearse and perform, try different combinations and see what works best for you.

Believable in the Plot

In addition to being appropriate for the role, an actor's characterization must be believable in the plot. Sadly, directors and actors sometimes fail in this area. Though *Hamlet* is a famous story, often evaluated in writing and frequently performed, many actors play Hamlet incorrectly. In one festival theater, an actor portrayed him to be mad or crazy from the first entrance. Somehow that actor missed the point—Hamlet *pretends* to be crazy to keep his uncle's spies, Polonius, Rosencrantz, and Guildenstern, from finding out that he has information about his father's death. Why should the audience sympathize with Hamlet if he is truly mad? Why would Ophelia have loved him? Little of the play makes sense if Hamlet's actions and wit are merely madness.

Natural for the World of the Play

If *The Importance of Being Earnest* were actually a serious drama, rather than a comedy, Lane would have to be played differently. Similarly, in the context of a **farce,** absurdity is the norm. Characterization must be handled appropriately. In Chekhov's play *A Marriage Proposal*, both the nervous young man coming to propose and his neighbor's daughter are willful people. More importantly, Chekhov has put them in a comic story line. When they begin arguing about which family owns the meadow between their properties, it should not make the audience fearful. The audience should be provoked to laughter. These characters must be played to suit the world of the play.

Definition

Farce is outrageous comedy.

Practical Approaches to Characterization

Once you understand what your character is doing and how he fits into the story, you can make decisions about how to characterize him. Of course, much of what you learned about characterization in oral interpretation can be applied. However, instead of suggesting several characters, you fully develop one. Review the information on characterization in Chapters 7 and 8.

One characterization technique that many actors find helpful is metaphor. Of course, in poetry a metaphor calls love a red, red rose and music the food of love. In the rehearsal process, an actor may consider what his character is similar to, since it is easier to concentrate on concrete, tangible objects than abstractions. If you find it difficult to think of a metaphor, give yourself a category such as "an animal" or "a type of tree" or "a color." Listed below are some descriptive words, one or more of which might fit a particular character. In the second column, there are possible metaphors, which are only suggestions. As you decide what adjectives (not necessarily from this list) apply to your character, choose an object that represents those characteristics. Several lines are blank for you to add your own ideas.

ROMEO, ROMEO, DOST THOU KNOW THY LINES? 243

Description	Metaphors
Gentle, sweet tempered, soft-spoken	A kitten; a peach
Energetic, vivacious	A puppy; neon green
Clever; dry sense of humor	A Siamese cat
Loud, brazen	An attack dog; a clanging iron bell
Highly motivated, stubborn	An unbroken colt
Jolly, warm-hearted	A life-sized teddy bear
Honest and strong; loyal	An oak tree; royal blue

CONCLUSION

As you approach your acting project, remember that a good actor is a good interpreter. Keep your interpretation tools handy. In this chapter, you have learned that acting requires constant attention to action; the background information allows you to make suitable performance choices; and the characterization makes the story real to the audience. As an actor, you do not just suggest the scene, as does the storyteller or reader; you must create it for the audience.

Character Metaphors

This activity should stimulate the students' imaginations as well as teach them a helpful tool for characterization. The chart on this student page lists various possible characteristics of a stage role as well as a possible metaphoric image for conveying it. Have students fill in the three blank lines. Then have them choose either one of their own ideas or one of the provided descriptions but with a new metaphor. Allow about five minutes of practice time for all of your students to move about the room and try to convey their chosen metaphor and the idea it represents. Have each student present his metaphor in turn. The class should be able to guess the metaphor and perhaps even the characteristic it represents.

Terms to Know

blocking	arena stage	action
proscenium stage	thrust stage	acting verbs
proscenium arch	crossing	stage directions
		farce

Ideas to Understand

True/False: **Write True or False for each statement. If false, cross out the word or words that make it incorrect and write in the word or words that make it true.**

True 1. Actions begin with goals.

True 2. A well-written story includes a hero meeting many obstacles.

False 3. ~~Only history~~ Many plays such as Shakespeare's *Henry V* have previous action.

True 4. Current circumstances can be understood from the dialogue and stage directions.

True 5. Dialogue conveys action in a play.

False 6. Stage directions are ~~seldom~~ usually worth reading.

True 7. Vocal warm-ups are helpful when speaking or acting for a large audience.

Short Answer: **Identify each of the following as proscenium, thrust, or arena stages.**

8. _Arena_ is also called theater-in-the-round.

9. _Thrust_ is actually a combination of the other two types of stages.

10. The audience sits on three sides. _thrust_

11. The audience sees through a "fourth wall." _proscenium_

12. Part of it resembles a picture frame. _proscenium_

13. The audience surrounds the stage. _arena_

14. The audience faces one direction. _proscenium_

15. Actors in dialogue must stand much farther apart than what is typical of natural conversation. _arena (thrust is also a reasonable answer)_

16. Center stage is the weakest position. _arena (thrust is also a reasonable answer)_

ROMEO, ROMEO, DOST THOU KNOW THY LINES? 245

DUO-ACTING WORKSHOP EVALUATION

Students _____

Scene _____

Characters _____

Note: You are ranked on a scale of 1-5, 1 being the lowest and 5 being the highest.

ELEMENT	COMMENTS	RANK
Interpretation		
Characterization		
Memorization		
Response to feedback		
Improvement		
Energy/Enthusiasm		
Overall prepared-ness		

Comments for individuals

SCORE

246 CHAPTER 10

Dramatistic Analysis of the Duo-Acting Scene

Play title, act and scene _____

Playwright _____

Characters (list of who is playing each) _____

Sources (list in bibliographical form) _____

_____

_____

_____

The Structure

1. **Whose story is it?** (personality and nature, purposes and goals, strengths and weaknesses of the central figure or figures)

   _____

   _____

   _____

   _____

   _____

   _____

   _____

2. **What are the circumstances?** (background, location, time, setting)

   _____

   _____

   _____

   _____

   _____

   _____

   _____

3. **What is the atmosphere of the scene?** (mood)

   _____

   _____

   _____

   _____

   _____

ROMEO, ROMEO, DOST THOU KNOW THY LINES? **247**

4. **What is the climax?** (of the whole play, if you know, and of your scene)

_____

_____

_____

_____

5. **What is the major dramatic question of the play?**

_____

_____

_____

_____

Evaluation

6. **What is the theme of the play?** (the moral or central truth)

_____

_____

_____

_____

7. **What is the worldview and tone?** (Refer to Chapter 3 if needed.)

_____

_____

_____

_____

8. **What is the purpose of the play?**

_____

_____

_____

_____

248 CHAPTER 10

Duo-Acting Assignment Sheet

Prepare

Due Dates

_____ Scene selection

_____ Teacher checks your manuscript

_____ Dramatistic analysis

_____ Title

_____ Introduction

_____ Performance

Resubmit your manuscript after performing. Your teacher will consult it while grading your work. Remember to mark your script with acting verbs and blocking notes and to submit it to your teacher! Write a rough draft introduction on the lines below.

_____

_____

_____

Practice

Evaluate yourself on a scale of one to ten in each of the following areas, rating your current effectiveness in each skill. One is weak, five is moderate or adequate, and ten is excellent. Explain your evaluation.

_____ Motivated actions _____

_____ Characterization _____

_____ Teamwork _____

Set goals for each practice session, such as "work on blocking" and "define characters more clearly." Chart your progress

DATE	GOAL	TIME minutes
	TOTAL TIME	

ROMEO, ROMEO, DOST THOU KNOW THY LINES? **249**

The Duo-Acting Project

If preparing for forensics is an important goal for your students, you may wish to repeat this project. Have all students choose a partner and a dramatic scene to perform. After completing the process, have your students switch to a new partner and choose a comic scene. (Of course, you may choose to have students work on comic scenes first.)

In addition to the selections in Appendix H, you will need to select scenes from other plays. Consult Teacher's Appendix 2 for titles. You may find it necessary to choose several three-person scenes to create more options for quality material and reduce the amount of time required for the additional project.

Appendix H

You may wish to select scenes of your own choosing to supplement the options provided.

Performance Days

The duo-acting scenes will probably require two class periods to perform.

Project Checklist

For the duo-acting project, you will need to select due dates for each of the following components:

(The assignment sheet and marked script could be checked on the day the student speaks.)

1. Several acting scenes surveyed (read)

2. Dramatistic analysis

3. Duo-acting workshop

4. Assignment sheet

5. Marked script

6. Duo-acting performance

The Evaluation Form

When comparing the evaluation form for the duo-acting script with the chamber theater script, you will find only one feature changed (and *focus* in now called *communication*). Under the general heading Interpretation, *narration* has been replaced by *action*. Since the acting scenes contain few or no narrative elements, you will probably not need to comment on the topic. On the other hand, action is primary to a play—without it there is no drama. You may wish to assign a higher point value to that category.

Play Title _____

Participants _____

Teamwork		Comments	Pts.
Unity	**4** Cast functions very well together **3** Cast functions reasonably well together **2** Cast functions adequately **1** Cast seems somewhat disjointed		
Focus	**4** Concentration very evident, very focused **3** Good level of concentration **2** Lacking concentration **1** Little or no concentration—unfocused		
Energy	**4** Excellent energy level; full of vitality **3** Adequate energy level **2** Inconsistent or low energy level **1** Inadequate energy level		
Communication	(Plot, conflict, exposition, theme, etc.) **4** All elements of the story clearly communicated **3** Most elements of the story communicated **2** Some elements of the story clear **1** Many elements not completely clear		
Staging	**4** Creative, effective, and improved from workshop **3** Adequately effective **2** Does not complement the text **1** Distracts from communicating meaning		

Interpretation			
Action	**4** Most or all of the dialogue communicates action **3** Some dialogue communicates action **2** Dialogue seems awkward at times **1** Weak viewpoint; weak style		
Characters	**4** Distinct, lifelike characters **3** Varied characters **2** Characters sometimes superficial **1** Characters not distinct or believable		

Individual Work			
Improvement	**4** Utilized feedback to improve significantly **3** Some improvement shown **2** Little change from workshop quality **1** No improvement shown		

You demonstrate good ability in . . .	You would benefit from more attention to . . .

Total Points _____   Grade _____

O for a muse of FIRE

ILLUSION

reality

nature MIRROR

MASK

TRUTH

drama

. . . each man in his time plays many

Chapter 11
Introduction

Because we live in a media-driven world, students need to be introduced to mass communication. Since this is a drama course, the text features radio broadcasting, with particular emphasis on scripted segments. If your schedule permits and your students display interest, certainly explore other aspects of radio as well as other forms of media. In a home education environment, you may wish to integrate this chapter with study of political communication, persuasion and other rhetoric, usage of the Internet, or related topics.

This chapter combines basics about radio broadcasting with simple playwriting techniques. The project can be a full-scale class production (15-25 minutes in length), or it can include only select segments with other portions omitted. If you do not plan to stage a play publicly, either as a class or as a school-wide production at least once during the current school year, fully developing this project would be ideal. Obviously, staging a play or musical in addition to this course may cause time constraints that would prevent this chapter's project from becoming a full production.

CHAPTER 11

Lesson Plan
Suggested homework is in **boldface**.

Lesson Description	Recommended Presentation	Performance Projects/ Written Assignments
I. Radio (p. 255)	ST—Practice Creating Perspective; Write a Script; Practice Scripts TE—Opening Discussion Questions; Field Trip; Hand Signals Game	Assign roles in the Radio Segment project
II. Playwriting (p. 265)	ST—Identify the Major Dramatic Question; Assign roles and responsibilities for the Radio Segment project TE—Café Scene; Practice Is the Key; Perfectionism	**ST—Assign Writing a Commercial** Radio Segment workshop
Assessment	Chapter quiz or unit test	Radio Segment performance. **Assign Journal 12**
Suggested teaching time: 12-13 class periods		

I Hear What You're Playing

You're on the air in five, four, three, two, . . .

Teaching Materials

- Public address system if available
- Recording equipment if available
- Recorded sound effects or materials for creating sound effects
- Workshop rubrics (students submit their own copy)
- Performance rubrics (students submit their own copy)

OVERVIEW

Know—*Concepts*

The purpose of radio
Producing radio segments

Grow—*Skills*

Playwriting
Creating and using sound effects
Reading scripts on the air

Show—*Performance*

Radio dramas
Commercials

Samuel received a clock radio as a Christmas gift. The next morning, his sleep was interrupted by voices instead of music. In half-wakefulness, he perceived that several people were having a conversation. This was followed by suspenseful music and the sound of a door banging shut. Samuel bolted upright in bed. Now fully awake, he wondered who had been in his room. Then a slight static noise drew his attention to the radio alarm clock. He laughed aloud to think he had begun picturing what he had heard as part of his dream. After adjusting the dial for better reception, he listened to the remainder of the episode, intrigued with the detective's ability to find evidence and draw conclusions. His thoughts were interrupted when his sister knocked loudly on his door. "Mom says you'd better hurry if you want any cinnamon rolls!" He heard her quick footsteps retreating down the staircase. Not wanting to miss either the fresh-baked cinnamon rolls or the rest of the story, Samuel dashed downstairs two steps at a time. He quickly returned to his room, rolls and a glass of milk in hand.

Perhaps you've never listened to a radio play or an audio book. This chapter will introduce you to the medium of radio, teach you how to perform a dramatic radio script, and explain the basic techniques of creating a script for radio, stage, or screen. In addition to performing a script, you will have the opportunity to create a short script on your own, applying what you have learned.

Opening Discussion Questions

Find out what your students are interested in. Ask the following questions:

1. Are you curious about a studio's atmosphere while the announcers are "on the air"?
2. Are you interested in the technical aspects of radio?
3. Have you ever called in to a talk-radio program? What was your experience?
4. Do you find radio a useful source of news?
5. When might you prefer television news to radio news and vice versa?
6. Have you listened to a radio broadcast via the Internet?
7. How do you imagine radio changing in the future—In five years? In ten?

RADIO

By the early 1930s, some people predicted that television would make the radio obsolete. After all, why listen if you can both listen and see? However, audio devices such as radios, cassettes, compact discs, and computer sound files are more popular today than ever. Remember, it's easier to listen than watch something if you're washing your car in the driveway, driving in traffic, or building a model airplane. As a student of drama, also consider the appeal of using your imagination. Have you ever had a friend describe a film or television feature only to reply, "But have you read the book?" As with reading, radio allows the audience members to participate in creating the scene in their minds. Let's look at the characteristics of radio and the process of producing radio broadcasts.

The Development of Radio

1895	Radio is born. Guglielmo Marconi of Bologna, Italy, places his transformer near his house and places his receiver almost two miles away on the other side of a hill. His servant receives a transmission in Morse code and fires a gun to indicate its arrival.
1896	Marconi demonstrates his invention to the British authorities and applies for a patent.
1898	Wireless telegraphy is first used in naval ships.
1899	Telegraphic communication occurs between England and France.
1901	Marconi's transmitting station in Cornwall, England, successfully transmits a signal across the Atlantic Ocean to Newfoundland, Canada—a distance of 2,175 miles.
1909	Marconi receives the Nobel Prize.
1914	Marconi transmits speech more than fifty miles.
1915	The spoken word is transmitted from Arlington, Va., to both Paris and Honolulu.
1920	The first commercial radio station, KDKA Pittsburgh, signs on.
1930	The FCC (Federal Communications Commission) recommends to Congress that profanity on the air be banned.
1932	A study shows that most stations' programming is 62.9 percent music, 21.3 percent educational, 11.8 percent literature, 2.5 percent religion, and 1.5 percent "novelties."
1930s	Television seems to threaten radio. First popularity charts begin appearing for "most played songs."
1940s	News flashes announce the events of World War II—such as the bombing of Pearl Harbor and the landing of troops at Normandy—making the war very personal on the home front.

I HEAR WHAT YOU'RE PLAYING 255

Much of television programming is classified as entertainment. Unlike reading, listening to the radio or a storyteller, or viewing a live drama, television does not stimulate active, mental participation. Though television entertainment is not inherently wrong, in large quantities it can inhibit imagination and thinking skills.

Lesson Motivator

Radio has played a significant role in modern culture and even politics. As the first practical form of mass communication, it revolutionized not only home entertainment but also advertising, political campaigning, the reporting of news and weather, and culture in general.

Find out what aspects of radio and broadcasting interest your students. Perhaps stimulate discussion with Opening Discussion Questions (below).

You may also wish to play prerecorded radio segments as samples for discussion concerning radio's "devices." For example, ask students how radio stations typically identify themselves. (Possible answer: a promo with thematic music and an announcement of the call letters and station slogan.) Then play an example of a promo.

PRESENTATION
Radio

Field Trip

A field trip to a local radio station would be an ideal complement to this study. If you have the opportunity to do so, consider planning the following:

1. Have students think of questions to ask. Tell your students they must see themselves as news reporters, gathering information for an informative radio or television segment. They should begin by asking who, what, why, when, where, and how. The students can also record any other questions that come to mind.

2. Collect the students' questions and make comments and suggestions as you see fit.

3. Have students bring their pre-approved questions with them on the field trip. Remind them that they are reporters, not tourists. They should actively participate in learning while on the field trip, not just traipse around enjoying the fact that they "got out of class."

If a field trip is not possible, consider having your students work as a class to develop a list of their top ten questions. Then you or a responsible student could submit those questions in writing to a radio station. When a reply is received, discuss it in class.

Lesson Objectives

The student will be able to

1. Identify the major events of radio history.

2. Explain both the historical and current significance of radio broadcasting.

3. Describe the key features of radio broadcasting.

4. Identify the personnel who produce scripted radio segments.

5. Describe the process of producing a radio segment.

6. Define radio terminology presented in the chapter.

7. Use basic hand signals to communicate while "on the air."

8. Format a radio script.

1960s	Radio drama declines in popularity.
1968	AM stations become endangered by stereo recordings they are not equipped to play.
1970s	The music selection process becomes more specialized. Programs and even entire radio stations focus on interest groups rather than trying to play something for everyone.
1980s	Various forms of talk radio gain popularity.
1990s	Radio stations begin broadcasting via the Internet, expanding their audience from local to international.

Characteristics of Radio

Radios have changed drastically in appearance and quality since KDKA Pittsburgh signed on the air in 1920. Radio broadcasting evolved technologically throughout the twentieth century. In the midst of these changes, radio has retained certain aspects: conveying information, creating for the mind's eye, and communicating with a natural style.

Conveying Information

Long before teens were carrying radios to picnics and volleyball games, workmen and military personnel used various types of radios to communicate with one another. Today, everything from winter storm watches to call-in advice programs to political coverage indicates that radio has the important role of providing information to the public. Radio also provides music, sports coverage, and other entertainment.

1. Give examples of radio programming that informs listeners. *Answers will vary but may include storm watches and warnings, school closings, and news.*

2. Give examples of radio programming that persuades (seeks to influence) listeners. *Answers will vary but may include commercials, infomercials, and political talk shows. (Students may list religious programming here as well as under inspirational.)*

3. Give examples of radio programming that inspires listeners (spiritually, ethically, or patriotically). *Answers will vary but may include announcements from charities, devotionals and sermons from various church groups, and service messages supporting the military.*

256   CHAPTER 11

Radio Station Visit

Your student could visit a radio station or compose a letter asking questions about the station. Be sure to check his letter for clarity, grammar, and usage before mailing it.

Creating for the Mind's Eye

Radio broadcasting is an art form intended for the ear, not the eye. Sometimes the expression *the mind's eye* is used to describe the relationship between aural (auditory) input and what the audience members "see." When producing anything from a radio commercial to an audio book of a classic novel, both the script and the presentation must appeal to the audience's imagination. The means by which this goal is reached will be discussed later in this chapter.

Communicating with a Natural Style

You may think that radio announcers have voices unlike those of other human beings—fuller and mellower, more resonant, and even musical. Announcing is not an acting job, however. Most radio announcers spend their college years and internships developing their voices to the fullest, not for the purpose of sounding like "radio people" but to sound pleasant to the ear and to be easily understood.

As you develop your voice, avoid imitating a "radio voice" if it results in a caricature of a radio personality. Instead, focus on improving your delivery. When practicing, set aside time to polish your diction, phrasing, and breath support. In the rest of your practice time and when you speak to an audience—including on the air—focus primarily on communicating conversationally. When on the air, picture someone in your audience. Talk *with* him, not *at* him. The radio broadcaster should strive for a natural style, similar to that of a public speaker.

For announcing, interviewing, and similar tasks, your language, diction, and usage should sound the same as natural speech. In a dramatized segment, whether a play or even a commercial, the dialogue should be interactive, without long speeches. Characters should speak for the same reason we speak each day in conversation—to clarify, to inform, to contradict, and so on. In other words, characters must be motivated to say their dialogue meaningfully in order for it to sound natural and convincing. Their message must have a real purpose. For dramatic segments, the level of naturalism in delivery depends on the type of story and the character.

The Production Process

Now that you understand the nature of radio broadcasting, consider the means by which broadcasts are produced. As in any other business, personnel use specialized skills to produce radio broadcasting.

I HEAR WHAT YOU'RE PLAYING 257

Personnel

Producing a radio broadcast is really a team effort, as you will see with the next project. You will have a vital role to fill, whether you are a cast member or a technician. Additionally, you can learn about the basic skills described below, even though you may not apply every skill in the chapter project.

The production of a dramatized segment includes the roles of director, sound person, music transition person, cast members, and engineer. The **director** is responsible to call every cue. He must be familiar with the script and stay alert throughout the rehearsals and airtime. The director uses hand signals to communicate with everyone present. The **sound person** is responsible to play prerecorded sound cues or even create some sound cues. The **music transition person** plays prerecorded musical interludes or creates musical transitions as needed. Obviously, the **cast members** read and dramatically interpret the roles in the commercial or play. The **engineer** controls the recording process and the broadcasting equipment such as mics (MIKES). His job is similar to that of an audio technician in a church who sets recording volumes for various portions of a worship service.

For the project at the end of the chapter, you should be able to get involved in one or more of these roles. You will need an engineer for the script only if you are using equipment such as a public address (PA) system.

definition

*The **director** supervises rehearsals and airtime, calling cues (prompts for the next line or sound) and leading the other participants.*

*The **sound person** plays and/or creates the sound effects.*

*The **music transition person** plays and/or creates musical interludes and background music.*

*The **cast members** enact the roles.*

*The **engineer** operates the broadcasting equipment, including mics, volume levels, and recording.*

Perspective refers to the sense of distance between a given character or noise and the audience as well as the distance between that character and other characters.

Specialized Skills

Many skills used on the air are the same as those used in public speaking, oral interpretation, and stage acting. In radio broadcasting, however, effective use of perspective and sound effects becomes more crucial, since the audience cannot see the speaker to gain understanding from his facial expressions or gestures. Both radio and television personnel use hand signals to communicate while on the air. In addition to creating perspective and sound effects, other vital skills for work in broadcasting include reading radio and television scripts and creating vocal characterization.

Perspective

Admittedly, radio is very one-dimensional because it is perceived by only one sense. The audience receives no visual input—only aural. Writers and producers of radio programming must create *perspective* to overcome this flat quality. **Perspective** refers to the sense of distance between a given character or noise and the audience as well as the distance between that character and other characters. Since radio programming is conveyed by sound equipment, actors and sound effects can be distanced from the microphone to create perspective. For example, if a character is "on" mic, the listeners will perceive him as close. Background noises and voices that slowly "fade on" mic give the sense of movement. The dialogue conveys whether the on mic character is moving or if the other characters are approaching him. The distance from the microphone may be described by phrases such as "slightly off" mic or "far off" mic. Of course, when a character is entering the scene, he will "fade on" and when leaving, "fade off."

Several terms are used to convey these ideas in scripts. "Up" means louder and may appear in phrases such as "fade up" (gradually getting louder) and "up and under" (louder at first and then fading to become a background sound). For example, to fade up you might begin recording slightly off mic and move to on mic. Also, the term "sting" refers to a sudden increase in volume. Often, *sting* refers to a musical interlude between scenes, and the instruction is "sting and under."

When producing a commercial or dramatic scene for radio, decide how the perspective will be conveyed. For every line of dialogue and every sound effect, determine where the action is taking place. If two women are having an on mic conversation and a knock is heard at a door in another room, the knock must be far off mic to convey the distance. However, if one of the women drops a glass, that sound effect must be much closer to the mic than the knock. In a different script in which the knock preceded dialogue, the sound effect needs to be on mic with an off mic voice calling, "Just a minute! I'm coming!" This voice moves closer to the mic during the line to convey movement toward the door.

In most cases you can change perspective simply by fading on and fading off mic. Never leave the mic with nothing on. This is called "jumping" mic and confuses the listener. To switch from one group of characters to another without following a character, use a transition device such as music fading on as the action leaves one scene and fading off as a new scene comes to the mic.

Remembering that radio occurs in the imagination and must have perspective will be the key to producing an effective radio segment for your project.

> ### *Perspective Jargon*
>
> - Mic—microphone
> - On mic—speech, music, or sound effect is made directly into the microphone. This gives a sense of proximity to the audience.
> - Slightly off mic; far off mic—speech, music, or sound effect is recorded at a specific distance from the microphone.
> - Fade on—speech, music, or sound effect slowly gets louder. This gives a sense of approaching the audience from a distance.
> - Fade off—speech, music, or sound effect slowly gets softer. This gives a sense of moving away from the audience.
> - Up—speech, music, or sound effect becomes immediately audible.
> - Fade up—speech, music, or sound effect slowly becomes audible.
> - Up and under—speech, music, or sound effect becomes immediately audible and then decreases in volume until it is only background noise.
> - Sting—speech, music, or sound effect suddenly increases in volume.

I HEAR WHAT YOU'RE PLAYING 259

Practice Creating Perspective

The brief script below presents the illustration about Samuel and his clock radio as though the story were occurring on the air. For the first few lines, margin labels identify whether the dialogue or sound effect (SFX) is on mic or not. Label the remaining lines with one of the following: *on mic, fade on,* or *fade off.*

Unknown Title	Page 1

SFX: 1. REGULAR BREATHING OF A SLEEPING PERSON. A

The boy's breathing is on mic and the bird is at least slightly off mic. The static is slightly off mic and the voices are far off mic.

2. BIRD IS HEARD CHIRPING. STATIC FROM A

3. RADIO (FADES UP). INDISTINCT VOICES ARE

4. HEARD.

SAMUEL: 5. (NOT REALLY AWAKE) Huh? Hmm.

Samuel's text is on mic.

MUSIC: 6. (STING AND UNDER)

Music suddenly increases in volume (on mic) and then fades to background (slightly off mic).

SFX: 7. A DOOR BANGS SHUT.

Door banging is slightly off mic.

SAMUEL: 8. (WAKING SUDDENLY) Who's there?

Samuel speaks on mic.

SFX: 9. STATIC (UP AND UNDER)

Static quickly fades on and slowly fades off to convey radio tuning.

SAMUEL: 10. (LAUGHS LOUDLY) I wasn't dreaming! It was

11. actually my new radio. Maybe I can improve the

12. reception. It's kind of fuzzy.

Samuel speaks on mic.

SFX: 13. STATIC (UP AND UNDER) VOICES UP

Static fades on and then fades off. The voices fade on as the static fades off.

You may have guessed that if the script were to continue, the sister's voice and footsteps would have to begin far off mic and slowly fade on when she arrives. As you can see, a great deal of thought goes into even a short radio segment.

Hand Signals

Obviously, neither radio nor television crews can speak out loud during a live broadcast to signal that they need to switch to a commercial in thirty seconds or to wrap up the idea for the end of a show. For these and many other frequent messages, the following **hand signals** are used.

Definition

Radio and television crews use **hand signals** *to communicate silently while on the air.*

Figure 1. The **attention** or **standby signal** is a simple wave of the hand, given by the director (called the stage manager in television).

Figure 2. Right after the standby signal, the director gives the **cue signal** by rapidly lowering his hand, pointing his index finger at the next speaker.

Figure 3. If the speaker needs to wrap up a thought for a break, the **break signal** is given.

Figure 4. When a speaker receives a **cut signal,** he should stop immediately because an emergency may have occurred.

Figure 5. If the director mimes pulling taffy, he is communicating that the speakers need to **slow down** when reading a script or **stretch** the conversation when ad-libbing until notified otherwise.

Figure 6. If the segment is running long, the director may use the **speed-up signal** to tell the speaker to quicken his delivery.

Figure 7. The **wrap-up signal** means to conclude the segment smoothly and promptly.

I HEAR WHAT YOU'RE PLAYING **261**

Hand Signals Game

Instructions. Begin by demonstrating each hand signal while verbally identifying it. Have your students stand and repeat each signal as you demonstrate. (They will be less likely to be inhibited about the action if they get out of their chairs. You may even want them to form a circle to get them out of "lecture/note-taking" mode.)

When you are confident that your students understand every signal, have them form pairs. Call out a signal. Have students compete to see who can initiate the hand signal faster. This will aid them in memorizing the motion with the meaning.

Then have the partners take turns doing hand signals for each other. The person watching should identify the signal as fast as possible. As soon as he has identified his partner's signal, he takes a turn giving a signal.

Sound Effects Suggestions

Many sound effects can be produced very simply. For example, to convey that characters are walking on a particular type of surface, use a cardboard box filled with an appropriate substance such as sand or pebbles. The sound effects person(s) can "walk" a pair or two of shoes in the box. Another cue might call for an indoor type of sound. Shoes with metal taps may be ideal for "walking" across tile or wood. Your sounds effects person should be free to roam about the room as needed if sounds are being recorded. Place the microphone near the hinges when opening or closing a creaky door to maximize the effect and near the sash if a window squeaks. To create the sound of banging shutters, strike together two thin boards. (The banging should be irregular, not rhythmic, in order to mimic the wind's effect.) Use your imagination when creating your own sound effects.

Sound Effects

Abbreviated SFX, **sound effects** play an integral role in dramatized radio segments. A stage production might need few if any sound effects, especially with a simple script and lighting cues that create transitions from scene to scene. However, radio depends on sound effects to convey everything from mood to transitions to crowds to singular noises, such as a train whistle. Sound effects may be live at the time of the broadcast or may be prerecorded, perhaps even from a digital sound-effects library.

definition

Sound effects include live and prerecorded sounds that become part of the action or are used to enhance the story as background noise.

Scripting

In Chapter 9 you learned some of the basic guidelines for adapting literature into a script format. In the second half of this chapter, you will learn basic principles of writing your own script or play. Only terms and rules specific to radio are introduced here.

In a radio script, each page has a header with the title left aligned and the word *Page* and the appropriate number on the right. The script is double-spaced.

Each music and sound effects (SFX) cue is underlined, beginning with the tag and continuing through the entire cue. These cues are in all caps, whereas dialogue lines have only their tags in all caps. Instructions about a cue appear in all caps and parentheses. A colon follows the tags, and the text is about two inches from the left margin. (See Figure 8 below.)

Figure 8. Two sample cues

Sample 1

SFX: 12. APPLAUSE—(UNDER AND FADE OUT)

Sample 2

MUSIC: 28. (STING AND UNDER)

-MORE-

Notice that each line begins with a number followed by a period. Each page begins with line 1. All lines, whether dialogue or cues, are numbered consecutively. In multiple-page scripts every page except the last must be marked "-MORE-" at the bottom.

When a cue occurs during a line, ellipses are used before and after the interruption. The character's name is not repeated after the sound effect. (See Figure 9.)

262   CHAPTER 11

Figure 9. An interrupted line

ANNCR:	11. Try new Bright Rinse . . .
MUSIC:	12. (STING AND UNDER)
	13. . . . the color-safe bleach that really works!

Obviously, radio does not use a physical stage. The stage directions are simply called *instructions to the actor*. These instructions appear in parentheses and all caps. They must be placed before the text during which the actor performs the task. (See Figure 10.)

Figure 10. Instructions to the actor

SFX:	6. DOOR CREAKS OPEN AND THEN BANGS
	7. SHUT.
MAN:	8. (ENTERS, CLEARS HIS THROAT) I've come
	9. to see you.
SFX:	10. CASH REGISTER DRAWER SHUTS.
STORE CLERK:	11. I thought I told you never to come back
	12. here—
MAN:	13. (INTERRUPTING) I don't wait around for a
	14. gilded invitation when I want to do
	15. something.

Write a Script

Arrange the following information into the form of a script as described above. You may or may not need all of the lines provided.

> Several men chatting amiably are heard in the background. The snipping sound of hair scissors is heard. The barber is whistling merrily. The sounds of a door opening and a door chime are heard. Footsteps are heard as Molly and Benjamin enter the shop. Molly says, "Come along, Benjamin." The barber calls out, "Well, hello there, Molly." She replies, "Hello, Mr. Smalley." "And how's the young Benjamin doing today?" A child's voice responds, "Very well, sir." The sounds of the scissors continues. Just then, the door and door chime repeat themselves.

I HEAR WHAT YOU'RE PLAYING 263

Experiment with Voices

Voices for radio dramas and commercials need to be especially distinct and interesting. Encourage your students to be creative in their development of character voices. Unique characters demand unique voices, whether dramatic or comic characters. Such skill emerges from diligent practice more than from natural ability.

Answers will vary but should be similar to the following example:

SFX: 1. *(SLIGHTLY OFF MIC) SEVERAL MEN CHATTING AMIABLY*

SFX: 2. *HAIR SCISSORS SNIPPING (UP AND UNDER) AS*

3. *BARBER WHISTLES MERRILY*

SFX: 4. *(SLIGHTLY OFF MIC) DOOR OPENS AND DOOR CHIME*

5. *RINGS: FOOTSTEPS OF A WOMAN'S SHOES AND A*

6. *CHILD'S SHOES (FADE UP AND UNDER)*

MOLLY: 7. *(FADES ON WITH FOOTSTEPS) Come along, Benjamin.*

BARBER: 8. *(CALLING OUT) Well, hello there, Molly.*

MOLLY: 9. *(FADES UP TO ON MIC) Hello, Mr. Smalley.*

BARBER: 10. *And how's the young Benjamin doing today?*

BENJAMIN: 11. *(A YOUNG BOY'S VOICE) Very well, sir.*

SFX: 12. *(OFF MIC) DOOR OPENS AND DOOR CHIME RINGS*

13.

14.

Characterization

When approaching a script as an actor, be certain that you understand the story and how your part fits. Knowing the genre will help a great deal. You will want to experiment with various vocal qualities because your voice will distinguish your character. Since you have learned to perform in front of an audience, communicating with your facial expression, gesture, and so on, the thought of a microphone alone may seem rather awkward. You need to relax and interpret your lines as you would otherwise.

Specialized Skills in Radio

- Creating perspective
- Hand signals
- Sound effects
- Scripting
- Vocal characterization

Perhaps you've heard someone say, "Answer the telephone with a smile on your face, and your voice will show it." This applies to radio as well. Though unseen, your facial expression will influence your vocal delivery. Go ahead and characterize physically as well as vocally. Just keep in mind that you cannot substitute a gesture for a voiced response. If the other actor says, "Do you know why your brother had to stay after school to clean the boards for Mr. O'Malley?" and you shrug your shoulders, you've lost the listeners. You can shrug your shoulders or stuff your hands in your pockets while saying, "Boy, I don't know, Dad." Your actions can help you stay focused on the story and your character. They may also enhance your communication with your fellow actors.

Process

For stage plays or live musical performances, whether orchestral or operatic, the actors and musicians have a series of rehearsals and then the performance. In contrast, radio rehearsals are followed by **airtime.** Segments may be prerecorded without rehearsing and then edited electronically. The editing process can add the music and sound effects as well as correct errors. However, since you will not have editing equipment, you will need to rehearse before airing your segment.

Airtime refers to the broadcasting of a segment on radio or television.

Practice Scripts

The scripts in Appendix I will give you the opportunity to produce a dramatic segment for an audience, whether you are performing live or via PA system or even prerecording your segment. Regardless of what role your teacher assigns you, decide to be a strong link in the chain of teamwork. You may not have the role that most interests you, but remember that this is a chance to practice and learn as a group.

PLAYWRITING

The play's the thing . . . !

—William Shakespeare, *Hamlet*

Lars tried writing stories when he was in junior high and ninth grade. Repeatedly, his teachers wrote on his papers, "Show, don't tell" and "Too much narration and description; too little action." He often thought to himself, "People like Charles Dickens sure wrote an awful lot of narration and description. Why can't I?"

Many novice authors struggle with balancing narration, description, and dialogue. Their stories move too slowly because they have overwritten them. Consider this example:

> The rays of moonlight were slowly disappearing as a slow-moving cloud gradually covered the moon. The shadows of the two figures faded until there was almost no light at all. Now they stood in total darkness. Grace never moved but stood tautly against the tree, trying to breathe quietly.

Small Roles

Encourage your students to accept small or less interesting roles even when they had hoped for a larger role. They should accept the role offered and portray that character to the best of their ability. Acting maturity and experience are gained more by eager involvement than through one or two leading roles. Often, an actor who successfully portrays a minor character will be more likely to receive a larger role in a future production.

Lesson Motivator

Writing a play is unlike writing in any other genre. Obviously, the formatting is unique, but the content is unique as well. The play script is only the skeleton of the play, waiting for actors to add muscle and voice, designers to add scenery, costumes, makeup, and lighting, and an audience to share the experience of the characters. Most writers speak directly to their audiences. The playwright must communicate with the director, cast, and crew, who must in turn communicate with the audience.

This fact has several ramifications. The playwright can and should be succinct. A good playwright usually understands poetic expression and uses it when necessary—not just in dialogue but also in descriptions. For example, a metaphor will more quickly communicate the personality of a character to the actor or the ambiance of a scene to the designers. The metaphor can also stimulate more creativity in the actors and designers than explicit instructions.

Next, the playwright must imagine the whole story but restrain himself to writing only dialogue and basic physical movement. If he takes the novelist's liberty to describe facial expression, mood, attitude, and even physical characteristics, he limits the play's producers. ("Her hair fell in waves of amber curls as she turned" makes an unrealistic demand on the actor and maybe even on the wig and makeup crews.) Too many such demands could discourage directors from even selecting that play for production.

Finally, the playwright has a strong obligation to communicate thought through dialogue, since actors are limited to the spoken word. Certainly some playwrights have written soliloquies effectively, but these are seldom found in modern realistic drama, since they wouldn't make sense. Practically speaking, a full-length play script may require as much time, effort, creativity, and intelligence to create as prose works containing more pages.

> "He must not find me," she said to herself with a slight gulp. "If only the moon would stay hidden, he wouldn't be able to find me."
>
> Grace thought she heard a rustle in the leaves, not far behind her. She stiffened again. Her mind reeled and tumbled as she thought about where she might run if he appeared in the shadows. . . .

Not only is this example tricky to follow, but not much has happened. What if the writer had condensed the first three paragraphs? Consider the following:

> Grace thought she heard a rustle in the leaves, not far behind her. She stiffened again. Even the darkness of a cloudy night could not make her feel safe from him.
>
> "Where can I run if he finds me? Can I outrun him?"* These and many other questions raced through her mind. The answers did not come. The rustling ceased. The only sound now was her heartbeat, which seemed to boom like thunder, announcing her presence.
>
> Then a low voice interrupted the silence. . . .

*By this point, the story has already covered all of the action in the two paragraphs above.

In fewer lines, more has happened. Writing a play is similar because the audience came to see something occurring. If the action drags, their heads will nod.

In the following pages, you will read about basic principles for playwriting. These principles apply to playwriting for all mediums—radio, television, motion picture, and stage. However, since your chapter project concerns radio, the activities will feature radio scripts.

Playwright and Dramatist

Those who write novels are called novelists. Those who write for newspapers and magazines are called journalists. Those who write plays are called dramatists or, more commonly, **playwrights.** Notice that the term is not *play-writer*. The suffix *wright* means a craftsman. Wheelwrights and shipwrights are those who craft wheels and ships. So a playwright crafts a play—a reminder of the importance of structure and creative work needed in playwriting.

definition

Playwrights, or dramatists, are craftsmen of dramatic literature.

Create Conflict

Remember that drama must have action. The action must lead to conflict. No conflict, no interest, no play.

Often a playwright sits down to write because of an idea or image that comes to mind. Sometimes the idea begins with a character, other times with a setting. Regardless of the source, the careful playwright quickly solidifies a central conflict.

266 CHAPTER 11

PRESENTATION

Playwriting

Don't Wander Spiritually

Ask the students to take out a sheet of paper. Read to them the following principle of playwriting: "The careful playwright quickly solidifies a central conflict. Otherwise, anything he writes will tend to wander." Pose this question: "What must a Christian solidify in his life in order not to wander

spiritually?" Allow three minutes for students to write an answer. You may want the students to place this in their journals.

Ask a Major Dramatic Question

An easy way to clarify the central conflict is to word it as a question. The major dramatic question (MDQ), discussed in Chapter 2, summarizes the central conflict for the reader or audience. For the writer, the major dramatic question is a guide. As the old adage says, "If you aim at nothing, you will surely hit it."

Hypothetically, let's assume that you are writing a dramatic script using this MDQ: "Can the new soccer coach make a real team out of the players who haven't won a game in three seasons?"

Define an Objective for the Protagonist

How will the new soccer coach build a better team? Obviously, he must create change in a team that plays poorly. If the coach is to succeed, he must determine why team members play poorly and fix that problem. Do they lack effective team strategies or even basic skills such as passing the ball? Do they lack team spirit or have low morale? Perhaps all of these problems exist. If so, each problem will be an obstacle to his objective: to get the varsity team playing well.

Sometimes the objective and MDQ are almost identical. However, the MDQ may describe what is necessary for the objective to be reached. In Shakespeare's *Romeo and Juliet*, the main characters marry in secret because of a family feud. They want to live happily ever after (objective). If you say that the major dramatic question is "Will they live happily ever after?" you do not describe their great obstacle and consequently fail to reveal conflict—a necessary ingredient in drama. Instead, identify the MDQ as "Can Romeo and Juliet convince their families to make peace?" They will never realize their objective without such reconciliation.

Identifing the Major Dramatic Question

Read through the following script and then identify the MDQ.

TKS Saves the Day		Page 1
MUSIC/SFX:	1. GENERAL CAFÉ NOISES—MOOD MUSIC,	
	2. PEOPLE TALKING, CLATTER OF DISHES	
	3. AND UTENSILS (UP AND UNDER)	
PHIL:	4. That club sandwich any good, Warren?	
WARREN:	5. Needs more mayo. (CALLING) Excuse me, Miss?	
SERVER:	6. Yeah, how kin I help ya?	
	-MORE-	

Café Scene

Have your students create the scene in the student text above. Assign the roles. Appoint several students to create specific sound effects. You might even help the cast members to focus and really imagine the scene by having the entire class arrange their desks like small two- and three-person café tables. The students not involved with a speaking role or specific sound effects should carry on low conversation and pantomime eating lunch. Be sure to have them imagine a specific food. Make it very real. Ideally, they should not become so caught up in their own improvisations that they ignore the formal scene. Good actors can create stage business while still following the primary action. Then they won't miss a cue—even if they haven't spoken for many lines or scenes. If you believe your students will not pay attention, run the scene more than once. Have the "extras" listen silently the first time and then create stage business. You might consider videotaping the scene as another possibility. Then the students can observe themselves.

The Role of Conflict

While real life involves avoiding and resolving conflicts, drama depends on a sustained central conflict for action.

WARREN:	1. Could I get some mayo?
SERVER:	2. Oh, soitenly [certainly], honey. I'll be right back
	3. with that.
PHIL:	4. (SIPPING HOT SOUP) Do you mind going over
	5. the report?
WARREN:	6. Sure. Hand it here.
SFX:	7. THUMP OF BRIEFCASE ON THE TABLE,
	8. CLICKING AS PHIL UNLATCHES IT,
	9. RUSTLE OF PAPERS
PHIL:	10. (HESITATING) Uh, your hands?
WARREN:	11. (LAUGHING) A little tomato and pickle juice
	12. wouldn't look too good on your report, would it?
PHIL:	13. (POLITELY CHUCKLES) No, I don't
	14. suppose—
SFX:	15. (FADE ON) FOOTSTEPS ON THE TILE
SERVER:	16. Here's yoah [your] mayo, mister.
SFX:	17. CLINK OF SMALL DISH ON THE TABLE
WARREN:	18. (ALMOST SHOUTING) Oh, watch out, Phil!
PHIL:	19. What? Huh? Oh!
WARREN:	20. Miss, before you go, could you get some extra
	21. napkins or maybe a damp cloth? Phil's got a
	22. presentation after lunch and doesn't want to be
	23. wearing his soup for it, I'm sure!

-MORE-

 CHAPTER 11

PHIL: 1. (MUTTERING) It never fails—just the time you

                    2. need to look your best you drag your tie through

                    3. the minestrone. (EXASPERATED) And my wife

                    4. gave me this tie for Christmas.

SERVER: 5. Aw, you don't want napkins, you want TKS

                    6. Spray Spot Lifter. Heah [Here], I keep some in

                    7. my apron for just this kind of emoigency

                    8. [emergency]. Just spray it on the spot and let it set

                    9. foah [for] a few minutes.

PHIL: 10. (IN DISBELIEF) You carry it with you?

WARREN: 11. (LAUGHING HEARTILY) Talk about service!

SERVER: 12. Soivice [service] is our pleasuh at Uptown Café.

                    13. (to Phil) Looky there now. Those tough

                    14. cleaning ingredients in the TKS lift doit [dirt]

                    15. right off the soiface [surface]. Now just brush off

                    16. the white residue.

PHIL: 17. Like that?

SERVER: 18. You got it.

PHIL: 19. Thanks, Miss.

SERVER: 20. No problem! Enjoy the rest of yoah [your] soup.

                    21. It tastes better than it weahs.

PHIL: 22. Yes—

WARREN: 23. Nice waitress. Smart too!

                    -MORE-

I HEAR WHAT YOU'RE PLAYING   269

Compare a Short Story

If your students have studied "The Masque of the Red Death" by Edgar Allan Poe, discuss the story. What activities inherent to a party are excluded because those details have little or nothing to do with the plot? *(Answers may include greetings, polite conversations, deep discussions, music, dancing, eating, and so on).*

Point out that the short story writer's task is not to imagine and record every aspect of an event. Rather, he must feature details inherent to a plot. The same is true for the playwright.

TKS Saves the Day   Page 4

PHIL: 1. I'm impressed. That was a potential disaster—but

                         2. thanks to TKS Spray Spot Lifter, the afternoon is

                         3. saved.

SFX: 4. <u>MUSIC AND BACKGROUND NOISES (FADE</u>

                         5. <u>OUT WITH THE VOICES)</u>

1. What do you think the MDQ is? <u>*Answers will vary but may include "Will Phil be*</u>
   <u>*ready for his presentation?"*</u>

2. Who is the central character? <u>*Phil*</u>

3. Each character's dialogue is distinct. Tell what the style of speech reveals about each individual.
   <u>*Answers will vary but may reflect the following: The server's speech suggests a*</u>
   <u>*city background, maybe from New Jersey or New York. Phil speaks professionally*</u>
   <u>*and seems to be tense as well. Warren is more jovial, hearty. He is there to enjoy*</u>
   <u>*his lunch, not just eat out of necessity.*</u>

As you can see, even a commercial may use characters in conflict to sell a product. Later in the chapter you will have the opportunity to practice your playwriting skills by writing this type of advertisement.

Write a Rough Scenario

The word **scenario** means an outline of a plot. The phrase *rough scenario* refers to a first draft or a rough draft of that outline. Unlike a speaking outline, the scenario doesn't need roman numerals, capital letters, and so on. Though not necessary, the rough scenario may be divided into major movements of action that will become acts or scenes.

definition

A **scenario** *refers to an outline of a plot, particularly a dramatic plot.*

To write a good rough scenario, think of the *plot* first. Try writing a fairly detailed description of that plot in paragraph form. Don't be too concerned about your spelling or punctuation in this first attempt. As you develop the plot, think through what characters will appear in the story. If you are writing about a soccer team, the tendency might be to try to have twenty or more characters, which is quite unnecessary. Choose just a few of these people as characters. You may want to work on two sheets of paper (or two parts of a computer document)—one for recording several paragraphs of plot and the other for recording a list of characters and descriptions.

Your first plot paragraph might look something like this example:

> We have played thirty-two soccer games since my freshman year and lost every single one of them. We've scored a couple of times, but usually on a penalty kick. The new soccer coach, Mr. Jamison, is replacing the old coach, who broke his leg during preseason soccer camp. I feel sorry for Mr. Jamison. He doesn't know anybody and hasn't even taught at Central before now. In a week and a half, we have our first game—or should I say our first *defeat.*

Many details are clarified in this paragraph: the viewpoint character, the name of one of the characters, a concept of previous action, and so on. Now you can develop this into a complete scenario, rather than just a summary. Your revision could resemble this example:

Setting

Central High, the present

Locations

Hallway lined with lockers, school gym, soccer field, and cafeteria

Characters

Mr. Jamison, the new soccer coach

Darryl, a senior, has played soccer for three years

Brandon, a senior, best friends with Darryl, has played soccer for three years

Winston, a junior, a new student at Central

"Stone" Johnston, a junior, a braggart who leads the school's basketball team well but doesn't play soccer because he won't "waste his time"

Vernon, a freshman, seems to have made the team only because so few tried out

Shirley, a junior, friendly and smart

Alex (Alexandra), a senior, Shirley's friend, quiet in groups

I HEAR WHAT YOU'RE PLAYING ⬤271

Action

Scene 1: The school hallway, lined with lockers

- The 2:50 bell rings.
- Students fill the hall.
- Brandon chats for a moment with Shirley in the hall.
- She quickly excuses herself when Alex calls to her from down the hall.
- Brandon wrestles with his gym bag, wedged in his narrow locker.
- Darryl and Winston approach, chatting.
- Darryl begins telling Winston about their losing streak of thirty-two games.
- Winston seems to think they must play some tough teams.
- He asks what their scores average.
- Darryl tells him they often lose about five to zero unless they make a penalty kick.
- As they join Brandon at the lockers, they discuss the possibilities of winning with new players and the new coach.
- Each guy expresses his opinion.
- Mr. Jamison approaches, greeting the boys—trying to remember their names.
- He forgets Darryl's name, calling him Barry.
- He apologizes.
- He tries to encourage the guys about the first game in a week and a half.
- To himself, Darryl mutters, "our first defeat."

Scene 2: The cafeteria, the next day

- Sounds of clinking of lunch trays and products dispensed from vending machines such as beverage cans and candy bars are heard.
- Alex and Shirley enter, deep in conversation over trigonometry.

Actions characterize the complete rough scenario. These consecutive actions follow logically. Scenes occur in real time, not hours or days apart, and at the same location. Still, there is no real dialogue.

Refine and Revise

Once you have worked from an opening to a resolution of the conflict in the form of a scenario, set it aside for a day or two. When you pick it up again, read it, asking the following questions.

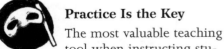

Practice Is the Key

The most valuable teaching tool when instructing students who are learning a new form of writing is practice that includes supervision and honest feedback. The text provides opportunity for students to practice scripting for radio, but you can add your own rough scenario writing assignment.

One simple approach is to choose a well-known story, either something your students have read recently or a popular children's tale such as "Goldilocks and the Three Bears" or "Little Red Riding Hood." Ideally, have students begin their assignment during class but complete it outside of class. Instruct them to write a scenario of the story. Remind them to include only blow-by-blow action, no narration, description, or dialogue. This would be a valuable assignment to peer-edit. Have students exchange papers and use a different color pen or pencil to "grade" their partner. Encourage them to look for a clear flow of action as well as extraneous material. They should make positive comments about the plot, as appropriate, and offer constructive criticism.

Have I written plot rather than story?

Remember that in an effective plot, one action leads to another. There must be progression. Try reading your scenario from the end to the beginning to see if there are unnecessary actions. In the example above, if you never develop a subplot involving Brandon and Shirley, you won't want to keep their brief conversation as an opener. It would be a source of confusion and a waste of time.

Have I created interesting obstacles?

Even in the brief example above, obstacles are present. Brandon wants to talk with Shirley but doesn't keep her attention. Winston wants to be positive about the soccer team, but Darryl insists on filling in all of the negative details. Think through each phase of your character's quest for a goal and see if there are one or more obstacles to challenge him appropriately.

Programming on radio and television is notorious for switching to a station break right after a new obstacle is introduced. Of course, this is intentional because it motivates the audience to stay tuned to the program. This is a good lesson for the prospective playwright—use goals and obstacles to create conflict and suspense. You will hold your audience's attention this way, even through interruptions.

Have I created at least one identifiable type of conflict?

Will the soccer story become Darryl's struggle against discouragement? Will the story focus on a team's learning to stand together against outside forces, such as other teams and even low expectations on the part of their fans? Review the types of conflict. One is man versus man. List the others below. Consult Chapter 2 if you need to review.

1. Man vs. *Himself*
3. Man vs. *Nature*
2. Man vs. *Society*
4. Man vs. *God*
  or the gods (Greek legends)

Make the major conflict sustain the attention of the audience and have most incidents further that struggle. As a beginning playwright, avoid subplots as much as possible. If you include one, make it very minor and simple so that the audience doesn't wonder what the main conflict is. Be clear!

Can a friend read the scenario and understand it?

Editing someone else's writing is always easier than correcting your own work. While taking a drama class or writing a play independently, try to get a peer who will read your writing. You will find the help to be worth the effort. Ask your friend to read your scenario and point out anything that seems unclear. Ask his honest opinion about the interest quality of the story as well.

Are the characters distinct?

Your friend may be able to give you feedback on this issue as well. Most stories profit from variety in the characters. Who wants to read a story or see a play about five shallow and materialistic characters or a half-dozen practical jokers? In

---

 Get a Friend's Opinion

Share Proverbs 27:17 with your students. ("Iron sharpeneth iron; so a man sharpeneth the countenance of his friend.") Engage them in a discussion with the following questions:

1. The right kind of friend can sharpen us spiritually, morally, and intellectually through his or her example, counsel, and criticism. Many people still cringe under even the most constructive criticism. Why is this? (*Answers may include that people are naturally proud, like their comfort zones, don't like failure, have competitive spirits, etc.*)

2. How can we more readily receive and act on constructive criticism? (*Answers may include humbling ourselves, realizing that everyone has room for improvement, and avoiding quick judgment when others present their ideas.*)

addition to variety, make sure that each character is developed fully enough in your mind for you to be able to write his dialogue to sound like an individual. Have you ever had a friend report an incident to you and you responded, "I can hear her saying that" or "I can see him doing just that"? Know your characters well enough to be able to test the plot and dialogue you create for them—would they really do or say that? If the answer is "no," then you should revise.

Practical Tips

For most would-be writers, a common theme is "I need more time!"—for example, "I could enter that essay contest if I weren't so busy" or "I would keep a journal if I had time to do it right!" Though this seems a compelling and popular concept, more time does not equal better writing. Especially as a novice playwright, consider *limiting* your time for writing dialogue. Try writing or typing triple-spaced on your first draft so you and others who read the script have plenty of room to write in ideas or additions. If you triple-space, try writing eight to ten pages in about an hour. Though this may sound impossible, many have succeeded using this method. When writing dialogue, don't stop for anything—ignore interruptions completely. Promise yourself a break at the end of the time period you choose and stick to your plan.

Limiting writing time helps in two areas: avoiding perfectionism and eliminating "rabbit trails." The perfectionist too often becomes the procrastinator. In addition to using the excuses described above, the procrastinator claims "writer's block." Writer's block means that a would-be writer is waiting for earthshaking

inspiration to descend. The blank page leads to a blank drawing board in the mind. Having a scenario should prevent you from drawing a blank. As for inspiration, Thomas Edison said, "Success is 99 percent perspiration and 1 percent inspiration." Don't wait for brilliance—write now. You can always revise when and if the "muse" arrives.

"Rabbit trails" usually occur when a playwright gets a grandiose idea about an intricate plot or very sophisticated characters. One way to avoid this is to begin with a one-act play, not a three-act. The one-act play isn't just shorter—it's simpler. Two or three one-acts can make an evening of fun too.

Writing a Commercial

Now that you understand basic principles of radio broadcasting and radio script format as well as basic playwriting techniques, you will have a chance to apply these. Businesses often hire advertisers to create commercials for their

 274 CHAPTER 11

Perfectionism

Initiate a discussion by asking the following questions:

1. Why does society hold up the perfectionist as an example for us to follow? (*Answers may include that he is ultra-organized; he never gives up; he does more than is necessary; he overachieves; he is the best in his field; and so on.*)

2. No one would argue with the merit of working diligently, but how could a perfectionistic attitude be damaging to the Christian life? (*Answers should describe various attitude problems such as success at any cost, love of power/control, an ambition to be better than others, impatience when dealing with a less accomplished individual, and so on.*)

Share I Corinthians 10:31: "Whether therefore ye eat, or drink, or whatsoever ye do, do all to the glory of God." A Christian with a mind directed toward the glory of God will work diligently without obsessions.

products. Choose one of the clients below and write your own radio script. Please keep all of the limits in mind, including length.

Fact Sheet 1

Client wants a humorous mood.

Length:	Sixty seconds
Client:	Finley's Pet Shop
Occasion:	Christmas Sale
Merchandise:	Goldfish—$1.99
	Aquariums—ten-gallon with filter—$25.99
	White mice—$1.49
	Hand-raised parakeets—$19.99
Dates:	December 15–Christmas Eve
Location:	Corner of North Main and Briarwood Avenue

Fact Sheet 2

Client wants an elegant mood.

Length:	Sixty seconds
Client:	Brownby's Fine Jewelry, since 1864
Occasion:	Valentine's Day Sale
Merchandise:	Diamond rings—starting at $399.99 (free sizing)
	Diamond earrings—starting at $79.99
	Ruby heart pendants—starting at $59.99
	10K and 14K gold lockets—starting at $39.99
	Deferred interest plan available
Dates:	January 10–February 14
Location:	Ogden Mall, Fulton

Fact Sheet 3

Client wants a patriotic atmosphere.

Length:	Sixty seconds
Client:	On a Roll Delicatessen
Occasion:	Picnic catering
Merchandise:	6" sub with three meats—$3.99
	Sub platter (any six 6" subs)—$19.99
	Party Pack (one sub platter, one quart of potato or pasta salad)—$22.99
Dates:	June 14 (Flag Day)–July 4
Location:	211 Elmer Park Street

CONCLUSION

You are now equipped to participate in a radio segment. You also know how to format a script of your own and how to create its drama. This will be your last opportunity to collaborate with other students, since your final project is a choice of solo projects. Make the most of this opportunity, because experience improves your ability onstage as well as on the air.

I HEAR WHAT YOU'RE PLAYING 275

CHAPTER 11 REVIEW

Terms to Know

director	hand signals	speed-up signal
sound person	attention/standby signal	wrap-up signal
music transition person	cue signal	sound effects
cast members	break signal	airtime
engineer	cut signal	playwrights
perspective	slow-down or stretch signal	scenario

Ideas to Understand

True/False **Write True or False for each statement. If false, cross out the word or words that make it incorrect and write in the word or words that make it true.**

True 1. Dramatized radio segments should capture the audience's imagination.

False 2. A beginning radio student should carefully imitate experienced announcers.
~~carefully imitate~~ *avoid imitating*

False 3. Using gestures is useless when reading a dramatic role on the air. ~~useless~~ *useful*
(What the audience cannot see may still improve vocal delivery.)

True 4. A dramatist writes plays.

True 5. Sound effects may be created live or played from a sound-effects library.

False 6. Radio serves mainly to entertain rather than to inform or to persuade.
~~mainly~~; ~~rather than~~ *or*

False 7. A rough scenario is necessary for only a first-time playwright. ~~only~~; ~~first-time~~

False 8. Subplots are always good additions to a script. ~~always~~ *sometimes* or just add *not*

True 9. The engineer at a radio station operates equipment.

False 10. Writing a first draft of dialogue is the most time-consuming step in the playwriting process. ~~most~~ *least*

False 11. Perfectionism is necessary to good playwriting. ~~necessary~~ *harmful (leads to procrastination)*

Short Answer

12. The _____director_____ calls all cues during rehearsals and airtime.

13. A _____cue_____ signal involves pointing at the next speaker.

Radio Segment Assignment Sheet

Prepare

Due Dates

———————— Workshop

———————— Performance

———————— Select one commercial for each client from the commercial-writing activity (may be done by a vote from the class).

———————— Write statements for news, sports, and weather broadcasts (can be fictitious, real school news, or community news).

———————— Schedule the commercials, news briefs, and the dramatic segments (Appendix I) into approximately fifteen minutes of programming.

———————— Find music for the dramatic segments.

———————— Find or create sound effects for the dramatic segments.

———————— Develop a slogan for your station's promos. (This should include your fictitious call letters.)

———————— Find or write a phrase of music to accompany the slogan and record it.

———————— Check that the PA system is in good working condition.

Practice   **List the student responsible for each portion of the segment.**

Newscast

General News ————————————————————————————

Sports ————————————————————————————

Weather ————————————————————————————

Other ————————————————————————————

Staff

Director ————————————————————————————

Sound Person ————————————————————————————

Music Person ————————————————————————————

Engineer ————————————————————————————
(if you are using a PA system)

Announcer ————————————————————————————
(greetings, announcements, possibly the slogan)

I HEAR WHAT YOU'RE PLAYING 277

Radio Segment Project

This type of project will not be accomplished without well-supervised delegation. Carefully evaluate your students' natural talents. Try to assign every student to a task that will be challenging but manageable for him. (You will only make the project harder for yourself and your students by assigning the least musical student to select music for the dramatic segment.) Of course, if a student is inexperienced or even weak in an area but shows interest in learning more and improving, you should certainly allow that student to participate. You may wish to assign him a partner if you have another student talented in that area who would be a good peer-tutor.

Project Checklist

For the radio segment, you will need to select due dates for each of the following components:

1. Writing a Commercial (activity)
2. Favorite commercial for each client chosen
3. News statements written
4. Broadcast elements (news, commercials, and so on) scheduled
5. Dramatic segment music selected
6. Dramatic segment sound effects found and/or created
7. Promo slogan developed
8. Promo music found or composed
9. Workshop (may require several class periods)
10. Performance

Also, don't forget to assign and announce which students will perform each task. Instruct them to write the appropriate names in the blanks that precede each task.

Commercials *Below your selected commercial, list characters and cast members.*

Client 1: Finley's Pet Shop

Characters	Cast members
_____	_____
_____	_____
_____	_____
_____	_____
_____	_____
_____	_____

Client 2: Brownby's Fine Jewelry, since 1864

Characters	Cast members
_____	_____
_____	_____
_____	_____
_____	_____
_____	_____

Client 3: On a Roll Delicatessen

Characters	Cast members
_____	_____
_____	_____
_____	_____
_____	_____
_____	_____

Dramatic Segments *Below each title, list characters and cast members.*

Title: The Latchstring

Characters	Cast members
_____	_____
_____	_____

Title: The Last Straw

Characters	Cast members
_____	_____
_____	_____

Set goals for each practice session, such as "refine characterization." Chart your progress here. Include individual and group rehearsals.

DATE	GOAL	TIME minutes
	TOTAL TIME	

I HEAR WHAT YOU'RE PLAYING 279

The Evaluation Form

When comparing the evaluation form for the radio segment project with that of the duo-acting project, you will find a couple of changes. *Communication*, *Staging*, and *Action* have been deleted. A category for rating *Technical* aspects has been added in the Teamwork section. Also, *Narration* is a new category in the Interpretation section.

As before, you can grade groups on one or just a few forms and then photocopy the sheet(s) on which your comments appear before writing anything for Individual Work on each student's form.

Student's name/role(s) _____

Teamwork	Comments	Pts.
Unity — 4 Cast functions very well together / 3 Cast functions reasonably well together / 2 Some cast members work well together / 1 Cast seems somewhat disjointed		
Focus — 4 Concentration very evident, very focused / 3 Good level of concentration / 2 Lacking concentration / 1 Little or no concentration—unfocused		
Energy — 4 Excellent energy level; full of vitality / 3 Adequate energy level / 2 Inconsistent or low energy level / 1 Inadequate energy level		
Technical — (Includes text, music, sound cues, etc.) / 4 Consistently accurate and prompt cues / 3 Generally accurate and prompt cues / 2 Some incorrect or delayed cues / 1 Many cues missed		

Interpretation		
Narration — 4 Clear viewpoint; compelling style / 3 Clear viewpoint; acceptable style / 2 Vague viewpoint; acceptable style / 1 Weak viewpoint; weak style		
Characters — 4 Distinct, lifelike characters / 3 Varied characters / 2 Characters sometimes superficial / 1 Characters not distinct or believable		

Individual Work		
Improvement — 4 Utilized feedback to improve significantly / 3 Some improvement shown / 2 Little change from workshop quality / 1 No improvement shown		

You demonstrate good ability in . . .	You would benefit from more attention to . . .

Total Points _____   Grade _____

RADIO SEGMENT WORKSHOP EVALUATION

Name _____ Scene _____

Note: You are ranked on a scale of 1-5, 1 being the lowest and 5 being the highest.

ELEMENT	COMMENTS	RANK
Cue pickups		
Interpretation		
Characterization		
Response to feedback		
Energy/Enthusiasm		
Overall preparedness		

Comments for individuals

SCORE

The Final Challenge Introduction

Often students and teachers approach the close of a semester or school year with mixed emotions. A time of vacation is well anticipated and well earned, yet the end of a chapter in life is always cause for reflection. Use the atmosphere surrounding this time as an educational advantage. Urge your students to make these projects the crowning achievement of their work in this course. You may wish to weight these final assignments with greater point values than previous assignments—enough to reward the students who show significant improvement. However, avoid weighting this project too much; some students have great difficulty concentrating at the end and should not see their grades plummet because of one weak project.

THE FINAL CHALLENGE

Our revels* now are ended. These our actors,
As I foretold you, were all spirits and
Are melted into air, into thin air;
And, like the baseless fabric of this vision,
The cloud-capp'd towers, the gorgeous palaces,
The solemn temples, the great globe itself,*
Yea all which it inherit, shall dissolve,
And, like this insubstantial pageant faded,
Leave not a rack* behind. We are such stuff
As dreams are made on,* and our little life
Is rounded with a sleep.*

—William Shakespeare, The Tempest

revels: entertainment, performance

the great globe itself: double meaning: the Globe Theater and the earth
rack: wisp of a cloud
We are such stuff / As dreams are made on: we are as imaginary and fantastical as dreams.
and our little life / Is rounded with a sleep: suggests that at death we awake from the dream of life into true reality.

The Tempest by William Shakespeare (Bob Jones University Classic Players)

Lesson Plan
Suggested homework is in **boldface.**

Lesson Description	Recommended Presentation	Performance Projects/ Written Assignments
Developing a Production Concept (p. 285)	ST—Think About It (two activities) **TE—A Little Competition**	**TE—Assign Christian Hero and Thematic Script projects** **ST—Assign Journal 13**
Assessment	Chapter quiz and/or final exam	Workshop Performance **ST—Assign Journal 14**
Suggested teaching time: 7-9 class periods		

Shakespeare's final play, *The Tempest*, is often regarded as his most masterfully crafted play. Duke Prospero temporarily holds an entire island under his command. Many people equate this temporary power with the influence of Shakespeare's plays upon each audience. Continuing that comparison, Prospero's speech describes not only the pageant (performance) he staged, but also the pageant Shakespeare staged for the duration of his career in theater. As Prospero's pageant is a play within the play, *The Tempest* is a play within the drama called life.

Thus, as Hamlet says, drama "holds the mirror up to nature," and the audience sees truths about life. As you conclude this study in drama, reflect on the truth you have seen in the literature and performances. For your final project, you will choose one of two assignments. Try to choose a topic or theme that summarizes what you personally have learned this semester.

THE PROJECTS

Your first option for a final project is a storytelling project. You will choose a Christian hero and read about one or more incidents in his life from two or more sources. One source may be a biographical sketch in a reference book, but the other source needs to be an actual biography or autobiography. Develop this story as you did the short story in Chapter 8. Outline the plot of one or more related incidents. You will practice telling the story in your own words before performing it. The story should clearly convey at least one truth about life.

The second option is a *thematic script*. You will choose a theme and three pieces of literature that develop that theme. Though these pieces do not need to be very long, they should represent more than one type of literature. For example, you might use a short or mid-length poem, a short story, and a scene from a play. Or you might select a portion from a famous speech, an article, and a biography. You can choose one piece that is humorous and another that is very serious. You can use well-written *published* letters or journal entries. However, the pieces of literature must fit well together in their shared theme.

Before choosing your project, read the guidelines outlined below and spend some time reading in the library. Equate the importance of this project with that of a music recital: it should showcase the progress you have made in your studies.

The Christian Hero Story

- **Content:** extemporaneous storytelling about a Christian hero's life
- **Length:** eight to ten minutes
- **Possible sources:** biographical sketches and summaries in reference materials; biographies; and autobiographies
- **Purpose**
  Learn about a hero's life in detail.
  Observe truths from real-life narratives.
  Present narrative through effective storytelling.
  Convey at least one truth about life as seen in the hero's testimony.

THE FINAL CHALLENGE 283

Teaching Materials
- Awards for A Little Competition (optional)

 A Little Competition

Have an oral interpretation contest using Prospero's speech from Shakespeare's *Tempest*. Give the students a few days to prepare for the contest. Each student will read or recite Duke Prospero's speech. Tell the students to be creative in their approach. On the contest day, consider having two other teachers join you in judging the contest. (Having either one or three judges is appropriate. Having two judges often creates ties, and it is difficult to break a tie in such a competition.) You may wish to award bonus points or some sort of prize for the contest winner, as well as one or two runner-up awards. (Appropriate first-place prizes might include a copy of Shakespeare's sonnets or famous lines from Shakespeare, note paper or stationery with a dramatic theme, a book of collected monologues, and so on. Remember, a great prize need not be an expensive prize. Even a computer-generated certificate of recognition would work well.)

- **Due dates**

  _____ Select hero

  _____ Complete reading

  _____ Submit rough draft outline

  _____ Submit performance concept worksheet

  _____ Complete final outline*

  _____ Workshop

  _____ Performance

* Your teacher may or may not require you to submit your final outline. Be certain to ask.

- **Additional guidelines**

  Performer must develop a production concept.

  See Chapter 8 to review principles for outlining a story.

The Thematic Script

- **Content:** three pieces of literature
- **Length:** eight to ten minutes
- **Possible sources:** biographies, novels, short stories, articles, poems, diary and journal entries, and letters (all must be published)
- **Purpose**

  Identify themes in various genres of literature.

  Develop a thematic program.

  Clearly present a truth about life based on the script's theme.

- **Due dates**

  _____ Choose theme and first piece of literature

  _____ Choose second and third pieces of literature

  _____ Submit performance concept worksheet

  _____ Submit written transitions

  _____ Complete final script**

  _____ Workshop

  _____ Performance

**Your teacher may or may not require you to submit your final script. Be certain to ask.

- **Additional guidelines**

  Prepare one memorized selection, one extemporaneous selection, and one manuscript selection.

  Write and memorize a short introduction and transitions that help the audience understand the program.

  Develop a production concept (see next section).

PRESENTATION

The Projects

Christian Heroes

Encourage your students to consider reading about and studying heroes of the faith as a hobby. Biographies, autobiographies, journals, and church history books provide a wealth of information about these faithful men and women. Studying Christian biography teaches valuable lessons from these heroes' personal lives in addition to creating a framework for comprehensible study of history.

Of course, knowledge of church history will help students understand why they believe what they believe. Additionally, they will appreciate the struggles that past saints endured and will be encouraged in any struggles that they face personally. For those who will be involved in preaching or teaching in their future ministries, these narratives will serve as excellent illustrations.

A recommended reading list includes biographies and autobiographies as well as the following books surveying church history:

Sidwell, Mark, ed. *Faith of Our Fathers: Scenes from American Church History.* Greenville, S.C.: Bob Jones University Press, 1991.

DEVELOPING A PRODUCTION CONCEPT

In Chapter 9, you learned that professional theater productions have a central idea for conveying meaning—a production concept. Sometimes the central idea is a simple motif, or style. One example given describes a staging of Mark Twain's short story "The Celebrated Jumping Frog of Calaveras County." The motif is simple—hillbilly. This concept governs choice of set, costumes, props, music, and certainly the acting style. A British dialect would be quite out of place, as would a character in a tuxedo.

Sometimes the production concept is more thought-provoking and conveys thematic elements. Guy de Maupassant's "The Necklace" needs more than a motif. The story has very strong thematic elements that must be featured to make the staging successful. The sample given describes two narrators appropriately wearing tuxedoes on an elaborate set. This supports a concept of wealth and luxury. Though this may sound just as simple as the hillbilly concept, the progression of the story soon proves otherwise. Rather than a humorous tale to entertain, "The Necklace" is a harsh commentary on the hypocrisy found in pretentious, upper-class circles and the foolishness of discontentment.

Professional play and opera productions may be scheduled two or more years in advance of the anticipated opening night. The director and staff immediately begin developing a production concept for the event. For either assignment in this chapter, you will follow many of the same steps producers do: study and analyze the material to be performed, research previous productions of that material, view current productions (if possible), and brainstorm for a suitable approach.

The Basic Steps

First, you must know the material very well, understanding the author's intentions and the meaning of the text. You must understand the parts well; but more importantly, you must have a clear understanding of the big picture. Think about the last time you prepared or watched someone prepare food. You may have had some interest in the ingredients, but you were probably eager to know what the finished product would be like—how would it taste and smell and look? This is the perspective you will need on a story, scene, or poem you plan to perform. You need a keen interest in the overall impression. Don't get lost in the details and miss the big picture!

I'm sure the forest is around here somewhere. I just have to find my way out of these trees!

THE FINAL CHALLENGE **285**

Lesson Motivator

Since this section deals with abstractions, you will want to find ways of making them more concrete. Like a poet who explains the seemingly indescribable (such as love or hope) through comparisons, you can compare these ideas with what is familiar to your students. See Designing Examples below for ideas.

Lesson Objectives

The student will be able to

1. Explain *production concept.*

2. Incorporate the basic steps recommended for developing a production concept.

3. Compare two productions of the same play.

Designing Examples

Theatrical productions, like all other products of human invention, must begin with a concept. Someone, somewhere, puts down ideas on a drawing board, so to speak.

Perhaps some of your students may be very interested in cars. If so, you might discuss a couple of popular models. You might contrast the design of a sports utility vehicle with the design of a sports car. Ask your students what the designer has in mind before designing the newest update on an SUV. How is that different from the purpose in designing a sports car? What about

---

————. *Faith of Our Fathers: Scenes from Church History.* Greenville, S.C.: Bob Jones University Press, 1989.

Sidwell, Mark. *Free Indeed: Heroes of Black Christian History.* Greenville, S.C.: Bob Jones University Press, 1995.

Philip Schaff. *History of the Christian Church.* Grand Rapids: Eerdmans, 1995.

PRESENTATION
Developing a Production

The Big Picture

Though we all must manage the details of life each day, a Christian must not let these details obstruct his view of the "big picture" of the Christian life.

Christ gave his followers a commission in Matthew 28:19-20. ("Go ye therefore, and teach all nations, baptizing them in the name of the Father, and of the Son, and of the Holy Ghost: Teaching them to observe all things whatsoever I have commanded you: and, lo, I am with you alway, even unto the end of the world. Amen.")

Not all of us will be called to a foreign land to witness for Christ, but this commission applies to our own nation, states, cities, towns, neighborhoods, and even our own homes. Throughout His earthly ministry, Christ never forgot the big picture—His purpose in

The Final Challenge   285

a family vehicle, such as a minivan, or a luxury vehicle? If your students understand the relationship between the vehicle designer's purposes and the product, they should be able to apply the same reasoning to developing a production concept. Other possible comparisons include clothing fashions, athletic equipment, and computer software.

Developing a Production Concept

1. Study and analyze the material to be performed.
2. Research previous productions of the material.
3. View current productions, if possible.
4. Brainstorm for a suitable approach.

A director tries to learn from previous and current productions to get a variety of perspectives; you can gain further insight into the meaning and purpose of your selection by doing the same. Attend plays and forensics meets to spark your creativity.

The director leads the production staff in brainstorming for a production concept; likewise, you must decide what element of the script to emphasize. In a play, this emphasis is applied as much as possible to the design of the set, the lighting, the music and sound, the costumes, and the makeup style. It also influences the casting and acting styles. Although you will not have all these elements in your project, apply the production concept to the ones that you do have.

Sample Productions to Consider

Shakespeare's frequently performed comedy *As You Like It* depicts two sets of brothers and two cousins. Duke Senior, whose power has been usurped by his brother, Duke Frederick, lives in exile in the Forest of Arden. A youth named Orlando, fearing his own evil brother, hides in the Forest of Arden. The usurping duke also turns against his niece Rosalind and threatens her life if she doesn't leave the court. His daughter chooses to run away with Rosalind to the Forest of Arden.

Since the Forest of Arden is a fictitious location and the play contains no references to historical figures or facts, *As You Like It* can be performed in a wide range of time periods and settings without straining the text whatsoever. Two productions of this play are described below. Notice how each has a production concept that emphasizes different features of one play. Your storytelling project and thematic scripts may also be handled several ways effectively.

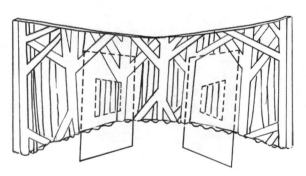

Production 1

Production concept: seasons of the heart

Time period: 1870 (country and continent are not identified—probably European)

Description: As the play progresses, the autumn set shown here adapts marvelously to the plot and the production concept. Scenes in the elegant 1870s court of Duke Frederick add a tapestry rug and furniture to what is shown. The

---

coming to earth. Though He healed diseases, walked on water, and raised the dead, these miracles were only details in His commission.

remainder of the play occurs in the forest. The two flats tilt back, becoming ramps that suggest paths leading into the forest. When the colorful curtain is drawn back, autumn comes to an end. Now the tree branches that had been silhouettes behind colorful foliage are dark and barren in appearance—an ideal setting for Duke Senior's speech about "the icy fang . . . of the winter's wind." This move from autumn to winter emphasizes mood for the banishment of Rosalind. Later, spring arrives as several romances develop. Finally, summer emphasizes life and growth when the brothers reunite and several weddings take place.

Production 2

Production concept: revelry vs. rivalry

Setting: Philadelphia, Pennsylvania: the "city of brotherly love" accentuates the importance of family relationships.

Time period: 1815: Pennsylvania was still largely forest region during the early nineteenth century. Also, close-knit families characterized the early nineteenth century as many pioneered into the uncharted West.

Description: Elegant Edwardian home furnishings shown here lend formality to the duke's court. The set and costumes give the impression of a black-and-white photograph, yellowed by the passing of time. This emphasizes the detachment of these first scenes.

When the story moves to the Forest of Arden, the backdrop is removed, revealing a forest scene that one might find in a child's coloring book—the grass and leaves are colored crayon-box green, and

the sky (backdrop), crayon-box blue. Costumes share this color scheme. In this simplified, almost storybook setting, the two pairs of brothers, having learned the lesson of brotherly love, forsake the *rivalry* known at court and join their friends in *revelry* at the conclusion of the play.

THE FINAL CHALLENGE 287

And fall into our rustic revelry.
Play, music! And you, brides and bridegrooms all,
With measure heap'd in joy, to the measures fall.

Application

Of course, neither production described above represents the "right way" to stage *As You Like It*. Any approach that reflects the intent of the author and presents the story within the boundaries of a unifying idea is generally very effective.

Production Concept
• Reflects the intent of the author
• Presents the story within the boundaries of a unifying idea

The Christian Hero Story

When you are planning your hero story, you will have to decide how to present your hero. For example, if you present a narrative from the life of hymn writer Fanny Crosby, you might choose one of her famous hymns as a theme for your story. Depending on which song and theme you choose, you may decide to wear a costume and actually play Crosby, or you might decide to be a narrator or family member. Obviously, you should choose costuming only if the character is your gender. Otherwise, you must be a neutral storyteller or an appropriate character in the hero's life.

For example, a young lady might tell about Jonathan Edwards and his family as his wife, Sarah Edwards, or as one of his daughters. Do not decide on features such as costuming, set, props, and so on without first deciding what message you need to convey. Once the message, or theme, is clear in your mind, decide how to convey that message and apply it to each area—costumes, set, props, and so on. You don't need a stage to create an interesting setting for your story. An electric candle or a small lamp, a table with a table covering, a cushioned chair, or any other simple prop can make a great difference in the effect of the program. In what setting do you imagine your character? If he or she has a desk, is it messy or neat, elegant or simple?

A Sample Plan For a Christian Hero Story

(female performer)

Note: a storytelling outline is not included here, though the Christian Hero Story project requires one. Refer to outlining principles and samples in Chapter 8 as needed.

Topic: Fanny Crosby

Theme: Spiritual light in a world of darkness

Explanation: Fanny Crosby was blind, but she met the true Light of the world, Jesus Christ. Though she continued in physical darkness, she walked in spiritual light. She knew that in eternity, she would enjoy both physical and spiritual light in the presence of her Savior.

Production concept: From darkness to light

Application: The performer, dressed like Crosby in somber-colored clothing, tells the narrative in first person. The set is a wooden chair and table. Props include a Bible, dark glasses, several very old books, loose papers, and a cane. Lighting is an old lamp on the desk at the beginning. At the end, the performer has a friend slowly open the blinds, creating a long shaft of sunlight on the acting area. The performer strives to convey a mood of hope and faith through her delivery.

Evaluation

This production concept supports the theme of the script, taken directly from the character's life. Depending on your situation and available resources, you may include other means of developing the concept than what is described in this sample. Let the sky be your limit as you brainstorm alone or with a friend to develop and apply a concept to your script.

Think About It

How might a male performer tell about the life of Fanny Crosby?

_____
_____
_____
_____
_____
_____

The Thematic Script

The thematic script may be approached in a similar fashion. Consider the general topic "The Civil War." First, narrow it down to a more specific topic, such as "Abraham Lincoln." Next, choose what theme in his life to develop. Possible themes include "humble roots to great dignity," "a man of character," and "in pursuit of peace."

THE FINAL CHALLENGE 289

Sample Thematic Script

(male performer)

Topic: Abraham Lincoln

Theme: In pursuit of peace

Explanation: Abraham Lincoln faced the task of governing a nation torn by political, economic, social, and moral issues. Amid a whirlwind of polarized views on these issues, Lincoln strove to create compromise in hopes of preserving the union—in hopes of bringing peace to a nation "conceived in liberty." Today, U.S. currency bears his image, and the Lincoln Memorial in Washington, D.C., stands as a tribute to his great leadership. Truly, Lincoln's consuming goal as president of the United States was "that this nation, under God, shall have a new birth of freedom, and that government of the people, by the people, for the people, shall not perish from the earth."

Production concept: In the eye of the storm

Application: Notations throughout the script describe application of the production concept for set, props, and technical aspects.

Script Outline

The presentation begins with a visual image and sound effects that suggest a physical windstorm. The performer, dressed in neutral modern clothing, places a desk and chair in the acting area of the room. A swirled pile of papers and an electric candle are on the desk. A friend turns off the lights in the room, but the candle is still "burning." The performer exits the acting area and turns on a recording with sounds of wind gusts. (Sound-effects CD libraries are often available at public libraries.) When the wind gusts become audible, the candle "goes out" (is unplugged). Now in near darkness, the performer approaches the desk. When he reaches it, the lights are turned on and then the sound-effects recording fades as the performer introduces the script.

Introduction: Whatever else may be said of the sixteenth president of the United States, Abraham Lincoln, all may agree that he had an indomitable spirit. Despite a humble background, division in his political party, and tremendous personal criticism from newspapers and politicians alike, Lincoln governed boldly and sincerely.

Vachel Lindsay's poem "When Abraham Lincoln Walks at Midnight" speaks not of the Civil War, but of the First World War, using Lincoln as a symbol for the American spirit that loves peace and freedom.

Acting: Throughout each portion of the performance in which Lincoln is characterized, the performer conveys dignity through posture, movement, and clothing.

Selection 1: "When Abraham Lincoln Walks at Midnight" by Vachel Lindsay (memorized)

Goal: to communicate a storm of personal sorrows.

Sitting in a chair turned sideways to the audience, the performer suggests a ride in a train with his bodily movement—the jostling of starts and stops. His demeanor conveys slight agitation throughout this introduction. However, when he stands to deliver the address, a sense of calm sweeps over him.

Transition: Some important political figures refused to attend the dedication of the cemetery at Gettysburg, insisting that the president would say nothing worth their hearing. Before Lincoln departed by train to Gettysburg, his child became ill. Then, on the train, an older man approached to say, "My son died at Gettysburg." Lincoln offered words of comfort and then remarked, "When I think of the sacrifices of life yet to be offered, and the hearts and homes yet to be made desolate before this dreadful war is over, my heart is like lead within me, and I feel at times like hiding in deep darkness."

Selection 2: "The Gettysburg Address" by Abraham Lincoln (manuscript)

Goal: to communicate a storm of public opinion

A friend plays another very brief recording of several voices exclaiming, "Mr. President," "Excuse me, Mr. President!" to convey a group of pushy newspaper reporters swarming Lincoln.

Transition: Lincoln's dedication at the Gettysburg cemetery received varied responses. Although the *Chicago Times* reported that "on the present occasion Lincoln acted the clown," the dedication's principal speaker, Edward Everett, wrote to the president the next day: "I should be glad if I could flatter myself that I came as near to the central idea of the occasion in two hours as you did in two minutes."

Despite criticism and the great burden of wartime leadership, Lincoln continued in the White House for a second term. He once said, "I destroy my enemies when I make them my friends."

Selection 3: Carl Sandburg's *Abraham Lincoln: The War Years*, Chapter 63: "The Second Inaugural" (extemporaneous storytelling)

Sound of the wind gusts is repeated and fades out slowly with the concluding speech.

Conclusion: (final paragraph of the inaugural address) "With malice toward none; with charity for all; with firmness in the right, as God gives us to see the right, let us strive on to finish the work we are in; to bind up the nation's wounds; to care for him who shall have borne the battle and for his widow, and his orphan—to do all which may achieve and cherish a just and a lasting peace among ourselves, and with all nations."

THE FINAL CHALLENGE 291

Christian Hero and Thematic Script Projects

As is emphasized in the student text, the final projects should be viewed with the gravity of a year-end music recital. The student should strive to demonstrate his progress as well as his best effort in the subject. If you find that your students need so much time for this project that they cannot prepare for a final exam, eliminate the test, not the project. If you want to give a final exam that is not cumulative, consider a test over Unit 3 with a few questions about production concept included.

You will notice that there are fewer recommended activities for this chapter compared with every previous chapter. You will need your class time to help students with their projects. If expected to complete all of the necessary tasks independently, the students will not only lack adequate time, but most of them will also become overwhelmed by the task and will never complete it satisfactorily. However, with your help and peer encouragement, such projects can challenge and develop your students. They will find preparing a forensics selection far less intimidating after success in this course.

Evaluation

Lincoln spent his terms as president pursuing peace for the American people. The script reflects that idea as a theme of his life and his legacy. The production concept, "In the eye of the storm," works as counterpoint to the theme, contrasting his pursuit with the struggles that surrounded his public service.

Think About It

How might a female performer tell about the life of Abraham Lincoln? (The literature and theme need not be the same as what is presented here.)

_____
_____
_____
_____
_____
_____

CONCLUSION

Though this project concludes your present course of study in performing literature, you have a lifetime of learning ahead of you. Keep reading for your own benefit and pleasure. Keep reading to others. Someone once said, "To learn to read to others is to have the pleasure of eating a good meal with friends at the table rather than to eat alone." This feast is available to all who open a volume of literature to share it with a friend or group. Bon appétit!

 THE FINAL CHALLENGE

 **A Lifetime of Learning**

Read the following line from the text to your students: "You have a lifetime of learning ahead of you." This line refers to communicating literature to others, but what does it mean in a broader sense? What implications does that sentence have for their future lives? (*Answers may include that you don't learn everything there is to know in high school and college; self-motivation in the learning process is necessary after high school and college; life is not long enough to learn all that there is to know; reading should be a major part of your life; and so on.*)

Final Project Assignment Sheet

Prepare

Carefully follow the checklist provided with your chosen project. Remember that good written work is the best foundation for an effective performance.

Practice

Set goals for each practice session, such as "refine characterization." Chart your progress here. Include individual and group rehearsals.

DATE	GOAL	TIME minutes
	TOTAL TIME	

WRITTEN WORK EVALUATION

Name _____   Scene _____

Note: You are ranked on a scale of 1-10, 1 being the lowest and 10 being the highest.

ELEMENT	COMMENTS	RANK

Performance concept is
  Clearly stated
  Appropriate for the script
  Applied effectively		

Script is presented
  In correct form
  Clearly and neatly		

Text or selections are well chosen and organized		
Comments		**SCORE**

THE FINAL CHALLENGE 293

Project Checklist

For the Christian hero project, you will need to select due dates for each of the following components:

1. Hero selected
2. Reading completed
3. Statements of theme and production concept*
4. Rough draft outline
5. Production concept worksheet
6. Final outline (optional)
7. Final Project assignment sheet
8. Christian hero workshop
9. Christian hero performance

For the thematic script project, you will need to select due dates for each of the following components:

1. Theme and first piece of literature selected
2. Second and third pieces of literature selected
3. Statements of production concept*
4. Rough draft script or written transition statements (optional)
5. Production concept worksheet
6. Thematic script workshop
7. Final outline (optional)
8. Final project assignment sheet
9. Thematic script performance

*You may wish to require students to submit tentative ideas for these before their production concept worksheet is due. That way you can redirect students as needed before they spend much homework time developing content for their projects based on a vague or unacceptable theme or concept.

WORKSHOP EVALUATION

Name _____ Scene _____

Note: You are ranked on a scale of 1-5, 1 being the lowest and 5 being the highest.

ELEMENT	COMMENTS	RANK
Interpretation		
Characterization		
Response to feedback		
Improvement		
Energy/Enthusiasm		
Overall preparedness		

Comments

SCORE

Production Concept Worksheet

Christian Hero Story

Name _____ *Score* _____

Topic _____

Theme _____

Explanation _____
_____
_____

Production concept
_____

Application _____
_____
_____

Introduction:

   I. _____

   II. _____

   III. _____

Conclusion:

THE FINAL CHALLENGE 295

Production Concept Worksheet

Thematic Script

Name _____ **Score** _____

Topic _____

Theme _____

Explanation _____

_____

_____

Production concept _____

_____

Application (Write neatly in the margin by each portion of the outline or include on a separate sheet of paper.)

Label each selection of literature as memorized, manuscript, or extemporaneous storytelling.

Introduction:

First selection: _____
Transition:

Second selection: _____
Transition:

Third selection: _____
Conclusion:

Name _____ Program Title _____

Selection(s) _____

Teamwork		Comments	Pts.
Narration	4 Clear viewpoint; compelling style 3 Clear viewpoint; acceptable style 2 Vague viewpoint; acceptable style 1 Weak viewpoint; weak style		
Characterization	4 Strong evidence that observations have been incorporated into characterization 3 Clear characterization communicated 2 Adequate characterization communicated 1 Unclear or weak characterization		
Word Color	4 Compelling imagery 3 Mostly vivid imagery 2 Some clear imagery 1 Flat, uninteresting imagery		
Illusion of First Time	4 Effectively communicated by concentration and realization 3 Adequately conveyed 2 Not sustained 1 Unclear, not compelling		

Delivery		Comments	
Poise	4 Excellent emotional control 3 Good emotion to control nervousness 2 Noticeable nervousness 1 Nervousness obvious		
Bodily Action	4 Aids communication 3 Usually enhances the message 2 Neither distracts from nor enhances the message 1 Distracts from the message		

Outline

Written
4 (5 check marks)
3 (4 check marks)
2 (3 check marks)
1 (1-2 check marks)

— Main points accurately reflect primary plot complications

— Supporting points facilitate movement from one main point to the next

— Introduction is well chosen

— Conclusion is well chosen

— If used, delivery cues are used correctly

You demonstrate good ability in . . .	You would benefit from more attention to . . .

Total Points _____   Grade _____

The Evaluation Form

Although this rubric bears little resemblance to the rubrics for the last few projects, it is identical to the rubric for the storytelling project. You may wish to attach additional comments to this last evaluation, describing each student's progress shown during the course. Every student, regardless of level of ability, should find this encouraging. Even just a sentence of encouragement added in the bottom margin can have a profound effect.

... an ever fixed mark, that looks on tempests and is never shaken

O for a muse of FIRE

ILLUSION

reality

MASK

nature MIRROR

TRUTH

drama

the quality of MERCY is

... each man in his time plays many ...

strained; it droppeth as the

tle falling

MERCY is not strained; it

DREAMS

APPENDIX A
THE PERFORMER'S JOURNAL

For this course you will generally have one or two assignments per chapter to write in a personal performer's journal. Sometimes you will be asked to critique your monologue or scene. Other times you will write about goals for yourself. Your teacher might not read every entry, but he will definitely check to be certain you have completed the assignments.

Though these entries may be informal in style, you should always practice correct grammar and usage in your writing. Also remember that your teacher would rather see clear, meaningful thought than great volumes of "fluff."

• Entry 1

Write three or four sentences evaluating your performance of "Story Without Words" and/or "Sing Your Story." (Your teacher may require both of these assignments.)

• Entry 2

This journal entry is very special and may be your longest entry. It could easily require a full page (front and back) or more. Most subsequent entries will be only one to three paragraphs.

Title this entry "My Performance Compass" or something similar. Discuss several key beliefs you hold. Then explain how you will protect these convictions as you "navigate" through fiction and drama to perform. Possible topics to discuss include religion, family, work ethic, and personal convictions.

• Entry 3

After reading Chapter 4, choose one piece of quoted literature and write a brief paragraph discussing its theme. Identify the literature by title, author, and genre (prose, poetry, or drama).

• Entry 4

Complete this activity after you present your Scripture story. Your entry needs to be just five or six sentences long. Your topic is "Using oral reading of Scripture in ministry." Be specific about how you can use oral reading of Scripture personally as you serve currently and/or in the future. (For example, will you read the story or tell it? Will you read narratives in junior church or a Bible club?)

The Performer's Journal

Introduction

You can use this journal as an opportunity to teach your students to record their progress. Emphasize thoughtful and honest evaluation on each assignment. Content is more important than format, spelling, and grammar.

Keeping the journal pages together throughout the semester, whether in a binder or a notebook, is strongly recommended. You may wish to have students reread their journals at the end of the semester to observe the ways they've grown.

Journal Entry 1

Make certain your students write a self-evaluation. Critiquing fellow actors has its place, but this journal entry should focus on what each student perceives he did well and what areas he needs to improve. You may wish to collect this assignment promptly to compare the students' self-evaluations to your diagnosis of their current performance level. If you see a large discrepancy, now is the time to meet with that student. Make certain he understands why he received the grade and comments you gave.

Journal Entry 2

Since this entry is much lengthier than any other, you may wish to require an essay format. Rather than just allowing students to record ideas as they think of them, encourage them to organize their thoughts first. They can list categories they wish to cover and then develop each category into a two- to three-sentence paragraph. If time permits, you may wish to ask students to back up their statements with Scripture. Encourage them to use resources such as Bible study software and Bible concordances.

Journal Entry 3

This assignment should help students begin to evaluate literature, preparing them for the dramatistic analysis assignments used in future chapters.

Journal Entry 4

This assignment is a simple and ideal way for your students to think about how their studies relate to their lives

• Entry 5

Complete this activity after the sonnet performances. Your entry needs to be just five or six sentences long. Your topic is "My favorite sonnet performance." Name the sonnet, author, and performer. Give several reasons you liked it. For example, tell what specific elements about your peer's delivery made you like it.

• Entry 6

Complete this activity after you perform your monologue. Your entry needs to be just six or seven sentences long. Choose one of the following topics. (Your teacher may require both of these assignments.)

1. In one brief paragraph, describe what types of roles you might play because of the style of your monologue. In a second paragraph, describe a contrasting role and what you might use to audition for it.

2. Describe a character in minute detail. Draw from the monologues you have just seen performed and the improvisational activities from this chapter. This character may be completely fictitious or based on a person you know. Either way, give your character a fictitious name. Describe his or her voice, posture, manners, and so on.

• Entry 7

Complete this exercise after presenting your storytelling project. Write a paragraph evaluating how you adapted to audience feedback as you told the story. For example, if your audience consisted of preschoolers, how did you adjust to squirming or miscellaneous comments about "new shoes," "baby brother" or the like?

• Entry 8

After participating in one or more readers theater scripts, write a paragraph describing your role(s) and what your experience was like. Read this paragraph to a friend who is unfamiliar with readers theater. Help him picture what happened.

• Entry 9

After your chamber theater workshop, brainstorm about what you personally or what your group can do to improve your scene. Form these ideas into a brief proposal that you can share with your fellow actors. Seek their feedback, whether your ideas are about your own performance or the group's performance.

 APPENDIX A

---

outside school. For many it may prompt an interest in participating in ministry as well.

Journal Entry 5

Journal entry 5 should help students begin to recognize the benefits of effective delivery as they associate an enjoyable presentation with good delivery.

Journal Entry 6

For option 1, students will probably describe how a humorous monologue may lead to a comic role or an emotionally intense selection might show their qualifications for portraying a tragic character.

For option 2, students should demonstrate ability to imagine a stage character with enough detail to make that character realistic and believable. Such an exercise should help students avoid generic or stock characters when they perform.

Journal Entry 7

Students need to learn to adapt to various audiences so that as parents, Sunday-school teachers, and professionals, they will suit their communication style to the situation. This assignment will be more valuable if your students tell their stories to a group of children rather than their classmates, but it is applicable either way.

• Entry 10

Complete this assignment after studying Chapter 10. Your entry needs to be just six or seven sentences long. Choose one of the following topics for an essay. (Your teacher may require both of these assignments.)

1. Compare the stage space your school provides with another type of stage. Identify each stage as proscenium, arena, or thrust, and then describe the advantages of each.

2. If you have seen a play or other dramatic presentation at your school, you may discuss how that drama worked on the available stage and what might be different on a different type of stage. Identify each stage as proscenium, arena, or thrust.

• Entry 11

Complete this assignment after performing your duo-acting scene. Your entry needs to be just six or seven sentences long. Evaluate your participation in the project as a team player. How did you interact in ways that helped your rehearsals to be effective? What might you do in a future duo-acting scene to be a better team player? (If your rehearsals were not very effective, tell why and how you might approach the process differently for better results.)

• Entry 12

Complete this assignment after performing the radio segment project. Your entry needs to be just six or seven sentences long. Choose one of the following topics for a paragraph discussion. (Your teacher may require two or more of these assignments.)

1. Describe your principal role in the project. What did you like or dislike about your role? What did you learn? What might you do better in the future?

2. After specifying what role(s) you played in the project, discuss what role you would like to play if you have another opportunity to participate in radio programming. Give reasons for your choice.

3. If you are interested in a career in radio, discuss what role you would be most interested in and why you would pursue such a career.

• Entry 13

Complete this assignment after choosing your topic and theme for your final project. State your topic and theme. Then in one or two paragraphs describe your goal(s) for your project. What effect do you want to have on your audience (provoke thought, cause laughter, inspire to virtue, and so on)? Also give reasons for your goal(s).

• Entry 14

Complete this assignment after all performances of the final project. Your topic is "The most important lesson I learned during my study of literature performance." Your entry should be about three paragraphs in length. You may title your entry if you wish.

Journal Entry 8

Look for clear, accurate, and vivid description with this assignment.

Journal Entry 9

This assignment permits the student to critique his personal performance or the performance of his group. You may wish to instruct students to cover both subjects.

If possible, allow a few minutes during class for students to meet with the other students in their scenes and share the feedback they recorded in their journals.

Journal Entry 10

This entry may require more time and thought than the others. Be sure to tell your students to allow more writing time as they budget their homework time.

For option 1, be sure to check for accuracy concerning your school's facilities. Also, when giving the assignment, you may need to recommend several other local stage spaces as a reminder to students. For example, if you know that a local performance center hosts theater troupes and orchestras and the like, mention its name. Some students may have attended an event there in the past.

For option 2, expect students to be thorough in their description of the production they saw and be creative about alternative staging possibilities.

Evaluate Your Intake

For the next three days, check each of the following categories.

Time in minutes		DAY ONE				DAY TWO				DAY THREE				TOTALS	GROUP TOTALS
		0-30	31-60	61-120	121+	0-30	31-60	61-120	121+	0-30	31-60	61-120	121+		
TELEVISION	educational														Television
	sports														
	weather/news														
	features														
	sitcoms/cartoons														
MUSIC	sacred														Music
	classical														
	other														
RADIO (NONMUSIC)	weather/news														Radio
	talk shows														
	sports														
	other														

Grand Total _____

Compare your grand total to the amount of time you have spent in prayer, Bible reading, and verse memorization. Most of us would have to hang our heads in shame. We are very likely spending more time each day listening to music, viewing sports, and performing other activities listed above than we are pursuing knowledge of God.

Though God does not demand that the majority of our day be spent in Bible study, He has commanded us to do several other things:

> Finally, brethren, whatsoever things are true, whatsoever things are honest, whatsoever things are just, whatsoever things are pure, whatsoever things are lovely, whatsoever things are of good report; if there be any virtue, and if there be any praise, think on these things. (Philippians 4:8)

> And be not conformed to this world: but be ye transformed by the renewing of your mind, that ye may prove what is that good, and acceptable, and perfect, will of God. (Romans 12:1)

302 APPENDIX B

Journal Entry 11

Since so many students desire to compete in duo-acting competitions, learning to work with a partner is particularly important. Remind students that honest evaluation can lead to personal growth and development.

Journal Entry 12

The feedback your students give on these questions concerning roles may prove useful to you if you teach this course again in future semesters. It may guide you in delegating responsibilities for this project.

Journal Entry 13

Unlike previous entries, journal entry 13 asks the student to set forth goals, not just evaluate past events. As part of a final project in the course, this should prompt students to realize that purposeful planning is an important part of maturity. The adult with a vision will be more likely to succeed—in college, in career, and in his personal goals.

Journal Entry 14

Look for a carefully thought-out and reflective answer. Urge your students to be thorough and honest. Tell students they may wish to retain this journal as well as their graded rubrics for a college portfolio. Those studying subjects related to education or communication may find these two items very useful.

APPENDIX C
SELECTED SONNETS

Note: Lines 1-8 develop an idea. Lines 9-14 draw conclusions about that idea. Notice that the phrasing is more fluid and conversational in the beginning but that the second part requires frequent pauses to match its more assertive content.

Sample Sonnet Script

Sonnet 54 by William Shakespeare

(O, how much more doth beauty) (beauteous seem

By that sweet ornament* which truth doth give!) /   *ornament: decoration*

(The rose looks fair,) (but fairer we it deem*   *deem: judge, evaluate*

For that sweet odour which doth in it live.) /

(The canker-blooms* have full as deep a dye   *canker-blooms: wild rose blossom or the blossom of a dog rose*

As the perfumed tincture* <u>of the roses,</u>)   *tincture: pigment*
of the roses: simile—canker blooms are the same color as roses

(Hang on such thorns) (and play as wantonly*

When <u>summer's breath</u> their masked buds discloses:*) /   *wantonly: in a frolicsome manner, teasingly*
summer's breath: metaphor—tenor is the warm weather of summer

(But, for their virtue only is their show,*) /   *summer's . . . discloses:* air (weather) that can open the closed buds
show: display

<u>(They live unwoo'd)</u> <u>(and unrespected fade,)</u>   **they live unwoo'd:** personification—as a woman is wooed
and unrespected fade: personification—ascribing character to the flowers

<u>(Die to themselves.)</u> / (Sweet roses do not so;) /   **Die to themselves:** personification—ascribing a will to the flowers

(Of their sweet deaths are sweetest odours* made:) //   *odours: scents, fragrances*

<u>(And so of you,)</u> <u>(beauteous and lovely youth,)</u>   **And so of you, beauteous and lovely youth:** apostrophe—direct address to the abstraction Youth

(When that shall fade,) / (my verse distills* your   *distills: purifies*

truth.)//

SELECTED SONNETS 303

Selected Sonnets

Introduction

With each poem mentioned below, you will find one possible theme or central truth. As students analyze these poems, they may easily make other valid conclusions. Encourage them to think on their own. Use this material as a guide, not a dictator.

Many of the poems include ideas and questions for discussion.

Student Resources

Emphasize the notes provided for each sonnet in the student text. These should aid the students' sonnet evaluation by saving time they would have used "looking up words." These notes fall into three categories: unfamiliar words, words used symbolically, metaphorically, etc., and literary and biblical allusions.

Encourage the students to read the entire sonnet first, without the aid of the marginal notes, attempting to define unfamiliar words based on contextual clues. After making a thoughtful attempt, the student should reread the text, referencing the meaning of any word with an asterisk (*).

Numerous sonnets, particularly Shakespeare's and these by modern (19th and 20th century) authors, employ familiar words that convey metaphor, simile, or other poetic devices. Since a

---

Teacher Resources

In Appendix C, you will find two basic tools to assist you in teaching and grading the students' work on the sonnet project.

First of all, since a thorough student analysis of a performance selection includes basic biographical details, brief biographical sketches are provided in the margin for your reference in grading the students' written work. Obviously, these are far from exhaustive.

Secondly, if your class size is small, some days scheduled for performance in the suggested teaching schedule may be used for class discussion instead. You will find some discussion questions on the following pages.

Finally, biblical and literary allusions are cited to enhance the students' understanding of context and to demonstrate integration of literature and other studies.

Since most sonnets use formal or even archaic diction, stress thoughtful pre-performance evaluation. Otherwise, the sonnet project will become a tedious drill in rote memorization. It should be an exciting opportunity to present one of the most popular and enduring poetic forms.

Edmund Spenser
(ca.1552-99)

Spenser, whose family was likely connected to prominent families in Lancashire, received a comprehensive education studying classics of literature and rhetoric as well as Latin, Greek, and Hebrew.

His *Amoretti* and *Epithalamion* reflect his marriage to Elizabeth Boyle. Spenser also authored the unfinished epic *The Faerie Queene* and other shorter works.

Ben Jonson reports that Spenser died "for lake [lack] of bread" in January 1599, though it seems unlikely for a popular poet to starve to death.

Spenser is buried in Westminster Abbey.

Sonnet 75 by Edmund Spenser

One day I wrote her name upon the strand,★

But came the waves and washèd it away.

Agayne I wrote it with a second hand,

But came the tyde and made my paynes his prey.

Vayne man, sayd she, that dost in vaine★ assay★

A mortal thing so to immortalize,

For I myself shall like to this decay,

And eke★ my name be wipèd out likewise.

Not so, quod★ I, let baser★ things devize

To die in dust, but you shall live by fame.

My verse your vertues rare shall eternize,

And in the hevens wryte your glorious name.

Where, whenas death shall all the world subdew,

Our love shall live, and later life renew.

strand: beach

in vaine: profitlessly
assay: attempt

eke: also

quod: said
baser: lower, worse

AMORETTI III: THE SOVEREIGN BEAUTY
by Edmund Spenser

The soverayne★ beauty which I do admyre,

Witnesse the world how worthy to be prayzed!

The light whereof hath kindled heavenly fyre

In my frail spirit, by her from baseness★ raised;

That being now with her huge brightness dazed,

Base thing I can no more endure to view;

But looking still on her, I stand amazed

At wondrous sight of so celestiall hue.

So when my tongue would speak her praises due,

It stopped is with thought's astonishment:

And when my pen would write her titles true

It ravisht★ is with fancies wonderment:

Yet in my heart I then both speake and write

The wonder that my wit cannot endite.★

soverayne: superlative in power, authority

baseness: he declares she has elevated him

ravisht: carried off

endite: proclaim, declare

(304) APPENDIX C

Edmund Spenser

Sonnet 75

Theme. Though many monuments are temporal, poetry can create a lasting monument.

Discussion. Spenser uses the sand to represent brevity. As children build sandcastles that the tide will easily level, so we too try to carve messages in the sands of time that may be easily forgotten.

1. Compare sands of the beach to sands in an hour glass. What influence does time hold over each? How are they different? (*Figuratively speaking, the passing of the hours changes these "sands." As time passes, the tide comes to manipulate the beach's surface, strewing it with plant and animal life; the passing of time permits sands to slip through the glass. Sands in the glass measure time, whereas time "measures" the sand of the beach, changing it from dry to wet and back, as well as altering its composition.*)

2. How is sand an appropriate symbol for mortality? (*Answers may vary. Sand depicts mortality well since we are formed from the dust [Gen. 2:7] and return to the earth.*)

Sonnet 68 by Edmund Spenser

Most glorious Lord of lyfe,* that on this day

Did'st make thy triumph over death and sin,

And having harrowd* hell did'st bring away

Captivity thence captive,* us to win:

This joyous day, dear Lord, with joy begin;

And grant that we, for whom Thou diddest die,

Being with thy dear blood clean washt* from sin

May live for ever in felicity!*

And that thy love we weighing worthily

May likewise love Thee for the same againe;

And for thy sake, that all lyke deare didst buy,

With love may one another entertayne.*

So let us love, deare love, lyke as we ought:

Love is the lesson which the Lord us taught.

Lord of lyfe: the resurrected Christ

harrowd: plundered
bring away / Captivity thence captive: allusion to Ephesians 4:8-9 "When he ascended up on high, he led captivity captive, and gave gifts unto men. (Now that he ascended, what is it but that he also descended first into the lower parts of the earth?)"

clean washt: washed completely

felicity: happiness, bliss

entertayne: harbor or maintain

Sonnet 1 from Astrophel and Stella

by Sir Philip Sidney

Loving in truth, and faine* in verse my love to show,

That she (dear She) might take some pleasure of my paine,

Pleasure might cause her read, reading might make her know,

Knowledge might pitie win, and pitie grace obtaine,

I sought fit words to paint the blackest face of woe;

Studying inventions* fine, her wits to entertaine,

Oft turning others' leaves,* to see if thence would flow

Some fresh and fruitfull showers* upon my sun-burn'd brain.

But words came halting* forth, wanting Inventions stay;*

Invention, Natures child, fled step-dame* Studies blowes;*

And others' feet still seemed but strangers in my way.

Thus, great with child* to speake, and helplesse in my throes,*

Biting my truant* pen, beating my selfe for spite,

Foole, said my Muse to me, looke in thy heart, and write.

faine: giving a false appearance

inventions: ideas

leaves: pages or books

showers: ideas
halting: wavering or moving with uncertainty
wanting Inventions stay: the desired (wanted) ideas are "stuck"
step-dame: stepmother
Studies blowes: as he flails away at ideas of what he might write, the ideas run away as a child runs from a spanking
great with child: literally, at the end of a pregnancy; here used to imply urgency
throes: severe pain, as occurs in childbirth
truant: lazy or idle

Sir Philip Sidney
(1554-86)

Sir Philip Sidney received his education at Christ Church College, Oxford. As a soldier, Sidney was eventually knighted by Elizabeth I. He was a model of the Renaissance gentleman.

In 1585, he became a governor in the Netherlands; he died of wounds received while fighting against a Spanish convoy.

All of his works were published posthumously. The best known are "The Defence of Poesie," the sonnet cycle *Astrophel and Stella*, and *Arcadia*.

Most Glorious Lord of Lyfe
Theme. Christ's death and Resurrection are an example to us concerning the sacrificial nature of love.

Discussion. Though we were sinners—enemies of God—Christ loved us enough to die in our place. His Resurrection provided a means by which we can enjoy eternal bliss rather than condemnation. We should follow Christ's example, loving as He loved.

1. The conclusion emphasizes what scriptural lesson? (*to love God and our neighbors* [Matt. 22:37-40] *and to be kind* [Eph. 4:32].)
2. Discuss the motives Spenser cites for fulfilling that command. (*Christ conquered death and sin for us, He bought us, etc.*)

Sir Philip Sidney

Sonnet 1 from Astrophel and Stella
Theme. Emotions are difficult to express.

Discussion. Imagine yourself in the following situations. When a friend hurts your feelings, is it hard to tell him so? After arguing with your sister, can you talk it out? How long after your parents refuse permission to attend an activity will it take for you to communicate profitably with them again—minutes? an hour? a day?

1. Why are certain subjects difficult to speak or write about? (*The scenes described above as well as the situation in the*

John Donne
(1572-1631)

Raised as a Roman Catholic in an Anglican Church environment, John Donne (DUN) spent his early years without a sincere faith. His early poetry, like his lifestyle, reflects the degenerate nature of fallen man. When his wife, Ann More, died, Donne's life changed direction. As can be seen in his *Holy Sonnets*, John Donne became a man with a broken and contrite heart, devoted fully to God.

His contributions to literature include metaphysical poetry, satire, songs, and the *Holy Sonnets*.

Holy Sonnet 2 by John Donne

As due by many titles* I resign*

My self to Thee, O God; first I was made

By Thee, and for Thee, and when I was decayed*

Thy blood bought that, the which before was Thine;

I am Thy son, made with Thy Self to shine,

Thy servant, whose pains Thou hast still repaid,

Thy sheep, Thine image, and, till I betray'd

My self, a temple of Thy Spirit divine;

Why doth the devil then usurp* on me?

Why doth he steal, nay ravish* that's Thy right?

Except Thou rise and for Thine own work fight,

O! I shall soon despair, when I do see

That Thou lov'st mankind well, yet wilt not choose me,

And Satan hates me, yet is loth* to lose me.

As . . . titles: owed by right of the many names, or positions
resign: submit, surrender

decayed: fallen, ruined by sin

usurp: seize by force without legal right

ravish: carry off forcibly

loth: loathe

Holy Sonnet 7 by John Donne

At the round earth's imagin'd corners*, blow

Your trumpets, angels, and arise, arise

From death, you numberless infinities

Of souls, and to your scatter'd bodies go;

All whom the flood did, and fire shall o'erthrow,

All whom war, dearth, age, agues,* tyrannies,

Despair, law, chance hath slain, and you whose eyes

Shall behold God and never taste death's woe.

But let them sleep,* Lord, and me mourn* a space,

For, if above all these my sins abound,

'Tis late to ask abundance of Thy grace

When we are there; here on this lowly ground

Teach me how to repent; for that's as good

As if Thou hadst seal'd my pardon* with Thy blood.

imagin'd corners: allusion to the four corners of the earth

agues: alternating chills, fever, and perspiring

let them sleep: allow them to remain in the grave, not yet resurrected
mourn: in repentance for one's sin

seal'd my pardon: ratified or made the pardon legal

306 APPENDIX C

poem [being "in love"] involve strong emotions.)

Emotions can be very difficult to communicate. Sometimes the depth of the emotion prevents us from communicating, and sometimes the person involved deters us.

2. What emotion is most difficult for you to express? Why? (*Answers will vary but may include anger, sorrow, and affection.*)

Holy Sonnet 10 by John Donne

Death, be not proud, though some have called thee
Mighty and dreadful, for thou art not so;
For those whom thou think'st thou dost overthrow
Die not, poor Death, nor yet canst thou kill me.
From rest and sleep, which but thy pictures be,
Much pleasure; then from thee much more must flow,
And soonest our best men with thee do go,
Rest of their bones, and soul's delivery.
Thou art slave to fate, chance, kings, and desperate men,
And dost with poison, war, and sickness dwell,
And poppy or charms can make us sleep as well,
And better than thy stroke;* why swell'st thou then?
One short sleep* past, we wake eternally,*
And death shall be no more; Death, thou shalt die.*

stroke: blow of death

one short sleep: time spent in the grave before the resurrection
wake eternally: live in heaven

Death . . . die: "He will swallow up death in victory;" (Isa. 25:8) "And God shall wipe away all tears from their eyes; and there shall be no more death." (Rev. 21:4)

Holy Sonnet 11 by John Donne

Spit in my face you Jews, and pierce my side,
Buffet, and scoff, scourge, and crucify me,
For I have sinn'd, and sinn'd, and only he
Who could do no iniquity* hath died:
But by my death can not be satisfied
My sins, which pass the Jews' impiety:*
They kill'd once an inglorious man, but I
Crucify him daily, being now glorified.
O let me, then, his strange love still admire:
Kings pardon, but he bore our punishment.
And Jacob came clothed in vile harsh attire
But to supplant,* and with gainful* intent:
God clothed himself in vile man's flesh, that so
He might be weak enough to suffer woe.

he / Who could do no iniquity: Christ

impiety: irreverence or piousness

supplant: trick, deceive
gainful: self-fulfilling

SELECTED SONNETS 307

John Donne

Holy Sonnet 10

Theme. Though all men eventually succumb to death, it will not have the final victory.

Discussion. Scripture depicts death as an outward or physical representation of what occurs spiritually when a man is unregenerate. A man is born dead spiritually, separated from God by his sins. "And you hath he quickened [made alive], who were dead in trespasses and sins" (Ephesians 2:1).

Our society often views death as the defeat of medical science. How does the Bible contradict this faulty worldview? (Philippians 1:21 and many other Scripture passages show that it is better to be with God than to remain physically alive on earth.)

George Herbert
(1593-1633)

Herbert was the son of Sir Richard Herbert. His mother, Magdalen, an heiress, was a patroness to John Donne, and Donne dedicated the *Holy Sonnets* to her.

When George was only three years old, Sir Richard died. He was survived by Magdalen and ten children.

As a teen, Herbert attended Westminster School, studying Latin, Greek, and music. He attended Trinity College, Cambridge, on a scholarship. By age twenty-three, he became a Fellow of Trinity, teaching Greek, rhetoric, and oratory.

Herbert became a parish minister in the Church of England when he was thirty-one. The preacher-poet was known for his acts of love and kindness toward his congregation. He was only forty when he died of consumption. He was survived by his wife, Jane Danvers, who later married Sir Robert Cook.

A friend, Nicholas Ferrar, had Herbert's poems published the year of his death. *A Priest to the Temple* (1633) created lasting recognition for Herbert, due to the quality of verse.

Holy Sonnet 14 by John Donne

Batter* my heart, three-person'd* God, for you
As yet but knock, breathe, shine, and seek to mend;*
That I may rise, and stand, o'erthrow me, and bend
Your force to break, blow, burn, and make me new.
I, like an usurped* town, to another due,
Labour to admit you, but O, to no end.
Reason, your viceroy* in me, me should defend,
But is captiv'd, and proves weak or untrue.
Yet dearly I love you, and would be loved fain,*
But am betroth'd* unto your enemy:
Divorce* me, untie or break that knot again,
Take me to you, imprison me, for I,
Except you enthrall* me, never shall be free,
Nor ever chaste,* except you ravish* me.

Batter: to strike repeatedly with force
three-person'd: reference to the Trinity
mend: improve or repair

usurped: illegally possessed by force

viceroy: a ruler who represents a monarch

fain: willingly

betroth'd: figuratively, sworn allegiance

Divorce: separate, pull apart what is bonded together

enthrall: captivate; emphasizes the irony of freedom found when a bondslave to Christ Jesus
chaste: pure, holy
ravish: contrasting with chaste to symbolize the entirety of Christ's possession

Redemption by George Herbert

Having been tenant* long to a rich Lord,
Not thriving, I resolvèd to be bold,
And make a suit* unto Him, to afford*
A new small-rented lease, and cancel th' old.
In heaven at His manor I Him sought:
They told me there, that He was lately gone
About some land, which He had dearly bought
Long since on earth, to take possessiön.
I straight* returned, and knowing His great birth,
Sought Him accordingly in great resorts—
In cities, theatres, gardens, parks, and courts.
At length I heard a ragged noise and mirth*
Of thieves and murderers; there I Him espied*
Who straight, "Your suit is granted," said, and died.

tenant: renter

suit: petition
afford: grant me

straight: immediately

mirth: a synonym for joy, particularly spiritual joy; used here ironically
espied: saw

George Herbert

Redemption

Theme. Christ had to leave the splendors of heaven and face the greatest evils of earth in order to purchase salvation.

Note: *Redeem* means "to purchase" and is applicable in the context of buying land.

Discussion. A dramatic "forward" is a clue in a text that makes you eager to find out what will happen next. Television programs often switch to an advertisement immediately following a dramatic forward because the viewer is compelled to keep watching. Playwrights use this technique at the end of a scene or act.

How does Herbert use this technique to give his final line the emphasis that makes his point so effective? (*Your emotions are built up on the facts he presents, and your anticipation heightens the realization that Christ did indeed "pay it all." Notice how he even saves the phrase "and died" for the end of the last line.*)

Sonnet 17 by William Shakespeare

Who will believe my verse in time to come,

If it were fill'd with your most high deserts?*   deserts: praises

Though yet, heaven knows, it is but as a tomb*   tomb: figuratively, the poetry "masks" or "buries"

Which hides your life and shows not half your parts.

If I could write the beauty of your eyes

And in fresh numbers number all your graces,

The age to come would say "This poet lies,

Such heavenly touches* ne'er touch'd earthly faces."   touches: qualities, features

So should my papers, yellow'd with their age,

Be scorn'd like old men of less truth than tongue,

And your true rights be term'd a poet's rage,

And stretched metre* of an antique song: stretched metre: outrageous or exaggerated verse

But were some child of yours alive that time,

You should live twice;—in it and in my rhyme.*   But . . . rhyme: forever remembered in the poem as well as reflected in his descendants

Sonnet 18 by William Shakespeare

Shall I compare thee to a summer's day?

Thou art more lovely and more temperate:*   temperate: moderate, balanced

Rough winds do shake the darling buds of May,

And summer's lease* hath all too short a date: summer's lease: the length of time summer influences

Sometime too hot the eye of heaven* shines,   the eye of heaven: the sun

And often is his gold complexion dimm'd;*   gold complexion dimm'd: clouds or fog obscure full sunlight

And every fair from fair sometime declines,*   every fair . . . declines: all physical beauty slowly fades from its original quality

By chance, or nature's changing course, untrimm'd;*   chance . . . untrimm'd: the elements, an accident, or eventually just the process of aging

But thy eternal summer shall not fade,*   thy . . . fade: your qualities of beauty won't end

Nor lose possession of that fair thou ow'st;

Nor shall Death brag thou wander'st in his shade,*   shade: "The shadow of death"; nearness to death (Ps. 23:4)

When in eternal lines to time thou grow'st:*   eternal lines . . . grow'st: aging

So long as men can breathe or eyes can see,

So long lives this and this gives life to thee.*   So long lives . . . thee: you live as long as this sonnet lasts to immortalize and praise you

SELECTED SONNETS 309

William Shakespeare
(1564-1616)

Though both of Shakespeare's parents, John and Mary Arden Shakespeare, were likely illiterate, they were well-respected and active members of their community. John served as chamberlain, alderman, and even in a mayor-like position in Stratford.

At 18, William married Anne Hathaway. By the late 1580s when he was in his mid-twenties, he emerged as a London actor.

Since his father's civil positions entitled William and his siblings to free education at the Stratford grammar school, it is likely that William studied Latin composition and literature extensively. Such studies would explain the imagery and plot of numerous plays rooted in Latin stories.

He performed in the Chamberlain's Men, whose audience included Queen Elizabeth. Many scholars report that he wrote some of his plays to fulfill Queen Elizabeth's requests, particularly *The Merry Wives of Windsor.* She reportedly wished to see the comic character Falstaff fall in love.

Many of the bard's plays were performed at The Globe, a theater in the suburbs of London.

Though Shakespeare was a man of the theater—writing,

William Shakespeare

Sonnet 18

Theme. A beloved one's beauty will live forever because it has been captured in a poem. (See Spenser's "Sonnet 75" for a similar theme.)

Discussion. Shakespeare compares his subject to the loveliness of "a summer's day," emphasizing that her beauty surpasses that of even the most beautiful day.

By choosing to compare his subject to a universally accepted beauty/pleasure such as summer, what resulting implication does Shakespeare make concerning the subject of the sonnet? (*Beginning with the phrase "But thy eternal summer shall not fade" and continuing to the end of the sonnet, the poet shows that he expects his verse [tribute] to extend the "summer" or even the very life of his subject.*)

producing, and acting seemingly without thought of publication—most of his work was published during his lifetime. Various actors in his troupe who needed extra cash reported many play texts to the printers. Because of this haphazard approach, often a modern Shakespearean production script is actually a thoughtful compilation based on several copies of that play.

Though most famous for his plays, which include comedies, tragedies, histories, and romances, Shakespeare radically influenced the sonnet form as well.

Soon after Shakespeare's death, two of his friends published about half of his plays in an edition known as the First Folio, considered more authoritative than the earlier copies.

Shakespeare's works comprise nearly 40 plays, including several collaborative efforts, 154 sonnets, and several long poems.

In 1623, Ben Jonson wrote of Shakespeare:

Triumph, my Britain, thou hast one to show
To whom all scenes of Europe homage owe.
He was not of an age, but for all time!

Sonnet 81 declares the immortality of the poet's verse, though he didn't publish his works himself. Such a theme was popular in the poetry of

Sonnet 19 by William Shakespeare

Devouring Time,* blunt thou the lion's paws,
And make the earth devour her own sweet brood;
Pluck the keen* teeth from the fierce tiger's jaws,
And burn the long-liv'd phoenix* in her blood;
Make glad and sorry seasons as thou fleets,*
And do whate'er thou wilt, swift-footed Time,
To the wide world and all her fading sweets:
But I forbid thee one most heinous crime:
O, carve not with thy hours my love's fair brow,
Nor draw no lines* there with thine antique pen;
Him in thy course untainted* do allow,
For beauty's pattern to succeeding men.
Yet, do thy worst, old Time: despite thy wrong,
My love shall in my verse ever live young.

Devouring Time: time personified and described as a predator

keen: savage

phoenix: mythical bird, supposed to have lived many centuries only to burn itself and emerge youthful
fleets: slips away; quickly moves or passes

lines: wrinkles

untainted: unblemished, not damaged

Sonnet 23 by William Shakespeare

As an unperfect actor on the stage,
Who with his fear is put besides his part,*
Or some fierce thing replete* with too much rage,
Whose strength's abundance weakens his own heart.
So I, for fear of trust, forget to say
The perfect ceremony of love's rite,*
And in mine own love's strength seem to decay,
O'ercharg'd with burden of mine own love's might.
O, let my books be then the eloquence
And dumb presagers,* of my speaking breast,
Who plead for love and look for recompense*
More than that tongue that more hath more express'd.
O, learn to read what silent love hath writ:
To hear with eyes belongs to love's fine wit.

Who . . . part: in nervousness, forgets his lines
replete: filled with

rite: ceremony, vow

dumb presagers: silent prophets

recompense: thanks, gratitude

(310) APPENDIX C

© 2002 BJU Press. Reproduction prohibited.

Sonnet 23
Theme. Fear can steal your tongue when you try to express love.

Discussion. Compare the theme of this sonnet to Sidney's "Sonnet 1" from *Astrophel and Stella*. (*Love is difficult to express sincerely in words.*) Contrast the imagery used to convey these similar ideas. (*The researcher of love poetry versus the "unperfect actor."*)

Sonnet 29 by William Shakespeare

When in disgrace with fortune and men's eyes,*

I all alone beweep* my outcast state

And trouble deaf heaven with my bootless* cries

And look upon myself, and curse my fate,

Wishing me like to one more rich in hope,

Featur'd like him, like him with friends possess'd,

Desiring this man's art,* and that man's scope,*

With what I most enjoy contented least;

Yet in these thoughts myself almost despising,

Haply* I think on thee,—and then my state,

(Like to the lark,* at break of day arising

From sullen earth) sings hymns at heaven's gate;

For thy sweet love remember'd such wealth brings

That then I scorn to change my state with kings.

When . . . eyes: unfortunate and scorned by his peers
beweep: weep for or despise
bootless: empty, helpless
art: skill
scope: purpose, aim
haply: by chance
lark: known for its early song

Sonnet 49 by William Shakespeare

Against that time, if ever that time come,

When I shall see thee frown on my defects,*

When as thy love hath cast his utmost sum,*

Call'd to that audit* by advis'd respects;*

Against that time when thou shalt strangely pass

And scarcely greet me with that sun, thine eye,

When love, converted from the thing it was,

Shall reasons find of settled gravity;

Against that time do I ensconce* me here

Within the knowledge of mine own desert,

And this my hand against myself uprear,*

To guard the lawful reasons on thy part:

To leave poor me thou hast the strength of laws,

Since why to love I can allege* no cause.

defects: faults
sum: amount, numeric figure
audit: examination of an account
advis'd respects: good (sound) reasons
ensconce: figuratively, fortify
uprear: lift up
allege: testify or argue for

SELECTED SONNETS **311**

Sonnet 29

Theme. Being loved is more valuable than talent, ambition, or power.

Discussion.

1. What turns the author's self-pity into gratitude? (He remembers the value of love.)

2. What does the Bible teach about despair vs. hope? (The word hope occurs 131 times in Scripture. In defining hope, the New Bible Dictionary uses Abraham as an example. His situation did not seem to support his hope that Sarah would have a child. However, he believed in God and could therefore "in hope" believe "against hope" [Rom. 4:18]. Faith in God is inherent to biblical hope. Most occurrences of the word hope also mention love, mercy, and/or man's dependence on God.)

Sonnet 53 by William Shakespeare

What is your substance,* whereof* are you made,

That millions of strange shadows* on you tend?

Since every one hath, every one, one shade,*

And you, but one, can every shadow lend.*

Describe Adonis,* and the counterfeit*

Is poorly imitated after you;

On Helen's* cheek all art of beauty set,

And you in Grecian tires* are painted new;

Speak of the spring and foison* of the year;

The one doth shadow of your beauty show,

The other as your bounty doth appear,

And you in every blessed shape we know.

In all external grace you have some part,

But you like none, none you, for constant heart.

substance: essence, often referring to deity
whereof: of which

strange shadows: delusive image or a
  phantom; what is left without the sub-
  stance
shade: shadow

can . . . lend: able to reflect the images de-
  scribed in lines 5-11

Adonis: allusion to a handsome man
counterfeit: false copy

Helen: Helen of Troy, a beauty in legends

Grecian tires: Grecian attire

foison: abundance, harvest

Sonnet 71 by William Shakespeare

No longer mourn for me when I am dead

Then you shall hear the surly sullen bell

Give warning to the world that I am fled

From this vile world with vilest worms to dwell.

Nay, if you read this line, remember not

The hand that writ* it; for I love you so

That I in your sweet thoughts would be forgot,

If thinking on me then should make you woe.*

O, if, I say, you look upon this verse

When I perhaps compounded am with clay,*

Do not so much as my poor name rehearse;*

But let your love even with my life decay:*

Lest the wise world should look into your moan*

And mock you with me after I am gone.

writ: wrote

woe: to weep or sorrow

compounded . . . clay: buried

rehearse: repeat

decay: dwindle away

moan: condition of grieving

Sonnet 116 by William Shakespeare

Let me not to the marriage* of true minds

Admit impediments.* Love is not love

Which alters* when it alteration* finds,

Or bends with the remover* to remove:*

O no! it is an ever-fixed mark*

That looks on tempests* and is never shaken;

It is the star to every wand'ring bark,*

Whose worth's unknown, although his height be taken.*

Love's not Time's fool, though rosy lips and cheeks*

Within his bending sickle's* compass* come:

Love alters not* with his brief hours and weeks,

But bears* it out even to the edge of doom.*

If this be error and upon me prov'd,

I never writ,* nor no man ever lov'd.

marriage: meeting or union

impediments: faults, shortcomings

alters: forcibly changes
alteration: peculiarity, irregularity
remover: one who changes place
remove: to send away
ever-fixed mark: never-changing position

tempests: figuratively, storms

wand'ring bark: lost ship

worth's . . . taken: nautical—sailors measure height above the horizon, but this implies that value cannot be likewise measured
rosy lips and cheeks: youth
sickle: like a reaping hook but having a serrated edge; possible allusion to the mythical "Grim Reaper" (death personified), carrying a sickle
compass: circle or extent of reach
alters not: changes not
bears: forbears, endures
edge of doom: doomsday

writ: wrote

On His Blindness by John Milton

When I consider how my light* is spent,

Ere half my days, in this dark world and wide,

And that one Talent* which is death to hide,

Lodg'd with me useless, though my Soul more bent

To serve therewith my Maker, and present

My true account, lest He returning chide,

"Doth God exact* day-labour, light deny'd,"*

I fondly* ask; But patience to prevent

That murmur, soon replies, "God doth not need

Either man's work or His own gifts; who best

Bear his mild yoke, they serve him best," His state

Is kingly. Thousands* at his bidding speed

And post o'er Land and Ocean without rest:

They also serve who only stand and wait.

light: personal gift, ability, etc.

Talent: literally, a coin, but here it is used figuratively to mean that which is worth investing, a natural gift; allusion to Matthew 25:14-30, the parable of the talents

exact: require
light deny'd: when illumination has been denied
fondly: foolishly

Thousands: angels

John Milton
(1608-74)

Milton is best remembered for his longer poetic works: *Paradise Lost*, published in 1667 and revised in 1674; *Paradise Regained*; and *Samson Agonistes*; but his sonnet "On His Blindness" is arguably as famous as Shakespeare's and Browning's best.

Milton received bachelor's and master's degrees from Christ's College at Cambridge, which qualified him for work in the church, but he chose to study and travel instead.

Milton outlived two of his three wives and died on November 12, 1674, in London.

Sonnet 116

Theme. Constancy and faithfulness characterize genuine love.

Discussion. What overwhelming virtue of love is extolled in this famous sonnet? (*Answers will vary but may include constancy or faithfulness.*)

John Milton

On His Blindness

Theme. Faithfulness and worship constitute service as much as action does.

Discussion. Sometimes people have a desire to do something, and God does not provide the means. A would-be missionary is deemed "too frail" for the mission or a would-be vocalist, to have too little talent. Frustration may result. Milton points out that frustration when God denies our requests should not be equated with wasting the gifts God has given.

1. To what do lines 3-6 allude? (*the parable of the talents*)

2. What was Milton's talent? (*as evidenced by the poem, the ability to write well—eloquence*)

3. The poem's focus at the beginning shifts by the end. Who or what is emphasized at the opening of the poem? Who or what is emphasized at the close? (*The poet begins by focusing on himself and his gifts. However, he soon realizes that God doesn't need him but desires his faithfulness and worship.*)

Elizabeth Barrett Browning

(1806-61)

E. B. Browning was the daughter of Edward Barrett, who was wealthy enough to afford a five-hundred-acre estate called Hope End. As a child, Browning directed her eleven siblings in productions of plays. Before the age of ten, she had read parts of *Paradise Lost,* various Shakespearean plays, and several histories. As a teen, she could read literature in Greek, Latin, and Hebrew. Though she was not recognized in print until 1838, she had written four books of rhymed couplets by the age of 12.

Browning became a recluse after her brother Edward drowned. Eventually, a friend, John Kenyon, urged a meeting between Elizabeth and an admirer of hers, Robert Browning.

Elizabeth's *Sonnets from the Portuguese* were personal—addressed to Robert, whom she had married. However, he convinced her to publish them, and her popularity increased until she was under consideration for poet laureate, an honor that was given instead to Tennyson.

Her most famous works include the verse novel *Aurora Leigh,* "How Do I Love Thee?" and an argument against child labor, "The Cry of the Children."

Sonnet 13 by Elizabeth Barrett Browning

And wilt thou have me fashion* into speech

The love I bear thee, finding words enough,

And hold the torch* out, while the winds are rough,*

Between our faces, to cast light on each?—

I drop it at thy feet.* I cannot teach

My hand to hold my spirit so far off

From myself—me—that I should bring thee proof

In words, of love hid in me out of reach.

Nay, let the silence of my womanhood

Commend my woman-love to thy belief,—*

Seeing that I stand unwon, however wooed,

And rend the garment of my life,* in brief,

By a most dauntless, voiceless fortitude,*

Lest one touch of this heart convey its grief.*

fashion: give form, make or mold

torch: light that illuminates by fire
while . . . rough: when one's feelings may be at risk

I . . . feet: I give up

Commend . . . belief: speak words of praise to yourself concerning my love

rend . . . life: the struggle is so great as to cause her to feel "torn"
dauntless, voiceless fortitude: brave, silent strength
Lest . . . grief: she chooses to suffer rather than be vulnerable

Sonnet 14 by Elizabeth Barrett Browning

If thou must love me, let it be for nought*

Except for love's sake only. Do not say

"I love her for her smile—her look—her way

Of speaking gently,—for a trick of thought

That falls in well with mine, and certes* brought

A sense of pleasant ease on such a day"—

For these things in themselves, Belovèd, may

Be changed, or change for thee,—and love, so wrought,*

May be unwrought so. Neither love me for

Thine own dear pity's wiping my cheeks dry,—

A creature might forget to weep, who bore

Thy comfort long, and lose thy love thereby!

But love me for love's sake, that evermore

Thou mayst love on, through love's eternity.

nought: nothing

certes (SUR teez): for certain

wrought: formed, created

Elizabeth Barrett Browning

Sonnet 13

Theme. Silent action can be as great a testimony to love as verbal declaration.

Discussion. Like Sidney in "Sonnet 1" of *Astrophel and Stella* and Shakespeare in "Sonnet 23," Browning expresses the inability to speak of love.

To what does she attribute her difficulty? (*shyness, fear of vulnerability, impropriety, maturity of womanhood, etc.*)

Sonnet 14

Theme. To be lasting, love must be based on an act of the will rather than on things that change over time (appearance, characteristics, and so on).

Discussion. Browning notes that love based on superficial qualities will disappear when those elements change.

1. Explain the qualities on which she does not wish affection to be based. (*Answers will vary and may include* her smile [favor], appearance or beauty, soft voice, etc.)

2. What proper basis does she propose for loving? (*"Love for love's sake"* [line 13], *suggesting that love must be volitional, a choice, rather than a whim or action based on a changing element such as beauty or even a deeper quality like a merciful nature.*)

Sonnet 43 by Elizabeth Barrett Browning

How do I love thee? Let me count the ways.
I love thee to the depth and breadth and height
My soul can reach, when feeling out of sight
For the ends of Being and ideal Grace.★
I love thee to the level of everyday's
Most quiet need,★ by sun and candle-light.
I love thee freely, as men strive for Right;
I love thee purely, as they turn from Praise.
I love thee with the passion★ put to use
In my old griefs, and with my childhood's faith.
I love thee with a love I seemed to lose
With my lost saints,—I love thee with the breath,
Smiles, tears, of all my life!—and, if God choose,
I shall but love thee better after death.

ends . . . Grace: at life's fullest, most glorious moments

everyday's / Most quiet need: small, mundane needs

passion: emotion, energy

An Hour with Thee by Richard Chenevix Trench

Lord, what a change within us one short hour
Spent in Thy presence will avail to make!
What heavy burdens from our bosoms take!
What parched grounds refresh as with a shower!
We kneel, and all★ around us seem to lower;
We rise, and all, the distant and the near,
Stands forth in sunny outline, brave and clear;
We kneel,★ how weak; we rise, how full of power!
Why, therefore, should we do ourselves this wrong,
Or others—that we are not always strong—
That we are sometimes overborne with care—
That we should ever weak or heartless be,
Anxious or troubled—when with us is prayer,
And joy and strength and courage are with Thee?

all: all things

kneel: kneel in prayer

In 1861, Elizabeth died in her husband's arms.

Richard Chenevix Trench
(1807-86)

Born in Dublin, Ireland, Richard Chenevix Trench was both an Anglican clergyman and an author. Though he authored many theological writings, Trench is best remembered for his writings that deal with philology and poetry. He authored *The Study of Words* (1851), *English, Past and Present* (1855), and *Collected Poems* (1865).

SELECTED SONNETS **315**

Sonnet 43

Theme. The speaker's love is all encompassing.

Discussion. Doubtless Browning's most famed sonnet, "How do I love thee?" contains contrasts that beautifully depict the diverse abilities of love. Identify and discuss them. Contrast lines 2-4 with 5-6. Contrast the beginning of 10 and the second half of 10. Contrast the items listed in 12-13.

Christina Rossetti
(1830-94)

Born in London on December 5, 1830, to Gabriele, a professor, and Frances (Polidori) Rossetti, Christina Georgina Rossetti seemed to absorb much of her father's talent and her mother's devout faith.

Twice Rossetti was in love, but she eventually rejected both men because neither shared her Christian faith. By the time Christina was in her early twenties, she and her mother tried to found a school to generate family income. (Her father's poor health had created a financial strain.) However, this attempt soon failed. Christina herself experienced chronic illness, which was sometimes diagnosed as angina and other times as tuberculosis.

Though she spent her time at home, Rossetti did interact with her brothers' friends, such as Charles Dodgson (Lewis Carroll), A. C. Swinburne, and James Whistler. Later in life, she participated in the Society for Promoting Christian Knowledge.

Rossetti died of cancer in December 1894.

In a Pass of Bavaria between the Walchen and the Waldensee by Richard Chenevix Trench

A sound of many waters!*—now I know
To what was likened the large utterance sent
By Him who mid the golden lampads went:*
Innumerable streams, above, below,
Some seen, some heard alone, with headlong flow
Come rushing; some with smooth and sheer descent,
Some dashed to foam and whiteness, but all blent
Into one mighty music.
            As I go,
The tumult of a boundless gladness fills
My bosom, and my spirit leaps and sings:
Sounds and sights are there of the ancient hills,
The eagle's cry, the mountain when it flings
Mists from its brow, but none of all these things
Like the one voice of multitudinous rills.*

sound . . . waters!: allusion to Revelation 1:15 "his [Christ's] voice as the sound of many waters."

Him . . . lampads: allusion to Revelation 1:13 "And in the midst of the seven candlesticks one like unto the Son of man."

rills: small streams or brooks

Sonnet 2 by Christina Rossetti

I wish I could remember that first day,
First hour, first moment of your meeting me,
If bright or dim the season, it might be
Summer or winter for aught* I can say;
So unrecorded did it slip away,
So blind was I to see and to foresee,
So dull* to mark the budding of my tree*
That would not blossom yet for many a May.
If only I could recollect* it, such
A day of days! I let it come and go
As traceless as a thaw of bygone snow;*
It seem'd to mean so little, meant so much;
If only now I could recall that touch,
First touch of hand in hand—Did one but know!

aught: whatever, anything

dull: lacking keenness of perception
budding . . . tree: beginning of life or life of romance

recollect: remember

traceless . . . snow: snow melts and is absorbed into soil

Sonnet 4 by Christina Rossetti

I lov'd you first: but afterwards your love
Outsoaring* mine, sang such a loftier song
As drown'd the friendly cooings* of my dove.
Which owes the other most? my love was long,
And yours one moment seem'd to wax more strong;
I lov'd and guess'd at you, you construed* me—
And lov'd me for what might or might not be
Nay, weights and measures* do us both a wrong.
For verily* love knows not "mine" or "thine";
With separate "I" and "thou" free love has done,
For one is both and both are one in love:
Rich love knows nought* of "thine that is not mine";
Both have the strength and both the length thereof,
Both of us, of the love which makes us one.

Outsoaring: exceed the height of

cooings: soft murmuring sounds characteristic of pigeons and doves

construed: interpreted, understood

weights and measures: comparisons

verily: for certain, truly

nought: nothing

Sonnet 5 by Christina Rossetti

O my heart's heart,* and you who are to me
More than myself myself,* God be with you,
Keep you in strong obedience leal* and true
To Him whose noble service setteth free,
Give you all good we see or can foresee,
Make your joys many and your sorrows few,
Bless you in what you bear* and what you do,
Yea, perfect* you as He would have you be.
So much for you; but what for me, dear friend?
To love you without stint* and all I can
Today, tomorrow, world without an end;*
To love you much and yet to love you more,
As Jordan at his flood* sweeps either shore;
Since woman is the helpmeet* made for man.

heart's heart: object or focus of one's emotions

more than myself myself: his life is more a part of her existence than her own activities, needs, etc.
leal: faithful or loyal

bear: burdens you carry

perfect: improve; sanctify

stint: restriction

world . . . end: "world without end" (Eph. 3:21)

Jordan . . . flood: common metaphor for death or dying
helpmeet: wife, allusion to Genesis 2:18, 20

SELECTED SONNETS **317**

Sonnet 6 by Christina Rossetti

Trust me, I have not earn'd your dear rebuke,
I love, as you would have me, God the most;
Would lose not Him, but you, must one be lost,
Nor with Lot's wife* cast back a faithless look
Unready to forego* what I forsook;*
This say I, having counted up the cost,
This, though I be the feeblest of God's host,
The sorriest sheep Christ shepherds* with His crook.
Yet while I love my God the most,
I deem that I can never love you overmuch;
I love Him more, so let me love you too;
Yea, as I apprehend it, love is such
I cannot love you if I love not Him,
I cannot love Him if I love not you.*

Lot's wife: allusion to Genesis 19:26: "But his wife looked back from behind him, and she became a pillar of salt."
forego: overlook, avoid
forsook: renounced, denied

shepherds: In John's Gospel, as well as other passages, Christ describes His leading of His people as shepherding. Sheep are known for minimal intellect.

I cannot love you . . . love not you: allusion to Matthew 22:37-39: "Thou shalt love the Lord thy God with all thy heart, and with all thy soul, and with all thy mind. This is the first and great commandment. And the second is like unto it, Thou shalt love thy neighbor as thyself."

Sonnet 8 by Christina Rossetti

"I, if I perish, perish"*—Esther spake:
And bride of life or death, she made her fair*
In all the lustre* of her perfum'd hair
And smiles that kindle longing but to slake.*
She put on pomp of loveliness, to take
Her husband through his eyes at unaware;*
She spread abroad her beauty for a snare,
Harmless as doves and subtle as a snake.*
She trapp'd him with one mesh* of silken hair,
She vanquish'd* him by wisdom of her wit,
And built her people's house that it should stand:—
If I might take my life so in my hand,
And for my love to Love put up my prayer,
And for love's sake by Love be granted it!

I, if I perish, perish: ". . . and if I perish, I perish." (Esther 4:16)

made her fair: made herself look beautiful

lustre: sheen, light reflecting softly

slake: cause a fire to burn less strongly

take . . . unaware: enchant or captivate the will through charming him by her appearance

Harmless . . . snake: allusion to Matthew 10:16: "Be ye therefore wise as serpents, and harmless as doves."
mesh: literally, a thread or cord of a net; figuratively, a device to ensnare
vanquish'd: defeated or banished

Christina Rossetti

Sonnet 6

Theme. Love for a person will not detract from love for God as long as you have right priorities.

Discussion. Describe the priorities Rossetti presents in her poem. (*Love God foremost, and all other loves will have their proper places.*)

Sonnet 13 by Christina Rossetti

If I could trust mine own self with your fate,*

Shall I not rather trust it in God's hand?

Without Whose Will one lily doth not stand,

Nor sparrow fall at his appointed date;

Who numbereth the innumerable sand,*

Who weighs the wind and water with a weight,

To Whom the world is neither small nor great,

Whose knowledge foreknew every plan we plann'd.

Searching my heart for all that touches you,

I find there only love and love's goodwill

Helpless to help and impotent* to do,

Of understanding dull,* of sight most dim;*

And therefore I commend* you back to Him

Whose love your love's capacity can fill.

fate: what will happen to you

one lily . . . innumerable sand: allusion to Luke 12:6, 7, 27; Genesis 32:12

impotent: powerless

dull: lacking understanding
dim: weak eyesight
commend: entrust, commit

Sonnet 14 by Christina Rossetti

Youth gone, and beauty gone if ever there

Dwelt beauty in so poor a face as this;

Youth gone and beauty, what remains of bliss?*

I will not bind fresh roses in my hair,

To shame a cheek at best but little fair,—*

Leave youth his roses, who can bear a thorn,—*

I will not seek for blossoms anywhere,

Except such common flowers as blow with corn.

Youth gone and beauty gone, what doth remain?

The longing of a heart pent up forlorn,*

A silent heart whose silence loves and longs;

The silence of a heart which sang its songs

While youth and beauty made a summer morn,

Silence of love that cannot sing again.

bliss: serene joy

fair: pretty

Leave . . . thorn: rose represents youthful-ness, capturing the height of passions with their corresponding dangers

forlorn: despair

SELECTED SONNETS 319

Sarah Knowles Bolton
(1841-1916)

As an author, Sarah Knowles Bolton is remembered for her poetry, biography, and children's literature. Bolton graduated from Hartford Women's Seminary and taught school. She was involved in various movements, including temperance, and she even traveled in Europe from 1881-83 to study women's education and labor conditions.

Gerard Manley Hopkins
(1844-1889)

Hopkins's parents, Gerard and Catherine Hopkins, were High-Church Anglicans. Though he dreamed of being a poet and painter, he instead became a Jesuit priest. For a period of time, he was convinced that it was not right for a priest to write poetry, so he destroyed what he had written. Later, with further study, he determined it was acceptable to compose verse. Hopkins borrowed features from the Welsh poetry he read. He invented what he called *sprung rhythm*, in which feet of one to four syllables in length contain "rising" or "falling" rhythm. This produces an irregular rhythm. Hopkins's style was certainly ahead of its day—a forerunner to modern poetry.

Other poems by Gerard Manley Hopkins include "Pied Beauty," "Thee, God, I

Remember by Christina Rossetti

Remember me when I am gone away,
Gone far away into the silent land;
When you can no more hold me by the hand,
Nor I half turn to go yet turning stay.
Remember me when no more day by day
You tell me of our future that you plann'd:
Only remember me; you understand
It will be late to counsel* then or pray.
Yet if you should forget me for a while
And afterwards remember, do not grieve:
For if the darkness and corruption leave
A vestige* of the thoughts that once I had,
Better by far you should forget and smile
Than that you should remember and be sad.

counsel: discuss, advise

vestige: memory

His Monument by Sarah Knowles Bolton

He built a house, time laid it in the dust;
He wrote a book, its title now forgot;
He rules a city, but his name is not
On any tablet graven, or where rust
Can gather from disuse, or marble bust.*
He took a child from out a wretched cot;
Who on the State dishonor might have brought;*
And reared him in the Christian's hope and trust.
The boy, to manhood grown, became a light
To many souls and preacher to human need
The wondrous love of the Omnipotent.
The work has multiplied like stars at night*
When darkness deepens; every noble deed
Lasts longer than a granite monument.

bust: statue of head and shoulders only

child . . . brought: orphan in a government facility

multiplied . . . night: multiplied in the same way stars appear beginning with a few at dusk and many more becoming visible when the sun has set

320 APPENDIX C

God's Grandeur by Gerard Manley Hopkins

The world is charged* with the grandeur of God.

It will flame out, like shining from shook foil;

It gathers to a greatness, like the ooze of oil

Crushed. Why do men then now not reck* his rod?

Generations have trod, have trod, have trod;

And all is seared* with trade; bleared,* smeared* with toil;

And wears man's smudge and shares man's smell: the soil

Is bare now, nor can foot feel, being shod.*

And for all this, nature is never spent;

There lives the dearest freshness deep down things;

And though the last lights off the black West* went

Oh, morning, at the brown brink eastward, springs—

Because the Holy Ghost over the bent

World broods* with warm breast and with ah! bright wings.

charged: saturated or filled with power, as a weapon may be filled with explosive power

reck: take heed of

seared: scarred or withered
bleared: blurred
smeared: made dirty

shod: wearing shoes

last . . . West: sunset

broods: hovering as a bird who is protecting or hatching eggs

Preacher's Prayer, A Sonnet by Bob Jones Jr.

Not every day the preacher's soul is fired,

But when the spark is there, foundations quake

And mountains move. Then sinful hearts, inspired

By judgment fears, to penitence* awake.

Spirit anointed, most imperfect clay

Becomes a golden vessel for God's Word,

Which, overflowing, heals and cleans away

Black doubt and hind'ring fear. Then Christians stirred

Know rushing mighty wind, baptizing fire,

Speaks such a preacher with a prophet's tone,

By love consumed, revival his desire,

Blessed beyond measure, pulpit then a throne.

Give to this preacher now the heavenly pow'r

My people wait. Make this the shining hour.

penitence: sorrow for one's sin

come from, to Thee Go," "The Wreck of the *Deutschland*," "The Leaden Echo and the Golden Echo," and "The Windhover: To Christ Our Lord."

Bob Jones Jr.
(1911-1997)

Bob Jones Jr., son of the well-known evangelist who founded Bob Jones University, demonstrated a great love of language throughout his lifetime. He often performed onstage in classic works of drama. His roles included Shylock in Shakespeare's *Merchant of Venice* and the title character in Rostand's *Cyrano de Bergerac*. As the second president of Bob Jones University and later as the chancellor, he preached frequently at Bob Jones University and around the world. Throughout his lifetime, Jones often recorded his thoughts in verse, a number of which have been set to music. He authored "The Bob Jones University Hymn" and "The Anniversary Hymn" ("Praise Ye Jehovah") as well as other hymns and gospel songs. Other poetic works include "My Song," "Sometime I Shall Not Care," and "Broken Things."

SELECTED SONNETS 321

Background Information

In most cases, a performer should be familiar with a play or novel in its entirety before even selecting a monologue to excerpt. However, for the sake of efficiency, this appendix provides introductory notes on each monologue to summarize the background circumstances. You may wish to provide this information to your students.

Resources on Shakespeare

For the Shakespearean monologues, encourage students to consult narrative summaries of the appropriate play to gain further insight into the characters that they are developing. Excellent sources include *Tales from Shakespeare* by Charles and Mary Lamb and *Beautiful Stories from Shakespeare* by E. Nesbit.

Comprehension

Remind students to consult the dictionary for any word that is unfamiliar to them.

Jaques (jay KWEEZ) [from *As You Like* It by William Shakespeare: Act II, Scene 7]

> *All the world's a stage;*
> *And all the men and women merely players;*
> *They have their exits and their entrances;*
> *And one man in his time plays many parts,*
> *His acts being seven ages. At first the infant,*
> *Mewling* and puking in the nurse's arms;*   *mewling: crying*
> *Then the whining school-boy, with his satchel*
> *And shining morning face, creeping like snail*
> *Unwillingly to school. And then the lover,*
> *Sighing like furnace,* with a woeful ballad*   *sighing like furnace: giving off sighs as a furnace gives off smoke*
> *Made to his mistress' eyebrow. Then a soldier, . . .*
> *Jealous in honour, sudden and quick in quarrel,*
> *Seeking the bubble* reputation*   *bubble: inflated, easily popped*
> *Even in the cannon's mouth. And then the justice,*
> *In fair round belly with good capon* lined,*   *capon: chicken*
> *With eyes severe and beard of formal cut,*
> *full of wise saws* and modern instances;*   *saws: clichés*
> *And so he plays his part. The sixth age shifts*
> *Into the lean and slipper'd pantaloon,**   *pantaloon: Pantalone, a commedia dell'arte character, who was old and easily deceived by other characers*
> *With spectacles on nose and pouch on side;*
> *His youthful hose, well sav'd, a world too wide*
> *For his shrunk shank;* and his big manly voice,*   *shank: leg*
> *Turning again toward childish treble, pipes*
> *And whistles in his sound. Last scene of all,*
> *That ends this strange eventful history,*
> *Is second childishness and mere oblivion;*
> *Sans* teeth, sans eyes, sans taste, sans everything.*   *Sans: without*

Petruchio (puh TROO kee yoh) [from *The Taming of the Shrew* by William Shakespeare: Act IV, Scene 1]

> *Thus have I politicly* begun my reign,*   *politicly: skillfully or craftily*
> *And 'tis my hope to end successfully. . . .*
> *She ate no meat to-day, nor none shall eat;*
> *Last night she slept not, nor to-night she shall not.*
> *As with the meat, some undeserved fault*
> *I'll find about the making of the bed;*
> *And here I'll fling the pillow, there the bolster,*
> *This way the coverlet,* another way the sheets:—*   *coverlet: bedspread*
> *Ay,* and amid this hurly* I intend*   *ay (aye): yes or yea*
> *That all is done in reverend care of her;*   *hurly: confusion*

 APPENDIX D

Jaques

A male or female can perform this speech. Jaques demonstrates how life is similar to a play in which we all perform a variety of roles. Though the other characters recognize the points he makes about life, none of them agree that life is meaningless simply because it ends with death. This monologue can be enacted in many ways with great success: to amuse (the audience), to sadden, to inspire, etc.

Petruchio

Baptista Minola has two daughters—the sweet and lovely Bianca and the beautiful but stubborn and ill-tempered Katherine. Bianca has three suitors, but Baptista declares that Bianca will not be able to get married until her sister Katherine marries. In this hilarious play, the three suitors of Bianca convince the rough-hewn, confident Petruchio, who happens to be in town seeking his fortune, to court Katherine. They agree to pay for the expenses of Petruchio's courting, and they inform him of the added incentive of the family money that comes with marrying Katherine. After marrying Katherine, Petruchio sets forth his plan to "tame" her. Notice lines 9 and 10 of Petruchio's soliloquy. Though he uses unusual measures, he has Katherine's best interest at heart. As a result, Katherine is drastically transformed by the end of the play.

And in conclusion she shall watch* all night: *watch: stay awake*
And if she chance to nod, I'll rail and brawl
And with the clamor keep her still awake.
This is a way to kill a wife with kindness;
And thus I'll curb her mad and headstrong humour.
He that knows better how to tame a shrew,
Now let him speak; 'tis charity to show.

KING HENRY V [from *Henry V* by William Shakespeare: Act IV, Scene 3]

This day is call'd the feast of Crispian:*   *Crispian: shortened form of Saint Crispinian*
He that outlives this day, and comes safe home,
Will stand a tip-toe when this day is nam'd,
And rouse him at the name of Crispian.
He that shall live this day, and see old age,
Will yearly on the vigil feast his neighbours,*   *Will . . . neighbors: dine with friends*
And say, "To-morrow is Saint Crispian":   *yearly on the eve of Saint Crispin's Day*
Then will he strip his sleeve and show his scars,
And say, "These wounds I had on Crispin's day."
Old men forget; yet all shall be forgot,
But he'll remember with advantages*   *advantages: exaggerations*
What feats he did that day. . . .
This story shall the good man teach his son;
And Crispin Crispian shall ne'er go by,
From this day to the ending of the world,
But we in it shall be remembered,—
We few, we happy few, we band of brothers;
For he to-day that sheds his blood with me
Shall be my brother; be he ne'er so vile,*   *be . . . vile: though he has a very low sta-*
This day shall gentle his condition:*   *tion in life*
And gentlemen in England now a-bed*   *gentle his condition: raise his rank in life*
Shall think themselves accurs'd they were not here,   *a-bed: in bed*
And hold their manhoods cheap while any speaks
That fought with us upon Saint Crispin's day.

Hamlet [from *Hamlet* by William Shakespeare: Act III, Scene 2]

Speak the speech, I pray you, as I pronounced it to
you, trippingly on the tongue: but if you mouth* it,   *mouth: to speak in an artificial way*
as many of your players do, I had as lief* the   *lief: readily or willingly*
town-crier spoke my lines. Nor do not saw the air
too much with your hand, thus, but use all gently:
for in the very torrent, tempest, and as I may say,
the whirlwind of passion, you must acquire and beget
a temperance that may give it smoothness. O, it
offends me to the soul, to hear a robustious
periwig-pated fellow* tear a passion to tatters, to   *periwig-pated fellow: a man wearing a wig*

SELECTED MONOLOGUES **323**

King Henry V

England prepares to fight mighty France. France's army outnumbers England's army by about five to one. Henry gives this speech just moments before the battle in order to inspire his English troops to greatness. Henry uses the words *Crispin* and *Crispian* interchangeably in this speech in order to refer to Saints Crispin and Crispinian, early Roman Catholic martyrs and the patron saints of shoemakers, who won converts through their trade. Emperor Maximian condemned them to death for their religious activities around A. D. 286. The Feast of Crispian had been celebrated on October 25 for centuries by members of French shoemaking guilds. When Henry defeated the French forces at the battle of Agincourt on October 25, 1415, Saint Crispin's Day came to be known as the annual celebration of this great victory.

Hamlet

A male or female can perform this speech. Hamlet seeks to coach the members of an acting company who have arrived at his residence. Hamlet wants them to perform a play called *The Murder of Gonzago*, in which he will insert a speech of about a dozen lines. Hamlet's purpose in having the play performed is to expose the guilt of his Uncle Claudius, the king of Denmark, who is the brother and murderer of Hamlet's father, the former king of Denmark.

very rags, to split the ears of the groundlings,* who
for the most part are capable of* nothing but
inexplicable dumbshows* and noise . . . pray you, avoid it. . . .
Be not too tame neither, but let your own discretion
be your tutor: suit the action to the word, the
word to the action; with this special observance, that you
o'erstep not the modesty of nature: for anything so
overdone is [away] from the purpose of playing, whose end,
both at the first and now, was and is, to hold, as 'twere, the
mirror up to nature; . . .

groundlings: people who stood in the low-admission area of an Elizabethan theater
capable of: able to understand
dumbshows: silent enactment of part of a play

SPEED [from *Two Gentlemen of Verona* by William Shakespeare: Act II, Scene 1]

VALENTINE
Why, how know you that I am in love?
SPEED
*By these special marks: first you have learned, like Sir Proteus,
to wreathe your arms, like a mal-content,* to relish a love-song,
like a robin-redbreast; to walk alone, like one that had the
pestilence; to sigh, like a school-boy that had lost his A B C;
to weep, like a young wench* that had buried her grandam; to
fast, like one that takes diet; to watch like one that fears robbing;
. . . You were wont,* when you laughed, to crow like a cock;
when you walked, to walk like one of the lions; when you fasted,
it was presently after dinner; when you looked sadly, it was for
want* of money: and now you are metamorphis'd* with a
mistress, that, when I look on you, I can hardly think you
my master.*

mal-content: dissatisfied person

wench: a girl or young woman

wont: accustomed to

want: lack
metamorphis'd: transformed

LAUNCE (LAWNS) [from *The Two Gentlemen of Verona* by William Shakespeare: Act II, Scene 3]

(Enter LAUNCE leading a dog.)
Nay, 'twill be this hour ere I have done weeping; all the kind*
of the Launces have this very fault: I have received my proportion,* like the prodigious* son, and am going with Sir
Proteus to the Imperial's court. I think Crab my dog be the
sourest-natured dog that lives: my mother weeping, my father
wailing, our maid howling, our cat wringing her hands, and all
our house in a great perplexity; yet did not this cruel-hearted
cur* shed one tear: he is a stone, a very pebble stone, and has
no more pity in him than a dog: . . . why, my grandam having
no eyes, look you, wept herself blind at my parting. Nay, I'll
show you the manner of it: this shoe is my father;—no, this left
shoe is my father;—no, no, this left shoe is my mother; nay, that
cannot be so neither: yes, it is so; it is so; it hath the worser
sole. . . . This hat is Nan our maid; I am the dog:—no, the dog
is himself, and I am the dog—O, the dog is me, and I am myself;*

ere: before
kind: kin or family
proportion: malapropism (humor-ous verbal error) for portion
prodigious: malapropism, prodigal

cur: a distasteful dog

(324) APPENDIX D

Speed

A male or female can perform this speech. Speed is a page or servant to Valentine. He is a lovable, comic character who is teasing the love-struck Valentine in this scene. Ironically, in the first act of the play Valentine had been lecturing his good friend Proteus about the debilitating aspects of love. Valentine's line is added to aid knowledge of the context.

Launce

A male or female can perform this hilarious speech. Launce is the quick-witted, clownish servant to Proteus. Proteus has been sent away by his father to the emperor's court. This soliloquy shows Launce's melodramatic grief in having to leave his home.

Jane

While the governess in Mr. Rochester's estate, Thornfield Hall, Jane falls in love with Mr. Rochester. He encourages this love, while holding a deep, dark secret in a remote part of his estate. Mr. Rochester is hiding his insane wife. He intends to marry Jane, but the truth that he has an insane wife is revealed. Jane flees Thornfield Hall in deep despair. Later, Jane learns that Rochester's wife has set fire to Thornfield Hall. When the smoke clears, Thornfield Hall is in ashes,

ay, so, so. Now come I to my father: "Father, your blessing."
Now could not the shoe speak a word for weeping. Now come
I to my mother: (O, that she could speak now!) . . . well, I kiss
her:—why there 'tis; here's my mother's breath up and down.*. . .   **up and down:** *exactly*
Now the dog all this while sheds not a tear nor speaks a word; but
see how I lay the dust with my tears.

Jane [from *Jane Eyre* by Charlotte Brontë: Chapter 37]

My spirits were excited, and with pleasure and ease I talked to him dur-
ing supper, and for a long time after. There was no harassing restraint, no re-
pressing of glee with him; for with him I was at perfect ease, because I knew
I suited him: all I said or did seemed either to console or revive him. De-
lightful consciousness! It brought to life and light my whole nature: in his
presence I thoroughly lived; and he lived in mine. Blind as he was, smiles
played over his face, joy dawned on his forehead: his lineaments* softened   **lineaments:** *shape of his face*
and warmed. After supper, he began to ask me many questions, of where I
had been, what I had been doing, how I had found him out; but I gave him
only very partial replies: it was too late to enter into particulars that night.
Besides, I wished to touch no deep-thrilling chord—to open no fresh well of
emotion in his heart: my sole present aim was to cheer him. Cheered, as I
have said, he was: and yet but by fits. If a moment's silence broke the conver-
sation, he would turn restless, touch me, then say, "Jane."

Mr. Rochester [from *Jane Eyre* by Charlotte Brontë: Chapter 37]

And there is enchantment* in the very hour I am now spending with   **enchantment:** *overwhelming*
you. Who can tell what a dark, dreary, hopeless life I have dragged on for   *charm*
months past? Doing nothing, expecting nothing; merging night in day; feel-
ing but the sensation of cold when I let the fire go out, of hunger when I for-
got to eat: and then a ceaseless sorrow, and, at times, a very delirium* of   **delirium:** *unrestrained excitement*
desire to behold my Jane again. Yes: for her restoration I longed, far more
than for that of my lost sight. How can it be that Jane is with me, and says
she loves me? Will she not depart as suddenly as she came? To-morrow, I
fear I shall find her no more. What is the use of doing me good in any way,
beneficent* spirit, when, at some fatal moment, you will again desert me—   **beneficent:** *kind*
passing like a shadow, whither and how to me unknown; and for me, re-
maining afterwards undiscoverable.

Mr. Darcy [from *Pride and Prejudice* by Jane Austen: Chapter 58]

I have been a selfish being all my life, in practice, though not in principle.
As a child, I was taught what was right; but I was not taught to correct my
temper. I was given good principles, but left to follow them in pride and con-
ceit. Unfortunately, an only son (for many years an only child), I was spoiled
by my parents, who, though good themselves, allowed, encouraged, almost
taught me to be selfish and overbearing—to care for none beyond my own
family circle, to think meanly* of all the rest of the world, to wish at least to   **meanly:** *low in importance or value*

SELECTED MONOLOGUES   325

---

the wife is dead, and Mr. Rochester is blind. Jane finds out where Rochester is now living and goes to visit him. This monologue is a soliloquy.

Mr. Rochester

Mr. Rochester expresses his hopes and fears to Jane upon her unexpected visit (refer to the previous *Jane Eyre* mono-logue for more details). Bear in mind that Mr. Rochester is blind and that one of his hands has been lost as a result of the fire. Rochester is now a weak and humble man after years of stubborn-ness and pride.

Mr. Darcy

When Elizabeth meets him, Mr. Darcy seems to be the ultimate aloof aristo-crat, presenting a demeanor of coldness and insensitivity. Elizabeth, allowing her dislike of Darcy's demeanor to prejudice her against him, unfairly judges his character to be poor. Darcy confesses his love to Elizabeth but is careful to point out that he is stooping to accept Elizabeth's low family connec-tions. Elizabeth rejects Darcy, blaming him for many faults. While Darcy learns to be more humble, Elizabeth discovers how badly she has misjudged him. This scene takes place when he returns to visit her.

think meanly of their sense and worth compared with my own. Such I was, from eight to eight-and-twenty; and such I might still have been but for you, dearest, loveliest Elizabeth! What do I not owe you? You taught me a lesson, hard indeed at first, but most advantageous. By you I was properly humbled. I came to you without a doubt of my reception. You showed me how insufficient were all my pretensions* to please a woman worthy of being pleased.

pretensions: excuses

Emma [from *Emma* by Jane Austen: Chapter 1]

I promise you to make [no matches] for myself, papa; but I must, indeed, for other people. It is the greatest amusement in the world! And after such success, you know! Everybody said that Mr. Weston would never marry again. Oh dear, no! Mr. Weston, who had been a widower so long, and who seemed so perfectly comfortable without a wife, so constantly occupied either in his business in town or among his friends here, always acceptable wherever he went, always cheerful—Oh no! Mr. Weston certainly would never marry again. Some people even talked of a promise to his wife on her deathbed, and others of the son and the uncle not letting him. All manner of solemn nonsense was talked on the subject, but I believed none of it. Ever since the day, about four years ago, that Miss Taylor and I met with him in Broadway Lane, when, because it began to drizzle, he darted away with so much gallantry, and borrowed two umbrellas for us from Farmer Mitchell's, I made up my mind on the subject. I planned the match from that hour; and when such success has blessed me in this instance, dear papa, you cannot think that I shall leave off matchmaking.

A Young Lady [adapted from "The Freshman Speaks Extemporaneously" by Lindsey Barbee]

I'm paralyzed with fright! Kate is flat on her back with the flu in the nurse's office, and she wants me to take her place in the debate, which begins in five minutes. [Pause] You have to do what a senior tells you to do, and, besides, Kate has been telling me for weeks that I have to learn to speak extemporaneously if I want a spot on the debate team. I don't even know what the topic is!—Did someone just call my name? Here goes nothing, and I mean nothing. [She rises, advances, and clears her throat.] Ladies and Gentlemen, [Giggles nervously] it is with great pleasure that I rise to speak to you about one of the most significant questions of our day [Long pause]: Is the intellect of a woman superior to that of a man? How can we hesitate in the consideration of such a proposition? [She hesitates and then becomes oratorical.] On one hand we have man—weak, childish man. What has man done to claim our slightest appreciation and gratitude? On the other hand—woman; woman—who has climbed from the lowest social position to the highest pinnacle of—[Hesitates]—well, to the highest pinnacle. Compared with such accomplishment, we can but see that man is—well—is not—a woman. Oh, my friends, can we stand idly by when the burning issue of such a question is at stake? No, I beg of you, rouse yourselves! [Ending with a flourish] Is the intellect of a woman superior to that of a man? No, I say, no! A thousand times, no! Oh—I mean yes—yes—a thousand times, yes!

Emma

Emma is excited that her wonderful friend and former governess, Miss Taylor, has married the widower Mr. Weston. Emma is even more excited that she was the matchmaker between them. Just before Emma makes the following remarks, her father says, "Ah! My dear, I wish you would not make matches and foretell things, for whatever you say always comes to pass. Pray do not make any more matches."

A Young Lady

In this monologue, *extemporaneously* means a speech that is delivered with little or no preparation—impromptu. Have you ever wondered why public speaking is the greatest fear of modern Americans? Well, this monologue may give you some insight.

Amy

Amy's older sister Beth has caught a horrible fever. Since Amy is the youngest of the four daughters, she is sent to her aunt's home to avoid catching the fever. While roaming the house with Amy, Esther, her aunt's maid, confides to Amy that her aunt has willed all of her jewelry to Amy and her sisters, adding that a beautiful turquoise ring will be given to Amy. Amy decides that she, too, should make a will "so that if she did fall ill and die, her possessions might be justly and generously divided." It should be noted that Amy is approximately eleven years old and has a bent toward the melodramatic. Amy's

Amy [from *Little Women* by Louisa May Alcott: Chapter 19]

I, Amy Curtis March, being in my sane mind, do give and bequeethe [sic] all my earthly property—to wit:—namely—To my father, my best pictures, sketches, maps, and works of art, including frames. Also my $100, to do what he likes with. To my mother, all my clothes, except the blue apron with pockets. To my dear sister Margaret, I give my turkquoise [sic] ring (if I get it). To Jo I leave my breast-pin, the one mended with sealing wax, also my bronze inkstand—she lost the cover—and my most precious plaster rabbit, because I am sorry I burnt up her story. To Beth (if she lives after me) I give my dolls and my new slippers—if she can wear them being thin when she gets well. To my friend and neighbor Theodore Laurence I bequeethe [sic] my clay model of a horse though he did say it hadn't any neck. Also in return for his great kindness in the hour of affliction any one of my artistic works he likes. And now having disposed of my most valuable property I hope all will be satisfied and not blame the dead. I forgive everyone, and trust we may all meet when the trump shall sound. Amen. To this will and testament I set my hand and seal on this 20th day of Nov. Anno Domino [sic] 1861.

Jo (female) [from *Little Women* by Louisa May Alcott: Chapter 35]

You'll get over this after a while, and find some lovely, accomplished girl, who will adore you, and make a fine mistress for your fine house. I shouldn't. I'm homely and awkward and odd and old, and you'd be ashamed of me, and we should quarrel—we can't help it even now, you see—and I shouldn't like elegant society and you would, and you'd hate my scribbling,* and I couldn't get on without it, and we should be unhappy, and wish we hadn't done it, and everything would be horrid! I don't believe that I shall ever marry. I'm happy as I am, and love my liberty too well to be in any hurry to give it up for any mortal man.

scribbling: writing, a favorite pastime

Mary Magdalene [adapted from John 20:1-16]

I hurried through the garden to Jesus' tomb this morning. When I arrived, I was surprised to find that the huge stone covering the opening of the tomb had been rolled away. I ran to where Peter and John were staying, and I told them that somebody had stolen away the body of Jesus. They both rushed to the tomb, and when they looked inside they saw only linen grave clothes. John realized that Jesus must have risen from the dead. Peter and John started home again, but I stayed by the tomb and wept. I didn't know what had happened to Jesus. I stooped down and looked into the tomb. What I saw, I couldn't believe! Angels, dressed in white robes, sat at the head and foot of where Jesus had lain. They both looked so kind. They asked me why I was crying. I told them that someone had taken away the body of Jesus and I didn't know where they'd put Him. I turned around suddenly and a man was standing close to me. He asked me why I was crying and who I was looking for. I assumed he was the gardener, so I asked him if he had taken Jesus somewhere else. He said my name. "Mary!" I looked at him again and that's when I knew—I knew that He was Jesus. He had risen from the dead!

misspelled words in the will are signaled by the word *sic*.

Jo

After many years of a close friendship, Laurie [Theodore Laurence] finally decides to confront Jo about his love for her. Moments before the following monologue by Jo, Laurie tells her that he has loved her since he first met her. Jo is merely fond of Laurie as a dear friend and nothing more. She has known that one day Laurie would propose, but Jo resolutely confesses to him that she does not love him truly—and never could.

Mary Magdalene

In early dawn on the third day after Jesus' Crucifixion, Mary Magdalene goes to visit Jesus' tomb. Mark 16:1 further reveals that she went to the tomb with two other women in order to anoint the body of Jesus with sweet spices. The surname Magdalene is most likely used to show that she was from the town of Magdala and also to distinguish her from the several other Marys who are named in the Gospels. Luke 8:2 reveals that Jesus had earlier cast seven demons out of her. Matthew 27:56 shows that she witnessed the Crucifixion of Jesus.

Martha [adapted from John 11:1-44]

My brother Lazarus was very ill. Mary and I tried to care for him—we did everything we knew to do. But he needed more help than we could give. We sent word to Jesus, who was teaching in a small town. The messenger told Him that Lazarus was very sick, but Jesus didn't return with the messenger. In fact, He stayed there for two more days. When He finally arrived, it was too late. Lazarus had died. I ran to greet Jesus, saying I wished He'd come sooner to save Lazarus. He told me that Lazarus would live again and then asked if I believed He was the Son of God. "Yes, of course!" I said. We went straight to the tomb, where we found Mary weeping. Jesus first asked where Lazarus had been laid and then wept. I'd never seen Him cry before, but I knew He loved my brother dearly. Soon He prayed and then loudly cried, "Lazarus, come forth." At those words, Lazarus appeared from his tomb, still bound by grave clothes, but very much alive, just as Jesus had promised!

Rhoda [adapted from Acts 12:1-16]

King Herod recently put the apostle James to death, and since this pleased the people so much, he decided to throw the apostle Peter in prison and execute him also. Many of us Christians gathered in a home to pray for Peter. We were huddled together, praying fervently, when I seemed to hear a knock at the door of the gate. Without disturbing the others, I crept to the door and asked who was there. Peter answered! I was so excited that I forgot to open the door for him. I quickly ran back to the others and told them that Peter himself was standing at the gate. One man raised up his head and told me that I was out of my mind. I tried to convince them that Peter really was standing at the gate. Another said that it must be Peter's angel. But the knocking would not stop, so the others went to the door and opened it. When they saw Peter for themselves, they were amazed!

Moses [adapted from Exodus 13:21–14:31]

After ten devastating plagues, Pharaoh finally released us from slavery. We were free but not alone, for God led our path—by day in an amazing glowing cloud, and by night in a breathtaking pillar of fire. We had traveled as far as the edge of the Red Sea when our sense of freedom began to slip away. Pharaoh's army was quickly closing in on us. My people became confused and panic-stricken. They let their frustration out on me, saying, "What have you done—have you brought us this far just to let us die? We were better off as slaves in Egypt. We should have stayed there." God told me to hold out my hand over the sea. Suddenly, a mighty rushing wind formed a wall of water on two sides with a completely dry path in between. Immediately, I led the people down this incredible path. Looking back, I saw the grand host of the Egyptians gaining rapidly. We had no chance. We were no match for the speed of their chariots. Just when I thought we were doomed, every single one of the Egyptians' chariots seemed to grind to a halt. Horses and men were flying in all directions. The chariot wheels had fallen off! They began a swift but confused retreat back toward the shoreline. God told me to stretch my hand back over the sea, and when I did, the two walls of water crashed together. Not one Egyptian escaped.

Martha

Martha's personality is perhaps best seen in Luke 10:38-42, in which she appeals to Jesus because she has to do all the serving while her sister Mary just sits at His feet. John 11:3 and 36 reveal that Jesus was a close friend of Lazarus, Martha and Mary's brother.

Rhoda

The grandson of Herod the Great, King Herod Agrippa I of Palestine, is mentioned in this monologue. He executes the apostle James and then sets his sights on the apostle Peter, whom he imprisons, chaining his hands and leaving four soldiers to guard him. In a miraculous event, God sends an angel to lead Peter out of the jail. Peter then goes to the very house where many Christians have gathered to pray for him. Rhoda sees him first. There is no other mention in Scripture of this young woman named Rhoda.

Moses

The children of Israel have been enslaved in Egypt for 430 years when God uses Moses to confront Pharaoh with the demand that the Israelites be set free. After nine hideous plagues Pharaoh finally calls for the departure of Moses and the children of Israel. Soon after the Israelites leave, Pharaoh regrets his decision to let them go and quickly pursues them with a host of soldiers, horses, and chariots.

Caleb [adapted from Numbers 13–14:9]

God had promised to give the Israelites the Land of Canaan, and now we were near that land. Joshua and I were among the twelve spies that were sent in to check it out. What a wonderful land—fertile soil, fruitful crops—it was like a paradise! However, the people of the land were like giants compared to us. The walled cities were massive. This didn't worry me, though. I was confident that we could overcome the people and take the land. Joshua agreed with me. But the other spies were afraid of these giants of Canaan. They said that such a mighty race of people would devour us if we tried to attack them. The Israelites believed them and began to cry and complain, saying that it would have been better to die in Egypt—or even in the wilderness. They wanted to choose a new leader to take them back to Egypt. Now we must plead with them to repent.

Paul [adapted from Acts 27–28:6]

A long voyage lay ahead from Caesarea to Rome, where I must stand before Caesar. At one point during the journey, I felt strongly that we would face some very dangerous seas. We could potentially lose cargo and even our lives, but the captain dismissed my warning. Just as I had suspected, a huge storm relentlessly tossed our ship! The passengers feared for their lives, but God told me that we would make it to Rome safely. The ship crashed into a sandbar near a beach. Some jumped overboard and swam ashore, while others floated to the beach on pieces of the ship. All of us managed to get to land safely. The inhabitants of the island were very friendly. The weather was cold, so they built us a fire. While I was putting more wood on the fire, a snake jumped out and locked its fangs into my hand. The natives froze. They fixed their eyes on me. As I stood there with the viper hanging from my hand, the people said to one another that I must be a murderer who had escaped death at sea only to receive justice on this island. I shook the beast into the fire. The people stared at me, expecting me to swell up or fall dead at any second, but the snake's bite had no effect on me.

SELECTED MONOLOGUES 329

Caleb

Three months after leaving the land of Egypt, Moses and the children of Israel arrive in the wilderness of Sinai. During the next ten months they receive the Decalogue, directions for constructing the tabernacle and for the numerous facets of the sacrificial system. Then they travel from Sinai to Paran, where one man from each of the twelve tribes of Israel is chosen to spy out the land of Canaan.

Paul

In Jerusalem, the Jews bring charges against Paul of being a troublemaker, and he is thrown into prison. Later he pleads his case effectively before Governor Felix, who nevertheless leaves him in prison. After two years, Festus succeeds Felix as governor. The Jews press Festus to send Paul to Jerusalem so that they can kill him in an ambush, but Festus decides that Paul should be tried in Caesarea. When the Jews come there to accuse Paul, he states his innocence and appeals to Caesar in Rome. Before Paul is sent to Caesar, King Agrippa II requests to hear his case. Paul explains that the Jews have accused him merely because he preaches the gospel of Jesus Christ. Agrippa concludes that Paul has done nothing to deserve imprisonment or death, but since he has appealed to Caesar, Paul boards a ship headed for Rome.

APPENDIX E
CHRISTIAN HEROES

Christian Heroes

Selection

If you prefer either that a student avoid choosing a particular individual or individuals from this list or choose only from the list to avoid having to evaluate other individuals, announce these rules before directing the students' attention to the list. This will prevent a student from becoming interested in a subject he will not have opportunity to pursue.

Numerous authors, artists, composers, statesmen, physicians, and others have left legacies of Christian faith. Many of these were not included on this list because a student might easily read a biography that featured the individual's contribution to culture or society without making much mention of faith. If a student wishes to pursue such an individual, have him submit his biographies to you for quick perusal before he reads them.

The following list is certainly not exhaustive. If you are interested in a Christian hero not included on this page, consult your teacher. If you do choose from this list, choose one or more alternates before looking for biographies. You may not find sufficient information available on the first individual. If that is the case, search for a different person.

Consider choosing an individual about whom you know little or nothing. This creates a real learning opportunity beyond your speaking and acting ability. Reading a biography is a fascinating means of learning history.

Men

Philip P. Bliss	Henry Knott	Ira Sankey
William Whiting Borden	John Knox	Billy Sunday
E. M. Bounds	C. S. Lewis	C. H. Spurgeon
David Brainerd	Eric Liddell	John Stewart
John Bunyan	George Liele	John Stam
John Calvin	David Livingstone	J. Hudson Taylor
Lott Carey	D. Martyn Lloyd-Jones	Charles Albert Tindley
William Carey	Martin Luther	William Tyndale
Oswald Chambers	John Marrant	Booker T. Washington
Jonathan Edwards	Clebe McClary	Isaac Watts
Jim Elliot	D. L. Moody	Charles Wesley
T. S. Eliot	G. Campbell Morgan	John Wesley
Christmas Evans	George Mueller	George Whitefield
Jonathan Goforth	John Newton	William Wilberforce
Bob Jones Sr.	Daniel Alexander Payne	John Wycliffe
Adoniram Judson	Nate Saint	

Women

Amy Carmichael	Ann Hasseltine Judson	Mary Slessor
Fanny Crosby	(first wife of Adoniram Judson)	Elisabeth (Betty) Scott Stam
Darlene Deibler Rose	Emily Chubbuck Judson	(wife of John Stam)
Sarah Edwards	(third wife of Adoniram Judson)	Sojourner Truth
(wife of Jonathan Edwards)	Sarah Boardman Judson	Narcissa Whitman
Elisabeth Elliot	(second wife of Adoniram Judson)	Susanna Annesley Wesley
(wife of Jim Elliot)	Isobel Kuhn (wife of John Kuhn)	(wife of Samuel Wesley,
Rosalind Goforth (wife of Jonathan	Florence Nightingale	mother of Charles and John
Goforth)	Elizabeth Prentiss	Wesley)
Lady Jane Grey	Christina Georgina Rossetti	Katherine (Kitty or Katie) von Bora
Frances Ridley Havergal	Pandita Ramabai	(wife of Martin Luther)

 APPENDIX E

Additional Notes

Students may have difficulty finding adequate information on several of the black heroes (Lott Carey, George Liele, John Marrant, Daniel Payne, John Stewart, Charles A. Tindley, Booker T. Washington, Sojourner Truth). *Free Indeed: Heroes of Black Christian History* by Mark Sidwell (BJU Press) provides some biographical information on the lesser-known heroes. You and your students may find this book a valuable resource.

Be aware that a few names on this list may belong to multiple individuals who are discussed in print or on the Internet. Remind the students to be certain they have found a Christian hero. For some individuals, the middle name has been included to reduce the probability of such a problem.

APPENDIX F
RECOMMENDED SHORT STORIES

Author	Title	Competition Categories			Topical Categories			
		Dramatic	Humorous	Adventure	Detective	Imaginative	Love	Western
Hans Christian Andersen	"The Brave Tin Soldier"	✓		✓			✓	
	"The Emperor's New Suit"		✓			✓		
	"The Happy Family"		✓			✓		
	"The Loveliest Rose in the World"	✓				✓		
	"The Old Street Lamp"	✓				✓		
	"The Princess and the Pea"	✓				✓		
	"The Snow Man"	✓				✓		
	"The Snowdrop"	✓				✓		
	"Thumbelina"	✓				✓		
	"The Top and the Ball"	✓				✓		
	"The Ugly Duckling"	✓		✓		✓		
	"What the Old Man Does Is Always Right"		✓			✓		
	"The Wild Swans"	✓				✓		
Ambrose Bierce	"An Occurrence at Owl Creek Bridge"	✓		✓				
	"The Man and the Snake"	✓		✓				
Richard Connell	"The Most Dangerous Game"	✓		✓				
Stephen Crane	"The Bride Comes to Yellow Sky"	✓		✓		✓		✓
Hamlin Garland	"The Return of a Private"	✓				✓	✓	
Brothers Grimm	"The Bremen-Town Musicians"					✓		

Recommended Short Stories

This list of stories is not exhaustive, but contains only a handful of the great stories that could be performed by your students. For instance, twenty-five O. Henry stories are listed; however, O. Henry wrote nearly three hundred short stories. By obtaining anthologies of some of the great short story writers, a speech teacher can greatly increase his students' ability to find excellent selections for class work and fine-arts competitions. Students should be able to find these selections at the school library or at a local public or university library. In fact, many of the selections can be found on the Internet. Although much thought and care went into choosing the stories, some do contain offensive elements that need to be cut. Many of the stories will definitely need to be shortened in length for performance purposes. Some stories are relatively short; they may be appropriate for class projects but not for fine arts competitions. Always make sure that your students time their cuttings accurately.

APPENDIX F
RECOMMENDED SHORT STORIES

Author	Title	Competition Categories		Topical Categories				
		Dramatic	Humorous	Adventure	Detective	Imaginative	Love	Western
Brothers Grimm	"The Fisherman and His Wife"	✓	✓	✓			✓	
	"The Frog Prince"	✓		✓		✓	✓	
	"The Golden Bird"	✓		✓		✓		
	"Hansel and Gretel"	✓		✓		✓		
	"Little Red Riding-Hood"	✓		✓		✓		
	"Rapunzel"	✓		✓		✓	✓	
	"Snow White and the Seven Dwarfs"	✓		✓		✓		
Nathaniel Hawthorne	"The Birthmark"	✓				✓	✓	
	"The Celestial Railroad"	✓		✓		✓		
O. Henry	"A Call Loan"	✓		✓				✓
	"A Chaparral Prince"	✓		✓				✓
	"A Double-Dyed Deceiver"	✓		✓			✓	✓
	"A Lickpenny Lover"		✓				✓	
	"A Retrieved Reformation"	✓		✓			✓	
	"The Adventures of Shamrock Jolnes"	✓		✓				
	"After Twenty Years"	✓		✓				
	"Art and the Bronco"			✓				✓
	"Buried Treasure"			✓				✓

APPENDIX F
RECOMMENDED SHORT STORIES

Author	Title	Competition Categories		Topical Categories				
		Dramatic	Humorous	Adventure	Detective	Imaginative	Love	Western
O. Henry	"Christmas By Injunction"		✓	✓				✓
	"The Cop and the Anthem"		✓			✓		
	"The Emancipation of Billy"	✓			✓			
	"The Gift of the Magi"	✓					✓	
	"The Guardian of the Accolade"	✓		✓				
	"The Indian Summer of Dry Valley Johnson"						✓	✓
	"Jimmy Hayes and Muriel"	✓		✓				✓
	"The Last Leaf"	✓						
	"The Love Philtre of Ikey Schoenstein"		✓				✓	
	"Mammon and the Archer"		✓				✓	
	"The Missing Chord"	✓					✓	✓
	"The Passing of Black Eagle"		✓	✓				✓
	"The Princess and the Puma"		✓	✓			✓	✓
	"The Ransom of Mack"		✓				✓	
	"The Ransom of Red Chief"		✓	✓				
	"Two Thanksgiving Day Gentlemen"	✓						
Shirley Jackson	"Charles"		✓					
W. W. Jacobs	"The Monkey's Paw"	✓						
Rudyard Kipling	"The Beginning of the Armadillos" from Just So Stories		✓			✓		

APPENDIX F
RECOMMENDED SHORT STORIES

AUTHOR	TITLE	Competition Categories		Topical Categories				
		Dramatic	Humorous	Adventure	Detective	Imaginative	Love	Western
Rudyard Kipling	"The Cat That Walked by Himself" from *Just So Stories*		✓			✓		
	"The Elephant's Child" from *Just So Stories*		✓			✓		
	"How the Camel Got His Hump" from *Just So Stories*		✓			✓		
	"How the First Letter Was Written" from *Just So Stories*		✓			✓		
	"How the Rhinoceros Got His Skin" from *Just So Stories*		✓			✓		
	"How the Whale Got His Throat" from *Just So Stories*		✓			✓		
	"Rikki-Tikki-Tavi" from *The Jungle Book*		✓			✓		
	"The Sing-Song of Old Man Kangaroo" from *Just So Stories*		✓			✓		
S. I. Kishor	"An Appointment with Love"	✓					✓	
Mary Macleod	*King Arthur and His Knights*	✓		✓		✓		
Guy de Maupassant	"A Piece of String"	✓						
	"The Necklace"	✓						
Patrick F. McManus	"A Road Less Traveled By"		✓					
	"The Bandage"		✓					
	"Another Boring Day"		✓					
	"The Big Woods"		✓					
	"I, the Hunted"		✓					
	"Kid Brothers and Their Practical Applications"		✓					
	"The Night the Bear Ate Goombaw"		✓					

APPENDIX F
RECOMMENDED SHORT STORIES

Author	Title	Competition Categories		Topical Categories				
		Dramatic	Humorous	Adventure	Detective	Imaginative	Love	Western
Patrick F. McManus	"Toe"		✓					
	"The Two Masked Raiders"		✓					
Herman Melville	"Bartleby"	✓						
Beatrix Potter	"The Roly-Poly Pudding"			✓		✓		
	"The Tale of Benjamin Bunny"			✓		✓		
	"The Tale of the Flopsy Bunnies"			✓		✓		
	"The Tale of Mr. Jeremy Fisher"			✓		✓		
	"The Tale of Peter Rabbit"			✓		✓		
	"The Tale of Timothy Tiptoes"			✓		✓		
Howard Pyle	The Merry Adventures of Robin Hood		✓	✓		✓		
	The Story of King Arthur and His Knights		✓	✓		✓		
Archibald Rutledge	"The Tomb"		✓	✓				
Saki (H. H. Munro)	"Dusk"		✓	✓				
	"The Interlopers"			✓				
	"The Lull"		✓					
	"Mark"		✓					
	"The Mouse"		✓					
	"Mrs. Packletide's Tiger"		✓					
	"The Phantom Luncheon"		✓					
	"The Wolves of Cernogratz"	✓						

RECOMMENDED SHORT STORIES 335

APPENDIX F
RECOMMENDED SHORT STORIES

Author	Title	Competition Categories		Topical Categories				
		Dramatic	Humorous	Adventure	Detective	Imaginative	Love	Western
Frank R. Stockton	"The Griffin and the Minor Canon"	✓	✓	✓		✓		
Jesse Stuart	"Split Cherry Tree"	✓	✓					
James Thurber	"The Car We Had to Push"		✓					
	"The Day the Dam Broke"		✓					
	"The Dog That Bit People"		✓					
	"Draft Board Nights"		✓					
	"The Macbeth Murder Mystery"		✓					
	"More Alarms at Night"		✓					
	"The Night the Bed Fell"		✓					
	"The Night the Ghost Got In"		✓					
	"The Secret Life of Walter Mitty"		✓					
	"University Days"		✓					
Mark Twain	"The Celebrated Jumping Frog of Calaveras County"		✓					✓
	"The Death Disk"	✓		✓				
	"Luck"		✓	✓				
	"The Private History of a Campaign That Failed"		✓					
Patrick Waddington	"The Street That Got Mislaid"	✓	✓	✓				
Oscar Wilde	"The Devoted Friend"		✓			✓		
	"The Model Millionaire"						✓	

APPENDIX G
READERS THEATER SCRIPTS

Be Still and Know

adapted from Psalms 33, 46, 89, 93, 95, and 96

Introduction

Many psalms—including 33, 46, 89, 93, 95, and 96—speak of God's power. A Christian never has to fear nature or any other force because he knows that God is mightier than all of these things. Paul emphasizes a believer's security in God when he writes, "For I am persuaded, that neither death, nor life, nor angels, nor principalities, nor powers, nor things present, nor things to come, Nor height, nor depth, nor any other creature, shall be able to separate us from the love of God, which is in Christ Jesus our Lord" (Romans 8:38-39).

1. After reading the script, describe the effect of the sound effects on the theme.

Answers will vary but may include that the sound effects reinforce the theme by creating an atmosphere that focuses attention on the idea of being still in the midst of a storm.

2. What element of the script do you think will be most attention-getting to the audience?

Answers will vary but may include the sound effects and/or the repeated phrases.

Dramatis Personae

GROUP 1 (G1), quite a few women (may include a few men)
GROUP 2 (G2), a few women
GROUP 3 (G3), men
All other assignments are individual speakers and are labeled "Man 1," "Woman 1," etc.

READERS THEATER SCRIPTS **337**

Script

G1: whhhhhhh-chhh, whhhhhhh-chhh, . . .
(*By softly blowing and making these sounds, create the sound of waves washing over the shore. Begins about twenty seconds before the text.*)

G2: (*Whispering*) Be still.
Be still.

G2, 3: (*Softly voiced*) Be still. (*With growing intensity*) Be still, and know. Be still, and know that I am God.

G1: (*Waves cease.*)

G3: The Lord reigneth.

G2: Be still.

G1: Whhhhhhhhoo . . . (*Create the sound of a soft wind until noted otherwise.*)

G3: He is clothed with majesty.

G2: Be still and know—

G3: The Lord is clothed with strength.

MAN 1: The earth is full of the goodness of the Lord.

MAN 2: By the word of the Lord were the heavens made; and all the host of them by the breath of his mouth.

G3: He gathereth the waters of the sea together as an heap: he layeth up the depth in storehouses. Let all the earth fear the Lord:

MAN 1: Let all the inhabitants of the world stand in awe of him.

MAN 2: For he spake,

G3: and it was done;

MAN 2: he commanded,

G3: and it stood fast.

WOMAN 1: Therefore will not we fear,

MAN 1: though the earth be removed,

G3: and though the mountains be carried into the midst of the sea.

G2: Be still.

G1: (*Wind and waves combine and grow louder progressively.*)

STAGING

"Be Still and Know"

Staging possibilities include—

1. No staging. Since this is an in-class project, you may wish to have students simply remain in their seats or move to different desks by groups so that they can listen to those around them.

2. Allow the students to incorporate stools, chairs, or other nondescript furniture. If using this selection for a performance with an audience (parents, perhaps), try having the students form a circle or square around the audience seating. Alternate speakers from each group so that the audience experiences a "live" version of surround sound.

3. Improvise your own staging.

traditional readers theater in solo speaking roles, use choric speaking for this selection and assign solo readers to perform the poem "The Leaden Echo and the Golden Echo" rather than the other way around.

Handling the Script

The success of this script depends primarily on two factors. First, the teacher or coach must introduce the theatrical elements as serious and appropriate. Otherwise, students may easily take creating sound effects as an opportunity to behave disruptively. The best way to introduce these theatrical qualities is to begin with an appropriate atmosphere for learning and then demonstrate each sound effect. If the teacher or coach takes the task seriously, the students will as well.

Secondly, this script must be approached with attention to its lyric qualities. Just as a beautiful musical composition requires good phrasing and appropriate use of crescendo and decrescendo, this selection demands attention to sounds. The volume, word color, and blending of voices in each group must be refined to create the desired effect.

Enjoy this piece. Help your students enjoy the words as well as the comforting truths they represent. The more effective the performance, the more memorable the

---

The Leaden Echo and the Golden Echo
by Gerard Manley Hopkins

Introduction

This lyric poem contrasts views on the inevitability of aging. The speaker asks, "Can beauty be kept in spite of the passing of time?" Two very different answers echo back to her.

1. After reading the poem aloud, think about what words were unfamiliar to you. Were there any whose meaning you could guess from context? If so, which ones?

Answers will vary.

2. What words should you look up in the dictionary to help you better understand? List them below with simple definitions.

Answers will vary.

Dramatis Personae

VOICE 1, expresses hope, optimism

VOICE 2, represents the thoughts of the speaker; also demonstrates a clear progression in wisdom and understanding

VOICE 3, expresses distress, discouragement

The Leaden Echo

VOICE 2:	How to keep—
VOICE 3:	is there any
VOICE 1:	any,
VOICE 2:	is there none such,
VOICE 3:	nowhere known
VOICE 1:	some, bow or brooch
VOICE 2:	or braid or brace,
VOICES 1, 2, 3:	lace,
VOICE 3:	latch or catch
VOICE 2:	or key to keep

MAN 1: Thou rulest the raging of the sea:

G2: when the waves thereof arise, thou stillest them.

G3: The heavens are thine, the earth also is thine: as for the world and the fullness thereof, thou hast founded them.

WOMAN 1: There is a river, the streams whereof shall make glad the city of God.

WOMAN 2: God is in the midst of her; she shall not be moved.

G1: *(Wind and waves cease.)*

MAN 2: Who is a strong Lord like unto thee?

G3: Thou hast a mighty arm: strong is thy hand, and high is thy right hand. Justice and judgment are the habitation of thy throne: mercy and truth shall go before thy face.

G2: Let thy mercy, O Lord, be upon us, according as we hope in thee.

G1: *(Waves begin again, growing quickly in volume.)*

G2: The floods have lifted up, O Lord, the floods have lifted up their voice; the floods lift up their waves.

G3: The Lord on high is mightier than the noise of many waters,

G1: *(Waves cease.)*

G3: yea, than the mighty waves of the sea.

G2: Let the heavens rejoice, and let the earth be glad; let the sea roar, and the fullness thereof: Let the field be joyful, and all that is therein: then shall all the trees of the wood rejoice before the Lord.

WOMAN 1: O come, let us worship and bow down: let us kneel before the Lord our maker.

MAN 1: Give unto the Lord the glory due unto his name.

WOMAN 2: O worship the Lord in the beauty of holiness.

MAN 1: All the earth shall worship thee, and shall sing unto thee; they shall sing to thy name.

G1: Be still.

---

(338) APPENDIX G

STAGING

"The Leaden Echo"

Staging possibilities include—

1. Create a set from neutral furniture such as boxes or stools. Have other students make suggestions about how to use these set pieces. One possibility would be to suggest a well with a black box. Have Voice 2 ask questions of the well and the other two speakers stand on either side or move about.

2. Any staging suggested for "Be Still and Know."

VOICE 3: Back beauty,
VOICE 1: keep it,
VOICE 2: beauty,
VOICE 1: beauty,
VOICE 3: from vanishing away?
VOICE 2: Ó is there no frowning of these wrinkles,
VOICE 3: rankéd wrinkles deep,
Dówn? no waving off of these most mournful messengers,

VOICE 1: still messengers,
VOICE 2: sad and stealing messengers of grey?
VOICE 3: No there's none,
VOICE 1: there's none,
VOICE 2: O no there's none,
VOICE 1: Nor can you long be,
VOICE 3: what you now are,
VOICE 1: called fair,
VOICE 3: Do what you may do,
VOICE 2: what,
VOICE 3: do what you may,
And wisdom is early to despair:

VOICE 1: Be beginning;
VOICE 2: since, no, nothing can be done
To keep at bay
VOICE 3: Age and age's evils, hoar hair,
Ruck★ and wrinkle,
drooping, dying,
death's worst, winding sheets, tombs and
worms and tumbling to decay;

VOICE 1: So be beginning,
VOICE 3: be beginning to despair.
VOICE 2: O there's none;
VOICE 1: no

Ruck: crease, fold

VOICES 1, 2: no
VOICES 1, 2, 3: no
VOICE 3: there's none:
VOICE 1: Be beginning to despair,
VOICE 2: to despair,
VOICE 1: Despair,
VOICE 2, 3: despair,
VOICES 1, 2, 3: despair,
VOICE 3: despair.

Spare: Let me speak!

The Golden Echo

VOICE 1: Spare!★
VOICE 2: There is one,
VOICE 1: yes I have one
VOICE 2: (Hush there!);
VOICE 3: Only not within seeing of the sun,
VOICE 2: Not within the singeing of the strong sun,
VOICE 1: Tall sun's tingeing,
VOICE 2: or treacherous the tainting of the earth's air,
VOICE 1: Somewhere elsewhere there is
VOICE 3: ah well where!
VOICE 2: one,
VOICE 1: [there is] Oné.
VOICE 2: yes I can tell such a key, I do know such a place,
VOICE 1: Where whatever's prized and passes of us,
VOICE 2: everything that's fresh and fast-flying of us,
VOICE 1: seems to us sweet of us and swiftly away with,
VOICE 3: done away with, undone,
VOICE 2: Undone,
VOICE 3: done with, soon done with,
VOICE 2: an'd yet dearly and dangerously sweet
VOICE 2: Of us,
VOICE 1: the wimpled★-water-dimpled,   *wimpled: creased, folded*

truths will be for both the readers and the audience members.

"The Leaden Echo"

Role Assignments

Voice 1—high, lighter voices (mostly sopranos)

Voice 2—medium, richer voices (mostly altos and tenors)

Voice 3—low and darker voices (mostly basses)

In a smaller group, women can read voices 1 and 2, men, voice 3. For an all-ladies group, voice 1 could be one or just a few sopranos; voice 2, several sopranos and altos; voice 3, a few with lower alto ranges. This selection is not ideal for an all-male cast.

Remind students on this script particularly not to pause at the end of a line but at the next punctuation mark. An example would be the phrase "to keep / Back beauty," which appears on two lines but is one thought.

Because this selection is abstract and emphasizes sound quality, the suggested production concept focuses on sounds. Experiment with reading the poem aloud several times before attempting to stage it, if you stage it at all.

VOICE 2: not-by-morning-matchèd face,
VOICE 1: The flower of beauty,
VOICE 2: fleece of beauty,
VOICE 3: too too apt to, ah! to fleet,
VOICE 2: Never fleets móre,
VOICE 1: fastened with the tenderest truth
To its own best being and its loveliness of youth:
VOICE 2: it is an everlastingness of,
VOICE 1: O it is an all youth!
Come then, your ways and airs and looks, locks,
VOICE 2: maiden gear,
VOICE 1: gallantry
VOICE 3: and gaiety and grace,
VOICE 1: Winning ways,
VOICE 2: airs innocent,
VOICE 1: maiden manners,
VOICE 3: sweet looks, loose locks,
VOICE 1: long locks,
VOICE 2: lovelocks,
VOICE 1: gaygear, * *gaygear: bright, lively attire*
VOICE 3: going gallant,
VOICE 1: girlgrace—
VOICE 2: Resign them,
VOICE 1: sign them,
VOICE 2: seal them, send them,
VOICE 1: motion them with breath,
VOICE 3: And with sighs
VOICE 1: soaring, soaring sighs
VOICE 2: deliver
Them;
VOICE 1: beauty-in-the-ghost,
VOICE 2: deliver it, early now,
VOICE 3: long before death

VOICE 2: Give beauty back,
VOICE 1: beauty,
VOICE 2: beauty,
VOICES 1, 2, 3: beauty,
VOICE 2: back to God,
VOICE 1: and beauty's giver.
VOICE 2: See; not a hair is,
VOICE 1: not an eyelash,
VOICE 2: not the least lash lost; every hair
Is,
VOICE 1: hair of the head,
VOICE 2: numbered.
VOICE 1: Nay, what we had lighthanded left in surly the mere mould
VOICE 2: Will have waked and have waxed
VOICE 3: and have walked with the wind
VOICE 2: what while we slept,
VOICE 1: This side, that side
VOICE 3: hurling a heavyheaded hundredfold
What while we,
VOICE 2: while we slumbered.
O then,
VOICE 3: weary then why
VOICE 1: When the thing we freely fórfeit
VOICE 2: is kept with fonder a care,
VOICE 1: Fonder a care kept than we could have kept it,
VOICE 2: kept
VOICE 1: Far with fonder a care
(and we, we should have lost it)
VOICE 3: finer,
VOICE 2: fonder
VOICE 1: A care kept.
VOICE 3: —Where kept?
VOICE 1: Do but tell us where kept,

N1: whose ideas, though somewhat polished and sharpened by the progressiveness of distant Latin neighbors,

N2: were still large, florid, and untrammeled,

KING: as became the half of him which was barbaric.

N2: He was a man of exuberant fancy, and, withal, of an authority so irresistible that, at his will, he turned his varied fancies into facts. He was greatly given to self-communing, and, when he and himself agreed upon anything, the thing was done.

N1: When every member of his domestic and political systems moved smoothly in its appointed course, his nature was bland and genial;

N2: but, whenever there was a little hitch, and some of his orbs got out of their orbits, he was blander and more genial still,

KING: for nothing pleased him so much as to make the crooked straight and crush down uneven places.

N1: Among the borrowed notions

N2: by which his barbarism had become semified was that of the public arena,

N1: in which,

N2: by exhibitions of manly and beastly valor,

N1: the minds of his subjects were refined and cultured.

N2: But even here the exuberant and barbaric fancy asserted itself.

KING: The arena of the king was built,

N1: not to give the people an opportunity of hearing the rhapsodies of dying gladiators,

N2: nor to enable them to view the inevitable conclusion of a conflict between religious opinions and hungry jaws,

N1: but for purposes far better adapted to widen and develop the mental energies of the people.

KING: This vast amphitheater was an agent of poetic justice in which crime was punished, or virtue rewarded, by the decrees of an impartial and incorruptible chance.

VOICE 3: where.—
VOICE 2: Yonder.
VOICE 1: —What high as that!
VOICE 2: We follow,
VOICES 1, 2, 3: now we follow.
VOICE 1: —Yonder,
VOICE 2: yes yonder,
VOICES 1, 2: yonder,
VOICES 1, 2, 3: Yonder.

The Lady or the Tiger?
by Frank Stockton

Introduction

Stockton transports the reader to the fictitious and implausible kingdom of a so-called semi-barbaric king. Though the setting is unrealistic, the question he poses is startlingly realistic. This humorous tale really evaluates motives in the human heart.

After reading the story, decide how you think it should end. Write a brief ending below.

Answers will vary.

Dramatis Personae

NARRATOR 1 (N1), the voice of dignity
NARRATOR 2 (N2), the voice of the barbaric
THE KING
THE PRINCESS
THE YOUNG MAN, who dared to fall in love with the princess

Script

N1: In the very olden time there lived

KING: a semi-barbaric king,

READERS THEATER SCRIPTS (341)

STAGING

"The Lady or the Tiger?"

Staging possibilities include—

1. This flamboyant story seems best presented as masterful storytelling rather than as a play. Consider allowing all readers to carry a script and move about, speaking directly to the audience as storytellers taking turns. Each reader might use a crown or some other hat to suggest a character.

2. "The Lady or the Tiger?" would be fun to use simple costumes for, if you decide to stage it in more of a chamber theater style. Anything that is flashy and a bit gaudy in style would work well. For example, for this story, no one will care if you costume with jewels that are obviously rhinestones, not gems.

N1: When a subject was accused of a crime of sufficient importance to interest the king, public notice was given that on an appointed day

YOUNG MAN: the fate of the accused person would be decided in the king's arena.

N1: When all the people had assembled in the galleries,

KING: and the king, surrounded by his court, sat high up on his throne of royal state on one side of the arena, he gave a signal,

N2: a door beneath him opened, and the accused subject stepped out into the amphitheater.

YOUNG MAN: Directly opposite him, on the other side of the enclosed space, were two doors, exactly alike and side by side.

N2: It was the duty and the privilege of the person on trial to walk directly to these doors and open one of them.

KING: He could open either door he pleased;

YOUNG MAN: he was subject to no guidance or influence but that of the aforementioned impartial and incorruptible chance.

N2: If he opened the one, there came out of it a hungry tiger, the fiercest and most cruel that could be procured,

YOUNG MAN: which immediately sprang upon him and tore him to pieces

KING: as a punishment for his guilt.

N2: The moment that the case of the criminal was thus decided, doleful iron bells were clanged, great wails went up from the hired mourners posted on the outer rim of the arena, and the vast audience, with bowed heads and downcast hearts, wended slowly their homeward way,

YOUNG MAN: mourning greatly that one so young and fair,

N1: or so old and respected, should have merited so dire a fate.

YOUNG MAN: But, if the accused person opened the other door, there came forth from it a lady, the most suitable to

YOUNG MAN: his years and station that his majesty could select among his fair subjects, and to this lady he was immediately married, as a reward of his innocence.

KING: It mattered not that his affections might be engaged upon an object of his own selection;

N1: the king allowed no such subordinate arrangements to interfere with his great scheme of retribution and reward.

N1: The exercises, as in the other instance, took place immediately; and in the arena. Another door opened beneath the king, and a priest, followed by a band of choristers, and maidens blowing joyous airs on golden horns and treading an epithalamic* measure, advanced to where the pair stood, side by side, and the wedding was promptly and cheerily solemnized. Then the brass bells rang forth their merry peals, the people shouted glad hurrahs, and the innocent man, preceded by children strewing flowers on his path, led his bride to his home.

epithalamic: suitable as wedding music

N2: This was the king's semi-barbaric method of administering justice.

KING: Its perfect fairness is obvious. The criminal could not know out of which door would come the lady; he opened either he pleased, without having the slightest idea whether, in the next instant, he was to be devoured or married.

N2: On some occasions the tiger came out of one door, and on some out of the other.

KING: The decisions of this tribunal were not only fair, they were positively determinate: the accused person was instantly punished if he found himself guilty, and, if innocent, he was rewarded on the spot, whether he liked it or not.

N2: There was no escape from the judgments of the king's arena.

KING: The institution was a very popular one.

N2: When the people gathered together on one of the great trial days, they never knew whether they were to witness a bloody slaughter

342 APPENDIX G

N1: or a hilarious wedding.

KING: This element of uncertainty lent an interest to the occasion which it could not otherwise have attained. Thus, the masses were entertained and pleased,

N1: and the thinking part of the community could bring no charge of unfairness against this plan,

YOUNG MAN: for did not the accused person have the whole matter in his own hands?

PRINCESS: This semi-barbaric king had a daughter as blooming as his most florid fancies, and with a soul as fervent and imperious as his own. As is usual in such cases, she was the apple of his eye, and was loved by him above all humanity.

YOUNG MAN: Among his courtiers was a young man of that fineness of blood and lowness of station common to the conventional heroes of romance who love royal maidens.

PRINCESS: This royal maiden was well satisfied with her lover,

YOUNG MAN: for he was handsome and brave to a degree unsurpassed in all this kingdom,

PRINCESS: and she loved him with an ardor that had enough of barbarism in it to make it exceedingly warm and strong.

N1: This romance moved on happily for many months,

KING: until one day the king happened to discover its existence. He did not hesitate nor waver in regard to his duty in the premises. The youth was immediately cast into prison, and a day was appointed for his trial in the king's arena.

N2: This, of course, was an especially important occasion, and his majesty, as well as all the people, was greatly interested in the workings and development of this trial.

KING: Never before had such a case occurred;

YOUNG MAN: never before had a subject dared to love the daughter of the king.

N1: In after years such things became commonplace enough,

KING: but then they were in no slight degree novel and startling.

YOUNG MAN: The tiger cages of the kingdom were searched for the most savage and relentless beasts,

N2: from which the fiercest monster might be selected for the arena;

PRINCESS: and the ranks of maiden youth and beauty throughout the land were carefully surveyed by competent judges

N1: in order that the young man might have a fitting bride.

N2: Of course, everybody knew the young man was guilty as charged.

YOUNG MAN: He had loved the princess, and neither he, she, nor any one else, thought of denying the fact;

KING: but the king would not think of allowing any fact of this kind to interfere with the workings of the tribunal, in which he took such great delight and satisfaction.

PRINCESS: No matter how the affair turned out, the youth would be disposed of,

KING: and the king would take an aesthetic pleasure in watching the course of events,

YOUNG MAN: which would determine whether or not the young man had done wrong in allowing himself to love the princess.

N1: The appointed day arrived. From far and near the people gathered, and thronged the great galleries of the arena, and crowds, unable to gain admittance, massed themselves against its outside walls.

KING: The king and his court were in their places, opposite the twin doors,

YOUNG MAN: those fateful portals, so terrible in their similarity.

N2: All was ready.

KING: The signal was given. A door beneath the royal party opened, and the lover of the princess walked into the arena.

YOUNG MAN: Tall, beautiful, fair, his appearance was greeted with a low hum of admiration and anxiety.

N1: Half the audience had not known so grand a youth had lived among them.

PRINCESS: No wonder the princess loved him!

YOUNG MAN: What a terrible thing for him to be there!

N1: As the youth advanced into the arena he turned, as the custom was, to bow to the king, but he did not think at all of that royal personage.

YOUNG MAN: His eyes were fixed upon the princess, who sat to the right of her father.

N2: Had it not been for the moiety* of bar-barism in her nature, it is probable that lady would not have been there, but her intense and fervid soul would not allow her to be absent on an occasion in which she was so terribly interested.

moiety: half

PRINCESS: From the moment that the decree had gone forth that her lover should decide his fate in the king's arena, she had thought of nothing, night or day, but this great event and the various subjects connected with it. Possessed of more power, influence, and force of character than any one who had ever before been interested in such a case, she had done what no other person had done—she had possessed herself of the secret of the doors.

PRINCESS: She knew in which of the two rooms, that lay behind those doors,

YOUNG MAN: stood the cage of the tiger, with its open front,

N2: and in which waited the lady.

N1: Through these thick doors, heavily curtained with skins on the inside, it was impossible that any noise or suggestion should come from within to the person who should approach to raise the latch of one of them.

KING: But gold, and the power of a woman's will, had brought the secret to the princess.

PRINCESS: And not only did she know in which room stood the lady ready to emerge, all blushing and radiant, should her door be opened, but she knew who the lady was.

PRINCESS: It was one of the fairest and loveliest of the damsels of the court who had been selected as the reward of the accused youth,

KING: should he be proved innocent of the crime of aspiring to one so far above him;

PRINCESS: and the princess hated her.

N2: Often had she seen, or imagined that she had seen, this fair creature throwing glances of admiration upon the person of her lover,

PRINCESS: and sometimes she thought these glances were perceived, and even returned.

N2: Now and then she had seen them talking together; it was but for a moment or two, but much can be said in a brief space; it may have been on most unimportant topics,

PRINCESS: but how could she know that?

N1: The girl was lovely,

N2: but she had dared to raise her eyes to the loved one of the princess; and, with all the intensity of the savage blood transmitted to her through long lines of wholly barbaric ancestors,

PRINCESS: she hated the woman who blushed and trembled behind that silent door.

YOUNG MAN: When her lover turned and looked at her, and his eye met hers as she sat there, paler and whiter than any one in the vast ocean of anxious faces about her, he saw that she knew behind which door crouched the tiger, and behind which stood the lady.

PRINCESS: He had expected her to know it.

YOUNG MAN: The only hope for the youth in which there was any element of certainty was based upon the success of the princess in discovering this mystery; and the moment he looked upon her, he saw she had succeeded, as in his soul he knew she would succeed.

N1: Then it was that his quick and anxious glance asked the question:

YOUNG MAN: "Which?"

PRINCESS: It was as plain to her as if he shouted it from where he stood.

N1: There was not an instant to be lost.

N2: The question was asked in a flash; it must be answered in another.

YOUNG MAN: Her right arm lay on the cushioned parapet before her. She raised her hand, and made a slight, quick movement toward the right.

PRINCESS: No one but her lover saw her. Every eye but his was fixed on the man in the arena.

YOUNG MAN: He turned, and with a firm and rapid step he walked across the empty space.

N1: Every heart stopped beating, every breath was held, every eye was fixed immovably upon that man.

YOUNG MAN: Without the slightest hesitation, he went to the door on the right, and opened it.

N2: Now, the point of the story is this: Did the tiger come out of that door,

N1: or did the lady?

N2: The more we reflect upon this question, the harder it is to answer.

N1: It involves a study of the human heart

N2: which leads us through devious mazes of passion, out of which it is difficult to find our way.

N1: Think of it, fair reader, not as if the decision of the question depended upon yourself,

N2: but upon that hot-blooded, semi-barbaric princess, her soul at a white heat beneath the combined fires of despair and jealousy.

N1: She had lost him,

KING: but who should have him?

PRINCESS: How often, in her waking hours and in her dreams, had she started in wild horror, and covered her face with her hands as she thought of her lover opening the door on the other side of which waited the cruel fangs of the tiger!

N2: But how much oftener had she seen him at the other door! How in her grievous reveries had she gnashed her teeth, and torn her hair, when she saw his start of rapturous delight as he opened the door of the lady!

N1: How her soul had burned in agony when she had seen him rush to meet that woman, with her flushing cheek and sparkling eye of triumph; when she had seen him lead her forth, his whole frame kindled with the joy of recovered life; when she had heard the glad shouts from the multitude, and the wild ringing of the happy bells; when she had seen the priest, with his joyous followers, advance to the couple, and make them man and wife before her very eyes;

PRINCESS: and when she had seen them walk away together upon their path of flowers, followed by the tremendous shouts of the hilarious multitude, in which her one despairing shriek was lost and drowned!

N2: Would it not be better for him to die at once, and go to wait for her in the blessed regions of semi-barbaric futurity?

N1: And yet, that awful tiger, those shrieks, that blood!

PRINCESS: Her decision had been indicated in an instant, but it had been made after days and nights of anguished deliberation.

YOUNG MAN: She had known she would be asked, she had decided what she would answer, and, without the slightest hesitation, she had moved her hand to the right.

N2: The question of her decision is one not to be lightly considered, and it is not for me to presume to set myself up as the one person able to answer it. And so I leave it with all of you: Which came out of the opened door—the lady, or the tiger?

The Open Window
by Saki

Introduction

Many of Saki's stories focus on elements of surprise, irony, and humor. "The Open Window" conveys all of these. What seems to be a very tragic account is actually an artful practical joke presented by a master storyteller.

1. After reading the script once or twice, give a brief description of each character listed below.

Answers will vary.

Narrator

dry humor, insightful, an outside observer who comments on the scene—not a part of the story

Mrs. Sappleton

proper, honest, cordial

Vera

coy, subtle, witty, playful

Framton Nuttel

nervous, anxious, fidgety

2. The word "romance" appears in the last sentence. What does it mean in this context?

the ability to tell fanciful tales

Script

Dramatis Personae

NARRATOR (SAKI) FRAMTON NUTTEL'S SISTER
MRS. SAPPLETON MR. SAPPLETON
VERA, her niece RONNIE, brother to Mrs. Sappleton
FRAMTON NUTTEL

NUTTEL: Framton Nuttel endeavored to say the correct something which should duly flatter the niece of the moment without unduly discounting the aunt that was to come. Privately he doubted more than ever whether these formal visits on a succession of total strangers would do much towards helping the nerve cure which he was supposed to be undergoing.

SISTER: "I know how it will be—"

NARRATOR: his sister had said when he was preparing to migrate to this rural retreat;

SISTER: "you will bury yourself down there and not speak to a living soul, and your nerves will be worse than ever from moping; I shall just give you letters of introduction to all the people I know there. Some of them, as far as I can remember, were quite nice."

NUTTEL: Framton wondered whether Mrs. Sappleton, the lady to whom he was presenting one of the letters of introduction came into the nice division.

NARRATOR: When she judged that they had had sufficient silent communion, the niece asked,

VERA: "Do you know many of the people round here?"

NUTTEL: "Hardly a soul. My sister was staying here, at the rectory, you know, some four years ago, and she gave me letters of introduction to some of the people here."

NARRATOR: He made the last statement in a tone of distinct regret.

VERA: "Then you know practically nothing about my aunt?"

NUTTEL: "Only her name and address." He was wondering whether Mrs. Sappleton was in the married or widowed state. An undefinable something about the room seemed to suggest masculine habitation.

VERA: "Her great tragedy happened just three years ago. That would be since your sister's time."

NUTTEL: "Her tragedy?"

VERA: "My aunt will be down presently, Mr. Nuttel."

NARRATOR: Said a very self-possessed young lady of fifteen.

VERA: "In the meantime you must try and put up with me."

STAGING

"The Open Window"

This story seems ideal for chamber theater. Try creating a living room set with whatever furniture you have available to you. Don't worry about realism, since you still have a narrator present. When characters deliver narrative lines, have them address the audience proper. Handle dialogue as you would in a play.

NARRATOR: Somehow in this restful country spot tragedies seemed out of place.

VERA: "You may wonder why we keep that window wide open on an October afternoon."

NARRATOR: She indicated a large French window★ that opened on to a lawn.

★ French window: also called a French door

NUTTEL: "It is quite warm for the time of the year; but has that window got anything to do with the tragedy?"

VERA: "Out through that window, three years ago to a day, her husband and her two young brothers went off for their day's shooting. They never came back. In crossing the moor to their favorite snipe-shooting ground they were all three engulfed in a treacherous piece of bog. It had been that dreadful wet summer, you know, and places that were safe in other years gave way suddenly without warning. Their bodies were never recovered. That was the dreadful part of it."

NARRATOR: Here the child's voice lost its self-possessed note and became falteringly human.

VERA: "Poor aunt always thinks that they will come back someday, they and the little brown spaniel that was lost with them, and walk in at that window just as they used to do. That is why the window is kept open every evening till it is quite dusk. Poor dear aunt, she has often told me how they went out, her husband with his white waterproof coat over his arm, and Ronnie, her youngest brother, singing 'Bertie, why do you bound?' as he always did to tease her, because she said it got on her nerves. Do you know, sometimes on still, quiet evenings like this, I almost get a creepy feeling that they will all walk in through that window—"

NARRATOR: She broke off with a little shudder. It was a relief to Framton when the aunt bustled into the room with a whirl of apologies for being late in making her appearance.

MRS. SAPPLETON: "I hope Vera has been amusing you?"

NUTTEL: "She has been very interesting."

MRS. SAPPLETON: "I hope you don't mind the open window. My husband and brothers will be home directly from shooting, and they always come in this way. They've been out for snipe★ in the marshes today, so they'll make a fine mess over my poor carpets. So like you menfolk, isn't it?"

★ snipe: long-billed shore bird

NARRATOR: She rattled on cheerfully about the shooting and the scarcity of birds, and the prospects for duck in the winter.

NUTTEL: To Framton it was all purely horrible. He made a desperate but only partially successful effort to turn the talk on to a less ghastly topic; he was conscious that his hostess was giving him only a fragment of her attention, and her eyes were constantly straying past him to the open window and the lawn beyond.

NARRATOR: It was certainly an unfortunate coincidence that he should have paid his visit on this tragic anniversary.

NUTTEL: "The doctors agree in ordering me complete rest, an absence of mental excitement, and avoidance of anything in the nature of violent physical exercise."

NARRATOR: Framton labored under the tolerably widespread delusion that total strangers and chance acquaintances are hungry for the least detail of one's ailments and infirmities, their cause and cure.

NUTTEL: "On the matter of diet they are not so much in agreement."

MRS. SAPPLETON: "No?" (*Yawns*) "Here they are at last! Just in time for tea, and don't they look as if they were muddy up to the eyes!"

NUTTEL: Framton shivered slightly and turned towards the niece with a look intended to convey sympathetic comprehension.

READERS THEATER SCRIPTS **347**

The Blue Cross

by G. K. Chesterton

Introduction

Chesterton wrote a collection of mysteries involving the character Father Brown and titled it *The Innocence of Father Brown*. In this story, Father Brown will seem like a minor character until the final scene. His involvement in the story will be revealed at that time.

As you read this through the first time, notice characterization cues in the dialogue. Once you have learned the ending, reread, looking for the clues that point to the final outcome.

1. As you read, when did you first realize what the outcome might be?

Answers will vary based on what clues the student notices.

2. When did the inspector appear to believe Valentin, in your opinion?

Answers will vary but may include that he never fully did until they reached the Heath or even until Flambeau revealed himself.

Locations

Harwich; London; and Hamstead Heath

Dramatis Personae

(In order of appearance)

NARRATOR
VALENTIN, the head of the Paris police
FLAMBEAU, an infamous international thief
FATHER BROWN, a clergyman
WAITER 1, an Italian
SHOPKEEPER, a common Englishman
INSPECTOR, a London police inspector
POLICE, a London officer
WAITER 2, a young Englishman
WOMAN, an elderly clerk in a sweetstuff shop (bakery)

VERA: Vera was staring out through the open window with a dazed horror in her eyes.

NUTTEL: In a chill shock of nameless fear Framton swung round in his seat and looked in the same direction.

NARRATOR: In the deepening twilight three figures were walking across the lawn towards the window, they all carried guns under their arms, and one of them was additionally burdened with a white coat hung over his shoulders. A tired brown spaniel kept close at their heels. Noiselessly they neared the house, and then a hoarse young voice chanted out of the dusk:

RONNIE: "I said, Bertie, why do you bound?"

NUTTEL: Framton grabbed wildly at his stick and hat.

NARRATOR: The hall door, the gravel drive, and the front gate were dimly noted stages in his headlong retreat. A cyclist coming along the road had to run into the hedge to avoid imminent* collision.

imminent: about to occur

MR. SAPPLETON: "Here we are, my dear," (Coming in through the window) "—fairly muddy, but most of it's dry; Who was that who bolted out as we came up?"

MRS. SAPPLETON: "A most extraordinary man, a Mr. Nuttel. Could only talk about his illnesses, and dashed off without a word of goodbye or apology when you arrived. One would think he had seen a ghost."

VERA: "I expect it was the spaniel."

NARRATOR: Vera spoke very calmly.

VERA: "He told me he had a horror of dogs. He was once hunted into a cemetery somewhere on the banks of the Ganges by a pack of pariah dogs, and had to spend the night in a newly dug grave with the creatures snarling and grinning and foaming just above him. Enough to make anyone lose their nerve."

NARRATOR: Romance at short notice was her specialty.

"The Blue Cross"

Possible Doubling

Narrator and Woman

Flambeau and Waiter 2

Shopkeeper and Police (also Father Brown if needed)

Waiter 1, Inspector

(348) APPENDIX G

STAGING

"The Blue Cross"

This story seems suitable for readers theater or modified readers theater.

Possibilities include:

1. This story could be presented as if it were a play with numerous asides. All characters could block scenes with onstage focus. Narrative lines could be delivered with offstage focus. If this method is used consistently, the audience will accept the convention.

2. You might also try staging this using simple stools or chairs. Experiment to see what you prefer.

Script

NARRATOR: Between the silver ribbon of morning and the green glittering ribbon of sea, the boat touched Harwich* and let loose a swarm of folk like flies, among whom the man we must follow was by no means conspicuous—nor wished to be.

VALENTIN: There was nothing about him to indicate the fact that his grey jacket covered a loaded revolver, that his white waistcoat covered a police card, or that the straw hat covered one of the most powerful intellects in Europe. For this was Valentin himself, the head of the Paris police and the most famous investigator of the world; and he was coming from Brussels to London to make the greatest arrest of the century.

FLAMBEAU: Flambeau was in England. The police of three countries had tracked him from Ghent* to Brussels* to the Hook of Holland.*

VALENTIN: It was thought that he would take some advantage of the unfamiliarity and confusion of the Eucharistic Congress,* then taking place in London.

FLAMBEAU: In his best days

NARRATOR: (I mean, of course, his worst)

FLAMBEAU: Flambeau was a figure as statuesque and international as the Kaiser.

VALENTIN: Almost every morning the daily paper announced that he had escaped the consequences of one extraordinary crime by committing another.

NARRATOR: Each of his thefts would make a story by itself.

FLAMBEAU: It was he who ran the great Tyrolean Dairy Company in London, with no dairies, no cows, no carts, no milk, but with some thousand subscribers.

NARRATOR: These he served by the simple operation of moving the little milk cans outside people's doors to the doors of his own customers.

Harwich: English port city on the North Sea Ghent: a city in Belgium Brussels: the capital city of Belgium Hook of Holland: outer port of Rotterdam, West Netherlands. From here, ships cross the English Channel to Harwich, England. Eucharistic Congress: assembly concerning the topic of communion (the Lord's Supper)

FLAMBEAU: He was also known to be a startling acrobat; despite his huge figure, he could leap like a grasshopper and melt into the treetops like a monkey.

VALENTIN: Hence the great Valentin, when he set out to find Flambeau, was perfectly aware that his adventures would not end when he had found him. But how was he to find him? On this the great Valentin's ideas were still in process of settlement.

FLAMBEAU: There was one thing which Flambeau could not cover with his disguises and that was his height.

VALENTIN: If Valentin's quick eye had caught a tall applewoman, a tall grenadier,* or even a tolerably tall duchess, he might have arrested them on the spot.

grenadier: member of the British Grenadier Guards, the first regiment of the royal household infantry

NARRATOR: But all along the train there was nobody that could be a disguised Flambeau, any more than a cat could be a disguised giraffe. There was a short railway official, three fairly short market gardeners picked up two stations afterwards, and a very short Roman Catholic priest.

VALENTIN: When it came to the last case, Valentin gave it up and almost laughed.

FATHER BROWN: The little priest had a face as round and dull as a Norfolk dumpling and eyes as empty as the North Sea. He had several brown-paper parcels, which he was quite incapable of collecting.

VALENTIN: Valentin had no love for priests. But he could have pity for them, and this one might have provoked pity in anybody.

FATHER BROWN: He had a large, shabby umbrella, which constantly fell on the floor. He did not seem to know which was the right end of his return ticket.

NARRATOR: He explained with mooncalf simplicity to everybody in the carriage that

FATHER BROWN: he had to be careful, because he had something made of real silver "with blue stones" in one of his brown-paper parcels.

NARRATOR: He continuously amused the Frenchman until arriving (somehow) at Tottenham.

VALENTIN: Valentin kept his eye open for someone else; he looked out steadily for anyone, rich or poor, male or female, who was well up to six feet; for Flambeau was four inches above it. He alighted at Liverpool Street, however, quite conscientiously secure that he had not missed the criminal so far. He then went to Scotland Yard* to regularise his position and arrange for help in case of need; he then went for a long stroll in the streets of London, walking through a square beyond Victoria.

*Scotland Yard: police headquarters in London

NARRATOR: It was a quaint, quiet square, very typical of London, full of an accidental stillness. One of the four sides was much higher than the rest, like a dais;* and the line of this side was broken by one of London's admirable accidents—a restaurant that looked as if it had strayed from Soho.*

*dais: raised platform   *Soho: entertainment district in London

VALENTIN: Valentin stood in front of its yellow-white blinds and considered them long

NARRATOR: All of Valentin's wonderful successes had been gained by clear and commonplace French thought. Because he understood reason, he understood the limits of reason.

VALENTIN: Flambeau had been missed at Harwich; and if he was in London at all, he might be anything from a tall tramp on Wimbledon Common to a tall toastmaster* at the Hotel Metropole.

*toastmaster: master of ceremonies

NARRATOR: When he could not follow the train of the reasonable,

VALENTIN: Valentin coldly and carefully followed the train of the unreasonable.

NARRATOR: Instead of going to the right places—banks, police stations, rendezvous—*

*rendezvous: meeting place(s)

VALENTIN: he systematically went to the wrong places; knocked at every empty house, turned down every cul-de-sac,* went up every lane blocked with rubbish, went

*cul-de-sac: street with no outlet; a dead-end street

round every crescent that led him uselessly out of the way.

NARRATOR: Something about the quietude and quaintness of the restaurant roused all the detective's fancy and made him resolve to strike at random.

VALENTIN: He went up the steps, and sitting down at a table by the window, asked for a cup of black coffee.

NARRATOR: It was halfway through the morning, and he had not breakfasted; the slight litter of other breakfasts stood about on the table to remind him of his hunger; and adding a poached egg to his order, he proceeded musingly to shake some white sugar into his coffee,

FLAMBEAU: thinking all the time about Flambeau. He remembered how Flambeau had escaped,

NARRATOR: once by a house on fire;

VALENTIN: once by having to pay for an unstamped letter,

NARRATOR: and once by getting people to look through a telescope at a comet that might destroy the world.

FLAMBEAU: He thought his detective brain as good as the criminal's, which was true. But he fully realised the disadvantage.

VALENTIN: "The criminal is the creative artist; the detective only the critic."

NARRATOR: He lifted his coffee cup to his lips slowly, and put it down very quickly. He had put salt in it. He looked at the vessel from which the silvery powder had come; it was certainly a sugar-basin. He looked to see if there were any more orthodox vessels.

VALENTIN: Yes; there were two salt-cellars quite full.

NARRATOR: He tasted it.

VALENTIN: It was sugar.

NARRATOR: Then he looked round at the restaurant with a refreshed air of interest, to see if there were any other traces of the artistic taste which puts the sugar in the salt-cellars and the salt in the sugar-basin. Except for an odd splash of some dark fluid on one of the white-papered walls, the whole place appeared neat, cheerful, and ordinary. He rang the bell for the waiter.

WAITER 1: When the official came, the detective asked him to taste the sugar and see if it was up to the high reputation of the hotel.

VALENTIN: "Do you play this delicate joke on your customers every morning—changing the salt and sugar?"

WAITER 1: The waiter, when this irony grew clearer, assured him there was no such intention; it must be a most curious mistake. "I zink it is those two clergymen that threw soup at the wall."

VALENTIN: "Threw soup at the wall?" (Aside) Surely this must be some singular Italian metaphor.

WAITER 1: "Yes, yes, threw it over there on the wall. Two clergymen came in here very early, as soon as the shutters were taken down. One of them paid the bill and went out; the other was some minutes longer getting his things together. But he went at last. Only, before he stepped into the street he threw the soup slap on the wall. I tried to catch the men, but they disappeared into Carstairs Street."

NARRATOR: The detective was on his feet with his hat settled and his stick in hand. It was fortunate that even in such fevered moments of pursuit his eye was cool and quick.

VALENTIN: Something in a shop-front went by him like a mere flash; yet he went back to look at it.

NARRATOR: The shop was a popular greengrocer, an array of goods set out in the open air and plainly ticketed with their names and prices. In the two most prominent compartments were two heaps, of oranges and of nuts respectively. On the heap of nuts lay a sign,

VALENTIN: "Oranges, two a penny." ★ *two a penny: two for a penny*

NARRATOR: On the oranges,

VALENTIN: "Brazil nuts, 4d. ★ a lb." *4d.: four pennies (pence)*

NARRATOR: Valentin drew the attention of the red-faced shopkeeper to this inaccuracy in his advertisements.

SHOPKEEPER: The shopkeeper said nothing, but sharply put each card into its proper place.

VALENTIN: "What connects the idea of nuts marked as oranges with the idea of two clergymen, one tall and the other short?"

SHOPKEEPER: The eyes of the tradesman stood out of his head like a snail's; he really seemed for an instant likely to fling himself upon the stranger. "I don't know what you 'ave to do with it, but if you're one of their friends, you can tell 'em from me that I'll knock their silly 'eads off, parsons or no parsons, if they upset my apples again."

VALENTIN: "Indeed? Did they upset your apples?"

SHOPKEEPER: "One of 'em did," said the heated shopman; "rolled 'em all over the street. I'd 'ave caught the fool but for havin' to pick 'em up."

VALENTIN: "Which way did these parsons go?"

SHOPKEEPER: "Up that second road on the left-hand side, and then across the square."

NARRATOR: Valentin vanished like a fairy. On the other side of the second square he found a policeman and displayed his badge.

VALENTIN: "This is urgent, constable; have you seen two clergymen?"

POLICE: "I 'ave, sir—They took one of them yellow buses over there, them that go to Hampstead." ★ *Hampstead: part of Camden, a borough of Greater London*

VALENTIN: "Call up two of your men to come with me in pursuit."

NARRATOR: In a moment, the French detective was joined on the opposite pavement by an inspector and the policeman.

INSPECTOR: "Well, sir—"

VALENTIN: (Valentin pointed suddenly with his cane.) "I'll tell you on the top of that omnibus."

READERS THEATER SCRIPTS **351**

NARRATOR: When all three sank panting on the top seats of the yellow vehicle,

INSPECTOR: "We could go four times as quick in a taxi."

VALENTIN: "Quite true, if we only had an idea of where we were going."

INSPECTOR: "Well, where are we going?"

VALENTIN: "If you know what a man's doing, get in front of him; but if you want to guess what he's doing, keep behind him. Stray when he strays; stop when he stops; travel as slowly as he. Then you may see what he saw and may act as he acted. All we can do is to keep our eyes skinned for an odd thing."

INSPECTOR: "What sort of odd thing?"

VALENTIN: "Any sort of odd thing."

NARRATOR: The yellow omnibus crawled up the northern roads for what seemed like hours on end. By the time they had left Camden Town,* the policemen were nearly asleep; at least, they gave something like a jump as Valentin shouted to the driver to stop.

> *Camden Town: an inner borough of Greater London*

VALENTIN: (Overlapping the narration) "Driver! Stop here!"

NARRATOR: They tumbled down the steps into the road, Valentin triumphantly pointing his finger towards a window on the left side of the road. This window, like all the rest in the hotel, was of frosted glass; but in the middle of it was a big, black smash, like a star in the ice.

VALENTIN: "Our cue at last, the place with the broken window."

POLICE: "What window? What cue? Why, what proof is there that this has anything to do with them?"

VALENTIN: Valentin almost broke his bamboo stick with rage.

"Proof! Why, of course, the chances are twenty to one that it has nothing to do with them."

NARRATOR: They were soon seated at a late luncheon at a little table, looking at the star of smashed glass from the inside.

VALENTIN: (To the waiter) "Got your window broken, I see."

WAITER 2: "Yes, sir. Two of those foreign parsons had a cheap and quiet little lunch, and one of them paid for it and went out. The other was just going out to join him when I looked at my change again and found he'd paid me more than three times too much. 'Here,' I says to the chap who was nearly out of the door, 'you've paid too much.' 'Oh,' he says, very cool, 'have we?' 'Yes,' I says, and picks up the bill to show him. Well, I'd have sworn that I'd put 4s.* on that bill. But now I saw I'd 4s.,* as plain as paint."

> *4s.: four shillings (twenty shillings equaled one pound at this time)*

VALENTIN: "Well? And then?"

WAITER 2: "The parson says, 'Sorry to confuse your accounts, but it'll pay for the window.' 'What window?' I says. 'The one I'm going to break,' he says, and smashed that blessed pane with his umbrella."

(All three inquirers make an exclamation.)

NARRATOR: "The man marched out of the place and joined his friend just round the corner. Then they went so quick up Bullock Street that I couldn't catch them."

The three made their journey now through bare brick ways like tunnels; streets with few lights and even with few windows. Dusk was deepening, and it was not easy even for the London policemen to guess in what exact direction they were treading. Valentin stopped an instant before a little garish sweetstuff shop.*

> *sweetstuff shop: like a bakery*

VALENTIN: After an instant's hesitation he went in.

WOMAN: An angular, elderly woman ran the shop.

INSPECTOR: When she saw the door blocked with the blue uniform of the inspector, her eyes seemed to wake up.

WOMAN: "If you've come about that parcel, I've sent it off already."

VALENTIN: "Parcel?"

WOMAN: "I mean the parcel the clergyman left."

VALENTIN: "Tell us what happened exactly."

WOMAN: "Well, the clergymen came in about half an hour ago and bought some peppermints and then went off towards the Heath.★ But a second after, one of them runs back into the shop and says, 'Have I left a parcel?' Well, I looked everywhere and couldn't see one; so he says, 'Never mind; but if it should turn up, please post it to this address,' and he left me the address and a shilling for my trouble. And sure enough, though I thought I'd looked everywhere, I found he'd left a brown-paper parcel, so I posted it to the place he said. I can't remember the address now; it was somewhere in Westminster.★

> **Heath:** *a wilderness area covered with shrubbery (heath or heather)*
> **Westminster:** *the abbey on the north bank of the Thames at London*

VALENTIN: "Is Hampstead Heath near here?"

WOMAN: "Straight on for fifteen minutes, and you'll come right out on the open."

VALENTIN: Valentin sprang out of the shop and began to run.

POLICE: The other detectives followed him at a reluctant trot.

NARRATOR: The street they threaded was so narrow and shut in by shadows that when they came out unexpectedly into the void common and vast sky they were startled to find the evening still so light and clear. A perfect dome of peacock-green sank into gold amid the blackening trees and the dark violet distances. Standing on the slope and looking across the valley,

VALENTIN: Valentin beheld the thing which he sought.

NARRATOR: Among the black and breaking groups in that distance was one especially black which did not break—

VALENTIN: the two priests. By the time he had substantially diminished the distance, he had perceived something else. Whoever was the tall priest, there could be no doubt about the identity of the short one. It was his friend of the Harwich train.

NARRATOR: Now, so far as this went, everything fit rationally enough. Valentin learned that morning that a Father Brown from Essex

FATHER BROWN: was bringing up a silver cross with sapphires, a relic of considerable value, to show at the congress.

FLAMBEAU: It was no surprise that when Flambeau heard of a sapphire cross, he should try to steal it. Surely he could deceive such a silly sheep as the man with the umbrella and the parcels.

VALENTIN: But what had the stealing of a blue-and-silver cross from a priest to do with chucking soup at wall paper? What had it to do with calling nuts oranges, or with paying for windows first and breaking them afterwards? Valentin had come to the end of his chase, yet missed the middle of it.

NARRATOR: The two figures that they followed were evidently sunk in conversation, going to the wilder and more silent heights of the Heath. As their pursuers gained on them,

INSPECTOR: the latter had to use the undignified attitudes of the deer-stalker, to crouch behind clumps of trees and even to crawl prostrate★ in deep grass.

> **prostrate:** *lying flat*
> **ramshackle:** *rickety*

NARRATOR: There was an old ramshackle★ wooden seat under which sat the two priests still in serious speech together.

VALENTIN: Valentin contrived to creep up behind the big branching tree, and, standing there in deathly silence, heard the words of the strange priests for the first time. After he had listened for a minute, he was gripped by doubt. The two priests were talking exactly like priests. The first he heard was the tail of the taller priest's sentence that concluded,

FLAMBEAU: "where reason is utterly unreasonable?"

FATHER BROWN: "No, reason is always reasonable. I know that people charge the Church with lowering reason, but it is just the other way."

FLAMBEAU: "Yet who knows if in that infinite universe—"

READERS THEATER SCRIPTS 353

FATHER BROWN: "Only infinite physically, not infinite in the sense of escaping from the laws of truth."

VALENTIN: Valentin behind his tree was tearing his fingernails with silent fury.

POLICE: He seemed almost to hear the sniggers of the English detectives whom he had brought so far.

FATHER BROWN: "Reason and justice grip the remotest and the loneliest star. Look at those stars. Don't they look as if they were single diamonds and sapphires? Well, you can imagine any mad botany or geology you please. Think of forests of adamant with leaves of brilliants. Think the moon is a blue moon, a single elephantine sapphire. But don't fancy that all that frantic astronomy would make the smallest difference to the reason and justice of conduct. On plains of opal, under cliffs cut out of pearl, you would still find a notice-board, 'Thou shalt not steal.'"

VALENTIN: Valentin was just in the act of rising and creeping away, felled by the one great folly of his life. But something in the very silence of the tall priest made him stop until the latter spoke.

FLAMBEAU: "Just hand over that sapphire cross of yours, will you? We're all alone here, and I could pull you to pieces like a straw doll."

VALENTIN: "No."

NARRATOR: Flambeau suddenly flung off all his pontifical pretensions and laughed low but long.

FLAMBEAU: "No! You won't give it me—Shall I tell you why you won't give it me? Because I've got it already in my pocket."

FATHER BROWN: "Are—are you sure?"

FLAMBEAU: "Really, you're as good as a three-act farce. Yes, you turnip, I am quite sure. I had the sense to make a duplicate of the right parcel, and now, my friend, you've got the duplicate and I've got the jewels. An old dodge, Father Brown—a very old dodge."

FATHER BROWN: "Yes, I've heard of it before."

NARRATOR: The colossus of crime leaned over to the little rustic priest with a sort of sudden interest.

FLAMBEAU: "You have heard of it? Where have you heard of it?"

FATHER BROWN: "Well, I mustn't tell you his name. He was a penitent, you know. He had lived prosperously for about twenty years entirely on duplicate brown-paper parcels. And so, you see, when I began to suspect you, I thought of this poor chap."

FLAMBEAU: "Did you really have the gumption to suspect me just because I brought you up to this bare part of the heath?"

FATHER BROWN: "No, I suspected you when we first met. It's that little bulge up the sleeve where you people have the spiked bracelet."

FLAMBEAU: "How did you ever hear of the spiked bracelet?"

FATHER BROWN: "Oh, one's little flock, you know! So I watched you, you know. At last I saw you change the parcels. Then, I changed them back again and left the right one behind."

FLAMBEAU: "Left it behind?"

FATHER BROWN: "I went back to that sweet-shop and asked if I'd left a parcel, and gave them a particular address if it turned up. Well, I knew I hadn't; but when I went away again I did. So, instead of running after me with that valuable parcel, they have sent it flying to a friend of mine in Westminster. (To the audience) We can't help being priests. People come and tell us these things."

NARRATOR: Flambeau tore a brown-paper parcel out of his inner pocket and rent it in pieces. There was nothing but paper and sticks of lead inside it.

FLAMBEAU: "I don't believe you. I don't believe a bumpkin like you could manage all that. I think you've still got the stuff on you, and if you don't give it up—why, we're all alone, and I'll take it by force!"

FATHER BROWN: "No, you won't take it by force. First, because I really haven't still got it. And, second, because we are not alone."

NARRATOR: Flambeau stopped in his stride forward.

FATHER BROWN: "Behind that tree are two strong policemen and the greatest detective alive. A man generally makes a

NARRATOR: small scene if he finds salt in his coffee; if he doesn't, he has some reason for keeping quiet. I changed the salt and sugar, and you kept quiet. A man generally objects if his bill is three times too big. If he pays it, he has some motive for passing unnoticed. I altered your bill, and you paid it."

FATHER BROWN: The world seemed waiting for Flambeau to leap like a tiger. But he was held back as by a spell; he was stunned with the utmost curiosity.

"Well, as you wouldn't leave any tracks for the police, of course somebody had to. At every place we went to, I took care to do something that would get us talked about for the rest of the day. I didn't do much harm—a splashed wall, spilt apples, a broken window; but I saved the cross.

FLAMBEAU: "How do you know so much about criminal thinking?"

NARRATOR: The shadow of a smile crossed the round, simple face of his clerical opponent.

FATHER BROWN: "Has it never struck you that a man who does next to nothing but hear men's real sins is not likely to be wholly unaware of human evil? I was sure you weren't a priest."

FLAMBEAU: "Why?"

FATHER BROWN: "You attacked reason; it's bad theology."

NARRATOR: The three policemen came out from under the twilight trees. Flambeau was an artist and a sportsman. *(Bowing)* He stepped back and swept Valentin a great bow.

VALENTIN: "Do not bow to me, mon ami.★ Let us both bow to our master." ★*mon ami: French for "my friend"*

NARRATOR: And they both stood an instant uncovered while the little Essex priest blinked about for his umbrella.

READERS THEATER SCRIPTS ⟨355⟩

APPENDIX H
SELECTED ACTING SCENES

Antigone
adapted by George Judy from the work of Sophocles

Dramatis Personae

ANTIGONE (an TIG uh nee)
ISMENE (ihz MEE nee)

Script

ANTIGONE: O sister! Dear sister Ismene!
How heavy the hand of God is upon us;
How we suffer for our father Oedipus. (ED uh puhs)
There is no pain, no sorrow, no dishonour
We have not shared, you and I,
And now there is more.

ISMENE: What is it Antigone? Are you mad?
Why do you pull me from the palace
Before dawn?

ANTIGONE: The battle is ended; our brothers
Both fallen and Creon (KREE ahn) is named king.
He comes now to proclaim orders to the city.
How can you sleep?! Have you heard nothing?

ISMENE: I have heard nothing of those we love.
My tears drove me to sleep.
The Argive army, I know was withdrawn
And Eteocles (iht EE uh kleez) and Polynices
(PAHL uh NEYES eez),
Our brothers, both dead.
What more could I know?

ANTIGONE: That's why I pulled you from your bed.
To tell you my news where we could speak alone.

ISMENE: What news, Antigone?!
What news could be more black
Than the death of our brothers
Or better than the end of the war?

ANTIGONE: O Ismene!
Our dearest treated like an animal!
Our brother . . . Eteocles is safe.
He is to be buried as a hero of state
With all observance due the noble dead.
But Polynices, just as unhappily fallen,
Still lies in danger and shame,
Uncovered, unblest, unwept.
A feast of flesh for carrion birds and
Ravaging beasts of the field.
He is not to be buried, not to be mourned.
No enemy of Thebes (THEBZ) has ever suffered so
Or ever deserved such a fate.
The noble Creon! Our own uncle makes this order,
Ismene;
Against you, against me . . . .
Against our family.
The penalty for disobedience
Is death.
Now is the time to show yourself
A true daughter of Oedipus.
To show yourself
Worthy of your high born blood.

ISMENE: My poor sister, if this is true,
What can I do, or undo, to help you?

ANTIGONE: The question is will you help me?

ISMENE: With what, Antigone? What do you want?

ANTIGONE: To cover the body;
We'll go together,
As sisters, you and I.

ISMENE: You mean . . . to bury him?
Against the order?

ANTIGONE: Is Polynices not my brother?
Is he not yours?
He fought against our city, yes,

ACTING SCENES **357**

STAGING
Antigone

If furniture is used, it could be modern, neutral, or suggestive of the historical setting—perhaps "stone" benches. Since Ismene asks, "Why do you pull me from the palace?" the setting will be most logical if it is a courtyard or garden.

Guide the actors in blocking the scene to give Antigone a clear sense of inner strength, while Ismene conveys hesitation and dependence. However, Ismene should not appear so weak that her dignity is questioned. Strive to keep both actors performing realistically, not melodramatically.

Selected Acting Scenes

The selections in Appendix H represent diverse styles and topics designed to be accessible to young actors. If you are a reader of plays, you will no doubt find numerous other scenes for two or three actors. Do not view these scenes as authoritatively the finest materials available but as representative of a much broader selection of excellent pieces. This appendix exists to help you get started. You may choose to use these same scenes every semester that you teach this course. However, it is quite valid for you to substitute other materials.

If you choose to use other materials, be sure to maintain a high standard concerning copyright laws. High-school students are very impressionable and may remember the testimony you establish more than any of the subject-related principles or facts you teach.

You will need to choose at least one three-person scene if you have an odd number of students.

Consult Teacher's Appendix 2 for ideas about plays from which to select alternative scenes.

Scene Content

In order to enable you to obtain reprint permissions, the scenes in this appendix have been presented as they would appear in the full text of the play. For an in-class practice scene, you can obviously choose to disregard music, sound, and light cues. Edit these and other elements (stage directions, for example) at your discretion.

Antigone

As was stated in Chapter 5, classic literature is timeless. Every thread of plot in *Antigone* seems as modern as it is ancient. Sophocles (SAH fuh KLEEZ) depicts Thebes as a great modern city of the Greek world, devastated by war. George Judy's adaptation makes a comparison with countless other cities whose notable skylines have been damaged or utterly destroyed by acts of war, particularly bombings.

Sophocles also depicts Antigone as an impetuous youth who places honor and justice above her own safety. Through his modern comparisons, Judy helps the audience see that today's youth face the same struggles against established rulers who prioritize practicality or politics above the ideals that young people embrace.

In this scene, Antigone reveals to her sister, Ismene, that their brother Polynices has been denied the honorable funeral granted to their other brother Eteocles, both of whom died in battle, though fighting in opposing armies.

ANTIGONE:
But his claim was as strong as that of Eteocles.
He dies in battle for what he believed.
That is punishment enough.
Our brother does not deserve
This dishonor before the gods.
I will never desert him; never.

ISMENE:
But Creon has ordered this.
The gods have made him our king.
How can we dare what is forbidden by the state?

ANTIGONE:
We dare because it is right!
How does our uncle dare keep me from my brother?

ISMENE:
O sister, beware your pride.
You forgot the shame of our father,
Killing his father, wedding his mother;
His awful crimes self-proved,
Avenged by his own stubborn hand.
You forget the death of our mother,
Hung in a noose of her own making.
And now our brothers, full of anger and pride,
Both boasting their claims to the throne,
Both dead in a single day; Blood for blood,
Both slain by the other's hand.
We two stand alone now, Antigone,
The last of the line of Oedipus.
How shall we end if we disregard the law?
If we defy our king? O sister,
Think what it costs to be always "right."
We are women; we should nurture men,
Not fight against them. We need our leaders.
Strong rulers offer strong protection
For our city, for ourselves . . .
We must obey this order, Antigone,
Even orders worse than this.
May the gods forgive me, I must do
As I am commanded; to do more is madness.

ANTIGONE:
Go your own way then, a helpless woman,
Waiting to be led by men.
I will bury my brother.
I will not ask again for your help
Nor would I thank you if you gave it.

ANTIGONE:
The gods, I know, will protect me but
If I should die, what happiness!
Convicted of loyalty and reverence.
I am content to lie beside my brother,
Rather than to stand here with you.
We have little time to please the living,
But all eternity to love the dead.
Live, Ismene, if you will, live;
And defy the holiest laws of heaven.

ISMENE:
I do not defy the laws of heaven.
I obey the laws of the state! I have no choice—

ANTIGONE:
There is always a choice.

ISMENE:
Is it wrong to choose to live?
I know I am weak, Antigone—

ANTIGONE:
(Still appealing.) A handful of earth is not heavy.

ISMENE:
(Pulling away.) No.

ANTIGONE:
Then let weakness be your excuse . . .
I will cover the body of my brother.
(She starts out.)

ISMENE:
I fear for you, Antigone! I fear—

ANTIGONE:
Fear for yourself. You need not fear for me.

ISMENE:
At least be secret. Go quietly.
I'll not betray you.

ANTIGONE:
You betray me already.
Do you think I care if the world
Knows I love my brother?
Proclaim it to the city, to all the world,
Or I shall hate you even more!

ISMENE:
How can you be my sister?
My heart is frozen at the thought of this
While yours burns blindly with madness—

ANTIGONE:
Is it madness to know
where true duty lies?
I know my duty—

ISMENE:
What good is your "duty" if you can't succeed?
The whole city is watching, Antigone!
You're doomed to fail—

ANTIGONE: When I have tried and failed,
I shall have failed.

ISMENE: But why start such a hopeless task?

ANTIGONE: Enough! You are not my sister.
I have no sister.
Leave me alone with my madness.

ISMENE: Antigone, wait—

ANTIGONE: No! Your words won't bury my brother.
I will kneel and put my hands in the earth.
There is no punishment that can make me
Fear that honor. I am proud of my love.

ISMENE: Go then, go! To your death if you can't listen to reason . . .
(ANTIGONE exits. ISMENE runs after her, then stops.)
But remember the living who love you . . .
And will love you still.

Antigone
adapted by George Judy from the work of Sophocles

Dramatis Personae
ANTIGONE (an TIG uh nee)
CREON (KREE ahn)
SENATOR (walk-on)

Script

CREON: Now tell me, "grown woman,"
In as few words as you can,
Did you know of the order forbidding this act?

ANTIGONE: The order was plain enough.
The word of the king is law.

CREON: Yet you think yourself above the law?

ANTIGONE: No one is above the law,
But some laws are made higher than others.
Do you think your orders strong enough
To overrule the unwritten laws of heaven?

CREON: The gods have delivered our city
From the bloody hands of your brother, Antigone.
They require no honor for such a traitor.

ANTIGONE: They require my family to mourn their dead.
The laws of man may change moment by moment
But the rules of the gods stand true
Yesterday, today and tomorrow.
I have honored the laws of heaven above the laws of man;
I have buried my brother.
As I stand guilty before you,
I stand innocent before the gods.

CREON: Your act, in itself, may seem righteous, child,
But you cannot turn the law into your own hands.
Would you place the desires of one
Above the protection of our city?

ANTIGONE: How does covering the body of my brother
Bring danger to our homes?

CREON: Our city will fall without respect for order.
Even an act committed in honor
Cannot stand above authority and rule.
You are the daughter of a king, a lawmaker.
No one should hold our laws more sacred,
Or no more truly bound by their rule.

ANTIGONE: Judge me then, if you will,
Enforce your order and let me die.
I will trust myself to the
Judgement of heaven.

SENATOR: She is her father's daughter,
She shares the spirit of Oedipus.

CREON: The pride of Oedipus!
Stubborn, foolish pride, Antigone.
I have no time to play this game.

ANTIGONE: There is no game, Uncle.

CREON: There is, child. You play the rebel, burning with passion,
And you would have me play the tyrant.
You would make me kill you to prove a point
When I would do nothing more than save your life and name.

ANTIGONE: I cannot make you a tyrant, Uncle.
You have chosen to be king,
As I have chosen to bury my brother.
We must do our duty.

Antigone
Please note that the character Senator has only one line. This need not be a rehearsed role. Just call upon a student to read the line for the workshop and performance days.

ACTING SCENES **359**

STAGING
Antigone

Try staging this scene between Antigone and Creon in a setting that suggests an executive office (or its equivalent in ancient Greece). Creon might begin the scene casually, treating Antigone like a welcome family member; but by the end of the scene, he should clearly establish himself as a powerful leader in contrast to her—a powerless convicted prisoner. Possible ways to depict this dynamic relationship could include use of set, props, and costuming. For example, if Creon wears modern clothing and leans against the front edge of a large desk as the scene begins, he could move behind his desk, put on and button his coat, and even appear to be summoning guards by the end of the scene.

CREON: My duty is to protect this city,
To protect these people,
To protect you . . . even from yourself.

ANTIGONE: You cannot protect me from what I believe.

CREON: Do you wish to die?

ANTIGONE: I wish to live. But not at any price.
Your punishment I can easily bear.
Leaving my mother's son to rot in the field,
Lying alone, unmourned, unburied,
This is the pain beyond bearing.
The death you threaten comes to me
As it must for every mortal.
If sooner rather than later,
I will thank you then for letting
Me join my family. To live each day
Without them, as I do, makes me glad to die.

CREON: (Softly at first; not as an attack, but with reason.) These proud
thoughts do not sit well
On the shoulders of children.
Who has punished you to commit this crime?
With whom do you conspire?

ANTIGONE: I have acted alone.
I conspire with the gods.

CREON: (Kneeling to touch her face.)
Repent this foolish act, child,
And grow to your full flower or
Stand as a woman, and face the judgement of the state.
(Nothing from ANTIGONE; she has forced his hand. He rises.)
People of Thebes!
My sister's child, this daughter of Oedipus,
With whom I share my home,
Has broken the law of our city.
She stands before us now, not in shame
But proudly boasting her deed.
In this act she names herself our enemy,
When she could have easily been our friend.
Before the gods and this city I have vowed
To protect you from our enemies,
To enforce the order of law.
The good of the many must stand
Before the willful desires of the one.
Even if that one were my own child.
(He looks. Still nothing from ANTIGONE.)
The full punishment of Thebes
Must fall to Antigone . . .
And to her partners in this action.
If you know more of this crime.
Stand forward and speak
Stand forward!
(Nothing. He tries a new tact.)
Call forth her sister. Bring Ismene here.
(ANTIGONE is suprised. SENATOR exits.)
She fills my house with weeping and wailing:
I thought, in mourning for her brothers,
But the thoughts of criminals often
Betray themselves after the deed is done.
If your sister knows of this act
She stands as guilty as you.

ANTIGONE: Will you do more than kill me?

CREON: Since death is your wish, no.
I can do nothing more.

ANTIGONE: Then why delay?
Nothing I say can weigh with you,
As nothing you say can reach my ear.
I have buried my brother.
It was an honorable act,
As anyone here would tell you
Were their lips not locked with fear.
None of these people think as you.

CREON: Yes, Uncle, they do.

ANTIGONE: Yet they dare not tell you so.
Only kings and rebels truly speak their minds.
Your people hold their tongues because they are afraid.

CREON: My only fear is that your willful passion
Will claim your life, child.

ANTIGONE: No, Uncle. I think I frighten you.
I frighten you because I can say "no."
It is easy to lead when all will blindly follow
But hard when someone stands up to say "no."

360   APPENDIX H

CREON: "No" is a word for children, Antigone.
It is easy to play the rebel; to find fault,
It is even easy to die. Death is escape.
What is hard is to live; to work,
To stare into days of sorrow and loss;
To accept responsibility and still to go on.
It costs much more to live than to die.
These citizens are not afraid.
They are wise in the ways of the law,
And a world filled with uneasy choices.
These people hear the practical voice of reason
While you cover your ears and scream.
You stand alone in your childish pride,
Unrepentant and unashamed.

ANTIGONE: There is no shame in honoring my brother.

CREON: Was not his enemy, who died with him, your brother?

ANTIGONE: Yes, both were my brothers, the sons of Oedipus.

CREON: In honoring one, do you not insult the other?

ANTIGONE: He that is dead will not accuse me so.

CREON: He will, Antigone, he will scream from the underworld
If you honor him no more than a traitor.

ANTIGONE: It was not a traitor but his brother that died.

CREON: Attacking his country, his home,
While the other defended!

ANTIGONE: Even so, we have a duty to the dead.

CREON: What of your duty to the living?!
Should we give equal honor to good and evil?

ANTIGONE: In the land of the dead
Perhaps that is the law!

CREON: An enemy can't be a friend, even when dead!

ANTIGONE: (Fighting to make sense of it all.) Must an enemy dead
remain forever an enemy?
Ready to rise in spirit
And turn our fears into war?
Is the land of the gods divided like ours,
With bloody lines between friend and foe?
I have no answers for your riddles,
I only know I follow my heart.

CREON: My way is to share my love,
Not to share my hate.
Go then, if you will hear no reason,
Share your love among the dead,
Where it can bear no fruit.
(Starts to exit.)
The gods save our city from the logic of women!

The Gift of the Magi
by Thomas Hischak, based on the short story by O. Henry

Dramatis Personae

JIM
DELLA

Script

It is the flat, empty. DELLA puts her head in from outside, cautiously. She wears her shawl over her hair. She calls softly.

DELLA: Jim?
(Sure that he is not there, she quickly comes in, puts a small package down on the table and goes to the mirror. She closes her eyes, removes the shawl and then looks into the mirror. Her hair is very short. She sighs and tries to run her hand through her hair to make it seem more full.)
Please, God . . . make him love me still.
(She remembers the package, goes to the table, picks it up.)
There you go, Jimmy! A gift deserving of the name . . .
(Jim enters below, and she hears him coming up the stairs. She puts the package away, goes once more to the mirror. Jim enters the flat. She turns to him and smiles.)

JIM: Della . . .

DELLA: Merry Christmas, darling.
(A pause; he stares at her awkwardly.)

JIM: You've cut off your hair.

DELLA: Yes. I did. (Pause; then she blurts out.) Please, Jim, don't look at me that way. I did it for you, really. I mean, I had my hair cut and sold it because I couldn't have lived through Christmas without giving you a present. I didn't know what else to do.

STAGING
"The Gift of the Magi"

If realistic furniture is used for this scene, a worn sofa, mismatched chair or rocker, and an outdated coffee table or end table would work well. The scene might use kitchen furniture instead. The set pieces should not be unsightly, but they need not be elegant either.

The stage directions mention the use of a mirror. Because of the brightness of stage lights and threat of glare, mirrors are seldom used onstage. Even though you will probably have students perform these scenes using normal indoor lights rather than stage lights, you may still want to have Della face the audience and pantomime looking in a mirror.

DELLA: I tried to save, Jim. Honestly I did but it amounted to practically nothing. Nothing at all! So I sold my hair. It'll grow out again, I promise. But I just had to do it, Jimmy. Besides, my hair grows fast, awfully fast, and before you know it . . .

JIM: (Numbly.) You've cut your hair?

DELLA: Cut it and sold it; yes, Jim. I did. I had to. Don't you like me just as much as you used to? Do you still love me without my long hair? I'm still me without it.

JIM: (Vaguely looks about the room.) You say your hair is gone.

DELLA: You needn't look for it. I sold it, I tell you. It's Christmas Eve, Jim. Don't be angry with me. We're going to have a lovely Christmas after all. Look at the wonderful gift I've got for you! (She gets the package, brings it to him.) I know you'll love it, Jim. You'll see. Everything will be all right then. You'll open my Christmas present for you and then I'll put the chops on the stove and we'll celebrate Christmas and we'll live happily ever after! (Brief pause.) Please say something, Jim.

JIM: (Still looks dumbfounded. Then he seems to snap out of it and laughs gently.) Of course I still love you. (Kisses her.) Without your long hair, of course! It's just that you had me going there for a moment. (He laughs again.)

DELLA: (Confused.) Jim?

JIM: It's all right, really. Just a joke. Here . . . (Takes a package from his pocket.) Take a look at that and you'll get the joke, too.

DELLA: A present? For me? Oh, Jim . . . where did you find the money?

JIM: Go ahead. Open it.

DELLA: You are a genius! All this time you had money put aside and I didn't even know it! (Opening the package) How you ever did it, I'll never know. I mean, you can't put off a butcher or save on the grocery bill or . . .

DELLA: (A shout of joy, then a cry of anguish as she looks into the unwrapped box.) The combs . . . ! (She lifts them up.) The Queen of Sheba's combs! But my hair . . .

JIM: You see why I was a little stunned.

DELLA: My beautiful, beautiful tortoise shell combs . . . With jewels on the rims. Better not let the old Queen find out. (Goes to mirror, holds the combs up against her short hair.) They're even lovelier now than in the shop window! Oh, and my hair all gone.

JIM: Like you say, your hair grows fast.

DELLA: Oh, it does, Jim. I promise you it will!

JIM: If it never grows an inch, you're still my girl. But we've forgotten all about your gift! Here. Open it. You'll have to agree it's the most perfect thing ever! I kept looking and looking and finally there it was in the window of this shop on Broadway. The second I saw it I knew that it was the perfect gift I'd been searching for. (Jim has opened the box, holds up a gold chain.) I said to myself, this is the gold chain that's worthy of the watch. Isn't it a dandy, Jim? You'll have to look at the time a hundred times a day now. And the chain is long enough so you can wear it like so . . . and it will show all the time. Just think what old Solomon's reaction is going to be! Give me your watch, Jim. I want to see how it looks on the chain. (Jim starts to move away.)

DELLA: Jim, give me the watch for a second. . . . (Pause.) What's the matter, Jim?

JIM: Della, let's put our Christmas presents away and keep them awhile. They're too nice to use just now.

DELLA: But, Jim . . .

JIM: I sold the watch to get the money to buy your combs.

DELLA: (A pause.) Oh . . .

JIM: So why don't we put our wonderful gifts away, and you can put the chops on the stove?

DELLA: Yes . . . I guess you're right. (Pause.) Oh, Jim!

(She starts to laugh, a laugh close to tears. He laughs, too, as THEY fall into each other's arms.)
Oh, how foolish we've been!

JIM: No . . . not foolish at all. They were perfect gifts. Maybe the most perfect gifts ever given at Christmas.

A Marriage Proposal: Western Style
by Tim Kelly

Dramatis Personae
NATALIE
LEM

Script

NATALIE: (Enters right, also wearing a work apron.)
Oh, it's you. Maw said there was someone to see me.

LEM: How do, Natalie.
(Sticks the flowers straight out.)
Wild flowers. Plucked 'em myself. By hand.

NATALIE: (Takes them.)
Thanks. That's thoughtful.
(Sniffs.)
Nice smell. You'll have to excuse me for wearin' this old apron. We're bakin' today.

LEM: I know. Your Maw told me.

NATALIE: You haven't been here for so long. Quite the stranger. Set yourself down.
(He sits on sofa, stiffly.)
You want a sandwich or somethin'?

LEM: Nope. Had lunch.

NATALIE: (She sits beside him.)
You're wearing a clean shirt. Aren't you workin' your spread today? And your boots are polished! (Impressed.) My, my.

LEM: Uh, I'll try to be brief.

NATALIE: Why so serious?

LEM: We've grown up together, you and me.

NATALIE: True.

LEM: Uh, our families have known each other a long time.

NATALIE: I reckon.

LEM: We like each other.

NATALIE: Uh-huh.

LEM: My property adjoins your own.

NATALIE: Where one ends, the other begins.

LEM: My meadow touches your grazing pasture.

NATALIE: (Surprised.) YOUR meadow?

LEM: Yes, it belongs to me.

NATALIE: What nonsense. The meadow belongs to us, not to you.

LEM: No, no. To me.

NATALIE: How do you figure that?

LEM: As far back as I can remember that meadow has always belonged to my family. It's true that at one time the title to the meadow was in dispute, but now everyone knows it belongs to me.

NATALIE: (Amazed.) You must be jokin'.

LEM: I don't joke about land.

NATALIE: (Stands, irritated.)
As far back as I can remember that meadow has belonged to MY family, not yours. What nerve!

LEM: The meadow isn't worth much. Besides, why get excited about a title that was confused?

NATALIE: You're the one who's confused.

LEM: The title clearly sez . . .

NATALIE: Title, title! What do I care about the title! All I know is that meadow belongs to us.
(Flings down the bouquet, folds her arms defiantly.)
That ends the matter.

LEM: (Stands.)
No, no, you don't understand. The meadow belongs to me. Under the title . . .

NATALIE: If you keep on explainin' about "the title", and wear a clean shirt every day of the week, that meadow would still

A Marriage Proposal: Western Style

This scene calls for extreme characterization in comparison with other scenes in this appendix. Natalie is a volatile person who is very expressive about her thoughts and emotions. She often is played as a woman who quickly changes from very sweet and demur on a line such as "your boots are polished" to angry by the line "As far back as I can remember that meadow has belonged to MY family, not yours." Lem is generally played as an anxious fellow who is prone to childlike hysterics. As the play progresses after this scene, physical humor often plays an increasingly predominant role. For example, Lem might stumble about the stage, clutching at his heart when he begins complaining of "palpitations." Though that portion does not appear in this scene, it follows soon after. This scene can and should build toward that climax of absurdity.

ACTING SCENES 363

STAGING
A Marriage Proposal: Western Style

If realistic furniture is used, be sure it is very plain and rustic. Of course, boxes or benches could be used representatively. Costumes are appropriate with the first choice, whereas the students could wear their regular clothing or neutral clothing (black or khaki) with the latter. Either way, realistic props such as an apron and a fistful of dandelions, daisies, and Queen Anne's lace could be used.

Encourage the actors to make full use of the stage space for this scene.

The Secret Garden

Your students may not be familiar with the Yorkshire dialect Dickon uses in this scene. Unless the actor has heard this particular accent, you may find it preferable to have him downplay the accent—just pronounce the words as they appear. Most of the abbreviated words are obvious, but *tha'* may be misleading. Be sure to explain to the actors that *tha'* means *thou* (you), not *that*.

LEM: be ours, ours, ours! I refuse to give up what belongs to my family.
(She turns her back on him.)
NATALIE: Ha!
LEM: Natalie, I don't need the meadow. It's the principle of the thing.
NATALIE: Look, if it's agreeable with you, let me give the meadow to you, as a gift.
LEM: You can't give me what's already mine. I think you've been in the sun too long. Until now we've thought of you as a good neighbor.
NATALIE: (Defensive.) I am a good neighbor.
LEM: Only last year we lent you our milking machine when yours broke down. Now you treat us like thieves!
NATALIE: Be reasonable.
LEM: Reasonable!
(Furious, she begins to circle the sofa, LEM trailing behind her.)
NATALIE: You offer to give me my own land! Excuse me, Lem, but neighbors don't treat each other that way.
LEM: I need some lemonade. I'm buildin' up a nervous sweat. Maybe I ought to take a vitamin pill.
(NATALIE sits in chair, right, with a defiant look to LEM. He goes to the table.)
LEM: That meadow is mine, Natalie. Please understand.
NATALIE: Mine.
LEM: Mine.
(Pours some lemonade, gulps.)
NATALIE: I'll prove it's our land. This afternoon I'm sendin' the hired man into the meadow for plantin'.
LEM: You do and I'll run him off.
NATALIE: You wouldn't dare!
LEM: Can't you understand? (Frantic.) That meadow is mine! Mine! Mine!
NATALIE: If you want to snort and rage like an angry bull, do it at home.
LEM: I'll tell you somethin', Natalie Taub. You can be a most provokin' female and that's a fact. Stubbornest woman I ever

---

NATALIE: knew, I'd deal with you differently if I wasn't feelin' so poorly today.
LEM: What's the matter with you?
NATALIE: I got the palpitations.
LEM: Then you'd better git home.
NATALIE: (Holds his side.) A pain in my side, too. I wonder if I brung along my bottle of liniment? (Searches, doesn't find it.)
LEM: You're a hypochondriac.
NATALIE: I don't hold with bad language!
LEM: It's not bad language, you idiot!
NATALIE: What's a . . . (Trouble with pronunciation.) "hypochondriac?"
LEM: It's what you are.
NATALIE: I'm gonna say it one more time. That meadow is mine! It belongs to me.
LEM: Us!
NATALIE: Me!

The Secret Garden
adapted by Sylvia Ashby from the novel by
Frances Hodgson Burnett

Dramatis Personae
DICKON
MARY

Script

(Downcast, MARY skips. Offstage whistling, DICKON appears.)
DICKON: (Hesitant.) Mornin', Miss.
MARY: Hello.
DICKON: Dickon's th' name.
MARY: (Quickly doffs cap.)
DICKON: (Thrilled.) Dickon!
MARY: (A bit shy.) I brung garden tools. An' packets o' seeds.

STAGING

The Secret Garden

Unless you want to stage this scene outdoors, you will probably find it advantageous to stage it abstractly. Encourage the actors to experiment with detailed pantomime and free movement on a bare stage. You may find sound effects (live or recorded) are more important than any set pieces.

MARY: Dickon, please show me!
(*Sits, inviting* DICKON. *He hesitates. She taps bench by way of encouragement.*)

DICKON: (*Sits.*)
Poppies come up pretty an' white. They bloom if tha' whistles to 'em.
(*Sound Cue #18—A chirp*)
Where's that Robin as is callin' us?

MARY: Is he really calling us?

DICKON: He's sayin', "See here. I wants a bit of a chat." Robin's took on thee. He'll tell all about thee in a minute.

MARY: Does he actually like me?
(*Sound Cue #19—Another chirp.*)

DICKON: Aye. He's makin' up to thee now, Miss Mary.

MARY: You understand everything birds say?

DICKON: Lived on th' moor so long—watchin' 'em break shell an' start fledgin' out—guess I'm one of 'em.

MARY: Perhaps you are!

DICKON: Sometimes I think I'm a bird or a beetle—an' don't even know it!
(*Shows.*)
These larkspur come up wherever tha' casts 'em. See here, I'll plant 'em for thee.

MARY: (*Alarm.*) Well, I—

DICKON: Mother says, "'Bout time they give Miss Mary a wee plot o' ground!" Where be this garden?

MARY: (*Trembles.*) I . . . I . . . don't . . . really.

DICKON: Tha' hasn't a bit o' garden? They wouldn't give thee none?

MARY: Can . . . can you keep . . . a secret? I . . . I don't know what I should do if someone found out. I think I might die!

DICKON: If I couldna' keep secrets 'bout hidin' places wild things run to, there'd be naught safe on th' moor.

MARY: (*Seizes his arm.*)
I've stolen a garden! Nobody wants it, nobody cares for it.

DICKON: (*Whispers.*) Stolen a garden?

MARY: The garden's mine now. Nobody has a right to take it from me! (*Agitated.*) I'm the only one who cares—the only one!

DICKON: Poor Miss Mary . . .

MARY: I've nothing to do. Nothing belongs to me. And I found it, just like Robin! They wouldn't take it away from Robin!

DICKON: How can tha' steal a garden?

MARY: Come. I'll show you. The wind swept aside a curtain of ivy along the wall. Suddenly I looked up and saw—
(*Pulls back ivy.*)

DICKON: (*Amazed.*) A door!
(*They enter.*)

MARY: My secret kingdom.

DICKON: (*Awed.*) Us heard 'bout a garden. Never thought I'd see th' place.

MARY: Inside these beautiful old walls—I might be a princess who falls asleep for a hundred years.

DICKON: Can tha' sleep for a hun'erd years?

MARY: (*Laughs.*)
I've no intention of sleeping. I'm more awake than ever!

DICKON: (*Stares.*) Aye, 'tis a pretty place . . . but strange, like a dream. Grey creepers climbin' over grey trees . . .

MARY: (*Eager.*) Will there be roses? Can you tell?

DICKON: Plenty o' wood needs cutin' out. Look! A snippet o' green!

MARY: (*Thrilled.*) Then it's still alive?

DICKON: Aye, 'tis wick all right.

MARY: Wick?

DICKON: Means stirrin' with life, like thee an' me.

MARY: I'm so glad! I want them all to be wick!

DICKON: (*Crosses.*)
I spy green in this 'ere wood. Aye, wick for sure! In summer, a fountain o' roses'll come splashin' from th' trees.
(*Turns.*)
Green shoots poppin' up! I figured tha' didn't know nothin' bout gardenin'!

ACTING SCENES **365**

The Secret Garden

As with the previous scene, the characters are children. However, you should not encourage your students to overplay this characterization. Certainly they should not try to have "high voices." Lighter (less resonant) voices would be fine.

MARY: (Wistful.) The bulbs were so little. I wanted them to feel welcome.

DICKON: They'll sprout up like Jack's beanstock!
(Looks out.)
Iris. Daffydowndillys. For a young wench, tha's done considerable!

MARY: (Skipping.)
I don't even get tired anymore.

DICKON: (Puzzled.) Seems like someone's been here since it were shut away. Looks to be a bit o' prunin' hither'n yon.

MARY: Dickon, will you help—help make the garden wick again?

DICKON: I've chased about th' moor in all weathers, same as rabbits. Soon as I'm done wi' chores, I'll come ever' day. Rain or shine!

MARY: Oh, I like you, Dickon! Never thought I should like four people!

DICKON: Only four?

MARY: You, Martha, Robin, and Ben. Though he is crabby at times.

DICKON: I knows tha' thinks me odd—a common moor boy wi' patched-up clothes. But tha'rt th' most peculiar lass I ever did see!

MARY: (A touch of Yorkshire.) Does tha' like me?

DICKON: Aye, an' so does Robin, I do believe.

MARY: That's two what likes me!

DICKON: (Staring.) Yonder tree—wi' th' branch broke—p'raps 'tis th' tree as Miss Lily fell from.

MARY: (Sudden.) Dickon, if Uncle found us here he'd send me away. I couldn't bear that.
(Sound Cue #20—Chimes ring. She crosses.)
Better go now.

DICKON: (Shows bundle.)
I'll stay a bit. Here's me dinner—bread an' a slice o' bacon.

MARY: (Returns, anxious.)
Whatever happens, you—you won't—ever tell?

DICKON: If a missel thrush showed me his nest, would I tell? Nay, Miss Mary. Tha'rt safe as a thrush on th' moor.

MARY: (Radiant.) Thank you, Dickon!
(Leaves garden.)
I've met Dickon! I've actually met Dickon!
(Exits. Sound Cue #21—Robin chirps.)

DICKON: I see thee showin' off, flirtin' thy tail feathers! Art tha' courtin' a bonnie miss? Tellin' lies 'bout bein' th' boldest cock robin on Missel Moor?
(Lights fade on DICKON.)

The Secret Garden
adapted by Sylvia Ashby from the novel by
Frances Hodgson Burnett

Dramatis Personae
COLIN
MARY

Script

(Night: MARY's room. Sound Cue #22—MARY is awakened by thunder.)

MARY: (Sits up.)
More rain. And wind too. Wuthering's such a mournful sound. (Hears crying.) That's not the wind I hear!
(Climbs from bed, lights candle.)
More like the crying I heard before.
(More thunder as she starts out.)
I think I remember the way. Down the long corridor—round a corner— (Louder crying.) Turn right. Or was it left? I wonder if Mrs. Medlock can hear the sound of my heart thumping?
(Upstage right, a shaft of light reveals a boy in bed.)
(Fearful whisper.) Who are you?

COLIN: (Terrified.) Mary Lennox. Who are you?

MARY: Colin Craven. Master of this house!

COLIN: (Blackout. Sound Cue #23—Music accent.)

***

ACT II

(Sound Cue #24—Music. The scene continues. COLIN lies in his bed, propped up by pillows.)

366 APPENDIX H

STAGING
The Secret Garden

Two elements in this scene recommend abstract staging: multiple locations and beds. Both would be difficult to present in a classroom setting. Consider using a large wooden box or a wide bench for Mary's bed at the beginning of the scene. Place it USC or perhaps slightly right of center. When she gets up and walks down the corridor, she could circle the stage, pantomiming the turns in the corridor. While Mary has the audience's attention, Colin should enter from the opposite direction as subtly as possible. The box can now represent the bed in Colin's room. A sound effect from offstage may help Mary's knock pantomime seem more believable.

COLIN: (Frightened.) Are you a ghost?

MARY: (Also frightened.) No. Are you?

COLIN: No. Who is Mary Lennox?

MARY: A girl from India. Andrew Craven is my uncle.

COLIN: He is my father.

MARY: Your father! I never knew—

COLIN: Come here.
(MARY approaches cautiously. He touches her.)
You are real, aren't you? Or am I a dreaming?

MARY: We're both awake. I think. (Offers.) I'll pinch you if you like.

COLIN: Where did you come from?

MARY: Down the corridor. No one said a word about you.

COLIN: They dare not. I won't have people staring.

MARY: What were you crying about?

COLIN: I can't sleep, my head aches. I have horrible dreams.

MARY: Why?

COLIN: Because I'm ill. Father thinks I'll be a cripple, like him. Therefore, servants aren't allowed to talk about me.

MARY: So many secrets in this house.

COLIN: Mother died when I was born. That's why Father hates me.

MARY: That's why he hates the garden . . . because she died.

COLIN: (Quickly.) What garden?

MARY: Oh, just a garden. (Changes subject.) Have you been locked up?

COLIN: Certainly not. I refuse to go anywhere!

MARY: You've stayed in this room . . . all these years?

COLIN: I was at the seaside once. People stared. One old lady patted my cheek so I bit her hand.

MARY: She probably thought you were a mad dog!

COLIN: I wore a brace to keep my back straight. Until a fancy London doctor said, "How stupid. Take the boy outside! Give him fresh air." But I won't go out! I hate fresh air!

MARY: (Crossing.) As you don't like people staring, shall I go?

COLIN: If you are real, sit down. We'll talk.

MARY: (Sits on bed.) When I first came I hated going out.

COLIN: Sometimes Father visits, when I'm asleep. Mainly he forgets I exist. Though he buys whatever I like. Tons of splendid books. A nurse taught me to read.

MARY: (Scornful.) And you do whatever you please? Like a little Rajah?

COLIN: Otherwise I get very ill. In fact, when I was born no one expected me to live!

MARY: (Stands.) That's when the garden door was locked.

COLIN: (Intrigued.) What's this garden you talk about?

MARY: (Nervous.) Oh, just a garden somewhere. Your father locked the door—buried the key.

COLIN: (Eager.) A locked garden? Where?

MARY: I'm not sure . . . no one is allowed in . . . I suppose there's a door, someplace.

COLIN: Ask the gardeners!

MARY: Perhaps they . . . aren't permitted . . . to answer questions.

COLIN: I can make them answer! I can make them obey!

MARY: (Fearful.) Can you? Can you do that?

COLIN: When Father's gone, I am Master here. Someday the Manor will be mine, if I live. But my doctor—Dr. Spencer—is Father's cousin. He wants me dead, of course.

MARY: Do you want to live?

COLIN: No. But I don't want to die. When I lie here thinking . . . I get dreadful headaches and cry and cry.

MARY: Let's talk of something else!

COLIN: (Imperious.) I want to see that garden. I'll make them dig up the key!
(Pounds.)
I'll make them open the door!

MARY: Oh no, no! You'll spoil everything!

COLIN: I will not!

MARY: The garden could be our special kingdom—if we can keep a secret!

ACTING SCENES 367

Pride and Prejudice

The humor in *Pride and Prejudice* hinges upon the atmosphere created by the actors (and set, when used). Both Lady Catherine and Miss Elizabeth Bennet have very refined manners, though Lady Catherine behaves more imposingly. To achieve the proper characterization, consider having both actors work to refine their stage movement. They could practice walking while balancing books on their heads. Both women should walk, sit, and rise with emphatically correct posture. Here, Elizabeth's characterization should stop. Lady Catherine's characterization could go on to refine detailed movements of the head and face.

COLIN: I've never had a secret. Not a happy one.

MARY: (Appeals.) Soon, perhaps very soon, I'll find a way in. Then we'll go together, the two of us.

COLIN: (Dreamy.) I should like that.

MARY: Let me tell you how I imagine it: Shut up so long, there may be a tangle of vines. Under the earth, roots and bulbs work with all their might . . . because it's warmer now.

COLIN: Sounds like you've been there already!

MARY: (Leaving, alarmed.) I'd better go—

COLIN: (Yells.) Mary Lennox!

MARY: (She stops.)

COLIN: We're cousins. I expect a visit every day! I'll send Martha for you.

MARY: (Crosses back, shocked.) Martha knows?

COLIN: She's next door, sleeping. When Nurse gives out, Martha takes over. If Mother hadn't died, perhaps I wouldn't be ill. Where is your mother?

MARY: Dead.

COLIN: See that silk cord? Pull it. (Mary pulls imaginary cord.)

MARY: (Studies picture.) Your mother's portrait?

COLIN: I don't know why she died. (Rages.) Sometimes I hate her for it!

MARY: Your eyes are so alike . . .

COLIN: Draw the cord. Quickly! (She does.)

MARY: (Starts out.) It's very late.

COLIN: Don't leave—not before I fall asleep. Know any songs? Did your mother sing to you?

MARY: She was always rushing off—dressed in lovely lacy things. Sometimes Ayah sang to me.

COLIN: Mary Lennox, I order you to sing!

MARY: (Mary keeps going.) Pleee-ase!

MARY: (Turns reluctant.) If you insist. (Sings Hindu lullaby.) So ja raj kumari, so ja raj kumari . . . (Gently arranges covers, exits as he drifts off. Sound Cue #25—Music takes up lullaby, and continues as CRAVEN enters to observe his sleeping son.)

Pride and Prejudice
adapted by Helen Jerome from the novel by Jane Austen

Dramatis Personae

ELIZABETH
LADY CATHERINE
HILL
MRS. LAKE (walk-on)

Script

(LADY CATHERINE examines the room, pictures, etc.; crosses to table L. of small fireplace, L., tapping it with her lorgnette to see if it is genuine. Sits at fireplace L.)

ELIZABETH: That piece is quite genuine—Lady Catherine. (Crosses to LADY CATHERINE) Is your chair comfortable?

LADY CATHERINE: Sit here— (Indicates other chair in front of fireplace) —Miss Bennet, where I can see you plainly. (ELIZABETH does so, LADY CATHERINE eyes her an instant.) You know why I am here?

ELIZABETH: No, indeed, I don't know what I have done to deserve this honor.

LADY CATHERINE: Has not your conscience told you?

ELIZABETH: My conscience?

LADY CATHERINE: Miss Bennet, I am not to be trifled with. I am celebrated for my frankness. Don't assume those innocent airs—I'm not a man! They will have no effect

368 APPENDIX H

STAGING

Pride and Prejudice

Any level of realism or nonrealism should work effectively with this scene. If only wooden chairs are available, the scene can still be highly theatrical and quite effective. If the actors are struggling with characterization, simple costumes might help. A garment's style really does influence physical demeanor.

If authentic costumes are not available, have Elizabeth wear a modern dress with an empire waist (preferably long, not knee-length) and pull her hair back, if it is long enough to do so. As a prop, she could use a long, slender scarf, draped behind her and over each elbow. A long string of pearls would be appropriate as well.

Lady Catherine might wear a dressy blouse, a tailored jacket, and a long A-line skirt. She might do well with a slightly oversized hat, gloves, and several strands of pearls.

Unlike scenes such as *A Marriage Proposal: Western Style*, blocking for this scene should be minimal.

LADY CATHERINE: whatever upon me. A report has reached me that you hope to be married to my nephew, Mr. Darcy. (ELIZABETH shows complete surprise.) I would not insult him by asking about the truth of this. I have come post haste from Rosings to let you know my exact sentiments.

ELIZABETH: What a long way to come for such a purpose, Lady Catherine. Especially as I know nothing of such a rumor.

LADY CATHERINE: Will you swear there is no foundation for it?

ELIZABETH: No, I do not pretend to be as celebrated for frankness as Your Ladyship. So there are certain questions I may not choose to answer—this is one of them.

LADY CATHERINE: How—how dare you? I insist on knowing! Has my nephew made you an offer of marriage?

ELIZABETH: But Your Ladyship has already declared that to be impossible.

LADY CATHERINE: It certainly should be! But your arts may have entangled him into forgetting what he owes to his family.

ELIZABETH: (Rises, curtseys and steps away from her) Then surely I should be the last to admit it.

LADY CATHERINE: (Furiously, rising) Miss Bennet, do you know who I am? I have not been accustomed—I am the nearest relative he has and entitled to know his dearest concerns.

ELIZABETH: (Calmly) Then question him. You certainly are not entitled to know mine.

LADY CATHERINE: This marriage to which you have the effrontery to aspire, will never take place. Never! Now what have you to say? (Steps down to face ELIZABETH.)

ELIZABETH: (Placidly) If there were no other objection to my marriage with Mr. Darcy—your commands would certainly carry little weight.

LADY CATHERINE: (Crosses and sweeps by ELIZABETH to table C.) Very well. If you persist—but don't expect to be received by his family—or his friends—

LADY CATHERINE: (Turns to ELIZABETH) Your name will never be mentioned by any of us!

ELIZABETH: I must confess to Your Ladyship that this will not give me a moment's concern.

LADY CATHERINE: (Amazed) Miss Bennet, I am ashamed of you. Is this your gratitude for my hospitality?

ELIZABETH: (Turns to her) Gratitude! But, Lady Catherine, I regard hospitality as a mutual grace, and by no means consider myself an object for charity.

LADY CATHERINE: (Coming down to ELIZABETH; pacing about) Understand, my girl, I came here determined—I am not used to submitting to any person's whims, nor brooking disappointments.

ELIZABETH: That is unfortunate. It is rather late in life for Your Ladyship to be receiving your first taste of it—

LADY CATHERINE: Be silent. The idea of you wanting to marry out of your own sphere!

ELIZABETH: (Smiling) Oh, I should not consider it so. Mr. Darcy is a gentleman—I am the daughter of one.

LADY CATHERINE: (Coming to ELIZABETH) And pray, what was your mother? A lady? (Laughs scornfully) The daughter of a shop-keeper, with a brother—an attorney!! (ELIZABETH turns away from her) You see, I am not deceived by your airs and graces.

ELIZABETH: (Turns to her) And you, Lady Catherine, the daughter of a peer! (Stepping away from her) It's strange how little birth seems to affect questions of taste—or—(To LADY CATHERINE)—gentleness of heart.

LADY CATHERINE: As if you could possibly know anything about such things. (Crosses to ELIZABETH) Answer me once and for all—Are you engaged to my nephew?

"The Ugly Duckling"

By the title of A. A. Milne's play, you may have anticipated a children's story featuring animal characters. However, the play's title is only an allusion to that tale. Camilla should be communicated to the audience as a simple but lovely young lady—a true princess, though lacking some of the frills. Whether staging just this scene or the entire play, there is no cause to make her or Prince Simon dowdy. They *do* need to be drastically different in appearance from the other cast members, however. This can be accomplished through use of style, color, and type of garment. It is advisable to make their costuming more appealing to the audience than the other cast members' costumes.

The Ugly Duckling
by A. A. Milne

Dramatis Personae

PRINCE
PRINCESS

Script

(PRINCE SIMON wanders in from the back unannounced. He is a very ordinary-looking young man in rather dusty clothes. He gives a deep sigh of relief as he sinks into the KING'S throne. . . . CAMILLA, a new and strangely beautiful CAMILLA, comes in.)

PRINCE: (surprised.) Well!

PRINCESS: Oh, hallo!

PRINCE: Ought you?

PRINCESS: (getting up). Do sit down, won't you?

PRINCE: Who are you, and how did you get here?

PRINCESS: Well, that's rather a long story. Couldn't we sit down? You could sit here if you liked, but it isn't very comfortable.

PRINCE: That is the King's Throne.

PRINCESS: Oh, is that what it is?

PRINCE: Thrones are not meant to be comfortable.

PRINCESS: Well, I don't know if they're meant to be, but they certainly aren't.

PRINCE: Why were you sitting on the King's Throne, and who are you?

PRINCESS: My name is Carlo.

PRINCE: Mine is Dulcibella.

PRINCESS: Good. And now couldn't we sit down?

PRINCE: (sitting down on the long seat to the left of the throne, and, as it were, wafting him to a place next to her.) You may sit here, if you like. Why are you so tired?

PRINCESS: (He sits down.)

PRINCE: I've been taking very strenuous exercise.

(Mrs. LAKE opens conservatory door; looks into living room in astonishment; makes a sign that there is too much noise. ELIZABETH nods.)

ELIZABETH: I must ask you to speak in a lower key. My sister is asleep out there.
(Walks away from her; crosses R. to bench)

LADY CATHERINE: No, I am not engaged to him.

ELIZABETH: (Crosses to sofa) And will you promise me you never will be?

LADY CATHERINE: (Turning to her; quietly) I will not.

ELIZABETH: Miss Bennet, I am shocked!

LADY CATHERINE: (Pompously; sits on sofa) Then I refuse to leave until you have given me that promise.

ELIZABETH: (Crosses to door R.C. and pulls bell cord) I trust Your Ladyship will have a pleasant journey back to Rosings.
(LADY CATHERINE rises in amazement. HILL enters R.C. from L.) Hill, Her Ladyship's coach, if you please.

HILL: It is waiting, Miss Lizzie.

LADY CATHERINE: (Pauses in amazement as she crosses to door R.C.) I take no leave of you. I send no farewell message to your mother! Miss Bennet, I am seriously displeased. (ELIZABETH is making a curtsey as LADY CATHERINE, without returning it, stalks out R.C. to R., followed by HILL, who leaves the door open)

STAGING
"The Ugly Duckling"

You may wish to employ some creativity to deal with the stage directions in this scene. Remember they are *instructions*, not mandates. Be sure to make choices that make the scene make sense and still maintain proper decorum for your students. In addition to school policies, the maturity of a given class may have some bearing on your choices.

PRINCESS: Is that part of the long story?

PRINCE: It is.

PRINCESS: (settling herself). I love stories.

PRINCE: This isn't a story really. You see, I'm attendant on Prince Simon, who is visiting here.

PRINCESS: Oh? I'm attendant on Her Royal Highness.

PRINCE: Then you know what he's here for.

PRINCESS: Yes.

PRINCE: She's very beautiful, I hear.

PRINCESS: Did you hear that? Where have you been lately?

PRINCE: Travelling in distant lands—with Prince Simon.

PRINCESS: Ah! All the same, I don't understand. Is Prince Simon in the Palace now? The drawbridge can't be down yet!

PRINCE: I don't suppose it is. And what a noise it makes coming down!

PRINCESS: Isn't it terrible?

PRINCE: I couldn't stand it any more. I just had to get away. That's why I'm here.

PRINCESS: But how?

PRINCE: Well, there's only one way, isn't there? That beech tree, and then a swing and a grab for the battlements, and don't ask me to remember it all— (He shudders.)

PRINCESS: You mean you came across the moat by that beech tree?

PRINCE: Yes. I got so tired of hanging about.

PRINCESS: But it's terribly dangerous!

PRINCE: That's why I'm so exhausted. Nervous shock. (He lies back and breathes loudly.)

PRINCESS: Of course, it's different for me.

PRINCE: (sitting up). Say that again. I must have got it wrong.

PRINCESS: It's different for me, because I'm used to it. Besides, I'm so much lighter.

PRINCE: You don't mean that you—

PRINCESS: Oh yes, often.

PRINCE: And I thought I was a brave man! At least, I didn't until five minutes ago, and now I don't again.

PRINCESS: Oh, but you are! And I think it's wonderful to do it straight off the first time.

PRINCE: Well, you did.

PRINCESS: Oh no, not the first time. When I was a child.

PRINCE: You mean that you crashed?

PRINCESS: Well, you only fall into the moat.

PRINCE: Only! Can you swim?

PRINCESS: Of course.

PRINCE: So you swam to the castle walls, and yelled for help, and they fished you out and walloped you. And next day you tried again. Well, if that isn't pluck—

PRINCESS: Of course I didn't. I swam back, and did it at once; I mean I tried again at once. It wasn't until the third time that I actually did it. You see, I was afraid I might lose my nerve.

PRINCE: Afraid she might lose her nerve!

PRINCESS: There's a way of getting over from this side, too; a tree grows out from the wall and you jump into another tree—I don't think it's quite so easy.

PRINCE: Not quite so easy. Good. You must show me.

PRINCESS: Oh, I will.

PRINCE: Perhaps it might be as well if you taught me how to swim first. I've often heard about swimming, but never—

PRINCESS: You can't swim?

PRINCE: No. Don't look so surprised. There are a lot of other things which I can't do. I'll tell you about them as soon as you have a couple of years to spare.

PRINCESS: You can't swim and yet you crossed by the beech-tree! And you're ever so much heavier than I am! Now who's brave?

PRINCE: (getting up). You keep talking about how light you are. I must see if there's anything in it. Stand up! (She stands obediently and he picks her up.) You're right, Dulcibella. I could hold you here for ever.

ACTING SCENES 371

(Looking at her)
You're very lovely. Do you know how lovely you are?

PRINCESS: Yes.
(She laughs suddenly and happily.)

PRINCE: Why do you laugh?

PRINCESS: Aren't you tired of holding me?

PRINCE: Frankly, yes. I exaggerated when I said I could hold you forever. When you've been hanging by the arms for ten minutes over a very deep moat, wondering if it's too late to learn how to swim—
(he puts her down)
—what I meant was that I should like to hold you forever.

PRINCESS: Why did you laugh?

PRINCE: Oh, well, it was a little private joke of mine.

PRINCESS: If it comes to that, I've got a private joke of mine. Let's ex-change them.

PRINCE: Mine's very private. One other woman in the whole world knows, and that's all.

PRINCESS: Mine's just as private. One other man knows, and that's all.

PRINCE: What fun. I love secrets. . . . Well, here's mine. When I was born, one of my godmothers promised that I should be very beautiful.

PRINCESS: How right she was.

PRINCE: But the other one said this:
I give you with this kiss
A wedding-day surprise
Where ignorance is bliss
'Tis folly to be wise.
And nobody knew what it meant. And I grew up very plain. And then, when I was about ten, I met my god-mother in the forest one day. It was my tenth birthday. Nobody knows this—except you.

PRINCESS: Except us.

PRINCE: Except us. And she told me what her gift meant. It meant that I was beautiful—but everybody else was to go on being ignorant, and thinking me plain, until my wedding-day. Because, she said, she didn't want me to grow up spoilt and wilful and vain, as I should have done if everybody had always been saying how beautiful I was; and the best thing in the world, she said, was to be quite sure of yourself, but not to expect admiration from other people. So ever since then my mirror has told me I'm beautiful, and everybody else thinks me ugly; and I get a lot of fun out of it.

PRINCE: Well, seeing that Dulcibella is the result, I can only say that your godmother was very, very wise.

PRINCESS: And now tell me your secret.

PRINCE: It isn't such a pretty one. You see, Prince Simon was going to woo Princess Camilla, and he'd heard that she was beautiful and haughty and imperious—all you would have been if your godmother hadn't been so wise. And being a very ordinary-looking fellow himself, he was afraid she wouldn't think much of him, so he suggested to one of his attendants, a man named Carlo, of extremely attractive appearance, that he should pretend to be the Prince, and win the Princess' hand, and then at the last moment they would change places—

PRINCESS: How would they do that?

PRINCE: The Prince was going to have been married in full armour—with his visor down.

PRINCESS: (laughing happily). Oh, what fun!

PRINCE: Neat, isn't it?

PRINCESS: (laughing). Oh, very . . . very . . . very.

PRINCE: Neat, but not so terribly funny. Why do you keep laughing?

PRINCESS: Well, that's another secret.

PRINCE: If it comes to that, I've got another one up my sleeve. Shall we exchange again?

PRINCESS: All right. You go first this time.

PRINCE: Very well. . . . I am not Carlo.

PRINCESS: (Standing up and speaking dramatically)
I am Simon!—ow!
(He sits down and rubs his leg violently.)

PRINCE: (alarmed). What is it?

PRINCESS: Cramp. (In a mild voice, still rubbing) I was saying that I was Prince Simon.

PRINCESS: Shall I rub it for you? (She rubs.)

PRINCE: (still hopefully). I am Simon.

PRINCESS: Is that better?

PRINCE: (despairingly). I am Simon.

PRINCESS: I know.

PRINCE: How did you know?

PRINCESS: Well, you told me.

PRINCE: But oughtn't you to swoon or something?

PRINCESS: Why? History records many similar rules.

PRINCE: (amazed). Is that so? I've never read history. I thought I was being profoundly original.

PRINCESS: Oh, no! Now I'll tell you my secret. For reasons very much like your own, the Princess Camilla, who is held to be extremely plain, feared to meet Prince Simon. Is the drawbridge down yet?

PRINCE: Do your people give a faint, surprised cheer every time it gets down?

PRINCESS: Naturally.

PRINCE: Then it came down about three minutes ago.

PRINCESS: Ah! Then at this very moment your man Carlo is declaring his passionate love for my maid, Dulcibella. That, I think, is funny. (So does the PRINCE. He laughs heartily.) Dulcibella, by the way, is in love with a man she calls Eg, so I hope Carlo isn't getting carried away.

PRINCE: Carlo is married to a girl he calls "the little woman," so Eg has nothing to fear.

PRINCESS: By the way, I don't know if you heard, but I said, or as good as said, that I am the Princess Camilla.

PRINCE: I wasn't surprised. History, of which I read a great deal, records many similar ruses.

PRINCESS: (laughing). Simon!

PRINCE: (laughing). Camilla! (He stands up.) May I try holding you again? (She nods. He takes her in his arms and kisses her.) Sweetheart!

PRINCESS: You see, when you lifted me up before, you said, "You're very lovely," and my godmother said that the first person to whom I would seem lovely was the man I should marry; so I knew then that you were Simon and I should marry you.

PRINCE: I knew directly I saw you that I should marry you, even if you were Dulcibella. By the way, which of you am I marrying?

PRINCESS: When she lifts her veil, it will be Camilla. (Voices are heard outside.) Until then it will be Dulcibella.

PRINCE: (in a whisper). Then good-bye, Camilla, until you lift your veil.

PRINCESS: Good-bye, Simon, until you raise your visor.

Cyrano de Bergerac
by Edmond Rostand

Dramatis Personae

CYRANO
CHRISTIAN

Script

(All have gone out by different doors, some by the staircase. CYRANO and CHRISTIAN are face to face, looking at each other for a moment.)

CYRANO: Embrace me now!

CHRISTIAN: Sir?

CYRANO: You are brave.

CHRISTIAN: Oh! But—

CYRANO: Nay, I insist.

CHRISTIAN: Pray tell me—

CYRANO: Come, embrace! I am her brother.

CHRISTIAN: Whose brother?

CYRANO: Hers i' faith! Roxane's!

CHRISTIAN: (Rushing up to him)
O heavens! Her brother . . . ?

ACTING SCENES **373**

You may wish to review the introduction and summary of *Cyrano* on pages 25-26 of the Teacher's Edition (bottom margin).

Picking Up Cues

This scene could easily become long and tedious if the cues are not "picked up" at the right time. If the actors struggle with making the scene flow smoothly and conversationally, two exercises may help. You can direct them to practice their own lines consecutively, hearing the other character's words in their minds and intentionally cutting them off (out loud). Also, they can practice the scene several times on different days using only paraphrase, not the wording provided. This will help them focus on the content and flow of the conversation rather than on timing.

Background Information

This scene from Act 2 occurs in a spacious restaurant-type bakery. Roxane has told Cyrano that she loves Christian, though they have never spoken. Christian has recently joined the cadets. Immediately preceding this scene, Cyrano has been telling the cadets the story of his bravery against a hundred men. Christian has repeatedly finished sentences for Cyrano, always using the word "nose" in some fashion. Rather than

---

STAGING
Cyrano de Bergerac

The physical location of this scene has little bearing on the action. The scene could be communicated clearly by use of a couple of wooden chairs and a table. In particular, Cyrano should make full use of open stage space. This is not a chat at afternoon tea. Cyrano promised Roxane that he would befriend Christian for her sake, and this is his opportunity to fulfill that promise. He also realizes that he can have the joy of winning Roxane's heart, though not the joy of winning her. He will be Christian's soul and Christian will be his mask. Cyrano can finally speak his love without fear of rejection because of his appearance.

Both the actors' characterizations and their stage business should reflect the fact that both men feel "on the verge" of achieving their mutual dream: wooing and winning the fair Roxane.

displaying rage, as Cyrano normally does when his nose is insulted, he commands all of the cadets out of the room and then speaks respectfully to Christian.

CYRANO: Cousin—brother! The same thing!

CHRISTIAN: And she has told you . . .?

CYRANO: All!

CHRISTIAN: She loves me?

CYRANO: Maybe!

CHRISTIAN: (Taking his hands) How glad I am to meet you, sir!

CYRANO: That may be called sudden sentiment!

CHRISTIAN: I ask your pardon—

CYRANO: (Looking at him, with his hand on his shoulder) True, he's fair, the villain!

CHRISTIAN: Ah, sir! If you but knew my admiration—

CYRANO: But all those noses—

CHRISTIAN: Oh! I take them back!

CYRANO: Roxane expects a letter.

CHRISTIAN: Woe the day!

CYRANO: How?

CHRISTIAN: I am lost if I but ope my lips!

CYRANO: Why so?

CHRISTIAN: I am a fool—could die for shame!

CYRANO: None is a fool who knows himself a fool.
And you did not attack me like a fool.

CHRISTIAN: Bah! One finds battle cry to lead th' assault!
I have a certain military wit,
But, before women, can but hold my tongue.
Their eyes! True, when I pass, their eyes are kind . . .

CYRANO: And, when you stay, their hearts, methinks, are kinder?

CHRISTIAN: No! for I am one of those men—tongue-tied,
I know it—who can never tell their love.

CYRANO: If I could be a musketeer, with handsome face!

CHRISTIAN: Roxane is clever. I'm sure to prove
A disappointment to her!

CYRANO: (Looking at him)
Had I but
Such an interpreter to speak my soul!

CHRISTIAN: (With despair) Eloquence! Where to find it?

CYRANO: (Abruptly) That I lend,
If you lend me your handsome victor-charms;
Blended, we make a hero of romance!

CHRISTIAN: How so?

CYRANO: Think you you can repeat what things
I daily teach your tongue?

CHRISTIAN: What do you mean?

CYRANO: Roxane shall never have a disilusion!
Say, wilt thou that we woo her, double-handed?
Wilt thou that we two woo her, both together?
Feel'st thou, passing from my leather doublet,
Through thy laced doublet, all my soul inspiring?

CHRISTIAN: But, Cyrano—

CYRANO: Will you, I say?

CHRISTIAN: I fear!

CYRANO: Since, by yourself, you fear to chill her heart,
Will you—to kindle all her heart to flame—
Wed into one my phrases and your lips?

CHRISTIAN: Will it please you so?
Give you such pleasure?

CYRANO: (Madly) It—(Then calmly, business-like)
It would amuse me!
It is an enterprise to tempt a poet.
Will you complete me, and let me complete you?
You march victorious—I go in your shadow;
Let me be wit for you, be you my beauty!

CHRISTIAN: The letter, that she waits for even now!
I never can—

CYRANO: (Taking out the letter he had written)
See! Here it is—your letter!

CHRISTIAN: What?

CYRANO: Take it! Look, it wants but the address.

CHRISTIAN: But I . . .

CYRANO: Fear nothing. Send it. It will suit.

CHRISTIAN: But why have you . . .?

374 APPENDIX H

CYRANO: Oh! We have our pockets full,
We poets, of love letters, writ to Chloes,
Daphnes—creations of our noddle-heads.
Our lady-loves—phantasms of our brains,
Dream-fancies blown into soap-bubbles! Come!
Take it, and change feigned love-words into true.
I breathed my sighs and moans haphazard-wise;
Call all these wandering love-birds home to nest.
You'll see that I was in these lettered lines
Eloquent all the more, the less sincere!
Take it, and make an end!

CHRISTIAN: Were it not well to change some words?
Written haphazard-wise,
Will it fit Roxane?

CYRANO: 'Twill fit like a glove!

CHRISTIAN: But—

CYRANO: Ah, credulity of love! Roxane
Will think each word inspired by herself!

CHRISTIAN: My friend!
(He throws himself into CYRANO's arms. They remain thus.)

Cyrano de Bergerac
by Edmond Rostand

Dramatis Personae

CYRANO
ROXANE

Script

CYRANO: (Twilight begins to fall.)
His letter! Ah! you promised me one day
That I should read it.

ROXANE: What would you? His letter?

CYRANO: Yes, I would fain,—today . . .

ROXANE: (Giving the bag hung at her neck)
See! Here it is!

CYRANO: (Taking it)
Have I your leave to open?

ROXANE: Open—read!
(She comes back to her tapestry frame, folds it up, sorts her wools.)

CYRANO: (Reading)
"Roxane, adieu! I soon must die!
This very night, beloved; and I
Feel my soul heavy with love untold.
I die! No more, as in days of old,
My loving, longing eyes will feast
On your least gesture—ay, the least!
I mind me the way you touch your cheek
With your finger, softly, as you speak!
Ah me! I know that gesture well!
My heart cries out!—I cry 'Farewell'!"

ROXANE: But how you read that letter! One would think . . .

CYRANO: (Continuing to read)
"My life, my love, my jewel, my sweet,
My heart has been yours in every beat!"
(The shades of evening fall imperceptibly.)

ROXANE: You read in such a voice—so strange—and yet—
It is not the first time I hear that voice!
(She comes nearer very softly, without his perceiving it, passes behind his chair, and, noiselessly leaning over him, looks at the letter. The darkness deepens.)

CYRANO: "Here, dying, and there, in the land on high,
I am he who loved, who loves you—I . . ."
(Putting her hand on his shoulder)

ROXANE: How can you read? It is too dark to see!
(He starts, turns, sees her close to him. Suddenly alarmed, he holds his head down. Then in the dusk, which has now completely enfolded them, she says, very slowly, with clasped hands)
And, fourteen years long, he has played this part
Of the kind old friend who comes to laugh and chat.

CYRANO: Roxane!

ROXANE: 'Twas you!

CYRANO: No, never; Roxane, no!

ROXANE: I should have guessed, each time he said my name!

CYRANO: No, it was not I!

Cyrano de Bergerac

Many years have passed since the events of the previous scene from *Cyrano*. Roxane married Christian as a result of Cyrano's letters and poetry. Both men left for battle immediately following the impromptu ceremony. When letters composed by Cyrano compel Roxane to visit the troop, Christian realizes that Roxane really loves Cyrano, not him. It is not his attractive appearance that has inspired her affection, but Cyrano's capacity to express love. He insists that Cyrano tell Roxane about his part in wooing her so that she can choose which man she loves. Christian is then fatally wounded in battle. Cyrano tells him that Roxane knows the truth (though she does not) and that she has chosen Christian.

In this scene, Cyrano pays Roxane a weekly visit to bring her news. She has never remarried and still carries the last letter from Christian, penned by Cyrano.

Subtext

Be sure the students portraying Cyrano and Roxane realize the need for great sincerity in this scene. Roxane has matured greatly during the course of the play. She does not accuse Cyrano of love, but instead encourages and implores him to confess it.

STAGING

Cyrano de Bergerac

Cyrano has a fatal head wound, which he conceals. He lacks the spirit and expressive movements that have always characterized him. The scene may work best if he is seated for most or all of it. Roxane may move about upstage of him at the opening of the scene. Upon learning that he is the true author of all that she has cherished, she would certainly move to the same area or even downstage of him. She would likely attempt eye contact, and he would repeatedly avoid it.

ROXANE: It was you!

CYRANO: I swear!

ROXANE: I see through all the generous counterfeit—
The letters—you!

CYRANO: No.

ROXANE: The sweet, mad love-words!
You!

CYRANO: No!

ROXANE: The voice that thrilled the night—you, you!

CYRANO: I swear you err.

ROXANE: The soul—it was your soul!

CYRANO: I loved you not.

ROXANE: You loved me not?

CYRANO: 'Twas he!

ROXANE: You loved me!

CYRANO: No!

ROXANE: See! How you falter now!

CYRANO: No, my sweet love, I never loved you!

ROXANE: Why have you kept silent these fourteen years,
Knowing he had no part in this letter—
Knowing the tears were yours?

CYRANO: (Holding out the letter to her)
The blood was his.

APPENDIX I
RADIO SCRIPTS

The Latchstring   Page 1

MUSIC:	1. SOMETHING "PIONEERISH" (UP AND
	2. CROSSFADE WITH)
SFX:	3. CRACKLING OF FIRE IN FIREPLACE
NARR:	4. Mary Tyler glanced with troubled eyes at
	5. the face of her husband as they sat before
	6. the fire in their little cabin. She knew that
	7. he, too, was living over the uncertain days
	8. since the outbreak of the war. Time and
	9. again there had been reports that the
	10. British soldiers had incited the Indians
	11. to burn the cabins of the settlers and
	12. massacre whole villages. Despite these
	13. reports, the Tylers lived as before, on
	14. friendly terms with their neighbors,

-MORE-

RADIO SCRIPTS 377

The Latchstring   Page 2

NARR:	1. both Indian and white. When the mas-
	2. sacres occurred in nearby settlements,
	3. they had continued to leave out the latch-
	4. string—that leather thong that enabled
	5. a person outside the door to lift the latch
	6. and enter. The Tylers trusted entirely in
	7. the protection of their heavenly Father,
	8. and had refused to arm themselves, or
	9. even to latch the door.
JAMES:	10. The word in town is that our settlement
	11. is next on the Indians' list.
MARY:	12. I heard it too. James, . . . perhaps . . .
	13. perhaps we ought to bar the door
	14. tonight—for the sake of the children.
JAMES:	15. Maybe so. It seems to me every man
	16. within ten miles has upbraided me for
	17. not trying to protect my family better.
MARY:	18. It's never been this near before. . . .
JAMES:	19. And at least we'll be doing what most
	20. people consider safest.

-MORE-

Radio Drama Scripts

The most important quality of radio drama for your students to bear in mind as they perform is this: radio drama is theater of the mind. The audience cannot see them. They communicate exclusively through sound—voice, music, and sound effects. You may want to have the students who perform the speaking roles in each script practice several times before any other students hear the scene. Then, have them perform for a small audience (perhaps the students performing the other script) without being visible to that audience. (If you have no physical dividers available, have the audience face away from the performers.) If the performers are effectively communicating vocally, the story will be clear and interesting to the audience. If they are not focusing their communication skills on vocal communication, the audience feedback will reflect confusion or disinterest. Peer feedback may be more convincing in this case than teacher feedback.

"The Latchstring"

Let this script have a vintage feel to it. The atmosphere is very traditional, reflecting the style of early radio drama. Rather than considering the script dated or antiquated, consider performing it an opportunity to survey a popular historical style. Background music that is slightly melodramatic may make the style more apparent to the students as well as to the audience.

The Latchstring   Page 3

SFX: 1. CRACKLING OF FIRE (UP AND UNDER),

NARR: 2. LOW MOAN OF WIND SNEAKS IN
3. For what seemed like a long time, they
4. sat gazing at the fire. The silence was
5. broken only by the moaning of the wind
6. in the pine trees and the crackling of the
7. logs on the hearth. For the first time in
8. all the dark days, Mary felt afraid. She
9. stirred uneasily and cast a furtive glance
10. around the shadowy room.

JAMES: 11. (STRETCHES AND YAWNS) Well, no sense
12. sitting here all night. Let's go to bed. I'll
13. latch the door.

SFX: 14. FOOTSTEPS ON WOODEN FLOOR,
15. LATCH DOOR AND BAR IT

MUSIC: 16. UNEASY TYPE (UP AND FADE OUT BY
17. LINE 3, PAGE 4.)

NARR: 18. For hours, James tossed restlessly. Every

-MORE-

The Latchstring   Page 4

NARR: 1. time one of the children stirred or a
2. branch scraped the roof, he would sit up
3. with a start and then fall back, unnerved.
4. He tried to calm himself by repeating
5. verses from Scripture, but instead of the
6. usual comfort, the words only brought
7. rebuke.

VOICE: 8. (FILTER) "Why are ye fearful, O ye of
9. little faith? Take the shield of faith,
10. wherewith ye shall be able to quench
11. all the fiery darts of the wicked."

JAMES: 12. Mary, are you awake?

MARY: 13. Yes, James, I haven't slept. I've tried to
14. pray, and always the answer has been,
15. "Behold the Lord's hand is not short-
16. ened that it cannot save."

JAMES: 17. And the verse that keeps coming to me
18. is, "Why are ye fearful, O ye of little
19. faith?"

-MORE-

The Latchstring   Page 5

MARY: 1. We did wrong to bring in the latchstring
2. and bar the door.

JAMES: 3. Well, that's easy to remedy.

NARR: 4. Quickly James stepped to the door, un-
5. bolted it, and pulled the leather thong
6. through to the outside. When he lay down
7. again, they both enjoyed a security that
8. they had not felt for hours. They drifted
9. off to a peaceful sleep—but not for long.
10. They were soon awakened by a
11. terrifying sound. . . .

SFX: 12. INDIAN WAR WHOOPS OUTSIDE

MARY: 13. (GASP) James! Listen!

JAMES: 14. Indians! They're all around us. . . .

SFX: 15. WAR WHOOPS QUIET TO MUMBLING . . . .
16. LATCH UNDONE (SLIGHTLY OFF MIC)

MARY: 17. (FRIGHTENED) They're pulling the
18. latch. . . .

JAMES: 19. Don't move, and don't make a sound.

-MORE-

RADIO SCRIPTS   379

The Latchstring   Page 6

JAMES: 1. Pray!

SFX: 2. DOOR OPENS, WHISPERED VOICES
3. (FADE ON)

NARR: 4. By the dim light streaming in from the
5. bedroom window, James could see seven
6. Indians in full war paint enter the room.
7. They motioned and talked to each other,
8. and then silently turned and left the
9. room. . . .

SFX: 10. WHISPERED VOICES (FADE OFF)
11. . . . A few seconds later they heard the
12. outside door pulled closed.

SFX: 13. DOOR PULLED CLOSED (OFF MIC)
14. It seemed an eternity had elapsed before
15. Mary heard James stir. . . .

JAMES: 16. (SIGHS OF RELIEF) It's all right now,

MARY: 17. Mary—they've gone.
18. Mercy, what a fright!

NARR: 19. In the morning, when James and Mary

-MORE-

"The Last Straw"

This script has a more modern, fast-paced style. Karl should be a very focused character—more machine than man. Though equally professional, John is more human in his actions and responses.

Either role could be male or female. Change the character names as needed for your situation—2 men, 2 women, or 1 man, 1 woman.

The Latchstring   Page 7

NARR: 1. looked out their door, they saw only the
2. smoking ruins of their neighbors' cabins.

MARY: 3. Oh, James, look—

JAMES: 4. Let us never doubt the protection of the
5. Lord again!

MUSIC: 6. "ALL IS WELL" MOOD (UP AND UNDER)

NARR: 7. Years later, when the war was over, the
8. government of the United States appointed
9. James Tyler as a representative to an Indian
10. conference. One day he told his remarkable
11. experience to the assembly—about the
12. latchstring and God's protection. After he
13. had finished, one of the Indians rose and
14. said:

INDIAN: 15. I was one of those warriors. We were on
16. a rampage that night. After imbibing Brit-
17. ish liqour, we went from village to village
18. wreaking havoc. . . . but when we found
19. the latchstring out, our leader said . . .

-MORE-

The Latchstring   Page 8

INDIAN LEADER: 1. "No burn this house; no kill these people;
2. they do us no harm; they trust the Great
3. Spirit."

MUSIC: 4. (UP TO FINISH)

The Last Straw   Page 1

SFX: 1. OFFICE DOOR OPENS.

JOHN: 2. Karl . . .

KARL: 3. (OFF MIC) Have you forgotten how to
4. knock?

JOHN: 5. Do you knock when you come into my
6. office? Look, something important has
7. come up.

KARL: 8. It'll have to wait.

JOHN: 9. I'm sorry Karl, this can't wait.

KARL: 10. Well, I'm sorry too, John, but I've got a
11. beastly headache. Some other time.

JOHN: 12. You're going to have a worse headache
13. when I get through.

-MORE-

The Last Straw   Page 2

KARL: 1. I haven't felt well all day. I don't want to

2. talk business.

JOHN: 3. Sorry, but this report just came up from

4. the lab. . . .

SFX: 5. REPORT LAID NOISILY ON DESK—KARL

6. RUMMAGES THROUGH IT.

7. . . . It says our last shipment of Diahexene

8. was polluted. It's toxic.

KARL: 9. You mean it's—poisonous?

JOHN: 10. The chemist said it'll attack the nerves. The

11. most pleasant thing that can happen is

12. blindness.

KARL: 13. How much did we ship out?

JOHN: 14. Only four cases so far, but enough to

15. blind a hundred people.

KARL: 16. Where did the cases go?

JOHN: 17. Two back East. One to Mexico. The other one

18. here in town. We'll have to notify the au-

19. thorities—then send out tracers immediately.

-MORE-

The Last Straw   Page 3

KARL: 1. Forget it!

JOHN: 2. Forget it? Are you crazy?

KARL: 3. Yes, crazy like a fox. Don't you know

4. what'd happen if we sent out tracers? It'd

5. be in every paper in the country. We'd lose

6. every account we've got. The Andrews

7. Pharmaceutical Company would be out of

8. business in two days flat.

JOHN: 9. Now, wait a minute, Karl. . . .

KARL: 10. No, you wait a minute. Tell me—the

11. chemist—does he know?

JOHN: 12. He only knows the Diahexene's polluted.

13. He doesn't know it's been sent out.

KARL: 14. Good. Then it's all settled.

JOHN: 15. Karl, for heaven's sake, don't you realize

16. what this means? It means that some

17. body's going to . . . yes, I guess you do

18. realize it and just don't care.

KARL: 19. But I do. I'm really very sorry for all

-MORE-

The Last Straw

Page 4

KARL: 1. those people. But I care more about us,
2. John—you and me. Now, just between
3. you and me, let's get one thing straight.
4. No one—and this includes you, John—
5. no one is going to breathe one word
6. about the Diahexene. Do you understand?

JOHN: 7. Oh, yes, I understand. For eight years
8. you've taken advantage of me every step
9. of the way. This has become your company,
10. and you've made me your errand boy.

KARL: 11. Now John, let's not get touchy.

JOHN: 12. I'm sick of it. I'm going to call the health
13. department. (FADE OFF) This is one time
14. we're going to do things my way.

SFX: 15. DOOR OPENS.

MUSIC: 16. TENSE (STING AND UNDER)

KARL: 17. John! What did you say?

JOHN: 18. (OFF MIC) I said, this is one time we're
19. going to do things my way.

-MORE-

The Last Straw

Page 5

KARL: 1. Yes, well—I don't think so.

JOHN: 2. I'd like to see you stop me.

KARL: 3. I could always foreclose on your stocks and
4. home mortgage. It would be a shame for
5. your wife to be reduced to a pauper's life.

JOHN: 6. Karl, you wouldn't!

KARL: 7. If you mention one word about this, I'll
8. see to it that you are bankrupt beyond
9. repair.

JOHN: 10. I—I can't believe it!

KARL: 11. Believe it. Now, shut that door so we can
12. plan our strategy.

JOHN: 13. (FADE ON) Karl, please. I'll make a deal.
14. I'll sell out my stock—give you complete
15. control of the company—if you'll just let
16. me call in the shipments before anyone
17. gets poisoned.

KARL: 18. As if the company would be worth any-
19. thing then. No thank you, John. No deal.

-MORE-

The Last Straw   Page 6

JOHN: 1. Isn't there anything I can say . . . ?

KARL: 2. No, now please . . .

SFX: 3. TELEPHONE RINGS.

KARL: 4. . . . now what . . . .

SFX: 5. PHONE CRADLE LIFTED.

KARL: 6. . . . Andrews Pharmaceuticals . . .

DOCTOR: 7. (FILTER) Hello, Karl, Dr. Hughes here. Just

           8. wanted to verify our appointment this

           9. afternoon and golf after.

KARL: 10. The appointment, yes. I don't know about

           11. the golf. I've had a bad headache all morning.

DOCTOR: 12. Really? I'm surprised to hear that—espe-

           13. cially after the shot I gave you yesterday.

           14. Diahexene is supposed to work miracles.

KARL: 15. What—did you say?

DOCTOR: 16. Diahexene. You should know about it. We

           17. just got a shipment from your company

           18. a couple of days ago. Matter of fact,

           19. you're the first person I've treated with it.

                        -MORE-

RADIO SCRIPTS   383

The Last Straw   Page 7

KARL: 1. (DAZED) No—No—

DOCTOR: 2. Karl? Is something . . .

SFX: 3. PHONE SLAMMED DOWN

MUSIC: 4. (STING AND UNDER)

JOHN: 5. Karl, what's wrong?

KARL: 6. Wrong? Everything's wrong! I think you'd

           7. better call the health department after all.

MUSIC: 8. (UP TO FINISH)

... an ever fixed mark, that looks on tempests and is never shaken

O for a muse of FIRE

ILLUSION   reality

MASK

nature   MIRROR

TRUTH

drama

... the quality of MERCY ...

... each man in his time plays many ...

MERCY is not strained; it droppeth as the gentle falling rain ...

... we are the stuff DREAMS are made of

ACKNOWLEDGMENTS

Antigone by Sophocles, adapted by George Judy. © Copyright 1997, by Pioneer Drama Service, Inc., Englewood, Colorado. All rights reserved. Used by permission.

"The Dinner Party" by Mona Gardner, copyright © 1942, 1970 by SATURDAY REVIEW reprinted by permission of Bill Berger Associates, Inc.

The Gift of the Magi based on the short story by O. Henry by Thomas Hischak. © Copyright, 1983, by Pioneer Drama Service, Inc., Englewood, Colorado. All rights reserved. Used by permission.

The Jungle Books by Rudyard Kipling. Used by permission of Random House.

A Marriage Proposal:Western Style by Tim Kelly. © Copyright, 1978, by Pioneer Drama Service, Inc., Englewood, Colorado. All rights reserved. Used by permission.

"The Mountain Whippoorwill" by Stephen Vincent Benét. Copyright © 1925 by Stephen Vincent Benét. Copyright renewed © 1953 by Rosemary Carr Benét. Reprinted by permission of Brandt & Brandt Literary Agents, Inc.

Pride and Prejudice by Helen Jerome dramatized from Jane Austen's novel. Used by permission of Samuel French Ltd.

The Secret Garden by Sylvia Ashby. © 1997 by Sylvia Ashby, by permission of the publisher, Baker's Plays.

"Silver" by Walter de la Mare. Used by permission of The Literary Trustees of Walter de la Mare and The Society of Authors as their representative.

"To Jesus on His Birthday" by Edna St. Vincent Millay. From COLLECTED POEMS, HarperCollins. Copyright © 1928, 1955 by Edna St. Vincent Millay and Norma Millay Ellis. All rights reserved. Reprinted by permission of Elizabeth Barnett, literary executor.

The Ugly Duckling by A. A. Milne. Used by permission of Samuel French Ltd on behalf of the Estate of A. A. Milne.

PHOTOGRAPH CREDITS

The following agencies and individuals have furnished materials to meet the photographic needs of this textbook. We wish to express our gratitude to them for their important contributions.

Billy Graham Center, Wheaton, Illinois
COREL Corporation
Digital Stock
Earle Publishing Company
Eastman Kodak Company
Library of Congress
National Oceanic and Atmospheric Administration/Department of Commerce

National Oldtime Fiddlers' Contest
PhotoDisc, Inc.
Herbert G. Ponting
Petty Officer Second Class Richard Rosser, U.S. Navy
Unusual Films
U.S. Department of Defense
Dawn L. Watkins
© 2001 www.arttoday.com

Front Cover
Unusual Films

Front Matter
Unusual Films iv

Unit 1
Unusual Films vi

Chapter 1
Unusual Films 2, 3 (both), 4, 14; U.S. Department of Defense, photo by Petty Officer Second Class Richard Rosser, U.S. Navy 13

Chapter 2
Digital Stock 20, 21 (both), 22; Unusual Films 24, 29

Chapter 3
Digital Stock 38, 39 (both), 40; Unusual Films 43, 53; Archives of the Billy Graham Center, Wheaton, Illinois 44; National Oceanic and Atmospheric Administration/Department of Commerce, photo by Herbert G. Ponting 46 (top)

Chapter 4
PhotoDisc 58, 59 (both), 60 (top); Library of Congress 66; Unusual Films 77; National Oldtime Fiddlers' Contest 78

UNIT 2
Unusual Films 88

Chapter 5
PhotoDisc, Inc. 90, 91 (both), 92 (top); Library of Congress 95; COREL Corporation 97; © 2001 www.arttoday.com 111

Chapter 6
PhotoDisc, Inc. 120, 121, 122 (rose); Dawn L. Watkins 120, 121, 122 (Christmas balls); © 2001 www.arttoday.com 125, 135; PhotoDisc, Inc. 138

Chapter 7
Unusual Films 148, 149 (both), 150, 152, 156, 159, 162

Chapter 8
PhotoDisc, Inc. 170, 171 (both), 172; Unusual Films 176

UNIT 3
Unusual Films 194

Chapter 9
Unusual Films 196, 197 (both), 198

Chapter 10
Unusual Films 220, 221 (both), 222, 225 (both), 226, 231, 236 (all), 237 (all), 240

Chapter 11
Eastman Kodak Company 252, 253 (both), 254, Unusual Films 257

The Final Challenge
Unusual Films 282; Photo from "Memoirs of 80 Years" by Fanny Crosby, Earle Publishing, Boston, 1906 289; PhotoDisc, Inc. 290

INDEX

A

acting verbs, 230
action
    definition, 230
    major components, 230
adapting, readers theater, 202-7
aesthetic distance, 134
age interests, 174
airtime, 265
alliteration, 76, 132
antithesis, 130
apostrophe, 130
arena stage, 225
    blocking, 228
assonance, 133
attention/standby signal, 261
audience, 17, 82
    audience proper, 82
    possible audiences, 83
    suitability, 80
    target audience, 17

B

background, 233
    current circumstances, 235
    previous action, 233
ballad. *See* poetic forms
blocking, 223
body, use in characterization, 183
brainstorming, 177
break signal, 261

C

cast members, 258
chamber theater, 200
characterization, 182, 239
    for radio, 264
    for stage acting, 239
    for storytelling, 182
characters, 25
    creation of, 182
choric speaking, 208
Christian hero story, 288
Christian worldview, 42
classics, 94

cliché, 127
climax, 29, 113
comedy, 156
communication apprehension
    (stage fright), 114
comprehension, 63
conflict, 23
connotative meaning, 66
consonance, 133
context, 68
crisis, 28
crossing, 228
cue signal, 261
current circumstances. *See* background
cut signal, 261

D

delivery cues, 107
demographics, 174
denotative meaning, 64
denouement (resolution), 31
design, 17
dialogue, 186
    direct dialogue, 186
    indirect dialogue, 186
    revealing action, 238
diction, 84
direct dialogue, 186
director, RTV, 258
drama, 4
    formal performance. *See*
      performance
    mimicry, 9
    role-play, 10
    social expectations, 12
    social roles, 11
dramatic "V", 185
dramatic compression, 76
dramatic literature, 202
dramatic poetry. *See* poetic forms

E

elements of a story, 23
    characters, 25

    conflict, 23
    exposition, 24
    plot, 26
    theme, 23
emphasis, 112
engineer, 258
ethics. *See* worldview,
    characteristics of
experience, 69
exposition, 24
extemporaneous, 186

F

falling action, 31
farce, 243
figurative language, 127
    figures of sound, 132
    figures of speech, 130
    figures of thought, 127
first-person narration, 186
flat characters, 182
forensics, 151, 162-64
frame of reference, 155

G

genres, 73
    drama, 79 (*See also* drama
    in the Bible, 94)
      sermons and declamation,
      100
    poetry, 76 (*See also* poetry)
    prose, 73 (*See also* prose)

H

habit. *See* worldview,
    characteristics of
haiku. *See* poetic forms,
    lyric poetry
hand signals, 261
humanism (humanistic
    worldview), 43
hyperbole, 110

INDEX

ILLUSION reality

nature MIRROR MASK

TRUTH drama

O for a muse of FIRE

... an ever fixed mark, that looks on tempests and is never shaken

it droppeth as the gentle falling rain. the quality of MERCY is not strained; it droppeth as the gentle falling rain. the quality of MERCY is not strained; it droppeth as the gentle falling

... each man in his time plays many

we are the stuff DREAMS are made on

TEACHER'S APPENDIX 1
DRAMA RESOURCES

Most of these resources are available online as well as by mail. All addresses are in the United States.

Forensics

Note: Many of the companies listed in the next category would also have some materials appropriate for competitions.

Edna Means Publications
PO Box 7336
Loveland, CO 80537-0336

Wetmore Declamation Bureau
PO Box 2695
Sioux City, IA 51106-0695

National Forensics League
125 Watson Street
PO Box 38
Ripon, WI 54971

Drama

Baker's Plays
1000 Chauncey Street
Boston, MA 02111

Broadman Press
127 Ninth Avenue North
Nashville, TN 37234

Dramatic Publishing Company
4150 North Milwaukee Avenue
Chicago, IL 60641

Dramatists Play Service, Inc.
440 Park Avenue South
New York, NY 10019

Eldridge Publishing Company
PO Box 1595
Venice, FL 34284

Lillenas Publishing Co.
PO Box 527
Kansas City, MO 64141

Pioneer Drama Service
2127 South Colorado Boulevard
PO Box 4267
Englewood, CO 80155-4267

Samuel French, Inc.
25 West Twenty-fifth Street
New York, NY 10036

TEACHER'S APPENDIX 2
RECOMMENDED PLAYS, MUSICALS, AND PROGRAMS

Please note that the inclusion of these titles is not a complete endorsement of their contents. Your church and school ministry must evaluate each dramatic script to determine whether or not to use that material.

Also, when publicly producing any portion of a play script under copyright, you must secure permission to omit or change portions of the text when you apply for royalties. Many playwrights will grant permission for minor changes to be made. This fact does not dismiss the need to ask permission. Honoring copyright regulations is a matter of testimony, not just legality.

DRAMA	
Title	*Author*
Anastasia	Marcelle Maurette and Guy Bolton
And Then They Came for Me: Remembering the World of Anne Frank	James Still
Anne of Green Gables	Sylvia Ashby
Antigone	Sophocles *Note: some English translations are not philosophically acceptable.*
Binding Ties	Sharon Woodruff (BJUP)
Diary of Anne Frank, The	Goodrich and Hackett
Heidi	Adapted by John Baldwin
I Never Saw Another Butterfly	Celeste Respanti
Little Women	Adapted by Roger Wheeler
Long Road Home, The	Earl Reimer
Miracle Worker, The	William Gibson
Not Far from the Gioconda Tree	Tim Kelly
Oliver Twist	Adapted by Robert Thomas Noll
Our Miss Brooks	R. J. Mann
Remember My Name	Joanna Halpert Kraus
Scarlet Letter, The	Adapted by Glover
Secret Garden, The	Adapted by Sylvia Ashby
Tale of Two Cities	Adapted by Joellen K. Bland
Young and the Fair, The	Richard Nash

COMEDY	
Title	*Author*
Adventures of Tom Sawyer, The	Adapted by Dave Barton and Matt Bond
Arsenic and Old Lace	J. Kesselring
Importance of Being Earnest, The	Oscar Wilde
Matchmaker, The	Thornton Wilder
Miscalling of Pastor Levitt, The	Dale Savidge (BJUP)
Open Window, The	Adapted by James Fuller
Pair of Lunatics, A	W. R. Walkes
Papa Was a Preacher	Adapted by John McGreevy
Pride and Prejudice	Adapted by Helen Jerome
Romancers, The	Edmond Rostand
Ugly Duckling, The	A. A. Milne

MYSTERY	
Title	*Author*
Elevator, The	Herbert Gardner
Mousetrap, The	Agatha Christie
Patient, The	Agatha Christie
Witness for the Prosecution	Agatha Christie

FARCE AND MELODRAMA	
Title	*Author*
Bear, The	Anton Chekhov *Note: Some English translations incorrectly title this play* The Boor.
Connecticut Yankee in King Arthur's Court, A	Adapted by Tim Kelly
Lost Elevator, The	Percival Wilde
Marriage Proposal, A	Anton Chekhov
Marriage Proposal: Western Style, A	Tim Kelly

ADAPTATIONS	
Title	Author
Adventures of Tom Sawyer, The	Mark Twain
Anne of Avonlea	L. M. Montgomery
Anne of Green Gables*	L. M. Montgomery
Charlotte's Web	E. B. White
Cheaper by the Dozen	Frank Gilbreth Jr. and Ernestine Gilbreth Carey
Christmas Carol, A	Charles Dickens
Connecticut Yankee in King Arthur's Court, A*	Mark Twain
Emma	Jane Austen
Five Little Peppers and How They Grew, The	Margaret Sidney
Great Expectations	Charles Dickens
Hansel and Gretel	Brothers Grimm
Heidi*	Johanna Spyri
Hobbit, The	J. R. R. Tolkien
Huckleberry Finn	Mark Twain
Jane Eyre	Charlotte Brontë
Johnny Tremain	Esther Forbes
Lion, the Witch, and the Wardrobe, The	C. S. Lewis
Little Princess, A	Frances Hodgson Burnett
Little Women*	Louisa May Alcott
Many Moons	James Thurber
Oliver Twist*	Charles Dickens
Papa Was a Preacher*	Alyene Porter
Pride and Prejudice*	Jane Austen
Prince and the Pauper, The	Mark Twain
Ramona Quimby	Beverly Cleary
Scarlet Letter, The	Nathaniel Hawthorne
Stuart Little	E. B. White
Tale of Two Cities, A	Charles Dickens
Trumpet of the Swan, The	E. B. White
Velveteen Rabbit, The	Margery Williams
Winnie-the-Pooh	A. A. Milne
Wuthering Heights	Emily Brontë

* One adaptation has been recommended, but others may better suit the needs of your group's production.

John Brown's Body
by Stephen Vincent Benét

Lincoln, six feet one in his stocking feet,
The lank man, knotty and tough as a hickory rail,
Whose hands were always too big for white-kid gloves,
Whose wit was a coonskin sack of dry, tall tales,
Whose weathered face was homely as a plowed field—
Abraham Lincoln, who padded up and down
The sacred White House in nightshirt and carpet-slippers,
And yet could strike young hero-worshipping Hay
As dignified past any neat, balanced, fine
Plutarchan sentences carved in a Latin bronze;
The low clown out of the prairies, the ape-buffoon,
The small-town lawyer, the crude small-time politician,
State-character but comparative failure at forty
In spite of ambition enough for twenty Ceasars,
Honesty rare as a man without self-pity,
Kindness as large and plain as a prairie wind,
And a self-confidence like an iron bar:

"So that was him," they★ say. "So that's the old man.　　　*they: the soldiers*
I'm glad we saw him. He isn't so much on looks
But he looks like people you know. He looks sad all right,
I never saw nobody look quite as sad as that
Without it made you feel foolish. He don't do that.
He makes you feel—I dunno—I'm glad we could see him.
He was glad to see us but you could tell all the same
This war's plumb killin' him. You can tell by his face.
I never saw such a look on any man's face.
I guess it's tough for him. Well, we saw him, for once."

Richmond is fallen—Lincoln walks in its streets,
Alone, unguarded, stops at George Pickett's house,
Knocks at George Pickett's door. George Pickett has gone
But the strange, gaunt figure talks to George Pickett's wife
A moment—she thinks she is dreaming, seeing him there—
"Just one of George Pickett's old friends, m'am."

They drove back to the White House, dressed and ate,
Went to the theatre in their flag-draped box.
The play was a good play, he liked the play,
Laughed at the jokes, laughed at the funny man
With the long, weeping whiskers.
                                   The time passed.
The shot rang out. The crazy murderer
Leaped from the box, mouthed out his Latin phrase,
Brandished his foolish pistol and was gone.
Lincoln lay stricken in the flag-draped box.
Living but speechless. Now they lifted him
And bore him off. He lay some hours so.
Then the heart failed.
The breath beat in the throat.
The black, formless vessel carried him away.

1. Who is the speaker?

(*The only characters who have dialogue in this cutting are a soldier and President Lincoln. The soldier is describing and commenting on Lincoln to another soldier or military personnel companion. Lincoln speaks to Pickett's wife in Richmond. The rest of the poetry is "spoken" by the omniscient narrator, Benét.*)

Note: This is an appropriate answer for in-class discussion but is too superficial for homework. Remind the students that the first four questions should be based not just on the poem but on library research. A sample researched answer follows.

(*In this case, the narrator appears to be the author, Stephen Vincent Benét. Born in Bethlehem, Pennsylvania, in 1898, Benét studied at Yale University. He received the Pulitzer Prize for John Brown's Body in 1929. Other well-known works include "The Devil and Daniel Webster," a short story, and Western Star (1943), an unfinished narrative poem for which he received his second Pulitzer Prize in 1944. Among American authors, Benét provides outstanding literature that depicts the history and culture of the nation.*)

2. Where is the speaker speaking?

(*The narrator transports us with ease to innumerable scenes of the war. Lincoln is described in all of the following scenarios: [1] the White House, [2] the presence of a group of soldiers—probably in their camp, [3] the streets of Richmond, [4] George Pickett's house, [5] and Ford's Theater [name not specified in the poem].*)

3. When is the speaker speaking?

(*Benét first published this Civil War poem in 1927. [Students will not be able to provide this in classroom discussion but should provide such details on a homework assignment.]*)

4. To whom is the speaker speaking?

(*He speaks to Americans in a very poignant manner. His depictions of Lincoln create a multi-faceted view of an austere historical figure. Benét helps the modern reader [his audience], who may tend to see Lincoln as larger-than-life, to see Lincoln as a normal man who faced many difficult decisions and bore a heavy responsibility. In describing Lincoln's common experiences such as wearing slippers and being worn out by responsibility, Benét creates a well-rounded, accessible hero in that elegant, flag-draped box of Ford's Theater. Benét knows that his audience would not pity a character it does not know.*)

5. What is being said?

   (Lincoln was an ordinary man with an extraordinary life. He is more than a face on a coin or a speech in Gettysburg to memorize and recite. He, among others, represents a struggle in American history that became a great defining point for the nation's character. [It is also acceptable for students to list details of "what is being said" on a literal level. However, after they have presented a number of facts, encourage them to draw conclusions, such as those given in the answer above].)

6. How is it being said?

   (Benét uses description and diction to portray Lincoln as both simple and profound. For description, he uses his own wit and point of view as well as those of the soldier. For example, in the White House, the narrator gently mocks and praises the president. On the battlefield, the soldiers' own commonness creates an effective vehicle to describe Lincoln as a real man behind the title. Diction would overlap with the function of the description. Have you ever wondered what the president of the United States might say to you at your front door? Lincoln's unassuming poise and casual but courteous manner of speech say volumes about him.)

7. Why is it being said?

   (Most of Benét's major works seem geared toward depicting the past in a personal sense that cannot be preserved in history books. He does more than report the facts. He makes it personal. It has been said that those who forget the mistakes of history are doomed to repeat them. Benét makes the facts of history memorable by making history live and breathe with three-dimensional characters and conflicts.)

SCENE: two siblings and a household servant in a kitchen. All roles may be played as male or female.

TIME: the present

(SERVANT *is preparing food. Enter* YOUNGER *sibling.*)

YOUNGER: Smells great in here! I'm sorry—I didn't mean to startle you.

SERVANT: I'm not usually so jumpy. It's just strange to hear your voice again.

YOUNGER: With the hours Dad has me working the ranch, you won't hear it often.

SERVANT: Supper will be ready by 6 P.M. as usual.

YOUNGER: I never appreciated your delicious meals until I didn't have them. You're an excellent cook.

SERVANT: Just comes from years of experience.

(*Enter* ELDER *suddenly.* YOUNGER *does not see* ELDER.)

YOUNGER: Maybe you can catch me up on all the neighborhood news. I know a lot has changed since—

ELDER: I wouldn't have guessed! You don't seem to have changed at all. Always talking when you were supposed to be working. You've been home two days, and you're at it again.

YOUNGER: I just came in for some water.

ELDER: Twenty minutes ago.

SERVANT: There's cold lemonade in the refrigerator. Why don't you both help yourselves?

ELDER: I think I will.

(ELDER *pours a glass and sets the pitcher on the table.* YOUNGER *reaches for it.* ELDER *pulls the pitcher, still mostly full, out of reach.*)

There doesn't appear to be enough for both of us.

(YOUNGER *moves to the sink, filling his glass with tap water.*)

YOUNGER: (to SERVANT) Looking forward to enjoying that dinner.

(YOUNGER *exits.*)

ELDER: What arrogance!

SERVANT: (*Aside*) Indeed.

ELDER: For a year now—no, for our whole lives, I've helped Dad around this place. I couldn't have been higher than the fence posts when I started working with the cattle and training the sheepdogs. Doesn't that mean anything?

SERVANT: Your dad appreciates all you've done. He's very proud of your hard work and accomplishments. He speaks highly of you.

ELDER: I'd like to believe that. My brother (sister) has always worked half-heartedly, in my opinion. He (She) would be living in the stables if I were Dad. He (She) doesn't deserve such a welcome.

The Prodigal Son
from *God's Trombones*
by James Weldon Johnson

Introduction

James Weldon Johnson was fascinated by the impact of the oratory of the black preachers of his day. Their use of storytelling and bold imagery arrested their audiences' minds.

The result of his interest was a project titled God's Trombones in which Johnson presented seven sermons in poetic style, ranging in topic from "Creation" to the final "Judgment Day." Perhaps no other narrative in Scripture has spoken more poignantly and clearly to men and women through the centuries than the parable of the prodigal son. Here, Johnson retells it, incorporating the culture to which his audience would best relate.

If you retold this story for your peers, what might you include to make the message most relevant to them?

_____

_____

What might you retain from Johnson's style?

_____

Were there any phrases that specifically the story come alive to you? If so, which ones?

_____

This script is supplementary to those provided in Appendix G. It has been withheld from the student text because Johnson's sermon poems are forthright in their descriptions. Some of the description may be too vivid for your students, depending on their level of maturity. If you choose to use this script, discuss the seriousness of the topic before reading the script. Emphasize that though this is a story poem, it is also representing a parable told by Christ. Descriptive lines about the temptations to which the prodigal yields need to be handled with maturity. You should preview the script before using it in class and adapt it as needed to suit the maturity of your students.

Staging

For staging this piece, less may be better. Readers theater format or modified readers theater format is recommended over chamber theater. Use of offstage focus is recommended when delivering the dialogue. Narrative lines could be directed toward the audience proper. Give the audience members the impression that the readers want to communicate with each of them.

Dramatis Personae

PREACHER
STORYTELLER
PRODIGAL
FATHER
MAN
WOMAN

Script

PREACHER:	Young man— Young man— Your arm's too short to box with God.
STORYTELLER:	But Jesus spake in a parable, and he said: A certain man had two sons. Jesus didn't give this man a name,
PREACHER:	But his name is God Almighty.
STORYTELLER:	And Jesus didn't call these sons by name,
PREACHER:	But ev'ry young man, Everywhere, Is one of these two sons.
STORYTELLER:	And the younger son said to his father, He said:
PRODIGAL:	Father, divide up the property, And give me my portion now.
STORYTELLER:	And the father with tears in his eyes said:
FATHER:	Son, Don't leave your father's house.
STORYTELLER:	But the boy was stubborn in his head, And haughty in his heart, And he took his share of his father's goods, And went into a far country.
PREACHER:	There comes a time, there comes a time When ev'ry young man looks out from his father's house, Longing for that far-off country.
STORYTELLER:	And the young man journeyed on his way, And he said to himself as he traveled along:
PRODIGAL:	This sure is an easy road, Nothing like the rough furrows behind my father's plow.
PREACHER:	Young man— Young man— Smooth and easy is the road That leads to hell and destruction. Downgrade all the way, The further you travel, the faster you go.

MAN:	No need to trudge and sweat and toil,
WOMAN:	Just slip and slide and slip and slide
PREACHER:	Till you bang up against hell's iron gate.
STORYTELLER:	And the younger son kept travelling along, Till at night-time he came to a city. And the city was bright in the night-time like day, The streets all crowded with people, Brass bands and string bands a-playing, And ev'rywhere the young man turned There was singing and laughing and dancing. And he stopped a passer-by and he said:
PRODIGAL:	Tell me what city is this?
STORYTELLER:	And the passer-by laughed and he said:
MAN:	Don't you know? This is Babylon, Babylon, That great city of Babylon. Come on, my friend, and go along with me.
STORYTELLER:	And the young man joined the crowd.
PREACHER:	Young man— Young man—
PRODIGAL:	You're never lonesome in Babylon.
PREACHER:	Young man— Young man— You can never be alone in Babylon, Alone with your Jesus in Babylon. You can never find a place, a lonesome place, A lonesome place to go down on your knees, And talk with your God, in Babylon.
PRODIGAL:	You're always in a crowd in Babylon.
STORYTELLER:	And the young man went with his new-found friend,
PRODIGAL:	And bought himself some brand new clothes,
STORYTELLER:	And he spent his days in the drinking dens,
PREACHER:	Swallowing the fires of hell.
STORYTELLER:	And he spent his nights in the gambling dens,
PREACHER:	Throwing dice with the devil for his soul.
STORYTELLER:	And he met up with the women of Babylon.
PREACHER:	Oh, the women of Babylon!
WOMAN:	Dressed in yellow and purple and scarlet, Loaded with rings and earrings and bracelets, Their lips like a honeycomb dripping with honey, Perfumed and sweet smelling like a jasmine flower:

PREACHER:	And the jasmine smell of the Babylon women Got in his nostrils and went to his head,
STORYTELLER:	And he wasted his substance in riotous living,
MAN:	(*Echoing*) wasted
WOMAN:	(*Echoing*) wasted
STORYTELLER:	In the evening, in the black and dark of night,
WOMAN:	With the sweet-sinning women of Babylon. And they stripped him of his money,
MAN:	And they stripped him of his clothes, And they left him broke and ragged In the streets of Babylon.
STORYTELLER:	Then the young man joined another crowd——
MAN:	The beggars and lepers of Babylon.
STORYTELLER:	He went to feeding swine,
PRODIGAL:	And he was hungrier than the hogs;
STORYTELLER:	And he got down on his belly in the mire and the mud And ate the husks with the hogs.
PREACHER:	And not a hog was too low to turn up his nose At the man in the mire of Babylon.
STORYTELLER:	Then the young man came to himself—— He came to himself and said:
PRODIGAL:	In my father's house are many mansions,
MAN:	Ev'ry servant in his house has bread to eat,
WOMAN:	Ev'ry servant in his house has a place to sleep;
PRODIGAL:	I will arise and go to my father.
STORYTELLER:	And his father saw him afar off,
FATHER:	And he ran up the road to meet him.
PRODIGAL:	He put clean clothes upon his back, And a golden chain around his neck,
FATHER:	He made a feast and killed the fatted calf, And invited the neighbors in.
PREACHER:	Oh-o-oh, sinner, When you're mingling with the crowd in Babylon——
MAN:	Drinking the wine of Babylon——
WOMAN:	Running with the women of Babylon——
PREACHER:	You forget about God, and you laugh at Death.

MAN: Today you've got the strength of a bear in your arms,

PREACHER: But some o' these days, some o' these days,
You'll have a hand-to-hand struggle with bony Death,
And Death is bound to win.
Young man, come away from Babylon,
That hell-border city of Babylon.
Leave

WOMAN: the dancing and gambling of Babylon,

MAN: The wine and whiskey of Babylon,

WOMAN: The women of Babylon;

PREACHER: Fall down on your knees,
And say in your heart:

PRODIGAL: I will arise and go to my Father.

Scripture Narrative Project

Prepare

Select a narrative. Choose something dramatic, with a strong conflict and a hero character.

Check the length. Time yourself while reading aloud. If the passage is too long, make a cutting using the guidelines outlined in this chapter. If it is too short, select a different narrative or consult your teacher about combining two incidents involving the same character.

Complete the dramatistic analysis (pp. 17-18). When you proofread this assignment, choose ideas to include in a thirty-second extemporaneous introduction (not memorized word-for-word).

Create your manuscript. Type your manuscript (double-spaced) and attach it in a folder. The folder should be a dark color (preferably black) for a professional look. Use one-inch margins to allow space for your notes. Assign a title that supports your story's message.

Mark your manuscript. Neatly make an asterisk (*) by any unfamiliar words. Write synonyms or brief definitions for each in the right margin. Also mark thought units with parentheses and pauses with slashes: one slash for a brief pause and two for a long pause. For example:

*(And Abraham took the wood of the burnt offering, and laid it upon Isaac his son; /
and he took the fire in his hand, and a knife; / and they went both of them together. //)*

[Isaac said] ("My father:"//)

Practice

Know your story. Familiarity with the text allows you to present the story fluidly and ener-getically. If you are attached to the script visually, you won't communicate effectively.

Take practicing seriously. It is the means by which you develop good interpretation technique. Practice sessions are as important as the actual performance. Practice makes permanent. Incorrect practice leads to a poor performance. Only correct practice leads to an excellent performance.

Fulfill requirements for practice sessions.
- Aloud ("In your head" isn't enough!)
- Loudly (Paint the back wall with your voice.)
- Repeatedly (Several repetitions on different days)

Set goals. Your practice goals need to include distinct diction for clarity and sincerity. The audience should have no doubt that the story means a great deal to you and your walk with the Lord.

Get feedback. Have a friend or family member serve as your audience for two rehearsals—one partway through the rehearsal process and one at the end. Ask him to give suggestions and help you evaluate your progress.

Perform

Stay calm and confident. When it is your turn to present your Scripture narrative, give your teacher your evaluation form and walk quietly to the front of the room. Focus primarily on your interpretation skills: intensity, sincerity, and poise. Be energetic! Be enthusiastic! Show your message as you speak.

Sonnet Project

Prepare

Select a sonnet. Appendix C contains almost forty sonnets from which you may choose. Read at least a dozen of the sonnets before choosing. Don't forget to read the notes in the margin.

Complete the dramatistic analysis (pp. 143-44). Be thorough. Skimping on the written work cheats yourself and your audience. Select an interesting fact about the writing of the poem, its purpose, or the author's life to use as an attention device in your introduction.

Prepare your script. For the Scripture narrative project, you used parentheses to mark whole thought units because in a narrative, thought units may or may not be divided into paragraphs. In a short poem such as a sonnet, there are seldom more than one or two thought units, so you will not need to mark them. Instead, mark phrases and clauses with parentheses. You may have to subordinate one phrase to another but not necessarily with a pause. Use a slash mark for pauses—one slash for a short pause and two for a long pause. Then examine each phrase individually. Underline figurative language and label it in the margin. (See the sample on p. 303.) Paraphrase as needed.

Practice

Memorize correctly. Practice numerous times without an explicit goal of memorization. While you cannot completely refine your presentation for the performance until you fully memorize the poem, you will not interpret well if you memorize before developing clear meaning and emotion.

Utilize interpretation. Work to maintain previously studied interpretation skills: phrasing, emphasis, and subordination. Then reach for the new tools in your toolbox: aesthetic distance, visualization, word color, and vitalization. Make as many notes on your script as needed. It can be crowded since you will not use it on the platform.

Fulfill requirements.

- Fully memorized; no notes or script permitted
- One-minute introduction consisting of the title, author, and a couple of sentences of description to "frame" the poem

Perform

Plan well. For example, you may wish to choose an appropriately dressy outfit a day or two in advance and be sure it doesn't need laundering or ironing on the day you need it.

Be confident. When your turn comes, give your teacher your evaluation form and script and walk quietly to the front of the room. Take a very brief moment to collect your thoughts. (Do not look down at the floor!) Check for correct posture and breathing as you begin your introduction. Speak directly to the audience for the introduction and then make as fluid a transition as possible to your role as a narrator or character. When you are finished, pause momentarily to allow the ideas to sink into the minds of the audience. Return to your seat with as little distraction as possible.

Monologue Project

Prepare

Select a monologue. You may select a monologue from Appendix D or choose another monologue with permission from your teacher. As you read through the appendix, keep three goals in mind. Your selection should interest you, suit your audience, and challenge your skills.

Complete the dramatistic analysis (pp. 167-68). Remember to proofread! Also, choose interesting details that you can include in your introduction.

Prepare your script. Mark your monologue as you marked your sonnet. Identify each phrase with parentheses and use one slash to denote a brief pause or two slashes for a sustained pause. Underline figurative language, identifying its type and meaning in the margin.

Practice

Work to communicate meaning and character. The audience should not be aware of you or your personality. The more you focus on the literature and the character you are presenting, the less nervousness will show.

Memorize only what you can already communicate effectively. If you struggle with memorization, review memorization methods (pp. 139-40).

Work to conceal your technique. For example, if you are switching from speaking directly to the audience to using aesthetic distance, you should practice that transition until it is smooth. Your tools should not be noticeable when your work of art is complete.

Perform

Adjust to the format. Your teacher may choose to have you perform this assignment in an auditorium, creating as much of the atmosphere of an audition as possible. He may allow a script, or he may require memorization.

Be confident. When your name is called, submit your "audition card" and proceed confidently to the platform. If your teacher calls "time" before you have completed your selection, stop immediately and return quietly to your seat. Remain quiet throughout the audition process, even if it seems that you are seated far enough away that you won't disturb the next speaker or your teacher.

Storytelling Project

Prepare

Select a short story. Appendix F contains a list of recommended stories. What stories interest you the most? For what age groups would your top five favorites be most ideal? On your assignment sheet (p. 189), list these five stories, their authors, and a description of the ideal audience.

Complete the worksheet "My Situation and My Audience" (p. 190).

Complete the dramatistic analysis (pp. 191-92) after finalizing your choice of a story. You will notice that the order and wording of the questions have changed slightly to better suit the context of a short story.

Prepare your outline. Remember to look for action as you write your practice outline. All of your main points must be key plot complications. Your supporting points should be minor complications or other actions that lead to complications. Don't consider your outline complete until you have identified the climax, selected sentences to use as the introduction and the conclusion, and carefully proofread your work.

Practice

Practice extemporaneous delivery. Unless directed by your teacher to memorize, plan to learn the plot and then repeatedly practice telling the story in your own words. (You may wish to loosely memorize the introduction and conclusion.)

Practice repeatedly over time. "Cramming" usually fails the extemporaneous storyteller. If you wait until the last minute to rehearse, you may remember snatches of the author's words but lack the ability to paraphrase the rest in a style that matches the author's. You will probably need to practice at least ten to twelve times total, spaced out over a week or more. Usually, practicing more than three times in one session becomes too tiring to be effective.

Perform

Captivate your audience in the story. Your teacher will tell you whether you will perform your story for class or as a guest storyteller for another group. In either case, seek to engage your audience in the story.

Adjust to the situation. Recognize the specific needs of your audience. For example, if you tell your story for the second grade late in the afternoon, expect them to be tired of sitting still. Perhaps you could begin by asking them a question that will lead into your introduction. The best type of question will encourage a group response ("How many of you have ever . . . ?"). Regardless of the audience's age, be energetic and focused.

Readers Theater Project

Prepare

Your teacher may assign you a role in one or both of the readers theater scripts in Appendix G. The size of your role will not affect your grade.

Strive to be a team player and communicate the literature.

Practice

Be ready to improvise! Your teacher may ask you to create live sound effects or human scenery (you may use your body to suggest a hat rack, for example, holding your arms like the hooks). Experiment with stage movement such as pantomime. Don't worry about what others will think.

Perform

Build rapport. Regardless of how many points your teacher gives for this assignment—do your best. You will be working with other students on the next several projects; you need to earn their respect and cooperation.

Chamber Theater Project

Prepare

You will choose or be assigned a role(s) in one or more of the chamber theater scripts found in Appendix G.

Complete the dramatistic analysis (pp. 215-16), which has been reworded to better suit the nature of the literature and this project. Completing this worksheet early in your preparation will help you understand the material you are practicing.

Practice

Explore the text. In class, you will rehearse these scripts three different ways. First, you will explore the text with help from your teacher. This will be your first workshop, and it will not be graded.

Utilize independent work time. Next, your teacher may allow you to rehearse while he coaches another group.

Workshop the script. This second workshop will involve performing at least half of your script in front of the rest of the students. (Unless your teacher specifies otherwise, plan to have the script memorized.) Your teacher will coach you during the workshop and then rank you individually for each category. (The workshop score is primarily an individual grade.)

Review your lines and stage movements independently.

Perform

Keep your fellow cast members in mind. Think like a team.

Don't let your mind wander between one of your lines and the next. Alertness allows you to rescue someone who "goes blank." Also, you must react appropriately to the other actors for your performance to seem real.

The performance score is primarily a group grade because most categories apply to your team's effort. However, your grade will reflect your personal effort and improvement since the workshop.

Duo-Acting Project

Prepare

Choose a script from Appendix H. Your teacher may assign a partner and/or script to you.

Complete the dramatistic analysis (pp. 247-48).

Create an introduction to your scene. Since your scene will be an excerpt from a play, use a brief introduction to clarify the context. You and your partner should develop a one-minute introduction that summarizes the plot and characters. Your teacher may require a written introduction.

Consider the subtext—the meaning behind the words—according to the context. Avoid reading something into a text. If the subtextual meaning doesn't make sense in the context of the whole play, it probably isn't really there. For example, subtext for "I'm going to die," might include "I've battled this illness for months and must face reality" (serious drama), "I'm very thirsty" (comedy), or even "If you don't let me win this petty argument, I shall collapse on your sofa!" (farce). Your subtext must make sense.

Practice

Warm up your acting instrument. Use various warm-ups for your body, voice, and diction to prepare yourself for each rehearsal.

Participate in improvisations. Improvisations develop good working relationships. Try repeating favorite improvisations learned in class. Also, try paraphrasing your scene—focusing on action rather than wording. This task will improve your interpretation as well as your memorization.

Evaluate what actions cause other actions to occur. Keep these actions foremost in your mind as you rehearse.

Choose a focus for each rehearsal: text meaning, interpretation, blocking, and acting chemistry. These elements may be rehearsed in almost any order.

Develop interpretation. Remember that action begins with a goal, meets an obstacle, and results in conflict. Find the motive behind each of your character's lines. Consult the activity on page 231 to guide you in marking verbs on your own script and submit it on your performance day.

Develop blocking. Blocking is most effective if developed during the process of interpreting. The movement is motivated by the actions of the text (rebuking, intimidating, encouraging, and so on).

Build teamwork. If your acting partner doesn't respond to your interpretation of a line, try something else. The audience will notice if you and your partner are not really communicating.

Perform

Remember your audience, not just your lines. Practicing with the methods given here should prevent your forgetting your lines in performance. However, you might forget about (ignore) either your partner or the audience proper. If you forget your partner, the scene will be ineffective because it lacks interaction. If you forget the audience proper, you will not project, enunciate, or communicate a clear message. The audience will become restless and bored. Think about the audience as you practice so that you will remember it when you perform.

Radio Segment Project

Prepare

Expect to be assigned multiple roles. Your teacher will organize students into positions typical of a radio broadcasting team for the purpose of creating fifteen minutes of radio programming. (Tasks are listed on p. 277.) This project's complexities will require careful planning.

Practice

Plan more rehearsal time for commercials and dramatic segments than the news flashes or station promos. Your teacher will assign specific tasks to you. One student may be responsible to find music cues for a dramatic segment and then portray a newscaster. Another may develop a station name and slogan and then serve as the sound person.

Practice independently. Though your teacher will guide you through rehearsals, you will need to practice your lines and interpretation individually as well.

Learn your role (speaking or nonspeaking) well, even though radio often involves reading from a script. After you have rehearsed several times, you will run through your scenes without stopping. Your teacher will evaluate this part of the project with a grade for each student.

Perform

Learn every skill you can. Your experience will vary greatly depending on what production role(s) you fulfill. Make the most of each opportunity. If your class airs your program with public-address equipment, try to learn as much as possible about that part of the process, even if you are not assigned a "tech" role. You will be evaluated primarily as a member of the cast and crew. However, you will also be graded individually on your personal improvement since your workshop.

Final Challenge

Prepare

Use your production concept worksheet as a guide, not just a homework assignment. Refer to examples in the chapter if you are uncertain about how to fill out the worksheet. Your preparation for this final project will of course be determined by which option you choose. Consult pages 283-84 for a detailed listing of your tasks and deadlines.

Plan ahead. Being prepared will mean not just keeping up with requirements but constantly planning ahead. Taking the initiative to look ahead to the next step and asking questions early in the process will ensure success.

Practice

Make excellent delivery a priority. By this point in the course, you may feel relatively comfortable with performing in front of your peers. Don't become so comfortable that you are not motivated to refine your delivery.

Ask for audience feedback. A well-chosen audience of one or two friends or family members while you are practicing is still very beneficial. Choose a person who will be honest and kind. President Woodrow Wilson once said, "I not only use all the brains that I have, but all that I can borrow." Don't be afraid to get critical feedback from people who can help you improve. Others can see weaknesses you cannot.

Perform

Make it your goal to captivate your audience. Everything you plan—visually and audibly—should command their attention.

Strive for vitality. As with any type of communication—from phone calls and sales presentations to presidential debates—keep your message vital. Vitality must be the driving force behind your performance.

Finish strong. Perhaps nothing is more satisfying than giving your last ounce of strength at the end of a race or competition. Even if you feel exhausted after months of effort, remember that this is the end. Rise to the occasion and give your very best. More than anyone else, you will enjoy the rewards of your effort—satisfaction in your accomplishment and most importantly, the blessing of utilizing God-given talents.

Semester at a Glance

Week	Day One	Day Two	Day Three	Day Four	Day Five
1	1: course introduction	1: Everyday Life	1: As We Grow	1: Formal Performance	1: quiz; improvisation
2	2: Elements of a Story	2: Elements of a Story, cont.	2: Basics of Communicating a Story (TE); rehearsal	2: quiz; rehearsal	2: **Performances**
3	3: Philosophy	3: Discernment	3: Analysis	3: quiz; activities	4: Reading Comprehension
4	4: Reading Comprehension, cont.	4: Reading Technique	4: Dramatistic Analysis	4: quiz or unit test	5: The Drama of the Ages
5	5: The Drama of the Ages, cont.	5: Interpretation Skills	5: Interpretation Skills, cont.	5: Standing Alone; quiz	5: **Scripture Narrative performances**
6	6: Lyric Poetry	6: Lyric Poetry, cont.; Figurative Language	6: Figurative Language, cont.	6: Interpretation of Poetry	6: rehearsal
7	6: activities, rehearsal	6: **Sonnet performances**	7: Acting; What It Is Not	7: Acting; What It Is	7: activities
8	7: quiz, rehearsal	7: rehearsal	7: **Monologue performances**	8: Preparing Your Story	8: Preparing Your Story, cont.
9	8: Practicing Your Story	8: quiz or unit test; rehearsal	8: **Storytelling performances** (or rehearsals, if stories will be told outside of class)	8: **Storytelling performances,** cont.	8: **Storytelling performances,** cont.
10	9: Understanding Readers Theater	9: introduce readers theater scripts; assign roles in chamber theater scripts	9: Scripting Readers Theater	9: Performing Readers Theater	9: quiz; readers theater workshops
11	9: **Readers Theater performances**	9: chamber theater workshops	9: chamber theater workshops, cont.	9: additional rehearsal for chamber theater	9: **Chamber Theater performances**
12	10: Stage wise	10: Stage wise, cont.	10: The ABCs of Acting	10: The ABCs of Acting, cont.	10: quiz; duo-acting workshops
13	10: duo-acting workshops, cont.	10: duo-acting workshops, cont.	10: duo-acting workshops, cont.	10: rehearsals	10: **Duo-acting performances**
14	10: **Duo-acting performances,** cont.	11: Radio	11: Radio, cont.	11: assign roles and tasks for radio segment; get organized	11: Playwriting
15	11: Playwriting, cont.	11: quiz or unit test, work on commercials	12: introduce/assign Final Challenge projects*	11: radio segment workshops	11: radio segment workshops, cont.
16	11: radio segment workshops, cont.	11: rehearsal	11: rehearsal	11: **Radio Segment performance**	12: Developing a Production Concept
17	12: Developing a Production Concept, cont.	12: Final Challenge workshops	12: Final Challenge workshops, cont.	12: Final Challenge workshops, cont.	12: Final Challenge workshops, cont.
18	12: **Final performances**	12: **Final performances,** cont.	12: **Final performances,** cont.	review	final unit test or final exam

*Please note, you will need to introduce and assign each chapter's major project on the first or second day you teach material from that chapter. For some chapters, particularly The Final Challenge, you will need to give the assignment during the preceding chapter so students have adequate preparation time.